INTRODUCING MASS COMMUNICATION

Michael W. Gamble
New York Institute of Technology

Teri Kwal Gamble
College of New Rochelle

McGRAW-HILL
BOOK COMPANY
New York
St. Louis
San Francisco
Auckland
Bogotá
Hamburg
Johannesburg
London
Madrid
Mexico
Montreal
New Delhi
Panama
Paris
São Paulo
Singapore
Sydney
Tokyo
Toronto

INTRODUCING MASS COMMUNICATION

Copyright © 1986 by McGraw-Hill, Inc.
All rights reserved. Printed in the United States
of America. Except as permitted under the
United States Copyright Act of 1976, no part of this
publication may be reproduced or distributed in any
form or by any means, or stored in a data base
or retrieval system, without the prior written
permission of the publisher.

2 3 4 5 6 7 8 9 0 DOCDOC 8 9 8 7

ISBN 0-07-022770-5

This book was set in New Baskerville Book by University Graphics, Inc. (ECU).
The editors were Marian D. Provenzano and James R. Belser;
the designer was Joan E. O'Connor;
the production supervisor was Diane Renda.
The drawings were done by Fine Line Illustrations, Inc.
R. R. Donnelley & Sons Company was printer and binder.
Cover and part illustrations were drawn by Linsay Barrett.

Library of Congress Cataloging in Publication Data

Gamble, Michael.
    Introducing mass communication.

    (McGraw-Hill series in mass communication)
    Includes bibliographies and index.
    1. Mass media. I. Gamble, Teri Kwal. II. Title.
III. Series.
P90.G298 1986   001.51   85-12755
ISBN 0-07-022770-5

INTRODUCING MASS COMMUNICATION

McGRAW-HILL SERIES IN MASS COMMUNICATION

CONSULTING EDITOR
Alan Wurtzel

Dordick: Understanding Modern Communications
Gamble and Gamble: Introducing Mass Communication

ABOUT THE AUTHORS

Both Teri and Michael Gamble received Ph.D. degrees in communication arts from New York University. Michael is a professor at New York Institute of Technology and Teri is a professor at the College of New Rochelle. Award-winning teachers, the Gambles have conducted seminars and short courses for numerous professional and business organizations. They have brought their involving and creative approach to textbook writing to a wide range of subjects in the communication arts; among their works are *Contacts: Communicating Interpersonally* (Random House), *InterMedia* (Moore Publishing), *Painless Public Speaking* (Macmillan), and *Literature Alive* (National Textbook). The Gambles have worked as consultants for Children's Television Workshop, Cablevision and National Public Radio as well as KPH&B Marketing in New York, and WLMW Advertising in New Jersey.

Teri and Michael have published in a wide variety of journals and have presented workshops in the communication arts for the Speech Communication Association, the National Council of Teachers of English, the New York State Speech Communication Association, and others. They are currently involved in research with the Computer Graphics Lab of New York Institute of Technology to develop computer-generated models for use in courses in mass communication.

The Gambles live in New Jersey with their favorite media consumers, 6-year-old Matthew Jon and 8-month-old Lindsay Michele.

For Matthew Jon and Lindsay Michele

CONTENTS

PREFACE xiii

PART ONE THE MEDIATED WINDOW: A BEGINNING 1

CHAPTER 1 COMMUNICATION, THE MASS MEDIA, AND YOU 3

- Defining Communication: The Wide-Angle View 4
- Defining Mass Communication: Focusing In 8
- What the Mass Media Do 10
- The Role of the Mass Media in Your Life 11
- Summary 14
- Key Terms 15
- Notes 15
- Suggestions for Further Reading 15

PART TWO THE PRINT MEDIA: THE WINDOW OPENS 17

CHAPTER 2 BOOKS: MADE TO LAST 19

- How Books Were Developed 21
- The Birth of the Popular Book 26
- The Modern Book Industry 28
- The Publishing Process 33
- Book Censorship 45

- Summary 50
- Key Terms 50
- Notes 50
- Suggestions for Further Reading 51

CHAPTER 3 NEWSPAPERS: THE MEDIUM AND ITS MAKERS 53

- The Early Years: Setting Precedents 55
- The Penny Press: A Mass Medium 60
- The Post-Civil War Period: Yellow Journalism 62
- The Twentieth Century: Objectivity Returns 67
- Newspapers Today: Something for Everybody 71
- The Organization of a Newspaper: Who Does What? 78
- Summary 84
- Key Terms 84
- Notes 84
- Suggestions for Further Reading 85

CHAPTER 4 NEWSPAPERS: THE CONTENT AND THE ISSUES 87

- What Is News? 88
- Gathering the News 89
- Writing the News 92
- A Look at Legal Restraints 95
- Ethical Considerations 109
- Summary 115
- Key Terms 115
- Notes 115
- Suggestions for Further Reading 116

CHAPTER 5 MAGAZINES: FORMS, FUNCTIONS, AUDIENCES 117

- The Way Things Were 118
- Magazines Target the General Audience 123
- Magazine Publishing in the Television Age 126
- Magazine Organization: Who Does What? 132
- Contemporary Magazine Editing 134
- Summary 141
- Key Terms 141
- Notes 142
- Suggestions for Further Reading 142

PART THREE RADIO, TELEVISION, AND FILM: THE ELECTRONIC WINDOW 143

CHAPTER 6 RADIO AND RECORDINGS: THE WINDOW HAS EARS 145

- Pioneers: Early Developments and Developers 146
- The Business Takes Shape 151
- Federal Regulation of Broadcasting 154
- Programming through the Years 156
- The Recording Industry 162
- Restructuring the Radio Medium 173
- National Public Radio 179
- Station Operation: Who Does What? 182
- Playing to Win: Radio and Ratings 184
- Summary 188
- Key Terms 188
- Notes 189
- Suggestions for Further Reading 189

CHAPTER 7 TELEVISION: THE IMAGE EMERGES 191

- Television: An "I" View 192
- Looking Backward 194
- The Emerging Structure 201
- The Control and Regulation of Television 204
- How the Station Operates 209
- The Promise of Public Television and Cable TV 210
- Summary 214
- Key Terms 215
- Notes 215
- Suggestions for Further Reading 215

CHAPTER 8 TELEVISION: ASSESSING THE IMAGE 217

- Programming: Principles, Practices, and Pressures 218
- Focus on Television News and the Electronic Journalist 225
- Television versus Real Life 232
- Is Television Taking Away Childhood? 234
- Television Violence and Children 235
- Advertising and Children 240

- Images of Women and Minorities 242
- Summary 243
- Key Terms 244
- Notes 244
- Suggestions for Further Reading 245

CHAPTER 9 MOVIES: THE WINDOW SCREEN 247

- Movies: The Personal Experience 248
- Movies: A Social and Psychological Happening 250
- The Beginnings of Cinema: From Dreams to Pioneers 252
- Modern Times 260
- Censorship: Too Close for Comfort 272
- The Movie Business 276
- Promoting the Film: Outside Influences 283
- Film Watching: A Viewer's Guide 285
- Documentaries and Short Films 287
- Film and Video: Two Mediums or One? 288
- Summary 290
- Key Terms 290
- Notes 290
- Suggestions for Further Reading 291

PART FOUR PERSUASION: MORE THAN WINDOW DECORATION 293

CHAPTER 10 ADVERTISING: THE PROPELLING POWER 295

- The Environment: Display Window for Advertising 296
- The Development of Advertising 300
- The Method Behind the Magic 304
- The Medium Behind the Message 317
- The Advertising Agency: Industry Nerve Center 325
- Who Watches the Advertisers? The Regulators 326
- Where Do You Stand? 329
- Summary 332
- Key Terms 333
- Notes 333
- Suggestions for Further Reading 334

CHAPTER 11 PUBLIC RELATIONS: THE PRACTICE OF COMMUNICATION 337

- Explaining Public Relations 338
- The Public Relations Practitioner 344
- Communication and Public Relations 348
- The Ethics of Public Relations 355
- A Message for Our Time 359
- Summary 360
- Key Terms 360
- Notes 360
- Suggestions for Further Reading 361

PART FIVE RESEARCH AND MASS COMMUNICATION 363

CHAPTER 12 RESEARCHING THE MASS MEDIA: LOOKING FOR ANSWERS 365

- The Role of Mass-Media Research 366
- Mass-Media Research: Key to Changing Theories 366
- Media Research: A Potpourri of Approaches 368
- Summary 378
- Key Terms 378
- Notes 378
- Suggestions for Further Reading 378

PART SIX THE FUTURE: THE WINDOW WIDENS . . . OR DOES IT? 381

CHAPTER 13 THE NEW TECHNOLOGY: DEMASSIFYING THE MEDIA 383

- The Changing Media Environment: Plugging In, Tuning Out 384
- The Home Video Revolution 385
- The Impact of the New Technology 396
- Summary 397
- Key Terms 397
- Notes 397
- Suggestions for Further Reading 398

CONTENTS   xi

CHAPTER 14 NOT THE LAST WORD: YOUR ROLE BEYOND THIS BOOK   399

- Where Do You Go from Here? Looking for a Career   400
- Where Will the Media Go from Here?   402
- Where Do You Go from Here? Living with the Media   424
- Summary   426
- Notes   427
- Suggestions for Further Reading   427

GLOSSARY   429
INDEX   437

PREFACE

Our goal in writing this book is not only to familiarize you with the theory and practice of mass communication but also to help you internalize key mass-communication principles and concepts so that you are in a position to become more effective media watchers, consumers, and practitioners. It is our belief that after reading this text, completing the Media Probes (exercises) contained in it, and "living" the course, you will develop a clearer understanding of mass communication. We made every effort to ensure that the text's content and special features work together systematically to precipitate your active participation both in and out of the classroom setting. The materials contained in the work have been tested on a variety of student groups and have succeeded in challenging students of all ages, from the traditional 18-year-old to the adult returning to college.

Introducing Mass Communication covers the major content areas of mass communication: the media scene, the communication process, radio, television, film, advertising, public relations, journalism, etc. However, this book distinguishes itself from its competition in a number of strategic ways. It alone provides you with a truly complete learning package, a work which not only presents content in a clear, understandable manner but also carefully integrates a series of exercises, interviews, and other features designed to maintain your interest. The following types of features are used in each chapter: Media Probes, Media Scopes, Media Views, and You Were There.

Media Probes are activities that can be used in and outside of the classroom. Recognizing that many introductory classes are often mass lectures, we designed the exercises so that they could be performed by a student working alone or with another person. The Media Probe experiences are there to help you look at mass communication, assess effects, and gain the insight and practice you need to become "media-wise." We do not expect your instructor to use all the Media Probes contained in the text in the course of the semester. Instead, your instructor will pick and choose from them to fit your needs as well as the time available. Each Media Probe that your instructor selects will focus your attention on a specific aspect of mass communication. We believe that these activities will help to make the study of mass communication active and experiential in nature and more exciting and rewarding for you than ever before.

In addition to Media Probes, we offer *Media Scopes*. Media Scopes are charts which chronicle the development of each area of mass communication. Rather than simply providing a series of boxes or a time line, we created a graphically alive format which acts to draw you into the life of the chart—thereby insuring that you do not ignore it or pass over it.

A third feature of our book is *Media Views*. Media Views offer you a series of opinions or behind-the-scenes descriptions of various mass-communication sets and happenings. We have conducted some original interviews for these spots in order to share with you the key insights and experiences of real-world media practitioners. In order to provide as varied a perspective as possible, we also selected statements from well-known representatives of the fields of television, radio, journalism, book and magazine publishing, film, advertising, and public relations.

To complement Media Views, we also offer *You Were There*. This series transports you back in time so that you can be privy to the thoughts and experiences of media figures of the past and have a firsthand eye-witness account of events that occurred. By building on historical research and biographical materials, we help bring yesterday to life for you today.

Introducing Mass Communication aids you in other ways as well. Each chapter begins with a *Chapter Preview* that serves to guide you through the text's content. The function of each preview series is to clarify exactly what you should be able to understand or do after completing a chapter; in effect, preview objectives illuminate and specify goals and help prepare you for what is about to occur. Also included at the end of each chapter are a *Summary* of content covered, a list of *Key Terms,* and an annotated list of *Suggestions for Further Reading.* Also since the mass-communication field has evolved a specialized vocabulary, a *Glossary* is provided at the end of the text for ready reference.

Introducing Mass Communication was designed for use in the introductory course in mass communication. We believe it meets the needs of all students, whether or not they are majoring in the field, since it presents a framework the media critic, the media viewer, and the hopeful media practitioner can respond to. The text requires no prerequisites.

The following aspects of mass communication are covered in the book:

Part One, "The Mediated Window: A Beginning," lays the foundation for your future study by defining key communication processes and examining the effects of today's media on the individual and society.

Part Two, "The Print Media: The Window Opens," guides you through the history, functions, and key issues surrounding the book, newspaper, and magazine industries.

Part Three, "Radio, Television, and Film: The Electronic Window," offers you a chance to explore the historical developments and present operation of each of these media forms.

Part Four, "Persuasion: More Than Window Decoration," provides a comprehensive treatment of two of mass communication's growing areas: advertising and public relations.

Part Five, "Research and Mass Communication," exposes you to research methodology and provides you with a survey of research opportunities.

Part Six, "The Future: The Window Widens ... Or Does It?" offers you the chance to examine today's media environment and read predictions about its survival.

The last chapter of the book presents you with a very special feature—a program for developing a life-long appreciation of the media and their impact on you and your world. This is the only text that contains suggestions and strategies for continuing your study of mass communication once the course has ended or for entering a media-related career. As such, we hope it helps to increase the relevancy and importance of the materials you have studied.

We believe that *Introducing Mass Communication* will permit you to learn by reading, doing, observing, and experimenting. We believe it will encourage you to learn by thinking and experiencing. We know it will permit you to learn by direct and immediate involvement.

We want to thank the people at McGraw-Hill for working so hard to ensure the book accomplished our goals. Marian Provenzano, our acquiring editor, played a key part in persuading us to tackle this project; for her enthusiasm we are most appreciative. Our editor, Stephen Wagley, played a major part in shaping our manuscript; we are very thankful for his critical insights and extremely close reading. And our project editor, James Belser, helped us to refine the work and move it expeditiously through the publication maze. To the designer, Joan O'Connor, goes credit for the book's visual appeal.

In addition, we want to offer a special thanks to James O'Brien for sharing his knowledge of film with us and preparing the first draft of that chapter. But most importantly, the following reviewers not only reinforced our belief in this book but also gave generously of their time and talent to ensure the book's accuracy and effectiveness: Stuart Bullion, Southern Illinois University; Juliette Lushbough Dee, University of Delaware; Sue K. Fathree, East Central University; Joseph Foley, Ohio State University; Bruce Garrison, University of Miami; Steve Goldman, Polk Community College; Garth S. Jowett, University of Houston; Cherie Lewis, University of California, Los Angeles; Val. E. Limburg, Washington State University; Marilyn J. Matelski, Boston College; Richard Peacock, Palomar College; Tina Pieraccini, State University of New York at Oswego; William Rugg, Oklahoma State University; James R. Saville, Albany Junior College; and Denise M. Trauth, Bowling Green State University. We are especially grateful to them.

Michael W. Gamble
Teri Kwal Gamble

PART ONE

THE MEDIATED WINDOW: A BEGINNING

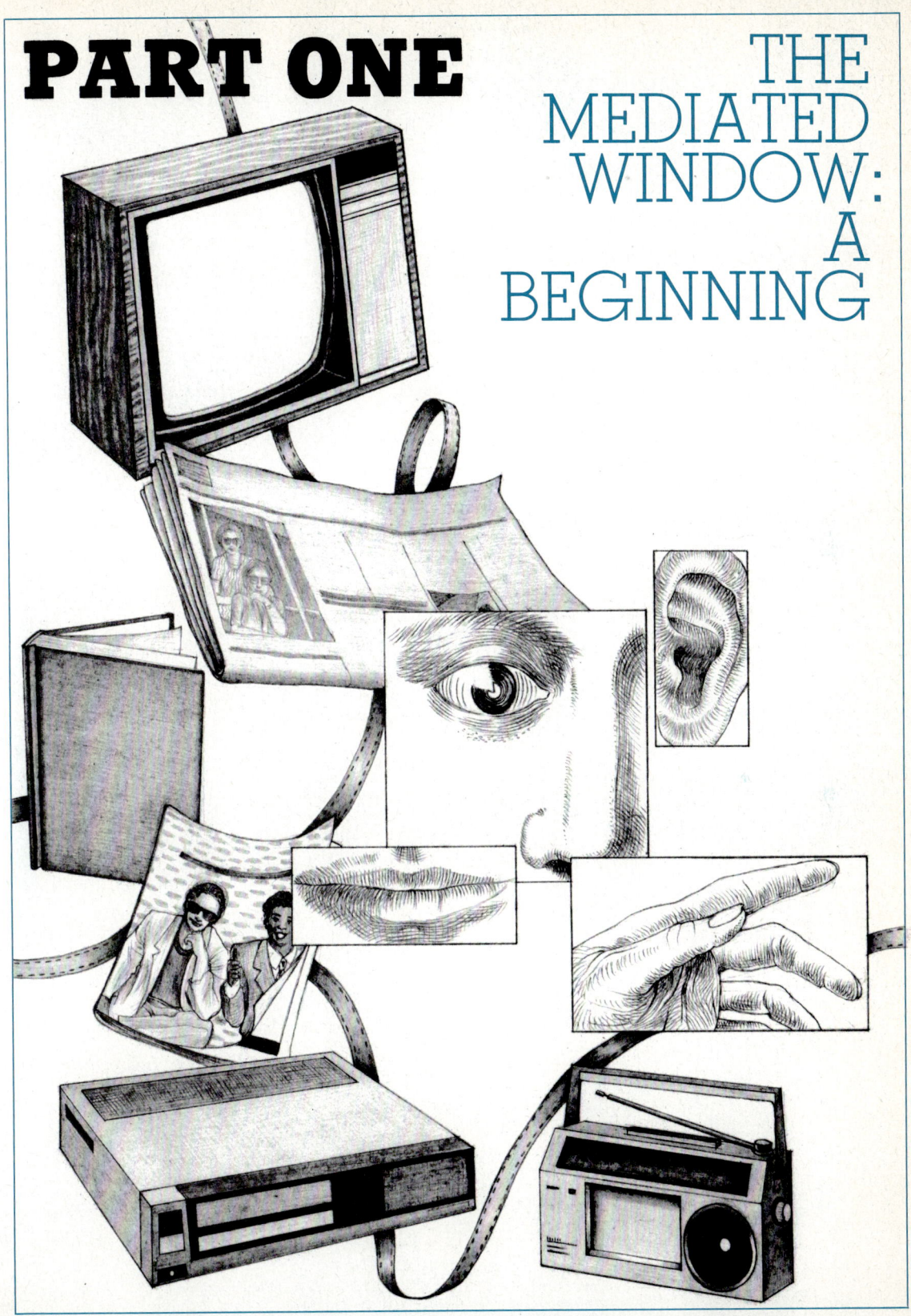

CHAPTER 1

COMMUNICATION, THE MASS MEDIA, AND YOU

As extensions of our psychic and sensory powers, the media have a way of shaping us even as we are shaping them. Understanding media has a lot to do with understanding me.
John Culkin

CHAPTER PREVIEW

After reading this chapter, you should be able to:
- Define "communication"
- Identify and discuss the essential ingredients of communication
- Define "mass communication"
- Compare and contrast mass communication with personal, group, and public communication
- Diagram the mass-communication process
- Explain the functions performed by the mass media
- Discuss the roles the mass media play in your life

A radio. A stereo. A newspaper. A magazine. A book. A film. An advertisement. A video cassette recorder. These are just some of the mass media that constitute the communication society of which you are a part. Headlines, promos, bulletins, flashes, hit records, hit shows, DJs, personalities, life glorified, life horrified, the real, the not-so-real, what we think, what we are now, what we want, what we get, the possible, the impossible, yesterday, tomorrow—all brought to you by the media.

This book is about you and your relationship to the media that permeate your world. The topics we cover will help you as you practice the routine of being human: thinking, learning, feeling, playing, working, relaxing, establishing relationships, and above all, communicating—sometimes alone, sometimes with others, but always in a context of a society that has made the mass media a central part of life. The role that communication in general, and mass communication in particular, play in your day-to-day life cannot be overemphasized. Whether you are 18 or 80, male or female, married or single, the media affect you in ways that you may only partially perceive. So whether you would like to use the media more effectively, not merely to survive but to thrive in a mediated world, or whether you intend to develop skills and acquire knowledge that will increase your chances of making your career in the mass media, the time to improve your understanding is now.

DEFINING COMMUNICATION: THE WIDE-ANGLE VIEW

From birth to death, all types of communication play an integral part in your life. Whatever your occupation or leisure-time activities, communication of one form or another has a role. In fact, if people were asked to analyze how they spend most of their waking day, the prime responses would be "communicating" or "being communicated to." In reality, communication is "the essential human connection."[1] Whether in pictures, or music, whether verbal or nonverbal, informative or persuasive, frightening or amusing, clear or unclear, purposeful or accidental, person-to-person or mediated, communication is our link to the rest of humanity. It pervades everthing we do.

But what is communication? And what is it we seek to accomplish with it? Let us begin to answer these questions by examining what we consider to be the essential ingredients of communication. Each of these ingredients is present during every communicative act, that is, every time a message is sent intentionally or accidentally from a source to a receiver via a channel.

Senders and Receivers

Communication involves people who send and receive messages, sometimes simultaneously. This means that the role of *sender* or *receiver* is not restricted to any one party to the communication process; instead, we play both roles. And this is a good thing, for if we were just senders, we might send message after message without ever stopping to consider whether the message was being received as we intended it to be. And if we were just receivers, we might be open to any and all messages that came our way. We would not stop to consider how we were being affected by what we were receiving, whether it was in our best interest, or, for that matter, how we should respond. There are times when it seems as if communication is predominantly one way: receivers of messages fail to react; senders of messages fail to consider the reactions of the receiver before sending another message. But for communication to be effective, the messages people send to others should, at least in part, be determined by the messages received from them.

Field of Experience

We each carry our *field of experience* with us wherever we go. When the people communicating have had similar life experiences, chances are they will be able to relate to each other in an effective way. However, to the extent that their life experiences have been different, they will probably have difficulty interacting with or understanding each other. As our storehouses of experience diverge, it becomes harder for us to share meaning. Conversely, as storehouses of experience converge, the sharing of meaning becomes easier.

Messages

The *message* is the content of a communicative act. People communicate a wide variety of messages. Some of these messages are private (a smile accompanied by an "I love you"), while others are directed at millions (a network television show, a mass-market paperback). Some messages are sent intentionally ("I want you to know"), while others are sent accidentally ("I didn't realize you were watching me"). But as long as someone is there to interpret the results of a sender's efforts, a message is being sent. Thus, we can say that everything a sender does or says has potential message value.

Of course, some messages are easier for the receiver to filter, censor, or ignore than others. A flip of the switch turns off the TV; a turn of the dial changes the radio station; a trash can stands ready to accept a discarded newspaper; and a sign of displeasure or boredom can terminate a conversation. But each of these actions is a message for behavior watchers, whether they are directly involved in the exchange or, like pollsters and ratings services, hired to watch. Consequently, whether you smile, listen, renew a magazine subscription, watch a particular TV program, or turn away from a person, you are communicating some message, and your message is having some effect.

The media—print and broadcast means of communication—actively mold our society's behavior and expectations. (Randy Matusow)

Channels

We may send our messages to receivers through a variety of sensory *channels*. We may use sound, sight, smell, taste, touch, or any combination of these to carry a message. Some channels are more effective at communicating messages than others, and the nature of the channel selected affects the way a message will be processed. For instance, what kind of message do you get from someone who has eaten onions? The impact of a message changes as the channel used to transmit it changes. Experience shows that most of us have channel preferences; that is, we prefer to rely on one or more channels while disregarding others. Which channels are you most attuned to? Why? Adept communicators are channel switchers who recognize that human communication today is an ever-expanding, multichanneled event.

Noise

Noise is anything that interferes with the ability to send and/or receive messages. Thus, while noise could be sound (static, for example), it does not necessarily have to be sound. It could also be physical discomfort (a headache), psychological makeup (a poor self-concept, an inflated ego, or a high level of defensiveness), semantic misunderstandings (as when people give different meanings to words and phrases or use different words and phrases to mean the same thing), a broken machine (the "Please Stand By" sign flashed across your television set, a malfunctioning turntable), or the environment (a sparsely furnished room, a dimly lit office).

The important point to remember is that noise can function as a communication barrier. As noise increases, the chances for effective communication usually decrease, and as noise decreases, the chances for effective communication usually rise.

Feedback

Feedback returns information to the sender of a message, thereby enabling the sender to determine whether the message was received or correctly understood. There are four ways of looking at feedback. First, it can be positive or negative. Positive feedback encourages sources to continue sending similar messages; it enhances or reinforces behavior in progress. In contrast, negative feedback discourages sources from encoding similar messages; it inhibits or terminates behavior in progress. Second, feedback can be internal or external. Internal feedback is derived from the sender's subjective perception of the effectiveness of the message sent; external feedback is derived from others who are party to the message exchange. A producer's belief that he has a hit TV show on his hands constitutes one form of internal feedback, while the show's actual ratings constitute one form of external feedback. Third, feedback can be immediate or delayed; and fourth, it can be free or limited. In an immediate and free feedback condition, the reactions of the receiver are directly and freely communicated to and perceived by the source. At a political rally a speaker knows immediately whether the audience in the hall is friendly or unfriendly. In contrast, if you want to communicate your opinion of a newspaper article or television news segment to the editor or the producer, before your views are received by the intended party, printed, or aired, several days or perhaps even weeks might elapse. This lack of direct and immediate feedback is one of the limitations of the traditional mass media.

Feedback serves useful functions for both senders and receivers: it provides senders with the opportunity to measure how they are coming across, and it provides receivers with the opportunity to exert some influence over the communication process. For example, if a receiver lets a sender know that a message was not received or was received incorrectly, the sender can take steps to alleviate the problem; he or she might send it in a different way, in the hope that the changes will facilitate receiver understanding.

Effect

Every communication has an outcome; that is, it has some *effect* on the persons who are a party to it, though the effect may not always be immediately observable. The consequence may be monetary, cognitive, physical, or emotional. For example, people may profit from the communication, or learn something, or alter their appearance or self-image.

Context

Finally, every communication takes place in some *context*, or setting. Sometimes, the context is so natural we fail to notice it; at other times, the context makes such an impression on us that we make a conscious effort to control our behavior because of it. For example, consider the extent to which your behavior would change if you were to move from a park to a political rally, to a movie theater, to

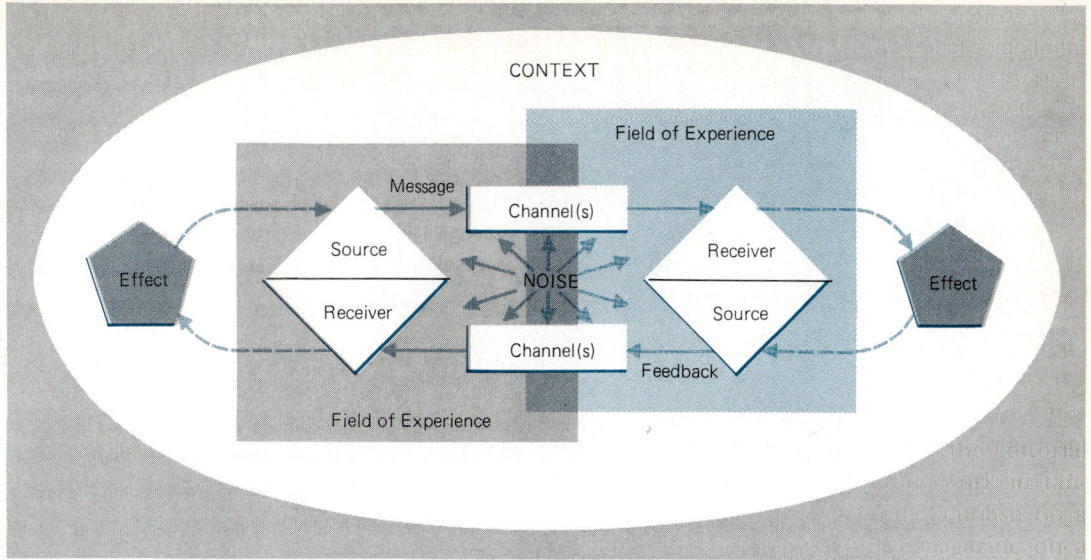

FIGURE 1-1 A model of communication.

a funeral home. Every context provides us with rules or norms for interaction. Take some time to consider how your present setting influences your behavior. In what ways, if at all, would your posture, manner of communicating, or attire change if you were in another setting? Sometimes place, time, and the people with us affect us without our being aware of it.

Figure 1-1 shows how all the elements we have discussed fit together.

Types of Communication

Although all types of communication include the variables pictured in Figure 1-1, the relationship of the variables changes as conditions and circumstances are altered. In this book, we will concentrate on mass communication, but first we must distinguish mass communication from three other types—personal, group, and public communication.

In *personal* communication, one individual communicates with himself or herself (intrapersonal communication) or with one other person (interpersonal communication). Silent conversations with the self (thinking about a movie you saw, planning how to respond to a question posed by your instructor) as well as person-to-person interactions (talking to someone about your job, discussing a new record with a friend) are examples of personal communication. It is as a result of personal communication that most friendships and, eventually, most intimate relationships are formed.

A large portion of our communication time is devoted to interacting in *group* settings. Here, several persons (for example, family members, organizations, or social groups) meet together to share leisure time, converse, solve a problem, or make a decision.

We also find ourselves called upon to speak in *public,* that is, to address others who are part of an audience.

We all participate in personal (one-to-one), group (one-to-few), and public (one-to-many) communication encounters, both as senders and receivers. And in each communication, messages are transferred between sender and receiver either deliberately or accidentally.

But communication in our society has an-

Interpersonal communications are the bedrock of friendships throughout life. (Hazel Hankin)

other dimension to it. It is rich in mass media, which have the power to influence us directly and indirectly, overtly and covertly, on a daily basis. This book is a first step in exploring the role the mass media play in our lives, and to do this, we need to address a number of questions. To what extent do the mass media enhance or impede the three other types of communication we identified? In what ways do the mass media bring us closer together? In what ways do they drive us further apart? How, if at all, do the mass media contribute to the education of our citizenry? How, if at all, do they affect our behavior and the meanings we share? It is the task of students of mass communication to analyze how the mass media influence us and our world, as well as the part we have played and will continue to play in determining and realizing those influences.

DEFINING MASS COMMUNICATION: FOCUSING IN

Mass communication is like the other forms of communication we have mentioned. It involves people, fields of influence, messages, channels, noise, feedback, effect, and context. But it is different from other types of communication in a number of ways.

First, mass communicators rely on technical devices or intermediate transmitters (mechanical or electronic media like newspapers, magazines, radio, television, film, or a combination of these) to disseminate their messages widely and rapidly to scattered audiences. And to some extent, the presence of each different medium changes the nature of the communication act.

Second, mass communicators attempt to share meaning with millions of human beings whom they do not know personally. Consequently, the vastness and anonymity of the mass-communication audience distinguishes it from other types of audience. Mass-communication senders and receivers simply do not really know each other; they merely possess each other's summary statistics. Thus, while we may know that other people are a part of the mass-communication act we are experiencing, we are not privy to what they look like or who they actually are.

Third, the message is public; it is intended to reach and be acceptable to many people.

Fourth, as sources, mass communicators are primarily composed of formal organizations like networks, chains, or conglomerates. In effect, a mass communication is the product not of one individual but of a group—usually a bureaucracy that under most circumstances exists to make a profit.

Fifth, mass communications are controlled by many *gatekeepers*. Whereas in personal, group, or public communication a single person usually controls the message that is transmitted, in mass communication a number of individuals can exercise control over the message that will travel through the mass medium to reach the public. Any person who has the ability to limit or expand, emphasize or deemphasize, interpret or reinterpret the information sent over or received from a mass medium may be thought of as a gatekeeper. Thus, a film editor, a reporter, and a network censor may each perform gatekeeping functions.

Sixth, feedback is more delayed than it is in other types of communication. Reducing the potential for feedback reduces both the sender's and the receiver's ability to know whether the message received was comparable to the message encoded

The modified version of our original model (Figure 1-2) should help you visualize some of the distinctions between communication in general and mass communication in particular.

Despite the differences between them, the mass media have expanded, not destroyed, personal, group, and public communication, for this media environment also serves as a backdrop for all of our other communication relationships. In addition, we are currently witnessing two media transformations: both the mass audience and the mass media are becoming more specialized. Consequently, we presently have a greater choice regarding how many mass audiences we belong to as well as how many of the mass media we use. What we must remember, though, is that each mass audience we belong to shapes us and our relation to society in its own way.

To summarize, mass media are tools, instruments of communication that permit us

FIGURE 1-2 A model of mass communication.

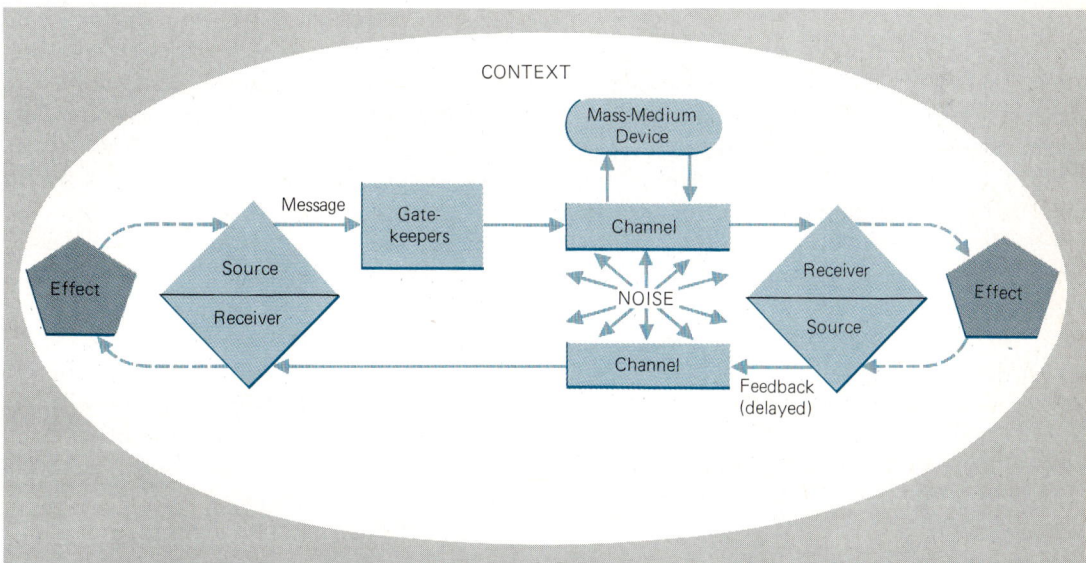

"*Amuse! Entertain! Inform!*"

(Drawing by Vietor, © 1983 *The New Yorker* Magazine, Inc.)

to record and transmit information and experiences rapidly to large, scattered, heterogeneous audiences; as such, they extend our ability to talk to each other by helping us overcome barriers caused by time and space. Because of the mass media we have been able to expand the types of communication that we engage in. Because of the mass media we are now able to transmit messages almost instaneously on a virtually unlimited scale. But a question still remains: Are we using the media wisely?

WHAT THE MASS MEDIA DO

There are a number of ways in which the mass media make daily life easier for us. First, they inform and help us keep a watch on our world; they serve a surveillance function. The media provide us with the news, information, and warning we need to make informed decisions. They gather and pass on information we would be unlikely or unable to obtain on our own. They also inform us about conditions or happenings that they determine could threaten our day-to-day existence. Of course, not all the information provided to us by the media is serious; much of the information they offer focuses on sources of entertainment, the home, fashion tips, or menu suggestions.

By relying on the media to perform the information and surveillance function, we reap benefits as well as risks. To be sure, we do find out things quickly, but the rapidity of the dissemination can itself lead to problems. For example, on January 4, 1984, the following warning went out across the state of Pennsylvania: "The USA is under attack." The warning, intended for use in case of a nuclear war, was relayed to forty-four of Pennsylvania's sixty-seven counties—all because a technician made a mistake while installing a computerized teletype system. Though the alert was canceled within four to five minutes, at least one county had already broadcast the news to the public.[2] Mistakes and distortions travel as quickly as accurate information.

Second, the media set our agendas and help structure our lives. By deciding what stories are given coverage in newspapers and magazines and what programs are aired on radio and television, the mass-media schedule what we talk about and what we think about; in other words, our conversations tend to be media-current. Along with this "selection" aspect, each medium also provides us with a specific perspective on each event. The range of analyses and evaluations we open ourselves to can affect whether or not we will be exposed to differing points of view and whether or not we will be in a position to evaluate all sides of an issue before we ourselves take a position.

Third, the mass media help us to connect with various groups in society. Although we may not get the same pleasure from them as we might get from interacting face-to-face with other human beings, the media do enable us to keep in contact with our politicians, keep a finger on the pulse of public opinion, and align ourselves with others who have the same concerns and interests.

Fourth, the media help to socialize us. Through the mass media we supplement what we have learned about behavior and values in direct encounters with other people. The media show us people in action; their portrayals help us assess what the preferred patterns of behavior and appearance are. By so doing, they teach us norms and values, and they participate in our socialization.

Fifth, the media are used to persuade us and to benefit the originators of messages. For example, advertising and public relations are filled with people whose task is to use the media to further their persuasive goals. Thus, the media provide platforms for idea and product advocates. It is their ability to persuade and sell so effectively that sustains and nourishes most of our media. Let us not forget that the media are predominantly industries that must turn a profit to stay in business.

Sixth, the media entertain. All of the media expend a portion of their energies trying to entertain their audiences. For instance, even though the newspaper is a prime medium of information, it also contains entertainment features; most newspapers offer their readers at least some of the following: comics, a crossword puzzle, games, and horoscopes. Television, motion pictures, recordings, fiction books, and some radio stations and magazines are devoted primarily (though not exclusively) to entertainment. As our free time increases—the typical adult now has almost thirty-four hours a week of leisure time—and people seek relief from boredom, escape from the pressures of daily life, or emotional stimulation and release, the entertainment function served by the mass media will become even more important than it is at the present time.

FUNCTIONS OF THE MEDIA
INFORM! SET AGENDAS! CONNECT! EDUCATE! PERSUADE! ENTERTAIN!

THE ROLE OF THE MASS MEDIA IN YOUR LIFE

We spend a lot of time with some form of mass communication each day and each week (see Figure 1-3). How many hours do you spend with the media?

Most people spend approximately seventeen hours, or one-half of all their leisure time, as well as a portion of their working hours consuming the mass media. They also have very specific media preferences. For example, when 223 college students were asked to rank books, newspapers, magazines, rec-

FIGURE 1-3 Use of media by teenagers. (*Teen-age Research Unlimited, reprinted from USA Today, November 29, 1983.*)

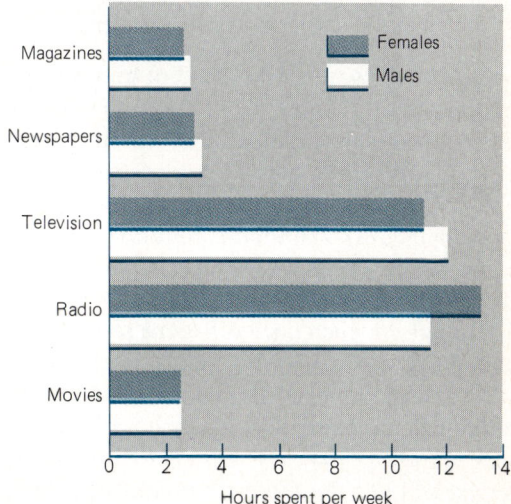

MEDIA PROBE

For the next week, survey your personal media habits. To do this, simply log the amount of time, in fifteen-minute units, you spend consuming each medium identified below. When the week is over, total your consumption units and divide by 4 to determine the number of hours you spend with each of the preceding media. To which medium or media did you devote the most time? the least time? Why do you think this was so? Finally, add the consumption hours together. The figure that results represents the number of hours you spend with the mass media during a typical week.

EXAMPLE

	MON.	TUE.	WED.	THU.	FRI.	SAT.	SUN.	Consumption Units	Hours
Newspapers	II	I	I		I	I	III	9	2 hrs. 15 min.

DAILY LOG

	MON.	TUE.	WED.	THU.	FRI	SAT.	SUN.	Consumption Units	Hours
Newspapers									
Magazines									
Books									
Radio									
Stereo									
Film									
Television									
Video recorder									

TOTAL _____

ords and tapes, television, radio, and movies on a scale of 1 (most liked) through 7 (least liked), the results revealed that the first preference of respondents was records and tapes, while their last preference was newspapers (see Figure 1-4).[3] To what extent do your personal media preferences support or contradict these findings?

Though we each have different media likes and dislikes and use the media in different ways, few of us can claim that we are independent of them. Every now and then, just to assure ourselves that it is we who control the media and not the media that control us, we may declare that we could get along just fine without them. But could we really?

For a moment try to conceive of our society without newspapers, magazines, or books. Imagine what it would be like to have no radio, records, television, movies, or tapes. Our flow of information would be curtailed; our appetite for entertainment would remain unsatiated. Though we may curse the mass media and periodically chant, as they did in the movie *Network*, "We're mad as hell, and we're not going to take it anymore," on the whole we fear being disconnected from the media, and most of us are much happier with

MEDIA PROBE

Some years ago, the British Broadcasting Corporation conducted a test designed to determine if viewers could live without television for a year. On hundred and eighty-four families were paid a fee *not* to use their sets. Despite the monetary incentive, families began dropping out of the study almost immediately; no one stayed with the experiment longer than five months. Researchers agreed that the subjects had suffered withdrawal symptoms similiar to those of drug addicts and alcoholics. Though a similar study conducted in Germany yielded comparable results, a more recent study done in the United States demonstrated that one-third of a Connecticut town's residents could successfully kick the TV habit for one month with little or no side effects.

Unlike the people described above, attempt to cut yourself off not just from television but from *all* mass media for a seventy-two-hour period. If you are successful, explain the steps you had to take. If you find the task impossible, also explain why. Describe how you imagine a media-poor environment would differ from a media-rich one.

---

them than we would be without them. So it is not surprising that, typically, a television set plays six hours and forty-five minutes a day, a radio plays twenty-two hours a week, over 100 million people read some part of a newspaper each day, and we each consume an average of fifteen books a year. Millions of our dollars and millions of our hours are spent on and with the mass media in a twelve-month period. For better or worse, we and the mass media are inextricably linked to each other. Usage patterns and media preferences and habits may change as the times change, but the mass media will remain our companions and an integral part of American life. Consequently, we can expect to be surrounded, immersed, and engulfed by a continual deluge of mass communication.

TheMedia Individual: Influences and Effects

As an individual, you are influenced by the media. Perhaps you can even program your day by them. You may rise to the sounds of music or news on the radio, dress while watching the *Today* show, *Good Morning America,* or CBS *Morning News,* eat breakfast while perusing the morning paper, travel to work while listening to favorite radio stations or tapes, eat lunch while reading a book or magazine, travel home again accompanied by the radio or tapes, eat dinner while listening to or watching the evening news, fill the evening hours and unwind by watching television or going to a movie, and finally fall asleep to the TV, stereo, or radio. But how does all this media consumption affect you?

We all know that the media individual

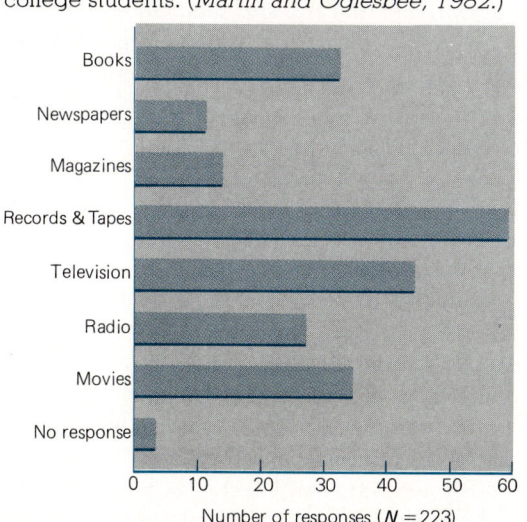

FIGURE 1-4 Media preferences of 223 college students. (*Martin and Oglesbee, 1982.*)

COMMUNICATION, THE MASS MEDIA, AND YOU   13

today differs from the media individual of yesterday. Those born into the age of VCRs are simply different from those born into the age of radio. VCR users, for example, need not structure their lives around the television schedule; they need not be present to tape a program they will view at a later time. The media that provide the fabric of an era also influence and affect the values, attitudes, and lifestyles of the people born into that era. With media technology there is no going backward. Thus, it makes sense for us to understand how the media of our age do what they do: how they reflect or set our priorities, how they alter or amplify our perceptions, and how they shape or modify our consciousness.

The mass media teach, and their lessons are cumulative. The mass media guide us in establishing, extending, or displacing meanings, lead us in approving or disapproving portrayals, and encourage us to reinforce or replace our system of values. Without our stopping to consider why they are such effective instructors, the mass media reveal the world and our place in it to us. Of course, as with any lessons, those offered by the media may be misinterpreted or distorted. Whatever their effects, however, because they help shape our being and our environment, they should never be glossed over or ignored. At the same time that they provide us with information and entertainment, the media also exert their persuasive power, sometimes overtly, but frequently so subtly that we do not consciously realize we are being worked over. For some of us, our immersion in the mass media is total: we come to believe what we have seen and heard and the media world becomes our real world. For others, there are barriers maintained between the real world and the media world, barriers we pass through time and time again. Sometimes we imitate what we see, while other times we reject it, depending on how accepting we are of the information and portrayals offered to us by the media. But because of the large audience to which the mass media are directed, they are still enormously powerful, and they cause critics to take sides. Some critics point to the media as forces that strengthen the character of consumers; others say they weaken them. Some critics say that the media support values; others say that they help erode them. Some citics say the media make our decisions for us; others say they give us the knowledge we need to make them. Whatever your position, it is a fact that today's children spend more time with the mass media than in the company of their own parents or in school. It is also a fact that the mass media are changing the way we behave as human beings.[4] Consequently, we believe it is time to answer the questions How? and To what end?

The Media Society: Pathways to Understanding

This book is about the growth and influence of the mass media in America. The media have become staples of daily life. Almost as necessary to us as food, clothing, and shelter, they help to define us and influence how we relate to our world. In this book we will look briefly at the history of the media, their place in modern society, and the extent to which they affect us all. During the course of our investigations, we will explore the current status of the media and speculate about their future. At all times, our primary aim will be to help you become more intelligent users of the mass media.

SUMMARY

Communication in general and mass communication in particular play significant parts in our lives. Whatever the activities we engage in, we can be certain that communication is playing a role. And whatever the nature of the communicative act, the following components are always present: people (single or multiple senders and receivers); mssages (the content of the communication); channels (message carriers); noise (anything that interferes with the ability to send and/or receive messages); feedback (information returned to the source); effect (communication outcome); and context (the communication setting). Several additional characteristics help to distinguish mass communication from other types of communication: (1) the presence of a technical device or intermediate transmitter; (2) the vastness and anonymity of the audience; (3) the public nature of the message; (4) the presence of a bureaucracy; (5) the presence of multiple gatekeepers; and (6) delayed feedback.

The mass media perform a number of essential functions in our lives. First, they serve an information or surveillance function. Second, they serve an agenda-setting and interpretation function. Third, they help us to create and maintain connections with various groups in society. Fourth, they help to socialize and educate us. Fifth, they persuade us to purchase certain items or accept certain ideas. And sixth, they entertain us.

The number of hours we spend each week consuming the media is mind-boggling. For better or worse, we are inextricably linked to the media. Developing an understanding of that linkage, that is, the interplay between individuals and the media, is a continuing process. This book explores the growth and influence of the mass media in America and in your life. By understanding the media you can become a more intelligent media processer, user, and evaluator.

KEY TERMS

Communication
Mass
   communication
Personal
   communication
Group
   communication
Public
   communication
Sender

Receiver
Field of experience
Message
Channel
Noise
Feedback
Effect
Context
Gatekeeper

NOTES

[1] Ashley Montagu and Floyd Matson, *The Human Connection,* McGraw-Hill, New York, 1979, p vii.
[2] "PA Nuke Alert Was Mistake," *USA Today,* January 5, 1984.
[3] Charles E. Martin and Frank W. Oglesbee, "Television Viewing Habits of College Students," *Feedback,* vol. 23, 1982, pp. 21–24.
[4] Frederick Williams, *The Communication Revolution,* New American Library, New York, 1982, p. 15.

SUGGESTIONS FOR FURTHER READING

Forsdale, Louis: *Perspectives on Communication,* Addison-Wesley, Reading, Mass., 1981. *A highly readable interdisciplinary approach to the study of communication.*

Gamble, Teri, and Michael Gamble: *Communication Works,* Random House, New York, 1984. *Provides an overview of communication environments exclusive of the mass media.*

Klapper, Joseph: *The Effects of Mass Communication,* Free Press, New York, 1960. *Though a quarter of a century old, this resource is still valuable.*

McCombs, Maxwell E., and Lee B. Becker: *Using Mass Communication Theory,* Prentice-Hall, Englewood Cliffs, N.J., 1979. *Pragmatic in approach, this book builds on what we know about the mass media.*

McKenna, George: *Media Voices,* Dushkin, Guilford, Conn., 1982. *Provides a variety of perspectives and viewpoints that can be used as starting points to examine the media.*

Monaco, James: *Media Culture,* Dell, New York, 1978. *An interesting collection of acticles that add up to an insightful guide on the roles the media play in society.*

Schramm, Wilbur: *Men, Women, Messages and Media,* Harper & Row, New York, 1982. *Analyzes human communication from a social science viewpoint; offers the reader an holistic perspective.*

PART TWO

THE PRINT MEDIA: THE WINDOW OPENS

CHAPTER 2

BOOKS: MADE TO LAST

Words may, through the devotion, the skill, the passion and the luck of writers, prove to be the most powerful thing in the world.
                                William Golding

Our young people constitute the greatest resource our country has—and books are the nourishment essential to their intellectual growth into thoughtful and informed citizens.
                                John F. Kennedy

CHAPTER PREVIEW

After reading this chapter, you should be able to:
- Explain the role books play in your life
- Identify and discuss key developments in the history of the book industry
- Discuss the role the bookseller played in the development of the book industry in America
- Assess the extent to which family ownership patterns have influenced the book-publishing industry
- Describe the evolution of copyright laws
- Account for the rise of the best-seller
- Explain why the paperback became a phenomenon
- Draw an organizational chart for a typical publishing company
- Identify the roles played by a typical editorial, production, and promotion department
- Explain how best-seller lists are formulated and how they influence the industry
- Compare and contrast arguments for and against book censorship

What role do books play in your life? Since you are currently a student, books probably are playing a key part in your education. Most likely, you have to purchase at least one book for every course you take;— hence, the book you are now reading. In addition, you probably have found that from time to time you have to consult both school and public libraries in order to obtain information to aid you in preparing papers and presentations. Speaking of the impact libraries have upon us, educator Gilbert Highet observes:

> Sometimes when I stand in a great library . . . and gaze around me at the millions of books, I feel a sober, earnest delight which is hard to convey except by a metaphor. These are not books, lumps of lifeless paper, but MINDS alive on the shelves.
>
> From each of them goes out its own voice, as inaudible as the streams of sound conveyed day and night by electric waves beyond the range of our physical hearing; and just as the touch of a button . . . will fill the room with music, so by taking down one of these volumes and opening it, one can call into range the voice of a man far distant in time and space, and hear him speaking to us mind-to-mind, heart-to-heart.[1]

Libraries open up to us bright worlds of ideas and information (Will McIntyre, Photo Researchers)

Although more than one-third of all books sold are textbooks, to be sure, books are not merely educational tools. Certainly, our education would be a far different experience without books, but for a large percentage of us so would life in general. Thus, in addition to influencing the student population, books also influence the public at large. Clarence Petersen, author of *The Bantam Story*, provides an example of the extent to which books pervade our lives:

> The average reader scurries through the downtown railroad terminal on his way to the 5:41, briefcase tucked under arm, feet aching, and he pauses at the paperback book rack, suddenly transported into a fairyland of bright colors and bold titles. He has not read a book review in five years. Of current literary themes, he is totally innocent. But he has eyes. . . . His hand reaches out tentatively to pick up a volume. Girls in dishabille, airplanes in flames, prisoners in torment . . . famous names, authors and familiar titles whirl before his eyes in a delightful blur. Then he chooses.[2]

Tens of thousands of people make similar choices each day. Some select a hardcover book from a bookstore shelf, some a paperback. Each month millions of readers who belong to various book clubs also select one or more books that will be shipped directly to their homes. Books are a transportable medium. Easy to carry and ready for use on de-

THE PRINT MEDIA: THE WINDOW OPENS

MEDIA PROBE

How many books have you purchased in the last year? _____
What percentage were school-related purchases? _____
What percentage were for leisure reading? _____

How often during the past year did you read a book? _____
How many hours a week did you spend reading books? _____
What percentage of the books you read were paperbound? _____
What do your choices reveal about your wants and needs? If given the option to watch television or read a book, which would you choose, and why?

mand any time, day or night, they also provide us with a convenient means of storing and retrieving information and scheduling escape or personal entertainment.

Despite the competition books face from television, a study conducted for the Book Industry Study Group in October 1983 revealed that more than half of American adults read books, and of these one-third were heavy readers. That is, they read at least one book a week and spend an average of fourteen hours a week reading books. Thus, it was concluded that "in the age of electronic entertainment and personal computers, books are thriving."[3] Yet, the survey also revealed a disturbing trend. It seems that heavy readers are reading more books, while light readers and young readers (aged 16 to 21) are reading fewer. Into which group do you fit?

Today, we tend to take books for granted. However, the book has not always been as accessible as it is now, nor has the book industry been as extensive as it appears to be at present. In order for us to identify how books have influenced us and our society, we must first understand how the book medium came to be, why it grew, and how it works.

HOW BOOKS WERE DEVELOPED

The roots of books extend far back in time, perhaps to the cave paintings of our prehistoric ancestors. By the year 2400 B.C. clay tablets were used to record and store informa-

MEDIA VIEW

99 MILLION OF US ARE BOOK READERS

More than half of us read a book in the past six months, says a survey released . . . by the Book Industry Study Group.

The nonprofit group of publishers, retailers, librarians, and others found in a recent interview with 1,961 people that:

About 99 million of the USA's adults—56 percent—are book readers, about the same as in 1978.
35 percent of them read at least a book a week. In 1978, it was 18 percent.

Source: Barbara Zigli, *USA Today*, April 12, 1984.

63 percent of those ages 16–21 are book readers, down from 75 percent five years ago.
The average person spends 11.7 hours a week reading books and other publications, compared with 16.3 hours watching TV and 16.4 hours listening to radio.
Book readers tend to be female, white, under 50, college-educated, and affluent.

MEDIA SCOPE

1450
Gutenberg uses movable type to print the Bible

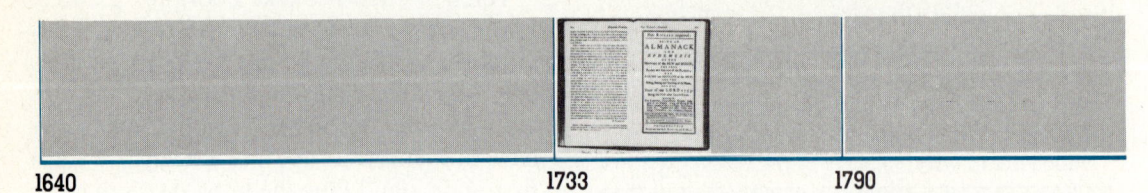

1640
First book printed in American colonies: The Whole Book of Psalmes

1733
Ben Franklin publishes Poor Richard's Almanack

1790
Congress enacts first federal copyright statute

1817
Harper Brothers begin publishing

1850
Beadle's Dime Novels (westerns) appear

1852
Uncle Tom's Cabin becomes one of the best-sellers

1909
McGraw-Hill founded

1913
Prentice-Hall formed

1924
Simon & Schuster established

1924
Book-of-the-Month Club formed

1925
Random House established

1939
Pocket Books begin revolution in American paperback publishing

1960s
Mergers and takeovers proliferate in the industry

1964
First paperback "extra" published: The Report of the Warren Commission

1978
Revision of the copyright law protects works from creation until fifty years after the author's death

1980s
Bookstore chains proliferate in high-density shopping malls

22   THE PRINT MEDIA: THE WINDOW OPENS

tion in Mesopotamia. While some were approximately the size of today's audiocassette, others were very heavy and cumbersome and therefore limited the spread of writing. In ancient Egypt, writing was done not on clay, but on *papyrus*. Smoother and easier to use than clay, and viewed today as the earliest form of paper, papyrus represented a key advance in writing. By the first century A.D., a material made from animal skins called *parchment* replaced papyrus as the chief writing medium. Parchment maintained this position for the next nine centuries, when the pulp of flax replaced it. But not only were innovations in writing of significance; of equal importance were developments in bindings. By the fourth century A.D., the Romans had developed a type of binding called *codex* in which a volume of parchment pages were bound on the left side much as books are today. Using a codex binding a reader could easily look through a book (as you have probably done with this one) rather than having to roll an entire scroll of parchment from one side to the other. This single advance indicated that books might well become an important communication medium. For many centuries, however, no additional significant strides were made. According to book industry analyst John Dessauer, one reason for the lack of progress was that up until the fifteenth century, books had to be transcribed by hand. As Dessauer notes, "religious and secular books then produced, mostly in monasteries, were often duplicated assembly line style with copyists, proofreaders, and illustrators each fulfilling separate, coordinated functions."[4] Thus, the book production process was a slow, arduous, and time-consuming one.

Although the Chinese had developed printing in the ninth century, the foundation of the modern book industry was actually laid in the fifteenth century by Johann Gutenberg, who combined movable type and a wine press to create the first printing system in the Western world. Gutenberg printed a book of masses, *The Constance Missal,* in 1450, and the famous Bible bearing his name in 1456. The idea of printing spread rapidly, and within fifty years over 30,000 books were printed. In 1501, Aldus Manutius designed a book which could be easily carried in a pocket—clearly a forerunner of today's mass-market paperbacks. During this same time period, books written in the vernacular began to replace works in Greek and Latin. Also, typography styles became less ornate, rendering books more readable and more in tune with the simplicity of the common person.

Still, printing procedures continued to be rather slow and cumbersome. It wasn't until 1800 that the French developed a machine that created paper in continuous rolls, thereby eliminating the need to insert sheets one at a time; this sped up the printing process considerably. By 1810 steam-powered presses were introduced; people or horses were no longer needed to turn the presses.

Another milestone occurred in 1884 when

MEDIA VIEW

THE HARPER HORSE

By 1833, the firm [Harper & Row] had installed a steam press, which had just been invented, and the horse who had walked for years in circles around Daniel Treadwell's horsepower press was retired to the Harper's Long Island farm, where he gave a classic demonstration of the conditioning process by walking around a tree in the pasture from seven in the morning until six at night, his usual working hours. When the noon whistle blew at a neighboring factory, he took off his customary lunch hour.

Source: John Tebbel, *A History of Book Publishing in the United States,* vol. 1, Bowker, New York, 1972, p. 275.

the German-born American Ottmar Mergenthaler developed the *Linotype* machine; this innovation meant that type could now be set mechanically instead of being laboriously inserted letter by letter by the printer.

Early American Books

In 1640 the first book was printed in the colonies; in that year the Puritan printer, Stephen Daye, published the *Whole Book of Psalmes* (also called the *Bay Psalm Book*) in Cambridge, Massachusetts. It was not until 1663 that the first American Bible appeared on the scene. Early American printers had to work under rigorous restrictions. Writing in 1671, Sir William Berkeley, the English-appointed governor of Virginia noted: "But I thank God there are no free schools or printing, and I hope we shall not have these hundred years, for learning has brought disobedience and heresy and sects into the world." The loyalties of printers to the crown were maintained through contracts afforded by the printing of sermons and the business of government.

It was the eighteenth century before popular books began to evolve. Between 1733 and 1758, Ben Franklin published *Poor Richard's Almanack*. Using the pseudonym Richard Saunders, Franklin sprinkled the book with humor, weather predictions, suggestions to farmers, and pithy sayings, including the now-well-known "Early to bed and early to rise, makes a man healthy, wealthy, and wise." Since the population at large could not afford to own books, only the elite were able to accumulate private libraries. Thus, books and status went together. Thomas Jefferson's private book collection was so extensive that it was purchased by the United States government in 1815 and became the nucleus of what is now the Library of Congress.

Bookbinding developed as a trade during this period as well. Sometimes done by the printer and sometimes by others, the binding business was a flourishing one. People of the

YOU WERE THERE

THOMAS BREND
BOOKBINDER AND STATIONER

Has for Sale, at his shop at the corner of Dr. Carter's large brick house, Testaments, Spelling Books, Primers, Ruddiman's Rudiments of the Latin Tongue, Watt's Psalms, Blank Books, Quills Sealing-Wax, Pocket Books, and many other articles in The Stationery Way. Old books rebound; and any Gentlemen who have paper by them and want it made into Account Books, may have it done on the shortest notice.

Source: Sign at Colonial Williamsburg

day often needed their Bibles rebound so that they could be passed down the family line from one generation to another. Continuity was important since births and deaths were often recorded in the family Bible, making it the major repository of a family's history. Business records in the form of ledgers were also bound for easy access and safekeeping.

Booksellers Become Publishers

Although many American publishers got their start as booksellers, they soon found it lucrative to combine the publishing and bookselling operations into one. In other words, they published books and also operated bookstores, so that the books they published had a ready market. The development of the book industry, as described by historian Luke White, was "characterized by greed, ruthlessness and small heed to the fundmental decencies of civilized business relations."[5] In time, however, the period of rapid and chaotic expansion ended, and the industry shed this image and replaced it with a facade of gentility.

Most publishing houses began as small family concerns, and their names still reflect this heritage. For example, we still have McGraw-

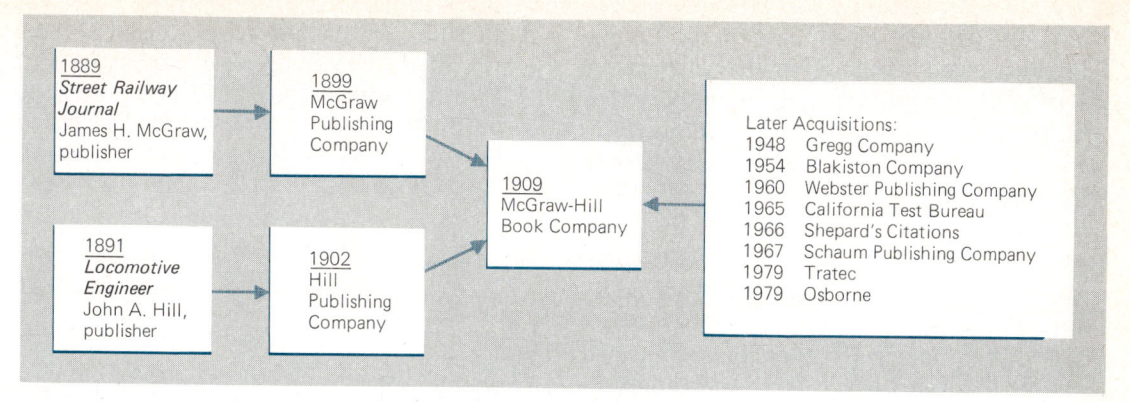

```
1889                1899
Street Railway      McGraw
Journal             Publishing
James H. McGraw,    Company
publisher                          1909            Later Acquisitions:
                                   McGraw-Hill     1948  Gregg Company
                                   Book Company    1954  Blakiston Company
                                                   1960  Webster Publishing Company
                                                   1965  California Test Bureau
1891                1902                           1966  Shepard's Citations
Locomotive          Hill                           1967  Schaum Publishing Company
Engineer            Publishing                     1979  Tratec
John A. Hill,       Company                        1979  Osborne
publisher
```

FIGURE 2-1 McGraw-Hill Book Company and its acquisitions. McGraw-Hill was formed by the merger of two independent publishing houses in 1909. A flip of the coin determined whose name would come first: James H. McGraw won; John A. Hill became president of the new company. In 1948 the company began to acquire other smaller publishing houses.

Hill, Harper & Row, and Charles Scribner's Sons, just to name a few. Let's briefly examine the origins of several of the nineteenth-century book companies that are still in existence today.

In the early years of the nineteenth century, bookseller Charles Wiley founded a publishing company, now called John Wiley & Sons. Charles had a back room in his bookshop which attracted many writers of the day, including notables such as William Cullen Bryant and James Fenimore Cooper. Wiley had met Cooper while on a sales trip and later published three of his books. While these books had done well, they had not made either man wealthy. In 1826 as Wiley lay dying, Cooper published his fourth novel—*The Last of the Mohicans*—with another publisher. The firm started by Charles Wiley was taken over by his son John; through the years it has been operated by a succession of Wiley family members.

John and James Harper began publishing in 1817. Joining them by 1825 were their brothers Wesley and Fletcher, and the firm's name was changed to Harper & Brothers. People would ask, "Who is the Harper?" The acceptable response was, "Any one of us is Mr. Harper, and all the rest are brothers." By the end of the Civil War, five sons of the original brothers were members of the firm as well.

Alfred Smith Barnes established the first publishing house to be run primarily as an educational endeavor. A. S. Barnes and Company chose to sell directly to teachers rather than to schoolbook agents, and by the end of the Civil War, their books were widely used; one series of math books sold over 5 million copies. Other New York publishers included Moses Dodd (now Dodd, Mead), Charles Scribner (Charles Scribner's Sons), and Edward Dutton (E. P. Dutton & Company). Similar family publishing operations were run in Philadelphia, Boston, and other cities.

The Copyright Laws and Book Piracy

Article 1, section 8, of the U.S. Constitution lays the foundation for copyright laws by stipulating that Congress shall have power "to promote the progress of science and useful arts, by securing for limited times to authors and inventors the exclusive right to their respective writings and discoveries." Although several states passed *copyright laws,* it was not until 1790 that the second session of the first Congress passed "an act for the encouragement of learning by securing copies of maps, charts, and books, to the authors and proprietors of such copies, during the times therein mentioned." Congress went on to give copyright to writers for a maximum of fourteen years. In time this was changed to twenty-eight years—fourteen years plus an additional fourteen years if the copyright was renewed. Then in 1901 another copyright act extended protection to fifty-six years—twenty-eight years plus a renewal period of twenty-eight years. The present law, in effect since January 1, 1978, protects an author's work during his or her lifetime and for half a century after his or her death.

Although the Copyright Act of 1790 protected the rights of American writers, it did not protect materials previously published outside of the United States. Consequently, American publishers found that it was quite lucrative to be the first to pirate books published in other countries. England became the prime target. According to historian John Tebbel, one such act of piracy involved the Philadelphia publishers Lea and Blanchard, who sent an advance copy of a new book called *Rienzi* over from England.

> Unfortunately, the ship that brought it carried a copy of the book destined for Harper and Brothers in New York, the Philadelphia company's chief rival. In a race to capture the New York market first, Lea and Blanchard rushed their copy to Philadelphia, distributed the sheets among a dozen printers, operated their presses all night, and had the reprinted sheets ready for the bindery by nine o'clock the next morning. Binding cases for the volumes had already been made and were waiting. By afternoon, Abraham Hart, another member of the firm, was on his way to New York in a mail stage in which he had hired every seat. He sat on only one; the others were fully occupied by five hunded copies of *Rienzi*.[6]

Persistence paid off for Lea and Blanchard; their book reached New York booksellers one day ahead of the version that Harper had pirated.

As we shall see, piracy met its demise because American publishers themselves finally demanded that the U.S. government forbid such tactics. The issue came to a head in 1842 when Charles Dickens began a lecture tour in which he demanded that America adhere to an international copyright law. Americans were slow to react; they enjoyed paying cheap prices for pirated British novels. By the 1860s, however, because war taxes had driven up production costs in this country, cheap British novels were being imported to America instead of being reprinted here. Then, in 1877, the Canadian government passed laws which made it possible for Canadian publishers to ship pirated American books into this country. And by 1884, Joseph Harper was chairing a copyright committee of publishers supporting international copyright protection. Finally, in 1891, President Benjamin Harrison signed a bill into law that allowed foreign authors to obtain copyright protection in this country. However, the issue was not actually fully resolved until 1955 when the United States finally joined the *Universal Copyright Convention*.

THE BIRTH OF THE POPULAR BOOK

The nineteenth century saw books emerge as a popular medium. By the end of the century, 90 percent of Americans were literate; thus, a truly mass audience for books existed for the first time. A major contributor to the de-

MEDIA PROBE

What do you think of copyright laws? In your opinion, should protection of a work have a time limit placed upon it, or should works be protected in perpetuity?

velopment of this mass market were McGuffey's *Readers*—a series of texts which taught generations of Americans how to read. One hundred and twenty-two of the readers were circulated, each carrying a moral message to the child. Other books like this excerpt from *Schoolmaster's Assistant,* first published in 1744, relied on riddles to teach math: "A farmer with a fox, a goose and a bag of corn has to cross a river in a boat so small that he can take only two of these three burdens with him at a time. How can he so handle matters that nothing will be destroyed, because he cannot leave the fox and the goose together, nor can he leave the goose and the corn."

Quick printing and cheap paper also helped to precipitate the popular book phenomenon by paving the way for the dime novel. No longer devoted exclusively to the classical liberal arts, these new works contained tales of adventure, romance, the wild west, and success; they now joined philosophy, science, and religion books on bookshelves. By the end of the century, a new ethic had taken hold: people would publish books only if they met a popularity criterion.

One of the early best-sellers, and a book which had tremendous social impact, was Harriet Beecher Stowe's *Uncle Tom's Cabin*. Published first in magazine serial form, and then as a two-volume novel in 1852, this work influenced contemporary thinking about slavery. Historian Philip Van Doren notes: "*Uncle Tom's Cabin* struck the world with explosive force. Its timing was just right, and it became not merely one of the greatest bestsellers, but a social document which influenced public opinion everywhere—even, in fact, in the South, where it had a clandestine circulation because its sale was forbidden there."[7] Later, the Uncle Tom story became the basis for plays enacted by theater troupes which toured the country. It was performed in the style of the "old-fashioned mellerdrama," with the audience cheering heros and hissing the villain.

Dime Novels

By 1850, publisher E. F. Beadle began publishing Beadle's Dime Novels. These books emphasized action and were often set in the west. During this same period, Horatio Alger (1834–1899) wrote 120 books, which sold 30 million copies. His books were rags-to-riches tales, stories of people who, because of hard labor and persistence, were able to attain success. The self-made individual theme is one tradition which has continued to this day—even though Alger stories, for the most part, have ceased to be read.

Best-Sellers

Between 1873 and the end of the nineteenth century, home libraries made up of books similar to today's Modern Library editions became an American phenomenon. Anxious to get on the home-library train, many American and British writers began to create "best-sellers," and writer fan clubs not unlike those devoted to today's rock stars began to spring up. Robert Browning and Rudyard Kipling were among those writers honored with fan clubs. In fact, Kipling created quite a "literary fever" among his 1890s "groupies" when he became ill and had to be rushed to a New York hospital, where fans thought he lay near death. In order to contain the crowd, officials had "the busy street roped off outside so traffic would not disturb him."[8] In addition, his doctors issued hourly bulletins. Suddenly, to the dismay of all the assembled fans, Kipling recovered and returned home. The public was so outraged that sales of his books dropped considerably! They never did forgive him for not passing on.

The best-seller list of the period spoke to the interests of a broad spectrum of the public. One book, nearly forgotten today, was *Trilby* by George du Maurier. Set in Paris, the book chronicles an Irish girl's adventures. The girl, Trilby, meets an evil hypnotist, Svengali, and creates something of a stir when she

BOOKS: MADE TO LAST 27

poses nude for student artists. Du Maurier's *Trilby* became as much a national phenomenon as Stowe's *Uncle Tom's Cabin.* Soon Trilby songs, circuses, plays, shoes (Trilby had beautiful feet), and even sausages became the rage.

The 1890s also saw the introduction of literary factories—organizations which existed to create novels almost by mass production. John Tebbel describes the process:

> Girls and women comprised most of the thirty or so employees of the factory... and "for the most part these girls were intelligent." They read all the daily and weekly periodicals in the country, bought by the pound from junk dealers. Any unusual stories of city life, especially those concerning the misdoings of city people, were marked by the girls and turned over to one of three male managers. The managers took the best of those submitted and turned them over to a corps of five women, who digested the accounts and made an outline for a story. Outlines were given to the chief manager, who distributed them to a list of a hundred or more writers entered in a large address book. A blank form that went with the outline read: "To _____ : Please make of the enclosed material a _____ part story, not to exceed _____ words for each part. Delivery of copy must be by _____ at the latest. A check for _____ will be sent to you upon receipt of manuscript. Notify us at once whether you can carry out this commission for us."[9]

Apparently, it didn't matter where authors found their material as long as what they wrote was popular with the masses. What was important was that dramatic and startling situations abound; two or three murders and a rescue or two in a single chapter was quite common.

THE MODERN BOOK INDUSTRY

The following comments were voiced at an annual convention of the American Booksellers Association:

> Shops and libraries... are crowded with publications whose value is of the very slightest, whose influence is positively harmful.... Books as they come from the press are in fact becoming what newspapers and magazines have always been—publications whose terms of life are ephemeral. They exist as the favorites of a week or a month, possibly the favorites of a year.[10]

Do you agree? Are bookstores filled with books which go out of style quickly only to be replaced by new fads? Do we discard some books almost as rapidly as we discard magazines? The preceding criticism could well have been written today, but in fact it was uttered in the year 1900. The point is that the book industry has stayed strangely the same. Even early comments made concerning book readership have a familiar ring. V. M. Schenck, a Massachusetts bookstore owner, made these satiric comments at the 1913 meeting of the ABA:

> The booksellers have a serious complaint. They say that people don't read books anymore.... Who has time to read books nowadays? Do our legislators read books? Can they teach our rulers in authority anything they didn't know before? Molders of public opinion may write books, but read them? Never![11]

More similarities can be found between the book industry then and now. First, as was true in earlier times, descendants of the original founders of the book industry still control many our publishing houses. Nelson Doubleday, for example, heads the Doubleday publishing house. Second, historian John Tebbel notes: "Computers may have been introduced to shipping and billing procedures, but there are still two major seasons for selling books, *royalties* are still paid twice a year, distribution problems are substantially the same and much else remains unchanged."[12]

The book industry has survived two world wars. During the first, many books were deemed to be inappropriate reading material for soldiers in the trenches, while others,

Bookstores are stocked with publications that themselves often have brief life spans. (Gabor Densen, Stock, Boston)

such as the novels of Zane Grey, flourished. Hundreds of thousands of books were sent to soldiers in a program sponsored by General Pershing and the American Library Association. Both before and after the war, new publishing houses were born: McGraw-Hill (1909), Prentice-Hall (1913), Simon & Schuster (1924), and Random House (1925), to name some of the major ones that still thrive today. And, as was the practice during the nineteenth century, these publishing houses were established by individuals, not faceless corporations. Among the major figures in the field were Bennett Cerf (Random House), Alfred Knopf, Richard Simon, and Max Schuster.

In his book *At Random,* Bennett Cerf describes the informal beginnings of Random House—an informality that characterized a number of the publishing houses of the day. Cerf recalls that he and his partner Donald Klopfer had been publishers of the Modern Library editions, a reprint series, but had been planning to expand into publishing originals as well. One day, commercial artist Rockwell Kent dropped in at the office. Cerf writes:

> He was sitting at my desk facing Donald, and we were talking about doing a few books on the side, when suddenly I got an inspiration and said, "I've got the name for our publishing-house. We just said we were going to publish a few books on the side at random. Let's call it Random House.
>
> Donald liked it, and Rockwell Kent said, "That's a great name. I'll draw your trademark." So, sitting at my desk, he took a piece of paper and in five minutes drew Random House, which has been our colophon ever since."[13]

Random House, of course, grew to be anything but a publisher-at-random. The name, however, survives to this day.

The Industry since World War II

Although book sales suffered during the years of the depression, they rebounded as the nation entered World War II. Once

YOU WERE THERE

BUSINESS AT RANDOM

In his book *At Random,* Bennett Cerf cites his dealings with the Book-of-the-Monh Club to illustrate the nature of "the gentlemanly profession" to which he belonged.

When a book club makes a selection it agree to pay, on each copy it distributes, a royalty that is always divided equally between the author and the publisher. It also guarantees to pay an advance against the sale of a specified number of books, and that advance is not returnable even if the club doesn't sell that many. If it sells more, of course, the royalty is paid on each additional copy.

At the time the Book-of-the-Month Club was quite young and small, and the guarantee for a selection was five thousand dollars, which was very little compared to what the club now pays. But when we got that check for the first trade book we published, we were delighted.

About a week later the Book-of-the-Month Club met in executive session, and we received a letter from Harry Scherman telling us that they had decided to raise their guarantee—to double it. And since our book had been selected only a week before, they felt that we shouldn't be shortchanged, so they were enclosing a check for an additional five thousand. Well, Donald and I thought about this for a while, and I wrote back: "Dear Mr. Scherman: This is really a fantastic thing to happen, and it renews one's faith in human nature. But I must tell you that if you had cut your guarantee from $5,000 to $2,500, I'm damned if I would have given you back $2,500. We made a deal at $5,000, and I must tell you we were so delighted we closed the office for the day. So with tears streaming down my cheeks, I am returning your check for $5,000."

Well, they were pleased with the letter, and the check came back with an admonition that we shouldn't be damn fools, but should cash it. And again we sent it back saying, "This is not businesslike at all." So we all decided we'd better meet for lunch—Harry Scherman, Robert Haas, Donald and I. By this time there was great mutual respect, and when that lunch was over we had become friends for life—all of us—and we finally settled on seventy-five hundred dollars, splitting the difference down the middle and everybody was happy about it.

Everybody was being decent, and when people are decent, things work out for everybody. That has been my theory all through life. If you're making money, let the other fellow make it, too. If somebody's getting hurt, it's bad, but if you can work a thing out so that everybody profits, that's the ideal business.

Source: Bennett Cerf, *At Random: The Reminiscences of Bennett Cerf,* Random House, New York, 1977, pp. 72–74.

---

again, the book industry shipped paperback "armed forces editions" of books to American soldiers stationed here and abroad. The war itself, followed by the aftermath of servicemen returning to college, and the baby boom had a tremendous economic impact on the book industry. Prior to the war, the industry fueled a relatively small part of the economy. After the war, however, the industry began to grow at a rate of 10 percent a year. In 1945, the industry was grossing $293 million. By 1980, gross sales exceeded $6.6 billion.

As the industry blossomed it became more and more attractive from an investment point of view. During the 1960s, mergers and takeovers began to proliferate. Publishers became public corporations. Random House merged with Alfred Knopf and Pantheon, only to then be purchased by RCA. The company has since been sold again. Holt, Rinehart & Winston became a subsidiary of CBS. Xerox purchased both Ginn and Company and R. R. Bowker. The list goes on and on; thus, today most major publishing houses are subsidiaries of other corporations. Mergers have had two primary effects. First, they have compelled the companies to develop orderly management systems, including budgeting, forecasting, and planning systems common to most industries but lacking to that point in the family-style publishing houses. Second, and perhaps less fortunately, the mergers have brought many non-book-publishing people into the business. Consequently, publishing decisions typically reflect the "bottom line" mentality that dominates American business in general. Yet, even with the upsurge it has experienced, the book industry remains to this day but a small part of the American economy. In *The Book Industry in Transition,* Benjamin Compaine points out that in 1976 the $4.2 billion in publisher's receipts for the entire industry would place it only forty-first on the Fortune list of the nation's largest industries. Still, the prestige factor inherent in books makes the industry's importance extend far beyond the photocopy and tire industries that precede it on the list.[14]

The Paperback Phenomenon

When Pocket Books inaugurated the modern American paperback book revolution in 1939, the concept on which they sought to capitalize was not really a new one. Actually, it dated back to colonial times, when sermons and government documents were bound between soft covers. The trend continued, and during the first half of the nineteenth century some newspapers also began inserting unbound books in the papers in order to avoid paying the higher postal fees on books. Also during the second half of this century, dime novels experienced a surge in popularity.

Later in the century, cheap libraries composed of reprints of pirated titles were in vogue—that is, until the copyright laws were changed. Then in the twentieth century, England's Penguin Books captured a corner of the mass market by being the first company to market hardcover reprints in more affordable paperback editions.

Robert Fair deGraff, a publisher who had been witness to the successes of Penguin Books in England, launched Pocket Books in association with Simon & Schuster. Soon all paperbacks were referred to as *pocket books* irrespective of their actual imprints. During World War II, Pocket Books alone shipped some 25 million softcover books overseas. In the years immediately following the war, the market became quite competitive: Bantam, Avon, New American Library, Signet, Berkley, Ace, and others sought to obtain a piece of the action. Today, many mass-market paperbacks are still reprints leased from the hardcover publisher for a five-to seven-year period. In addition, many paperback publishers now also print originals—paperback books which have never appeared in hardcover.

For example, let's briefly examine the phenomenon of the romance novel. According to *Forbes* magazine in 1982 these "bodice-ripper" paperbacks yielded $250 million in annual sales. Harlequin puts the figure somewhat higher at $493 million. Whichever figure is right, it has been estimated that if just the Harlequin books sold in a single day were stacked one on top of the other, the pile would be sixteen times as high as New York City's World Trade Center. Approximately half of the paperbacks sold in this country are romances. One reader has been quoted as saying, "I don't smoke. I don't drink. I don't play golf. If I want to buy romance novels, I owe it to myself. It's a cheap way to forget your problems."

Writing romances pays handsomely. *Forbes* did a survey in 1982 which estimated the author's income from one of these books at

BOOKS: MADE TO LAST 31

MEDIA PROBE

The following passage parodies the style of the romance. What do you think of it?

> John selected a grapefruit, delicately exploring its luscious roundness with the tips of his fingers. Then he thrust his paring knife deep into the grapefruit once, then again, then again and again and again, until finally, suddenly, he stopped, satisfied that the grapefruit was properly sliced. Lighting a cigarette, he looked over at Jessica. "That was marvelous, John," she sighed.

Source: Dave Barry, "To Cook Up Best Seller, Use Equal Portions of Diet and Sex," *The Record*, January 16, 1983, pp. C1, C8.

Next, examine an actual romance novel. How can you explain the appeal of such a book?

$30,000. Many writers generate ten books a year. Why do they sell so well? The formula "boy meets girl, boy loses girl, boy and girl are reunited" is an old one, but one that contemporary romance writers have capitalized on. An interesting mix of sensuality and sweetness, violence and gentleness, and past and present settings, the genre offers a wide choice to its readers. Although readers of romances are predominantly women, men read them as well.

Paperback books are distinguished from hardbacks as much by their printing and distribution systems as by their soft covers. It was the high-speed and rubber-plate rotary presses that made paperback mass production a reality. Clarence Petersen, book editor for the *Chicago Tribune*, described one such machine:

> The Strachan and Henshaw printing press is one of man's mightiest works, as big as a house, its flanks festooned with decks and ladders so the pressmen can clamber about it and poke at its innards.... When ready to work, the rubber printing plates are fastened in place, the web of paper is threaded down and around and over and under, the fountains are full of ink which descends through pipes from a tank high overhead, the pressman pushes the button on the control console, and the press begins to roll, slowly at first, with a subdued clop-clop-clop from the cutting mechanism. As it gathers speed, the roar increases and the clopping of the cutter runs together in a continuous blast.[15]

Papers go through the press at 1200 feet per minute. Bantam alone uses 1800 tons of paper per month.

Printing a large number of books—several hundred thousand in one printing—is one thing. Selling those books is quite another! Distribution is a problem for hard-and soft-cover books alike, but it is especially critical for the paperback publisher. Part of the publisher's problem is the vast number of books being produced. In 1980, for example, mass-market publishers printed an average of 423 titles per month.[16] From these 423 titles, owners of the nation's 90,000 outlets needed to fill but 70 to 100 available spaces, or pockets, making the choice of which books to select a challenge.

In addition to choosing new titles, outlet owners also try to save pocket space for backlist best-sellers, which they know move reasonably well. Each fall as the school year starts, they also reserve additional space for reference items like dictionaries and thesauruses. Thus, space is one major problem which the industry has not yet been able to solve. More than 500 independent wholesalers exist to stock the nation's newsstands. Many of these are magazine operators who handle paperbacks on the side. Consequently, just as unsold magazines are returned for full credit, so are unsold paperbacks. Inefficiency appears to reign. The immediate space problem is solved by the shredding machine. Shredders automatically rip covers off books. The covers are then sent back to the publisher for full credit, while the denuded books themselves are turned into confetti. As Roger Smith observes, "For one who loves books, it is a painful sight."[17]

Long-range waste problems have also gone unsolved. While computers have been used to keep better records regarding how many books are available and where they are in the distribution system, an effective means of forecasting consumer demand still does not exist. Projections that are made are simply not accurate. Still, most publishers prefer having too many books on the racks than too few. Smith notes: "Mass market paperbacking is an industry populated by incurable optimists."[18] All are hoping for a big seller; in paperback publishing one best seller is the only way to offset the many books that make marginal profits or none at all.

Paperback Extras! Having an established tradition of working with magazine and newspaper distributors, it was only a matter of time before paperback publishers would try to publish "instant books"—works almost as timely as newspapers and magazines. The first *paperback extra* was produced in 1964 when Bantam published the *Report of the Warren Commission on the Assassination of President Kennedy* only eighty hours after the original document was released to the public. Freed from federal hands at 9 A.M. on Friday, September 25, the document was immediately flown to New York. Petersen recounts: "Most of Friday afternoon was devoted to copy fitting pages, estimating length and size of type. Not until 9 P.M. did eleven linotype machines begin setting the text, a job that continued for twenty-one hours. Galleys were proofed, read and corrected, then fit into page forms and corrected again by twenty-four proofreaders, some hired especially for the project, working in three shifts."[19] The presses were rolling in Chicago by Monday morning, producing 1200 books per hour; by 5:30 the next morning, books were already being shipped.

MEDIA PROBE

Imagine that you run one of the nation's 90,000 paperback book outlets—perhaps a newsstand or drugstore. What criteria would you use to select books to fill your store's 70 to 100 "pockets"? Keep in mind that it is highly unlikely that you would have an opportunity to read the books prior to selecting them.

The resulting 1.5 million copy sale was so successful that other companies began publishing instant books as well. Over the next decade, Bantam alone published fifty-six paperback extras, including *The White House Transcripts* some six days after the Nixon version of the White House tapes was released, and *The End of the Presidency,* a book which followed immediately upon the heels of Nixon's resignation. What extras have you noticed on newsstands recently?

THE PUBLISHING PROCESS

It is a given that books do not magically appear on bookstore shelves, in magazine racks, in grocery stores, or at your home via the mail on their own. A system had to be developed to get them there. In a preceding section of this chapter we looked briefly at the paperback book. Let us now examine the entire industry, concentrating on how it is organized, how it operates, and where its machinery needs oiling.

How Book Publishers Are Organized

Book publishers vary greatly in size and form. Some houses publish only one or two books a year—operating what is, in effect, a mom-and-pop business with headquarters in a basement. Major publishers, however, turn out hundreds, and sometimes thousands, of

BOOKS: MADE TO LAST 33

YOU WERE THERE

EXTRA! EXTRA!

Following is a chronology of an "extra"—the edited Watergate tapes that Bantam published under the title, *The White House Transcripts.*

April 29, 1974. President Nixon tells the nation that he is releasing the edited tape transcripts.

April 30. The transcripts, a 1308-page document, are issued by the Government Printing Office.

May 2. Bantam announces that it will publish the transcripts as a paperback, in collaboration with the *New York Times.* (Dell, on the same day, announces that it, too, will publish a paperback edition, with the *Washington Post* as collaborator.)

That afternoon, 1300 pages of copy for Bantam's edition arrive at the W.F. Hall Printing Company's Diversey Avenue plant in Chicago. Hall has already scheduled overtime shifts. Bantam has notified Hall, which prints most of Bantam's books, that paperbacks already in production can be set aside for the Watergate Tapes paperback.

By Delta Airlines jet, Hall sends the copy to the typesetter, the E.T. Lowe Publishing Company in Nashville. An hour after the copy arrives, it is being set by four tape-driven Teletype linecasters and five manual linotypes.

May 4. At 4 A.M., Lowe finishes setting the transcripts' more than 250,000 words. All the type proofs have been read twice by a team of seven proofreaders. The typesetters pause to await arrival of the book's introduction by R.W. Apple of the *New York Times,* and other editorial material from New York.

At 9 A.M., Ray Little, Bantam's vice-president for production, arrives in Nashville.

At 6 P.M., Bantam editors Judy Knipe and Jean Highland arrive in Nashville with the remaining copy. In Chicago, mechanicals for the cover arrive at Regensteiner Press.

May 5. By early morning, typesetting is completed. Lowe starts making up page forms. Bantam editors supervise last-minute changes and OK page proofs. Lowe begins making the first of 148 six-page bakelite molds.

In Chicago, Regensteiner completes separations for the cover. Plates are made in the evening.

May 6. The first group of molds is finished, but there will be no commercial jet to Chicago until tomorrow. A private jet is chartered and takes off from Nashville at 8 P.M. with the first molds. The jet makes a round trip, returning to Nashville to pick up Little, the two editors and the rest of the molds.

May 7. The jet lands in Chicago shortly after midnight. The molds are rushed to Hall's Diversey plant, where last-minute typesetting and mold preparation are completed. In eight hours, four men and two machines turn out the book's rubber plates—an average of 110 plates an hour. Hall rushes the rubber plates to its Normandy Avenue plant. (This plant produces an average of 1.5 million paperbacks every 24 hours, five days a week.)

Between 1 A.M. and 4 A.M., Regensteiner prints the covers—32-up—on a four-color, 77-inch Miehle offset press. Covers are shipped to Hall, where they are varnished and cut apart.

The rubber molds are mounted on Mylar sheets, and the sheets are wrapped around the cylinders of most of Hall's two-unit Strachan & Henshaw flexographic presses. Each press prints two-up 32-page signatures, or 128 separate pages. The plates go on the presses at 8 A.M. The first books come off the Sheridan patent-binding lines at 6 P.M.

Source: Roger M. Smith, *Paperback Parnassus,* Westview Press, Boulder, Colo, 1976, pp. 62–63.

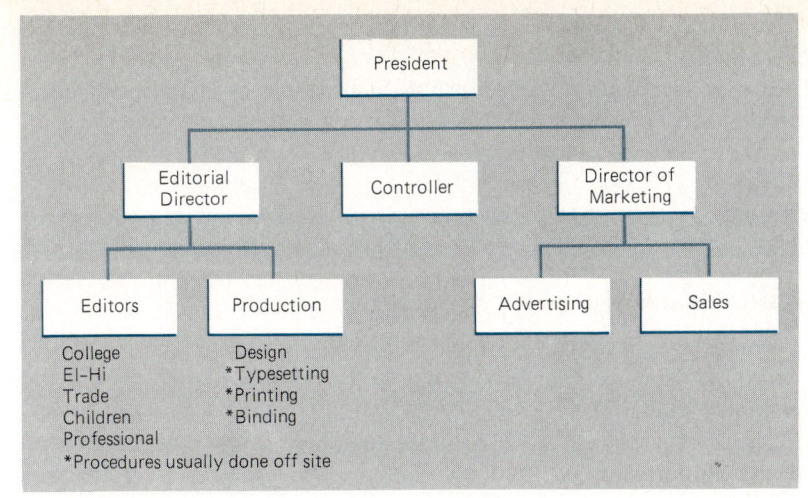

FIGURE 2-2
Organization chart of a typical publishing house.

books each year, books that are targeted to meet the needs and wants of different markets.

A ride up the building elevator of a major New York publishing house like Holt, Random House, or McGraw-Hill reveals part of the book story. One floor is most likely devoted to the college department, another to the elementary–high school (ElHi) department. Trade books and children's books probably occupy a floor or two, while other floors may be devoted to accounting, personnel, and executive offices. Thus, a typical company's organizational chart might well resemble the one depicted in Figure 2-2.

Although the topic areas may overlap somewhat, books are generally categorized as either trade, educational, or professional in nature. *Trade books* are sold primarily through public bookstores, though they are also frequently marketed through book clubs. Contained in the trade category are works of fiction and nonfiction, including how-to books, self-help books, and children's books, as well as religion and reference works. Reference books and encyclopedias are also often sold door-to-door. Educational books comprise approximately 30 percent of the publishing field. College texts like the one you are now reading, texts for grades K–12, and professional books, which will be marketed to doctors, lawyers, managers, etc., are included in the educational book category. While textbooks are usually sold in college bookstores or directly to school systems, professional books are traditionally sold via direct mail or through trade bookstores; professional books are also usually priced somewhat higher than other types of books.

The Editorial Department

Someone has to make the decision whether or not to publish a book. To be sure, an author (if he or she has the money) can contract directly with a printer to self-publish, but most do not. Instead, most authors leave it to major publishing houses to publish their works for them. The procedure starts with an editor or a team of editors, often called acquiring editors. According to editor and publisher John Farrar, these editors are very special people:

> Many editors, even the most scholarly, read widely and with catholicity of taste. They must if they are to keep their jobs. They are aware of fads and fancies as well as world events, politics and philosophies. Editorial departments watch

BOOKS: MADE TO LAST   35

for good writers wherever they appear. They read other publishers' books and catalogues. They read newspapers and magazines—all sorts of magazines. They follow the theatre, the radio and television. They must follow, too, not only creative writing but critical writing, and watch closely the publications of their own trade, the reviews, the book announcements.[20]

MEDIA VIEW

THE TEXTBOOK-PUBLISHING PROCESS

Most people are aware of the textbook only as a finished product. The chart in Figure 2-3 chronicles a text's development.

In 1982 the idea for the text you are reading was born. How long did the publishing process take? To find out take a look at the copyright date listed in this book's front cover.

FIGURE 2-3 Typical process by which a grade school or high school textbook is produced. The complete process, from conceptualization to preparation of a revision, can take several years. (*Adapted from the School Division of the Association of American Publishers.*)

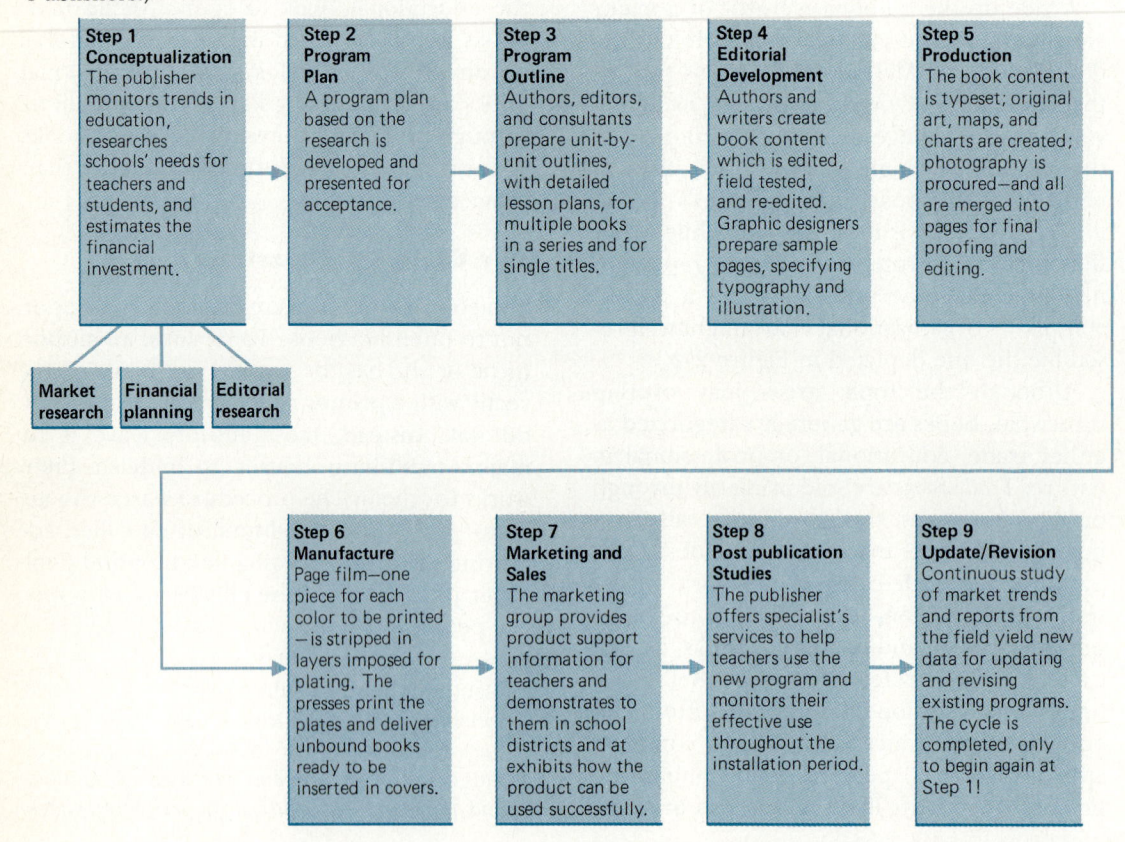

Step 1 Conceptualization
The publisher monitors trends in education, researches schools' needs for teachers and students, and estimates the financial investment.
- Market research
- Financial planning
- Editorial research

Step 2 Program Plan
A program plan based on the research is developed and presented for acceptance.

Step 3 Program Outline
Authors, editors, and consultants prepare unit-by-unit outlines, with detailed lesson plans, for multiple books in a series and for single titles.

Step 4 Editorial Development
Authors and writers create book content which is edited, field tested, and re-edited. Graphic designers prepare sample pages, specifying typography and illustration.

Step 5 Production
The book content is typeset; original art, maps, and charts are created; photography is procured—and all are merged into pages for final proofing and editing.

Step 6 Manufacture
Page film—one piece for each color to be printed—is stripped in layers imposed for plating. The presses print the plates and deliver unbound books ready to be inserted in covers.

Step 7 Marketing and Sales
The marketing group provides product support information for teachers and demonstrates to them in school districts and at exhibits how the product can be used successfully.

Step 8 Post publication Studies
The publisher offers specialist's services to help teachers use the new program and monitors their effective use throughout the installation period.

Step 9 Update/Revision
Continuous study of market trends and reports from the field yield new data for updating and revising existing programs. The cycle is completed, only to begin again at Step 1!

MEDIA PROBE

THE NOVELIST OF TODAY AS SEEN BY KURT VONNEGUT

I am a member of what I believe to be the last recognizable generation of full-time, life-time American novelists. We appear to be standing more or less in a row. It was the Great Depression which made us similarly edgy and watchful. It was World War II which lined us up so nicely, whether we were men or women, whether we were ever in uniform or not. It was an era of romantic anarchy in publishing which gave us money and mentors, willy-nilly, when we were young—while we learned our craft. Words printed on pages were still the principal form of long-distance communication and stored information in America when we were young.

No more.

Nor are there many publishers and editors and agents left who are eager to find some way to get money and other forms of encouragement to young writers who write as clumsily as members of my literary generation did when we started out. The wild and wonderful and expensive guess was made back then that we might acquire some wisdom and learn how to write halfway decently bye and bye. Writers were needed that much back then.

It was an amusing and instructive time for writers—for hundreds of them.

Television wrecked the short-story branch of the industry, and now accountants and business school graduates dominate book publishing. They feel that money spent on someone's first novel is good money down a rat hole. They are right. It almost always is.

So, as I say, I think I belong to America's last generation of novelists. Novelists will come one by one from now on, not in seeming families, and will perhaps write only one or two novels, and let it go at that. Many will have inherited or married money.

Source: Kurt Vonnegut, *Palm Sunday*, Delacorte Press, New York 1981.

In your opinion, is Vonnegut right in saying that the publishing industry is no longer able to support the development of novelists? If so, how will this affect the reading public? The viewing public? Do you think the writing of novels should be left to the idle rich? Why or why not?

Many authors send unsolicited manuscripts—or "over the transom"—to such editors. While the acceptance rate of unsolicited manuscripts is small for trade works, it is larger for texts. Trade authors have a much better chance of having their manuscript published if they submit it to the acquisitions editor through a literary agent. It is the literary agent's job to seek out authors, select manuscripts, help authors fine-tune their proposals to suit the demands of the marketplace, and submit them to an editor or editors. Editors usually take about thirty days to respond positively or negatively. If the response is positive, the agent also serves as the liaison between author and publisher during contract negotiations. He or she negotiates royalty rates, the size of the advance against royalties, and subsidiary rights packages, including television and film sales. The agent also orchestrates the auctions that are used to sign books by famous authors, personalities, or political figures. When such an auction is held, the agent submits the proposal or manuscript to several publishers, and on a given day, each publisher is given the opportunity to bid via the telephone for the right to publish that particular work.

Most publishing contracts award a 10 percent royalty rate to the author, although some authors do command more than that, When the paperback rights of a hardcover

YOU WERE THERE

MAX PERKINS

Maxwell Evarts Perkins was unknown to the general public, but to people in the world of books he was a major figure, a kind of hero. For he was the consummate editor. As a young man he had discovered great new talents—such as F. Scott Fitzgerald, Ernest Hemingway, and Thomas Wolfe—and had staked his career on them, defying the established tastes of the earlier generation and revolutionizing American literature. He had been associated with one firm, Charles Scribner's Sons, for thirty-six years, and during this time, no editor at any house even approached his record for finding gifted authors and getting them into print. . . .

His literary judgment was original and exceedingly astute, and he was famous for his ability to inspire an author to produce the best that was in him or her. More a friend to his authors than a taskmaster, he aided them in every way. He helped them structure their books, if help was needed; thought up titles, invented plots; he served as psychoanalyst, lovelorn adviser, marriage counselor, career manager, money-lender. Few editors before him had done so much work on manuscripts, yet he was always faithful to his credo, "The book belongs to the author.". . .

Partly because Perkins was the preeminent editor of his day, partly because many of his authors were celebrities, and partly because Perkins himself was somewhat eccentric, innumerable legends had sprung up about him, most of them rooted in truth. . . . It was said that Perkins had agreed to publish Ernest Hemingway's first novel, *The Sun Also Rises,* sight unseen, then had to fight to keep his job when the manuscript arrived because it contained off-color language. . . .

Perkins had never spoken to a group like this before. Every year he received dozens of invitations, but he turned them all down. . . . He believed that book editors should remain invisible; public recognition of them, he felt, might undermine readers' faith in writers and writers' confidence in themselves. . . .

Hooking his thumbs comfortably into the armholes of his waistcoat, speaking in his slightly rasping, well-bred voice, Perkins began. "The first thing you must remember," he said, without quite facing his audience, "an editor does not add to a book. At best he serves as a handmaiden to an author. Don't ever get to feeling important about yourself, because an

Authors have to be published to be famous. Maxwell Perkins, the eminent editor at Charles Scribner's Sons, discovered talents such as F. Scott Fitzgerald, Ernest Hemingway, and Thomas Wolfe. (Charles Scribner and Sons)

editor at most releases energy. He creates nothing." Perkins admitted that he had suggested books to authors who had no ideas of their own at the moment, but he maintained that such works were usually below their best, though they were sometimes financially and even critically successful. "A writer's best work," he said, "comes entirely from himself." He warned the students against any effort by an editor to inject his own point of view into a writer's work or to try to make him something other than what he is. "The process is so simple," he said. "If you have a Mark Twain, don't try to make him into a Shakespeare or make a Shakespeare into a Mark Twain. Because in the end an editor can get only as much out of an author as the author has in him."

Source: A. Scott Berg, *Max Perkins: Editor of Genius*, E. P. Dutton, New York, 1978, pp. 3–7

---

book are sold, the standard split is 50-50 for author and publisher; the Author's League, however, suggests that a graduated scale, which would split the payment 70–30 in the author's favor would be more equitable.

John Dessauer notes that once a contract is signed, the editor's job is to "work with an author to help him or her achieve the best organization, the most appropriate emphasis, the right tone, the optimal length, and the proper slant for the work."[21] In other words, the editor's job is to shape the work. Copy editors are hired to insure that appropriate punctuation and grammar are used. Dessauer emphasizes, "Nowhere is the essential midwifery of publishing more apparent than at the point where the editor must literally inhabit an author's soul and whisper as though from within, seeing the subject with the author's eyes and hearing the cadences of language with the author's ears."[22] One of the most famous examples of such a relationship was the one between editor Maxwell Perkins and novelist Thomas Wolfe.

Many stories about Perkins concerned the untamed writing and temperament of Wolfe. It was said that as Wolfe wrote *Of Time and the River* he leaned his 6-foot, 6-inch frame against his refrigerator and used the appliance's top or a desk, casting each completed page into a wooden crate without even reading it. Eventually, it was said, three husky men carted the heavily laden box to Perkins, who somehow shaped the outpouring into books.

Production

The production process follows the editorial process (though at times they work in tandem). While a newspaper may publish on a daily or weekly basis, and a magazine on a weekly, biweekly, or monthly basis, a book often takes months or even years to produce. Why is book production so time-consuming? What differentiates most books from magazines and newspapers?

Magazines or newspapers usually trim most of their stories to fit standard layouts or designs. *Time* magazine, for example, always has the same cover design with a new photo or drawing inserted into it. Newspapers always use the same layout, type size, etc. At least to some degree, however, books are individually designed. Books begin with an author's manuscript. In other words, with books the design emerges from the content. John Dessauer describes what he perceives to be the "cumbersome" steps involved in the book production process.

> The process begins with the designing of the book and, often, the ordering of sample pages from the compositor. The design must be reviewed and approved, decisions must be made regarding processes and suppliers, and a definite schedule must be prepared. This schedule will allow for the time needed to set the text and prepare any missing illustrations, for first proofs to be read by editors and author, for corrections to be made by the compositor, for final proofs

to be read by editors and author, and for the index to be prepared. Only then can reproduction proofs be furnished. Negatives and plates need to be made, arrangements for paper must be completed, all before the presses can roll. Press time itself is not always easy to come by, particularly if one has in mind to use certain equipment, and there are long waiting lists for some presses. Finally, books must be bound and jacketed.[23]

Although space does not allow us to explore the entire production process in detail, let's examine two key components in the process; typography and printing. The most common typeface available to the book designer is a variation of that used by the ancient Romans. Roman letters are distinguished by their cross strokes at the ends of lines. These are known as *serifs*.

serif

The second most frequently used typeface does not have the serif and thus is referred to as *sans serif,* that is, without the serif.

sans serif

Because the serif style is considered easier to read, it is the one used in the body of a text. Sans serif type, in contrast, is used for headlines and headings, Take a moment to examine the book you are reading. What typefaces did the designer use?

Originally, type was set by hand, one letter at a time. Today, however, much of this work is performed by a computer. The actual printing of the book may be accomplished in one of three ways: letterpress, offset, or gravure. In a *letterpress,* ink is applied to a raised surface, which then contacts the paper. Plastic or rubber plates usually provide the forms for this type of printing. *Offset printing* is a photographic process employed by most publishers, with the exception of mass-market paperback publishers. The *gravure* process is usually reserved for art books and other heavily illustrated volumes.

Color separations are necessary if color photographs and artwork is to be included in a book. That is, cameras equipped with red, green, or blue filters photograph the original art in order to extract the primary colors from them. In essence, a series of dots are used to blend the colors together during the printing process itself. Careful coordination between photographer and printer is necessary to insure that the final product contains an appropriate color balance. This process is expensive. Thus, it is not surprising that many books are printed in only one or two colors; this one, for example, is printed in two colors of ink with a full-color cover. You will notice that all photographs in the text itself are black-and-white.

Selection of appropriate paper is another key step in the printing process. There are three basic types of paper usually used: groundwood, free-sheet, and rag-content. The *groundwood paper* is used for mass-market paperbacks. It is of comparatvely low quality and tends to turn brown. *Free-sheets* are "free" of the less desirable impurities found in groundwood; they are also treated to last longer. Free-sheet paper is used in hardcover trade editions. *Rag-content paper* is quite expensive and used primarily in Bibles.

The actual binding of a book may occur as the pages come off the press, or the pages may be sent to another location. Most papers will not fold well if the sheet contains more than thirty-two pages. Thus, the average *signature* is a small booklet composed of thirty-two pages or less. The thirty-two pages are then either sewn together and bound in a hard cover or glued together and bound with a soft cover in what is called "perfect" binding. Before the cover is placed on the book, the edges of pages are cut to make them fit the specified trim size.

As you can see, the production process for a book is quite an involved one. Adding to the

Author tours are a time-honored book promotion technique. Here Harlem photographer James van der Zee autographs his book for a young admirer. (Ann McQueen, Stock, Boston)

complexity of producing a book with either simple or complex design features are the demands of the various printers' unions, equipment maintenance problems, delivery schedules, plant locations, and the possibility of human error.

Book Promotion

How to successfully promote a book is a problem which the industry has yet to solve to its satisfaction. Most trade books are promoted by author tours during which the author whistle-stops from city to city, making appearances in a number of bookstores (for autograph hours) and on a variety of local radio and television talk shows. Though such methods yield success, they also frequently present problems. Dan Green, publisher of Simon & Schuster, recalls that many years ago when he was employed as a publicist he flew from New York to Chicago to meet an author from California, whom he had booked to appear on a TV talk show. "The writer and I were so dumb. . . . We both forgot to change our watches and we didn't meet one another." Some time later, Green had scheduled Jessica Mitford, author of *The American Way of Death,* to appear on a Cleveland show, which to his dismay turned out to be not an adult but a children's program.[24] Even today books often arrive at bookstores after the author has left a city. Such complications occur despite the fact that publicity departments have grown in size in recent years. Esther Margolis, former publicity director at Bantam notes: "When I went to Bantam in November 1962, the entire promotion department was five people. When I left in 1980, there were five departments, 35 people, and a $3.5 million budget!"[25]

Talk show producers—always on the lookout for potential show topics like exercise, diet fads, or other self-help–related items—now attend the American Booksellers Association meeting in droves. Once there, they research both nonfiction and fiction offerings with an eye toward booking the authors for

"I know a lot of people will say 'Oh, no—not another book about cats.'"

(Drawing by Leo Cullum, © 1983 *The New Yorker* Magazine, Inc.)

upcoming programs. Fiction writers who are less well known than name personalities like Truman Capote or Gore Vidal are more difficult to book. But the author tour has become a staple of the industry; in fact, it is so much a part of the book business that publicity escort services exist in many cities just to fill the function of transporting traveling authors from program to program. By the way, it should be noted that one appearance on *The Phil Donahue Show* alone can sell as many as 50,000 book copies.

Although television and radio advertising are used to market books, most marketing efforts are directed toward purchasing newspaper advertising space and obtaining book review coverage. The influence of book reviews on sales is noteworthy; hence, publishers do what they can to have their books reviewed in pretigious publications like *The New York Times* and *Publishers Weekly* in addition to local publications. Getting on a best-seller list is perceived to be so critical to a book's success that tales abound of motion picture companies buying up hundreds of copies of those books for which they have purchased film rights. Individual authors work to sell their books as well. Wayne Dyer, the pop psychologist, is reported to have filled a van with his first self-help book and driven cross-country, personally marketing them to bookstores in towns where he was to appear on talk shows.

The timing of a book's publication is another factor affecting whether or not it will make "the list." If few major authors are coming out with books during a particular time period, a book with a printing of 25,000 copies might well make the list. Stuart Applebaum, director of publicity for Bantam Books calls the lists, "more of a barometer than a thermometer." By that Applebaum means that the lists tend to show trends in book publishing rather than providing a precise accounting of the number of copies sold during any given week.

Of late, writers and publishers have used contests to promote books. The novel *Who*

MEDIA VIEW

THE PUBLICITY ESCORT

Tired of your humdrum existence? Want to meet fascinating people and make some extra money? If you own a car, the book publishing and gossip industries have a job for you. The nation's radio and television stations would have terrible trouble filling up their air time without the unpaid assistance of hundreds of authors who regularly turn up, coats brushed, tails wagging and tongues hanging out, to do the tricks that sell their books. . . .

There are a handful of bona fide professionals in the publicity escort business, and they are worth more than the publishers pay them. Detroit's Paul Stewart, a husky man in his late 20's, started doing publicity after he was laid off the Chrysler assembly line at the height of the recession.

While driving part-time for a limousine company, Mr. Stewart noticed that most of his passengers were authors. "I'd see them," he said, "appearing on absolutely the wrong shows for their books, like the author of some serious history on a talk show with an audience that's only interested in astrology. And I thought, well, I can give the publishers everything a limousine service can and maybe some sensible advice besides."

Mr. Stewart did indeed know everything about the media in Detroit; he shook his head sadly when a television host made an escape without mentioning the title of my book. "I've warned the people in New York about that show," he said, "but they don't listen. They only look at the size of the audience." He is also buying a limousine from his profits to insure that no author will be stuck on the freeway in the middle of a midwinter snowstorm.

Source: Susan Jacoby, "The Publicity Escort: New Job in the Lit Biz," *The New York Times Book Review,* May 13, 1984, p. 32.

MEDIA VIEW

HOW THE BEST-SELLER LISTS ARE MADE

While the major national best-seller lists—appearing in *The New York Times, Publishers Weekly* and *Time*—are often similar, they almost never are exactly the same because the three use different methods of gathering information.

'TIME'

No independent bookstores are polled by *Time* magazine, says Sharon Lauver, who helps compile the computerized list. "We call several chains of bookstores and get exact figures, so we deal in number of books sold." But, because the chains deal mainly in titles with mass appeal, any book that sells well in independent stores but isn't bought by the chains probably won't make the list.

'THE NEW YORK TIMES BOOK REVIEW'

The New York Times has an elaborate—and controversial—system for compiling its best-seller list. Although the paper refuses to confirm it, insiders say that each week, about 2,000 bookstores around the USA receive a printed list of 36 titles, including those already on the paper's best-seller list and others it considers leading contenders.

Booksellers are asked to fill in the number of

each title sold for that week, and there is space at the bottom to include books not on the list. Chains such as B. Dalton Bookseller, with 680 stores, and Waldenbooks, with 819 of its 850 stores reporting, make their own best-seller lists based on computerized sales records and pass their information along to *The Times* to be factored in with information from the independents.

'PUBLISHERS WEEKLY'

Publishers Weekly contacts "more than 1,600 bookstore outlets," including independently owned stores in major cities and chain stores and asks for the top five to 15 best-selling books in order, says senior editor Daisy Marylas. "We don't give the booksellers a preconceived list of titles."

Stores are given a point value so that smaller stores carry less weight than the large chains, such as B. Dalton or Waldenbooks. "But, we don't want to give (the chains) so much weight that a book that just sells there can make the list.

"It's not an exact science, far from it. It's a reflection of what's selling best, not a reflection of what's selling in order. I would say the top five are the top five. The bottom ones might be in a different order."

Source: Anita Manning, "Blatty and the Brouhaha over the Best-Seller List," *USA Today*, Sept. 13, 1983, p. 6D.

Which of these methods seems fairest to you? Why? If you were a bookstore owner, what method would you rely on to target best-sellers? Would your answer change if you viewed the question from the publisher's perspective? Why or why not?

YOU WERE THERE

CREATING BEST-SELLERS

Making a best-seller in today's crowded publishing field—where just one-third of new titles return any profit at all—is an art and a science, with little guarantee of success. "Unless you're publishing a brand name, especially in fiction, there's no way to predict how it will do," says Simon and Schuster publisher Dan Green.

Best-seller status is just the first link in a profit chain that includes lucrative paperback contracts, mega-bucks TV miniseries and movie sales. The selling of *The Warlord* by Malcom Bosse demonstrates the levers publishers can pull to get the most out of a book they believe has best-seller potential.

Bosse's novel was tagged for success from the time Simon and Schuster senior editor Herman Gollob saw the first half of the manuscript in April 1982. "I started to read the damn thing and I couldn't believe how good it was," he recalls. "I had that feeling of exultation."

Gollob raved about *The Warlord* to his boss Green, who told him to calm down, took the manuscript to read during his vacation—and came back convinced the editor was right. The mission was clear.

"We had to sell it in the house, in the industry and in the street," recalls Green. As at many publishing houses, major decisions at Simon and Schuster are made by a marketing committee that includes the publisher, top editors and heads of sales, marketing and subsidiary rights departments. After the committee gave the go-ahead, Simon and Schuster allocated $150,000 for a "major promotional effort"—one of the few mounted each year. That was a supreme vote of confidence: Promotion budgets for most books (if there is one) run from $5,000 to $20,000, say industry sources.

Then Frank Metz, Simon and Schuster Vice President and director of art and design, was called in to oversee *Warlord's* cover.... The final choice: an eyegrabbing Chinese axe on a blood-red background. "If a cover is well-designed, it has a life of its own," explains Metz.

The promotion budget was put to work:

Simon and Schuster printed 2,500 slick paper, soft-cover "special reading copies" instead of the bound galleys normally sent to industry mouths—reviewers and book sellers whose good words about *The Warlord* could stimulate sales.

A presskit touting "an extraordinary novel... designed to become a popular classic" went out with a letter from Bosse, a map of China and personal notes from Simon and Schuster executives.

A two-page spread in *The New York Times Book Review* (cost $20,688.50) was taken out.

By publication day, the book had been chosen as a Main Selection of the Book-of-the-Month Club by a literary board acting on recommendations from staff editors and free-lance readers, and it had won a rave review in *Publishers Weekly,* the industry trade journal.

Simon and Schuster ordered a first printing of 80,000—"an enormous number for an author without a record of blockbusters," admits Green; novels by authors without strong sales histories commonly get print orders of 5,000 to 10,000 copies....

Some believe a major promotional campaign helps a few good books at the expense of others. "The fixation on the best seller is one of the weaknesses of the publishing industry," says publishing consultant Leonard Shatzkin.

Source: Joel Dreyfuss, "Publishers Push Books and Pray," *USA Today,* June 17, 1983.

Killed the Robins Family, created by Bill Adler and written by Thomas Chastain, was a mystery with a gimmick: it contained no solution. Instead, the book promised a $10,000 reward for the reader who solved the murders of the eight members of the Robins clan. The solution, kept in the United States Safety Deposit Corporation in Manhattan, was not removed until May 28, 1984, when the winner of the contest was announced at the annual convention of the American Booksellers Association in Washington, D.C. The play propelled the book to a number of best-seller lists. Other writers and publishers have since devised other types of contests. For example, one book contained clues to the whereabouts of a buried treasure; another had no title—it was left to readers to come up with the title but without using words.

MEDIA PROBE

Bill Adler said of the book he created (*Who Killed the Robins Family*) "There's so much boredom, what with people spending their time watching TV and playing video games. This is a good book.... It's going to be fun for people." In your opinion, is the book contest fad going to continue? What type of individual do you think will be attracted to such ploys? Do you believe it will enhance or detract from the quality of books? Why?

BOOK CENSORSHIP

Czechoslovakian dissident Milan Simecka has written that there are countries where you can "go to a public library and borrow any book you want."[26] Do you think that this is the case in the United States? Have you ever been formally restricted from reading certain works? Journalist Richard Bernstein notes: "Censorship in our age may appear, at first,

MEDIA PROBE

LITERARY TARGETS

Here are the ten books most frequently targeted for censorship.

1. Catcher in the Rye, J.D. Salinger
2. Go Ask Alice, Anonymous
3. Of Mice and Men, John Steinbeck
4. The Grapes of Wrath, John Steinbeck
5. 1984, George Orwell
6. Lord of the Flies, William Golding
7. Forever, Judy Blume
8. Our Bodies, Ourselves, The Boston Women's Health Book Collective
9. The Adventures of Huckleberry Finn, Mark Twain
10. To Kill a Mockingbird, Harper Lee

Source: National Council of Teachers of English
Do you feel there are valid reasons for banning any of these books? What possible rationale do you believe individuals might use to justify making such decisions?

---

to have lost its element of controversy. It would probably be difficult to find respectable figures from any part of the political spectrum proclaiming support for censorship—except in the single area of pornography, which many in this country believe goes beyond the boundaries of what should be legally permissible."[27] It takes little courage for politicians of today to support freedom of expression openly. Additionally, both the American Library Association and the Association of American Publishers have developed a freedom-to-read statement, which contains the following pronouncement: "It is in the public interest for publishers and librarians to make available the widest diversity of views and expressions, including those which are unorthodox or unpopular with the public." Yet, *censorship,* though not as severe as the kind found in some countries, does exist in the United States.

USA Today reports that between the years 1980 and 1984, censorship complaints increased from 300 per year to almost 1000 per year.[28] *FOI,* a publication of the Society of Professional Journalists, also comments: "Censors are building a Library of Condemned Books that may soon become the world's fastest-growing but unused collection."[29] Efforts to censor books occur in a fifth of our nation's schools each year—and half succeed. In one two-year period alone—between 1982 and 1983—there were twenty-two book burnings in seventeen states.[30]

How does book banning affect the publishing industry? If limited in scope, censorship can actually have a boomerang effect; that is, it can result in increasing interest in a book. During the nineteenth century, *The Adventures of Huckleberry Finn* was banned by a New England library because it was thought to be littered with faulty grammar and to be of low moral quality. Mark Twain responded to this action by noting that it would probably insure the sale of 25,000 copies. More recently, attempts at government suppression of works like *The Pentagon Papers* have resulted in increased public attention being given to them. This is not to suggest that censorship is a positive phenomenon. It is not.

Books are attacked by a variety of different groups. The Moral Majority and other New Right groups are often targeted as being the most diligent censors. But they are not alone. In fact, one famous example of book censorship is attributed not to such groups but to college professors:

On April 1, 1950, Macmillan published Immanuel Velikovsky's *Worlds in Collision,* a book that attempted to explain the origins of the universe by references to the Old Testament, world literature and ancient mythology. Widely condemned by the scientific community, the book nevertheless soared onto the *New York Times* best-seller list, where it remained for 31 weeks. Yet two months after publication, at the height of its popularity, Macmillan literally gave the lucrative Velikovsky title to Doubleday without cost and dismissed the editor who had signed up the book. Moreover, Gordon A. Atwarer, who wrote an article praising the author's approach, even while disagreeing with many of his conclusions, was summarily dismissed as chairman of the astronomy department of the American Museum of Natural History and as curator of the Hayden Planetarium. The reason? An influential group of scientists, led by the late Harlow Shapley of the Harvard College Observatory, were so enraged by what they considered the "crackpot" ideas of Dr. Velikovsky, who was a psychoanalyst, that they threatened to boycott Macmillan's textbook department unless the company ceased publishing the book. Since textbooks accounted for some 60 percent of the besieged company's sales, Macmillan executives decided to give the book to a publisher that did not have a textbook department and could not therefore be pressured by academics.[31]

Does it surprise you that teachers and scientists would pressure a publisher to suppress ideas with which they do not agree? Would you ever behave similarly?

It should also be noted that censorship is not always instigated from outside the book-publishing field. In 1983, William Morris, editor of the first edition of *The American Heritage Dictionary* warned an audience at Harvard University Graduate School: "Beware of a new dimension of censorship: censorship inside the publisher's office, hidden censorship that only authors, editors, and, the ultimate control, the sales department, know about. This may well be more insidious and more dangerous than all the censors put together."[32] One example of Morris's fears occurred that same year when Dodd, Mead canceled two novels after its parent publisher, Thomas Nelson (the world's largest publisher of Bibles), noted that it considered some of the language contained in them to be inappropriate.[33] To do this, Nelson broke a contract.

One of the more highly debated questions regarding censorship is that of censorship of school books. The policies of the state of Texas are central to this controversy. Even though its $66 million textbook-buying budget comprises but 6 percent of the national market, Texas has sufficient clout to demand changes in texts. *USA Today* notes: "Texas has enough buying power to tell publishers 'Change the book or we won't buy it.' In most cases, publishers don't fight back."[34] In Texas, it is the state legislature that oversees textbook adoptions. When a book is adopted in Texas, it is adopted statewide. In other words, the state has to give its approval before school districts can purchase books. Getting a book adopted in Texas has been compared to receiving a license to go hunting. In each subject area, five publishers receive formal state approval to market their books to school districts. Not making the list precludes a publisher's right to do this. Consequently, having a book "approved" is critical from the publisher's perspective. Today, state adoption practices are in effect in some twenty-two states.

Texas is not alone in limiting access to certain books. In 1984, the Associated Press reported that the schoolboard in Lindenwald, New Jersey "has voted to limit access to three books it considers inappropriate for some children—one about an overweight youngster and the others dealing with divorce and family relations."[35] To be sure, the list of similar book casualties is a lengthy one. For example, journalist Christine Moore notes:

—John Wallace, a black administrator at the Mark Twain Intermediate School in Fairfax County, Va., is revising "Huckleberry Finn" to

BOOKS: MADE TO LAST 47

Its textbooks largely determine what a nation becomes and where it goes. (Erika Stone, Photo Researchers)

delete "offensive racist" remarks and predicts that his new version will someday supplant Mark Twain's original.

—In a Baton Rough, La. suburb, evangelists burned "Satanic" material that included the books "Cinderella" and "Snow White" and the records of Olivia Newton John. . . .

—After claiming credit for the defeat of the ERA, Phyllis Schlafly announced her Eagle Forum would devote itself to purifying school textbooks of feminist influences. In St. David, Arizona, the group succeeded in removing works by Conrad, Hawthorne, Hemingway, Homer, Poe and Steinbeck from required reading lists.[36]

Besides affecting texts and novels, censorship also affects dictionaries and references works. In 1982, for example, the Texas Education Agency demanded that a "short" list of forty-one words be deleted from *Webster's New World Dictionary*. Writing about this occurrence, reporter Nat Hentoff states: "At issue were definitions of such words as: ass, ball, bed (the verb), cunnilingus, fag, horny, hot, piece, queer, rubber, screw. You know, the kind of talk that goes on when the President and the National Security Council get together."[37] Although Simon & Schuster refused to amend the dictionary, there are reports that such actions have been taken by other dictionary publishers in order that their works might qualify for adoption.

To an extent, the school censorship issue has been transformed into an annual confrontation between Mel and Norma Gabler, who head the organization Educational Research in Texas, and Norman Lear's organization, People for the American Way, a group founded to fight censorship. Mel Gabler traditionally sets the stage for the discussions by noting: "The kind of textbooks we have largely determine what a nation becomes and where it goes."[38] At the state textbook committee hearings both public interest groups receive six minutes to discuss the merits of proposed books. Commenting on his work, Gabler states:

> Contrary to what our critics claim, we have no control over the textbook selection process in Texas or in any other state. All we want, all we've been working for over the past 22 years, is to let the public see what's in textbooks. . . . And every time we reveal what's in the textbooks they holler at us for censoring. . . . When they do it they call it constructive input; when we do it they call it censorship.
>
> This year we concentrated on world history. . . . We were concerned with world history because we wanted to make sure that besides the problems of capitalism, the books emphasized the problems of socialism and Marxism as well. . . .
>
> In the past, we also sought more balance in the teaching of man's origins, between creationism and evolution. In all areas textbooks are becoming better balanced.[39]

Is there any way to resolve the censorship issue? Ultimately, the courts will make a determination—as will the marketplace. Professor Morris Freedman of the University of

MEDIA PROBE

In your opinion should textbooks be revised so that they present a "balanced" treatment of content, or is this practice itself a form of censorship? Before answering, consider these statements:

"My money is purchasing these textbooks and my grandchild will use them, so I have a right to do this." (Norma Gabler, Educational Research analyst)

"The Gablers are not content to decide what their children should read and study; they want to decide what your children read and study in public schools." (Barbara Parker, People for the American Way)

"I feel the Gablers are doing a great service. They're ferreting out slang, vulgarities, and also things that are unpatriotic." (Paul Mathews, Texas Board of Education)

"Textbook critics . . . perceive the planet and government and all of humankind in one particular way, and they want to impose that on all children." (Edward Jenkinson, author of *Censors in the Classroom*)

"Censorship, like charity, should begin at home, but, unlike charity, it should end there." (Clare Booth Luce, American diplomat)

Now, where do you stand on the issue of textbook censorship?

Maryland, and himself a textbook author, suggested in an article in *The Christian Science Monitor*: "Politically sensitive committees should not shape the nature of textbooks. Responsible professionals should—the specialists who write or edit them, the teachers who use them. The free market of democratic education will determine the sound and successful titles." Freedman argues that "when Germany banned Jewish science and Jewish scientists, it lost the atom bomb and much of its cultural heritage. Soviet citizens remain puzzled and ignorant about the real world, because their textbooks and news media exaggerate socialist achievements and capitalist failures."[40] In a 1982 Supreme Court decision (*Pico v. Island Trees Board of Education*) Associate Justice William Brennan, Jr., argued for access to ideas, an access that "prepares students for active and effective participation in the pluralistic, often contentious society in which they will soon be adult members." The debate over which approach best prepares students for participation in society is sure to continue.

As we hope you now realize, the book, or "TV of the mind," as Librarian of Congress Daniel Boorstin calls it, is a vital medium of mass communication. More than 38,500 new book titles are published each year. As Clarence Day wrote, "The world of books is the most remarkable creation of man. Nothing else that he builds ever lasts. Monuments fall; nations perish; civilizations grow old and die out; and, after an era of darkness, new races build others. But in the world of books are volumes that have seen this happen again and again, and yet live on, still young, still as fresh as the day they were written, still telling men's hearts of the hearts of men centuries dead."[41]

MEDIA PROBE

Examine our discussion of textbook censorship. Do you believe it was well-balanced? Would you favor deleting any of the ideas presented here? Are there others that we have failed to include which could tend to sway the argument one way or the other? In other words, do you think that any portion of our discussion of this issue should be censored? Why or why not?

BOOKS: MADE TO LAST

SUMMARY

Today, books play a part in the lives of most literate Americans. It was not always this way, however. Although writing extends far back in history, it wasn't until the eighteenth century that popular books began to evolve. In addition, in contrast to other mass media, most book-publishing operations started as family-run concerns. Not until the 1960s did corporate America perceive book publishing as a real investment opportunity. Today, while the names of many of the family-run businesses remain, publishing houses are more likely than not to be subsidiaries of large conglomerates.

The road traveled by books and their authors has never been a particularly smooth one. For example, through the years unfair copyright laws and pirating problems have plagued the industry. So has the need to create best-sellers. The blockbuster book on the shelf in today's local bookstore traces its heritage back to dime novels and works like *Uncle Tom's Cabin*. And, although paperback books have long been printed, they really came into their own during World War II, when millions of soft-cover armed forces editions were shipped to our troops here and overseas. Following the war, the paperback revolution continued. In time, "instant books," more commonly referred to as "paperback extras," also became popular moneymakers.

Most modern-day publishing operations rely on their editorial, production, and promotion departments to develop and distribute their books. Interestingly enough, while book houses rely on their sales forces and advertising efforts to sell titles, they also make use of two types of mass media once thought to be in competition with books—television and radio. Increasingly, these two media are used as promotional outlets.

Though alive and well, the book industry does come under siege now and again from would-be censors. Statistics reveal that efforts to censor occur in one-fifth of our nation's schools, and that 50 percent of these attempts are successful. Abetted by forces both outside and inside the industry, the censor is a force to be considered. Still, despite such attempts, almost 40,000 new book titles are published each year. Thus, whether packaged in a soft or a hard cover, whether read for informational or entertainment value, it looks like the book is here to stay.

KEY TERMS

Papyrus
Parchment
Codex
Linotype
Copyright law
Universal Copyright Convention
Dime novels
Royalty
Pocket books
Paperback extras
Trade book
Serif
Sans Serif
Letterpress
Offset printing
Gravure
Groundwood paper
Free-sheet paper
Rag-content paper
Signature
Censorship

NOTES

[1] Gilbert Highet, *The Immortal Profession: The Joys of Teaching and Learning*, Weybright and Talley, New York, 1976, p. 5.

[2] Clarence Petersen, *The Bantam Story: Thirty Years of Paperback Publishing*, Bantam, New York, 1975, p. 1.

[3] "Books Hold Their Own," *The Bergen (NJ) Record*, Apr. 12, 1984, p. A9.

[4] John P. Dessauer, *Book Publishing: What It Is, What It Does,* 2d ed., Bowker, New York, 1981, p. 1.

[5] Luke White, Jr., *Henry William Herbert and the American Publishing Scene, 1831–1858*, Cartaret Book Club, Newark, 1943, p. 8.

[6] John Tebbel, *The Media in America*, Crowell, New York, 1974, pp. 117–118.

[7] Philip Van Doren, ed., *The Annotated Uncle Tom's Cabin,* Eriksson, New York, 1964, p. 7.

[8] John Tebbel, *A History of Book Publishing in the*

[8] *United States,* vol.1, Bowker, New York, 1972, p. 276.

[9] John Tebble, *A History of Book Publishing in the United States,* vol. 2, Bowker, New York, 1975, p. 8.

[10] Francis W. Halsey, *Publishers Weekly,* April 7, 1900, p. 717.

[11] V. M. Schenck, *Publishers Weekly,* May 17, 1913, p. 1757.

[12] John Tebbel, *A History of Book Publishing in the United States,* vol. 3, Bowker, New York, 1978, p. 382.

[13] Bennett Cerf, *At Random: The Reminiscences of Bennett Cerf,* Random House, New York, 1977, p. 65.

[14] Benjamin Compaine, *The Book Industry in Transition,* Knowledge Industry Publications, White Plains, N.Y., 1978, p. 2.

[15] Petersen, op. cit., p. 94.

[16] Dessauer, op. cit., p. 47.

[17] Roger M. Smith. *Paperback Parnassus,* Westview, Boulder, Colo., 1976, p. 25.

[18] Ibid., p. 59.

[19] Petersen, op. cit., p. 57.

[20] John Farrar, "Securing and Selecting the Manuscript," in Chandler B. Grannis (ed.), *What Happens in Book Publishing,* Columbia University Press, New York, 1957, p. 35.

[21] Dessauer, op. cit., p. 39.

[22] Ibid., p. 40.

[23] Ibid., p. 97.

[24] Edwin McDowell, "Pblishing: Rising Importance of Book Publicity," *The New York Times,* October 7, 1983.

[25] Ibid.

[26] Richard Bernstein, "Opening the Books on Censorship," *The New York Times Magazine,* May 13, 1984, p. 36.

[27] Ibid.

[28] Barbara Palmer, "Censorship: The Battle Is Heating Up," *USA Today,* June 21, 1984, p. D1.

[29] Christine Moore, "Textbook Censorship Multiplying," *FOI '82,* 1982, p. 70.

[30] Barbara Palmer, op. cit.

[31] Edwin McDowell, "Publishing Censorship Can Take Indirect Forms," *The New York Times,* February 18, 1983, p. C25.

[32] Nat Hentoff, "Selling the American Heritage for Big Texas Bucks," *The Village Voice,* October 4, 1983, p. 6.

[33] Herbert Mitgang, "Publisher Rejects Offensive Books," *The New York Times,* September 1, 1983.

[34] "If Books Are Gutted, Education Will Bleed," *USA Today,* August 9, 1983.

[35] Associated Press, March 16, 1984.

[36] Moore, op. cit.

[37] Hentoff, op. cit.

[38] Ibid.

[39] Mel Gabler, "Textbooks Need Fairness and Balance," *USA Today,* August 9, 1983, p. 8A.

[40] Morris Freedman, "Who Shall Choose the Textbooks?" *The Christian Science Monitor,* reprinted in *The Record,* April 27, 1983.

[41] Clarence Day, quoted in *Book Publishing in America,* by Charles Madison, McGraw-Hill, New York, 1966. p. 2.

SUGGESTIONS FOR FURTHER READING

Bailey, Herbert S.: *The Art and Science of Book Publishing,* University of Texas Press, Austin, 1980. *Examines the rational and irrational nature of publishing. Specific problems of the editorial, production, and business aspects are considered.*

Berg, A. Scott: *Max Perkins: Editor of Genius.* E. P. Dutton, New York, 1978. *A readable biography of one of America's most important editors.*

Cerf, Bennett: *At Random: The Reminiscences of Bennett Cerf,* Random House, New York, 1977. *As a leader of the industry, Cerf's recollections provide us with both an insightful and entertaining view of its development.*

Compaine, Benjamin M.: *The Book Industry in Transition,* Knowledge Industry Publications, White Plains, N.Y., 1978. *A comprehensive look at the trends in the business of books. Must reading for anyone interested in this side of the industry.*

Dessauer, John P.: *Book Publishing: What It Is, What It Does,* 2d ed., Bowker, New York, 1981. *A thorough examination of the book-publishing business. Valuable for anyone considering a career.*

Exman, Eugene: *The House of Harper,* Harper

& Row, New York, 1967. *A carefully compiled description of the birth and development of one of America's leading publishing houses.*

Grannis, Chandler, ed., *What Happens in Book Publishing,* Columbia University Press, New York, 1957. *A valuable collection of essays by people who were prominent in the industry during the 1950s.*

Gross, Gerald, ed., *Publishers on Publishing,* Grosset & Dunlap, New York, 1961. *A fascinating compilation of first-person accounts by many of the pioneers of publishing in America. Well worth reading.*

Petersen, Clarence: *The Bantam Story: Thirty Years of Paperback Publishing,* Bantam, New York, 1975. *An important view of the paperback phenomena as seen through the eyes of one of the major paperback publishing houses.*

Publishers Weekly, Bowker, New York. *The primary periodical for the book business. Recent copies are readily available in libraries. This magazine will bring you up to date on what is happening in the industry today.*

Smith, Roger M.: *Paperback Parnassus,* Westview, Boulder, Colo., 1976. *An intriguing and inventive look at the scope of the paperback and its impact on the industry as a whole.*

Tebbel, John: *A History of Book Publishing in the United States,* vols. 1–3, Bowker, New York, 1972, 1975, and 1978. *The most comprehensive view of the book industry available. The scholarly approach is quite readable.*

CHAPTER 3
NEWSPAPERS: THE MEDIUM AND ITS MAKERS

Put it to them briefly so they will read it, clearly so they will appreciate it, picturesquely so they will remember it, and, above all, accurately so they will be guided by its light.
Joseph Pulitzer

Presented a copy of his family tree yesterday, President Carter said of his genealogical history: "We've uncovered some embarrassing ancestors in the not too distant past. Some horse thieves, and some people killed on Saturday nights. One of my relatives, unfortunately, was even in the newspaper business."
The New York Times

CHAPTER PREVIEW

After reading this chapter, you should be able to:
- Assess the role newspapers play in your life
- Explain the functions served by newspapers
- Enumerate and explain key events in the development of the newspaper
- Identify and discuss the roles played by the following key figures in the development of the newspaper: Johann Gutenberg, Benjamin Harris, John Campbell, James and Benjamin Franklin, John Peter Zenger, Horace Greeley, Benjamin Day, Henry Raymond, Joseph Pulitzer, William Randolph Hearst, Edward Wyllis Scripps, Adolph S. Ochs, and Allen Neuharth
- Describe the part newspapers played in the American Revolution
- Explain how the penny press changed the newspaper business
- Define "yellow journalism"
- Compare and contrast yellow journalism with the tradition of "objective journalism" championed by Adolph S. Ochs
- Explain how consolidations affected the newspaper industry
- Define "jazz journalism"
- Compare and contrast dailies, weeklies, supermarket tabloids, special-interest, and alternative newspapers
- Describe how a typical newspaper is organized
- Discuss the functions performed by the business, production, news, and editorial departments of a newspaper

Have you seen today's newspaper? Did you read it? Are you familiar with today's news events and news makers? Professor Henry Labrie of Boston University reports that when he tested his students on current news events, wrong answers prevailed. What is even more distressing is that Professor Labrie's students were journalism majors. Professor Labrie now requires his students to read two newspapers daily. He adds, "Many students have told me this is the first time in their lives they have read newspapers."[1]

What role does a newspaper play in your life? What does a newspaper mean to you?

What is the primary function of a newspaper? Many people would say to keep the public informed. To this end, newspapers may contain information about what is happening in the world, the city, or the local community; they may contain information about the weather, entertainment, sports, self-improvement, and society. Given this range of information and diversity, people can use the newspaper to educate themselves, to discover something to do, or to find out how to do something. They can use it to fill leisure time, to avoid boredom, or to forget their own problems by becoming immersed in the problems of others. Over 100 million American adults read at least one newspaper every day, and they talk about it, too. So newspapers serve both a social and an informational function; in effect, they act as conversation catalysts. Most people who read the newspaper (53 percent) start by reading the front page and then proceed through the rest of the paper. The remainder turn to specific items first and then go through what is left.

Writing in his book on the news industry, journalist Gay Talese described the work his associates do as follows:

> Most journalists are restless voyeurs who see the warts on the world, the imperfections in people and places. The sane scene that is much of life, the great portion of the planet unmarked by madness, does not lure them like riots and raids, crumbling countries and sinking ships, bankers banished to Rio and burning Buddhist nuns—gloom is their game, the spectacle their passion, normality their nemesis.[2]

Like Talese, many people complain that too much of the news we are exposed to is unhappy news. They ask, "Where are the happy stories?" (Research shows that the public is overly sensitive to unpleasant stories, which actually make up a small fraction of the paper's content.) Others complain that too many of our current newspapers have adopted a fast-food approach to journalism, replacing important issues and concerns with fluff—information that is of little consequence. What do you think? Before you give a definitive answer, let us take a step back in time, and examine the roots of journalism as we know it today.

MEDIA PROBE

How many days a week do you read a newspaper?

Which sections of the newspaper do you like best? Why?

Which section of the newspaper do you read first? Why?

Which section(s) of the newspaper do you avoid reading? Why?

In your opinion, does your local newspaper supply you with sufficient information for you to make decisions or take positions regarding local, national, and international issues? Explain your answer.

Do you ever discuss what you read in the newspaper? How often? With whom?

Newspapers are the lifeblood of the print media, but readership is declining in many areas. (Anestis DiaKopoulos, Photo Researchers)

THE EARLY YEARS: SETTING PRECEDENTS

Johann Gutenberg's 1440 invention of the movable-type printing press in Germany paved the way not only for printed books, as we discussed in the previous chapter, but for newspapers as well. Following the invention of printing, the desire to create a medium that would disseminate information to large numbers of people surfaced. By the 1620s occasional (but primitive) news sheets appeared on the streets of London. Specializing in foreign news, these forerunners of newspapers, called "corantos," were sold by newsboys. Some years later, in 1641, the corantos were followed by daily reports of local events called "diurnals." And by 1644 poet John Milton was warning the people of his day about the need to keep the press free; writing in his now-famous *Areopagitica,* Milton called for a press free from government control and censorship: "Though all the winds of doctrine were let loose to play upon the earth, so Truth be in the field, we do injuriously, by licensing and prohibiting, to misdoubt her strength. Let her and Falsehood grapple; whoever knew Truth put to worse, in a free and open encounter?" In years to come Milton's appeals for a free press would serve as the basis for all who championed the cause of freedom of expression.

Edwin Emery in his book *The Press in America* points out that even the term "news" emerged from the advent of printing: "Up to about 1500, 'tydings' was the usual word used

MEDIA SCOPE

1440 — Johann Gutenberg develops movable-type printing press

1620s — Occasional primitive news sheets appear in London

1665 — Newspapers printed in England

1690 — Publick Occurrences Both Forreign and Domestick becomes America's first newspaper; only one issue was ever published

1721 — James and Ben Franklin published the New England Courant

1735 — John Peter Zenger acquitted for publishing articles which criticized the government

1765 — Stamp Act of 1765 provokes wrath of publishers and the legal profession

1783 — Pennsylvania Evening Post becomes America's first daily newspaper

1798 — The Sedition Act is passed; its goal is to suppress the press

1828 — Freedom's Journal America's first black newspaper, is founded

1833 — The New York Sun heralds in the Penny Press era

1841 — Horace Greeley starts The New York Tribune

1848 — Associated Press is formed

1851 — The New York Times begins publication

1883 — Joseph Pulitzer takes over the New York World; yellow journalism is born

1895 — William Randolph Hearst buys New York Morning Journal to compete with Pulitzer

1904 — The Daily Mirror—a newspaper for women started

1906 — The Gannett Chain is begun

1907 — E.W. Scripps organizes United Press

1914 — The New York Times contributes to objectivity by publishing important documents in their entirety

1933 — The American Society of Newspaper Editors adopts its statement on ethics: "Cannons of Journalism"

1950 — Photo-offset printing becomes possible

1955 — The Village Voice, the first alternative newspaper, begins publication

1958 — United Press and International News Service combine to form United Press International

1960 — Major newspapers begins to merge to cut expenses; computers used extensively for type setting

1962-63 — Tom Wolfe and Jimmy Breslin begin using New Journalism techniques for the New York Herald Tribune

1972 — Bob Woodward and Carl Berstein expose the Watergate Scandal in the Washington Post

1975 — The Wall Street Journal begins publishing via satellite

1983 — Bob Maynard becomes the first black publisher of a major newspaper, The Oakland Tribune

1983 — USA today, launched by the Gannett chain, becomes the first national daily produced via satellite for a general readership

56   THE PRINT MEDIA: THE WINDOW OPENS

YOU WERE THERE

BEN FRANKLIN: THE PRINTER'S APPRENTICE

From my infancy I was passionately fond of reading, and all the money that came into my hands was laid out in the purchasing of books.... This bookish inclination at length determined my father to make me a printer, although he had already one son of that profession. In 1717 my brother James returned from England, with a press and letters, to set up his business in Boston.... I was to serve as an apprentice till I was twenty-one years of age, only I was to be allowed a journeyman's wages during the last year. In a little time I made a great progress in the business and became a useful hand to my brother. I now had access to better books....

My brother had, in 1720 or 1721, begun to print a newspaper. It was the second that appeared in America and was called the *New England Courant*.... I remember his being dissuaded by some of his friends from the undertaking as one not likely to succeed, one newspaper being in their judgment enough for America. At this time, 1771, there are not less than twenty-five. He went on however, with the undertaking. I was employed to carry the papers to the customers after having working in composing the types and printing off the sheets....

One of the pieces in our newspaper on some political point, which I have now forgotten, gave offense to the Assembly. He was taken up, censured, and imprisoned for a month by the Speaker's warrant, I suppose because he would not discover the author. I, too, was taken up and examined before the Council; but though I did not give them any satisfaction, they contented themselves with admonishing me, and dismissed me, considering me perhaps an apprentice who was bound to keep his master's secrets. During my brother's confinement... I had the management of the paper; and I made bold to give our rulers some rubs in it, which my brother took very kindly, while others began to consider me in an unfavorable light as a youth who had a turn for libeling and satire.

My brother's discharge was accompanied with an order, and a very odd one, that "James Franklin should no longer print the newspaper called the *New England Courant*." On a consultation held in our printing office among his friends what he should do in this

Benjamin Franklin, once a printer's apprentice and always a champion of a free press, is toasted by colleagues on a post-Revolutionary visit to England. (Mary Evans Picture Library, Photo Researchers)

NEWSPAPERS: THE MEDIUM AND ITS MAKERS

conjuncture, it was proposed to elude the order by changing the name of the paper. But my brother, seeing inconveniences in this, came to a conclusion, as a better way, to let the paper in the future be printed in the name of Benjamin Franklin.... A very flimsy scheme it was; however, it was immediately executed, and the paper was printed accordingly, under my name, for several months.

Benjamin Franklin, *The Autobiography of Benjamin Franklin,* 1868.

to describe reports of current events. The word 'news' was coined to differentiate between the casual dissemination of information and the deliberate attempt to gather and process the latest intelligence."[3] Once news in print form became available to everyone who could read, becoming literate suddenly became important. Thus, the demand for education increased. Newspapers were printed first in Germany and Holland, spreading to England by 1665. Since newspapers were licensed by the crown, publishers who printed materials which were considered offensive to the ruling classes were placed in the stocks. By 1686, Benjamin Harris, a printer who had his differences with the crown, arrived in America and, in 1690, set up the first American newspaper, *Publick Occurrences Both Forreign and Domestick.* Only one issue was published; after it was released, Harris's operation was shut down and a second issue never appeared.

In 1704, Boston printer John Campbell published the second American newspaper: the *Boston News-Letter.* Campbell was the first of many printers who obtained a crown appointment as postmaster in addition to holding a job as printer. However, the dual appointment encouraged him, and others like him, to print only materials favorable to the government.

The next newspaper established in Boston was the *New England Courant,* operated first by James Franklin and later by his younger brother, Benjamin. During the years he served as publisher of the paper, young Ben Franklin was moved to comment: "Without freedom of thought there can be no such thing as wisdom; and no such thing as public liberty without freedom of speech, which is the right of every man." Franklin went on to start the *Pennsylvania Gazette;* many believe it was he who established newspaper publishing as an important and respected profession.

Newspapers Contribute to the Revolution

During the colonial period, newspapers printed the grievances of colonists and the replies of the British government. As such, they helped shape the opinions of the people. A number of specific controversies influenced the feelings of Americans regarding freedom of the press and contributed to the call for revolution.

The John Peter Zenger Case In 1733, John Peter Zenger began the publication of the *New York Weekly Journal.* Zenger, a German immigrant printer, was persuaded by powerful New Yorkers to use his newspaper as a medium through which to battle the royal governor, William Cosby. As a result of his antiadministration articles, Zenger was imprisoned on charges of "false, scandalous and seditious *libel.*" He was defended by Andrew Hamilton, who zeroed in on the word "false." Hamilton noted that if the words printed were true, they could not be libelous. During the course of the trial, Hamilton denounced lawless power and appealed to the jury for liberty.

As you see, I labor under the weight of many years, and am borne down with great infirmities of body; yet old and weak as I am, I should think it my duty, if required, to go to the utmost part of the land where my service could be of any use in assisting to quench the flame of prosecutions upon informations set on foot by the government to deprive People of remonstrating and complaining, too, of the arbitrary attempts of men in power. . . .

The question before the court and you gentlemen of the jury is not of small or private concern. . . . No! It may, in its consequence, affect every freeman that lives under a British government on the main of America. It is the best cause. It is the cause of liberty . . . the liberty both of exposing and opposing arbitrary power by speaking and writing Truth.[4]

Much to the astonishment of Governor Cosby, the jury delivered a verdict of not guilty, and Zenger was set free in 1735. His trial furthered the call for liberty and freedom of speech among Americans.

The Stamp Act of 1765 The Stamp Act of 1765 was implemented because the British needed funds to pay debts incurred in the Seven Years' War with the French. The act imposed a penny tax per issue on newspapers. Editors who interpreted the tax as an attempt to put them out of business were vocal in their opposition to it. Lawyers, who also objected to the act because it placed a tax on the paper they used to draw up legal documents, added their voices to the cry for repeal. Working together, the publishers and lawyers were successful in transforming the tax into an issue with the battle cry "No taxation without representation." The public outcry that ensued was sufficient to force Parliament to withdraw the act the following year.

The Revolutionary Period

During the revolutionary period, newspapers became quite political; that is, they openly took one side or the other in disputes. Thus while some championed the call for revolution, others remained loyal to the crown. Unlike today, editorials did not appear on a separate page, so the advocacy journalists of yesteryear simply wrote their opinions into the stories they covered. For example, Isaiah Thomas, used his paper, the *Massachusetts Spy,* to issue the cry: "Americans! Forever bear in mind the BATTLE OF LEXINGTON!" and, in 1776, Thomas Paine wrote these words in the first issue of his publication, *Crisis:* "These are the times that try men's souls. The summer soldier and the sunshine patriot will, in this crisis, shrink from the service of his country; but he that stands it *now,* deserves the love and thanks of man and woman." Newspapers also helped to create our first military hero, George Washington, as they reported his triumphs and played down his defeats.

The year 1783 marked the advent of a daily newspaper, the *Pennsylvania Evening Post,* an endeavor of Benjamin Towne, which lasted only a year and a half. But others followed, and by 1820, 20 of the 512 papers printed were dailies. However, the dominant feature of most of these papers was a lack of *objectivity;* many were partisan in nature, and personal attacks on political leaders were commonplace. Thomas Jefferson, for one, was branded the "infidel Jefferson" and in the *New England Palladium,* the people were warned that if they elected Jefferson, "our churches will be prostrated." As the years passed, many newspapers were brought to court on charges of seditious libel. It was Noah Webster (later of dictionary fame) who first separated traditional news articles from opinion articles by placing the latter on a separate editorial page—a practice that continues to this day.

After the war, newspapers focused on issues such as the treaty with England and the new Constitution, which included the First Amendment: "Congress shall make no law . . . abridging the freedom of speech, or

MEDIA PROBE

Would you support the enforcement of a sedition law today? Why or why not? To what extent, if any, do you believe that people in power would abuse such a law if it existed? How? Why?

of the press." By the 1790s, however, press freedom was again under attack. Tired of press criticism of his administration, President John Adams, engineered the passing of the Alien and Sedition Acts of 1798. These acts stated:

> That if any person shall write, print, utter or publish . . . any false, scandalous and malicious writing . . . against the government of the United States or either house of the Congress . . . or the said President . . . or to excite against them the hatred of the good people of the United States . . . shall be punished by a fine not exceeding two thousand dollars, and by imprisonment not exceeding two years.

Due to the public outcry resulting from convictions achieved under the acts, it was allowed to expire after two years.

THE PENNY PRESS: A MASS MEDIUM

In order to become a truly mass medium, newspapers had to be made available to a mass audience. Prior to 1833 newspapers were aimed mainly at society's elite and sold mainly by yearly subscriptions that were priced beyond the range of most of the people. Then, on January 1, 1833, Horace Greeley began publishing the *New York Morning Post*, the first attempt at a mass newspaper—one that was sold by the issue and cost 2 cents. Even though the price was soon cut to 1 cent, the paper failed within two weeks. The idea of a *penny press* did not die, though. The idea, a natural reaction to the increased industrialization, urbanization, democritization, and literacy of America, was kept alive among printers, and on September 3, 1833, Benjamin H. Day, a young job printer, launched the *New York Sun* with the motto, "It Shines for All." The *Sun* focused not on complex political issues but on human interest stories and sensational events. Within four months it was able to claim a circulation of 5000—more than all other New York newspapers combined. At the cost of only 1 penny, the street sales of this paper were brisk from the start.

As circulation increased for the *Sun* and its many imitators, editors began experimenting with various methods of news gathering. Day, for example, sent a reporter to night court to cover its proceedings. One sample news article read:

> Bridget McMunn got drunk and threw a pitcher at Mr. Ellis, of 53 Ludlow Street. Bridget said she was the mother of three little orphans—God bless their dear souls—and if she went to prison they would choke to death for want of something to eat. Committed.

Truth was not always a major concern of the penny presses. In 1835, for instance, the *Sun* reported the discovery of life on the moon:

> They averaged four feet in height, were covered, except on the face, with short and glossy copper-colored hair, and had wings composed of a thin membrane.

Although the story was later revealed to be a hoax, readership rose as a result of its appearance.

Owing to the penny press's popularity, advertisers began to flock to the new medium, and a new street sales distribution system was devised. Because of the increased competition between penny newspapers, editors began to use various techniques in an effort to "scoop" each other. Reporters would be

MEDIA PROBE

Think of a recent news event. How many hours after the event were you able to read about it in the newspapers? How do you imagine life in the United States would change if you had to wait up to a month to hear about important events and their outcome?

sent out in speedboats to meet incoming ships in an attempt to get the foreign news first; even carrier pigeons and horses were used in order to obtain news stories more quickly. By the mid-1840s most newspapers were equipped with the telegraph; this innovation further enhanced the newspaper's ability to speed information to the public. Gone were the days when a week or more would elapse before the death of a famous person could be read about in city newspapers, as had occurred when the first president of the United States, George Washington, had died. News would now be diffused to the masses in a timely fashion.

Horace Greeley and the *Herald Tribune*

After his earlier unsuccessful start with a penny newspaper, in 1841 Horace Greeley launched the *New York Tribune*. In contrast to the *Sun*, the *Herald*, and his other penny-press competitors, Greeley's *Tribune* had a

YOU WERE THERE

THE *TRIBUNE* IS BORN

On the tenth day of April, 1841 . . . I issued the first number of *The New York Tribune*. It was a small sheet, for it was to be retailed for a cent, and not much of a newspaper could be retailed for that price. I had been incited to this enterprise by several Whig friends, who deemed a cheap daily, addressed more especially to the laboring class, eminently needed in our city, where the only two cheap journals then and still existing—*The Sun* and *The Herald*—were in decided, though unavowed, and therefore more effective, sympathy with the Democratic Party.

My leading idea was the establishment of a journal removed alike from servile partisanship on the one hand and from gagged, mincing neutrality on the other. . . . I believed there was a happy medium between these extremes—a position from which a journalist might openly and heartily advocate the principles and commend the measures of that party to which his convictions allied him, yet frankly dissent from its course on a particular question, and even denounce its candidates if they were shown to be deficient in capacity or (far worse) in integrity. . . .

The *Tribune*, as it first appeared, was but the germ of what I sought to make it. No journal sold for a cent could ever be much more than a dry summary of the most important or the most interesting occurrences of the day; and such is not a newspaper, in the higher sense of the term. We need to know, not only what is done, but what is purposed and said; and to this end, the prompt perusal of the manifestoes of monarchs, presidents, ministers, legislators, etc., is indespensible. . . .

I cherish the hope that the journal I projected and established will live and flourish long after I shall have mouldered into forgotten dust . . . and that the stone which covers my ashes may bear to future eyes the still intelligible inscription, "Founder of the New York Tribune."

Horace Greeley, *Recollections of a Busy Life*, J. B. Ford, New York, 1868, p. 28.

less sensational tone, leading Greeley to claim that the paper had attained a higher ethical stature than its competition. Greeley believed in education and work opportunities for all, civil rights and equal pay for women, the abolition of slavery, and the elimination of imprisonment for debts. The *Tribune* became the vehicle by which he communicated these ideas to the public. As is seen in the following statement from one of his lectures, Greeley was a publisher firmly committed to social reform:

> Legislators! Philanthropists! Statesmen! There *must* be some way out of this social labrinth; for God is good, and has not created men and women to starve for want of work. The precept "Six days shalt thou labor" implies and predicts work for all; where is it? and what shall supply it? If you cannot or will not solve this problem, at least do not defame or impede those who earnestly seek its solution!
>
> The great, all-embracing Reform of our age is therefore the SOCIAL REFORM—that which seeks to lift the Laboring Class, as such,—not out of labor, by any means,—but out of ignorance, inefficiency, dependence, and want.[5]

Having been started with a mere $3000, the *Tribune* was so popular by the end of its second year, that Greeley was able to raise the price to 2 cents per issue. Many of the issues Greeley championed, among them women's rights, are still talked about today. At his funeral it was said, "Today, between the two oceans, there is hardly an intelligent man or child that does not feel the influence of Horace Greeley." An editor who appealed to the intellect of his readers, Greeley respected his readers and chose not to talk down to them.

The New York Times of Henry Raymond

Henry Raymond had worked as a reporter and editor for Greeley's *Tribune*. After a stint in politics, in the fall of 1851 Raymond decided to publish his own conservative newspaper, *The New York Times*. Raymond's *Times* was characterized by a calm, restrained style of reporting and featured single-column headlines. Within a few weeks the paper's circulation rose to 10,000 copies; by 1857 circulation averaged 40,000 copies. The Civil War spurred the demand for up-to-date news—a demand Raymond and his competitors eagerly responded to. Raymond personally covered the first battle of Bull Run. Though he was able to be present for only a portion of the battle, Raymond confidently wrote that the union forces had won. Unfortunately, this report proved to be wrong.

Raymond spent the remainder of the war in his office, relying on his reporters to cover it for him. Like reporters of today, reporters of Raymond's time were keenly interested in obtaining first-hand information. Gay Talese reports the following incident as an example: "One night when Generals Grant and Meade were conversing privately in a tent, they heard noises in the bushes which, upon inspection, turned out to be a *Times* man lying on his stomach scribbling notes."[6]

In 1869, while visiting the apartment of a New York actress, Henry Raymond died. At the time of his death the *Times* had established a reputation for delivering objective journalism. Historian Frank Luther Mott notes: "The *Times* may be regarded as the culmination and highest achievement of the cheap-for-cash newspaper which was begun by the *Sun*. . . . The *Times* became, under Raymond's management, preeminently a newspaper. Its news was well balanced, well edited and copious."[7] Without the leadership of Raymond the *Times* fell on hard times but was saved from bankruptcy in 1896 by Adolph Ochs. *The New York Times* is operated to this day by Ochs's family.

THE POST-CIVIL WAR PERIOD: YELLOW JOURNALISM

The Civil War affected American journalism in a number of ways. For the first time journalists were forced to consider how they could inform the public without aiding "the enemy." Northern journalists were given guidelines regarding types of stories that, in the interest of public security, should not be written. The telegraph made it possible for reporters to send stories that contained information of military value. Because the telegraph transmission lines of the time were unreliable, military censorship was deemed necessary. In light of this, reporters felt compelled to summarize the important facts in the story's first paragraph. This *summary lead* was then followed by a more detailed explanation of the event being reported. Thus, it was reasoned, if the telegraph lines did break down, at least the main point of the reporter's story would reach newspaper offices. Because of this practice, what has become known as the inverted-pyramid style of writing became a journalistic standard. Also, as editors competed for street sales, larger and larger headlines were used to attract the customer's attention.

This period also saw the development of a more objective reporting style as newspapers started to rely on information received from *news cooperatives* or associations. The first such association was established in 1848 when six New York newspapers, all of whom had correspondents in Boston, recognized it would save them money if a cooperative agency were formed to cover that city for them. This agency became known as the Associated Press of New York. Because the Associated Press serviced a number of different papers—papers that endorsed a variety of political points of view—its reporters had to write to satisfy the ideological preferences of all client papers. For this reason, an impartial writing style became the goal. In time, this style also became the ideal that newspapers aspired to.

In post-Civil War years newspapers also became big business. By the turn of the century. the number of newspapers in the United States had quadrupled. Still highly competitive, newspaper editors were determined to

Joseph Pulitzer was the first of the press magnates who revolutionized journalism, building circulation through sensationalized news reporting. The competition between Pulitzer's *New York World* and William Randolph Hearst's *New York Journal* is alleged by some to have caused the Spanish-American War. (Culver Pictures)

outsell each other. The prime journalistic figures of the period were Joseph Pulitzer and his number one rival, William Randolph Hearst.

Joseph Pulitzer

Born in Hungary in 1847, Joseph Pulitzer attempted unsuccessfully to join military units in Europe. Unable to fulfill his dream of becoming a professional soldier, Pulitzer came to this country and served in the Union Army during the Civil War. Finally admitting his lack of professional military ability, he made his way to St. Louis, Missouri, where he held several jobs. In time, he began working as a journalist and also became active in politics.

NEWSPAPERS: THE MEDIUM AND ITS MAKERS   63

Then, in 1878, while attending a sheriff's auction, he purchased the bankrupt *St. Louis Dispatch*. Pulitzer succeeded in turning the paper around, and five years later he did the same for the *New York World*. Writing about Pulitzer, his biographer, W. A. Swanberg, noted that Pulitzer "wanted to sell millions of newspapers. He wanted to elect a President. He aimed for wealth and power—not an uncommon impulse—but to his great credit he wanted to help everyone to prosperity."[8]

Pulitzer's political and journalistic drive is reflected, in part, in the May 11, 1883, opening statement he wrote to his *World* readers: "There is room in this great and growing city for a journal that is not only cheap, but bright, not only bright but large, not only large but truly democratic—dedicated to the cause of the people rather than that of the purse-potentates." An immigrant himself, Pulitzer worked to ensure that his 2-cent paper would be attractive to the millions of new Americans who had been flooding the country's shores. He succeeded in appealing to them by stressing sensationalism. Headlines in the paper were hyped to emphasize sex, violence, scandal, crime, gossip, and disasters. For example, a story about convicted killer Angelo Cornetti written the night before his execution had this headline:

CORNETTI'S LAST NIGHT
Shaking His Cell Door and Demanding Release

Another headline described a murderer at the moment of execution:

WARD MCCONEY HANGED
Shouting From Under the Black Cap That His Executioners Are Murderers

And still another revealed the plight of a burgler who was arrested on his wedding day:

MARRIED AND TAKEN TO JAIL

Other headlines of the day included "Was He a Suicide?" "Maddened by Marriage," and "While the Husbands Were Away."

Ever eager to increase readership, Pulitzer even had erotic descriptions included in drama reviews. In this article a Pulitzer reviewer is discussing a production of *Romeo and Juliet*:

> Just imagine a divine girl with real warm blood glowing in every vein of her body, and a flush of health on her beautiful up-turned face, her red lips protruding in the slightest possible pout, and her whole attitude meaning expectancy and waiting, and then fancy how that ripe, tender mouth would taste when you begin to feed on it, young man.... How would it strike you to play Romeo to Miss Emma Abbott's Juliet?

On the other hand, Pulitzer's newspapers did crusade against large corporations and fight for the rights of the poor. He instructed his reporters to walk the streets in an effort to discover stories that could be made interesting to readers; one such effort produced a story that described the fate suffered by Kate Sweeney, an impoverished New Yorker.

> She lay down in the cellar to sleep and the sewer that runs under the house overflowed and suffocated her where she lay. No one will ever know who killed Kate Sweeney. No one will ever summon the Sanitary Inspectors.... Nobody seems to have thought it worth an investigation.

Pulitzer's papers also attacked crooked politicians, gambling, and police corruption and even printed lists of wealthy tax dodgers.

Still, *circulation* was always uppermost in Pulitzer's mind. He featured readership figures on the front page of the *World*, and he pioneered the use of stunts or contests to build circulation. Pulitzer's most famous stunt involved sending a reporter who used the byline "Nellie Bly" around the world, and holding a contest to see which reader would come closest to guessing how long it would take her to complete the journey. Could she do it in less than eighty days? Nearly 1 million estimates of her elapsed time were received before the contest's end. Bly made it in seventy-two days—traveling from San Francisco to New York in a special train. Of course, throughout her travels she sent in stories of the adventure, which also helped spur newspaper sales.

William Randolph Hearst

A second newspaper magnate of the period was William Randolph Hearst. Hearst developed a serious interest in newspapers while he was a student at Harvard. He started his paper in San Francisco a few years after Pulitzer had begun his newspaper in St. Louis. The son of a wealthy family, Hearst apparently decided he did not actually need to graduate from Harvard to succeed in the newspaper business. So, during Hearst's Junior year at Harvard:

> A messenger called at the home of each of his instructors, leaving a large package which, when opened, proved to contain a chamber pot with the recipient's name ornamentally lettered on the inside bottom. Perhaps Hearst did not deliberately plan his dismissal from Harvard, but it cannot be said that he tried earnestly to stay, and the effect was the same. He was expelled.[9]

In 1887 Hearst's father presented him with the *San Francisco Examiner* as a gift. Having worked briefly for Pulitzer, Hearst was able to use many of Pulitzer's techniques to help double his paper's circulation in just one year. He then took on Pulitzer directly by purchasing the ailing *New York Journal* (which had been founded by Pulitzer's brother, Albert). The resulting circulation war helped spur advances in printing and speed the delivery of news. Hearst's splashy approach to journalism—called *"yellow journalism"*—gained its name from a popular cartoon of the day, "The Yellow Kid." The cartoon told about a young child in a tenement who wore a yellow night-shirt. The Yellow Kid cartoonist, who first worked for Pulitzer, was lured to the *Journal* by Hearst. Pulitzer then started to print a competing Yellow Kid cartoon, and soon both papers were being referred to as "the yellow papers," and finally as yellow journalism.

Hearst is not fondly remembered by many historians. In his book *Newsmongers,* Robert Rutland reports:

> Left to a life of dilenttantism and political dabblings Hearst would have been fairly harmless. It was the combination of Hearst and journalism that made him appear to be a formidable force in American life for nearly 40 years. With more perspective it is obvious that Mr. Hearst was a self-indulgent egocentric who was rich enough to buy a number of newspapers. He inherited his wealth and proceeded to spend most of it, and his journalistic impact after 1904 was negligible.[10]

Nevertheless, by 1920 Hearst owned twenty daily newspapers, two wire services, six magazines, a newsreel motion picture company, and the King Features Syndicate. And supposedly the journalist featured in the film *Citizen Kane* was modeled after Hearst, depicting him as an editor who fought for the public's rights. "People are going to know who's responsible," says Kane. "And they're going to get the news—the true news—quickly, and simply and entertainingly. And no special interests will be allowed to interfere with the truth of that news." The image of an editor as a crusader for the people has survived to this day.

Edward Wyllis Scripps

While Hearst and Pulitzer had focused on capturing audiences in major cities, E. W. Scripps developed his newspaper empire by concentrating on the smaller but growing industrial towns of the country. Scripps's overriding goal was to be perceived as working for the common person: "I have only one prin-

NEWSPAPERS: THE MEDIUM AND ITS MAKERS   65

YOU WERE THERE

DID THE PULITZER-HEARST RIVALRY SPARK THE SPANISH-AMERICAN WAR?

The "ifs" of history are usually more amusing than profitable, but there seems to be a great probability in the frequently reiterated statement that if Hearst had not challenged Pulitzer to a circulation contest at the time of the Cuban insurrection, there would have been no Spanish-American War. Certainly the most powerful and persistent jingo propaganda ever carried on by newspapers was led by the *New York Journal* and the *World* in 1896–98, and the result was an irresistible popular fervor for war which at length overcame the long unwillingness of President McKinley. . . .

It was not until General Valeriano Weyler was appointed Captain-General of the Spanish forces in Cuba early in 1896 that atrocity stories became prominent in American papers. Weyler was nicknamed "the Butcher," and sensational descriptions were sent home of the sufferings of Cubans in concentration camps. Cuban atrocity stories proved to be good circulation pullers. However, one Hearst reporter and photographer sent a telegram to Hearst:

> HEARST, JOURNAL, NEW YORK
> EVERYTHING IS QUIET. THERE IS NO TROUBLE HERE.
> THERE WILL BE NO WAR. WISH TO RETURN.

To which Hearst is reported to have replied:

> PLEASE REMAIN. YOU FURNISH THE PICTURES
> AND I'LL FURNISH THE WAR. HEARST.

The War with Spain was, as wars go, almost ideal for newspaper treatment. It was near at hand. American commanders allowed unusual freedom to correspondents. It was a small war and thus not too difficult to cover. American arms on land and sea met with a series of successes which could be reported brilliantly. It was a short war, so that the public interest could be fully maintained until its end. Probably no greater army of correspondents had ever been mobilized for any war. . . . Some observers estimated there were as many as 500 writers, photographers and artists, representing scores of newspapers and magazines.

James Creelman, of the *New York Journal,* led an attack on a small fort at El Caney. The place was taken, and Creelman seized the Spanish flag as a trophy for his paper, but he was struck by a Mauser bullet which smashed his arm and tore a hole in his back. He was carried, half delirious, to the rear. He later wrote:

> Some one knelt in the grass beside me and put his hand on my fevered head. Opening my eyes, I saw Mr. Hearst, the proprietor of the *New York Journal*, a straw hat with a bright ribbon on his head, a revolver at his belt, and a pencil and notebook in his hand. The man who had provoked the war had come to see the result with his own eyes, and, finding one of his correspondents prostrate, was doing the work himself. Slowly he took down my story of the fight. Again and again the tinging of Mauser bullets interrupted, but he seemed unmoved. The battle had to be reported somehow.
>
> "I'm sorry you're hurt, but"—and his face was radiant with enthusiasm—"wasn't it a splendid fight? We must beat every paper in the world!"

In the war weeks, the *Journal* went to a circulation of 1,500,000, and the *World* went almost as high. Even after the signing of the peace protocol in August, the circulations of these papers remained above the million mark for several months. Other papers gained in circulation as well.

From Frank Luther Mott, *American Journalism*, Macmillan, New York, 1941, 527–537.

ciple and that is represented by an effort to make it harder for the rich to grow richer and easier for the poor to keep from growing poorer." Consequently, he became known as the "people's champion," and he supported labor unions and the right to strike while actively opposing utilities and other corporate interests. Scripps's business approach was simple. He would send an editor and business manager to a small town with $25,000 and instructions to start a newspaper. If the individuals succeeded they received 49 percent of the company's stock. If, on the other hand, their money ran out, others were sent to replace them. If the paper did not show a profit within a decade, the entire venture was scrapped. Many people, initially supported by Scripps, amassed considerable wealth in this way. Like other papers of the period, sensational stories tended to predominate. Most of Scripps's funded papers contained stories that protested against everything there was to protest against; in fact, Scripps himself noted that his motto was, "Whatever is, is wrong." Like Hearst, by the 1920s, Scripps' empire included a wire service, a news picture organization, and a feature business.

THE TWENTIETH CENTURY: OBJECTIVITY RETURNS

As the nineteenth century drew to a close, the newspaper business was dominated by yellow journalism. However, many editors were becoming convinced that things did not have to be this way. Among them was Adolph S. Ochs. In 1896, Ochs bought *The New York Times* and inaugurated an objective-journalism tradition that continues to the present. When Ochs purchased the *Times,* daily circulation was down to 9000 copies—less than it had been when the *Times* was originally started in 1851. But by Ochs's death in 1935 daily circulation was 465,000. If you were to visit the Times Building in New York City today you would see Ochs's credo on display:

"To Give the News Impartially, Without Fear or Favor." It is this principle that still guides the paper. In his book *The Kingdom and the Power,* journalist Gay Talese describes the atmosphere that prevailed: "*The New York Times* was a timeless blend of past and present, a medieval kingdom within the nation with its own private laws and values and with leaders who felt responsibility for the nation's welfare but were less likely to lie than the nation's statesmen and generals."[11]

Ochs had purchased the *Times* with but $75,000. For that amount he received 1125 shares of stock. His arrangement with the stockholders specified that if he ran the paper for three years without going into debt he would receive a total of 5001 shares—or a majority. After three years, Ochs was the newspaper's major stockholder. In order to obtain his goal, Ochs created a newspaper of record. Eliminating romantic fiction and what he deemed to be examples of trivia, he demanded that financial news, real estate, court proceedings, and governmental activities be given their due. In effect, he turned the *Times* into a bible of information for its readership. When news appeared in the *Times,* people assumed it to be true. For his part, Ochs demanded total accuracy and completeness:

> Many years ago, after a task force of Timesmen had acquitted themselves very well on a big story, the editors sat around at a conference the following day extending congratulations to one another; but Adolph Ochs, who had been sitting silently among them, then said that he had read in another newspaper a fact that seemed to be missing from *The Times'* coverage. One editor answered that this fact was minor, and added that *The Times* had printed several important facts that had not appeared in the other newspaper. To which Ochs replied, glaring, "I want it all."
>
> It is this thinking rigidly enforced, that has created an odd turn of mind and fear in some Timesmen, and has created odd tasks for others. For several years there were clerks in *The Times'*

newsroom assigned each day to scan the paper and count each sports score, each death notice, making sure that *The Times* had them all, or at least more than any other newspaper. At night there were *Times* editors in the newsroom pacing the floor waiting for a copyboy to arrive with the latest editions of other newspapers, fearful that these papers might have a story or a few facts not printed in *The Times*.[12]

Though the traditions adhered to by Ochs are still in force today, sometimes even *Times* reporters make exceptions and sacrifice accuracy for timeliness.

Newspapers Consolidate

Although newspaper circulation increased between 1910 and 1930, the number of newspapers declined. In response to the fact that advertisers sought to place their ads in papers with the highest circulation figures, newspaper chain owners like Hearst, Scripps, and Gannett shut down a number of their publications and merged others in order that they might maximize their profits. One result of mergers was that many newspapers now acquired two names: for example, the *Standard-Star*, the *Globe-Times*, the *Herald-Statesman*, the *Journal-News*, the *Statesman-Journal*, the *Register-Star*, the *Gazette-Reporter*, and the *Sun-Times*.

During the first twenty-five years of this century, newspaper mergers and *newspaper groups* or *chains* became commonplace. Historian Frank Mott reports, "There was nothing new about newspaper consolidations except the large numbers of them."[13] Mott uses as an example Frank A. Munsey, whom he labels the "Grand High Executioner." In 1903, Munsey had written, "In my judgment, it will not be many years . . . before the publishing business of this country will be done by a few concerns—three or four at most."[14] By 1916, Munsey was attempting to become one of the few publishing concerns he had envisioned. Some of his mergers included the *New York Press* and the *New York Sun* in 1923. In 1924 the *Mail and Express* was merged with the *Evening Telegram*. Finally, Munsey merged the *New York Herald* with the *New York Tribune*. Having completed his consolidations in New York City, he developed a comparable arrangement with Chicago papers. Similar consolidations occurred in cities from coast to coast.

Jazz Journalism

With wire services providing the same stories to each newspaper, journalism became more standardized. Even the comics and feature stories were similar. Suddenly, with look-alike journalism as the vogue, it became increasingly difficult to distinguish one paper from another; consequently, there was little reason to buy or read more than one paper. To combat this tendency, in 1919 the *Illustrated Daily News* (later *The Daily News*) launched a new cycle of sensationalism, dubbed "*jazz journalism*." *The Daily News*, like the other jazz journalism papers, was a *tabloid* that relied on vivid photographs for impact. For example, one typical front page of the paper spotlighted a picture of a woman convicted of murder at the moment she was electrocuted in the electric chair. Written in an easy-to-understand style, the paper was an instant success. Hearst's *Daily Mirror* (1928) and McFadden's *Daily Graphic* (1924) attempted to capitalize on *The Daily News's* success and adopted an even more sensational approach, running not just an abundance of photographs, but cosmographs (faked composite shots of events that might have occurred) as well. However, neither were successful in replicating the popularity of *The Daily News*, and by 1932 both had ceased publication. *The Daily News* exists to this day, still a tabloid (it is approximately half the size of *The New York Times*) but in a somewhat modified form. Though sensationalism would appear again from time to time, the jazz journalism trend

YOU WERE THERE

A *TIMES* REPORTER RELIVES THE ASSASSINATION OF PRESIDENT JOHN F. KENNEDY

Tom Wicker was riding in a press bus a few vehicles behind President Kennedy's limousine as the president's motorcade passed the Texas School Book Depository from which the fatal shots were fired. Suddenly he was the only *Times* reporter on the scene to report the story. The next day the paper ran his 106-paragraph story, yet only slightly more than one of those paragraphs described what Wicker had actually seen with his own eyes.

That day, a reporter had none of the ordinary means or time to check and double-check matters given as fact. He had to go on what he knew of people he talked to, what he knew of human reaction, what two isolated "facts" added to in sum—above all on what he felt in his bones.

It began, for most reporters, when the central fact of it was over. As our press bus eased at motorcade speed down an incline toward an underpass there was a little confusion in the sparse crowds that at that point had been standing at the curb to see the President of the United States pass. As we came out of the underpass, I saw a motorcycle policeman drive over the curb, across an open area, a few feet up a railroad bank, dismount and start scrambling up the bank. The press bus in its stately pace rolled on to the Trade Mart where the President was to speak. Fortunately, it was only a few minutes away.

At the Trade Mart, rumor was sweeping the hundreds of Texans already eating their lunch. It was the only rumor that I had ever seen; it was moving across that crowd like a wind over a wheatfield.

With the other reporters—I suppose thirty-five of them—I went on through the huge hall to the upstairs press room. We were hardly there when Marianne Means of Hearst Headline Service hung up a telephone, ran to a group of us and said, "The President's been shot. He's at Parkland Hospital."

We ran for the press busses. I barely got aboard a moving bus. Fortunately again, it was only a few minutes to Parkland Hospital. There at its emergency entrance, stood the President's car, the top up, a bucket of bloody water beside it.

Throughout the day, every reporter on the scene seemed to me to do his best to help everyone else. Information came only in bits and pieces. Each man who picked up a bit or a piece passed it on. I know no one who held anything out. Nobody thought about an exclusive; it didn't seem important. . . .

I wandered down a corridor and ran into Sidney and Chuck Roberts of *Newsweek*. They'd seen a hearse pulling up at the emergency entrance and we figured they were about to move the body.

We posted ourselves inconspicuously near the emergency entrance. Within minutes they brought the body out in a bronze coffin.

Mrs. Kennedy walked by the coffin, her hand on it, her head down, her hat gone, her dress and stockings spattered. She got into the hearse with the coffin. That was just about the only eyewitness matter that I got with my own eyes that afternoon.

Hawks came in and told us Mr. Johnson would be sworn in immediately at the airport. We dashed for the press buses still parked outside. Many a campaign had taught me something about press buses and I ran a little harder, got there first and went to the wide rear seat. That is the best place on a bus to open up a typewriter and get some work done.

On the short trip to the airport, I got about five hundred words on paper. As we arrived at a back gate along the airstrip, we could see Air Force One, the Presidential jet, screaming down the runway and into the air.

Left behind had been Sid Davis of Westinghouse Broadcasting who with another reporter had prepared a "pool" report on the swearing in. Davis read it off, answered questions, and gave a picture that so far as I know was complete.

I said to Douglas Kiker of the *Tribune*, "We'd better go write. There'll be telephones in the terminal." He agreed. Kiker and I ran a half mile to the terminal, cutting through a baggage handling room to get there. I went immediately to a phone booth and dictated my five hundred word lead, correcting it as I read, embellishing it too.

I would write two pages, run down the stairs across the waiting room, grab a phone and dictate. Miraculously, I never had to wait for a phone booth or to get a line through. Dictating each take, I would throw in items I hadn't written, sometimes whole paragraphs.

Shortly after 7:00 p.m. I finished. So did Kiker. When I left the airport, I knew the worst of it was over. The story was filed on time, good or bad, complete or imcomplete, and any reporter knows how that feels. They couldn't say I missed the deadline.

From Tom Wicker, *On Press*, Viking, New York, 1978, 115-122.

---

was brought to an end by the onset of the depression.

The Decline of Newspapers

The depression adversely affected the newspaper industry, causing the total income of the industry to decrease 20 percent during the 1930s. This drop in revenue precipitated the closing of a number of papers; quite simply, those that were marginally profitable were forced to cease publication. As if worsening economic conditions were not enough of a blow, the newspaper industry was also faced with a new competitor for advertising dollars—radio. Intrigued with the potential of the new medium, advertisers were putting increasingly large percentages of their dollars into the popular new audio medium rather than into print. Since newspaper publishers had adhered to the practice of purchasing competing papers, they now decided to purchase competing radio stations as well, and by 1940 one-third of the radio stations operating in the United States were owned by newspapers. Some years later, when television also

---

MEDIA PROBE

1. Select a paper which is publishing in your home state today. Using both library sources and direct contact with the newspaper's public relations department, answer these questions:

    When did the paper begin? Who started it? Who currently owns it?
    Is the paper that exists today a result of a consolidation? If so, when did this occur? Why? What changes, if any, were made after a consolidation or ownership change?

2. Using a local library, conduct an investigation of a newspaper that once existed in your area but no longer exists today. This time attempt to answer these questions.

    When did the newspaper begin publication?
    When did it cease publication? Why?
    What happened to its staff? Were they fired? Absorbed elsewhere?

began to take away newspaper readers, the publishers, acting again to protect their interests, began purchasing television stations as well.

But owing to an infusion of revenue from local advertisers, newspapers are still very much a part of the media scene today. Let us next examine how and why they have managed to survive.

NEWSPAPERS TODAY: SOMETHING FOR EVERYBODY

Current newspapers come in a variety of shapes, sizes, and colors. Some are printed daily, while others come out weekly. Though traditionally tied to newsprint and prepared with the aid of high-speed printing presses, contemporary newspaper giants have now moved into the technological age of satellites and computers. Journalism professor Ernest Hynds in his book *American Newspapers in the 1980's* points out that today "newspapers must think of themselves as information providers and their audiences as information consumers."[15] Anthony Smith in *Goodbye Gutenberg* expands on this concept when he suggests that newspapers should be termed "an information collection industry with a number of new electronic as well as old print outlets developing over time."[16] In order to make sense out of this increasingly complex industry, let us begin to explore the types of newspapers that exist today.

Dailies

To be considered a daily, a newspaper must publish at least five issues per week. Today there are some 1710 such publications in the United States. Since advertisers—the major source of revenue for any newspaper—are concerned with the number of people who will be exposed to their messages, a newspaper's circulation is a key factor in determining whether or not the paper will be an economic success. Today daily newspapers that have a combined circulation of approximately 62.4 million copies have been experiencing changes. Several metropolitan dailies, including the *New York Herald Tribune,* the *Chicago Daily News,* and the *Washington Star,* have folded. As you can see in Figure 3-1, major afternoon newspapers have recently found themselves in financial trouble, while morning dailies have been gaining in numbers. Some people suggest this is because today we have more time to read in the mornings but less time to read at night. Do you agree? Additionally, Americans have been spending more of their time with Sunday papers. Sunday editions rose from 586 in 1970 to 786 in 1982. William Marcil, the chairman and president of the American Newspaper Publishers Association claims: "Our business is strong and competitive and thriving." One reason for this health has been the advent of national dailies.

National Dailies The year is 1975; satellites have entered the newspaper industry and by so doing have made the concept of a national newspaper a reality. In 1975 *The Wall Street Journal* opened a plant in Florida that was equipped to publish the newspaper by printing full-page images that had been trans-

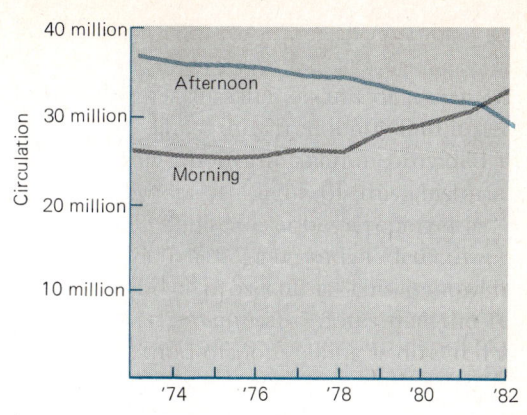

FIGURE 3-1 The decline of afternoon dailies. Figures for 1982 are preliminary. (*Editor and Publisher Yearbook and Newspaper Advertising Bureau; The New York Times, April 24, 1983.*)

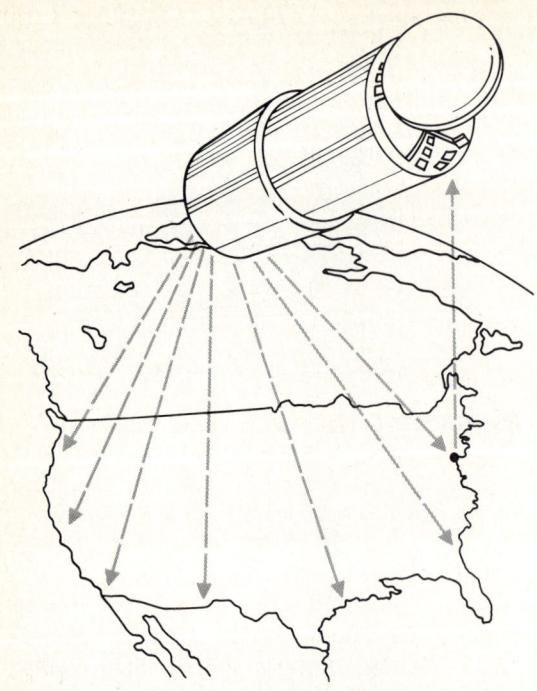

FIGURE 3-2 How satellites carry the news. Electronic signals carrying made-up pages of a magazine or newspaper are beamed to a satellite 22,300 miles above the earth. The signals are then beamed down to receiving stations across the United States, where the publications are printed and distributed. (*USA Today*, December 21, 1982.)

mitted by satellite. By 1983 four regional (eastern, midwest, southwest, and western) editions of *The Wall Street Journal* were being printed at seventeen plants nationwide. Though the news content of each edition is identical, the advertising varies from region to region. *The Wall Street Journal* was followed into space by other newspapers including the west coast, Chicago, and Florida editions of *The New York Times, The Christian Science Monitor,* and the international edition of the *Herald Tribune.*

Then, on September 15, 1982, *USA Today,* the country's first general-interest national newspaper was delivered via satellite. Unlike *The Wall Street Journal* and other national

MEDIA PROBE

After examining copies of both *The Wall Street Journal* and *USA Today,* compile a list of their differences and similarities. Which paper, in your opinion, is designed to meet your needs? Why? You may be surprised to find that only 73 percent of *The Wall Street Journal's* readers have attended college; *USA Today's* readers are not far behind—68 percent having attended college.

Neuharth believes that there is room for two more national dailies in this country. If you were chairperson of a national news organization, would you be in favor of establishing a national newspaper that would compete with *USA Today?* Why or why not?

---

dailies, *USA Today* is designed to carry only national advertising. Thus its various plants are able to print identical newspapers. In spite of the technological prowess used to put it together, *USA Today* is not without its critics. Having been termed "junk-food journalism," it is seen by some as the McDonald's of the dailies. Developed by Gannett chairman Allen Neuharth, following a detailed market research effort to determine what people wanted in a daily newspaper, the paper is a splashy product which specializes in short articles. Most of the paper's stories do not jump from page to page as is common in most newspapers. Neuharth says: "We finally had to make a rule that there would only be four stories a day that could jump. Those are the front page feature stories in each section."[17] *USA Today* is envisioned as a "second buy" for the newspaper reader; thus, it is not expected to interfere with the sales of local newspapers, including those owned by the Gannett chain.

Hodding Carter, in the PBS program "Inside Story" voiced the thoughts of many when speaking of *USA Today.*

The new publication is a highly professional product which has already taught a lot of old

What is a mass transit commute without newspapers? (Barbara Alper, Stock, Boston)

dogs some new tricks in the newspaper world. But newspapers have responsibilities as well as rights, and particularly a responsibility to print hard news along with the black ink. Newspapers should give people what is important as well as what is interesting. They must be more than the mirror image of each shift in public taste and opinion. That's where *USA Today* in particular, and Gannett in general, go wrong. But it's also where much of the newspaper business seems to be heading. And that's bad news for all of us.[18]

And critic Ben Bagdikian, in a recent issue of the *Columbia Journalism Review,* echoed Mr. Carter's lament: "Unfortunately, the country's first truly national daily newspaper of general circulation is a mediocre piece of journalism."[19] To what extent do you support the views expressed by Mr. Carter and Mr. Bagdikian? Why?

Suburban Dailies As people and merchants moved into the suburbs, so did newspapers. Although today many major papers such as *The New York Times* do include suburban sections, the suburban dailies have also been quite successful in targeting their editorial content to their particular readers and in attracting advertisers in their own right. Circulation among suburban dailies in communities of 100,000 to 500,000 grew 20 percent during the 1970s and has continued its surge in the 1980s. National advertising is solicited for the suburban press by two trade associations: the Suburban Newspapers of America and US Urban Press. Among the suburban dailies, Long Island's *Newsday* is one of the best-known. *Newsday* utilizes a tabloid format and has grown with Long Island since the paper's inception in 1940, with present-day readership estimated at the half-million mark. Today many suburban newspapers are owned by chains; Gannett, which

MEDIA PROBE

Many people feel that suburban dailies are little more than glorified bulletin boards. Do you agree or disagree? Why? How would you evaluate a suburban daily that serves your area or an area near you? Do you find it interesting to read? Why or why not? Are there any types of articles your paper does not have that you wish it would? If so, what are they?

NEWSPAPERS: THE MEDIUM AND ITS MAKERS

| MEDIA VIEW |

THE WALL STREET JOURNAL.

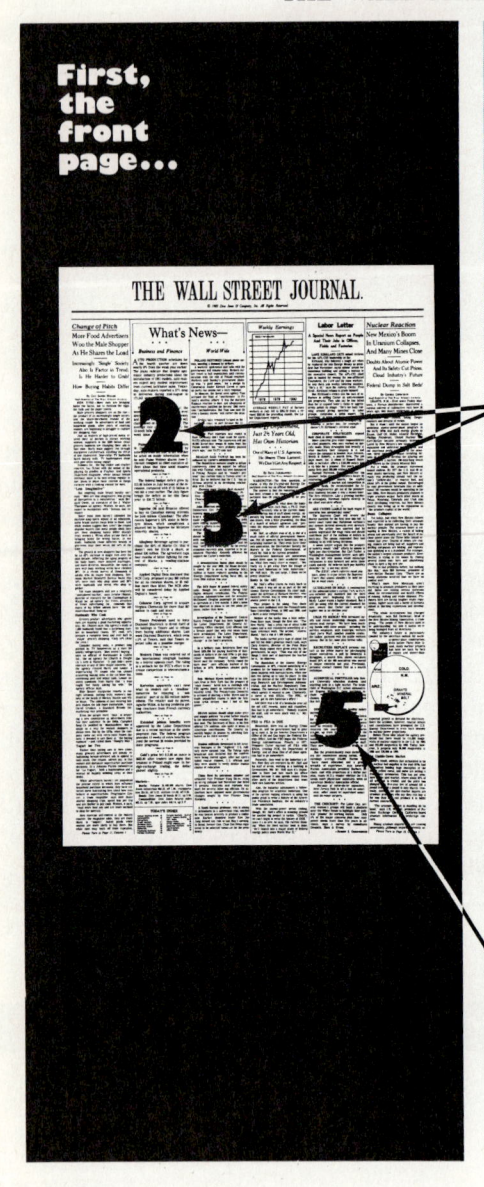

First, the front page...

Black & white and full of color.

The Journal's front page is considered a classic. A standard of excellence for the communications industry. A model studied by journalism schools. This front page combines fast news with in-depth feature reporting. Every phase of business news is covered for the busy people who rely on The Wall Street Journal to keep them informed in as short a time as possible. Here's what you'll find on page one:

Columns 2-3: What's News

Perhaps the most readable set of news capsules available in any newspaper. It takes our editors 14 hours to prepare it so it won't take you more than 10 minutes to read it. Spend 10 minutes or less with these columns and you'll be up-to-the-minute on the important news of the day.

Business and Finance (column two) is a distillation and index of the major news concerning corporate, industrial and economic activities in the U.S. and around the world. A concise summary of each story is followed by a page reference to the complete story in that issue.

World-Wide (column three) briefs readers on the national and international political scene. Boldfaced headings key each item with the most significant nonbusiness news listed first. If you haven't time to read your metropolitan newspaper, the World-Wide column fills you in with a quick, yet thorough overview of the day's news.

Column 5: Special Reports

Since most managers must stay current in a variety of areas, The Journal runs five spe-

74   THE PRINT MEDIA: THE WINDOW OPENS

THE WALL STREET JOURNAL.

Columns 1, 4, 6: Feature Stories

The three daily features on page one help to distinguish The Journal and its special brand of journalism.

Front page features offer comprehensive, deftly crafted, detached interpretations of the world. Subject matter runs the gamut, from rock-jawed investigative stories to erudite economic analyses of government policy to tongue-in-cheek looks at the lighter side of life.

The goals are clear:

"Our purpose is to inform and enlighten our readers. The feature story, by definition, is separate from a spot news story in that it allows you to stand back and take a broader look at an ongoing news development. We wrap in a lot of detail, history and general information that you might not have time to do in the daily news that runs inside the paper."

Glynn Mapes
Front Page Editor

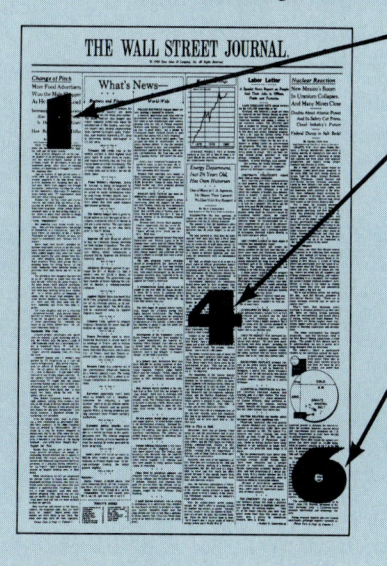

The reporting approach used in features depends on the type of story required. For instance, most stories are written by a single reporter who has delved deeply into the subject matter, taking an overview approach that can require weeks — even months — to complete.

Some features are co-reported; others are the result of "round-ups" — thematic pieces woven together by The Journal's rewrite staff from material submitted by the news bureaus. Occasionally, a series of feature articles sharing a common theme (such as: "Blacks in America") will be published.

These feature stories appear in slots that have developed their own personalities:

Column one. For the most part these are general interest stories, many of them sociological in nature. Subjects may include law, education, politics or foreign affairs. Typical features: an examination of archaeology in the U.S.; a report on how more states are monitoring judges for improper conduct; a personality profile of an ex-salesman who struck it rich by founding two heart-device firms; a comprehensive analysis of the Russian presence in Afghanistan.

Column four. Articles are apt to be about anything — from a treatise on playing Blackjack in Atlantic City to the methods used by the Treasury Department to dispose of worn-out bills. To the reader discovering The Journal for the first time, column four comes as a real surprise.

Column six. Typically, this is a hard news story on business, economics or finance. Occasionally, there will be an investigative report known as a "cops and robbers" story. Some recent features: A miniseries on plant closing procedures in Britain and the U.S.; the business climate of South Korea; a thorough review of the President's economic program; a report on top executives who have "retired" but still wield considerable influence.

NEWSPAPERS: THE MEDIUM AND ITS MAKERS

owns ninety papers, Hearst, Knight-Ridder, and W. O. Scripps dominate the suburban daily market.

Weeklies

About 7500 weekly newspapers in this country serve small towns and suburbs. Designed to provide a sense of identity for local communities, these papers compete for advertising dollars with the dailies. Today weekly newspapers have a combined circulation of 40,243,795.

The Throwaway Shopper The throwaway shopper is one variety of weekly publication. Advertising occupies an average of 74 percent of the paper. Popular with advertisers because they enable them to reach 100 percent of the households in a specified area, they are delivered free of charge to consumers. Both the shopper and the weekly local newspaper are usually nonunion operations. These types of papers may constitute the last opportunity for people to start small in the newspaper business. The more than 1500 shopper papers yield a combined revenue of $500 million.

Supermarket Tabloids

Did you realize that aliens may be visiting Earth? That John Wayne may have returned from the dead? That you may diet while consuming pizza after pizza? If not, you probably have not been reading *The National Enquirer* or its clone, *The Star*. Many people have, however. In 1982 the Newspaper Readership Project reported that these two publications were reaching 20 million readers each week.

Generoso Pope purchased the Florida-based *National Enquirer* in 1952, establishing a "I Cut Out Her Heart and Stomped on It" cannibalism and gore approach to journalism. In 1968 the paper's format was altered in order to make it suitable for supermarket check-out rack distribution. It was followed to those racks in 1974 by Rupert Murdoch's *Star, The National Tattler,* and *Midnight,* among others.

Media critic Hodding Carter has called the supermarket tabloid type of newspaper a "journalistic mutt."[20] Although the reporters who write for these papers utilize techniques similar to those of recognized journalists—and claim to publish the truth—they do so in a rather sensational fashion.

Who reads these publications? Mostly lower-income females with no college education. Fully 65 percent of *National Enquirer* readers are women. Eight out of ten readers have not received more than a high school education, and 25 percent of the readers are in the 18 to 24-year-old range. However, 72 percent of the paper's readership are also newspaper readers—this figure is higher than the national average.[21]

In large measure, the "tabs" concentrate on reporting celebrity stories (often these precipitate lawsuits), diet tips, sensational medical breakthroughs, and psychic phenomenon. In fact, many of the tabloids employ psychics on their payrolls and use them to check out various leads.

Hodding Carter emphasizes that whether we are willing to face up to it or not, "respectable" media folk not only read the tabloids but also watch *Entertainment Tonight* and *Real People*. He further notes that *Good Morning America* conducts interviews not far removed from those featured in the tabloids and states that, in his opinion, *People Magazine* is but a step above them. Carter sums up his position: "If the tabs were the only game in town, it would be a bad thing—just as it would be if Twinkies were the only thing on food shelves. But they're not." He believes that "taken with a grain of salt," the tabs are harmless entertainment and represent the "twilight zone of American journalism." To what extent do you agree or disagree with Carter?

Special-Interest and Alternative Newspapers

Special-interest newspapers are newspapers directed at particular segments of the newspaper-reading audience. Primary target groups for special-interest papers include college students and minorities.

College Papers Many colleges support student-run daily, weekly, or monthly newspapers. Circulation of these papers range from a high of 40,000 for some down to a monthly readership of but a few hundred. Some colleges offer competing newspapers—one a laboratory publication of a journalism or communications department, and the other a semiautonomous publication emanating from the student government. Because surveys have shown that 96 percent of a college's population read at least part of the campus paper, college papers attract advertisers. Examine the college paper available on your campus. Who controls its publication? Who funds it? Would you consider volunteering your time to work for it? Do you read it regularly? Why or why not?

The Alternative Press *Alternative newspapers* are said to have begun with the 1955 publication of *The Village Voice*. When first published, the *Voice* offered its readership slanted political and cultural news. According to Robert Glessing, author of *The Underground Press in America,* the *Voice* was "the first newspaper in the history of modern American journalism to consistently report news with no restriction on language, a policy widely adopted by underground editors to shock the authority structure." *The Village Voice* was followed by a number of other underground or alternative papers (each the product of Americans who felt alienated from the mainstream); prime among these was *The Los Angeles Free Press*. For example, during the Vietnamese war era, hordes of young Americans who felt cut off from the establishment also felt themselves alienated from establishment presses. The needs of these people were met by alternative newspapers. The underground press attacked society and the war, frequently advertised sex, and included pleas from parents seeking runaway children. In addition, the underground press also relished attacking the mainstream press.[22] Today, most offerings of the underground press have vanished. *The Village Voice* does still exist, but under the ownership of newspaper magnate Rupert Murdoch.

The Minority Press The 1979 *Editor and Publisher Yearbook* listed 215 foreign-language newspapers in this country. Most prominent among these were the offerings of the Spanish-language press. *El Diario-La Prensa* has become a common sight in New York City, with a daily circulation of 69,000, as has *Diario Los Americas* in Miami, where the daily circulation is 55,000. Spanish-language newspapers in Texas and California are also growing with the Hispanic populations of these states.

Black-owned and operated newspapers date back to the publication of *Freedom's Journal* in 1827 by John B. Russwurm. Russwurm published the weekly to oppose exploitation and support equal rights. Over 3000 black newspapers have appeared since that time. Orator Fredrick Douglass, for example, published a number of newspapers including *Fredrick Douglass's Paper* and *The New National Era*. Through his editorial policies, Douglass let it be know that he supported "free men, free soil, free speech, a free press everywhere in the land. The ballot for all, education for all, fair wages for all."[23] From the late nineteenth century on, the black press grew in numbers, peaking at 275 papers in the 1960s. In recent years, however, the black press has experienced a decline. As the "white" press gave more coverage to minority issues in general, the audience for black-owned presses diminished correspondingly. Professor Phyl Garland of the Columbia

Graduate School of Journalism believes that the readership of the black presses has changed as well: "the black reader has grown far more sophisticated and is one of the major factors the black newspaper publisher is going to have to address if he is going to be successful today."

Black newspapers are making efforts to adapt. In the early 1980s, the *Sacramento Observer, Winston-Salem Chronicle,* and the *Pittsburgh Courier* were all making changes in layout and content in order to better their chances of reaching the more upscale black readership. Researcher Roland Wolsey believes there will always be a black press, "unless fully integrated means the complete eradication of the black experience, culture and personality."[24]

In Oakland, however, the minority press story underwent a new twist as Robert Maynard became the first black owner-publisher of a general-circulation metropolitan daily. In May 1983, Maynard purchased the ailing *Oakland Tribune* from the Gannett chain. Prior to that date, Maynard had served as the paper's editor and publisher. Upon becoming the paper's owner, Maynard hired additional nonwhite reporters in an effort to attract readers from the city's 54 percent black and Hispanic majority.[25] Thus, Maynard assumed the task of publishing a paper that appeals to minority groups as well as to the general public.

THE ORGANIZATION OF A NEWSPAPER: WHO DOES WHAT?

In order to operate effectively, a newspaper, like any media organization, must be organized in a systematic way (Figure 3-3). Although there is no one scheme used across the board, and not all newspapers can afford to staff each department separately, all newspapers fulfill news and opinion and production and business functions. Heading the newspaper is the owner. He or she appoints a publisher, who oversees the newspaper's

MEDIA PROBE

Examine current issues of your local newspaper. On what day does the newshole appear to be the largest? What sections of the paper contain the most ads? Where on the paper's pages are advertisements typically placed?

operation; in small operations, however, the owner may also function as the publisher.

The Business Function

The newspaper's business department performs advertising, circulation, promotion, and personnel functions. As with any organization, this department is concerned with payments that go out and revenues that come in. Much of the newspaper's incoming revenue is supplied by the advertising group.

Since advertising is expected to bring in approximately three-quarters of a newspaper's income, it is of major concern to the paper. Because newspapers rely so heavily on advertising, more and more of the paper's space is devoted to it. The advertising in a typical newspaper consumes from 23 to 70 percent of the paper's available column space. In most papers, the average space consumed by advertising is 60 percent. Newspapers print local (about 60 percent), national (about 10 percent) and classified (about 25 percent) advertising. National advertising usually comes to the paper from an advertising agency in camera-ready form. Classified advertisements are used extensively by people looking for jobs, organizations looking for people, and real estate buyers and sellers. Newspapers also distribute preprints—those fliers which are printed elsewhere and inserted into the paper prior to sale.

After all the advertisements are set, the remaining space available in the paper is called the *news hole*. Thus, it is the news, and not the advertising, that is made to fit the available space. Seldom are pages added to a paper so

MEDIA PROBE

Have you or anyone whom you know served as a newspaper carrier? Some people believe that since the newspaper pays its carriers no benefits such as social security or health insurance, it exploits them. Do you agree? Why or why not?

---

that more news can be printed. Pages are added regularly, however, to accommodate additional advertising.

On certain days of the week newspapers increase in length. Since Wednesday and Sunday are heavy advertising days, the papers published on these days will be longer. Keep in mind that as the amount of advertising increases, the size of the news hole may increase as well.

Approximately 25 percent of the income a newspaper receives is developed through circulation or sale. Newspapers are sold in a number of different ways. Newsstands or vendors, once popular in cities, have recently experienced a decline in use. Some newspapers, especially weeklies, are now sold entirely by subscription. Boxes or containers on street corners are another method of circulation. According to the Newspaper Advertising Bureau, 77 percent of all newspapers sold are home-delivered. This system depends for the most part on youngsters aged 12 to 16 who deliver the product to homes and apartments. Proponents of this medium believe that since each carrier operates as an independent distributor, this system helps them acquire basic business practices.

Lately, a number of newspapers have ex-

FIGURE 3-3 Organization chart of a typical newspaper.

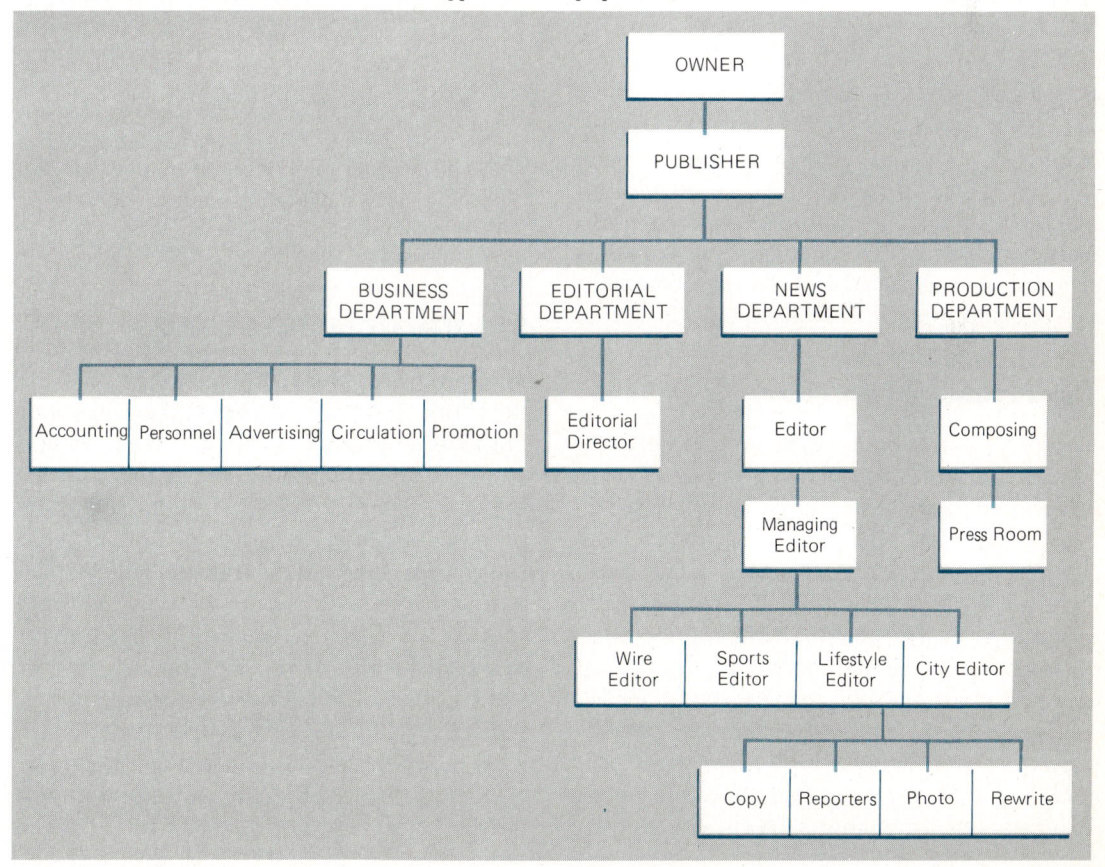

NEWSPAPERS: THE MEDIUM AND ITS MAKERS

perimented with hiring delivery personnel as staff members. Other papers have assumed the carrier's billing responsibilities so that the carrier is not forced to make extra house calls in order "to collect." In some locations like apartment houses or colleges, newspapers are now placed in a locked container to which only the subscribers have a key. This enables such subscribers to receive the daily paper and deposit the subscription charge in the box at the same time. While electronic means of delivery may affect traditional circulation methods in the future, the hand-delivered system seems to be well-entrenched.

Newspaper promotion people perform public relations functions for their organization. They aim to communicate a positive image of the newspaper organization to the general public so that circulation will be increased. To achieve this goal, the people in promotion sponsor athletic leagues, concerts, or other community-oriented events designed to encourage readers and potential readers to view the paper as a "human" enterprise. Of late, games have also been utilized as promotional devices. Wingo-Zingo-Zappo lottery-type games are used to entice people to purchase a particular newspaper. On a more academic note, "newspaper in education" programs are also used as a way to encourage and promote student readership.

The Production Function

The job of a newspaper's production department is to transfer words and photographs to the printed page. This task is accomplished in three phases: the first phase occurs in the composing room, where the page is laid out; the second phase occurs in the platemaking room, where the plates that produce the printed page are prepared; and the last phase occurs in the pressroom, where the paper is actually printed on high-speed presses. Computers, offset printers, and lasers have all combined to increase the speed and efficiency of newspaper production. Recently, changes have occurred in large and small newspapers alike. In 1982, for example, *The Record,* a medium-sized suburban daily, invested $62 million in new production equipment:

> Two high-speed offset presses have come all the way from Tokyo to take up residence in the plant's brand-new four-story pressroom. This awesome installation, designed by Tokyo Kikai Seisakusho (TKS), provides high-quality offset printing and more color printing capability than any other daily currently being published in this country. Completely computer-controlled, the 41-foot-high presses have little resemblance to the Scott letterpresses already being dismantled in the original pressroom. The new presses account for $23 million of the total project cost—the largest item on the books, consistent with the role they play at the core of the operation.
>
> The pioneering TKS presses are linked to an equally unusual inserting and storage system, displaying its Swiss-made precision as it handles the flow of newspapers to *The Record's* enlarged and renovated mail room. Designed by Ferag, this system is also a pilot installation for the United States. Completely computerized, it not only hastens the collating of newspaper sections and advertising inserts, but also increases geographic and demographic zoning capabilities for *The Record* and its advertisers.[26]

The News/Opinion Function

The news and editorial departments provide the product of the newspaper. You will notice in the organizational chart that the news and editorial departments of the paper are distinct and separate, with both reporting to the publisher. In this way, the news department can remain "objective" while the editorial department presents opinions. The editorial function is designed to help readers make sense out of the news and draw conclusions about topics of importance to contemporary society. In addition to the printing of editorials, the editorial function includes the selection and printing of letters to the editor, and on the op-ed or page opposite the editorial page, regular and guest columnists are given the opportunity to voice their views on issues of controversy.

The news division is headed by a managing editor or editor-in-chief. He or she is responsible for coordinating the operation of the news room. In addition, a number of editors work for this person and are charged with more specific responsibilities:

The wire editor is responsible for regional, national, and international news from the wire services.

The city editor is responsible for local events.

The sports editor is responsible for sports news.

The lifestyle editor is responsible for entertainment, society, food, and other features.

Since we like to think that news is at the heart of a newspaper, we believe it is important that we consider the reporter at work.

YOU WERE THERE

REPORTERS AT WORK: TWO VIEWS

VIEW ONE

June 17, 1972. Nine o'clock Saturday morning. Early for the telephone. Woodward fumbled for the receiver and snapped awake. The city editor of the *Washington Post* was on the line. Five men had been arrested earlier that morning in a burglary at Democratic headquarters, carrying photographic equipment and electronic gear. Could he come in?

Woodward had worked for the *Post* for only nine months and was always looking for a good Saturday assignment, but this didn't sound like one. . . .

Woodward left his one-room apartment in downtown Washington and walked the six blocks to the *Post*. The newspaper's mammoth newsroom—sound-absorbing carpet—is usually quiet on Saturday morning. Saturday is a day for long lunches, catching up on work, reading the Sunday supplements. As Woodward stopped to pick up his mail and telephone messages at the front of the newsroom, he noticed unusual activity around the city desk. He checked in with the city editor and learned with surprise that the burglars had not broken into the small local Democratic

Party office but the headquarters of the Democratic National Committee in the Watergate office-apartment-hotel complex. . . .

As Woodward began making phone calls, he noticed that Bernstein, one of the paper's two Virginia political reporters, was working on the burglary story, too.

Oh God, not Bernstein, Woodward thought, recalling several office tales about Bernstein's ability to push his way into a good story and get his byline on it. . . . Bernstein had begun a series of phone calls to everybody at the Watergate he could reach—desk clerks, bellmen, maids in the housekeeping department, waiters in the restaurant.

Bernstein looked across the newsroom. There was a pillar between his desk and Woodward's, about 25 feet away. He stepped back several paces. It appeared that Woodward was also working on the story. That figured, Bernstein thought. Bob Woodward was a prima donna who played heavily at office politics. Yale. A veteran of the Navy officer corps. . . . Bernstein was a college dropout. He had started as a copy boy at the *Washington Star* when he was 16, become a full-time

Carl Woodward and Robert Bernstein, the Watergate reporting team, at their *Washington Post* newsroom. The third party is probably not "Deep Throat." (Mark Godfrey, Archive Pictures)

reporter at 19, and had worked at the *Post* since 1966....

They had never worked on a story together. Woodward was 29, Bernstein 28.

The five men arrested at 2:30 a.m. had been dressed in business suits and all had worn Playtex rubber surgical gloves. Woodward learned that the suspects were going to appear in court that afternoon for a preliminary hearing. He decided to go....

Woodward had been to the courthouse before. The hearing procedure was an institutionalized fixture of the local court's turnstile system of justice: A quick appearance before a judge, who set bond for accused pimps, prostitutes, muggers—and, on this day, the five men who had been arrested at Watergate. At 3:30 p.m. the five suspects still dressed in dark business suits but stripped of their belts and ties, were led into the courtroom by a marshall. They seated themselves silently in a row and stared blankly toward the bench, kneading their hands. They looked nervous, respectful and tough.

Judge James A. Belsen asked the men their professions. One spoke up, answering that they were anticommunists, and the others nodded in agreement. The tallest of the suspects, who had given his name as James W. McCord, Jr., was asked to step forward. He was balding with a large, flat nose, a square jaw, perfect teeth and a benign expression that seemed incongruous with his hard edged features.

The Judge asked his occupation.

"Security consultant," he replied.

The Judge asked where.

McCord, in a soft drawl, said that he had recently retired from government service. Woodward moved to the front row and leaned forward.

"Where in government?" asked the Judge.

"CIA," McCord whispered.

The Judge flinched slightly.

Holy shit, Woodward said half aloud, the CIA.

He got a cab back to the office and reported McCord's statement. Eight reporters were involved in putting together the story under the byline of Alfred E. Lewis. As the 6:30 deadline approached, Howard Simons, the *Post's* managing editor, came into the city editor's office at the south side of the newsroom. "That's a hell of a story," he told the city editor, Barry Sussman, and ordered it onto Sunday's front page.

The first paragraph of the story read:

Five men, one of whom said he is a former employee of the Central Intelligence Agency, were arrested at 2:30 a.m. yesterday in what authorities described as an

82   THE PRINT MEDIA: THE WINDOW OPENS

elaborate plot to bug the offices of the Democratic National Committee here. . . .

On January 30, 1975, the President had delivered his annual State of the Union Message to a joint session of the House and Senate. . . .

"One year of Watergate is enough. . . . I want you to know that I have no intention whatever of walking away from the job that the American people elected me to do for the people of the United States."

Carl Bernstein and Bob Woodward, *All The President's Men,* Simon & Schuster, New York, 1974, pp. 13–19.

VIEW TWO

The day started at 6 a.m.: I was the first person in the building. I turned on the lights, along with the waxing machines, and sometimes the typesetter computers. We had an old-time chief composer who was a real bear—he didn't like women and especially young ones.

The wire—just AP—turned on by an electric timer at 1 a.m. We ran two tape machines and two printers because the editor, who was then near retirement, remembered too many times when the machines had jammed. They were old when I got there, and among my chores was being a minor league mechanic. They took a lot of kind words to keep running. Anyway, there were two enormous piles of computer tape awaiting me every morning. The trick was to go through the printed copy, pick out what I wanted to save after assessing my space needs, and then wind all the tapes and match them up with the copy. . . . Mondays were especially fun because I not only had that day's tape to contend with, but I also had miles of Sunday tape.

The next chore was to distribute the copy I had left from the previous afternoon to the punchers. They started at 7 a.m. From then on—every 20 minutes until 3:30—I ran a constant path from the desk through the wire room to make certain the reluctant machines were still working. Then I went through the composing room to collect whatever insults or problems the union shop might throw out. Then I would go the puncher's room to check their progress, shuffle the copy piles because some worked faster than others. Finally, I went through the proofroom to pick up corrections, then back to the composing room.

It was also invaluable because survival as a news editor depended on getting the paper out on time, and I could affect that in my little trip. It never failed that one of the punchers had put the important Page One story on the bottom of the Pleasant Gap personals that weren't going to run for a week.

From 7 to 8 I read, edited, and wrote headlines on whatever copy I had for that day. The editor had a special place in his heart for the four-inch light stories that came in on the wire every day. During that same hour I decided what needed to be written locally that hadn't been planned the day before.

The reporters would come in at 8 a.m. and I would talk with each reporter about story content, lengths, leads and the like. Also, at 8 a.m., the phones started ringing.

The editor wanted to see the page layouts and the day's plans by 9 a.m. We talked about what the day would bring, and we tried to plan for it. . . . Early deadlines on some stories were 10 a.m. and the little things, like hospital notes and accident reports, were due then. By 11 a.m. I usually started prodding the reporters.

We had two bureaus and also telecopter copier—which was a machine that was kept together with spit. The final piece of copy was, allegedly, to be given to the punchers no later than noon, but we often had to push that deadline back because of a late-breaking story or an errant reporter. But the paper had to be pasted up no later than 1 p.m. The last story was punched one page at a time, often while the reporter was still writing the final page. . . .

From about 1:30 to 3:30 I worked on the next day's paper: processing people page copy, features, Hints from Heloise, horoscopes, Dear

Abby, personals from 35 little towns . . . and anything else anyone wanted to place in a community paper. . . .

About 3—but usually closer to 4 or 5—the dummy for the next day's paper was on my desk. Although that was supposed to be the end of the day, it never was. The ad person who made up the dummy forgot to put in a full-page ad at least one or two days a week. Because the dummy from the advertising department filled only the ads, I dummied in the news, features, pictures, notes and records we already had. The dummy then went to the composing room workers the next day—and, like the type, untouchable for us. . . .

Ellen Findley, quoted in William L. Rivers, *News Editing in the '80s,* Wadsworth, Belmont, Calif:, 1983.

SUMMARY

In this chapter we explored the emergence of the newspaper. From the corantos to the diurnals, from the days of Benjamin Harris's *Publick Occurrences* to Allen Neuharth's *USA Today,* we saw how changes in the newspaper industry reflected changes in the world and influenced how people thought about the press.

Newspapers played a role in many of the key events of our country. They printed colonists' grievances during the revolutionary period, sparked the cry for freedom of speech as a result of the John Peter Zenger case, and advanced the political-journalism movement. Becoming a truly mass medium once the penny press came on the scene, newspapers attracted advertisers and also became big business. Competition became fierce. As the years passed, the pendulum swung from sensationalism to objectivity, from cries for social reform to cries for war, but one thing remained constant: publishers were ever attentive to the bottom line—the circulation figure. Eventually, this concern would precipitate an increasing number of consolidations.

Spreading from the major cities to growing industrial centers, from suburbia to small towns, the newspaper industry made a concerted effort to provide something for everybody. Having entered the technological age of satellites and computers, the newspaper is once again in a state of transition. However, even with all the changes, all newspapers still share common purposes: they all perform both news and opinion and production and business functions.

KEY TERMS

Libel
Sedition
Objectivity
Penny press
Summary lead
News cooperative
Yellow journalism
Circulation
Jazz journalism
Tabloid
Alternative newspapers
News hole
Freedom of the press
Newspaper group or chain

NOTES

[1] Associated Press, April 30, 1983.
[2] Gay Talese, *The Kingdom and the Power,* New American Library, New York, 1969, p. 1.

[3] Edwin Emery, *The Press in America: An Interpretative History of the Mass Media,* Prentice-Hall, Englewood Cliffs, N.J., 1972, p. 3.

[4] Frank Luther Mott, *American Journalism: A History—1690–1960,* 3d ed., Macmillan, New York, 1962, p. 37.

[5] Horace Greeley, *Recollections of a Busy Life,* J. B. Ford, New York, 1868, p. 161.

[6] Talese, op. cit., p. 161.

[7] Mott, op. cit., p. 280.

[8] W. A. Swanberg, *Pulitzer,* Scribner's, New York, 1967, p.70.

[9] W. A. Swanberg, *Citizen Hearst,* Scribner's, New York, 1961, p. 33.

[10] Robert A. Rutland, *Newsmongers: Journalism in the Life of the Nation,* Dial, New York, 1973, p. 263.

[11] Talese, op. cit., p. 6.

[12] Ibid., p. 31.

[13] Mott. op. cit., p. 635.

[14] Frank Munsey, *Munsey's Magazine,* February 1903, p. 664.

[15] Ernest C. Hynds, *American Newspapers in the 1980's,* Hastings House, New York, 1980, p. 11.

[16] Anthony Smith, *Goodbye Gutenberg,* Oxford University Press, New York, 1980, p. 42.

[17] "Life on the Fast Track With Allen Neuharth," *AdWeek,* April 1983, p. 13.

[18] Hodding Carter, *Inside Story,* Public Broadcasting Service, transcript of Program 305, p. 8.

[19] Ben Bagdikian, "Fast Food News—A Week's Diet," *Columbia Journalism Review,* March/April 1983, p. 32.

[20] Hodding Carter, *Inside Story,* Public Broadcasting Service, May 1983.

[21] Newspaper Readership Project, "Readers of *The National Enquirer* and *The Star* are Daily Newspaper Readers, Too!" Newspaper Advertising Bureau, New York, February 1982.

[22] See for example, S. B. Rudnick, "A Fifth Estate," *Orpheus,* August 1968, p. 3.

[23] Roland E. Wolsey, *The Black Press, USA,* Iowa State University Press, Ames, 1971, p. 23.

[24] Wolsey, op. cit., p. 332.

[25] Denise Kalette, "Black Press is Changing with Times," *USA Today,* May 25, 1983.

[26] "The Record," *Commerce Magazine,* October 1982, pp. 33–34.

SUGGESTIONS FOR FURTHER READING

American Newspaper Publishers Association: *News Research Reports,* American Newspaper Publishers Association, Washington, D.C., 1984. *A collection of reports on specific issues relating to newspaper publishing. A listing of current reports may be obtained from ANPA.*

Bogart, Leo: *Press and Public: Who Reads What, Where and Why in American Newspapers.* Lawrence Erlbaum Associates, Hillsdale, N.J., 1981. *A comprehensive examination of newspapers and their audiences.*

Columbia Journalism Review: Published bimonthly, this periodical contains discussions of current issues facing the newspaper industry.

Emery, Edwin, and Michael Emery: *The Press in America: An Interpretative History of the Mass Media,* 4th ed., Prentice-Hall, Englewood Cliffs, N.J., 1978. *A comprehensive text that presents the history of newspapers.*

Hynds, Ernest C.: *American Newspapers in the 1980's,* Hastings House, New York, 1980. *An informal discussion of the current newspaper industry and the problems confronting it.*

Mott, Frank Luther: *American Journalism: A History—1690–1960,* Macmillan, New York, 1962. *A classic text which chronicles the development of the newspaper industry in this country.*

Pitts, Alice Fox: *Read All About It: 50 Years of ASNE,* American Society of Newspaper Editors, Easton, Pa., 1974. *More than a history of the society, it provides first-hand accounts of the development of the newspaper industry.*

Rutland, Robert A.: *Newsmongers: Journalism in the Life of the Nation,* Dial, New York, 1973. *A provocative examination of journalism and the development of our society.*

Smith, Anthony: *Goodbye Gutenberg,* Oxford University Press, New York, 1980. *A fascinating look at newspapers today and tomorrow.*

Talese, Gay: *The Kingdom and the Power,* New American Library, New York, 1969. *A thor-*

ough examination of the development of The New York Times.

Williams, Herbert: *Newspaper Organization and Management,* Iowa State University Press, Ames, 1978. *A discussion of newspapers from a management point of view.*

CHAPTER 4

NEWSPAPERS: THE CONTENT AND THE ISSUES

Do anything. Go anywhere for a byline.
                Bernard Weinraub
                         Bylines

The function of the press in society is to inform, but its role is to make money.
                A. J. Liebling
                The Press

CHAPTER PREVIEW

After reading this chapter, you should be able to:
- Define "news"
- Enumerate and explain the criteria that make an event newsworthy
- Discuss the role that wire services, local, and investigative reporters play in gathering the news
- Describe the pressures that face reporters during the development of news articles
- Explain the rationale behind the inverted pyramid
- Assess the effectiveness of news article headlines
- Define and identify examples of "new journalism"
- Compare and contrast the authoritarian, libertarian, and social-responsibility theories of the press
- Define libel and assess how libel suits affect the way the press operates
- Discuss how the privacy principle affects the newspaper's ability to cover the news
- Describe the conflict between the First and Sixth Amendments
- Explain how prior restraint affects a reporter's ability to do his or her job
- Assess the extent to which the Freedom of Information Act has facilitated the reporter's job
- Discuss how conflicts of interest can interfere with a reporter's objectivity
- Explain the problems that the fair-play principle might precipitate
- Discuss under what conditions, if any, keeping secrets serves the public interest

One newspaper editor notes, "When a dog bites a man, that is not news; but when a man bites a dog, that is news." Fortunately, this is not the only credo adhered to.

WHAT IS NEWS?

In a 1982 report issued by The Newspaper Readership Project, researchers Judee Burgoon, Michael Burgoon, and Charles Atkin asked 489 working journalists how they defined *news*.[1] The responses they received included: "What raises eyebrows." "The flux of events." "Blood, sweat, war, and games." "What I want to write about." One of those replying, journalist Chris Koch, was somewhat more specific in phrasing his definition: "News generally involves an event which is observed either by the journalist or another individual, and this observation is recreated or reported to an audience." Thus, from Koch's perspective, news is the report of an event, not the event itself. Consequently, events that are unnoticed, events that are not recorded by a medium of mass communication, would not be considered news.

The size of the news hole also exerts an influence on what is considered news. As editors make decisions regarding what stories there will and will not be room for, they shape and define the news. Every day, editors receive a dummy, or layout, of pages for the following day's edition of the paper. The editor's job is to fill the space exactly. Too much or too little content for the news hole can cost the paper money, as unionized employees go on overtime while they wait to run and then deliver the completed product.

MEDIA PROBE

Working alone or with a group develop your own definition of "news."

Traditionally, journalists have been taught that an event becomes news or newsworthy if it fulfills one or more of five basic criteria: prominence, proximity, consequence, timeliness, and human interest. The first quality, *prominence*, refers to the concept that some people are simply better-known than others; hence, they become the newsmakers. Who might make the national news with the birth of a child: a well-known film star or your authors? If someone is well-known, what he or she does or accomplishes becomes of interest to readers. The second quality, *proximity*, serves as a measurement of the closeness of a story to the newspaper's readers. The local newspaper will cover local fires and accidents, but an accident that occurs in another state or country will have to be quite unusual or affect the future of readers if it is to be picked up outside of the locale in which it took place. This brings us to the third quality, *consequence;* consequence refers to whether or not an event will significantly affect the lives of the newspaper's readers. For example, usually events leading up to war are judged to be more newsworthy than events that lead up to a supermarket opening. The fourth quality, *timeliness*, is that which makes news "news" and not "olds." Current happenings and trends fall into this category. As Ben Bagdikian points out, however, our system of news reporting actually favors older information at times. This is because the earlier the story reaches an editor, the better the story's chances of being used. Thus, if you were planning to run a press conference in a community that had an afternoon newspaper, it would be better to schedule it for 10 A.M. than for 4 P.M. The fifth quality, *human interest*, relates to whether or not a story is emotionally appealing or unusual. The fact that 4000 students at a local college go diligently about their studies is not news; the fact that they riot is, however. Stories that are heart-tuggers, or that reveal the human side of events usually also find eager readers.

In a report prepared for the American Newspaper Publishers Association, researcher Michael Singletary put newsworthiness tests into perspective:

> When editors contemplate the newsworthiness and therefore the 'play' of a news story, their judgment is colored not just by the tried and true tests of timeliness, consequence, proximity, prominence and human interest, but also by their own professional publishers' preferences. The size of the newspaper, the nature of the competition, links with other news organizations, the kind of play the competition gives the same story and even a kind of follow-the-leader relationship with the larger newspapers.[2]

One additional news determinant worthy of our attention is conflict—either physical or intellectual. Two points of view on the value of a new drug, a dispute over the value attributed to a type of therapy, or a debate on the worth of a teaching technique can be a factor contributing to the selection of a story as newsworthy. As we know, violence is a form of conflict, and seen from this angle, it too becomes a newsworthy event.

GATHERING THE NEWS

Newspapers rely on three basic sources for news: the wire services; local reporters who cover regular beats, and more specialized investigative reporters.

The Wire Services

Pick up a copy of your local daily newspaper. How many articles in it are credited to the Associated Press (AP) or United Press International (UPI)? Your research will probably demonstrate that a large percentage of stories originate with these and other news services, including The New York Times News Service and Reuters. Quite simply, local newspapers are able to gather much of the in-

A reporter talks to her source. To become news, an event must be discovered, authenticated, and professionally reported. (Michael Hayman, Photo Researchers)

formation they make available to you because of the satellite hookups they have established with the *wire services*.

AP and UPI both have some 200 bureaus operating worldwide; it is the task of the bureaus to gather and transmit information. UPI, for example, sends 13 million words per day. Competition from other services and radio and television has made speed essential for the wire reporters—even when they face danger as a result.

At the local newspaper, a wire service editor is charged with selecting appropriate stories from the thousands that are sent over the various satellite and wire distribution systems each day. AP and UPI both compile a "budget," or list of important stories to be transmitted that day. The wire editor assembles the stories or "slugs," making note of the most important; these are submitted to the

NEWSPAPERS: THE CONTENT AND THE ISSUES 89

YOU WERE THERE

MAD DASH FOR THE PHONES

The pressure for speed is inherent in wire service work. A UPI man who witnessed two assassination attempts was Dean Reynolds. In 1972, covering a George Wallace speech in Laurel, MD, he was 25 feet away and saw Wallace recoil from the shots and fall, and Wallace's wife throw her body over his. As Reynolds sprinted for a pay phone, he worried that police might mistakenly shoot at him.

In 1981 Reynolds was 10 feet from President Reagan when the president was outside the Washington Hilton. Reynolds took off so fast that people he ran by were still crouched on the sidewalk. Again he feared being shot. Inside he bowled over several people who began cursing him and finally found a phone in an office.

Later, police seeking a "mystery man" who some said had run from the scene, realized it was Reynolds.

H.D. Doc Quigg, "UPI . . . As It Was and As It Is," *Editor and Publisher,* September 25, 1982, pp. 17–18.

---

news editor. This process is described by one wire editor for *The Miami News:*

> The bulk of the stories should move to the news editor by 5 a.m. Late-breaking and page-one stories should be through by 5:30 a.m. The afternoon weather story usually moves about this time; the AP story slugged "Nation's Weather" gives this information. If things are particularly bad (earthquakes in California, blizzards in the West, ice storms in New England), AP usually moves a separate story. The wire editor will flag the news editor if something like this should happen.

The wire editor views each story as a separate piece to be sent to the news editor or other departmental editors, for instance, lifestyle, sports, or business. Today, the articles distributed over the wire can be delivered directly into typesetting machines. Since the cheapest way to edit a wire story is to cut it off at the bottom, local rewriting occurs less and less frequently, contributing to a sense of sameness in our nation's newspapers.

The Reporter's Beat

Newspapers can cover local events at less cost than television and radio can. The person who supervises the collection of local information is the city editor; it is his or her job to assign reporters to sections, or beats, within the area to be covered. Typical beats include city hall, the criminal courts, and various police precincts. General-assignment reporters cover a variety of stories ranging from local disasters to food fairs.

Whatever the nature of his or her assignment, a reporter's job is to gather facts and assemble them so that a coherent view of what transpired is presented. Columbia University Professor Melvin Mencher in his book *News Reporting and Writing* notes: "A reporter's job is to look beneath the surface for the underlying reality." Doing this is not easy, however. Much of the news the reporter works with begins with a press release, a press conference, a speech, a decree, or a court decision. Such examples all have one element in common: they originate with and are controlled by the source. Reporters who deal exclusively with such source-controlled information run the danger of turning into rewrite men and women who simply verify delivered facts and put the material into a form acceptable to their newspaper.

One specific kind of source-controlled event that is fabricated just so the reporter can cover it has been termed a *pseudo-event* by social historian Daniel J. Boorstin. According to Boorstin, a pseudo-event "is not spontaneous, but comes about because someone has planned, planted or incited it." For example, during the hostage crisis in Iran, protest rallies were often timed to coincide with the presence of the media. More recently, one senatorial candidate sought to sustain media interest in her by running across her home state throughout the campaign period. Pseudo-events include demonstrations and marches—events that are scheduled to prompt media coverage. Often, once the press has left the scene, the "event" disbands.

Investigative Reporting

Reporters move into a deeper level of information gathering when they attempt to cover events that are beyond the control of "event managers." This type of reporting work involves extensive digging and checking, and it is the realm of the *investigative reporter*. Investigative reporting traces its roots to the muckraking practices of Lincoln Steffens and Upton Sinclair (see Chapter 5). The 1971 publication of *The Pentagon Papers* and the subsequent Watergate scandal increased the public's support of the investigative journalist.

Investigative journalists are often freed from other duties and are allowed to pursue a single story. The *Washington Post,* the *Philadelphia Inquirer,* and *Newsday* are among those papers that have a dozen staff members assigned to investigative projects. The expense of such work is compounded by the fact that months and months of researching and digging may fail to yield a publishable piece. According to reporter Jonathan Friendly, investigative reporters are now turning their eyes away from disclosures of corrupt individuals or businesses and are focusing on public and governmental agencies like prisons or hospitals: "Articles about public agencies pose little risk of a libel suit, compared with exposing individual dishonesty or

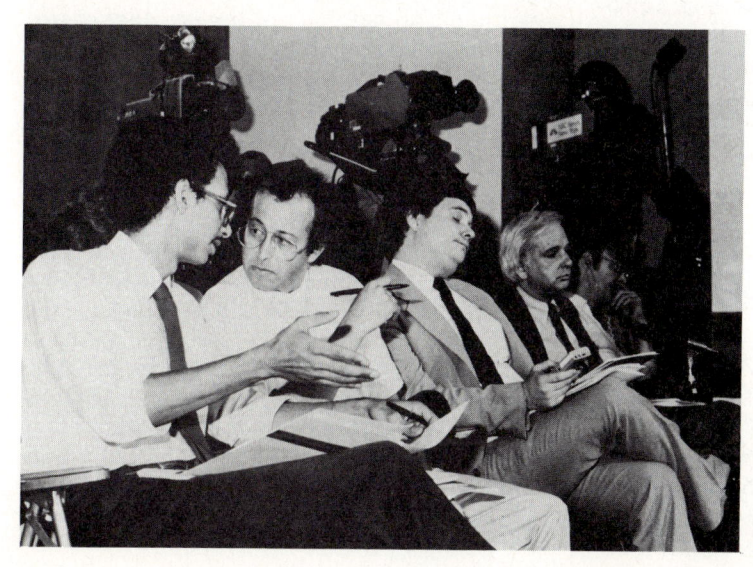

MEDIA PROBE

Using the same day's issues of two different newspapers, attempt to identify those stories which you believe emanated from source-controlled information. What cues can you use to distinguish planted stories from real news?

Investigative journalism often requires patient waiting and painstaking research with little immediate payoff in publishable leads. (Randy Matusow)

MEDIA VIEW

WHEN YOU WRITE SOMETHING YOU LOVE, IT DIES SO SOON

Dave Behrens
Newsday

How frustrating to write for a medium in which most words die in a day.... Perhaps it is this transitory nature of the craft which has bequeathed us a necrology of newspaper writing, a language of death. Reporters write on DEADLINE. Editors hold meetings called POST-MORTEMS. Old stories are kept in a MORGUE. Editors KILL stories (how true).

Language reflects attitudes, and in some cases determines them. The jargon of journalism reveals much about the values and perceptions of generations of writers and editors.

Take the hideous newspaper ... BRITE. That's spelled b-r-i-t-e. For years the only interesting writing, the only humor, the only relief from the banality of daily American journalism was in something called the six-inch brite.

Conversation overheard in newsroom:

"I've got space for a six-inch brite."

"How about several 20-inch dulls?"

Consider the language we use to describe the effects of newspaper writing on the reader. I once heard a city editor say something like: "The lead should have a news hook and should grab the reader and be filled with buzz words. Then after the jump, there should be a kicker at the end."

Pity the poor reader. All she wants is to relax with her newspaper. All we want is to grab, hook, buzz, jump and kick her.

Peter Roy Clark, ed., *Best Newspaper Writing, 1981*, Modern Media Institute, St. Petersburg, Fla., 1981.

---

corporate corruption." Friendly also notes that journalists have begun to work hand in hand with government prosecutors as a project is started. In your opinion is this practice appropriate or does it succeed in turning the journalist into yet another branch of our law enforcement system?

WRITING THE NEWS

Once information has been gathered and judged to be newsworthy, it needs to be turned into an acceptable news article. The actual process of writing the news is shaped by three variables: the pressure of time, the traditional inverted-pyramid writing style, and the need for eye-catching headlines. Let us examine each of these factors.

The Pressure of Time

Time is a factor which affects all newspaper writing. Thomas Plate of the *Los Angeles Herald-Examiner* compared his approach to writing under the pressure of deadlines with the problems faced by the relief pitcher in a baseball game:

The newspaper is a beautiful, imperfect instrument of information. You know that and try to minimize the imperfection. So you say, OK, this piece must move to Los Angeles in an hour and ten minutes. If you're experienced, you know what you're capable of doing in that time. You must be within yourself. It's like a pitcher coming in with three innings to go. He knows how many batters he's going to face, how many hits are likely to be against him, how many pitches he's going to throw, which batters are dangerous. He must command the arsenal that he has in the most effective way and be within himself.[3]

The Inverted Pyramid

The need to cover all the important information as efficiently as possible is another requirement facing the news writer. Journalists have long used the *inverted pyramid* (or upside-down triangle) to facilitate their job.

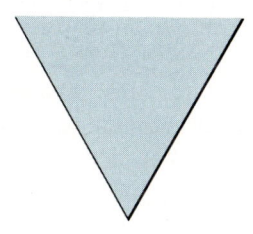

The structure indicates that the most important information is to be placed at the outset of a piece in what is termed the *lead*. For example, on October 7, 1981, Patrick Sloyan of *Newsday* began his story on the assassination of Anwar Sadat in this manner: "CAIRO—Egyptian President Anwar Sadat, a modern day pharoah who attempted to lead the Arab world toward a permanant Mideast peace with Israel, was assassinated yesterday by a band of soldiers who attacked a military parade reviewing stand with automatic rifles and hand grenades." This lead contains the following information: *who*—Sadat; *what*—assassinated; *when*—yesterday; *how*—automatic rifles and grenades; *where*—military parade reviewing stand. An example of what journalists call a "who" lead, the excerpt emphasizes the person by placing the name first. In like fashion, a "what" lead would emphasize the key thing in the story, a watermain break, for example. Other approaches used when writing leads include the direct use of quotes, epigrams, and description.

Creating the Headline

Because the headline writer may have limited space, writing headlines requires special skill. With a very few words the headline must capture the essence of an entire article, interest readers, and motivate them to continue reading. Three basic rules should be followed. First, the headline should support the lead of the story. Second, in most cases the headline should be written in the present tense: "President Sends Troops," rather than "President Sent Troops." Third, whenever possible, headlines should contain action verbs in order to help attract the reader's attention.

Headlines range in tone from the somber and serious ones found on the editorial page to the often-frivolous mood of those found on the sports pages. Whatever their mood,

MEDIA PROBE

1. Examine today's newspaper. Find an example of a "who" lead and a "what" lead. Note other types of leads that are used also.
2. Then either alone or with a group choose one news article to work on. However, before you read it, fold over the lead so that you are able to read only the remaining portions of the article. Your task is to write a lead for the story. When finished, compare the lead you wrote with the one contained in the original article.

MEDIA PROBE

Working alone or with others, try your hand at headline writing. Without reading the articles, cut headlines off several news stories. When you have done this, read the articles and devise your own headlines. How do the headlines you created stack up against those of the experienced headline writer? Does your headline support the story's lead? Does it contain an action verb? Is it written in the present tense?

however, all headlines must fit within a set structure of column width and typeface sizes. Today, most newspapers use computer systems which immediately tell the writer if the headline will fit the available space. For those instances when it does not, the writer must begin a search for appropriate but shorter synonyms.

New Journalism

Traditionally, journalists are taught to keep themselves out of their articles by writing in the third person and presenting the essential facts only: "Four people were killed yesterday when a private plane crashed in the hills of South Dakota." But perhaps it was inevitable that journalists would begin to revolt against this who-what-when-where-how-and-why standarized style of journalism. *New journalism* began to emerge during the early 1960s; it burst fully-grown onto the journalistic scene in 1965 with the publication of Tom Wolfe's collection of articles; *Kandy-Kolored Tangerine Flake Streamline Baby.*

New journalists focus on journalism as an art form. Writing as novelists do, they incorporate dialogue, flashbacks, the thoughts of people, and their own opinions into the articles they write. By recreating entire scenes, they tell a story. Yet, unlike the work of novelists, new journalism is not merely a product of the imagination; rather, it is derived from actual people and events. Tom Wolfe describes the form: "In the early 1960's a curious new notion, just hot enough to inflame the ego, had begun to intrude.... It was in the nature of a discovery. This discovery, modest at first, humble, in fact deferential, you might say, was that it just might be possible to write journalism that would read like a novel. *Like* a novel, if you get the picture."[4]

Truman Capote's *In Cold Blood,* a work that describes and recreates the murder of a family, has been termed a "nonfiction novel" and an example of new journalism. The list of journalists who turned to this style of writing includes Gay Talese, Rex Reed, Norman Mailer, John Gregory Dunne, George Plimpton, Joan Didion, and Hunter S. Thompson, to name a few. In an effort to probe for thoughts and emotions in addition to facts, new journalists interview people and then "reconstruct" dialogue to weave into their story. Wolfe says: "It seemed all important to *be there* when dramatic scenes took place, to get the dialogue, the gestures, the facial expressions, the details of the environment. The idea was to give the full objective description plus something that readers had always had to go to novels and short stories for, namely, the subjective or the emotional life of the character."[5] The result is a style of writing that is colorful, dramatic, and highly personal. Gay Talese adds: "I'm like a director and I shift my own particular focus, my own cameras from one [event] to the other."

It is possible that the competition with other media precipitated the rise of new journalism by giving the writer new freedom; in effect, it enables the writer to provide a personal perspective on a story in a manner that television, radio, and traditional print journalism simply cannot do. In the following excerpt, Tom Wolfe describes fellow new journalist Jimmy Breslin at work:

> Breslin made a revolutionary discovery. He made the discovery that it was feasible for a columnist to actually leave the building, go outside and do reporting on his own, genuine legwork. Breslin would go up to the city editor and ask what stories and assignments were coming up, choose one, go out, leave the building, cover the story as a reporter, and write about it in his column. If the story were big enough, his column would start on page one instead of inside. As obvious as this system may sound, it was unheard of among newspaper columnists....
>
> But Breslin worked like a Turk. He would be out all day covering a story, come back in at 4 p.m. or so and sit down at a desk in the middle of the city room. It was quite a show. He was a good-

looking Irishman with a lot of black hair and a great wrestler's gut. When he sat down at his typewriter he hunched himself over into a shape like a bowling ball. He would start drinking coffee and smoking cigarettes until vapor started drifting off his body. He looked like a bowling ball fueled with liquid oxygen. Thus, fired up, he would start typing. I've never seen a man who could write so well against a daily deadline.

Breslin made it a practice to arrive on the scene long before the main event in order to gather the off-camera material, the by-play in the makeup room, that would enable him to create character. It was part of his modus operandi to gather "novelistic" details, the rings, the perspiration, the jabs on the shoulder, and he did it more skillfully than most novelists.[6]

Breslin's work permitted him to have contact with people who made history. In *How the Good Guys Finally Won,* Breslin describes the setting for the sentencing of the Watergate conspirators Haldeman, Erlichman, Mitchell, and Mardian.

> It was 4:25 p.m. of an empty New Year's Day, 1975, and now it was all coming to an end.
>
> The windowless courtroom was too bright, the neon ceiling lights glaring off the blond-paneled walls. This type of American ceremony has no richness to it; dark tragedies are played out in flat, harsh civil-service surroundings. The five defendants already were in the courtroom when the doors were opened for reporters. There were less than a dozen ordinary spectators. At the start of the sequence of trouble, there are large crowds of the curious and knots of close friends shielding you from the curious. As the case wears on, and the next week becomes next month, the curious go elsewhere and the close friends live their own lives, and at the end you always are alone with fear. . . .
>
> Minutes went by. It was 4:40 now. Reporters were standing, looking at the defendants, making notes of what they were seeing, their hands shaking in the tension.
>
> The door knob rattled again. Silence in the room. Now the click. An immense black marshal, head shaved, looked into the room.
>
> "All ready?" he said to the gray-haired clerk.
>
> "All ready," the clerk said.
>
> The marshal went out the door but did not shut it entirely. Now, without a sound, the door swung open. The marshal slammed his hand on the wood.
>
> "All rise," the gray-haired clerk said.
>
> Into the harsh light came the judge, John Sirica.

A LOOK AT LEGAL RESTRAINTS

What should be the relationship between the press and the government? The answer to this question depends in part on the time, the place, and the philosophical and political orientation of the responder. In England, for example, an *authoritarian press* system prevailed from the fifteenth to the eighteenth centuries. That is, the press was looked upon as a mass medium that operated solely with the permission of, and to serve the purposes of, the ruling government. To this end, public dissent was viewed as harmful and was not tolerated. Since papers were required to pay exhorbitant fees in order to secure licences entitling them to print, few printers were willing to risk arousing the wrath of the authorities. Still in operation in many countries today, this particular theory of the press ensures that neither criticism of government nor views embarrassing or harmful to government are published.

In contrast, during the formative years of the United States, a *libertarian press* was popular. Libertarians assumed that since people were rational and capable of making their own judgments, no press controls needed to

MEDIA PROBE

Is new journalism fact or fiction? Do you believe it should complement or replace traditional journalistic techniques? Why?

be exerted. Their premise was that the people needed to be exposed to all sides of an issue in order to make informed decisions; in other words, in the eyes of the libertarian the press existed to serve the people, and the government was not to interfere with the operation of this medium. As Thomas Jefferson wrote in 1787, "were it left to me to decide whether we should have a government without newspapers, or newspapers without a government, I should not hesitate a moment to prefer the latter." This sentence has frequently been quoted by editors and reporters in defense of freedom of the press.

As times changed and new technologies appeared on the scene, a variation of this theory, now referred to as the *social-responsibility theory* of the press, emerged. In 1947, The Commission on Freedom of the Press explained the assumptions upon which this press theory was built. Social-responsibility theorists assert that the press has a right to criticize the government, but it also has the obligation to inform the citizenry properly and to respond to societal needs and interests. Emphasizing that people need to have access to information, adherents of this theory require that the press work to ensure that all aspects of the political and social spectrum are covered. Also, advocates of social-responsibility theory believe that the press should be charged with the task of developing and enforcing ethics in the public interest. The legal basis for both the libertarian and social-responsibility theories are found in the First Amendment of the Constitution: "Congress shall make no law . . . abridging the freedom of speech, or of the press." Originally designed to protect and sustain a free press in this country, these words have provided much heated debate. What exactly do they mean? The courts have been considering this question for almost 200 years. Let us examine some of the issues and conflicts that have arisen over their interpretation.

MEDIA PROBE

The saying "Sticks and stones will break my bones, but names will never harm me," is in direct opposition to the charge of libel. In your opinion, what names would harm you? Compile a list of words or charges that you would consider a libelous attack on your good name or reputation.

Libel: Reputation! Reputation!

The concept that you as an individual have a right to compensation if you are damaged by untrue statements written about you comes to us via the British legal system. Called *libel*, this law protects the individual against the publishing of defamatory statements that injure his or her good name or reputation or diminish the esteem, respect, or good will due him or her by holding him or her up to contempt, ridicule, or scorn. Slander, the label applied to spoken defamation does not pose as many problems for the media as libel does; in fact, today in many states, if a defamatory statement is broadcast, it is still treated as if the words uttered were written words and handled as libel. In general, characterizing people by using any of the following words—incompetent, corrupt, disreputable, a cheater, a fool, a slacker, a thief, ignorant, a deadhead, a tax evader, bankrupt, unethical, a communist, or the carrier of a disease (just to name a few)—is grounds for libel.

In order to sue a newspaper for libel the injured party (the plaintiff) must prove that the publication that printed such material was truly at fault for printing it; when the publication of such material is due to an error, the news medium cannot be held responsible. The principle was first enunciated by the Supreme Court in 1964 and resulted from a lawsuit in which it was alleged that *The New York Times* had printed untruthful statements about the Montgomery Alabama Police Commissioner, H. B. Sullivan. In its landmark ruling, the Supreme Court stated that a public official has to prove that the false statement made about him had been made with malice—that is, with "reckless disregard" for the falseness of the statement. In other words, the newspaper had to know that it was printing a lie. Unless this could be proven, the plaintiff could not prevail and a judgment that an individual had been libeled could not be sustained. This ruling has since been extended to apply to public figures as well as government officials. That is actors, sports figures, representatives of causes, and others who have thrust themselves into the public limelight also must prove malice before they can prevail in a court of law. For example, in 1981, actress Carol Burnett sued the *National Enquirer* over an item it had published that had portrayed her as being drunk while dining in a Washington restaurant. Burnett won the suit by proving that the newspaper had shown a reckless disregard of the facts; although the case is being appealed, the Burnett victory stirred a rash of public personality suits against tabloids like the *Enquirer*.

It should be noted that in a 1976 case involving Mary Alice Firestone, the court did differentiate between the type of proof needed by "ordinary people" and the type of proof required of celebrities by ruling that ordinary citizens do not have to prove malice in order to win a libel suit. However, it was noted that it was incumbent upon the "ordinary" plaintiff to prove that the press did not exercise "reasonable care" in determining the truth of the libelous statement. Also, it has been determined that a reporter can safely rely on statements made by police officers without fear of being sued for libel. If the statement provided by the law enforcement official ultimately turns out to be false, the paper is protected; it is not held responsible.

The press is able to protect and defend itself against libel suits in two basic ways. Its first and most effective defense is "the truth." If it can prove that the statement printed in the newspaper was true, the paper cannot be found to be at fault. Second, the press can rely on a defense of privilege and fair comment. The press has the right to report activities of public officials when they are acting in an official capacity, and it has a right to report what transpires during the meeting of governmental bodies including town councils, the House of Representatives, and the United States Senate. Comments made during such meetings are considered privileged and are not subject to legal action as long as a reporter gives a fair and accurate account of the event. In addition, criticism of public performances of entertainers and politicians are also judged to be exempt. In other words, people who invite attention are considered to be fair game for comment. Were it not for this, you would rarely be able to find a play or movie review in or on your local media. Again, this type of defense applies only to criticism and opinions, not to misrepresentation. Even with these defenses, attorneys frequently counsel smaller newspapers to refrain from printing material that, though defensible, might still result in a lawsuit. As a case in point, in the September 29, 1983, issue of *The Wall Street Journal* it was noted that after making a $1.4 million settlement in a $10.5 million libel suit first filed against it eight years earlier, the crusading spirit of the small Illinois newspaper the *Alton Telegraph* had all but been zapped. The paper, once famous for its investigations that led to the arrest of Illinois supreme court justices for accepting gifts of stocks, now deliberately avoids investigative journalism. Says the paper's editor and publisher Stephen A. Causley, "Wouldn't you be gun-shy if you nearly lost your livelihood and your home?"[7] Mushrooming libel awards have placed increased pressure on small publications "to sell out or

MEDIA PROBE

Noted attorney Gerry Spence takes the position that the press has far too much power under the First Amendment: "When the press hides itself behind the First Amendment, what it really does is ask us to give it a gun—a loaded gun that it has a right to use.... They can point the gun at my client, if they wish." In a 1983 CBS report "Eye on the Media," Spence discussed how he would present the case of a client he felt had been libeled to a jury:

> I'd talk to the jury about what a man's reputation is. What does it mean to him? This country has laid down its life and the life of its young people for its reputation. I think of the dangers—the sacrifices that we put ourselves in every day for reputation.
>
> For most of us, our reputations are worth more than money. Would you rather have money or reputation? And if you take away my reputation, wouldn't you give me money?

If you were a jury member, how would you react to such an argument? In your opinion are we holding the media too accountable in libel cases, or not accountable enough? Why?

---

close up." As a result, controversy is avoided, papers become timid, and free discussion of ideas is restricted. In contrast to smaller newspapers, larger newspapers do have the funds needed to fight libel cases. Thus, the *Louisville Courier-Journal* has established the policy of refusing to settle any suit out of court because they have found such a practice discourages the filing of suits. The paper also uses extensive discovery or investigative-reporting procedures to determine the truth inherent in the statement being defended. This helps to discourage suits as well. However, the fact remains that the threat of a libel suit poses serious problems for all newspapers, big and small alike.

Privacy versus the Right to Know

Found neither in the Constitution nor the Bill of Rights, the right of privacy is a relatively new concept in American law. It was first advanced in 1890 by a young lawyer, Louis Brandeis (later Supreme Court Justice Brandeis), and his law partner, Samuel Warren, in an article they wrote for the *Harvard Law Review*. Writing that the press had overstepped the bounds of "propriety and decency," Brandeis and Warren argued that citizens should be provided with a legal remedy in order to be able to protect themselves adequately from the prying and gossiping media. Today, the public appears to agree, and as a result nearly every state has adopted a *privacy law*.

In 1982, ABC News polled people in order to determine the public's attitude toward media practices that could infringe on a person's right to privacy: 64 percent of the people disapproved of reporters questioning families of air disaster victims, and 66 percent disapproved of reporters lying in wait outside of the homes of people whom they would like to interview. To what extent, if any, do you believe these opinions are in contradiction with the First Amendment, which guarantees the press the right to report the news?

The courts recognize four ways the press may be judged to be guilty of invading your privacy. The first is intrusion into someone's domain. Telephoto pictures or photographs taken of someone while he or she is on private property fall into this category. The second is the publication of what is considered to be private information. In other words, unless the person written about is a public figure, the material is of interest to the public, or the material was obtained from an of-

MEDIA VIEW

FREEDOM OF THE PRESS VERSUS INVASION OF PRIVACY

JOHN MARTIN: Do the relatives of passengers on an airliner that has crashed have a right not to be questioned as they try to learn why the plane hasn't arrived?

REPORTER:
Who are you waiting for, sir?

DR. JOSEPH KRZANOWSKI:
I'm waiting for my brother.

REPORTER:
We understand the flight has gone down. They haven't told you anything?

DR. KRZANOWSKI:
They haven't told us anything.

REPORTER:
Have you asked?

DR. KRZANOWSKI:
I asked them at the counter if there was any information, and they said that we had to go to the main terminal.

MARTIN: Does a presidential advisor who is under investigation have a right not to be hounded by reporters waiting at all hours outside his house?

RICHARD ALLEN,
former National Security Advisor: One night as we were being driven home, I saw the crowd on the step, near the curb. I got out of the car; these blinding lights were turned on, and I went to the back of the car, opened the trunk, and had the suit coat in my hand. I began to walk to the house, which is just a short distance, a few feet from the street. I crossed the lawn, I walked and stepped right into a box of food garbage. As I took my foot out of the box I gave it a drop-kick and knocked it clean across the lawn, and I said, "What is this?" I said, "Will you please get the garbage off my lawn immediately?" and went inside where our children were, almost I'd say, huddled by the front door, waiting for us to come home, feeling that they had been under seige.

MARTIN: Does the fiancee of a future king have the right to be left alone, especially in the last days of her private life outside the royal family? Does the family of a young man under investigation for murder have a right not to face constant scrutiny by network camera crews living in a van outside their house?

MARY WELCOME,
Wayne Williams' attorney: Our client's life, and the lives of his family and friends, have become a virtual nightmare. We ask that you cease staking out their home, following them, or otherwise affecting their right to live peacefully.

MARTIN: Crime, tragedy, scandal, and celebrity—fascinating to journalists and the public, but they involve real people. What about their privacy? This may surprise you, but strictly speaking, none of the four people we've mentioned here has a legal right not to be questioned or photographed in public. None of them.

"Freedom of the Press vs Invasion of Privacy," ABC News *Viewpoint,* August 12, 1982.

---

ficial governmental record, the public disclosure of private facts is considered to be an invasion of privacy. With regard to this requirement, the "newsworthiness" of its material almost always exempts a newspaper from this type of invasion of privacy suit. The third basis for a privacy suit involves the publishing of information that places a person in a false light. For example, what if a photograph were taken of you and then used to illustrate the "typical college dropout"? What if your name was identified as the name of the computer thief who had obtained thousands of dollars by fraudulent means? In each instance you would have been presented in a false light and thus you would be in a position to sue for damages. Finally, commercial exploitation is also considered to be an invasion

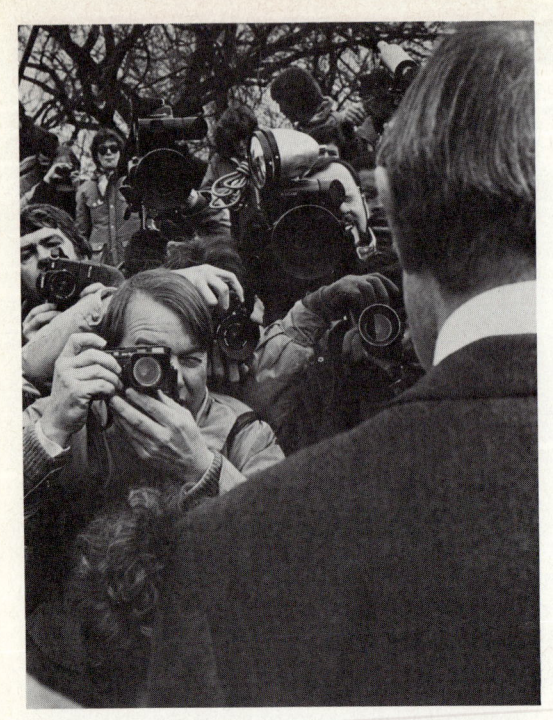

What constitutes a news event and how to cover it are mostly matters of media self-restraint in our society. (Art Stein, Photo Researchers)

of privacy. Let's assume that you go to see a preview of a film and are photographed smiling in the lobby. If the picture taken of you turns up in an advertisement for the film, the advertiser must have obtained your permission to print such an advertisement prior to the ad's publication; otherwise, this too is considered an invasion of your privacy. The threat of invasion of privacy suits, like the threat of libel suits, may serve to restrain the actions of the news media to some degree.

Trials and the Press: The First Amendment versus the Sixth Amendment

While the *First Amendment* to the Constitution guarantees freedom of the press, the *Sixth Amendment* to the Constitution guarantees a defendant the right to a fair trial before an impartial jury. To what extent, if any, are these two constitutional guarantees in conflict? And can a case be tried before an impartial jury if it has been thoroughly reported and discussed in the media? In order to answer these questions we need to explore the relationship existing between the courts and the press. Specifically, we must seek to determine how pretrial publicity affects the defendant's right to a fair trial and whether or not a reporter has a right to conceal the identity of his or her sources.

Pretrial Publicity To what extent does someone's familiarity with stories appearing in the news media about a defendant affect his or her ability to serve as a juror?

The fact that pretrial publicity adversely affects jurors has not been established conclusively. However, courts have acted to reduce the impact of such publicity. In 1961, Leslie "Mad Dog" Irwin was arrested and charged with committing six murders; newspapers reported that he confessed to all six slayings. When queried during the selection process, 90 percent of the 430 prospective jurors stated that they had formed an opinion of Irwin's guilt. Although Irwin was eventually found guilty and sentenced to death, the Supreme Court later ruled that pretrial publicity had ruined his chances for a fair trial, and it ordered that the case be retried. (Irwin was again found guilty; this time, however, he was sentenced to life in prison.)

The most famous pretrial publicity case was that of an Ohio osteopath, Dr. Sam Sheppard. In 1954, Sheppard's wife was found bludgeoned to death in their home. Sheppard was tried and convicted of the crime. But twelve years later his conviction was overturned because of the publicity attendent upon the trial. It seems that the newspapers had convicted Dr. Sheppard before the jury, in part because of Sheppard's refusal to take a lie detector test. Though Sheppard himself had willingly participated in an interview for a news article entitled "Loved My Wife, She Loved Me," and written a number of feature articles about the case, it was ruled that the press—by running headlines like "Why No

100   THE PRINT MEDIA: THE WINDOW OPENS

MEDIA PROBE

In your opinion, should privacy laws be strengthened? Before answering, consider these viewpoints. Harvard Law School professor and right to privacy advocate Arthur Miller states:

> In a democracy such as ours, no right can be absolute; every right must be balanced against other rights. And the right of every American to be let alone, the right of every American to have privacy, is a right of enormous social significance. It is wrong to dismiss it as some eccentric Greta Garbo or Howard Hughes syndrome. People who have been put into the spotlight of the media and have stood naked in the glare of publicity have suffered enormous emotional and social prices. And these people range from the families of the American hostages in Teheran, to other American heroes, to criminally accused, to governmental officials, to victims of air disasters. Ironically, the press claims that it's threatened by the right of privacy. Ironically, the press feels that it won't be able to report the news if we give too great a berth to the right of privacy. Sometimes they sound like a terrified hemophiliac hit by a pinprick of criticism. They demand immunity to publish anything as long as it is true, regardless of how they got it, how intrusive their behavior, and how sensitive the material is. That's just too glib—it's too glib to say, "Editing is for the editors." It's too glib to say, "We benefit the public, no matter how intrusive our techniques may be."
>
> The press should begin to realize that they are not merely conveyors, conduits for the news. They decide what the news is. They decide which story to report. They decide which fact goes in the first "graph." They decide which word to use. They cannot ignore or evade their responsibility for the people they report on. They cannot act, in Tom Lehrer's immortal line, like Werner von Braun, the rocket scientist: "I just send the rockets up, where they come down is not my department." No, dear journalists, you hold my privacy in your hands, so please, every once in a while, close the notebook, and put down the pencil.

In contrast, Floyd Abrams, freedom of press advocate, asserts:

> I think what we've really got to focus on is, what is it we want journalists to do? How much do we want them to do? There are excesses, there are always excesses of all of us, but we've got to keep the journalists free to inform us about what's going on. And if we push the notion of privacy too deeply into what has historically been First Amendment protected turf, the right of the press, as Professor Miller said, to decide for better or worse what to print and what to broadcast, we risk losing things, not for the press but for all of us—and that's our right to know what's going on.
>
> They turn off the lights, they take away the notebooks, they put the pencils away all around the world routinely, every night, too often, in societies in which people don't get the news. . . . It is more important, if you want to really strike balances, that the public be informed about critical matters of state, and even such issues as what kind of man an alleged mass murderer is. That's news; it should be news. It is an important thing for us to know, for us to hear. It's all too easy to say throw it away, turn out the lights, turn off the cameras. We're used to that around the world, and we ought not to be used to it here.
>
> The real question is, are we going to pass laws, are we going to have Congress act, are we going to have the courts involved in this area? Self-restraint is the answer; self-restraint is the only answer, but self-restraint within the context of press freedom, and that, I fear, is something we have to all protect. Not for the press; the press can always do other things, report about other subjects. They should report about important subjects, and we ought to be very careful before we start imposing legal limits on their rights to do so.

"Freedom of the Press vs. Invasion of Privacy," ABC News *Viewpoint*, August 12, 1982.

Now, what do you think? Should laws protecting our right to privacy be strengthened? Or should they be weakened? And what effect would this have on the press? The public?

YOU WERE THERE

MARK TWAIN ON PRETRIAL PUBLICITY

I remember one of those sorrowful farces, in Virginia which we call a jury trial. A noted desperado killed Mr. B., a good citizen, in the most wanton and cold-blooded way. Of course the papers were full of it, and all men capable of reading read about it. And of course all men not deaf and dumb and idiotic talked about it. A jury list was made out, and Mr. B.L., a prominent banker and valued citizen, was questioned precisely as he would have been questioned in any court in America:

"Have you heard of this homicide?"

"Yes."

"Have you held conversations upon the subject?"

"Yes."

"Have you formed or expressed opinions about it?"

"Yes."

"Have you read the newspaper accounts of it?"

"Yes."

"We do not want you."

A minister, intelligent, esteemed, and greatly respected; a merchant of high character and known probity; a mining superintendent of intelligence and unblemished reputation; a quartz-mill owner of excellent standing, were all questioned in the same way, and all set aside. Each said the public talk and the newspaper reports had not so biased his mind but that sworn testimony would overthrow his previously formed opinions and enable him to render a verdict without prejudice and in accordance with the facts. But of course such men could not be trusted with the case. Ignoramuses alone could mete out unsullied justice.

When the preemptory challenges were all exhausted, a jury of twelve men was impaneled—a jury who swore they had neither heard, read, talked about, nor expressed an opinion concerning a murder which the very cattle in the corrals, the Indians in the sagebrush and the stones in the streets were cognizant of! It was a jury composed of two desperadoes, two low peer-house politicians, three barkeepers, two ranchmen who could not read, and three dull, stupid human donkeys! It actually came out afterward that one of these latter thought that incest and arson were the same thing.

The verdict rendered by this jury was Not Guilty. What else could one expect?

Mark Twain, *Roughing It*, Penguin Books, New York, 1981.

Inquest?" and "Why Isn't Sam Sheppard in Jail?"—had prejudiced his ability to receive a fair trial. The press had taken an active role in seeking what it deemed to be "justice" by playing up inconsistencies in statements made by Sheppard and directly appealing for his arrest. In addition, during the actual court proceedings, the trial judge used his position as a pulpit from which to campaign for reelection. In light of all this, one federal judge was moved to note: "If ever there was a trial by newspaper, this was a perfect example."

In the 1966 opinion that overturned Sheppard's conviction and ordered a new trial, Justice Thomas Clark took time to comment upon the trial scene that prompted the action:

The courtroom in which the trial was held measured 26 by 48 feet. A long temporary table was set up inside the bar, in back of the single counsel table. It ran the width of the courtroom, parallel to the bar railing, with one end less than three feet from the jury box. Approximately 20 representatives of newspapers and wire services were assigned seats at this table by the court. Behind the bar railing there were four rows of benches. These seats were likewise assigned by the court for the entire trial. The first row was occupied by representatives of television and radio stations, and the second and third rows by reporters from out-of-town newspapers and magazines. . . .

The jurors themselves were constantly exposed to the news media. Every juror, except one, testified . . . to reading about the case in Cleveland papers or to having heard broadcasts about it. . . . During the trial, pictures of the jury appeared over 40 times in the Cleveland papers alone. The court permitted photographers to take pictures of the jury in the box, and individual pictures of the members in the jury room. . . . The day before the verdict was rendered—while jurors were at lunch and sequestered by two bailiffs—the jury was separated into two groups to pose for photographs which appeared in the newspapers. . . . All of the newspapers and radio stations apparently interviewed prospective witnesses at will, and in many instances disclosed their testimony.

In order to avoid such problems in the future, the court identified a number of safeguards that judges could invoke to prevent undue publicity before and during a trial. Among these safeguards were sequestering the jury, moving the trial to another county, and restricting the statements that could be made to the press both by lawyers and witnesses.

The Sam Sheppard case also precipitated the imposition of *gag orders* by judges. (Gag rules restrain participants in a trial from divulging information to the media or prevent the media from covering court events.) But by 1979 the Supreme Court had issued rather conclusive rulings that asserted that journalists could report what happens in open court; however, it was noted that pretrial proceedings could be closed to the public in order to protect the defendant's right to a fair trial. In your opinion, to what extent does this apparent compromise protect the right secured in both the First and Sixth Amendments?

Protecting the Reporter's Sources Reporters, like most of us, are seldom "at the scene" when a disaster occurs or a crime is committed. Thus, they frequently find it necessary to rely upon information provided to them by others. In light of this, historian Theodore H. White describes a reporter as "a cross between a beggar and a detective, a wheedler and a prosecutor. This is how he collects facts." White also notes that the reporter's method of note taking is directed at doing what he or she must to obtain information. "Most of us take notes as we go. Or, if note-taking cramps the person we are talking with, we jot down notes as soon as we can get away and catch our breath. We take notes on stenographer's pads, folded copy paper, margins of dinner menus. Sometimes we take notes with ostentatious flourish, either to bully people or to flatter them. Sometimes after feigning uninterest, we take notes surreptitiously—on a paper napkin under the table, even on a toilet paper in the washroom."[8] Given the difficulties they face when attempting to obtain information, reporters assert that their sources would dry up unless they are able to promise them anonymity. Without this ability, they contend, the public's right to know would be placed in jeopardy. For example, in all likelihood, the My Lai massacre probably would have gone undetected if a reporter had not been able to convince members of the United States Army to tell the truth by promising not to betray the confidence placed in him. Watergate might never have been uncovered were it not for the protection reporters Woodward and Bernstein were able to guarantee to their, to this day anonymous, source, "Deep Throat." Were a journalist to reveal the name of an informant or source, it is unlikely that others would trust the reporter again. Would you?

Although government informers may be granted anonymity and immunity from prosecution, no such privilege is traditionally accorded to sources of news reporters. Consequently, a number of reporters have been sentenced to jail for failing to reveal their sources. In 1959, for example, *New York Herald Tribune* television columnist Marie Torre was jailed for ten days when she refused to name the source of a story she had written about Judy Garland. In 1972, in *Branzburg v. Hayes* (a case resulting from reporter Paul Branzburg being permitted to witness the production of hashish in exchange for promising to keep the identities of those involved secret) the Supreme Court ruled that the First Amendment does not protect reporters from testifying before grand juries. However, the court did suggest that states could establish their own "*shield laws,*" which would protect reporters from having to reveal the sources of information given to them in confidence. Over half of the states have passed such laws. The New York law, for instance, reads in part: "no professional journalist or newscaster . . . should be adjudged in contempt by any court, the legislature or other body having contempt powers for refusing or failing to disclose any news or the source of any such news coming into his possession in the course of gathering or obtaining news for publication."

The law is not always in the reporter's favor. In 1978, in the case of *Zurcher v. The Stamford Daily* (a case involving a student newspaper that had covered a demonstration at a hospital which resulted in injuries to police officers), the Supreme Court ruled that the police could make surprise raids on reporter's homes and newsrooms if they had a court-approved warrant to search for evidence involving a crime committed by someone else. In 1980, however, Congress passed a law requiring that a subpoena, and not a warrant, was needed to conduct such searches; a subpoena is more limited in scope than a search warrant.

The problem involving reporters and their sources reached its apex in the 1976 murder case of Dr. X. One decade prior to this date, Riverdell Hospital, located in New Jersey, had been plagued by a series of unexpected deaths among patients who had been recovering successfully from surgery. A subsequent investigation uncovered eighteen empty vials, which were reported to have contained the lethal drug curare; they had been found in the dressing room locker of Dr. Mario Jascalevich, who was originally called Dr. X by the media to protect his identity. Myron Farber, reporter for *The New York Times,* was assigned to investigate the case. His work resulted in a series of front-page articles on Jascalevich and Riverdell Hospital. Ultimately, the defense, contending that it needed the information Mr. Farber was privy to in order to adequately defend Dr. Jascalevich, subpoenaed Farber's notes from both his home and *The New York Times*. When they were not delivered, both Farber and the *Times* were held in contempt of court. Farber was ordered to pay a $1000 fine; he also spent forty days in jail (the time needed to conduct the trial). *The New York Times* had to pay $285,000 in fines. Although the Supreme Court refused to review the case, the State of New Jersey ultimately passed a shield law, and Farber was pardoned.

Whether or not reporters have the right to conceal their sources is still open to question. Presently, the rights accorded to reporters depend upon the state in which they happen to be working. Thus, while reporters are protected in some states, in others they still face jail sentences if they opt to protect a source's identity. The government argues that shield laws impede the defendant's ability to receive

MEDIA PROBE

Does your state have a shield law? If so, read and summarize the law's provisions.

Do you believe reporters' sources deserve protection? Why or why not?

Who, in your opinion, should make the final judgment regarding what best serves the public interest, newspersons or judges? Why?

YOU WERE THERE

MYRON FARBER'S STATEMENT TO THE COURT PRIOR TO BEING SENTENCED

I would like to explain to the Court, and to the public, why I am refusing to surrender my reporter's file on the case of Dr. Mario E. Jascalevich. As serious as this matter is, and as highly technical as are the legal arguments, my position is not all that complicated. What is at issue here is not Dr. Jascalevich's right to a fair trial; he has access to the same people that I interviewed, and more. Nor is the issue my "right" to place myself above or outside the law. I have no such right, and I seek none. The issue, I believe, is the right of the public to be informed through its press, in accordance with the First Amendment of the United States Constitution.

I have been a newspaper reporter for fifteen years, twelve of them with *The New York Times*. Like anyone who has been a journalist that long, I have embraced certain standards. They are accuracy, fairness, impartiality, thoroughness. I have tried to live up to those standards. . . .

A reporter has only so many tools with which to work. His strength lies in his readiness and ability to reach out and listen to people on every side of an issue, people with greatly varying views of "the truth" or the facts. But sometimes, people who have done no wrong yet who have information that is useful to a rounded understanding of an issue are reluctant to speak out. They may be afraid of losing their jobs, or incurring the displeasure of a governmental agency, or drawing unaccustomed attention to themselves or to their families. They may agree to provide information only on a confidential basis. And if I, as a journalist, accept information on those terms, I cannot disavow that agreement later. Not without destroying my integrity. If I was willing to permit any devaluation of my ethical currency, I would soon find that my worth had eroded completely. And I could not work that way.

Myron Farber, *Somebody Is Lying,* Doubleday, New York, 1982, pp. 270–271.

---

a fair trial. Reporters argue that shield laws protect their right to publish the news. Again, the First and the Sixth Amendments appear to be in conflict.

Prior Restraint

In August 1983, the Reagan administration issued an unprecedented contract, to be signed by all government officials with access to high-level classified information. The contract will require them, for the rest of their lives, to submit for governmental review any articles or books they write. Though the purpose of this contract is to prevent unauthorized disclosure of classified information, critics note that its effects are likely to go far beyond that. As Floyd Abrams, a specialist in constitutional issues, states: "It will give those in power a new and powerful weapon to delay or even suppress criticism by those most knowledgeable to voice it. The new requirement, warns the American Society of Newspaper Editors, is 'peacetime censorship of a scope unparalleled in this country since the adoption of the Bill of Rights.'"[9] Asserting that this attempt at information control is hostile to the First Amendment's premise that a democracy needs an informed citizenry to argue and shape policy, Abrams and his supporters warn we will pay a high price if it is adhered to. Until this point in time, the United States government has seldom attempted to halt publication of material before it was printed. Termed "*prior restraint,*" this type of censorship, if widely practiced, could seriously diminish the public's right to know.

In 1931, the Supreme Court ruled in *Near v. Minnesota* that prior restraint was indeed a violation of the First Amendment. Somewhat more recently, however, this belief has been questioned, illustrating that the provisions of the First Amendment are far from absolute. On June 13, 1971, for example, *The New York Times* announced that it had obtained a "massive study of how the United States went to war in Indochina." This study summarized in "The Pentagon Papers" had been made available to the *Times* by Daniel Ellsberg, one of thirty-six authors who had worked on the project. In an effort to stop the publication of "The Pentagon Papers" on the grounds that the information contained in it was damaging to the United States, the Department of Justice brought a suit against both *The New York Times* and the *Washington Post*. Only seventeen days later, however, the Supreme Court ruled that the papers could be published. The publication of "The Pentagon Papers" did much to influence the tide of public opinion against the Vietnamese war. And it is interesting to note that in his book *Between Fact and Fiction,* media critic Edward Jay Epstein makes the case that *The New York Times*'s version of "The Pentagon Papers" was organized to show "the disparity between what political leaders say in public and in private." In retrospect, it is Epstein's view that the Pulitzer Prize-winning series was designed to present the material in an antiwar format.

Other cases involving the prior-restraint issue have arisen subsequent to "The Pentagon Papers" case. In 1974, the book *The CIA and the Cult of Intelligence* was printed containing blank spaces with the word "Deleted" inserted as a result of the government's having convinced the courts that the book's author, a former CIA agent, had agreed some nineteen years earlier not to reveal classified information upon leaving the agency. And in 1979, an attempt was made to restrain a magazine, *The Progressive,* from publishing what

> **MEDIA PROBE**
>
> What do you think? Are there instances when a newspaper should be restrained—that is, stopped—from publishing information? If not, why not? If yes, under what circumstances? How, in your opinion, would such "legal censorship" affect the relationship that exists between the government and the press?

was described as a do-it-yourself manual for making a hydrogen bomb. The case was dropped, however, when the information contained in the article was shown to have been previously published elsewhere. Again, we see that while the government carries a heavy burden of justification for imposing restraint, the reporter's rights as stated in the First Amendment are subject to certain restrictions. Whether or not they should be is the issue.

The Freedom of Information Act: Who Can Know What?

On July 4, 1967, the *Freedom of Information Act* (FOIA) became law. The act's premise is that the public has a right to know what is happening in the government—not merely what officials *say* is happening. As a consequence, government records are open for public inspection to any person for whatever purpose unless agencies can give specific reasons for withholding the documents from such inspection. Exempted from the law are trade secrets, oil-well maps, files of law enforcement investigations, and matters of national defense. In 1974, Congress plugged a number of holes in the act by requiring agencies to establish procedural guidelines, set uniform research and duplication costs, and make indexes of their files available to the public.

The law appears to be simple enough, yet it has sent governmental officials scrambling. James J. Cohn Jr., an Environmental Protection Agency inspector general has been quoted as saying: "We have to start thinking about what to get rid of before an FOIA request catches us with our pants down.... We can no longer duck materials in our desks and private workpaper files and hope to exempt them from disclosure.[10] How would you feel if you requested a document from the Federal Bureau of Investigation under the FOIA and received the information contained in Figure 4-1? To what extent, if any, do you believe the FBI has complied with the act's spirit?

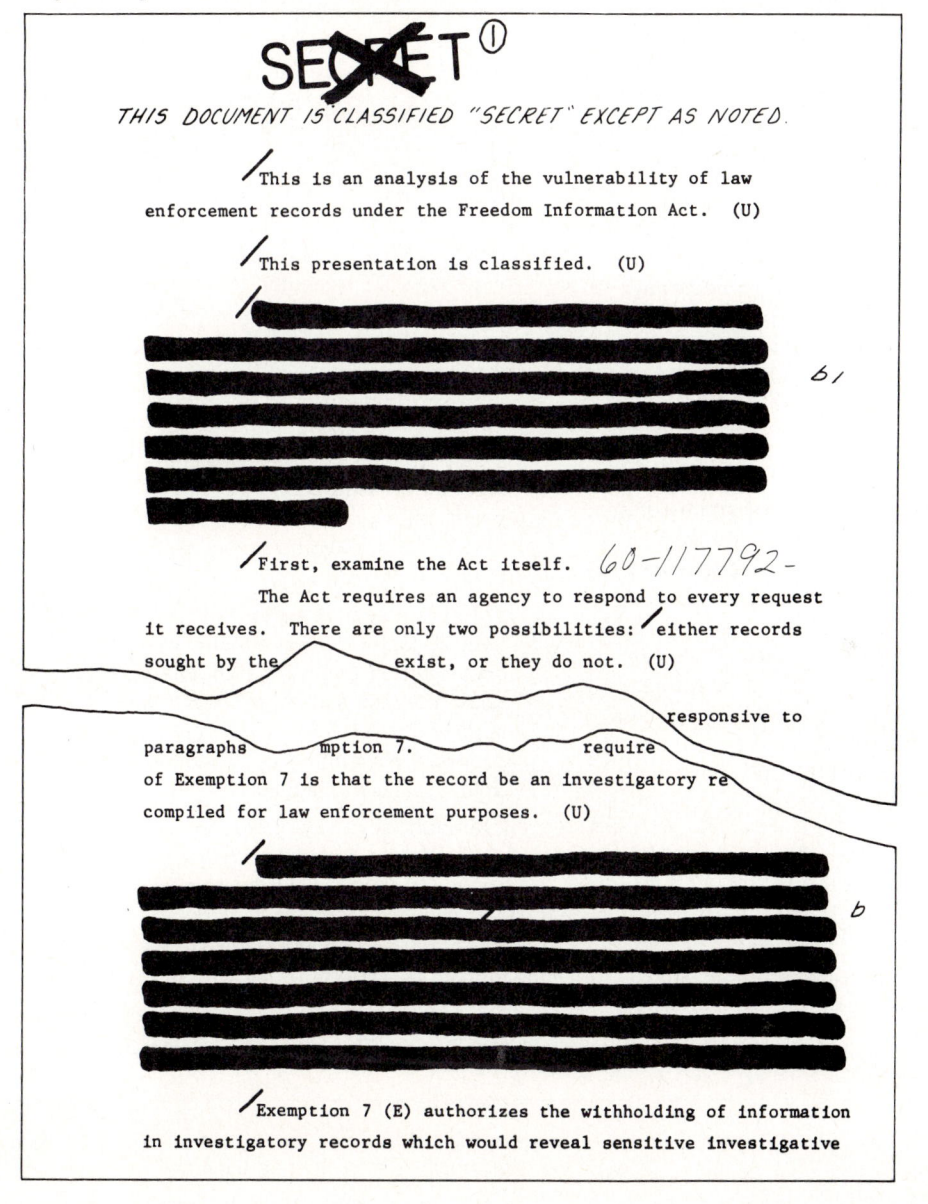

FIGURE 4-1 Freedom of information. A Federal Bureau of Investigation document on how to respond to requests for information is itself heavily deleted before being released as required by the Freedom of Information Act.

```
SECRET ①
THIS DOCUMENT IS CLASSIFIED "SECRET" EXCEPT AS NOTED.

   This is an analysis of the vulnerability of law
enforcement records under the Freedom Information Act. (U)

   This presentation is classified. (U)

   [REDACTED]                                              b1

   First, examine the Act itself.   60-117792-
   The Act requires an agency to respond to every request
it receives. There are only two possibilities: either records
sought by the        exist, or they do not. (U)

                                              responsive to
paragraphs      mption 7.           require
of Exemption 7 is that the record be an investigatory re
compiled for law enforcement purposes. (U)

   [REDACTED]                                               b

   Exemption 7 (E) authorizes the withholding of information
in investigatory records which would reveal sensitive investigative
```

YOU WERE THERE

DETROIT REPORTERS USE FOIA AND WIN PULITZER

When a healthy ex-football star from Michigan died of a heart attack aboard the aircraft carrier USS Ranger in 1981, all the Navy would tell his grieving family was that he died from an unfortunate accident during routine punishment. Paul Trerice's parents demanded to know more, but the Navy refused. *Detroit News* reporters Sydney P. Freedberg and David L. Ashenfelter began tracking down Trerice's shipmates to find out what they knew. The reporters pieced together more than a dozen eyewitness accounts of the mental and physical battering Paul Trerice suffered as a prisoner aboard the Ranger.

The Federal Freedom of Information Act is "simple, quick, and easy to use," according to the FOIA Service Center's how-to handbook. Well, there was nothing quick or easy about our efforts last year to obtain investigation reports and other documents about six Navy deaths.

For the better part of a year, Navy officials in Washington repeatedly tried to scuttle our attempts to help six families learn the truth about how their sons died in the peacetime Navy.... From June through September 1981, we spent most of our time writing FOIA requests.... But by late September, the reports still had not arrived. Based on information contained in the few documents we had obtained—and details supplied by witnesses... we published the first two installments of our series.

The first story described the difficulties five families and the *Detroit News* encountered when they asked the Navy over a period of months to provide details about the deaths.

The second story described how the Navy treated an Oklahoma family after their son vanished off the USS Ranger in the Pacific Ocean in 1976. The Navy told the family their son died while serving his country when he was blown overboard by jet exhaust during flight operations.

But documents obtained by *The News* told a far different story: Terry Colum, brig prisoner, jumped overboard during strenuous exercises after being denied water in the ship's jail. Unbeknownst to the family, his death had been listed as a suicide....

Getting around the Navy denials required a few tricks. When the Navy refused to tell us how many deaths it recorded in 1980, or provide us with any names, we gleaned the "in memoriam" pages of dozens of dusty naval yearbooks stored in a warehouse in Washington. Then, using the FOIA, we asked the Navy to provide uncensored death certificates for the sailors we identified. The Navy planned to delete the names and addresses of the next of kin, citing the Federal Privacy Act. When we protested over a period of two days, the Navy agreed to identify the sailors' relatives and their hometowns.

Based on this information, we contacted more than 70 families—more than half of whom claimed the Navy was withholding key details about their sons' deaths. The information established that there was a pattern of unresponsiveness in the way the service provided death details to families.

Although there have been vigorous attempts since Watergate to make government more accountable to the public, our experience with the Navy leads us to conclude that there are sufficient legal loopholes in the FOIA to enable bureaucrats to subvert the spirit and letter of the FOIA.

"Detroit Reporters Use FOI to Crack Navy Stonewall, Win Pulitzer Gold," *FOI '82*, Society of Professional Journalists, 1982.

Actually, securing information under the FOIA is a timely process—time which most journalists do not have. Thus, social scientists and other researchers who do not usually need information in a hurry will probably use the materials more frequently than will most journalists.

ETHICAL CONSIDERATIONS

The newspaper industry is a large and powerful mass medium. Speaking of this power, Kurt M. Luedtke, former executive editor of the *Detroit Free Press* and author of the screenplay for *Absence of Malice,* told the 1982 convention of the American Newspaper Publishers Association:

> On your discretionary judgments hang reputations and careers, jail sentences and stock prices. Broadway shows and water rates. You are the mechanism of reward and punishment, the arbiter of right and wrong, the roving eye of daily judgment. You no longer shape public opinion, you have supplanted it. There are good men and women who will not stand for office, concerned that you will find their flaws or invent them. Many people who have dealt with you wish that they had not. You are capricious and unpredictable, you are fearsome and you are feared, because there is never any way to know whether this time you will be fair and accurate or whether you will not. And there is virtually nothing we can do about it.[11]

Since reporters must be able to make quick decisions regarding what to report and what not to, they are frequently called upon to make snap ethical or moral judgments. Reacting to the pressures placed upon their people, a number of newspaper and journalistic societies have drawn up ethical codes of conduct; one such code is the Statement of Principles of the American Society of Newspaper Editors. In the coming pages we will examine a number of the ethical issues which journalists and the public need to take time to consider; these include conflict of interest, fair play, and responsibility.

Conflict of Interest

You open a newspaper and turn to the travel section. You find yourself reading an article in which a reporter reveals the virtues of vacationing on a particular Caribbean island. In the article the reporter mentions that his expenses were paid for by the island's government. In your opinion, does this constitute a conflict of interest? Every year hundreds of contests are run for the best article on a particular product or service. To what extent could the writing of journalists who are aware of these contests be biased by the desire to win the prizes offered by the sponsors? Representative Charles Gubser of California claims: "There is no greater group of free loaders in the world than the press. They will take anything they can get."[12] Garrett Ray, contributing editor for *The Littleton Colorado Independent*, addresses this problem:

> I know a lot about freeloading. Most journalists have an instinctive feel for it. Those who do not—well, they learn fast.
>
> The freeload is an American institution. It is ideally suited to a nation that exalts selling (products, services, ideas, politicians, religions) and that also underpays journalists. The illegitimate offspring of this liaison is the cocktail party for the press, heavy on the hors d'oeuvres.
>
> Every sales campaign begins with a party designed to cajole the American press into accepting the odd notion that the Chairman of the Board's announcement is really news. Broadcasters, newspaper reporters and magazine writers mingle just as if they were all part of the same profession. They momentarily submerge their differences out of respect for the importance of the occasion, and for the boiled shrimp, caviar and miniature shish kebabs.
>
> Even without a journalism course, novice reporters quickly learn the system. After only a month of on-the-job training, a beginner can balance a bourbon and water and a paper plate

AMERICAN SOCIETY OF NEWSPAPER EDITORS

A STATEMENT OF PRINCIPLES

PREAMBLE

The First Amendment, protecting freedom of expression from abridgment by any law, guarantees to the people through their press a constitutional right, and thereby places on newspaper people a particular responsibility.

Thus journalism demands of its practitioners not only industry and knowledge but also the pursuit of a standard of integrity proportionate to the journalist's singular obligation.

To this end the American Society of Newspaper Editors sets forth this Statement of Principles as a standard encouraging the highest ethical and professional performance.

ARTICLE I Responsibility

The primary purpose of gathering and distributing news and opinion is to serve the general welfare by informing the people and enabling them to make judgments on the issues of the time. Newspapermen and women who abuse the power of their professional role for selfish motives or unworthy purposes are faithless to that public trust.

The American press was made free not just to inform or just to serve as a forum for debate but also to bring an independent scrutiny to bear on the forces of power in the society, including the conduct of official power at all levels of government.

ARTICLE II Freedom of the Press

Freedom of the press belongs to the people. It must be defended against encroachment or assault from any quarter, public or private.

Journalists must be constantly alert to see that the public's business is conducted in public. They must be vigilant against all who would exploit the press for selfish purposes.

ARTICLE III Independence

Journalists must avoid impropriety and the appearance of impropriety as well as any conflict of interest or the appearance of conflict. They should neither accept anything nor pursue any activity that might compromise or seem to compromise their integrity.

ARTICLE IV Truth and Accuracy

Good faith with the reader is the foundation of good journalism. Every effort must be made to assure that the news content is accurate, free from bias and in context, and that all sides are presented fairly. Editorials, analytical articles and commentary should be held to the same standards of accuracy with respect to facts as news reports.

Significant errors of fact, as well as errors of omission, should be corrected promptly and prominently.

ARTICLE V Impartiality

To be impartial does not require the press to be unquestioning or to refrain from editorial expression. Sound practice, however, demands a clear distinction for the reader between news reports and opinion. Articles that contain opinion or personal interpretation should be clearly identified.

ARTICLE VI Fair Play

Journalists should respect the rights of people involved in the news, observe the common standards of decency and stand accountable to the public for the fairness and accuracy of their news reports.

Persons publicly accused should be given the earliest opportunity to respond.

Pledges of confidentiality to news sources must be honored at all costs, and therefore should not be given lightly. Unless there is clear and pressing need to maintain confidences, sources of information should be identified.

These principles are intended to preserve, protect and strengthen the bond of trust and respect between American journalists and the American people, a bond that is essential to sustain the grant of freedom entrusted to both by the nation's founders.

—adopted by the **ASNE** board of directors, Oct. 23, 1975.

stacked with chilis relleños, olives and pâté sandwiches, while still keeping the fingers of the right hand free to greet corporate nabobs.[13]

Of course, conflicts of interest go beyond press cocktail parties. Sports writers, for example, are often assigned to serve as official scorers at baseball games. And all-expense-paid trips to training camps—offered to journalists to cover practice sessions—are also common. Nor are conflicts of interest limited to writers of the sports or travel pages. To be sure, potential areas for conflicts of interest abound in all sections of the paper.

Should an editor or publisher run for public office? Can business writers write fairly about a corporation in which they have invested thousands of dollars? Should personal friendships be maintained with news sources? Should reporters accept coffee, a drink, dinner, or a bottle of expensive scotch from some person or corporation that they are researching?

How can the "opportunities" for conflicts of interest be reduced? Journalists offer one answer. They believe their salaries and expense accounts should be increased. For example, the *Los Angeles Times* gives a $20,000-a-year expense account to its travel editor Jerry Hulse, who has described Atlantic City as "the Skid Row Riviera. The nicest thing about visiting Atlantic City is the drive out of town. Visiting Atlantic City is like taking your vacation in military boot camp." Do you think Hulse would have written such a scathing review if his trip had been funded by the Atlantic City chamber of commerce?

Many newspapers have ethics codes which prohibit reporters from accepting free gifts, travel bonuses, meals, or offers of outside employment in order to diminish conflicts of interest. The extent to which these codes are adhered to, however, is open to question.

Fair Play

The ASNE principles state that a journalist should respect the rights of people involved in the news, observe common standards of decency, and give a fair and accurate portrayal of events. To this end, it is felt that people or organizations attacked in the news are due the right of simultaneous rebuttal. But, in fact, it is the newspaper editors who decide whether or not a news article will appear in print.

A football star dies of a heart attack in the company of a prostitute. Should that item be printed? A hometown girl is killed in a campus fire. Unfortunately, the fire occurred at 3 A.M. in a campus fraternity house. Should the location be divulged? A man wrestled a weapon from the would-be assassin of President Gerald Ford. To the man's dismay, newspapers covering the story exposed the fact that he was a homosexual. Should they have done that?

Fair-play problems also have arisen because of statements given "off the record." If a person agrees to speak off the record, is it fair to reveal that person's identity? Most reporters would not. However, if you make a statement to a reporter, do not expect to then be able to say, "Let's make that off the record." Once you divulge the information, it is too late to negotiate its use. Fair play works both ways.

Fair play is also related to the privacy issue. How sensitive should a reporter be to the right of individual privacy? Is what is newsworthy synonymous with what the public might find interesting? What do you think?

The Responsibility to Inform the People

Finally, a journalist's responsibilities include serving the general welfare of the people by keeping them informed so that they are able to make judgments on issues of the day. Sometimes, however, the welfare of the people may be better served if the journalist refrains from revealing all that he or she knows. For example, after the Iranian terrorists seized the United States embassy in Tehran in 1979, a number of reporters were privy to

MEDIA PROBE

FAIR PLAY?

Bus driver John Doe is transporting grade school pupils from the school to their homes. A car driven by a teenager cuts directly in front of Doe's bus. In trying to avoid hitting the car, Doe swerves, and the bus overturns into a ditch.

Fearing an explosion, Doe starts removing unconscious youngsters from the bus. He becomes almost exhausted but continues to remove the bus occupants in a heroic fashion. Just as he has finished removing the last bus passenger, Doe is badly burned as the bus does indeed explode.

The next morning the local newspaper runs a story telling how Doe may have saved two dozen lives. The next day the newspaper learns from an anonymous source that Doe is a closet homosexual. It checks out the information and learns that Doe was arrested 20 years earlier on a charge of taking indecent liberties with a minor. He would have been 21 at the time of the charge.

The newspaper further checks some sources in the gay community and learns that Doe is a homosexual, that he lives with a 30-year-old male and that he has always concealed his lifestyle from his employers.

Doe picks up the Sunday edition and reads a story about his alleged homosexuality. He walks to the window of the hospital room, and he is killed in the 11-story leap.

QUESTIONS

1. Should the newspaper have run the story alleging that Doe was a homosexual?
2. If it planned to run a story, should it have given Doe an opportunity to comment?
3. Did the public nature of his job justify the newspaper study about his sexual preference?
4. Under what circumstances, if any, should Doe's secret be revealed?
5. What kind of policy should the newspaper have about privacy in such matters as this?

Dennie Hall, "Guidelines for Case Study Programs," *Journalism Ethics Report*, Society of Professional Journalists, Sigma Delta Chi, 1982, p. 30.

---

the information that a group of six Americans had managed to escape the U.S. compound and were being sheltered in the Canadian embassy. The press held the story, choosing not to release it until all six Americans had been safely and secretly escorted out of Iran.

Deciding whether or not to reveal a secret is a decision that members of the press confront with increasing frequency. In her book *Secrets*, Sissela Bok emphasizes "Control over secrecy and openness gives power: it influences what others know and thus what they choose to do." Since journalists function, at least in part, as gatekeepers—separating information we will be privy to from information we may not share—they possess this power. The members of the press need to continually evaluate whether they are using the power they are entrusted with in a wise and responsible fashion.

Another aspect of the responsibility issue involves whether the names of CIA agents should be revealed by the news media. In a WRFM commentary, journalist Jim Branch noted:

> Philip Agee, ever since he left the CIA, has become the world's best known revealer of American CIA agents . . . though it's not likely that

MEDIA PROBE

THE RIGHT TO PRIVACY

It was early in the spring about 15 years ago—a day of pale sunlight and trees just beginning to bud. I was a young police reporter, driving to a scene I didn't want to see. A man, the police-dispatcher's broadcast said, had accidentally backed his pickup truck over his baby granddaughter in the driveway of the family home. It was a fatality.

As I parked among police cars and TV-news cruisers, I saw a stocky, white-haired man in cotton work clothes standing near a pickup. Cameras were trained on him, and reporters were sticking microphones in his face. Looking totally bewildered, he was trying to answer their questions. Mostly he was only moving his lips, blinking and choking up.

After a while the reporters gave up on him and followed the police into the small white house. I can still see in my mind's eye that devastated old man looking down at the place in the driveway where the child had been. Beside the house was a freshly spaded flower bed, and nearby a pile of dark, rich earth.

"I was just backing up there to spread that good dirt," he said to me, though I had not asked him anything. "I didn't even know she was outdoors." He stretched his hand toward the flower bed, then let it flop to his side. He lapsed back into his thoughts, and I, like a good reporter, went into the house to find someone who could provide a recent photo of the toddler.

A few minutes later, with all the details in my notebook and a three-by-five studio portrait of the cherubic child tucked in my jacket pocket, I went toward the kitchen, where the police had said the body was.

I had brought a camera in with me—the big, bulky Speed Graphic which used to be the newspaper reporter's trademark. Everybody had drifted back out of the house together—family, police, reporters, and photographers. Entering the kitchen, I came upon this scene:

On a Formica-topped table, backlighted by a frilly curtained window, lay the tiny body, wrapped in a clean white sheet. Somehow the grandfather had managed to stay away from the crowd. He was sitting on a chair beside the table, in profile to me and unaware of my presence, looking uncomprehendingly at the swaddled corpse.

The house was very quiet. A clock ticked. As I watched, the grandfather slowly leaned forward, curved his arms like parentheses around the head and feet of the little form, then pressed his face to the shroud and remained motionless.

In that hushed moment I recognized the makings of a prize-winning news photograph. I appraised the light, adjusted the lens setting and distance, locked a bulb in the flashgun, raised the camera, and composed the scene in the viewfinder.

Every element of the picture was perfect: the grandfather in his plain work clothes, his white hair backlighted by sunshine, the child's form wrapped in the sheet, the atmosphere of the simple home suggested by black iron trivets and World's Fair souvenir plates on the walls flanking the window. Outside, the police could be seen inspecting the fatal rear wheel of the pickup while the child's mother and father leaned in each other's arms.

I don't know how many seconds I stood there, unable to snap that shutter. I was keenly aware of the powerful story-telling value that photo would have, and my professional conscience told me to take it. Yet I couldn't make my hand fire that flashbulb and intrude on the poor man's island of grief.

At length I lowered the camera and crept away, shaken with doubt about my suitability for the journalistic profession. Of course I never told the city editor or any fellow reporters about that missed opportunity for a perfect news picture.

Every day, on the newscasts and in the papers, we see pictures of people in extreme conditions of grief and despair. Human suffer-

ing has become a spectator sport. And sometimes as I'm watching news film, I remember that day.
I still feel right about what I did.

James Alexander Thom, "The Perfect Picture," *Reader's Digest,* August 1976, p. 113.
Would you have acted as reporter Thom did? Why or why not?

Mr. Agee is very up to date on such topics now, since so many spies have come and gone since he went.... But he still likes to pretend he knows a lot.... And perhaps he has become a funnel of information for others. Louis Wolf publishes and edits a newsletter called The Covert Action Information Bulletin, which names CIA names. Since it all began Richard Welch ... an identified CIA operative ... was murdered in Greece ... an alleged CIA operative in Jamaica ... and his family were terrorized ... and other diplomats were harrassed in Nicaragua on similar allegations.[14]

Since these words were spoken in 1982, President Reagan has signed a law making it a crime to disclose the names of covert agents. The law, however, applies to private citizens—not to members of the press. Consequently, many newspapers including *The Wall Street Journal,* still print the names of CIA operatives. In your opinion, should the press continue its practice of revealing some secrets the government does not wish to be made public? Why or why not?

While quite a number of responsibility-related issues confront the press, the final one we will consider is terrorism. When terrorists seize hostages and make demands, how should reporters respond? To what extent does the news coverage accorded to terrorists encourage others to commit similar acts? Media critic Hodding Carter believes "media coverage encourages more violence, it encourages more terrorism, it encourages more demagogues." But Carter also goes on to note that media coverage also "encourages more freedom, it encourages more of almost everything which is basic to an open, pluralistic society." Thus, Carter believes, "There is no way that you can say "be responsible" without defining by government the ways that people are to be responsible."

An ABC News poll revealed that three out of five persons questioned believed news cameras should be banned by law from the scene of an act of terrorism; if this were done, it was hoped, terrorists would realize they would not get TV coverage to further their cause. But the question is, to what extent would this policy interfere with what is viewed as the public's right to know?

We have now examined a number of dilemmas journalists confront on a daily basis; however, we have in no way solved them: the problems are far too complex. Nevertheless, these issues are worthy of your time and consideration, and we do hope they are clearer than they were before you thought about them.

As we see, whether journalists perform their job as their job should be performed is subject to debate. When journalists do their job inadequately or recklessly, they should be taken to task. But when they perform well, they should be applauded. We believe that, above all else, it should be kept in mind that unless reporters are free to probe and willing to do so, the public's need to learn about matters that affect its welfare could go unfulfilled.

MEDIA PROBE

In the early weeks of the Iranian takeover of the U.S. embassy, NBC made a deal with the students holding the hostages: they agreed to permit one of the students to broadcast an unedited lengthy statement in exchange for an interview with a hostage that would be recorded under terrorist supervision. Do you think the network should have made such a deal? Why or why not?

SUMMARY

When asked to define "news," journalists supplied a multitude of responses ranging from "what raises eyebrows" to "the report of an event." However, most journalists agree that before an event becomes newsworthy, it must meet the following criteria: prominence, proximity, consequence, timeliness, and human interest. In addition, what is newsworthy depends at least in part on publisher preferences and the size of the news hole.

Newspapers rely on three key sources to gather the news: the wire services, reporters who cover regular beats, and investigative reporters. For much of the information they are supplied with, reporters are dependent on source-controlled information—that is, information that originates with the source. When reporters are able to cover events that are beyond the control of such "event managers," they enter the realm of investigative reporting.

Once information has been gathered and deemed newsworthy, it still needs to be transformed into an acceptable news article. Again, three key variables shape the process: the pressure of time, the inverted-pyramid style of writing, and the need for eye-catching headlines.

Journalists who object to the traditional "facts only" style of writing find comfort in new journalism. New journalism adherents write like novelists, incorporating dialogue, flashbacks, and personal opinions into their articles.

Through the years, the press and the courts have tried to come to terms on a number of issues. Among the issues they have debated are libel, privacy versus the right to know, freedom of the press versus a defendant's right to a fair trial, the problems posed by prior restraint, and the ramifications of the Freedom of Information Act.

In addition to debating legal issues, in the course of performing their jobs, reporters are also faced with a number of moral dilemmas. What constitutes a conflict of interest? What does fair play entail? Under what circumstances should a journalist conceal rather than reveal information? To be sure, whether journalists have handled the legal and ethical problems facing them effectively is itself subject to debate.

KEY TERMS

News
Wire service
Beat reporter
Investigative
  reporter
New journalism
Authoritarian press
Libertarian press
Social-responsibility
  theory
Pseudoevent
Inverted pyramid

Lead
Libel
Privacy law
First Amendment
Sixth Amendment
Gag order
Shield law
Prior restraint
Freedom of
  Information Act

NOTES

[1] Judee K. Burgoon, Michael Burgoon, and Charles K. Atkin, *The World of the Working Journalist,* Newspaper Readership Project/Newspaper Advertising Bureau, New York, 1982, p. 7.

[2] Michael Singletary, "What Determines the News?" in *News Research Report,* American Newspaper Publishers Association, New York, August 12, 1977, p. 1.

[3] Thomas Plate, "A Conversation With Thomas Plate," in Roy Peter Clark (ed.), *Best Newspaper Writing, 1981,* Modern Media Institute, St. Petersburg, Fla., 1981, pp. 103–104.

[4] Tom Wolfe, *The New Journalism,* Harper & Row, New York, 1973, p. 9.

[5] Ibid., p. 21.

[6] Ibid., p. 12.

[7] John Curley, "How Libel Suit Sapped the Crusading Spirit of a Small Newspaper," *The Wall Street Journal,* September 29, 1983, p. 1.

[8] Theodore H. White, "Why the Jailing of Farber Terrifies Me," *The New York Times Magazine,* November 26, 1978, p. 28.

[9] Floyd Abrams, "The New Effort to Control Information," *The New York Times Magazine,* September 25, 1983, pp. 22–27, 72–73.

[10] Bob Lewis, "Feds Urged to Destroy Records So

Requesters Don't Find 'Pants Down,'" *FOI'82,* Society of Professional Journalists, 1982, p. 9.

[11] Kurt M. Luedtke, "So How Do You Think the Referendum Will Go?" Speech delivered at the National Convention of the American Newspaper Publishers Association, May 1982.

[12] J. R. Wiggins, "Gifts, Favors and Gratuities," *Bulletin of the American Society of Newspaper Editors,* August 1, 1958, p. 1.

[13] Garrett Ray, "Freeloading: An American Institution," *Journalism Ethics Report,* Society of Professional Journalists, Sigma Delta Chi, 1982, p. 29.

[14] Jim Branch, "Prosecuting the Identifiers," New York: WRFM Radio, June 14, 1982.

SUGGESTIONS FOR FURTHER READING

American Society of Newspaper Editors: *ASNE Proceedings,* American Society of Newspaper Editors, Easton, Pa. *A yearly publication of the speeches and discussions held at the national convention of the American Society of Newspaper Editors. Excellent for current material on issues of legal and ethical controls on journalists.*

Anderson, Jack, and James Boyd: *Confessions of a Muckraker,* Random House, New York 1979. *An interesting account of Anderson's entry into investigative journalism.*

Burgoon, Judee K., Michael Burgoon, and Charles K. Atkin: *The World of the Working Journalist,* Newspaper Readership Project/Newspaper Advertising Bureau, New York, 1982. *A fascinating first-hand account of journalists on the job.*

Epstein, Edward Jay: *Between Fact and Fiction: The Problem of Journalism,* Vintage, New York, 1975. *A collection of highly readable essays on the ways the press handled Vietnam, the Pentagon Papers, Watergate, and other issues.*

Gillmore, Donald, and Jerome Barron: *Mass Communication Law,* West, St. Paul, Minn., 1979. *A comprehensive examination of the legal restraints on the press.*

Hulteng, John: *Playing It Straight,* Globe Pequot, Chester, Conn., 1981. *Case studies of the ethical principles facing journalists assembled for the American Society of Newspaper Editors.*

Johnstone, John, Edward J. Slawski, and William Bowman: *The News People,* University of Illinois Press, Urbana, Ill., 1976. *Three sociologists examine the process and product of American journalism.*

Mencher, Melvin: *News Reporting and Writing.* Wm. C. Brown, Dubuque, Iowa, 1979. *A comprehensive text on the process of newswriting.*

Rivers, William L.: *News Editing in the 80's,* Wadsworth, Belmont, Calif., 1983. *Exercises and theory are combined to introduce the reader to the news-editing process.*

Schudson, Michael: *Discovering the News,* Basic, New York, 1978. *An examination of the history of American newspapers from a social perspective.*

Weber, Ronald, (ed.): *The Reporter As Artist: A Look at the New Journalism Controversy,* Hastings House, New York, 1974. *A fine collection of works by new journalists.*

Wicker, Tom: *On Press,* Viking, New York, 1978. *A respected* New York Times *writer looks at his craft.*

Wolfe, Tom: *The New Journalism,* Harper & Row, New York, 1973. *A fascinating account of the development of new journalism by one of its chief proponents.*

Zinsser, William: *On Writing Well: An Informal Guide to Writing Nonfiction,* 2d ed., Harper & Row, New York, 1980. *A readable approach to writing for newspapers that should be valuable for anyone considering journalism as a profession.*

CHAPTER 5

MAGAZINES: FORMS, FUNCTIONS, AUDIENCES

I consider such easy vehicles of knowledge more happily calculated than any other, to preserve the liberty, stimulate the industry, and meliorate the morals of an enlightened free people.
George Washington

WANTED

A few sensible correspondents who will condescend to clothe their ideas in plain prose.
The Port Folio, *1822*

CHAPTER PREVIEW

After reading this chapter, you should be able to:
- Assess the role magazines play in your life
- Identify and discuss key developments in the history of magazines
- Compare and contrast general-interest magazines, women's magazines, and special-interest magazines
- Account for the rise in general-interest magazines following both the Civil War and World War I
- Explain how the muckrakers used magazines
- Discuss how the magazine industry adapted to the age of television
- Describe the ownership patterns that characterize the magazine industry
- Draw an organization chart for a typical medium-sized magazine
- Identify and discuss the functions performed by the magazine publisher, the editor-in-chief, and the editorial, advertising, circulation, and production departments
- Compare and contrast micro- and macro-editing
- Define "editorial concept"
- Describe the role research plays in magazine planning
- Explain how titles and articles are used to sell magazines
- Compare and contrast the design and layout of various magazines

Imagine that your local newsstand carried no magazines. Or worse, that there were no magazines to which you could subscribe. How might such a situation affect your lifestyle? From the 1950s to the early 1970s the possibility that magazines might vanish appeared to be a very real threat. A number of favorite weekly magazines ceased to exist—*Life, Look, Collier's,* and *The Saturday Evening Post* all closed their doors. What medium filled the void left by these popular magazines? Network television. Advertisers and readers alike turned in droves to the newer medium. All the indications were that magazines were on the way out. William G. Dunn, publisher of *U.S. News & World Report,* comments that even today, "most media directors at advertising agencies will spend money in broadcasting. After all, it is difficult to fill a blank page. It is more fun to go on location and create a TV commercial."[1] What he does not mention, however, is that it is also more expensive.

Of course, the magazine industry has not died. Instead it seems to have heeded the Queen's advice to Alice in *Through the Looking Glass:* "Now, *here,* you see, it takes all the running you can do, to keep in the same place. If you want to get somewhere else, you must run at least twice as fast as that!" Magazines have run hard, indeed. In August of 1980, the Magazine Publishers Association (MPA) reported that magazine circulation had grown twice as fast as the nation's population.[2] And by 1982, the MPA was able to state: "Magazines have become such an integral part of our lives that, today, nine out of ten adults read at least one of the measured consumer magazines during the average month."[3] The average reader examines eight magazines per month on 3.2 different days. The average page is viewed 1.7 times.[4] Magazines still play a formidable role in the lives of Americans. While a number of factors, including better demographics, may account for the resurgence of advertiser interest in the magazine business, one key factor was re-

MEDIA PROBE

Develop a list of magazines you have read or looked at during the past month. Why did you choose to read each magazine? Are there some publications you read more regularly than others? Why? What magazines would you not want to read at all? Why?

ported in a study done for the National Association of Broadcasters: 49 percent of the respondents reported that they were now watching less television than they had in previous years. The implication is that they have more time to spend consuming other media, including magazines.

What is a magazine? How does it differ from a newspaper? Usually, magazines are published periodically (traditionally, less frequently than newspapers) in a bound format, have a durable paper cover, and contain better-quality paper. Of course, while a trip to your local newsstand may produce exceptions, for the most part these guidelines can be relied upon to help you to distinguish magazines from other media.

Why do people read magazines? We will attempt to answer this question by examining the roots of magazines, the fragmenting of the audience for magazines, current industry patterns, and the editorial process.

THE WAY THINGS WERE

Although similarities in printing made early magazines in England difficult to distinguish from newspapers, the first magazine was probably *The Review,* published in 1704 and written for nine years by Daniel Defoe of *Robinson Crusoe* fame. Consisting of four pages, the magazine appeared three times each week at first, and as a biweekly in later years. Included in it was a column entitled "Advice from the Scandalous Club," in which Defoe

MEDIA SCOPE

1704 — Daniel Defoe begins publishing The Review in England

1741 — The American Magazine and Ben Franklin's General Magazine and Historical Chronicle become America's first magazines

1789 — Children's Magazine is published for young readers

1794 — Postal regulations altered to favor magazines

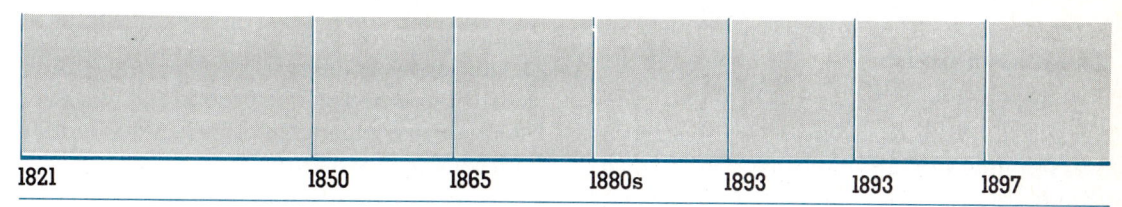

1821 — The Saturday Evening Post is founded

1850 — Harper's Monthly is founded

1865 — The magazine boom begins; E. L. Godkin founds The Nation

1880s — Ladies' Home Journal and other women's magazines appear

1893 — McClures Magazine becomes the first inexpensive periodical

1893 — Munsey's Magazine sells for 10 cents

1897 — Cyrus Curtis takes over The Saturday Evening Post

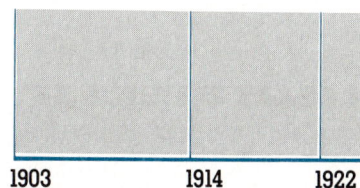

1903 — McClure's Magazine exposes Standard Oil, and muckraking begins

1914 — Audit Bureau of circulation founded

1922 — Reader's Digest is founded

1923 — Time magazine becomes a overnight success

1925 — The New Yorker is founded

1936 — Life magazine founded

1937 — Look appears, imitating Life

1945 — Ebony is born

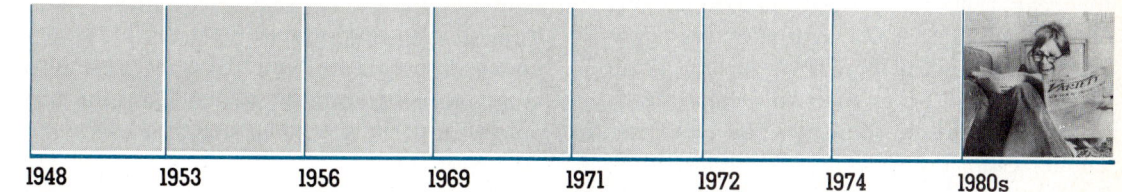

1948 — TV Guide founded; later expands nationwide

1953 — Hugh Hefner founds Playboy

1956 — Collier's ceases publication

1969 — The Saturday Evening Post dies

1971 — Look dies

1972 — Life prints final issue; MS Magazine is founded

1974 — TV Guide surpasses Reader's Digest as nation's largest-selling magazine

1980s — Specialized audiences are key to magazine success

MAGAZINES: FORMS, FUNCTIONS, AUDIENCES

discussed literature, etiquette, and other topics of interest. Then in 1709, Richard Steele created the fictitious Isaac Bickerstaff and made him the publisher of *The Tatler.* By relying on humor, *The Tatler* was able to handle serious topics and attack human foibles. A few years later, in 1711, Joseph Addison, who had been working with Steele, joined forces with him and the two began to publish *The Spectator,* an offering which contained humor, essays, and even short stories.

Magazine Roots

Numerous imitations of these publications sprang up in England, but in this country it was not until January 1741 that the first magazines were available. In that month and year *The American Magazine or a Monthly View of the Political State of the British Colonies* appeared and was followed in short order by Benjamin Franklin's *General Magazine and Historical Chronicle for the British Plantations in America. The American Magazine* ran but three issues and Franklin's folded after six. A great deal of the materials contained in these magazines and the ones that came after them had been reprinted from other sources. In addition, magazines of the times also had to contend with high postal rates and slow, primitive printing methods. So although a number of magazines started during the 1700s, most failed: historian John Tebbel reports that by the year 1800 only twelve magazines were being published in the United States. However, things began to pick up slowly. While there were still fewer than 100 magazines in 1825, 600 were in publication by 1850, and Tebbel estimates that 5000 to 6000 others had started and ceased publication.[5] Thus, the early to mid-nineteenth century saw the magazine industry in America really begin to come alive.

One editor who embodied the style and tone of this particular period was Joseph Dennie. Beginning his career with the New Hampshire weekly, *The Farmers Museum* in 1793, Dennie went on to publish *The Port Folio,* a high-quality magazine that featured articles and "lay sermons" by such figures as John Quincy Adams and Gouverneur Morris.

Magazine Boom: 1820 to the Civil War

Improved printing technology and compulsory education both contributed to the growth of the magazine medium. In fact, so evident was the development of the industry that Edgar Allan Poe was moved to write, "The whole tendency of the age is magazineward." And in 1828, reflecting the magazine boom taking place, the following was written in the *New York Mirror:*

> These United States are fertile in most things, but in periodicals they are extremely luxuriant. They spring up as fast as mushrooms, in every corner, and like all rapid vegetation, bear the seeds of early decay within them.... They put forth their young green leaves in the shape of promises and prospectuses—blossom through a few numbers—and then comes a "frost, a killing frost," in the form of bills due and debts unpaid. This is the fate of hundreds, but hundreds more are found to supply their place, to tread in their steps, and share their destiny.[6]

General-Interest Magazines One important development during this period was the growth of monthly general-interest magazines. In 1821, Samuel Atkinson and Charles Alexander began publishing *The Saturday Evening Post;* by 1826, they were also publishing a second popular general-interest magazine, *The Casket: Flowers of Literature, Wit and Sentiment.* In 1839, Atkinson sold *The Casket* to George Graham, who also purchased another magazine from actor William Burton and in 1840 combined the two into *Graham's Magazine.* Graham was one of the first magazine publishers to pay reasonable fees to his contributors, thereby attracting the likes of such writers as Poe, Bryant, Longfellow, and Holmes to his fold.

YOU WERE THERE

JOSEPH DENNIE: EDITOR AND WRITER

A glimpse of early American magazines can be derived from Joseph Buckingham's description of writer-editor Joseph Dennie. Buckingham—later a prominent editor in his own right—was employed as a printer's devil for *The Farmer's Museum*, where he had the opportunity to observe Dennie at work. Dennie was a Harvard graduate who had studied and practiced law before turning to magazine publishing and editing.

> In person he was rather below than above the middle height, and was of slender frame. He was particularly attentive to his dress, which, when he appeared in the street on a pleasant day, approached the highest notch of the fashion. I remember, one delightful morning in May, he came into the office dressed in a pea-green coat, white vest, nankin small-clothes, white silk stockings, and shoes, or pumps, fastened with silver buckles, which covered at least half the foot from the instep to the toe. His small clothes were tied at the knees with ribbons of the same color, in double bows, the ends reaching down to the ankles....
>
> Dennie wrote with great rapidity, and generally postponed his task until he was called upon for copy. It was frequently necessary to go to his office, and it was not uncommon to find him in bed at a late hour in the morning. His copy was often given out in small portions, a paragraph or two at a time; sometimes it was written in the printing-office, while the compositor was waiting to put it in type. One of the best of his lay sermons was written at the village tavern, directly opposite to the office, in a chamber where he and his friends were amusing themselves with cards. It was delivered to me by piecemeal, at four or five different times. If he happened to be engaged in a game when I applied for copy, he would ask someone to play his hand for him while he could give the devil his due. When I called for the closing paragraph of the sermon, he said, "Call again in five minutes." "No," said Tyler, "I'll write the improvement for you." He accordingly wrote the concluding paragraph and Dennie never saw it till it was put in print.

Joseph Buckingham, quoted in Frank Luther Mott, *A History of American Magazines, 1741–1850*, Appleton, New York, 1930.

Another important general-interest magazine of the times was *Knickerbocker*, started in 1833 and edited after 1834 by Lewis Gaylord Clark. Clark, like Graham, was willing to pay well to use the original works of major writers of the day. Clark's major innovation was to include an "Editor's Table" in each issue; in it he discussed fashion and New York City–related topics, much as the "Notes and Comments" section of *The New Yorker* does today. As the century progressed, other general-interest magazines, including *McClure's Magazine* (1893) and *Munsey's Magazine* (1897), established large circulations by selling their issues at 10 to 15 cents each.

Women's Magazines The first successful women's magazine was started in 1828 by Sara Josepha Hale. Titled *Ladies' Magazine*, Hale's publication campaigned both for women's rights and the need for women to become schoolteachers. After nine years Hale and her chief competitor merged their magazines, creating *Godey's Lady's Book*. Louis Godey's periodical as edited by Hale attained an impressive circulation of 40,000 monthly

The Saturday Evening Post, founded in 1824, typified mass cultural tastes for generations of Americans. (The Bettman Archive)

copies in 1850. Graham and other publishers also experimented with their formats in an effort to appeal to the growing women's audience. Today, among the magazines we see serving this market, are the *Ladies' Home Journal, Family Circle,* and *Woman's Day.*

Special-Interest Magazines During the first half of the nineteenth century, publications which were directed at special-interest audiences also became available. For example, magazines for children were a popular offering. Nathaniel Willis started *Youth's Companion* in 1827, and *Parley's Magazine* was begun by Samuel Goodrich in 1833. Goodrich wrote under the name of Peter Parley and delighted children for many years. *Youth's Companion* continued publication until the stock market crash in 1929.

Other special-interest magazines were targeted to appeal to groups of readers of the day. For example, *The National Police Gazette,* which you can still find on your newsstand, offered its readers a storehouse of violence-filled criminal acts. And *Turf Register,* begun in Baltimore in 1829, foreshadowed the sports magazines of today.

Legitimate and pseudoscience had followings as well. Phrenology, for instance, was a popular pseudoscience of the period; it was based upon the belief that certain intellectual and personality characteristics could be determined by examining the shape of a person's skull. In 1838, Nathan Allen, a medical student, began the *Phrenology Review.* Finding that he had many adherents, Allen also began a phrenology institute. Although Edgar Allan Poe was among the famous of this movement, the field certainly had its detractors as well:

> Thou has a noble cranium; what remains
> To make thee a great genius? Only brains.

The *Phrenology Review* survived until 1911, when the so-called science was finally rejected by both the scientific community and the general public.

The Professional Magazinist Emerges
Nathaniel Willis, a prolific writer of the day, is recognized as America's first professional magazine writer, or magazinist. Willis wrote for many publications, including his own children's magazine, *Graham's Magazine,* and *Godey's Lady's Book.* Willis, a writer of both fiction and nonfiction, began one of his humorous stories as follows:

> I have a passion for fat women. If there is anything I hate in life, it is what dainty people call a *spirituelle.* Motion—rapid motion in a smart, quick squirrel-like step, a pert, voluble tone—in short, a lively girl—is my exquisite horror! I would as lief have a *dioble petit* dancing his infernal hornpipe on my cerebellum as to be in the room with one.[7]

He went on to describe his heroine—a rotund girl whose name was Albina McLush.

Another name of the period, Edgar Allan Poe, was a prolific if poorly paid magazine writer and editor. During his troubled life, Poe served in an editorial capacity with five different magazines and contributed to more than thirty. He was paid $780 per year as editor of the *Southern Literary Messenger* (approximately what a male schoolteacher was paid at that time). Poe's work sold for $4 a page and his famous poem "The Raven" was purchased for but $10.

Another writer, Lydia Sigourney, wrote over 2000 magazine articles during a span of fifty years. Other women writers were hard at work as well. Top among them were two sisters, Alice and Phoebe Cary, who claimed, "We write with great facility." Reportedly, the Cary sisters produced two or three poems a day and wrote every day. Of course, much of what was written by them has long since been forgotten. However, other writings of the period, including the stories of James Fenimore Cooper have become an integral part of American culture.

Though the Civil War precipitated a break in magazine development, the antislavery issue was aided in part by abolitionist writings of the period, as well as by the serialization of Harriet Beecher Stowe's *Uncle Tom's Cabin*. Following the end of the war, the industry began to grow again.

MAGAZINES TARGET THE GENERAL AUDIENCE

Once the Civil War was over, general-interest magazines were on the rise, increasing their numbers from 260 in the year 1860 to 1800 in the year 1900. A number of events contributed to the dramatic growth of these large-circulation magazines. First, improvements in printing technology and production techniques made it possible to reduce the cost of magazines, thereby placing them well within the buying range of most people. Second, the *Postal Act of 1879* gave special mailing rates to magazines and enabled editors and publishers to aim for national rather than regional markets. With the founding of the *Ladies' Home Journal* in 1881, Cyrus Curtis became the first publisher to succeed in attracting a national audience. Curtis demonstrated that magazines could be sold below cost and thus attract large audiences for advertisers. By 1893, the *Ladies' Home Journal* had amassed a circulation of 700,000. In 1897, Curtis also purchased *The Saturday Evening Post* for a mere $1000. Then, in 1899, George Horace Lorimer became the magazine's editor, and an effort was begun to fine-tune the magazine to popular tastes. Lorimer focused on the considerable and growing middle class, providing them with entertainment, advice, and political sentiment. Convinced that "the business of America was business," Lorimer also made sure that the *Post* dealt with business concerns in both fiction and nonfiction articles. He had a keen ability to sense the national mood and reflect it in his publication. *McClure's, Munsey's,* and *Cosmopolitan* were three more inexpensive general-interest magazines of the period which, like the *Ladies' Home Journal,* were able to attract large audiences and many advertisers.

Muckrakers

The reform movement that characterized the press of the period was also reflected in the policies of the magazine industry. Reacting to those who used their writing to expose the corrupt practices of businesses of the day, President Theodore Roosevelt dubbed Lincoln Steffens, Ida Tarbell, Upton Sinclair, and others like them *muckrakers*. It was muckraking that enabled a number of magazines to attract the attention of the public, build strong reputations, and sell copies. Among the magazines that took the plunge into muckraking was *McClure's Magazine*.

YOU WERE THERE

A MUCKRAKING SAMPLER

Yet considering the remarkable abilities of John D. Rockefeller, who headed the Standard, it may well be asked whether the company had needed to resort to unfair methods of competition in order to gain preeminence in the field. Rockefeller was a man who gave himself entirely to his business, saw it as a whole, its tiniest detail as well as its largest possible ramification. He knew how to select and handle his associates, knew what to tell them and what to conceal. He took deep satisfaction in economies, hated waste whether in small or great things. Combined with these qualities was a genius for organization which it would be difficult to parallel in the history of American industry. With such an equipment nothing could have prevented him from becoming one of the leaders, probably the greatest, in the oil business.

But Rockefeller detested and feared free competition and the disorder and uncertainties which attended it. It interfered with stable prices and profits; it glutted the crude and refined markets; it was wasteful. He had seen no way to bring order and stability into the industry but for him and those with him to take over the entire oil-refining and marketing business of the country. By this means it could be run economically, efficiently and profitably for those in the combination. This could be done most expeditiously by getting special rates from the railroads. It was fair to ask them, he held, because the Standard would be the biggest and the most regular shipper. Aided by these special advantages over competitors, the Rockefeller group had acquired, through stock purchase or through direct or indirect property purchase, some seventy-four refining concerns, including many of the most successful in their districts. Contracts limiting the quantity of oil to be refined had also been made with certain firms strong enough to refuse to sell. In 1878 the Standard Oil Company was manufacturing over ninety per cent of the output of the country.

In securing mastery of the refining industry the Standard had been aided by its success in carrying out one of the most farsighted policies in its history, that of controlling the pipe lines which carried oil from the wells to the railway shipping points as well as to the tanks in which surplus was stored. So great had become its power over transportation facilities that in 1879, on representation of the Petroleum Producers' Union, the state of Pennsylvania, which produced the bulk of the world's oil, brought suit in equity against the Pennsylvania Railroad and the several pipe lines which the Standard owned or controlled. The upshot was an indictment in April of John D. Rockefeller and seven of his associates. The indictment charged a conspiracy to secure a monopoly of the oil business through the control of transportation.

Ida M. Tarbell.

"TWEED DAYS IN ST. LOUIS," OCTOBER 1902

The corruption of St. Louis came from the top. The best citizens—the merchants and big financiers—used to rule the town, and they ruled it well. They set out to outstrip Chicago. The commercial and industrial war between these two cities was at one time a picturesque and dramatic spectacle such as is witnessed only in our country. Business men were not mere merchants and the politicians were not mere grafters; the two kinds of citizens got together and wielded the power of banks, railroads, factories, the prestige of the city, and the spirit of its citizens to gain business and population. And it was a close race. Chicago, having the start, always led, but St. Louis had pluck, intelligence, and tremendous energy. It pressed Chicago hard. It excelled in a sense of civic beauty and good government; and there are those who think yet it might have won. But a change occurred. Public spirit became private spirit, public enterprise became private greed.

Lincoln Steffens.

> **MEDIA PROBE**
>
> Locate examples of muckraking authored by either Sinclair, Steffens, or Tarbell. Compare the work of these writers with the work accomplished by television-oriented investigative reporters today (as seen on *60 Minutes,* for instance). In what ways have the topics and the way they are handled changed through the years? In what ways have they remained the same?

Harold Wilson sums up the attitude held by these writers: "If the muckrakers viewed themselves as prophets, they also saw themselves as young scientists accumulating data on lawlessness."[8] International Harvester, patent medicine scams, and even the United States Senate were prime muckraker topics. The movement lost steam when Teddy Roosevelt decided not to run for the presidency in 1908, lost the 1912 race, and the country began to slide slowly toward World War I. Popular for a period, by 1910 a number of the problems had been remedied, business organized counterattacks, and advertising was becoming too important for magazines to continue fighting; the muckraking movement was pretty well spent.

Post-World War I

Large general-interest magazines continued to be popular during the postwar era, but new trends were also emerging.

Reader's Digest In 1922, DeWitt and Lila Wallace began clipping and editing articles from other magazines and reprinting them in their *Reader's Digest.* Based on the theory that busy people will pay for condensed versions of articles from other sources, *Reader's Digest* has survived to this day. Currently, however, it does include some original material in addition to its staple of reprints.

Newsmagazines The year 1923 witnessed the birth of another magazine for the busy reader. By compartmentalizing information in various departments—for example, national affairs, foreign news, books—*Time* turned itself into the first successful newsmagazine. Created by Henry Luce, *Time* set out to keep people well-informed by providing them with a perspective on and understanding of the world's events. By 1930 the magazine was showing a profit, and in 1933 two competitors, *Newsweek* and *U.S. News & World Report,* were also on the newsstands. *Time* has been quite successful with the reading public. In 1982, John A. Meyers, the magazine's publisher stated:

> When *Time* . . . was invented in March of 1923 it began with a total capitalization of $86,000 and a circulation of less than 10,000 copies. Today the current U.S. circulation is 4.5 million copies. When you include the international issues of *Time* which are received by people in 190 countries around the world, *Time's* circulation reaches 5.8 million copies a week—and its weekly audience totals nearly 30 million men and women worldwide. The first issue of *Time* was printed at one plant on West 36th Street in Manhattan. Now it takes fifteen plants around the globe to print the more than 235 regional, metropolitan and demographic editions that serve *Time's* readers and advertisers.[9]

The newsmagazines provide other media with leads; stories covered in them are often picked up for coverage by radio and television news teams and other magazines.

Picture Magazines By 1936, Henry Luce had begun yet another type of magazine—the photo magazine. *Life* and its competitor, *Look* (which appeared two months later), gave Americans pictures of major events. Functioning as a window on the world for millions of Americans in the days before television, the magazines gained in popularity. This new development in photojournalism was successful in attracting millions of readers each week. In the following passage, writer Dora

Jane Hamblin describes the initial surprise experienced by readers:

> It is difficult to explain, to those too young to remember the stunning impact of its size alone. Opened out flat, the magazine measured 13½ by 21 inches, a display space larger than many of today's television screens and in pre-television 1936 a revelation. Furthermore its images held still, fixed forever for perusal and study.
>
> What ensued when *Life* hit newsstands and mailboxes that first week was near-riot. News dealers across the nation telephoned and telegraphed for more copies. Presses creaked, groaned and broke down trying to keep up with the demand. Reserve paper stocks dwindled and ran out, occasioning frantic telephone calls for "more paper, find more paper." All other activity stopped in high school study halls as kids devoured the first issue of the first big picture magazine they had ever seen.[10]

Life was on the newsstands for thirty-six years, ceasing publication in 1972; its rival, *Look,* had died the previous year. Both *Life* and *Look* found themselves replaced by pictures that moved—television. However, owing to increased interest in photography and the increased expense and competitiveness advertisers face when buying TV time, *Life* has been able to resume publication on a monthly basis.

An Exception: *The New Yorker* One magazine which was targeted to meet the tastes of a sophisticated segment of the reading public was and still is *The New Yorker*. Founded in 1925 by Harold Ross, it counted among its stable of writers such names as James Thurber, Ogden Nash, and S. J. Perelman. Historian Theodore Peterson claims, "Certainly over the years *The New Yorker* influenced American journalism all out of proportion to its relatively small circulation. . . . Perhaps no other magazine in a similar period published as many articles, cantos and verses that later appeared in any book form."[11] The magazine raised the level of American humor to new heights. Combining cartoons and fiction with insightful profiles and commentaries, the magazine is in a class by itself.

MAGAZINE PUBLISHING IN THE TELEVISION AGE

People had relied on mass-circulation magazines to provide them with information and pictures about World War II. With the end of the war came television, however; and television would soon precipitate a change in the way mass-circulation magazines operated. Television was able to provide advertisers with a much larger audience than magazines. Suddenly, 30 to 40 million people could be exposed to an advertiser's message on television when only a few million might see it in a magazine. And to complicate things further, the cost per thousand for the television advertiser was less than it had been for the magazine advertiser. So magazines had to adapt. They had no choice, and they knew it. If you were a major advertiser, would you buy one page of advertising in *Life* or *Look* for $7.75 per thousand readers, or would you prefer to spend $3.60 for a one-minute commercial that would reach those same thousand people? Advertisers left magazines in droves, opting instead for the economy, motion, and sound of the television medium. Many magazines died, among them *Collier's* in 1956, *The Saturday Evening Post* in 1969, and, as we noted previously, *Life* and *Look* in 1971 and 1972.

What has happened since 1972? How are magazines doing today? According to the Magazine Publishers Association, average circulation for the top magazines was up 1.4 percent in the first six months of 1982. In this same period the number of magazines with a 1 million plus circulation increased from 63 to 65. And the circulation for the entire top 100 magazines increased by 8.1 percent. It is also significant that magazine cir-

YOU WERE THERE

A HIGH-FLYING MAGAZINE

At 1:03 A.M., January 30, aircraft No. N 801SW revved up for take-off. The thirty-four bus passengers were the only ones aboard the yawning DC-8 except the crew, but the moment the "No Smoking" sign went off they managed to fill the entire plane. One group rushed forward to a flying darkroom just behind the command cabin and began uncrating developing tanks and chemicals. Behind them another group connected light-tables and arranged boxes of paper, layout pads, pencils, cutters, glue and type samples.

Four young women and a man slid reference books into temporary shelves installed above long work-tables: Debrett's *Peerage,* Shakespeare's *Henry V,* a concise history of World War II, the collected works of Sir Winston Churchill.

Others sat down to typewriters on stands bolted to the floor and pecked away tentatively.... No two eyes met another two on the plane without a gleam of near conspiratorial pleasure.

We were off to do a dazzler, to be the first, best, and most flamboyant magazine on earth—LIFE. This time it was a high-wire act, touch and go at 33,000 feet, a race against time and distance. Our mission was to get to London just after the funeral of Sir Winston Churchill, pick up the film our photographers had shot that day, then turn tail and chase the setting sun across the Atlantic to the printing plant in Chicago. En route we would develop the color film, make the layouts, write the captions and text, submit to checking pages, make the pesky headlines fit. We would, in brief, "put the magazine to bed" as we raced through the sky at 600 miles per hour.

There was never a doubt in our minds that we could do it. It was in the proud tradition of the magazine, and it was our kind of story: from its very first issue, November 23, 1936, LIFE had been fascinated by spectacle. State funerals like John F. Kennedy's or Sir Winston's, Rose Bowl parades, debutante balls, floods, Hollywood extravaganzas, all were the stuff of great visual impact.

On the cover of the first issue was the massive Fort Rick Dam being built in Montana by the WPA. Inside was an aerial view of Fort Knox, the first aerial ever published of that repository of the nation's gold, and another spectacular on the brand-new Bay Bridge in San Francisco. But there also were some intimate scenes of Fort Rick Dam builders whooping it up on a Saturday night in the sleazy beer joints and shanty towns where they lived. And there was a startling full-page picture of an obstetrician holding up a newborn baby by its heels, with a coy headline "LIFE BEGINS."

Dora Jane Hamblin, *That Was the Life,* Norton, New York, 1977.

---

culation today is divided among many more titles than it was in the past. This specialization permits editors to target readers more effectively. Diversity characterizes today's magazine industry. And it is because of its diversity that the industry has been able to survive television.

What is somewhat ironic is that the magazine with one of the largest circulations today is built around television—*TV Guide.* This pocket-sized listing of schedules has become such a part of our media world that even the Time-Life empire could not compete with it when they tried to market a similar but larger offering. In many ways, *TV Guide* represents the contemporary magazine industry: it fills the specific needs of a specific audience. People turn to it as a ready reference that they need to consult when watching television. In like fashion, some of the other needs and wants in our lives have been filled by other magazines. Thus, the current magazine audience is divided into many different groups.

The Audience Fragments

Although many modern general-circulation magazines were forced to cease publication, hundreds of other magazines filled the void left by their demise. Why is this? Why are magazines with small audiences able to survive when those with large general audiences were not? Let's attempt to answer this question.

In what William Dunn, publisher of *U.S. News & World Report,* has characterized as a "kneejerk reaction," the large-circulation magazines increased their circulation in an attempt to "fight back" against television. But since each magazine had to be manufactured, this battle tactic increased costs. Television, on the other hand, was able to increase its audience without significantly adding to its production costs. Magazines next attempted to cut circulation by eliminating subscribers who lived in economically deprived areas. For example, when Martin Ackerman became president of the Curtis Publishing Company in 1968, *The Saturday Evening Post* was deeply in debt. Ackerman attempted to save the magazine by cutting circulation from 6.8 million readers to 3 million readers; his objective was to transform the periodical into a "high class magazine for a class audience." For this reason he ordered that all readers living in Nielsen A counties and some readers living in Nielsen B counties (the most affluent counties in America) be maintained, while all readers living in the Nielsen C and D areas and some living in the Nielsen B areas be dropped. Form letters were sent to dropped subscribers telling them the *Post* would no longer be serving them. Among those receiving such a form letter was Arkansas governor Winthrop Rockefeller. Now put yourself in the place of a dropped reader. Would you have been angered if your magazine subscription was canceled because you happened not to live in an affluent neighborhood? Many people were, and, as we noted, the *Post* died.

It became evident that advertisers liked television because of its ability to reach a mass audience. However, the magazine industry did offer something that television could not; magazines could specialize and bring a specific readership to the seller. For example, a television advertisement brings a commercial for a high-priced automobile to many people who are simply not in the market for such a product. Consequently, advertisers pay for viewers who are of no use to them. On the other hand, advertisers might well find a prime upper-income audience among the readers of a magazine targeted to meet the needs of physicians or lawyers. In similar fashion, an in-flight magazine provides a generally affluent audience of people who have little to do except read the magazine provided in the pouch of the seat in front of them; for this reason, advertisers are willing to pay handsomely to appear in such volumes. Thus, the magazine industry has become successful once again by reaching out—this time to smaller, more specialized audiences.

Magazines Specialize

What is the ultimate in specialized magazines? One that is written just for you and is a perfect match for your needs and interests. To date, while no one has marketed such an individualized magazine, *Farm Journal* has come pretty close to providing readers with a custom-made one. How is this accomplished? *The Wall Street Journal* reports: "Hog farmers don't want to hear about calves growing fat on souped-up alfalfa. And cattlemen don't care that sows farrow sooner when the lights are on."[12] To help solve this problem *Farm Journal* publishes supplements targeted to meet the needs of five different kinds of farmers in twenty-six different regions of the

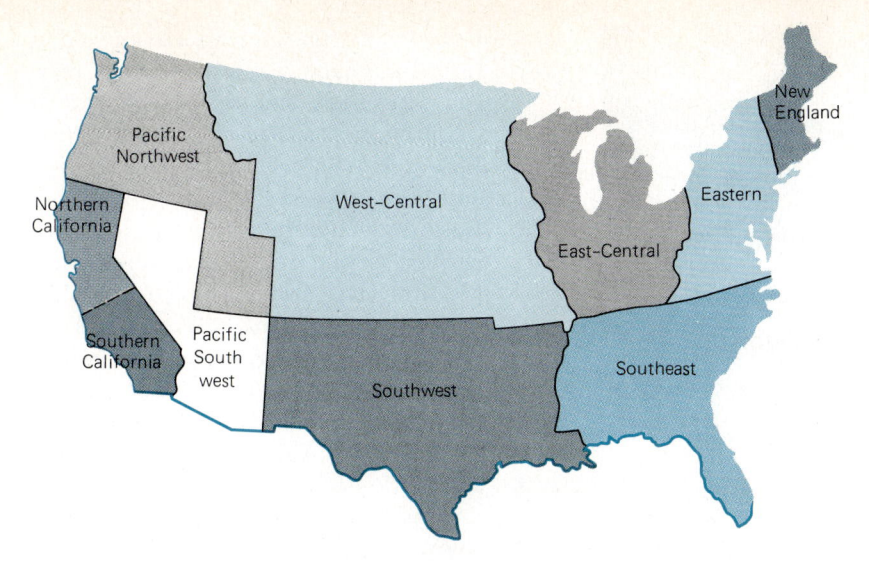

FIGURE 5-1 *Time* magazine has eleven regional editions in the United States alone. (*The World of Time,* Time-Life Publications.)

country. A "Top Producer" supplement is used for all large farms. The printing system works with a computer that reads each subscriber's interests and orders the bindery to include just those pages that are relevant to his or her needs. As a double check, the machinery measures the thickness of each magazine in an effort to ensure that the correct issue has been produced. The subscriber's name and address are placed on a card and inserted inside the magazine in addition to being printed directly on the front cover for mailing. All of this for a subscription price of $8 per year. Although some of the more than 1 million subscribers who fill out subscription questionnaires may check many more items than they are really interested in, Dale Smith, president of *Farm Journal* notes: "A farmer doesn't pick up a farm magazine to be entertained."

Although not as specialized as *Farm Journal,* other large-circulation magazines, especially newsmagazines like *Time* and *Newsweek,* also publish *regional and demographic editions* in an effort to speak to the interests of particular readers and attract advertisers. (See Figure 5-1 and Table 5-1).

Types of Magazines Today The modern magazine industry is so diverse that it is difficult to categorize it. *The Writer's Market,* for example, lists over 100 categories, including women's poetry, sports, and outdoors, just to name a few. Benjamin Compaine in *The Business of Consumer Magazines* groups magazines according to sex, locality, profession, hobbies, age, and ethnic background. J. W. Click and Russel Baird provide a somewhat more useful classification consisting of six categories.

TABLE 5-1 **Demographic Issues of *Time* Magazine**

Time A+	Ultra high income professional and managerial households
Time B	Business edition
Time S/E	Student and educator edition
Time T	Top management
Time Z	High-income zip-code areas

MAGAZINES: FORMS, FUNCTIONS, AUDIENCES 129

There is a vast market for highly specialized journals. *Byte* is a computer magazine. (Randy Matusow)

1. Consumer magazines, which are sold at newsstands and are available to everyone. Included among these are such publications as *Reader's Digest, Time, Newsweek, MS Magazine, Working Woman,* and *Science Digest.*
2. Business magazines or trade journals, which service particular industries. McGraw-Hill, for example, publishes *Architectural Record, Aviation Week, Graduating Engineer, Chemical Engineering, Electrical Construction and Maintenance, Power, Coal Age, Modern Plastics, Fleet Owner,* to name a few.
3. Association-related offerings. Among the more than 600 association magazines published are *The American Legion, The Rotarian, National Geographic,*

TABLE 5-2 Top Fifty Magazines in Circulation

Reader's Digest	18,171,628	Globe	2,044,193
TV Guide	17,516,896	Field & Stream	2,016,637
National Geographic	10,474,030	Glamour	2,011,207
Better Homes & Gardens	8,053,460	Smithsonian	1,987,062
Modern Maturity	8,037,000	Popular Science	1,812,654
AARP News Bulletin	7,410,273	V.F.W. Magazine	1,710,892
Family Circle	7,010,192	Workbasket	1,700,473
Woman's Day	7,007,909	Elks Magazine	1,636,426
McCall's	6,201,777	Popular Mechanics	1,635,126
Good Housekeeping	5,352,428	Parents	1,634,307
Ladies' Home Journal	5,205,413	Mechanix Illustrated	1,619,242
National Enquirer	5,069,224	Today's Education	1,557,831
Playboy	4,851,363	Changing Times	1,530,928
Time	4,555,610	True Story	1,530,730
Redbook	4,292,627	Boy's Life	1,529,131
Penthouse	4,022,034	Outdoor Life	1,528,729
The Star	3,802,516	Life	1,479,360
Newsweek	3,000,596	Seventeen	1,471,579
Cosmopolitan	2,802,494	Sunset	1,419,598
American Legion	2,578,901	Motorland	1,324,424
Prevention	2,485,156	Organic Gardening	1,310,948
People Weekly	2,471,122	Ebony	1,290,621
Sports Illustrated	2,452,049	American Rifleman	1,260,798
Southern Living	2,106,641	Bon Appetit	1,255,145
U.S. News & World Report	2,089,706	Vogue	1,223,800

Source: Audit Bureau of Circulation, p. 4. Based on average circulation per issue, 1st six months of 1982; includes general and farm magazines.

THE PRINT MEDIA: THE WINDOW OPENS

Journalism Quarterly, and the *Journal of the American Medical Association.*

4. Farm publications. In addition to *Farm Journal* (mentioned earlier), other farm-oriented publications are *California Farmer, Rice Farming,* and *American Fruit Grower.*
5. Public relations magazines, which provide a means for business and not-for-profit organizations to relate to one or more of their publics—for example their employees, customers, stockholders, or dealers. Among the more than 10,000 such magazines are Exxon's *The Lamp* and *Friends* published by General Motors.
6. One-shot magazines, which capitalize on a hot topic or idea. Rock-group magazines, *Star Trek,* and volumes on Elvis Presley fit into this category.

Magazine Ownership

The magazine industry today is dominated by giants like *Reader's Digest* and *TV Guide.* The top fifty magazines in circulation are identified in Table 5-2.

Who actually owns the magazines you read? To what extent are you surprised by the fact that *United, Pan Am Clipper, Continental, Eastern Review, Western's World,* as well as other in-flight magazines are all published by the East/West Network? According to East/West Network they are "publishers of magazines that dominate the sky." Over 1,700,000 copies are run each month for American air carriers, with an additional 1,486,000 copies run for eleven major international carriers. East/West prides itself on being able to tell advertisers that "each East/West magazine has its own editorial format directed to a specific audience. Each focuses on a basic theme of executive service and is edited to provide features that our readers can use and take action upon in their business and personal lives. Our editors in New York and Los Angeles create over 500 unduplicated pages each month. The easy chair environment of a jetliner is naturally most conducive to reading." This network of give-away magazines is marketed to advertisers as a means of reaching top-level decision makers—well-paid corporate executives. Advertisers are free to sell their products or services in one or all in-flight magazines; either way East/West wins, since it owns them all.

As Table 5-3 shows, most of our consumer magazines are owned by eleven leading pub-

TABLE 5-3 Largest Consumer Magazine Publishers in the United States, by Revenue, 1980

	REVENUE FROM MAGAZINE PUBLISHING (MILLIONS)	NUMBER OF DOMESTIC CONSUMER MAGAZINES
1. Time Inc.	$747	7
2. Triangle Publications	494	2
3. Hearst Corporation	324	14
4. CBS Inc.	298	10
5. Washington Post Company	262	2
6. Reader's Digest Association, Inc.	214	2
7. Newhouse (Condé Nast)	195	7
8. New York Times Company	192	3
9. Meredith Corporation	167	8
10. Ziff-Davis Publishing Company	165	17
11. Playboy Enterprises Inc.	162	2

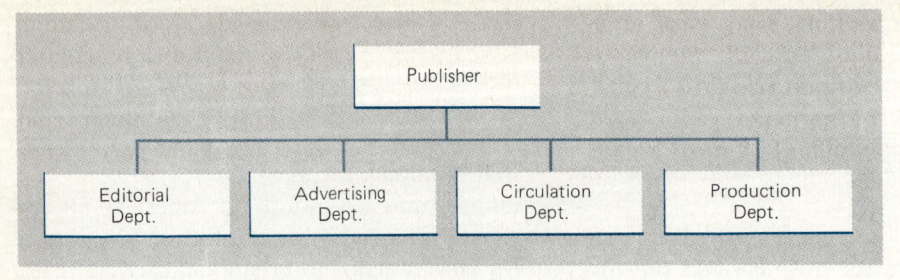

FIGURE 5-2 Organization chart of a typical magazine.

lishers. For example, Time Inc. owns seven magazines, including *Time, Life, Sports Illustrated, Money, People,* and *Discover.* CBS owns *Field & Stream, Woman's Day, Cycle World,* and *Road & Track,* among others. Ziff-Davis owns *Backpacker, Yachting* and *Stereo Review,* and Conde Nash publishes *Vogue, House & Garden, Glamour,* and *Mademoiselle.* While Triangle Publications, publisher of *TV Guide,* is not identified as a group owner because *Seventeen* magazine technically has a separate corporate publisher, for all practical purposes these two magazines are of the same ownership.

Even with these multiple listings, the magazine industry as a whole is characterized by a less concentrated ownership pattern than the broadcasting, newspaper, and film industries. In part, this may be due to the fact that the magazine industry is considered to be an easy-access industry. Because a small-circulation magazine can be operated out of a home by a very small staff, a wide variety of people are encouraged to publish magazines; unfortunately, however, hundreds fail every year.

MAGAZINE ORGANIZATION: WHO DOES WHAT?

Magazines, like other industries, have developed corporate structures to facilitate their operation. A typical organizational chart for a medium-sized magazine is shown in Figure 5-2.

Though magazine publishers have formal responsibility for the editorial aspects of the magazine, most publishers are business people and tend to leave editorial decisions to the editor-in-chief. They do, however, oversee the budgeting and advertising functions of the magazine.

The editor-in-chief is the individual responsible for the nonadvertising content of the magazine. The managing editor is usually in charge of the day-to-day business of getting a magazine completed and to the printer. Assisting the managing editor are other editors whose task it is to oversee particular departments within the magazine. All editors work jointly with art directors to design not only the articles appearing in the magazine but the magazine's cover and logo as well. Later in this chapter, we will explore the editorial process in more detail.

The advertising department is responsible for selling space in the magazine. Research staffs facilitate this effort by compiling information about the magazine's audience, which is then shared with advertisers and editors alike. In 1980, *Folio* magazine reported that approximately 54 percent of the average consumer magazine's revenues are derived from advertising. Today magazines are less advertisement-dependent than they were in earlier days when the reader who purchased a copy paid for but a small fraction of the magazine's production costs.

Subscriber and newsstand sales are the responsibilities of the circulation director. If

With postage increases cutting into subscription circulation, supermarket check-out counters have become lucrative magazine outlets. (Randy Matusow)

readership is down, the circulation director is the person who must take steps to discover why. The circulation department is divided into three sections: (1) subscription sales, containing the people charged with the job of obtaining and renewing subscribers; (2) single-copy sales, containing the people whose task it is to deal with retailers; and (3) fullfillment, containing the people who are responsible for ensuring that subscribers do indeed receive their copies. Fulfillment personnel update subscriber change of addresses, renewals, etc. Owing to the complexity of the task, the fulfillment function is sometimes handled by an external service agency.

Since seeking new subscribers is a prime function of the circulation department, let us briefly explore a number of the techniques circulation people use to encourage people to subscribe to a magazine. One common technique is to employ 3 x 5 blow-in cards, which are traditionally found in all magazines. A second strategy is to use sweepstakes sponsored by such organizations as Publisher's Clearing House and *Reader's Digest.* Heavy television promotion and recognized stars like Ed McMahon help promote the success of these endeavors. Jim Phelps, circulation director of *Reader's Digest,* when discussing his responsibility to "get the subs," noted that the Reader's Digest Sweepstakes gives readers a reduced rate on subscriptions, and then four to six months before the expiration of that subscription the magazine sends out renewal cards. It is interesting to note that it usually takes four to five years of renewals until the sweepstakes-solicited customers are paying full subscription price for the magazine. Phelps employs a third technique, the newsstand, as a means of attracting subscribers to *Reader's Digest.* One lucrative location for newsstands is the checkout

MAGAZINES: FORMS, FUNCTIONS, AUDIENCES   133

counter. In fact, Phelps reports that in 1983, 85 percent of *Reader's Digest* newsstand sales were made at checkout counters. Examine the checkout counter display in a store that you frequent. How many different publications are available there?

Circulation is also solicited through direct-mail lists, franchising programs of nonprofit organizations, and catalog agents. Magazines also attempt to market themselves as Christmas gifts.

It should be noted that prevailing postal rates do affect magazine circulation. In 1974 postal rates were amended in order to make them more favorable to magazines. Of late, however, magazine postal rates have skyrocketed. Because of this, many magazines unable to handle the increasing mail costs have had to shut down. *Reader's Digest* now advertises a basic subscription price noting that postage is additional. To be sure, postage increases will continue to pose problems for the industry in the years to come.

Finally, the production department is responsible for facilitating the printing and binding of the magazine. Since the quality of the printing, paper, and binding can influence a magazine's success in the market place, the decisions made by the production staff are critical.

CONTEMPORARY MAGAZINE EDITING

In his book *Magazine Editing in the '80s*, William Rivers tells the following story. "Pasted on the wall at eye level above a typewriter in the office of a movie-fan magazine editor is a picture of a young girl, a salesclerk in a Woolworth's store. The editor has never met her; he keeps the picture in view to remind him of his primary readership. When he is choosing and editing articles and photographs, he thinks of this young girl's tastes."[13]

The editor described in the preceding passage, like most editors today, is responsible

MEDIA PROBE

In your opinion, should the federal government subsidize magazines to a greater extent than they are by providing significantly reduced postage rates for them? What alternative delivery systems would you consider using if you were a magazine circulation director?

---

for ensuring that his or her magazine is addressed to a particular audience. Tom Lashnits, associate editor for *Reader's Digest,* speaking before a Center for Communication Seminar held in New York City, reflected this practice when he noted, "The key is to keep people buying the magazine." Lashnits went on to explain that magazines that fail—like the ill-fated *Families* magazine published by Reader's Digest—do so because they "often miss their niche in the marketplace." What steps do editors take to create magazines that sell? In order to answer this question, let's explore the editorial process in some detail.

The Editorial Concept: Creating the Formula

A magazine must have a concept or *formula* that guides it through the editorial process. In effect, the guiding concept or formula represents the magazine's personality, its unique mixture of editorial material and content. Do you think *Time* has such a personality? Can you compare *Time*'s personality with that of *Newsweek? U.S. News & World Report? MS Magazine? Working Woman? Gentleman's Quarterly?* To be sure, each of these magazines has a distinct editorial focus, one that differentiates it from other magazines on the market. Some editors, such as Norman Cousins, claim to edit to their own interests: "edit to please yourself, as I do, and hope that enough people share your enthusiasm and concerns to make the magazine a success."[14] Others note that this practice is neither the rule nor possible on a regular basis.

MEDIA VIEW

THE ART OF EDITING

The editor's job has sometimes been likened to that of an orchestra conductor. There he stands at the podium, or sits behind his desk, waving his arms in all directions. At his downbeat, reporters report and writers write and words pour in from near and far and pictures are assembled and headlines are written. And all these disparate elements come together harmoniously—we all hope—until they are finally formed into one symphonic whole. My predecessor as editor-in-chief of Time Inc., Hedley Donovan, once put it this way: "The editor doesn't make the news, except occasionally, but he does interpret it and shape it, as the conductor does. Above all," Donovan concluded, "he selects what's going to be on the program, which is one hell of a power."

Being an inveterate armchair conductor, I naturally like this comparison very much and enjoy seeing myself as a sort of Toscanini or at least a Solti of the press. But I was deeply shaken one day when I talked to a violinist and found that the fellow didn't think a conductor necessary at all. He thought most of the gyrations on the podium were done for show, and that most orchestras could play the score perfectly well on their own. And quite a few people feel the same way about editors. They suspect that most writers and reporters could do very nicely without all the arm waving by some maestro. In fact, some even feel, and I am horrified to report this, that editors just louse up good ideas, mess up stories and repress individuality. So in the dark night of the soul we sometimes face the question: Are editors necessary?

I know that you can hardly bear the suspense of trying to figure out what my answer to that question is. Well, it is, yes, editors are necessary. . . .

Of course there are different kinds of editing. To borrow a phrase from economics, there is micro-editing and macro-editing. The first has to do with words and meanings, style and structure. It involves the age-old battle to get meanings clear and structure as logical as possible, and to encourage a style that is attractive without being ornamental for its own sake. The purpose of journalism with very few exceptions is not self expression. If you want self expression, become poets. It's all right to show off in your journalistic writing and to be a little dazzling, if you can be, but never at the expense of clarity and communication. An editor can truly help a writer to say what he means. Something that may be perfectly clear and understandable in the writer's mind is not necessarily so when it reaches paper.

An editor serves his writer when he, in fact, represents the reader. The editor must ask all the questions that the reader is likely to have and he must ask them with the relentless insistence and single-mindedness of a five-year-old. . . .

An editor also must know his audience. In that respect I always admired General Charles Taylor, an early editor of the Boston *Globe*, who was an unabashed provincialist and wanted each citizen to see his name in the paper at least once a year. When he was informed that the rival Boston *Herald* had signed up another London correspondent, General Taylor cried: "Then, by God, we'll have to get another reporter in South Boston."

An editor should be a guardian of the language, uncompromising enemy of cliche and jargon and faulty grammar and bad syntax—all sins which are widely committed these days even by college graduates and even, I dare say, by editors. . . .

Anyway, language aside, an editor should have an engineer's eye for the structure of a story. I find that I sometimes have to read a story many times and, as it were, live with it for a while before the true or the most effective structure becomes clear to me. Often in such a case a story has to be taken apart and reassembled. But an editor fails completely if he merely rewrites a story himself.

This practice of rewriting has not been unknown at *Time* magazine, though it is much less frequent than is usually assumed. A good deal of writing, however, goes on in the margins of *Time* copy where criticisms, comments and suggestions for revisions appear in great profusion. Composing marginal notes is itself an art form. Eric Hodgins, an editor of *Fortune*, could be devastating with the observation: "This story *subtracts* from the sum of human knowledge." A former managing editor of *Time*, T. S. Matthews, would write: "This is Choctaw. Now try it in English."...

Let us move on to macro-editing—the matter of setting an agenda and a tone, or, to revert to my opening image, deciding what the orchestra should play and how. An editor must assume an often contradictory role either by restraining emotions or stirring them up. Sometimes he must calm things down and keep his staff from chewing up the score. More often he must allow himself to get excited and in turn excite those around him. He must be something of a showman and react viscerally to the drama of events. "Stop the presses—tear up the front page" is the oldest cliche of all newspaper melodrama. I have stopped the presses and torn up a cover many, many times; I have torn up entire issues and started over from scratch—and I've almost never been sorry afterwards.

Henry Anatole Grunwald, speech presented at the meeting of the American Society of Magazine Editors, New York, December 9, 1983.

J. W. Click and Russel N. Baird in *Magazine Editing and Production* note that magazine formulas can be divided into three key categories: (1) departments (containing sections like "Food," "Traveling," "Managing Your Money"); (2) articles within departments (containing articles like "Home Decorating," "This Month," "Win Money for your Recipes"); and (3) general types of contents (for example, Fiction, Editorials, Cartoons).[15]

Magazine formulas or publication policies are summarized in the *Consumer Magazine & Farm Publication Rates & Data*. A magazine may be described in the following manner:

> *Psychology Today* is edited to present scientifically accurate psychological information meaningful to the educated layman.
>
> *Redbook* is edited for young women 18–34 with special emphasis on the problem and challenges they face in forming their lives, careers and marriages.[16]

The *Redbook* entry goes on to discuss topics such as politics, medicine, and education, as well as the fact that one-third of the magazine's space is devoted to services like food, nutrition, fashion, needlecrafts, and the like. In addition, it is noted that a complete novel and short stories are projected for each issue. A magazine formula statement should iden-

MEDIA PROBE

In July 1984, Geraldine Ferraro became the first woman to run as a major party candidate for vice president. Do some library research to determine how this event was treated in each of the following magazines:

Time
Newsweek
U.S. News & World Report
MS Magazine
Gentleman's Quarterly
Glamour
Working Woman
Good Housekeeping
Cosmopolitan

Next, conduct a similar study on a subject of your choice.

tify the purpose of the magazine, its market, the standard of living and education of its readership, and the publication's competition.

Planning through Research

In order to produce a weekly or monthly product which interests readers, editors need to plan effectively. They may solicit ideas during formal editorial meetings and informal meetings with staff and free-lance writers. But when they need help in answering the question, How am I doing? they turn to research. Ruth Whitney, editor-in-chief of *Glamour* emphasizes that although magazines are a mass medium, the editor's job is to establish a one-to-one relationship with the reader: "Knowing your reader and his/her needs as well as you know your best friend is where good editing begins."[17] *Glamour,* for example, asks 400 readers to evaluate the content of the magazine each month. More specifically, readers are queried regarding what they found useful and interesting in an issue. In fact, each of the 400 "critics" is asked to rate every article in the magazine on a 10-point effectiveness scale. Editors use the resulting information to look for surprises and help them spot taste trends; in this way they are able to stay one step ahead of their general readership with respect to likes and dislikes on such matters as hairstyles, computers, or new sports fads. In like fashion, Dunn & Bradstreet uses the audit rating form to provide them with reader feedback on one of their technical publications.

Editors and Writers

Frequently, writers will themselves supply magazines with ideas for articles. In fact, many magazine editors find themselves flooded with hundreds, if not thousands, of unsolicited manuscripts each month. Most professional writers, however, save themselves and the editors a great deal of time and trouble by sending queries rather than completed articles to editors. In other words, the writer develops a brief but intriguing portion of his or her article and follows it with a succinct description of the remaining material the article will cover. It has even become a popular practice for writers to develop lists of ideas and take what is called "apple-peddling expeditions" to New York in order to call on a series of magazine editors. Then at meetings or over lunch, writer and editor are able to sift through the ideas in order to identify those meriting a *query letter* or further consideration. Thus, for all practical purposes, writers are really in the idea-selling business and editors are really in the idea-buying business. And they both have a mutual interest in searching for stories that provide readers with information, advice, and entertainment. Whether developed by the editor and given to a writer or brought in by the writer, in order to be selected for inclusion in a magazine the story idea must be judged potentially exciting and interesting to the readership of the magazine. Just as editors must be familiar with their magazine, so writers must immerse themselves in a magazine's back issues, reading them from cover to cover, looking for

---

MEDIA PROBE

Working individually or in groups, select a magazine, examine a few issues, and write a statement that succinctly describes the magazine's concept, audience, and competition. Compare your efforts with the one contained in *Consumer Magazine & Farm Publication Rates & Data.*

Select two or three competing magazines. Write a statement that represents each magazine's formula. Again compare your perception of each magazine with the one contained in *Consumer Magazine & Farm Publication Rates & Data.*

MEDIA PROBE

1. The following is a sample query letter that resulted in a publication for former *Time-Life* editor, and now free-lance writer, A.B.C. Whipple. Why do you think it was successful?

December 23, 1981.

Mr. Joseph Gribbons
Nautical Quarterly 373 Park Ave. South
New York, NY 10016

Dear Mr. Gribbons,

As an admirer of your handsome magazine, I'd like to suggest an article, partly because the subject would provide an excuse for the sort of illustrations you do so well.

The Odyssey. Yes, *The Odyssey*—as the first and foremost sailor's yarn. Besides its acknowledged merits as a work of literature, Homer's classic is also an eminently practical account of ancient seafaring. But it is more than that; anyone who has spent any time aboard a ship readily recognizes that, through Odysseus (or Ulysses, as the Romans later called him), Homer is spinning just the sort of tall tale for which mariners have been famous down all the centuries since. Odysseus is not just the literary progenitor of Vergil's Aeneas, Coleridge's Ancient Mariner and Melville's Ishmael; he is the legendary yarn-spinner, fixing his listeners and readers with a beady eye and transfixing them with his preposterous yet eerily believable narrative.

The text, then, would be a sailor's view of *The Odyssey*. How Homer vividly evokes the mariner's most dreaded danger, storm at sea. His precise descriptions of adverse currents heading Odysseus off course. His striking protrait of the treacherous riptide between the surf-beaten rocks of Scylla (Sicily) and the whirlpool of Charybdis (Scylla and Charybdis are still on charts of the Mediterranean); the sailor's romantic, wishful fables: sirens beckoning him ashore, an island seductress casting her spell, lotos (hashish); and even some pragmatic advice: Odysseus belatedly realized, when his sailors opened Aeolus' bag of winds, that the skipper can never sleep for long.

And so on. As you probably know, maritime experts have tracked Odysseus' course and pin-pointed many of his landfalls—the volcanic mountains of "one-eyed" Polyphemus, for example. One or two photographers have followed this course and taken spectacular pictures of the islands and the waters through which Odysseus must have sailed. The best collection I have seen is that of Erich Lessing. I have a copy of his massive and beautiful *The Voyages of Ulysses*, if you cannot readily locate one.

The combination of Lessing's photographs and an article (partly tongue-in-cheek) on Homer the ancient mariner and yarn-spinner might make an intriguing story for *Nautical Quarterly*. As for my qualifications, I have been writing about maritime history for a good many years, and can submit a sample or two from my books if you'd like to see them. Bud Lovelace knows of my work.

If all this sounds interesting to you, I can be reached by phone, and can come into New York any time during January. (I'll be away during February.)

Sincerely,

2. Next, for practice, create a list of six stories that you think might interest a particular audience. Then, targeting a magazine for each idea, write a query letter in which you aim to capture the attention of the magazine's editor.
3. Acting as an editorial review board, determine which student queries are the most promising and why.

ways to make ideas more appealing to the magazine's readers.

Selling through Titles and Covers

Click and Baird emphasize: "Pound for pound, line for line, and word for word, titles which are both eye catching and informative are the most effective sales tool an editor has for selling the content of a magazine." The newsstand and supermarket checkout counter feature so many competing magazines that to help sell a magazine its article titles must excite and interest the casual reader enough for him or her to be motivated to purchase the magazine then and there. Of course, titles come in all shapes and sizes. They can be descriptive: "Learning to Like New Zealand," or "A Dry Basement." They can involve the reader through the use of the word "you": "Help on Your Tax Return" or "How to Drive Your Children Sane." They can create suspense by posing questions: "Does More Class Time Help?" or "Is Our State Going Broke?" Or they can incorporate figures of speech, puns, and coined words: "The Pill in Perspective," or "The Age of Shovelry." Titles that sell magazines are said to have marquee value, that is, they attract attention just like the marquee of a movie theater does. Ruth Whitney reports that editors at *Glamour*, just like their counterparts at many other magazines, make an effort to develop sharp and clearly focused working titles for articles. For example, rather than titling an article "When the Love Affair Is Over" they might choose to call it "It's Over. How to Heal Your Emotions and Your Sex Life," or "What to Do When You Want Him Back." Rather than selecting a vague working title like "Abortion," they might instead begin with one like "Why I Ended My Baby's Life" or "The Man's View of Abortion." Thus, we see that the working title's purpose is to define as clearly as possible the specific subject of the story.

MEDIA PROBE

It is time for you to try your hand at creating working titles. Select a general topic such as money or prostitution or public speaking, and brainstorm possible working titles appropriate to your subject. What magazines do you imagine would be interested in receiving articles with your titles?

Covers also sell. According to Fred Bernstein, a free-lance writer for *People* magazine, a picture of a movie star on the cover sells the most magazines; next in spurring sales are pictures of TV stars, followed by pictures of sports figures and politicians.

Editors Work with Design and Production

An editor's job entails much more than selecting and copyediting stories. To be sure, editors make many decision which affect the nature of the completed product. It is editors who *break the book*. That is, they decide how the space of a magazine will be used. For example, it is up to editors to determine which articles warrant several pages, which are worthy of only a single page, and what the cover story or cover article will be. In addition, editors need to work cooperatively with the magazine's art department to set the layout and design of an issue. They must also be knowledgeable about typography because it is the editor's job to provide the printer with

MEDIA PROBE

Examine recent or current issues of several magazines. Note five covers which seem particularly effective or provocative to you. Explain why you like them.

Graphic design plays a large role in creating a magazine's identity in its desired market. (Christopher Morrow/Stock, Boston)

> **MEDIA PROBE**
>
> Select two newsmagazines. Compare the layout and design of each. Where, for example, are major stories placed? How is color used? Do stories contain boxed inserts? How do their typefaces differ? In what ways, if at all, are photo captions, charts, graphs, and maps used?
>
> If you were shown pages from each magazine and didn't know the magazine's title, do you think that, based on page appearance, you would be able to identify the magazine? How?

marginal notes which describe the various size types to be used for body text, headlines, and titles.

Locating photographs, deciding how to layout each page, and getting the camera-ready copy to the printer are all part and parcel of the editorial process; these tasks may be assigned to one or two people if a publication is small or to hundreds of people if we are dealing with a major news weekly.

To be sure, magazine design is a tricky business. It can help increase sales or it can detract from sales. As a case in point, noted magazine designer Walter Bernard reports that during his tenure with *New York Magazine* he decided to use design in a novel way: he turned the logo upside down in an effort to capture reader attention. Unfortunately, however, the effort backfired; the ploy did not attract buyers. Subsequent research revealed that because of the upside-down logo people were unable to recognize the magazine and consequently did not even realize that the issue was on the newsstand!

Given all the decisions, hard work, and coordination involved, it is not surprising that it may take an editor some six months to assemble just one issue of a magazine. Many editors, however, have tighter deadlines. Whatever the time limit, all welcome the challenge.

According to Peter Diamandis, president of CBS Magazines, a good editor is like a proficient surfer. By that Diamandis means that the editor must always try to ride the crest of a wave. If he is too far ahead of the wave it will break over him; if she is too far behind the wave, she'll miss it completely. What causes a publisher to miss the wave? Peter Derow, president of the CBS Publishing Group, attributes it to the fact that most mediocre publishers are uncomfortable doing things differently. Diamandis, his associate, believes that this is unfortunate since what's being called for is "not revolution, but evolution." Noting that most good magazines evolve about 10 percent a year in format, Diamandis reports that the 1980 version of a particular magazine should be totally replaced by the 1990 version of that magazine. This gradual evolution is necessary if the magazine is to keep pace with changes in the marketplace. Given this precept, what do you imagine your favorite magazine will be like in ten years? To what extent do you think it will effectively anticipate and reflect societal pressures?

Although there is no set rule of thumb that guarantees success in the magazine business, it is fun to speculate about factors that contribute to success. The magazine business, as we have seen, is a creative business, and the creative process is the heartbeat of the product. And what kind of shape is the "heartbeat" in? John Veronis, an investment banker in communications and publishing, believes the industry is extraordinarily healthy. He states: "I believe you will find as many opportunities for magazines in the next 10 years as in the last 10." Time will tell if he is right. After all, as Peter Diamandis is fond of noting: "Magazines are people. Magazines are ideas. Magazines are goals."

SUMMARY

Although they have experienced periods of difficulty, magazines today are generally healthy and have become an integral part of our lives.

Though magazines started slowly at first, improvements in printing technology and the institution of compulsory education contributed to the growth of the magazine industry in the first half of the nineteenth century. It was this period that also witnessed the emergence of the professional magazinist and monthly general-interest magazines like *The Saturday Evening Post* and *Knickerbocker*, women's magazines like *Godey's Lady's Book*, and special-interest magazines like *Youth's Companion*. Though the Civil War interrupted the development of the magazine industry, following the war magazines were again on the rise and used as forums for numerous writers, including the muckrakers.

Following World War I general-interest magazines like *Reader's Digest* and newsmagazines continued to be popular. In 1936, they were joined by picture magazines. One particular magazine that was not a general-interest magazine but nonetheless grew in popularity and continues to be popular to this day is *The New Yorker*.

After World War II, the magazine industry found itself faced with a new form of competition—television. Seeking to adapt to this new medium, magazines tried to appeal to smaller, highly fragmented audiences rather than to large general audiences. Magazines had in fact discovered that they could do something that television could not do: they could specialize and bring a specific readership to advertisers. Our present magazine industry has become so diverse that it almost defies categorization.

Considered to be an easy-access industry, the magazine industry as a whole is characterized by a less concentrated ownership pattern than that which characterizes the broadcasting, newspaper, and film industries. Still, by 1980, Time Inc., Hearst Corporation, CBS Inc., Newhouse, Meredith Corporation, and Ziff-Davis together own sixty-three domestic consumer publications.

Whatever the nature of its content, a magazine starts with people. The following are essential positions in the operation of a magazine: the publisher, the editor-in-chief, the advertising director, the circulation director, and the director of production. It is the task of these people and their staffs to speak to the needs and interests of a specific audience so that they create a magazine that sells. Guiding them in their efforts is their magazine's formula or concept.

KEY TERMS

Postal Act of 1879
Muckrakers
Regional and demographic editions
Magazine formulas

Query letter
Break the book

NOTES

[1] William G. Dunn, "Magazines: The Advertising Side," American Society of Magazine Editors Seminar, New York City, December 9, 1983.

[2] "Taking the Measure of Magazines," *Magazine: Newsletter of Research*, August 1980, p. 1.

[3] "Magazine Almanac," *Magazine: Newsletter of Research*, July 1982, p. 1.

[4] *MPX: A Study of Magazine Page Exposure, Audits and Surveys, 1983*, Magazine Publishers Association, New York.

[5] John Tebbel, *The American Magazine: A Compact History*. Hawthorne, New York, 1969, pp. 47–56.

[6] Quoted in John Tebbel, *The Media in America*, Crowell, New York, 1974, p. 163.

[7] Quoted in John Tebbel, *The Media in America*, op. cit., p. 172.

[8] Harold Wilson, *McClure's Magazine and the Muckrakers*, Princeton University Press, Princeton, 1970, p. 210.

[9] John A. Meyers, *Time: 1923-1982*, Time, New York, p. 1.

[10] Dora Jane Hamblin, *That Was the Life*, Norton, New York, 1977, pp. 18–20.

[11] Theodore Peterson, *Magazines in the Twentieth Century*, 2d ed., University of Illinois Press, Urbana, Ill., 1964, pp. 253–254.

[12] Jeffrey H. Birnbaum, "With 1,134 Editions, *Farm Journal* Labors to Please All of Its Readers," *The Wall Street Journal*, January 21, 1983.

[13] William L. Rivers, *Magazine Editing in the '80s*, Wadsworth, Belmont, Calif., 1983, pp. 2–3.

[14] "Newspaper Enterprise Association Interview with Norman Cousins," *Columbus Citizen Journal*, April 11, 1972.

[15] J. W. Click and Russell N. Baird, *Magazine Editing and Production*, 3d ed., Brown, Dubuque, Iowa, 1983.

[16] *Consumer Magazine & Farm Publications Rates & Data*, June 27, 1981, pp. 212, 570.

[17] Ruth Whitney, "Enhancing Your Editing Skills," American Society of Magazine Editors Seminar, New York City, December 9, 1983.

SUGGESTIONS FOR FURTHER READING

Click, J. W., and Russell N. Baird: *Magazine Editing and Production*, 3d ed., Brown, Dubuque, Iowa, 1983. *An excellent text; covers the responsibilities of magazine editor from concept through to production.*

Compaine, Benjamin M.: *The Business of Consumer Magazines.* Knowledge, White Plains, N.Y., 1982. *A comprehensive look at the business of magazines, including size, circulation, advertising, research, entrepreneurship, ownership, and outlook for the industry.*

Gill, Brendan: *Here at The New Yorker,* Random House, New York, 1975. *Richly illustrated with anecdotal information derived from the author's long career at* The New Yorker.

Hamblin, Dora Jane: *That Was the Life*, Norton, New York, 1977. *A look at* Life *from the perspective of an insider.*

Mott, Frank Luther: *A History of American Magazines 1741–1850,* Appleton, New York, 1930. *The most complete source of information on our early magazines; presents detailed descriptions of the more significant publications.*

Peterson, Theodore: *Magazines in the Twentieth Century,* 2d ed., University of Illinois Press, Urbana, Ill., 1964. *Presents a history and assessment of the American magazine industry from 1900 to the early 1960s. Scholarly yet readable.*

Rivers, William L.: *Magazine Editing in the '80s,* Wadsworth, Belmont, Calif., 1983. *Full explanation of the editor's role; provides a much-needed overview of the many facets included in the editor's job. Interesting examples.*

Tebbel, John: *The American Magazine: A Compact History,* Hawthorn, New York, 1969. *A readable and entertaining summary of major events in the history of magazines.*

Wilson, Harold S.: *McClure's Magazine and the Muckrakers.* Princeton University Press, Princeton, N.J., 1970. *Details the origin of McClure's and its reliance on muckraking to attract readers.*

PART THREE

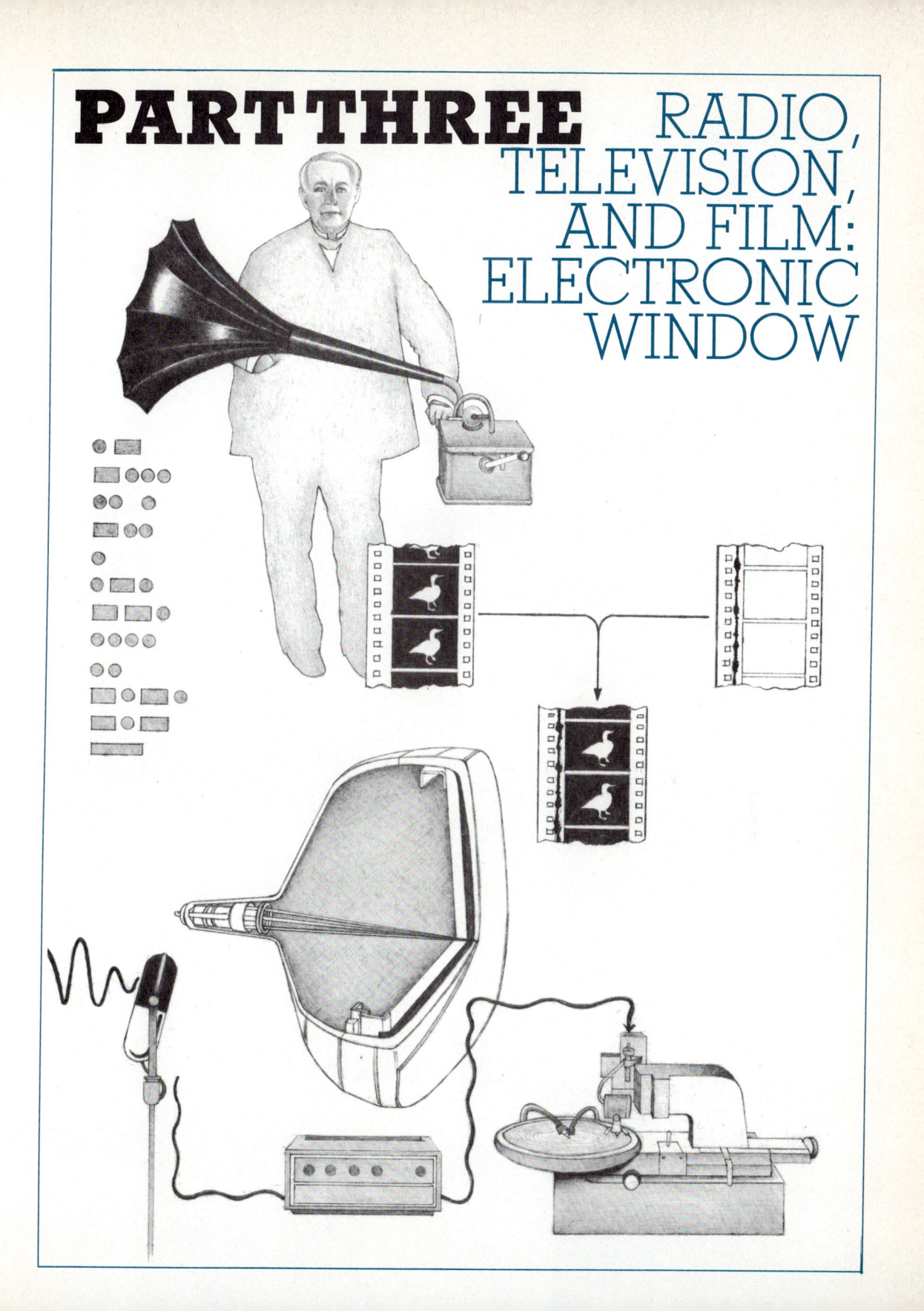

RADIO, TELEVISION, AND FILM: ELECTRONIC WINDOW

CHAPTER 6

Radio . . . is really a subliminal echo chamber of magical power. . . .
                          Marshall McLuhan

RADIO AND RECORDINGS: THE WINDOW HAS EARS

CHAPTER PREVIEW

After reading this chapter, you should be able to:
- Assess the role played by radio in your daily life
- Enumerate and explain key happenings in the development of the radio medium
- Explain how the Radio Acts of 1912 and 1927 and the Communications Act of 1934 affected the radio medium
- Compare the types of programming offered on radio in pre- and posttelevision America
- Discuss the development of the recording industry
- Describe the relationship existing between the recording industry and radio in pre- and post-MTV America
- Identify the four key phases of the recording process
- Explain how the recording business operates and define the functions essential to the operation of any recording company, large or small
- Describe the development of popular music in America
- Explain the past and present roles of the radio DJ
- Distinguish between the following radio formats: top 40, album-oriented rock, middle of the road, beautiful music, country and western, ethnic, classical, all news, all talk, and religious
- Describe the AM versus FM battle
- Identify the strengths and weaknesses of National Public Radio
- Discuss the functions performed by the following: the general manager of a radio station, the sales department, the programming department, the news department, and the engineering department
- Explain the role performed by Arbitron

How did you tell it was time for you to get up this morning? Did the sun wake you? Did the alarm go off? Did a person who lives with you nudge you or shake you? Or did the radio start to play?

What is today's weather forecast? Did you step outside to look at the sky and assess conditions for yourself or did you check the radio? When you were a teenager living at home, were you ever admonished to "turn down that radio," or "turn off that stereo"?

Radio, together with its close cousins the record and the audio tape, is a permanent fixture in the lives of the American people, having found a place in 99 percent of American homes and 95 percent of American cars. The *Arbitron* rating service estimates that persons 12 and older typically listen to their radios at least twenty-two hours each week. Indeed, for some the radio or the cassette player has even become a garment; it is worn or carried lest the individual be caught "naked" without it.

Today's listeners have a wide choice: they can tune themselves into a talk show, a news show, or music; they can change channels as their needs change or as their moods change; they can listen to what is being broadcast, or, by slipping a cassette into their recorder, they can personalize their sound environment further by programming their own selections. Wherever you go today, there is radio. Radios now outnumber people in this country more than two to one. Currently over 457.5 million sets are in operation. We are truly a "sound" society.

Of course, things weren't always this way. A day in the United States did not always begin or end with a top 40 station blaring the latest tunes, a talk show psychologist providing easy-access therapy, an all-news station reporting on the latest events, or advertisers hawking wares and services. No man, woman, or child who lived in a prehistoric society was privy to such a warning as this one: "The Galvanic Tribe has just moved warriers closer to our borders—more after this commercial message from. . ." The more than 9000 radio stations in this country do have an interesting history, however; a history that has been marked by years of expansion, years of turmoil, and years of change. Let us examine the development of this portable, movable, adaptable survivor medium.

PIONEERS: EARLY DEVELOPMENTS AND DEVELOPERS

It is hard to believe that prior to May 24, 1844, the words "transportation" and "communication" were for all practical purposes synonyms. Until that time information could only be moved from one point to another if it was carried—transported—by rail, horse, pigeon, or foot. This relationship was altered when Samuel Morse succeeded in opening the first telegraph line between Baltimore and Washington, D.C. His newly devised symbol system of long and short dashes was dubbed the Morse Code. Americans were both intrigued and frightened by the "lightning lines" as they contemplated Morse's first message, "What hath God wrought?" In time, telegraph offices opened across the country, and people dropped by simply to watch the process in operation. It was as if communication had become a form of free entertainment. And in many ways it had, for the telegraph office of the nineteenth century probably shared many similarities with the computer store of the twentieth century.

As is the case with many technological breakthroughs, not everyone was pleased with the new development. In his 1854 publication *Walden*, Henry David Thoreau argued that the telegraph was "an improved means to an unimproved end. . . . We are in great haste to construct a magnetic telegraph from Maine to Texas, but Maine and Texas may have nothing important to communicate." Do you agree? Can the same argument be made today about mass communication? Is

In this "sound" society, the radio accompanies us almost everywhere, even into this New York City park. (Hazel Hankin)

it simply an "improved means to an unimproved end"?

The work of many inventors was pooled to create what eventually became radio. In 1876, for instance, Alexander Graham Bell first demonstrated his invention, the telephone. It is likely that he visualized it as a means of mass communication, since he transmitted dramatic readings, concerts, and even a revival meeting over it. However, the resulting telephone company, commonly referred to as "Ma Bell," began making such profits simply by transmitting the conversations of individuals that the phone's potential as a mass communication medium was not explored. In the late 1880s, the German physicist Heinrich Rudolph Hertz demonstrated that energy could be sent through the air without the use of wires. Today, the numerical designation of radio stations such as "101 on your dial" refers to the cycles per second, called Hertz, at which the station broadcasts. Around the same time a 21-year-old Italian experimenter, Guglielmo Marconi, began his exploration of radio. When Italian authorities took no interest in his work, Marconi moved to England, where he negotiated an agreement with the British government. In 1896, his Marconi Wireless Telegraph and Signal Company was formed, and by 1901 he had successfully sent the first wireless signals across the Atlantic.

As the technology progressed, a maze of patents were produced. However, it was not until 1906 when American Lee De Forest developed the audion, an improvement on John Fleming's vacuum tube, that it became easier to receive voice and music transmissions. For this reason De Forest is often referred to as the father of radio. A visionary who saw radio as a medium that could educate as well as inspire an audience, De Forest arranged for Enrico Caruso to broadcast from the Metropolitan Opera House in New York City. By 1916 De Forest was also broadcasting election returns from the offices of the *New York American*. During his lifetime, De Forest obtained over 200 patents, but owing to a series of poor business decisions and bankruptcies, the rights to these patents were acquired by RCA. However, De Forest did live until 1961, and thus he was able to see his invention develop, change, and change again.

When the United States entered World War I in 1917 there were over 9000 radio transmitters in operation; most were owned by what we would call amateur, or "ham," operators. All were either shut down by the

MEDIA SCOPE

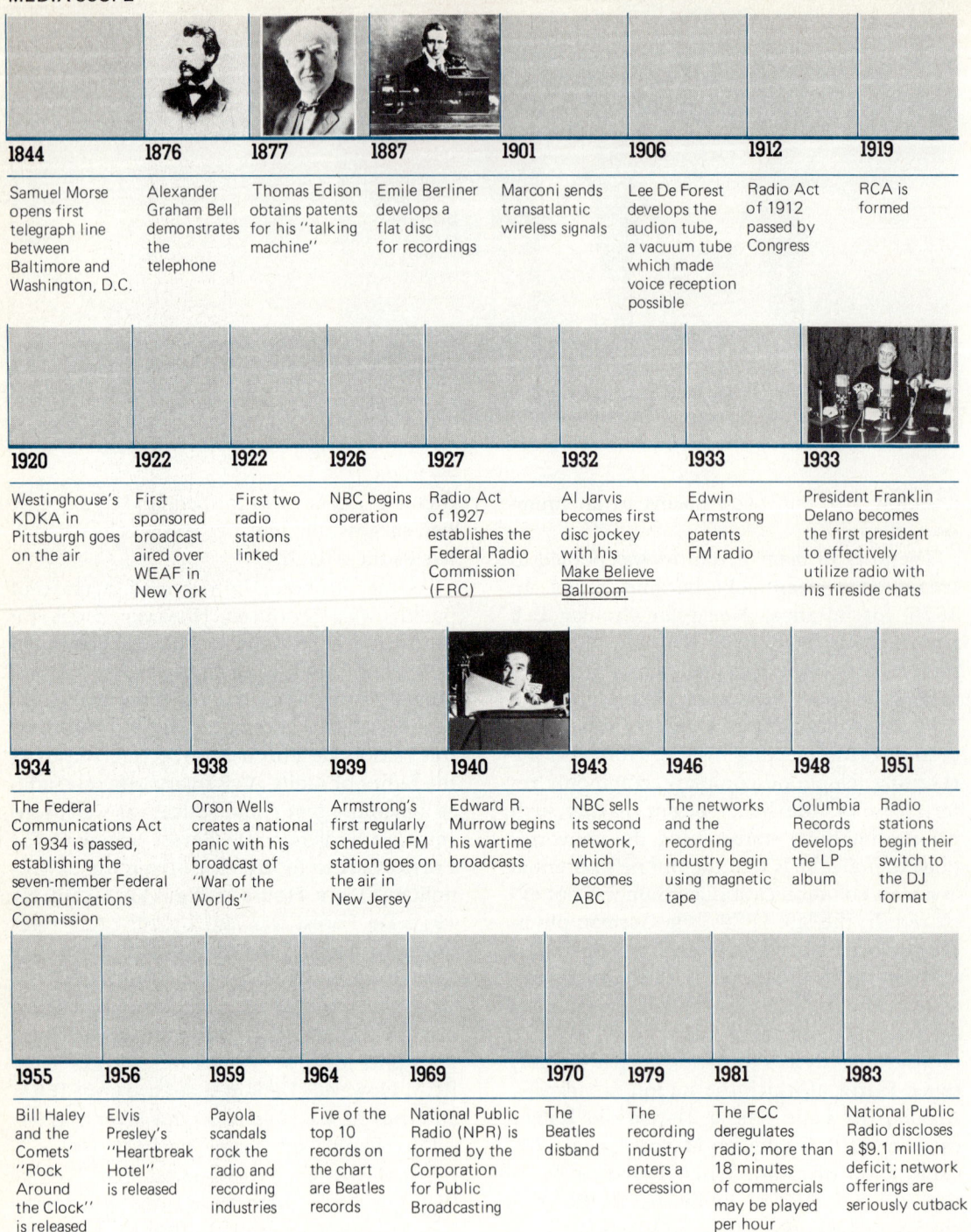

1844 — Samuel Morse opens first telegraph line between Baltimore and Washington, D.C.

1876 — Alexander Graham Bell demonstrates the telephone

1877 — Thomas Edison obtains patents for his "talking machine"

1887 — Emile Berliner develops a flat disc for recordings

1901 — Marconi sends transatlantic wireless signals

1906 — Lee De Forest develops the audion tube, a vacuum tube which made voice reception possible

1912 — Radio Act of 1912 passed by Congress

1919 — RCA is formed

1920 — Westinghouse's KDKA in Pittsburgh goes on the air

1922 — First sponsored broadcast aired over WEAF in New York

1922 — First two radio stations linked

1926 — NBC begins operation

1927 — Radio Act of 1927 establishes the Federal Radio Commission (FRC)

1932 — Al Jarvis becomes first disc jockey with his Make Believe Ballroom

1933 — Edwin Armstrong patents FM radio

1933 — President Franklin Delano becomes the first president to effectively utilize radio with his fireside chats

1934 — The Federal Communications Act of 1934 is passed, establishing the seven-member Federal Communications Commission

1938 — Orson Wells creates a national panic with his broadcast of "War of the Worlds"

1939 — Armstrong's first regularly scheduled FM station goes on the air in New Jersey

1940 — Edward R. Murrow begins his wartime broadcasts

1943 — NBC sells its second network, which becomes ABC

1946 — The networks and the recording industry begin using magnetic tape

1948 — Columbia Records develops the LP album

1951 — Radio stations begin their switch to the DJ format

1955 — Bill Haley and the Comets' "Rock Around the Clock" is released

1956 — Elvis Presley's "Heartbreak Hotel" is released

1959 — Payola scandals rock the radio and recording industries

1964 — Five of the top 10 records on the chart are Beatles records

1969 — National Public Radio (NPR) is formed by the Corporation for Public Broadcasting

1970 — The Beatles disband

1979 — The recording industry enters a recession

1981 — The FCC deregulates radio; more than 18 minutes of commercials may be played per hour

1983 — National Public Radio discloses a $9.1 million deficit; network offerings are seriously cutback

RADIO, TELEVISION, AND FILM: THE ELECTRONIC WINDOW

government or operated in the defense of the country during the war years. As World War I drew to a close, the question of what to do with the radio equipment and the newly acquired technology became an important issue. Marconi's company, which in this country was called the American Marconi Corporation, was very much in control of radio equipment manufacturing. Military leaders and executives from General Electric feared that the British-dominated Marconi Company might gain control of world communications. The Radio Corporation of America (RCA) was created to prevent this from occurring: General Electric, Westinghouse, and American Telephone and Telegraph (AT&T) pooled their various patent rights for broadcasting equipment and receiving hardware. Thus, RCA came to dominate communication in this country and abroad. Continued American control of RCA was ensured by the company's articles of incorporation, which stated that all members of the board of directors were required to be American and that at least 80 percent of the company's stock had to be held by U.S. citizens.

One problem that had faced the prewar industry was how to get radio equipment into people's homes and incorporated into their daily lives. Initially, radio stations were owned and operated by radio manufacturers, who used the medium to further sales of their own products. Early radios were sold in kits to be assembled at home by enthusiasts as a hobby or game. But that was prewar radio; the postwar years were different. Broadcasting historian Erik Barnouw has pointed out that by the war's end over 100,000 people had been trained in the use of radio. And radio really began to boom in the 1920s, when radio receivers requiring no assembly were marketed. Each month, the number of receivers sold steadily increased. Thus, the various corporations found a large home market primed and ready to accept the new medium.

The size of the market created another problem, however—the need for continuous programming. Once people owned radios they wanted something to listen to. In 1920, Frank Conrad, a Westinghouse engineer who was experimenting in radiotelephony, began broadcasting from his home in Pittsburgh under the call letters 8XK. Because Conrad found it tiring to talk all the time, he connected his phonograph to the transmitter, borrowed records from a music store, and began sending music by radio. Conrad's broadcasts fascinated listeners, who began sending him postcards requesting that he play certain selections and refrain from playing others that were scratched and of poor quality. Conrad's broadcasts helped to stimulate a tremendous demand for radios—so much so that Westinghouse began selling its war surplus radios in department stores. Eventually, Westinghouse built a more powerful transmitter and had Conrad broadcast his program from a studio constructed atop a building owned by Westinghouse. Conrad's Westinghouse station, KDKA, had its inaugural broadcast on November 2, 1920, when

YOU WERE THERE

It is November 1920. The first radio station in America to offer continuously scheduled programming, Westinghouse's KDKA, is about to broadcast the Harding-Cox election returns. Let's spend a few minutes with history and "listen" to that first broadcast.

In just one moment now, KDKA, in cooperation with the *Pittsburgh Post and Sun,* will present the latest presidential election returns. It is now apparent that the Republican ticket of Harding and Coolidge is well ahead of Cox and Roosevelt. At the present time Harding has collected more than 16 million votes against some 9 million for the Democrats.

We'll give the state vote in just a moment. First, we'd like to ask you to let us know if this broadcast is reaching you. Please drop us a card addressed to station KDKA, Westinghouse, East Pittsburgh, Pennsylvania.

MEDIA PROBE

THE FIRST RADIO COMMERCIAL

ANNOUNCER: This afternoon the radio audience is to be addressed by Mr. Blackwell of the Queensboro Corporation, who through arrangements made by the Griffin Radio Service, Inc., will say a few words concerning Nathaniel Hawthorne and the desirability of fostering the helpful community spirit and the healthful unconfined home life that were Hawthorne ideals. Ladies and Gentlemen, Mr. Blackwell.

BLACKWELL: It is 58 years since Nathaniel Hawthorne, the greatest of American fictionists, passed away. To honor his memory the Queensboro Corporation, creator and operator of the tenant-owned system of apartment homes at Jackson Heights, New York City, has named its latest group of high-grade dwellings "Hawthorne Court."

I wish to thank those within sound of my voice for the broadcasting opportunity afforded me to urge this vast radio audience to seek the recreation and the daily comfort of the home removed from the congested part of the city, right at the boundaries of God's great outdoors, and within a few minutes by subway from the business section of Manhattan. This sort of residential environment strongly influenced Hawthorne, America's greatest writer of fiction. . . .

Let me enjoin upon you as you value your health and your hopes and your happiness, get away from the solid masses of brick, where the meagre opening admitting a slant of sunlight is mockingly called a light shaft, and where children grow up starved for a run over a patch of grass and sight of a tree. . . .

Imagine a congested city apartment lifted bodily to the middle of a large garden within twenty minutes' travel of the city's business center. Imagine the interior of a group of such apartments traversed by a garden court stretching a block, with beautiful flower beds and rich sward, so that the present jaded, congested section dweller on looking out of his windows is not chilled with the brick-and-mortar vista, but gladdened and enthused by colors and scents that make life worth living once more. Imagine an apartment to live in at a place where you and your neighbor join the same community clubs, organizations and activities, where you golf with your neighbor, tennis with your neighbor, bowl with your neighbor and join him in a long list of outdoor and indoor pleasure-giving, health-giving activities. . . .

Let me close by urging that you hurry to the apartment home near the green fields and the neighborly atmosphere right on the subway without the expense and the trouble of the commuter, where health and community happiness beckon the community life and friendly environment that Hawthorne advocated.

Quoted in Gleason L. Archer, *History of Radio,* American Historical Society, New York, 1938, pp. 397–399.

Compare this excerpt with radio commercials of today. How is it similar? How is it different? Do you feel that today's audience would have considered purchasing these apartments based on this message? Why or why not? (Remember, in 1922 two were sold.)

---

it announced the Harding-Cox presidential election results. Because of the success of this initial operation Westinghouse executives constructed similar stations on top of corporate buildings in other cities. The sale of Westinghouse receiver parts also skyrocketed.

By 1921, RCA had begun to mass-produce home sets, as well as to build radio stations of its own. AT&T entered the picture in 1922 with New York station WEAF. WEAF was the first station to sell advertising time. On August 28, 1922, at 5:15 P.M., the Queensboro Corporation, a real estate firm, became the

The need for sufficient quality programming was critical in early broadcasting. (The Bettman Archive)

station's first paying customer. As a result of a 10-minute spot, during which they told listeners about available properties and for which they paid $100, two apartments were sold. Commercial radio advertising was born. By 1926, WEAF was grossing $750,000 annually. Other stations would emulate the model it provided.

THE BUSINESS TAKES SHAPE

Imagine that the year is 1922 and you are the owner or manager of a small radio station. It is your job to fill the air for several hours each night with programming that attracts and interests listeners. On Monday evening you start by playing some recordings. But then your collection is exhausted, and there is still time to fill so you decide to permit people to come into your studio and tell their favorite joke or sing their favorite song. You simply request your eager talent to line up outside. One at a time your announcer ushers them in, recites their names, and they are "on the air." To culminate the evening, someone from a local college gives a lecture and then you sign off. Before you know it, it is Tuesday, and you again face the same problem—filling the air time. People again line up outside the studio awaiting a chance "to do their own thing." Is it any wonder that radio station owners and managers quickly recognized that they had a need to band together in order to ensure that quality programming was broadcast? Is it any wonder that they quickly came to understand that it would be impractical to continue the practice of broadcasting whoever showed up at the door? Unfortunately, early radio programming often resembled the *Gong Show* minus the gong!

In 1922, the first attempt at such a linkage occurred when WGY in New York City and WJZ in New Jersey were joined together through AT&T telephone lines so that they could both carry the World Series. By 1925, twenty-six stations coast-to-coast were linked to broadcast President Coolidge's inaugural address to the nation. And to this day, sports and politics still occupy prominent roles in radio programming efforts. In days past, they provided the impetus that led to the creation of radio networks.

In 1925, David Sarnoff—then with RCA—suggested that all RCA stations be combined into a network. In 1926, the first NBC *network* was formed "to provide the best programs available for broadcasting in the United States." A second network was established the next year; it was composed of stations RCA acquired when it purchased AT&T's stations and broadcast assets. The first network came to be known as the Red network, the second as the Blue network—

YOU WERE THERE

DAVID SARNOFF: A YOUNG HERO AND HIS VISION

David Sarnoff came into leadership in radio and later television by way of the telegraph. At the age of 21, in April 1912, Sarnoff became a national hero while demonstrating the telegraph at a Marconi Wireless Telegraph Company of America booth in Wanamaker's Department Store in Manhattan. Suddenly through the static he began to hear distress signals from the *S.S. Olympic* nearly 1500 miles away: the *S.S. Titanic* was sinking! Sarnoff stayed at his telegraph for seventy-two hours, relaying information about the tragedy to other ships which might help save the survivors, to the press, as well as to relatives and friends of the passengers. Subsequently, Sarnoff rose to positions of importance in the Marconi company and later became the driving force of RCA and NBC until his death in 1971.

David Sarnoff was a man of vision. In 1915 or 1916 he sent a memo to his boss at Marconi. At a time when radio as we know it did not exist, Sarnoff wrote:

I have in mind a plan of development which would make radio a "household utility" in the same sense as the piano or phonograph. The idea is to bring music into the home by wireless.... The "Radio Music Box" can be supplied with amplifying tubes and a loud-speaking telephone, all of which can be neatly mounted in one box. The box can be placed on a table in the parlor or living room... events of national importance can be simultaneously announced and received. Baseball scores can be transmitted in the air by use of one set installed at the Polo Grounds.... By purchase of a Radio Music Box people could enjoy concerts, music, recitals, etc.

David Sarnoff, *Looking Ahead: The Papers of David Sarnoff,* McGraw-Hill, New York, 1968, pp. 31–33.

Reflecting an early view of radio, Sarnoff told his boss, "The main revenue to be derived will be from the sale of 'Radio Music Boxes' which if manufactured in quantities of one hundred thousand or so could yield a handsome profit."

What prime source of revenue did even Sarnoff fail to foresee when radio was still in its infancy?

---

both after the color of the pens that were used to show them in the annual stockholders' reports and meetings.

A year later, a music promoter named Arthur Judson became upset when he was denied the right to do business with NBC, so he tied together twelve stations and founded his own network, the United Independent Broadcasters Network. Judson's network eventually became the Columbia Phonograph Broadcasting System when it merged with the recording company. It was also the forerunner of the Columbia Broadcasting System (CBS). From the start, the CBS network suffered from a lack of funds and weak professional leadership, until it received both in the form of William S. Paley, heir to a tobacco company fortune.

The fourth network came into being in 1934. It was composed of four stations—one in New York City, one in Chicago, one in Detroit, and one in Cincinnati—which wanted to lure advertisers by providing them with more exposure for the most popular program in each city—*The Lone Ranger.* Since the stations were coming together for their mutual

MEDIA VIEW

WILLIAM S. PALEY: MY START IN NETWORK RADIO

The first radio I ever saw was a primitive crystal set. A friend clamped the earphones on me and I was dumbfounded. It was hard to believe that I was hearing music out of the air, and I never got over the surprise and the fascination.... [In 1926] my father was approached by one of his very close friends, Jerome Louchheim, a well-known and highly successful building contractor in Philadelphia, with a personal appeal that [my father's company] Congress Cigar advertise its La Palinas on a small radio network in which he had recently bought a controlling interest. The network, called the United Independent Broadcasters, was still in financial difficulties in New York City and Louchheim asked for my father's advertising as a token of his personal friendship. So, my father agreed to advertise and put me in charge of organizing a program.

I put together a program called "The La Palina Smoker," a half-hour show that featured an orchestra, a female vocalist whom we called "Miss La Palina," and a comedian as a master of ceremonies.... Over the next six months I made frequent trips to the United Independent Broadcasters' offices in New York and became rather well acquainted with this little network and its activities. UIB had been formed by Arthur Judson, the celebrated concert manager as a vehicle for putting the classical musicians he represented on the air. Incorporating the network on January 27, 1927, Judson had arranged with the Columbia Phonograph Company that in exchange for financial backing the network would be known on the air as the Columbia Phonograph Broadcasting System. [Louchheim later bought an interest in the network.]

In its first year of operation UIB had taken in $176,737 in net sales and had paid out $396,803. Louchheim had failed in all his efforts to turn the company around... he approached my father... and told him he had bought "a lemon," that the network's books were a mess, and he wanted out. But my father did not want to invest his money in such a venture.

I became tremendously excited at the prospect and the network's shaky condition did not deter me. It was the great promise of radio itself that impelled me to act and to act immediately.... I had about a million dollars of my own and I was willing to risk any or all of it in radio.... On September 26, 1928, I was elected president of a patchwork, money losing little company called United Independent Broadcasters.

My office high above the Paramount movie theatre was geographically at the hub of the playland of Broadway, but only geographically. In comparison with stage and screen, radio then ranked nowhere in show business.... But I had the gut feeling that radio was on the threshold of a great awakening, that marvelous things were about to happen and that I had come to the medium at the right moment.

William S. Paley, As It Happened: A Memoir, Doubleday, New York, 1979, pp. 32–40.

---

benefit, they chose the label Mutual Broadcasting System for their title. By the early 1940s, 160 stations were MBS affiliates. Unlike NBC and CBS, however, MBS owned no stations. Instead, Mutual pioneered the cooperative programming concept whereby local advertisers were able to sponsor quality programs distributed nationally.

The network picture as we know it today was completed in 1943 when the federal government forced NBC to sell its Blue Network—precipitating the birth of the American Broadcasting Company (ABC).

FEDERAL REGULATION OF BROADCASTING

You will recall that Marconi brought his wireless company to the United States during the early part of this century. At the time, one of his prime customers was the United States Navy, which needed to be able to communicate accurately and effectively with ships at sea. If you ever listened to a CB radio or wireless walkie-talkie when several people were trying to talk to several other people at the same time, you know that the resulting jumble of sound is almost impossible to decipher. This is precisely what was happening to Navy communications officers, who found themselves competing for airspace with the hundreds of amateur (ham) radio operators who were broadcasting in this country. In effect, their communications were drowning in a sea of interference.

The Radio Act of 1912

The United States participated in the International Wireless Conference held in Berlin in 1903 and 1906, and in London in 1912. The Radio Act which was passed by Congress in 1912 was designed in part to honor treaties resulting from those conferences. The act provided for some uniformity among radio operators and also required that anyone who wanted to operate a radio had to obtain a license. Amateurs were up in arms over this provision—after all, they argued, no one regulated newspapers or magazines! The act also specified that transmissions must be supervised by a licensed technician who had proven his competence by passing an examination. Also, the act empowered the president to shut down radio stations during wartime, if necessary; this power was used during World War I. In addition, the act gave the Secretary of Commerce the power to assign a specific wavelength or frequency to each broadcaster.

In practice, however, the act contained one fatal loophole; the Secretary of Commerce could not refuse to grant a license. Thus, as World War I ended, more and more stations applied for and received licenses, and the airwaves again became overcrowded. Though stations attempted to share the frequencies by dividing up the broadcast time, eventually there were just too many competing stations for that procedure to work. In fact, by 1924 more than 5000 stations were broadcasting regularly. Stations were even known to leave their transmitters on during their competitors' broadcasts, thus obliterating their programming.

For example, though WDAF (the station owned by the *Kansas City Star* newspaper) was scheduled to leave the air at 7 P.M. to let WHB broadcast from 7 to 9, they somehow learned that a local politician who was to appear on WHB was going to criticize the *Star;* so instead of vacating the airwaves, WDAF left their transmitter on; all station listeners were able to pick up on their receivers that evening was noise—high-pitched, ear-shattering noise. But WDAF was not alone in committing airwave piracy. A number of competing radio stations who shared the same frequency would even attempt to broadcast their respective church services at the same time to their respective listeners. The output was far from biblical. It was clearly time for Congress to act again. According to broadcast historian Erik Barnouw, radio was in real danger of becoming "a tower of Babel."

The Radio Act of 1927

On January 27, 1927, President Calvin Coolidge signed the *Radio Act of 1927* into law. In part, the act specified:

> This Act is intended to regulate all forms of in-

MEDIA PROBE

The year is 1930. As members of the Federal Radio Commission your job is to regulate the airwaves in the "public interest, convenience or necessity" while at the same time protecting the freedom of speech guaranteed citizens under the First Amendment of the Constitution.

Dr. John R. Brinkley has come before the FRC requesting the renewal of a station license (KFKB), which had been issued to him in 1923. Dr. Brinkley's medical credentials consist of an "honorary degree" from an unaccredited medical school in Kansas. His medical specialty is the insertion of goat sex glands into older men, which he declares renews their vigor and vitality. He performs this procedure in the Brinkley Hospital in Milford, Kansas.

As a commissioner, your concern is over Dr. Brinkley's use of his radio station and its relationship to the Brinkley Pharmaceutical Association. It seems that during the *Medical Question Box*, a half-hour program aired over KFKB three times each day, Dr. Brinkley prescribes medicines for patients who have written to him. Since he prescribes his medicines by means of code numbers, the "patients," and any other listeners who wish to do so, may take the prescribed number to participating pharmacists and have the prescription filled. Here are samples:

Exhibit A: She states her case briefly.... She had an operation, with her appendix, ovary and tubes removed a few years ago; she is very nervous and has dizzy spells.... In my practice in such cases as this I have many years used prescription number 61. I think if you go on a vegetable diet, a salt-free diet, for awhile and use Prescription numbers 64, 50, and 61, you would be surprised at the benefit you would gain.

Exhibit B: Here's one from Tillie. She says she had an operation, had some trouble ten years ago. I think the operation was unnecessary and it isn't very good sense to have an ovary removed with the expectation of motherhood resulting therefrom. My advice to you is to use Women's Tonic Numbers 50, 67, and 61.

What is your stance? Should the Federal Radio Commission grant a renewal of his license to Dr. Brinkley? Does he have a right to deliver such messages to the public over the airwaves? Is he broadcasting in the public interest? If you were a member of such a commission today, would there be any type(s) of radio programming you would consider banning? Why or why not? (Note: The Commission revoked Dr. Brinkley's license in 1930. Undaunted, he moved his operation across the border into Mexico, where he beamed his advice and prescription numbers into the United States via a high-powered transmitter for another decade.)

---

terstate and foreign radio transmissions and communications within the United States ... to maintain the control of the United States over all the channels of interstate and foreign radio transmission; and to *provide for the use of such channels, but not the ownership thereof,* by individuals, firms or corporations for limited periods of time, under *licenses granted by Federal authority.* (Emphasis added.)

Thus, the airwaves were considered a natural resource which had to be conserved and protected, just as Congress at the time was preserving public ownership of land, trees, water, and other natural resources. The act also formulated the concept that the radio stations must operate in the "public interest, convenience or necessity" rather than solely for the benefit of the broadcaster. In addition, the act created a five-member Federal Radio Commission to carry out the act's provisions, including, in part, classifying radio stations, prescribing the nature of service, and assigning frequencies.

The first person to test the new act was Dr. John Brinkley, a practicing Kansas physician with questionable credentials who had built a

RADIO AND RECORDINGS: THE WINDOW HAS EARS

small radio station and used it to broadcast messages to patients who were recovering from surgery or other illnesses. Other people, in addition to his patients, however, tuned in and listened to the advice readily dispensed by Brinkley. After a fire destroyed the original station, Dr. Brinkley built one with even greater power and used it to spread the word about himself to all who were willing and able to listen. Brinkley had even worked out a deal with druggists throughout the Midwest to dispense prescriptions he prescribed for patients over the air. The American Medical Association vigorously protested to the FRC.

The Radio Act of 1927 also established what we now refer to as the equal time provision for political candidates. Section 18 of the act states:

> If any licensee shall permit any person who is a legally qualified candidate for any public office to use a broadcasting station, he shall afford equal opportunities to all other such candidates for that office in the use of such broadcasting station.

Although the act did succeed in restoring some order and decorum to the radio medium, the fact that the FRC did not have authority over telephone and telegraph traffic would prompt Congress to again take action.

The Communications Act of 1934

When he became president, Franklin Delano Roosevelt ordered a review of all governmental regulatory agencies, including the Federal Radio Commission. As a result of this review, one of his recommendations to Congress was that a new agency be created to replace the FRC. This new agency would be responsible for regulating all aspects of communications and would be called the *Federal Communications Commission*. Thus, the *Communications Act of 1934* replaced the five-person FRC with seven FCC commissioners, who took office on July 11, 1934. No significant change in philosophy was incorporated into this act, other than the addition of wire. The FCC is still the major regulatory agency for wire and radio to this day. However, it presently has five commissioners.

PROGRAMMING THROUGH THE YEARS

During the depression of the 1930s, more and more people found themselves unable to afford outside entertainment. Since many people owned radios, they transformed their living rooms into home entertainment centers. In fact, almost 50 percent of all American households (12 million homes) had radios in 1930. By 1940, that figure would swell to 81 percent of American homes. Thus, radio would survive the depression and emerge relatively unscathed. In fact, in the period 1930–1940, radio advertising revenues actually rose from $25 million to more than $70 million. Also, by 1935, new research organizations had been created to provide data on audience size and composition. Program ratings were about to become an important factor.

Just as you scan today's television guide in order to determine what is available to watch, radio's audiences consulted guides that were printed in local newspapers. What types of programs did they find to listen to?

Convinced that radio was a good sales tool, companies like Eveready and Palmolive Soap began sponsoring comedy and variety shows that featured their names in the titles: *The Eveready Battery Hour* and *The Palmolive Soap Hour*. Radio became an amalgam of variety shows, mysteries, dramas, and comedies. Seeking to offer relief from the hard times of the depression, comedy programs provided hours of laughter. Jack Benny, Fred Allen, George Burns and Gracie Allen, Edgar Bergen and Charlie McCarthy, and Eddie Cantor all found friendly ears awaiting them each week. *Fibber McGee and Molly,* a situation

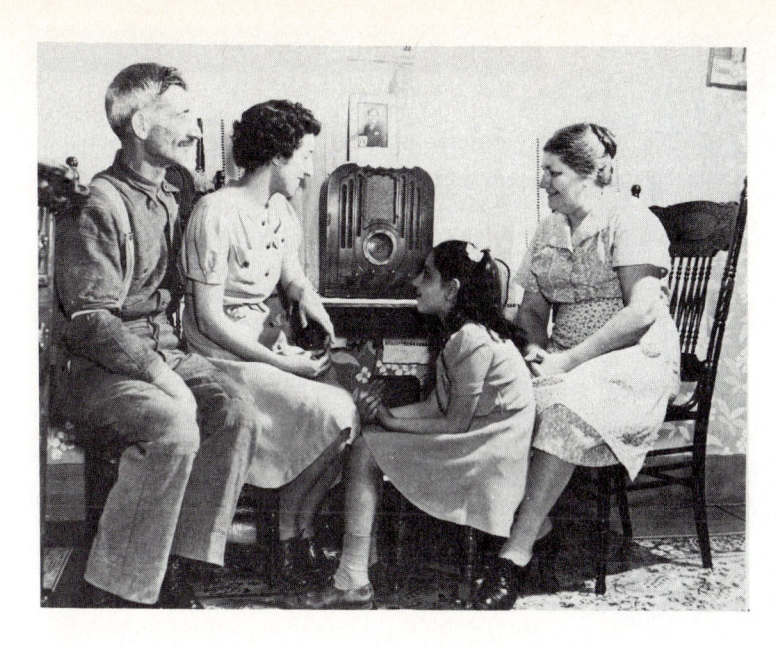

Radio, both as a focus of family entertainment and as a source of advertising revenues, actually thrived during the Depression. (The Bettman Archive)

comedy that aired weekly also attracted listeners. This show's enthusiasts anticipated the weekly opening of Fibber's closet, at which point a cascade of items, including the final tinkling bell, would invariably spew forth, producing a cacophony of sound pleasurably visualized in each listener's mind. The interest in comedy also sparked *Amos 'n' Andy,* an NBC hit and the most popular situation comedy during the late 1920s. Unfortunately, the program stereotyped blacks and used two white men to provide the voices of the lead characters. Despite its racist overtones, during its run *Amos 'n' Andy* was so popular that President Coolidge never missed a week's installment even changing his speaking schedule to accommodate it. The show affected the American public at large too; because of it dinner times were altered, the closing times of factories were adjusted, and theater curtains were raised late.

Probably the most popular type of radio program during radio's golden age was the mystery-adventure series. Among the very successful shows were *The Shadow* ("Who knows what evil lurks in the hearts of men—the Shadow knows"), *Gangbusters,* and *Inner Sanctum.* Also popular was radio's fantasy world, peopled with characters like Tom Mix, the Lone Ranger, the Green Hornet, Terry and the Pirates, and Superman. Drama came to the airwaves with *Lux Hollywood Theatre* and *Mercury Theatre of the Air.* The Orson Wells Mercury Theatre broadcast of "War of the Worlds" precipitated a national panic. Broadcast on Halloween eve in 1938 at a time when Hitler had invaded Czechoslovakia and war loomed on the horizon, the program describing an invasion, this one from Mars, caught Americans off-guard. They were taken in by the script's intermingling of story and "fictionalized" news bulletins about the Martian invasion. The national panic that ensued caused the FCC to ban the airing of fictionalized news announcements.

Today's popular television soap operas also had their roots in radio. Called "soaps" because various brands of soaps and detergents sponsored them, episodes dealt with the daily intrigues of the characters who inhabited their world; *Ma Perkins, Stella Dallas, The Romance of Helen Trent, Portia Faces Life,* and a

RADIO AND RECORDINGS: THE WINDOW HAS EARS

Orson Welles' 1938 broadcast of *War of the Worlds* so panicked the audience that the FCC banned the airing of fictionalized news. (Culver Pictures)

MEDIA PROBE

Spend some time listening to recordings of pre-television radio programs. (These are often available in school or public libraries.) Then compare the types of programming featured on radio with the types of programs you watch today on television. How have comedy, variety, and mystery programs changed? In what ways have they remained the same? Do you feel there is an audience for such programming on radio today? Why or why not?

---

host of others all had followings. Since soap segments always ended with an unresolved situation, people were enticed to tune in day after day. Listeners came to think of the characters on the soaps as members of their immediate family. When a baby was born gifts arrived at the station; when a character died, messages of sympathy would be sent. After commiserating and empathizing with the trials and tribulations of soapland's characters, listeners said they felt better equipped to solve their own problems.

Also included in radio's wide spectrum of programs were quiz shows like *The $64 Dollar Question,* children's shows like *Little Orphan Annie,* and talk shows.

In 1933, President Franklin Delano Roosevelt became the first president to make extensive and effective use of the radio. The week after his inauguration he went on the air with the first of many "fireside chats." In contrast to the formal public oratory of most politicians, Roosevelt used radio to create the illusion that he was speaking informally or chatting with each individual listener. Beginning with the phrase "My friends," Roosevelt would use simple, direct language to explain the problems the country was facing and the steps he was taking to solve them. In his first chat, for example, Roosevelt explained the conditions that had precipitated the bank "holiday" (closing). He told them of his plans for reopening the banks and assured people that their funds would be safe. If the doors of your bank were closed tomorrow, would you be concerned? At a time when millions of Americans were frightened that they had lost their life savings, Roosevelt told them, "I can assure you that it is safer to keep your money in a reopened bank than under the mattress." He closed the broadcast with an appeal for support:

> You people must have faith; you must not be stampeded by rumors or guesses. Let us unite in banishing fear. We have provided the machinery to restore our financial system; it is up to you to support and make it work. It is your problem no less than it is mine. Together we cannot fail.[1]

The next day as banks reopened, people did not run to withdraw their funds as had been predicted. In fact, more money was deposited than was taken out. In New York alone, the increase was some $10 million. Roosevelt had used radio to help stabilize the economy and move the depression-ridden country along the road to economic recovery. Roosevelt provided politicians who would follow him with a lesson in effective media usage.

News also had its place on the radio dial. Prior to World War II, radio stations would buy the early morning and evening papers and broadcast summaries of their contents. Then they began purchasing news directly from the United Press and the International News Service. But newspapers objected on the grounds that airing news on radio would bring about a decrease in newspaper sales. Eventually, the papers brought enough pressure to bear on the news services that they stopped selling their news to broadcasters. Some papers even boycotted radio by refusing to print program schedules. In time, however, the press's grip on news was loosened, and as World War II approached, radio was on its way to becoming an effective news medium, broadcasting events of the day within minutes or hours of their occurrence.

In the days before Pearl Harbor, radio news kept Americans abreast of the problems developing in Europe. In September of 1938, as Hitler threatened Europe, CBS and NBC radio crews covered events for America. Among the reporters on the scene for CBS was Edward R. Murrow; Murrow had been sent to Europe with the request that he transmit "talks" back to the network. And he did. Murrow gained fame for his at-the-scene broadcasts. Alexander Kendrick, in his book *Prime Time: The Life of Edward R. Murrow,* provides an example of a Murrow talk from London that was made during an air raid:

> The Battle of Britain had begun. German planes were over blacked-out London. It was 11:30 by Big Ben. "This is Trafalgar Square," reported Ed Murrow. "The noise that you hear at this moment is the sound of the air-raid siren. A searchlight just burst into action, off in the distance, an immense single beam sweeping the sky above me now. People are walking along very quietly. We're just at the entrance of an air-raid shelter here, and I must move the cable over just a bit, so people can walk in."

America's living rooms heard antiaircraft guns in the background. In Trafalgar Square, Murrow moved from the steps of St. Martin-in-the-Fields and the entrance to the church crypt which had become a shelter, and sat on the edge of the sidewalk. He said nothing. His open microphone picked up the sound of unhurried footsteps. Directly above him, two men stopped to talk. One casually asked the other for a light. The sirens and guns kept working.[2]

Thus, Murrow demonstrated through sound that even after all the bombings and the fall of France, England still stood calmly ready to continue the battle against Hitler's armies. Murrow's reports from all over Europe helped prepare the American public for America's entry into the war and carried us through the war years to its termination. Murrow continued his work as a journalist into the age of television, always ending his broadcasts with the famous closing line: "Good night . . . and good luck." He died in 1965.

Posttelevision Radio

The emergence of television signaled that radio would have to change significantly if it was to survive as a communication medium. Television had captivated and intrigued the radio audience, and TV had picture as well as sound. Media consumers were no longer content listening to their favorite personalities—now they could see them too. Television was perceived to be a more complete mass medium. In effect, radio had set the stage for television; the American people already liked to listen, and now they could also watch.

How would you feel if you were a post-World War II owner of a radio station who saw television stations springing up all around you? What do you think your reaction would have been? Would you have sold out and run? Would you have screamed and ranted? Or would you have searched for ways to fight back? At the time, many people in radio were convinced that their medium would simply die. Some felt that the radio system had simply been overpowered by a newer technology, that television was radio with pictures, and that, consequently, advertisers would no longer find radio an attractive vehicle for their messages. Of course, these fatalist views proved to be erroneous. In fact, according to the Radio Advertising Bureau's *Radio Facts,* today more than 80 percent of adults in this country are reached by radio every day and 95 percent are reached each week. Additionally, 99 percent of American households have at least one radio, with the typical household owning 5.5 sets.[3] Radio did not wither and die in the face of competition from television, as many had predicted. Quite the opposite, over the years radio has grown and prospered as a mass medium. However, for it to survive and thrive, radio was forced to assess its strengths and learn to capitalize on them. Radio had to find ways to differentiate and distinguish itself from television.

It was reasoned that radio demanded less attention of its listeners than television did of its viewers; the consumer of radio could perform other activities while still attending to the medium. Likewise, it was felt that the greater channel capacity of radio as compared to television also gave it the potential for greater diversification. And it was believed that radio was superior to television as a music medium. (Note: Music Television—MTV—has only recently emerged as a force.) Based on these perceived strengths, an effort was made to discover formulas that would permit radio to coexist with television.

If you were spending a few days visiting a city you had never been to before and you wanted to listen to country and western music, would you have to consult the local radio guide in order to determine the time at which the music you wanted to hear would be broadcast? Of course not. You could simply turn your AM or FM radio dial until you located a country and western station. The same holds true for other types of music as well as for talk shows and news shows. With the exception of a few smaller communities, radio stations have survived and prospered in the age of television by specializing in a particular type of programming; in other words, they have created an identification for themselves. They have no trouble answering the question, Who are you?

Technology has also aided radio's adaptation to the television age. If you compare a radio set built in the 1930s with one in your home today, the most striking differences are probably its size and weight. Most old-fashioned radios were fairly large and heavy; some were even large floor models that listeners "watched." The radio sets in your home today are probably significantly smaller, much more compact, and quite a bit lighter. They are probably scattered throughout your home: some may be perched on night tables and the kitchen cabinet, others may be housed as one component in a stereo system, and still others may be carried in your hand or clamped to your head. The emergence of the transistor as the replacement of large vacuum tubes has helped shape the role radio plays in our life today. In fact, the Radio Advertising Bureau reports that 470 million radios were in operation in 1982—up 47 percent since 1970. Eight million walk-along sets are now in use and that number is still growing. It is interesting that nearly 50 percent of all walk-along owners are adults in the 18–34 year old range.[4] The size and the weight of the equipment has contributed to the personalization of the radio medium.

During television's formative years, the ABC, NBC, and CBS networks were busy establishing themselves in television programming. As television started dominating the evening hours of Americans, network executives began to reduce the scope of their radio offerings; this was done to ensure that they were not competing with their own products. Eventually, network radio affiliates dwindled from 97 percent in 1947 to only 50 percent by 1955. By 1960, the last network programming form, the soap opera, went off the air.

YOU WERE THERE

RADIO REPORT BY EDWARD R. MURROW

April 15, 1945... Permit me to tell you what you would have seen, and heard, had you been with me on Thursday. It will not be pleasant listening. If you are at lunch, or if you have no appetite to hear what Germans have done, now is a good time to switch off the radio, for I propose to tell you of Buchenwald. It is on a small hill about four miles outside Weimar, and it was one of the largest concentration camps in Germany, and it was built to last. As we approached it, we saw about a hundred men in civilian clothes with rifles advancing in open order across the fields. There were a few shops; we stopped to inquire. We were told that some of the prisoners had a couple of SS men cornered there. We drove on, reached the main gate. The prisoners crowded up behind the wire. We entered.

And now, let me tell this in the first person, for I was the least important person there, as you shall hear....

A German, Fritz Kersheimer, came up and said, "May I show you round the camp? I've been here ten years." An Englishman stood to attention, saying, "May I introduce myself, delighted to see you, and can you tell me when some of our blokes will be along?" I told him soon and asked to see one of the barracks. It happened to be occupied by Czechoslovakians. When I entered, men crowded around, tried to lift me to their shoulders. They were too weak. Many of them could not get out of bed. I was told that this building had once stabled eighty horses. There were twelve hundred men in it, five to a bunk. The stink was beyond all description.

When I reached the center of the barracks, a man came up and said, "You remember me. I'm Peter Zenkl, one-time mayor of Prague." I remembered him, but did not recognize him.

As I walked down to the end of the barracks, there was applause from the men too weak to get out of bed. It sounded like the hand clapping of babies; they were so weak. The doctor's name was Paul Heller. He had been there since 1938.

As we walked out into the courtyard, a man fell dead. Two others—they must have been over sixty—were crawling toward the latrine. I saw it but will not describe it.

In another part of the camp they showed me the children, hundreds of them. Some were only six. One rolled up his sleeve, showed me his number. It was tattooed on his arm. D-6030, it was. The others showed me their numbers; they will carry them till they die.

An elderly man standing beside me said, "The children, enemies of the state." I could see their ribs through their thin shirts. The old man said, "I am Professor Charles Richer of the Sorbonne." The children clung to my hands and stared. We crossed to the courtyard. Men kept coming up to speak to me and touch me, professors from Poland, doctors from Vienna, men from all Europe. Men from the countries that made America.

We went to the hospital; it was full. The doctor told me that two hundred had died the day before... Dr. Heller pulled back the blankets from a man's feet to show me how swollen they were. The man was dead. Most of the patients could not move....

I asked to see the kitchen; it was clean. The German in charge had been a Communist, had been at Buchenwald for nine years, had a picture of his daughter in Hamburg. He hadn't seen her for almost twelve years, and if I got to Hamburg, would I look her up? He showed me the daily ration—one piece of brown bread about as thick as your thumb, on top of it a piece of margarine as big as three sticks of chewing gum. That, and a little stew, was what they received every twenty-four hours....

Dr. Heller, the Czech, asked if I would care to see the crematorium. He said it wouldn't be very interesting because the Germans had run out of coke some days ago and had taken to dumping the bodies into a great hole nearby. Professor Richer said perhaps I would care to see the small courtyard. I said yes . . . The wall was about eight feet high; it adjoined what had been a stable or garage. We entered. It was floored with concrete. There were two rows of bodies stacked up like cordwood. They were thin and very white. Some of the bodies were terribly bruised, though there seemed to be little flesh to bruise . . . I tried to count them as best I could and arrived at the conclusion that all that was mortal of more than five hundred men and boys lay there in two neat piles.

There was a German trailer which must have contained another fifty, but it wasn't possible to count them . . . It appeared that most of the men and boys had died of starvation . . . But the manner of death seemed unimportant. Murder had been done at Buchenwald. God alone knows how many men and boys have died there during the last twelve years. . . .

As I left that camp, a Frenchman who used to work for Havas in Paris came up to me and said, "You will write something about this, perhaps?" And he added, "To write about this you must have been here at least two years, and after that—you don't want to write any more."

I pray you to believe what I have said about Buchenwald; I have reported what I saw and heard, but only part of it. For most of it I have no words. . . .

Edward Bliss, Jr., ed., *In Search of Light: The Broadcasts of Edward R. Murrow 1938–1961*, Knopf, New York, 1967.

As a result, most radio programming was simply left to the discretion and the imagination of the local station manager.

Cost became the overriding factor among the owners and operators compelled to face the television challenge. In an attempt to present large blocks of programming cheaply, radio management began to turn to a natural ally in sound, the recording industry. Relations between the two media had not always been good. Executives of the recording industry would not even permit some phonograph records to be played over the air, since they believed that playing a record on the radio would hurt its sales. Similarly, singing stars like Bing Crosby had expressed the fear that the playing of their recordings would reduce the audience for their weekly radio shows. However, by the early 1950s radio stars were moving into television, and it had been shown that radio could provide the exposure that a recording needed to become a top selling hit.

MEDIA PROBE

Identify the location of every radio in your home. Record the time of day each radio is in use, the nature of the stations listened to, and the duration of each listening experience. Which radios are used most often? Which radios are seldom used? Compare your family's use of radio with that of other members in your class.

MEDIA PROBE

Assume that you are a station owner whose primary source of programming for your small operation has been network shows. To date, your prime activity has been selling advertising time for the programs supplied to you. Then one morning you arrive at your office to find that all such programming has been or soon will be canceled. How would you fill the programming gap? What criteria would you use to help you assess your programming options?

Since most radio stations, at one time or another, have based their formats or programming strategies on the talents of an omnipresent disc jockey and recorded music, it is important for us to explore the record industry.

THE RECORDING INDUSTRY

Radio serves as a prime outlet for and promoter of recordings. In fact, since music is a critical element in much of today's radio programming, some would say that a significant portion of radio is simply an extension of the record industry.

The Industry Develops

The sound recording of music was predated by printed sheet music, which was popular in homes in the eighteenth and nineteenth centuries. Does anyone in your home play the piano or the harpsichord in the parlor while family members "sing along" to the latest hits? Prior to 1877 this was a popular pastime, as people created their own home stereo systems composed of live "performances" by family and friends. This particular version of home entertainment experienced a reduction in popularity soon after December 1877, when Thomas Edison sang "Mary Had a Little Lamb" into a hand-cranked mechanism which included a cylinder wrapped in tinfoil. By 1890, Edison's phonograph and two competing devices, the gramophone and the praphophone, were on the market. In addition, by 1899, the *nickelodeon,* a coin-operated phonograph, was a popular attraction found in American penny arcades and amusement parks. The nickelodeon spurred the demand for the home phonograph in much the same way that the computer games in today's video arcades have helped create a demand for home video game systems.

While the turn of the century found the Columbia Phonograph Company pitted against Edison's North American Phonograph Company, Emile Berliner's U.S. Gramophone Company developed the flat disk that became the standard for records. Eventually, Berliner also formed the Victor Talking Machine Company, which took as its trademark the picture of a dog looking into the horn of a phonograph and the caption, "His Master's Voice." This new company was also the developer of the hand-cranked victrola.

World War I was a boom time for records. While 27 million records were manufactured in 1914, over 100 million were manufactured in 1919. However, the 1920s were dominated by radio, and during this period records fell on hard times. By 1929 the Victor Talking Machine Company had merged with the Radio Corporation of America to form RCA Victor. CBS's purchase of Columbia Records in 1938 symbolized the start of their lasting interest in the recording industry.

The depression years were a difficult period for the industry. Many people simply did not have money to spend on records. Edison's company went out of business, as did a number of other labels. Sales dropped from 46 million in 1930 to under six million just three years later. The nickel is credited with saving the industry; this time, however, instead of being used to feed nickelodeons, it was used to feed juke boxes that had been installed in restaurants and drug stores; this helped rekindle the demand for sound recordings. During World War II the growth of the recording industry was again slowed; shellac, then an essential ingredient in the manufacture of records, was declared vital to national defense, and supplies available to record manufacturers dropped significantly. During this difficult period record companies began sending free records to radio stations in exchange for free air play. The experiments demonstrated that radio could indeed sell records. This cooperative approach became the philosophy which, in effect, saved both industries as the war come to a close and audiences found themselves distracted by and fascinated with their new toy—television.

Prior to World War II, recordings had been made in "real time"; that is, an artist sang a song which was recorded directly onto a master disc. This disc was then used to "cut," or press, the records that would be sold in record shops. The process was plagued by an inability to correct errors, fine-tune volume, or eliminate annoying background noises. After the war an American army officer discovered a magnetic tape recorder in a German radio station. He displayed it at recording industry conferences in this country. Soon the recorder was being duplicated by the Ampex Corporation, and the 3M Company started manufacturing magnetic recording tape in 1947.

The use of magnetic tape recorders meant that audio could now be placed on several tracks and engineered or adjusted for appropriate levels. Artistic mistakes would be corrected, segments from different recording sessions could be edited together. Records would no longer have to be made in real time.

In 1948, the 78 revolution per minute (rpm) recording speed used for old records was replaced by RCA Victor's 45 rpm and Columbia's 33⅓ rpm speeds. For the next few years, the record-buying public was faced with a dilemma regarding what size record to purchase, hence the label "battle of the speeds." In 1950, RCA also began issuing 33⅓ records. But Columbia's victory was not total. The 45 would, in time, dominate the single pop-recording disc market. The 33⅓ would dominate album sales. In time, the 78 became obsolete. Starting in 1954, high-fidelity record players were sold. Stereophonic sound systems became available in the late 1950s.

Today's record industry keeps economic and demographic realities in mind as it goes about its business. The year 1978 was a huge one for the recording industry, with a record $4.2 billion in sales. By 1982, however, sales had slumped to $3.6 billion. Even though cassette sales have climbed consistently since 1976, the Record Industry Association of America reports that they have not offset the losses they experienced when sales plummeted from 212 million in 1979 to 137 million in 1982. Album sales have dropped as well. During this sluggish sales period, a number of small companies were forced to go out of business and larger firms were compelled to tighten their belts.

A constant thorn in the industry's side has been piracy. In 1983 eight large companies, including RCA, MCA, Capitol, and Atlantic, filed suit against 130 record distributors charging them with bootlegging records in North Carolina. They sued under the Sound Recording Act of 1972, which brought music counterfeiters under federal jurisdiction. The industry claims that at least 10 percent of all records and tapes sold in this country are pirated. Piracy today is made possible by the rapid development of recording devices which can produce high-quality copies.

Video games and home taping of music have also been blamed for the record industry's sales slump. However, while this industry was able to do little about the games except to wait for the initial craze to wear thin, it was able to take some practical steps against home taping. For example, have you ever wondered why disc jockeys talk into the instrumental opening of your favorite song? One reason is that they are encouraged to do so by the record companies, who use this ploy to diminish the likelihood that you will tape off the air rather than purchase records.

Another competitive strategy surfaced in 1982, the year *Music Television (MTV)* became widely available. By turning one cable channel into a video version of the top 40, the recording industry had succeeded in promoting their products through two media, television and radio, at the same time. *Time* magazine described the arrangement: "MTV and the record companies have developed a relationship that suits all of them just fine. In exchange for free air time, the companies provide eye-catching video tapes of artists performing their latest songs."[5] These promotional pieces, reminiscent of work pioneered by the Beatles, can cost $30,000 and up to produce. Despite the cost, MTV has become a staple for pop music promotion and three-minute video versions of songs are now shown repeatedly on cable television. The film *Flashdance*, which capitalized on the strategies popularized on MTV, was the first film to incorporate these video techniques.

According to Mark Kirkeby, a music critic, MTV serves a number of functions:

> The rise of promotional video has coincided with—and in part resulted from—the decline of the single. You remember the single, a seven-inch 45 r.p.m. record with a big hole in the middle and one song on each side? Ah, nostalgia. Most people have stopped buying singles (they are no longer a real profit center for any but the tiniest record companies), and most stations are less concerned with "breaking" records than with personalities, contests and image. Radio has also largely abandoned the prime record buyers of the 12-to-24 year old audience in favor of older, more affluent adults who presumably have little interest in the search for new talent. For record promotion people who still have jobs, that Tuesday afternoon appointment (with a radio station programmer) is more often a token hello than a real chance to get records added to a playlist. What's an attention-starved record label to do?
>
> Enter video. One-song promotional videotapes or films are far from new: the Beatles were making them 15 years ago, and such programs as Midnight Special and Don Kirshner's Rock Concert have been relying on videos since the middle of the seventies. But for years most of the artists featured were well known stars. The success of these videos . . . combined with the need to find some new way to promote rock artists, has led the major record companies to produce promotional videos on a much broader scale.[6]

The Australian group Men at Work hit the record charts after they were seen jumping kangaroo-style across an open beach on an MTV promotional piece. The use of MTV has also

MEDIA PROBE

Why do you think it is important for new groups to get exposure? To what extent is the search for new talent part of the strategy to deliver audiences to advertisers? What, if any, are the advantages of having new groups debut on MTV in contrast to radio? What do you see as radio's role in the promotion of new talent? To what extent, if any, does the constant emergence of new talent and change in musical taste contribute to communication problems for people of different age groups? What, if anything, should we or can we do about it?

forced radio stations to begin opening up their play lists to lesser-known groups. Once again, radio is being forced to compete with and adapt to television.

Record companies keep their eyes on record buyers. According to a study released in 1983 by the Record Industry Association of America, "There are growing indications that the age profile is changing." In other words, America is growing older. Sales to people 15 to 19 have fallen, while sales to people 20 to 35 have increased. Men are now purchasing a higher percentage of records than in the past—57 percent of all records bought in 1981 were purchased by men. This demographic information has also caused some radio stations to alter their "sound" by adjusting the recordings they play accordingly.

Recording Techniques

Making a sound recording no longer means setting up a microphone and singing a song onto a tape or a record. Recording today has become a contemporary art of self-expression. In recording studios, feelings and emotions are merged with technology; they become one. When working with musicians and producers, the recording engineer uses recording tape as his or her canvas, and music, microphones, mixers, limiters, equalizers, sound generators, and other technological tools as paint brushes.

In "high-tech" recording the producer, who controls the mixing process, can make or break a record's sales. (Randy Matusow)

There are at least four phases to the recording process: the recording session, mixing, mastering, and stamping. First, let's briefly examine the recording session. Professional sound studios today can handle four to forty-eight tracks of tape. That is, each microphone records sound onto a separate track or line on the tape, providing the ultimate flexibility when the sound is later combined or mixed. Thus, if someone in the studio makes an error, the engineer is able to replace just that track without affecting the remainder of the work that has been recorded. Musicians who appear on the same record may not even record in the studio at the same time, or if they are recording together, they may be separated by soundproof barriers in order to keep their recording track clean of music from other instruments or voices. Musicians wear headphones to hear what has been recorded before. Many wear one phone on and one off so that they are able to hear themselves as well as the sounds of others. This system provides for unique possibilities. For example, Stevie Wonder is known to have played all of the instruments for a number of his recordings.

Mixing is the second step in the process. In order to approach the mixing process with a "clean ear," those involved in the production of a record will often get away from the project for a few days after the taping sessions have been completed. Mixing involves combining the various tracks down to two. This can be done by either operating the mixing equipment manually or utilizing a computer to speed the process. During mixing, each track is equalized, echo or special effects are inserted, and decisions are made regarding where to place each track in the stereo spectrum.

Once the mix is completed, the next step is for the record to be *mastered* from tape to disc. Producers find it helpful to attend the masterings because it gives them the chance to listen for possible defects like skipping, sticking in the grooves, surface noises, or other problems.

After problems have been eliminated, the record is ready to be *stamped*. It is at this point that the actual phonograph record is molded. Then the discs are labeled, boxed, and shipped to various record distributors.

High technology has changed and is continuing to change the record-making process. Presently, digital equipment is able to record sound onto each track of a tape in a form that the computer can "read" and play back.

Newsweek describes this breakthrough: "During the recording process, the sound is 'sampled' at a very high rate of speed, 44,100 times a second, and converted into a digital code. The binary bits of information—a series of ones and zeros—are recorded on a master disc by a high-powered recording laser that inscribes billions of microscopic pits in a dense 2½ mile-long spiral pattern on the disc's surface."[7] Digital techniques help reduce, if not eliminate, quality loss during the mixing process—a problem commonly experienced when traditional mixing methods are used.

The year 1983 marked the introduction of digital techniques into the home sound system. Known as CDs, or *compact discs,* these recordings are played by a laser instead of a stylus (see Figure 6-1). The compact or digital system eliminates pops, ticks, and surface noise. Since nothing touches the record, there is virtually no record wear. According to home audio expert Mike Wilburt, "The difference between stereo and digital sound is like the difference between black-and-white TV and color TV." As compact disc recordings grow in popularity, the industry will have made its first real technological advance since stereo was introduced in the 1950s.

How the Business Operates

Today's recordings are manufactured and marketed by major corporations, like RCA, MCA, Columbia, or Warner Brothers; large independents like Motown; or one of hundreds of small specialty houses. In all cases certain functions including locating talent, making the recording, promoting the product, and distributing the product must be performed. In addition, accurate records must be kept. The typical recording company's organization scheme may look something like the one shown in Figure 6-2.

The Artist and Repertoire Department

The A&R department is responsible for de-

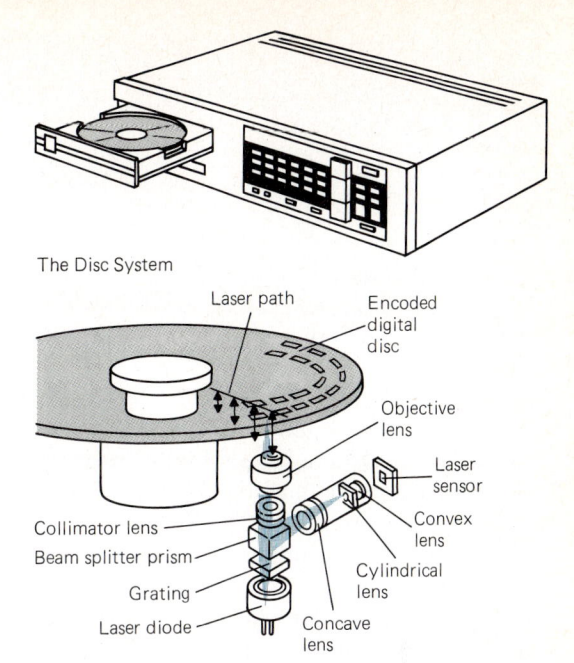

FIGURE 6-1 The compact disc player. A laser beam focuses on a spinning disc and transforms the reflections into a digital code that emerges as sound. (*Phillips Industries and Polygram Records.*)

veloping the product. Just as a book company's acquisitions editor is responsible for locating authors and developing books, so the A&R function is carried out by producers whose task it is to locate artists and oversee the preparation of the recording. Clive Davis, formerly of CBS Records and now president of Arista, describes this function:

> A record executive's job . . . is to spot emerging artists, nurture them (the right manager, booking agency, producer) and then launch, merchandise and showcase them. He must know the ingredients of musical excitement and be able to feel the potential for commercial success. It is dangerous to be too progressive or too far ahead of your time—but it is far more disastrous to lag behind it. The difference can be as subtle as defining what is coming . . . and what is arriving. Errors in judgment can cost millions.[8]

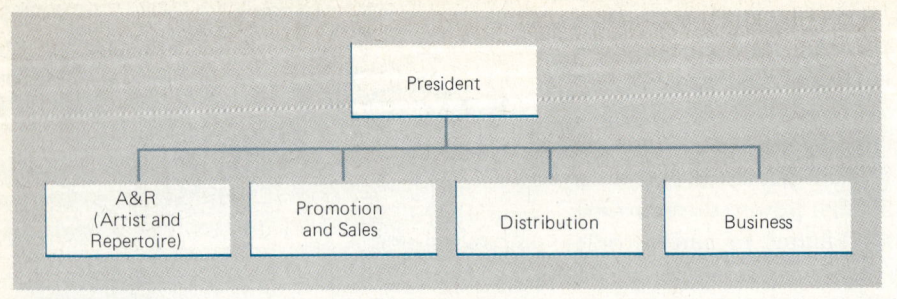

FIGURE 6-2 Organization chart of a typical recording company.

Some A&R people are musicians with creative abilities. Others have sales and management backgrounds but are able to do A&R work as well. In addition to producers, the A&R department employs people who listen to the hundreds of unsolicited demo tapes that individuals and groups constantly submit for consideration.

The Promotion Department Advertising and publicity are handled by the promotion or sales department. The promotion director's job is to help create an image for the artist or the group and to see that this image is firmly implanted in the mind of the record-buying public. Promotional devices include large displays for record stores and personal appearances by the artist. In addition, sample records may be given away to stores as well as to various radio stations, and buttons, banners, and posters may be distributed to radio station programmers as well. Company representatives also visit the programmers and DJs regularly in order to keep them apprised of the upcoming releases that will be available to them. One additional function of the promotion department is to generate publicity for clients; one aspect of this task is to keep the press informed of the impending arrival of a particular star or group. For example, the simple release of the day, time, and place where the Puerto Rican group Menudo was to arrive in midtown Manhattan produced enough young teenage girls to snarl afternoon traffic. The event was carried by all three network affiliates and made the front-page headlines in two of the three major dailies. A promotion department had done its job well.

The Distribution Department The distribution system of the record industry is composed of record stores, one-stops, independent distributors, and rack jobbers. The record store manager or owner may purchase recordings from individual manufacturers. This, however, requires that the owner or the manager work with a lot of different record companies and it is time-consuming. In addition, the owner does not want to wait weeks for the shipment of an album that a consumer wants now. If asked to wait, the purchaser will probably simply locate another local outlet that stocks the item she or he desires. For this reason, the industry has instituted one-stops, distributors who stock inventory from all record companies, especially the major labels. Purchasing from one-stops saves the store manager time and bookkeeping hassles. A third kind of record distributor is the independent distributor. This type of wholesaler stocks and, to some degree, promotes the records of smaller specialty labels, together with the records of some of the larger independent companies as well. The fourth type of promoter, the rack jobbers, supply records to supermarkets, variety stores, department stores, drug stores, and other outlets. With a 100 percent return policy, the rack jobber finds it easy to keep the retailer's racks filled with current recordings. By actually selecting the records to be displayed, the rack jobber also frees the manager from having to become involved in choosing records from the hundreds that are released every month. Jobbers account for 70 percent of all records sold. *Billboard* bases its surveys on information obtained from the above groups as well as on data derived from radio stations; in this way the weekly top 40, country and western, and other charts are formulated. Additional distribution is accomplished through record clubs such as RCA Record Club, and CBS's Columbia House. Direct advertising on television accounts for additional sales, as does direct-mail advertising.

Popular Music: The Lifeblood of the Medium

When TV came on the scene, radio stations began searching for ways to replace the fast-disappearing programming provided by the networks. Some turned to the popular music of the time—the Big Band sounds represented by band leaders Tommy Dorsey, Les Brown, and Mitch Miller and popular singers like Frank Sinatra, Peggy Lee, and Dinah Shore. As competition with television increased and continued into the mid-1950s, new bait was needed to attract young audiences to radio. In 1954 that bait burst upon the scene in the form of rock and roll.

Rock music conflicted with traditional middle-class standards of taste; since it was associated with antisocial values, rock and roll and the dances that accompanied its so-called strident sounds were banned in many cities coast to coast. The embodiment of youthful rebellion, rock's lyrics were condemned by some for offering a vicarious sexual experience, promoting juvenile delinquency, and appealing to unsavory people. For example, on July 23, 1956, *Time* magazine reported: "In San Antonio, rock 'n' roll was banned from city swimming pool jukeboxes because, said the city council, its primitive beat attracted undesirable elements given to practicing their spastic gyrations in abbreviated bathing suits." And in its February 16, 1958, issue, *Music Journal* noted: "Aside from the illiteracy of this vicious music, it has proved itself definitely a menace to youthful morals, and an incitement to juvenile delinquency." A number of observers felt rock and roll would lead to the downfall of civilization, while others counseled moderation, noting that its music provided listeners with a means of emotional release—a way to let loose.

Music and dance styles set the pace for the MTV generation just as they did for the rock 'n rollers of the 1950s. (A.P./Wide World)

MEDIA PROBE

If you were a parent during the mid-1950s, do you think you would have advocated that rock and roll be banned? Why or why not? Are there any songs or videos you think should be banned from the air today? If so, what are they? If not, why not?

RADIO AND RECORDINGS: THE WINDOW HAS EARS   169

In any case, rock provided the youth culture with a means to distinguish itself from the establishment. In some ways, rock came to symbolize a sense of rebellion, in others it came to symbolize a growing sense of community. The roots of this phenomenon were many and varied and included black rhythm and blues, country and western, and jazz as well as popular music. Rock's past is almost as interesting as its effects.

Its roots go back to African music, which was preserved in Southern Afro-American churches, where whole congregations would join in singing the fast-paced emotional songs. After World War II, rhythm and blues was popularized by Clyde McPhatter and others. Bo Diddley specialized in a bump and grind, and Little Richard used wild gyrations as well.

Like blues, country and western music also occupies a place in the heritage of rock. In 1925, station WSM in Nashville began broadcasting the *WSM Barndance*. Later dubbed the *Grand Ole Opry*, it soon became a symbol of success for country musicians.

Add some jazz and popular music to this mixture and it simply was a matter of time until someone combined the forms into a style that would interest the mainstream of American radio listeners. A country and western group, Bill Haley and the Comets, was the first group to bring it together for the general public. Haley, however, merely exposed the public to the new form. It was left to others to exploit its possibilities.

In 1954, Elvis Presley ventured into a small recording studio in Memphis and cut two songs. Sam Phillips, the studio's owner, had driven all over the South looking for new talent and had heard some of the demo cuts that Presley had made earlier for his mother. Phillips, believing that the rhythm and blues and country styles could be successfully combined perceived Elvis to be his answer. The records "Don't Be Cruel," "Heartbreak Hotel," "Love Me Tender," "Jailhouse Rock," "Hound Dog" and others followed. Elvis had studied James Dean in *Rebel without a Cause;* he had also watched Bo Didley bump and grind at the Apollo Theatre in Harlem. In time he would incorporate what he had seen into his own act. When Elvis appeared on *The Ed Sullivan Show* on September 9, 1956, he changed the course of popular music. His slick-down hair and unusual dress appealed to the young people of the day. Though televised only from the waist up in an attempt to nullify any fears of impropriety, his magnetism came across. Over the years Americans watched him go into the army, make a number of films, and die under questionable circumstances—overweight and into drugs.

Buddy Holly followed in the path that Elvis had blazed. Holly, however, is often looked to as the actual innovator of rock and roll. But it was Elvis's success that gave Holly the opportunity to explore the medium. With such songs as "Peggy Sue," and "That'll Be the Day," Holly developed into a true performer-producer, controlling the writing, recording, and production aspects of his work. Between 1957 and 1958 he had seven hits, all recorded in a studio in Clovis, New Mexico. Before his death at the age of 22, he had been the first to put his guitar and voice on separate recording tracks, the first to use strings in a rock and roll record, and the first white star to write his own material. When he died, it was much like Don McLean said—"the day the music died."

Jerry Lee Lewis, Chuck Berry, the Big Bopper, and a host of others filled the top 40 charts through the 1950s. Also during this period, "cover" records were popular. That is, black songs would be re-recorded by white singers. For example, the song "Work with Me Annie," containing overtly sexual lyrics like "Annie please don't cheat . . . gimme all my meat," was eventually recorded by Georgia Gibbs as "Dance With Me Henry." This version contained more palatable lyrics and was much more in tune with the tastes of the white, middle-class, record-buying public.

By the early 1960s, Elvis was in the army,

MEDIA VIEW

If you open a new radio station or, for that matter, any establishment where music will be played, you probably will receive a booklet in the mail: *ASCAP Music and the Law*. The booklet reads, "Since you are furnishing music for your patrons and may not know about the *American Society of Composers, Authors and Publishers (ASCAP)* we would like to tell you about ASCAP and how we can serve you." ASCAP was founded in 1914 by Victor Herbert to combat the lack of compliance with the 1906 copyright laws. Today's organization now has over 30,000 members.

Why should a station pay ASCAP 2 percent of its gross income? One answer is that joining ASCAP is cheaper and easier than trying to contact each publisher and song writer in order to obtain permission to play each piece of music you want to. The copyright law specifies that music cannot be publicly performed without permission of the copyright owner. Thus the need for ASCAP and its sister organization *Broadcast Music Incorporated (BMI)*. BMI was formed by the broadcasting industry in 1940 as an alternative to ASCAP. BMI has slightly fewer members and charges stations only 1 percent of their gross earnings. Together, these two nonprofit music licensing organizations account for about 98 percent of the songs performed today and provide a practical and economical music licensing service.

ASCAP and BMI survey music played in the following forums: on AM and FM radio, on television, in films, on cable broadcasts, on Muzak, and during concerts and band recitals. They then distribute royalties collected to members on the basis of the number of times a piece of music has been played or aired. Not all organizations pay up willingly, however, and to protect the rights of its members, the ASCAP quarterly magazine identifies those companies and institutions against whom ASCAP has instituted law suits because of their refusal to obey the copyright laws.

Buddy Holly was dead, and Jerry Lee Lewis had married a 14-year-old relative and was not being heard on the air. Rock music, now big business, became increasingly, but predictably, commercial. Ricky Nelson, Paul Anka, and Connie Francis were popular singers working with acceptable but not original material. With the exception of the Motown label, which featured artists like The Supremes and Stevie Wonder, rock was said to have gone stale. The time was ripe for a change. That change reached our shores in 1964—just one decade after Elvis had recorded in that small Memphis studio.

The Beatles Arrive John Lennon, Ringo Starr, Paul McCartney, and George Harrison were all born in the early 1940s. By 1963 they had formed The Beatles, and Beatlemania was sweeping England. By April of 1965 their songs held the first five slots on *Billboard's* top 40 chart. The work of the Beatles had an impact on musicians and the general public alike. Singer Bob Dylan recalls:

> We were driving through Colorado [and] we had the radio on and eight of the Top Ten songs were Beatles songs.... "I Want to Hold Your Hand," all those early ones.
>
> They were doing things nobody was doing. There chords were outrageous, just outrageous, and their harmonies made it all valid.... I knew they were pointing the direction where music had to go.
>
> It seemed to me a definite line was being drawn. This was something that never happened before.

Like Elvis a decade earlier, the Beatles appeared on *The Ed Sullivan Show;* as 73 million

RADIO AND RECORDINGS: THE WINDOW HAS EARS   171

MEDIA VIEW

COVERING UP THE ORIGINAL

In every case the "original" sounded much better than the copies I heard over the radio. I felt outraged and cheated by a system which had kept these hidden from me. The piano introduction to Joe Turner's "Shake, Rattle and Roll" was the perfect setup for Joe's opening shouted command: "Get out of that bed and wash your face and hands." Get out of that bed? Bill Haley had never sung that line. A world opened up in which recorded songs were representations of everyday scenes in an adult life, not teenage bubblegum fantasies.

Charlie Gillett, *Making Tracks: Atlantic Records and the Growth of a Multi-Billion-Dollar Industry*, Dutton, New York, 1974, pp. 2–3.

---

people watched, they captured the youth of this country. Greil Marcus, now an editor for *Rolling Stone*, described the reaction he observed in one college dormitory: "Four hundred people sat transfixed as the Beatles sang 'I Want to Hold Your Hand,' and when the song was over the crowd exploded. People looked at the faces (and the hair) of John, Paul, George and Ringo and said Yes . . . they heard the Beatles' sound and said Yes to that too."[9] The Beatles adapted their name from Buddy Holly's group, the Crickets, and in many ways followed the lead he set in developing rock music. The impact of their work was brought sharply into focus in 1980, when John Lennon was murdered in New York City. His death prompted people of all ages to think about the tremendous influence the Beatles had had on popular music, society, and the world. The Rolling Stones and the Animals, who had followed the Beatles to this country from England, brought with them a much rougher, more aggressive style of rock.

During the late 1960s Bob Dylan and a number of other folk singers were also popular. Born Robert Zimmerman in Minnesota, Dylan's most memorable songs included "Mr. Tambourine Man," "Like a Rolling Stone," and "Blowin' in the Wind." Folk musicians, influenced by rock, developed a hybrid folk-rock type of music. Country music, too, began to reach for a wider audience with another rock hybrid, country-oriented rock. During the 1970s, Nashville became a major recording center as Glenn Campbell, John Denver, the Mandrell Sisters, Olivia Newton John, and others were able to move in and out of country and rock seemingly at will. And the country sound had finally been accepted by mass audiences; singers like Kenny Rogers and Dolly Parton were commanding more money per week in Las Vegas than many popular noncountry singers.

The music philosophy of the 1970s can be summed up by the verse from the Mamas and Papas:

> You gotta go where you wanna go
> Do what you wanna do
> With whoever you want to do it with

The popular recording artists of the decade experimented with a wide variety of musical forms and styles. The Who created the rock opera *Tommy*. Taking their cue from the *Sergeant Pepper* album of the Beatles, groups like Blood, Sweat and Tears explored more stylistic combinations. Heavy-metal sound entered the scene; huge amplifiers and electronic equipment shared the stage with performers. Gradually, lighting and special effects were emphasized in concerts. But Carly Simon,

MEDIA PROBE

Are there particular Beatles songs that have influenced you and the way you think about life? If so, how? Which groups or singers of "yesterday" or "today" speak to you most clearly? What is there about the group or singers and their music that you are able to identify with?

Joni Mitchell, and Simon and Garfunkel chose to retain a calmer, gentler sound. Reflecting the "do your own thing approach" and sparked by the film *Saturday Night Fever*, people put aside dungarees and dressed up to dance in carefully choreographed patterns to the hard, faceless, "thump thump thump" of disco. Disco's reign ended when punk rock appeared. Punk, however, was short-lived and was soon replaced by New Wave music. Blondie, The B-52's, and Elvis Costello brought the sound of New Wave to millions. It has been said that New Wave acts like an aspirin and alleviates the pain of the individual in society. Do you agree?

Bob Marley was instrumental in bringing Jamaican reggae music to this country. Though the lyrics of reggae may be incomprehensible to Americans, the primeval beat is not. The sound of reggae has been incorporated into the music of Eric Clapton, Paul Simon, and the Rolling Stones.

In the early 1980s, Menudo arrived; designed to appeal to members of the Hispanic community, and carefully packaged, Menudo's music highlights the talents of boys fifteen and under; singers are phased out of the group as their voices change, ensuring that the group will sustain its teenie-bopper appeal.

Rock music began by creating a barrier between many parents and children. Rock today, however, both spans and binds the generations. The current rock market is splintered with different groups recording to meet the likes and needs of different audiences. Don Hibbard and Carol Kaleialoha comment that rock "has become an accepted part of American civilization, as much in tune with daily life as Barbie dolls, Budweisers, Ban Roll-On and Big Macs. Assimilated into the ebb and flow of middle-class society, stripped of its antagonist role, rock has evolved into a respectable, albeit superficial element within the larger matrix that is America."[10] Accounting for 50 to 65 percent of the income derived from record sales, today's rock music permeates jazz, country, soul, and even classical music. Radio, too, has been influenced by its presence; today, rock and its many variations provide much of the material for a number of radio formats.

RESTRUCTURING THE RADIO MEDIUM

Let's backtrack now. Imagine that you are a radio station manager attempting to survive the onslaught of television, what steps would you take? How could you put the recordings you were receiving to use? Certainly you could play them. But one right after another? How would you incorporate commercials? History helped stations managers answer such questions. In the early 1930s, Martin Block of New York's WNEW borrowed an idea which had been used successfully in Los Angeles by Al Jarvis of KFWB. Jarvis was the creator of the *Make Believe Ballroom* concept; he spun records, interspersing them with commercials and talk. By imitating this concept, Block was able to develop an audience of 4 million within just a few months and a waiting list of potential sponsors.

By the 1950s the disc jockey and the music he or she played became the replacement for network radio programs. How can the role of the disc jockey be defined? In practice, DJs are salespeople who spin records between

MEDIA PROBE

It has been argued that rock and roll is simply a medium designed to nullify or keep the masses entertained. By walking around with our radios in hand or clamped to our ears, some say we are being kept "passive" so that we will not think too deeply about issues that we ought to be considering. To what extent do you think this is true, if at all? To what extent do you think rock helps you escape reality? To what extent do you think it helps you confront reality? Explain.

The early disc jockey's sole control over what records were aired led to the "payola" scandals of the 1950s and 1960s. (Jeff Jacobson/Archive Pictures)

commercials. Their function is to entice you to purchase clothes, patronize a local store, eat at a restaurant, send away for free offers, et cetera, et cetera, et cetera. From the point of view of the recording industry, DJs attract listeners, and listeners purchase recordings.

Of course, the disc jockey's job is far from easy. DJs do much more than simply chatter idly. They may also select recordings from a station playlist, manipulate turntables, carts, and audio boards, as well as ready commercial copy or scripts. In addition, these days DJs jobs are far from secure. Each time a station changes its format, it usually also finds it necessary to hire new on-the-air personalities. DJ hours are long; they are filled with repetition and can be tiring. One young disc jockey lost his first job when after several hours on the air he could no longer stand to listen to a certain soft-drink commercial that he was playing consistently. During one of his air checks, or talk sessions between records, he explained to his listening audience that that particular soft drink would eat the paint right off a car. He was fired so swiftly that his replacement went on the air immediately after the next record!

Payola: the Mid-1950s Scandal

Experience showed that the amount of airtime or play a record received was correlated with the amount of income it would earn. During the early 1950s, decisions regarding what records to play were made by disc jockeys. It was common practice for recording-industry representatives to call on local stations and their DJs in order to acquaint them with up-and-coming releases. And with millions of dollars at stake, it appeared to be cost-effective to offer disc jockeys special favors in exchange for airtime.

Some DJs in major markets may have made $50,000 or more a year because of this prac-

MEDIA PROBE

From the stations in your area select three disc jockeys with contrasting air styles. Keep a log of the language they use and the topics they discuss. Then, using your notes and a stack of records, emulate the way each DJ fills an "air check" or break between records.

tice, called *payola*. When payola came to the attention of the public, the resulting outrage precipitated a congressional hearing, which led to Section 508 being added to the Federal Communications Act of 1934.

> . . . any employee of a radio station who accepts or agrees to accept from any person . . . or any person . . . who pays or agrees to pay such employee any money, service, or other valuable consideration for the broadcast of any matter over such station shall, in advance of such broadcast, disclose the fact of such acceptance or agreement to such station. . . .
>
> Any person who violates any provision of this section shall, for each such violation, be fined not more than $10,000, or imprisoned not more than one year, or both.

Although this regulation did curtail the dispensing of payola, or "plugola" as it was alternately called for a time, during the 1970s another scandal surfaced; unfortunately, payola is a phenomena which will probably continue to exist in a variety of forms for years to come.

As a result of the payola scandals, stations took the power of selecting music away from individual disc jockeys and gave it to station managers or program directors. By controlling a playlist, the manager-program director was able to design a unique sound which would be played throughout the day; the disc jockeys would now provide talk and intersperse live commercials. In recent years program directors have begun to rely on consultants and consulting organizations to help them determine the kind of sound their station should be identified with. In effect, the programmer now works to attract a particular segment of the listening marketplace and then airtime is sold to advertisers who believe that their products or services will be of interest to the people in that group. Do such consultants receive favors from recording companies? Kal Rudman, one such consultant whom you may have seen during his frequent appearances on *The Merv Griffin Show*, admits he has. But since Rudman is not a radio station employee, he is not in violation of the Federal Communications Act. He claims, however, that the money he receives does not influence the records he chooses to promote or recommend.

The Formats Emerge

Radio has become an exciting and competitive business as professionals battle for audience share and advertising dollars. As has been noted in the magazine *Channels of Communication:* "Each station now has its own sharply focused brand of entertainment, its own mood and identity, and thus its own segment of the listening audience." The authors of *The Radio Format Conundrum* acknowledge this when they observe "only when a station has a monopoly is it always possible for a station to be all things to all people. Anytime a market has more than one station, each attempts to appeal to listeners of different economic and cultural status."[11] As in any competitive situation, some people win and some people lose. Some people even win the losers; companies exist today whose only business is to sell stations whose owners have lost the game in a particular market.

Much as a football team changes plays and adapts its approach for various opponents, radio stations are constantly adapting their formats in an effort to win ratings and gain an edge over competing stations. In general, today's formats can be categorized as follows: top 40, album-oriented rock, and middle of the road, which spans the distance between rock and highly orchestrated beautiful music, country and western, ethnic, classical, all-news, all-talk, and religious programs.

Top 40   The top 40 format (sometimes also called "contemporary hit radio") is based on

ZIGGY™

"...AND NOW IT'S GOLDEN OLDIES TIME! HERE ARE THE TOP TEN HITS OF LAST MONTH!"

(© 1983 Universal Press Syndicate. Reprinted with permission. All rights reserved.)

the premise that not only do young people like to listen to recorded music, they like to listen to some recordings more often than others. Notes Larry Berger, program director at New York's WPLJ, "I think the success of the Top 40 has a lot to do with consumer confidence. In bad economic times, people seem to be more reflective, to look backward. During the seventies, you could play old music and be very successful. Top 40 is very present tense—what's happening now—and that's what people seem to want when times are good." Thus, in this format the records *Billboard* lists on its top 40 chart are played repeatedly, with some room left for a few new songs to be played as well. Today's top 40 format is fast-paced and youth-oriented, attempting to create a feeling of vibrant, electric motion combined with a sense of urgency. Commercials are lively and punctuated with jingles or fast-talking DJs. Since sales of singles are on the decline, many top 40 stations are also including album cuts that appeal to the younger segment of the market on their playlist.

Album-Oriented Rock The educated young-adult audience is the prime target of the album-oriented rock (AOR) format. On AOR stations, the DJ is more laid-back or restrained than the top 40 DJ, and the more extensive playlist includes new as well as more established artists and groups.

Middle of the Road A middle-of-the-road (MOR) station plays a mixture of rock, soft rock, and popular music. Nothing too abrasive is aired on these stations, but the sound is usually upbeat. MOR formats base much of their appeal on the personalities of their disc jockeys. These DJs often serve as driving companions to commuters who listen to the radio on their way to and from work. The target audience for MOR music is 25 to 48-year-olds.

Beautiful Music The beautiful-music (easy-listening) format consists mainly of highly orchestrated versions of older popular songs, show tunes, and even semiclassical music. Sometimes termed "radio wallpaper," this format is often automated or run by computer and contains few commercial breaks; thus, it holds its audience for extended periods of time. Beautiful music is designed for easy listening and as such is often played in business offices, doctors' waiting rooms, and elevators. Traditionally, it appeals to older adults, although today the programmers are hoping to span the 25- to 54-year-old spectrum of the market. The midday core of listeners for this format is, for the most part, women. In the early 1980s, beautiful-music listenership declined. *Radio Only* magazine described the problem: "Beautiful music is unique. It is mostly programmed by non-local syndicators. There are exceptions, but in this format, the syndicators control the programming. In the past, that has meant they got the credit. Today they get the blame. If the format is to survive, they must also be its salvation."[12] The format has failed to add much new music to its repertoire in nearly a decade. Programmer Dave Verdery told *Billboard:* "As long as I could remember, beautiful music has always been a format of instrumentals with a percentage of vocals by artists such as Tony Bennett, Frank Sinatra, Jack Jones, the Ray Charles Singers. When we went to the new tapes and started looking for suitable vocals, we all woke up and realized, Hey, nobody's recording this stuff anymore."[13] One major syndicator in the field, Bonneville Broadcasting Systems, chose to hire a conductor-arranger and record its own versions of contemporary music. John Patton, its president, says that the test will be to see how "contemporary" beautiful music can become and still be true to its nature. As with any format, the listeners will be the ultimate judge of its success or failure.

Country and Western   The country and western stations of the 1980s sound much like the top 40 stations except that they focus on the top 40 country tunes. They are alive and aggressive. Originating in the South, country and western has spread across the nation and now appeals to a wide audience. Today the format is being subdivided further into Nashville, Blue Grass, and progressive styles.

Ethnic   A format that appeals primarily to one group is generally classified as ethnic. The Black format is a popular ethnic format, although it often attracts many nonblacks as well. The music ranges from rhythm and blues to gospel and jazz. Unfortunately, few black stations are actually owned and operated by blacks. Thus, station policies are set by people outside of the intended audience. Two networks serve black stations: the National Black Network and the Mutual Black Network. Black stations now program public-affairs topics as well as music. The 1983 election of Harold Washington, the first black mayor of Chicago, has been attributed in part to the role played by black radio stations in the area. Kerney Anderson, general manager of black station WBMX, has said, "We are the medium through which the black community finds out what is going on."[14] The city's black stations actively worked to promote a voter registration effort, which proved to be an essential ingredient in Washington's election.

Other minorities are also represented on radio. One popular format is the Hispanic format in which all music and talk is in Spanish. Although the number of Hispanic stations in certain parts of the country is growing, the language barrier seems destined to keep this format's audience limited.

All News   As FM radio has begun to dominate the music market, AM stations have started to turn away from recordings altogether. In place of a musical format they have substituted all-news, an expensive format and one which seems to appeal to older audiences. "Give us twenty minutes and we'll give you the world," is a commonly spouted theme of all-news stations. The format includes hard news, weather, traffic reports, feature stories, sports, and commentary—all within a twenty-minute time period.

All Talk   The all-talk format is dominated by the call-in show pattern. A group of sports experts, psychologists, home-improvement specialists, and others work in revolving shifts to talk to listeners about information pertaining to their fields, information they believe can benefit the listener. An estimated 234 million of us tune in and participate in call-in radio talk shows, revealing without hesitation the financial, sexual, and health problems that plague us. All-talk radio is proliferating on the AM dial, as broadcasters discover that the format attracts a large, dedicated following among 35- to 65-year-olds. The format now commands a healthy 9.32 percent share of the market, according to Arbitron. All

MEDIA PROBE

The Larry King Show debuted with 28 affiliates on the Mutual Broadcasting System, January 30, 1978. Today it serves 272 stations. Questions are King's trade. His show which airs live via satellite from midnight to 5 a.m. each weeknight has become as popular as the guests he interviews. His lineup is studded with politicians, entertainers and authors. King says he doesn't bone up for his interviews because he wants "to be in the same boat" with his audience. King believes that if he has a lead over his audience regarding his guest or the information the guest will reveal then he may miss asking an obvious question.

King's five hour show is divided between a three hour guest interview and a two hour "Open Phone America," where King presides over a national call-in smorgasbord of comment, questions and sports trivia. . . . King enjoys the free-for-all call in segment of his show as much as interviewing guests. While some may think it peculiar to solicit opinions from strangers in the early morning hours, King revels in it.

"Mutual's Larry King," *Broadcasting,* February 7, 1983, p. 103

In order to explore the difficulties inherent in all talk radio, divide into pairs. One of you should play the role of host, the other the role of caller. The caller should select a topic, and it is then up to the host to ask appropriate questions and keep the interview alive and interesting for three to five minutes.

---

signs indicate that it will also be the growth format of the future.

On June 18, 1984, KOA's Alan Berg, a controversial radio call-in host in Denver was shot to death. *New York Times* reporter Peter W. Kaplan notes that his murder, whether or not it was caused by an angry listener, "served to remind talk broadcasters not only of their power, but also of the risk they face in taking on the unseen viewers and listeners."

Religious Syndicated religious formats are becoming popular choices for smaller stations. National Religious Broadcasters is an association that works to promote such broadcasts. It has grown from a few hundred members to thousands. The organization consists of representatives to the Protestant, Catholic, and Jewish faiths. The 600 religious stations use a direct-response method of fund raising. Listeners are urged to send in money to help spread "the word." Programming is normally provided free, with the programmer receiving the funds derived from the direct appeals.

AM versus FM

In December 1933 the United States Patent Office issued a patent on a new form of broadcasting—*FM*—to Edwin Howard Armstrong, a professor of electrical engineering at Columbia University. Armstrong spent the remainder of his life fighting for the development of his invention.

Before Armstrong's time, all commercial radio had been amplitude-modulated, or *AM;* on AM radio the amplitide, or height, of the carrier wave is altered to fit the characteristics of the sound. With Armstrong's invention, it became possible to keep the amplitude of the wave or its power constant while varying the frequency of the carrier wave in order to transmit the changes in sound. In contrast with the AM signal, the frequency-modulated, or FM, signal operates free of unwanted static and noise. It also offers the capability of stereo broadcasting. Yet, despite the better fidelity of FM, for some reason it did not catch on quickly. FM was destined to be the poor cousin of AM radio for years to come.

178 RADIO, TELEVISION, AND FILM: THE ELECTRONIC WINDOW

> **MEDIA PROBE**
>
> Identify at least ten stations on your AM and FM dials. Listen to each and determine the format each one uses. Which of the formats was the easiest to identify? Which were more difficult? How do stations in the same format category vary their sound?

A number of factors kept FM from developing. First, more people had AM receivers than FM receivers, and it was not possible to pick up FM on a standard AM radio. Second, many of the same people who owned AM stations owned FM stations; to facilitate the programming effort, they would broadcast the same show over both frequencies. Third, after World War II, the FCC moved FM from the place it had originally occupied on the broadcast spectrum; this rendered all existing FM radios obsolete.

Despondent over the fate of FM, upset because although FM sound was to be used for TV, RCA had not paid him royalties for the sets it built, and exhausted after years of court battles with RCA and others, Armstrong committed suicide in 1954. After his death, FM continued its slow development. It was not until 1961 that the Kennedy administration FCC began to encourage FM's growth. In 1961, the FCC authorized stereophonic sound transmission for FM. FM grew in popularity as people were able to buy AM-FM radios. And in 1965 another FCC ruling made it mandatory for owners of both AM and FM stations in cities with populations of over 100,000 people to program their stations differently at least 50 percent of the time. This led to programming innovations on FM that attracted listeners. In 1977 this rule was extended; now only 25 percent duplication of services was permitted for stations in cities of over 100,000 people, and only 50 percent duplication was allowed for stations in cities of between 25,000 and 100,000 people. By 1979 more listening hours were being spent with FM than with AM.

With their roles suddenly reversed, AM went on the offensive. In 1980 the FCC approved a Magnavox AM stereo system as the industry standard. In 1982 under the deregulation philsopy of the Reagan administration, the FCC reversed itself and in effect threw the door open to all types of AM stereo systems. The various systems, however, are not compatible. Therefore, the industry is proceeding cautiously. Among those eagerly awaiting the introduction of AM stereo are automobile owners—especially those who use a car to commute to and from work. AM has a longer range than FM, which makes it less subject to distortion and fading over long distances. What is the status of the AM-FM battle in your area today?

NATIONAL PUBLIC RADIO

In Lee De Forest's eyes radio had the potential to educate as well as to entertain the public. While most of today's stations have developed the entertainment function of radio, only a few educational and community-based stations still share De Forest's dream.

Educational radio began as early as 1917, when WHA started broadcasting from the University of Wisconsin. By 1922, seventy-four such stations were on the air. The number decreased through the late 1920s owing to increased competition from commercial broadcasters. Then, as now, the major problem facing noncommercial radio was funding.

Following World War II the FCC reserved twenty FM channels for noncommercial use. As the number of stations increased, a so-called bicycle network was formed, and programming tapes were mailed from station to station under the aegis of the National Association of Educational Broadcasters. Then, in 1969, the *Corporation for Public Broadcasting* (CPB) created *National Public Radio* (NPR).

According to *Newsweek,* NPR was a product of an afterthought: "when the Carnegie Commission first looked at public broadcasting . . . it focused exclusively on television, but because of the persistence of a few radio buffs present at the Congressional hearings, the final version of the Public Broadcasting Act mandated the Corporation for Public Broadcasting to encourage the growth of non-commercial radio as well as TV."[15] In 1970, CPB identified 80 of the 400 noncommercial stations on the air which met the minimal criteria they had established for NPR stations: they each had at least one full-time staff member and were offering forty-eight hours of programming forty-eight weeks per year.

National Public Radio functioned as a program distribution service controlled by member stations. By 1983, 276 stations were NPR affiliates. Each member station pays annual dues, which entitle it to any or all of the programming NPR offers. NPR gradually replaced the bicycle network with a more up-to-date distribution system, and in 1979 it became the first radio network to distribute programs by satellite. Even with such a wide distribution area, and despite the extensive exposure it has received, only 20 percent of Americans are able to recall ever hearing about National Public Radio.[16]

NPR Programming

During the 1970s and early 1980s, NPR produced a variety of programming for member stations. *JazzAlive* was a weekly offering of five concerts; both the New York City Opera and the Los Angeles Philharmonic were given regular airings. In addition, original dramatic material was commissioned, including Arthur Kopit's play *Wings,* which later ran on Broadway. But NPR's real claim to fame was *All Things Considered* and its companion piece, *Morning Edition.* These programs were unique in broadcasting and became important assets for affiliates during their fund-raising campaigns. *All Things Considered* earned a reputation as one of the finest news programs on the air. With a comparatively modest news budget—for instance, just $4.3 million dollars in 1981—*All Things Considered* was able to assemble a small but dedicated staff.

ATC has only one full-time reporter in Chicago and one in London. However, the satellite broadcast system enables local stations to file or transmit stories to the Washington, D.C., headquarters for possible inclusion in the day's broadcasts. NPR news is really a cooperative effort.

The host of *All Things Considered,* Susan Stamberg, joined the staff in 1971 and became the on the air cohost ten months later. Stamberg told *Newsweek,* "we're trying to create a new kind of radio that never existed—smart, sassy, irreverent." In her own book, *Every Night at Five,* she explains the program's philosophy in greater detail: "This was not to be only a news program. We would also pay attention to the arts, humanities, science and everyday life. *All Things Considered* would take its name seriously. Celebrate the human experience is how our first director of programming, Bill Siemering, put it."[17] During the 1983 budget crisis, station managers and the network agreed that *All Things Considered* and *Morning Edition* were the two programs that had to be saved.

Not everyone believes that NPR is doing its job effectively—or that it should be doing it at all, for that matter. Should tax dollars be used to support the public broadcasting of operas, symphonies, and live jazz concerts when only a small percentage of the population is interested in listening to such programs? Is the news programming offered by NPR politically biased? Some people would

MEDIA PROBE

Identify the public radio station that serves your area. Spend some time listening to *All Things Considered* or *Morning Edition.* How do they differ from traditional radio news shows? Do you agree that they are unique? Why or why not?

YOU WERE THERE

A DAY IN THE LIFE OF *ALL THINGS CONSIDERED*

"All right crew. It is now close to ten-thirty. Let's figure out what we've got for today."

Program editor Jim Angle runs the morning meeting. He's the newest member of the staff, new enough to show up at ten wide awake. He'll learn. The rest of us are grunting and gulping coffee.

Everyone is listening to Angle, but no one is looking at him. Our eyes are scanning the newspapers now spread across the conference table. We sift through our papers, searching for ideas, unanswered questions that *All Things Considered* might answer by tonight.

"Did you see what ABC did on El Salvador last night?"

"Yeah. Good film, but they didn't tell you anything."

In this room each morning at ten o'clock the world is compressed onto a long sheet of white paper on the table in front of the producer. This is not the time for philosophical or academic discussion. It is the time for good ideas that will work on the air. We at this table are facilitators. Pragmatists. Dealers in information. Sometimes I long for more dreamers. But dreams rarely drift into this discussion.

Mondays are the worst days in this room, just as they are in many rooms. Monday radio programs are rarely worth listening to. Like cars on the assembly line, news programs get better by Wednesday. Thursday tends to be the best broadcast day of the week. Words flow well; originality spills from typewriters and microphones. Friday's a toss up. Either we get sloppy, or something exciting happens because the momentum has been building all week.

The list is growing. It's definitely Thursday.

"Listen, we've got enough for four programs. We may as well stop."

There are forty-two story ideas on the long sheet of white paper. About twenty of them will get on the air tonight. The rest either drop out (the guest was inarticulate . . . there wasn't a story there after all . . . the tape didn't arrive on time) or get held over because something new and unpredictable will happen in the next few hours that must be reported tonight.

The meeting is over. The room empties. It's eleven-thirty. The next five and a half hours will be spent making tonight's program. At least three-quarters of these pieces on *All Things Considered* are taped and edited before the five o'clock broadcast. Everything the staff does now is aimed at getting the tapes ready for airing.

Three-thirty. Everyone is screaming for decisions. The map (of stories for the evening) must be finished.

Three-forty-five. No one is at a desk. We're in the studio mixing sounds, or in small booths editing tape.

Four o'clock. Most of tonight's tapes are in house and being edited. Director Jo Miglino is typing the rundown, a brief description of every item on tonight's program.

Four-fifteen. Sandy (co-host) and I use the rundowns to write our opening billboards, quick summaries of what listeners will hear.

Four-thirty. We go into the studio to record the billboards. They must fill a precise block of time. Recording usually assures that they do, and that they're flawless.

Four-forty-five. The billboards are taped. We make tea.

Four-fifty. Back in the studio, Sandy and I read and rewrite copy, call for clarifications and fact checks. It's very quiet here, too, and will be until six-thirty. The studio is an oasis of calm. Outside, the corridors are exploding as everyone scrambles to deliver finished tapes to the control room.

Four-fifty-nine. In the control room, Jo cues Lorraine "Ready with tape one. . . . Stand by . . . Hit it!"

Five o'clock. "Good evening, From National Public Radio in Washington, I'm Susan Stamberg." "And I'm Sanford Ungar, with *All Things Considered.*"

From Susan Stamberg, *Every Night at Five,* Pantheon, New York, 1982.

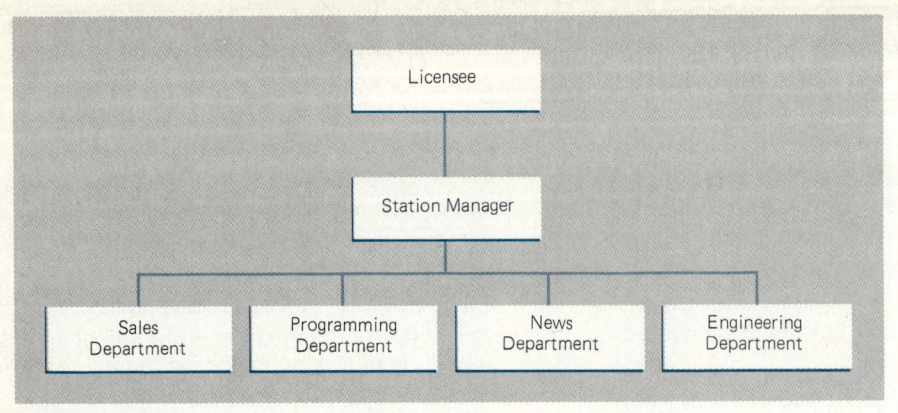

FIGURE 6-3 Organization chart of a typical radio station.

answer no to the first question and yes to the second question. What is your answer?

Unlike television, the educational uses of radio have not been explored. Although some attempts were made by individual stations, and a 1950s NBC radio series even brought literature to the air, no long-term use has ever been established. National Public Radio is attempting to remedy this. In 1981, NPR published its first catalog of audiocassettes. Suitable for classroom use, the materials are organized under topics like the humanities, education, science, and the social sciences. NPR staffers created the thirty- and sixty-minute cassettes by using the vast audio archives of the network. This catalog is now widely distributed to educators.

Despite NPR's financial problems, Brian Brightly, a former director of educational services for the network envisions an exciting future for full-scale audio courses offered both over-the-air and in cassette formats for college students. Thus, National Public Radio hopes to develop the long-neglected educational potential of radio.

STATION OPERATION: WHO DOES WHAT?

Like any other business, radio stations are owned by individuals or corporations. The owner or licensee obtains permission from the FCC to operate a station; the same party may own no more than seven AM and seven FM stations. In addition, no two AM or two FM stations under the same ownership may serve the same community. Hence, it has become common practice for owners to have one AM and one FM station operating in a particular community.

The licensee or owner hires a station manager to supervise the running of the station on a day-to-day basis. The station manager is responsible for overseeing key station functions, including sales, programming, news, and engineering. The departmental structure of a radio station depends on the station's size. Small stations with five or six employees will rely on the same people to fulfill a number of different tasks; in large stations responsibilities will be more dispersed. Most stations are divided into four departments, as shown in Figure 6-3.

Although most listeners probably consider programming to be the prime output of radio, from a management point of view it is the advertising output or sales that is critical. Only by generating advertising revenue can a commercial station compete successfully in the radio marketplace. The sales director is in charge of a sales staff or group of account executives; together they work to sell airtime to sponsors. Each station has a rate card which gives its prices for ten-, thirty- and sixty-second commercials. Rates vary according to the time of day—morning *drive times* are probably more expensive, for example—size of the market, and the amount of time purchased. Thus, ad rates can range from a few dollars to several hundred dollars per minute.

Payment variations also abound. For example, sometimes sale representatives "go off the card" and offer preferred clients more attractive rates. Stations may also barter or trade for services they need. As a case in point, ads for an automobile repair shop might be provided in exchange for repair of company vehicles. Coop advertising is also used; this form of advertising brings together a nationally sold product and a local store.

Generic advertising, another service available to stations—is a concept that appeals to smaller business operations. TM Companies of Dallas, for example, supplies stations with what they call their "master plan," that is, generic advertisements which can be combined with copy targeted to meet the needs of specific clients. For instance, "Better than Ever in Every Way," or "Great Deals in the USA" are slogans that have wide applicability. TM provides station sales representatives with a sample series of such ads to aid them in attracting advertisers. With this ammunition the station is able to help the local advertiser create an impressive, professional-sounding advertisement.

The programming department is composed of the program director and a staff of announcers and disc jockeys. The director is the person responsible for the station's "sound" as well as the station's standing in

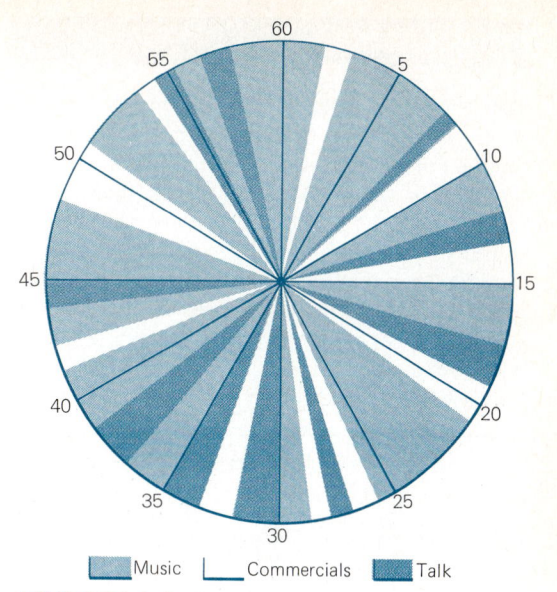

FIGURE 6-4 Program clock. The clock shows programming for one hour during early drive time for a top 40 format station.

MEDIA PROBE

Work with a partner to create 3 one-line jingles or slogans such as "The Best Service in Town," or "Super Savings This Week." Then identify local concerns or businesses which could use your generic jingles and create an ad for each.

the market. The process of programming a radio show is complicated. Programmers must work with a programming clock in mind; they have a limited amount of time within which to incorporate a number of different programming elements, including music (if that is the station's dominant format), talk, news, station IDs, weather, and commercials. A top 40 format **program clock hour** during early drive time might look something like Figure 6-4.

The sound of the station depends on the emphasis given to the various elements from which the program director has to choose. Simply varying the amount of time devoted to a particular type of music can affect the station's sound. Thus programmers must alter or fine-tune their station's clock so as to attract the maximum number of people in the listening audience.

Satellite distribution and computerized programming have helped to make automated and syndicated formats popular among radio stations—especially FM stations. When such a system is in place, the

MEDIA PROBE

Listen to a local station for a sixty-minute period. While you listen to it attempt to produce a sixty-minute time clock that reflects the programming elements in operation during that segment. How effective was the programmer in creating a sound you enjoyed listening to? How would you change the clock if given the chance? Design a clock that reflects the programming decisions you would make. Remember, the station is a commercial one and must sell sufficient advertising time to stay in business.

---

functions traditionally performed by a programmer are now performed by a consultant or consulting firm. Drake Chenault in California, Burkhart, Abrams, Michaels, Douglas and Associates in Atlanta, Bonneville Broadcasting in New Jersey, and United Stations in New York are leading programming consulting groups; they pretape programs that will be syndicated to stations that avail themselves of the service. United Stations, for example, releases three programs weekly: *The Great Sounds,* which features hits of the 1930s to the 1960s; *The Weekly Country Music Countdown,* which spotlights the top 40 country list and also integrates interviews with singers and the stories behind the songs; and *Rock, Roll and Remember,* a show hosted by Dick Clark that is an effective blend of nostalgia, history, and interviews. Each of the syndicated programs is carefully timed and has space left to incorporate six 60-second commercial positions in each hour to be sold by the stations. In addition, United Stations also sells six network positions and includes these in the tape the station receives. Under the arrangement worked out with stations, United Stations retains all national advertising revenues and supplies the programs to stations free of charge.

While some stations intermix automation with live programming, other stations are fully automated and use programming provided by consulting groups that require no station input. Automated systems use a computer and several tape players to replace the live DJ. Among the fully automatic formats available to stations are these offered by the Tanner Company: *Red Satin Rock, Tanner Country, Pacific Green* (beautiful music), and *Bright Blue* (middle of the road).

The news department of the radio station is composed of anchorpeople, DJs, copywriters, editors, and reporters. Radio news efforts range from a "rip and read" approach, in which the DJ simply takes the information from the Associated Press or United Press International wires and reads it, to the complete and intensive all-news approach, in which news is broadcast twenty-four hours each day. All-news operations require an extensive staffing and equipment commitment and are thus quite expensive to run. Since many stations simply cannot afford to maintain the large news staffs required of sophisticated news operations, they simply choose to use either network news feeds, such as those provided by Mutual, RKO, AP, ABC, CBS, and NBC, or they rewrite the wire service report for national and regional news and rely on their own people to provide local news only.

The members of the engineering department are responsible for keeping the station on the air and for maintaining the station's equipment. The engineer of a large station will also operate the turntables and tape equipment during broadcasts, while in small stations, this function is performed by the disc jockey.

PLAYING TO WIN: RADIO AND RATINGS

Is anyone out there listening? Who? How many? Where do they live? How old are they? Can we prove it? How do you spell "success" in radio? The answer: R-A-T-I-N-G-S! Stations and advertisers need to be able to answer questions like those we posed above. If the programs a station offers do not attract sufficient numbers of listeners who belong to the advertiser's target groups, there is little reason for the advertiser to purchase time on that station. Consequently, radio stations—like television stations—subscribe to ratings services.

The major company servicing the radio industry is Arbitron (ARB), a subsidiary of the Control Data Corporation. Arbitron's job is to measure the audiences of radio stations and report how well each commercial station is doing in its quest for ratings. In order to do this, Arbitron has divided the nation into approximately 175 nonoverlapping geographic areas or markets. Participating households are selected at random from a listing of all telephone numbers in the market, and once they agree to become part of the Arbitron sample, persons age 12 and over in each of the selected households are given diaries and asked to record their radio listening experiences for a week, beginning Thursday and ending Wednesday (see Figure 6-5). The diaries participants receive are compact and have been designed to go where the listeners go; in this way, Arbitron is able to measure radio listening both in the home and out of the home regardless of whether the listeners themselves turned on the radio or were merely present at a location where a radio was playing. When completing their diaries participants are instructed to indicate the time they spent listening to the radio as well as the station listened to. Space is left at the back of the diary for demographic data, including age, sex, ethnic background, and employment information. Arbitron samples approximately 3000 to 4000 people in each of their markets. About 50 percent of the diaries Arbitron distributes are returned.

Once tabulated, the results of the returned diaries will provide the station manager with specific information about the station's average quarter-hour estimates including (1) *average persons;* (2) *average-persons ratings;* and (3) *share of audience. Average persons* tells you the estimated number of persons listening to a station at least five minutes during any quarter hour in a time period. The *average-persons rating* is the ratio of the number of people listening to a particular station to the number of people in the entire market. *Share of audience* is the ratio of listeners to a particular station to the total radio listening audience at the time of the sample. Arbitron measures all its markets once a year and large markets such as New York and Los Angeles four times a year. A sample Arbitron report is shown in Figure 6-6. For example, if a total market consists of 100,000 people, and 10,000 of those people listened to station KPPP from 6 A.M. to 10 A.M., a time when a total of 50,000 people are listening to the radio, KPPP's average-person estimate would be 10,000, meaning that this is the estimated average number of persons listening to KPPP in any quarter hour beginning with 6 A.M. to 6:15 A.M. and ending 9:45 A.M. to 10 A.M.; KPPP's rating would be 10,000/100,000, or 10 percent, and its share would be 10,000/50,000, or 20 percent.

Arbitron also provides demographic breakdowns on listeners, for instance, women 18+; women 18–34; women 18–49; adults 18+; adults 18–34; adults 18–39. Such information can help guide advertisers in deciding which stations offer them the greatest potential audience for a particular product or service.

In addition to these quarter-hour estimates, Arbitron provides cumulative (*cume*) estimates. In contrast to quarter-hour estimates which reveal how many people are listening at a given moment, cume figures reveal the total number of people who have tuned in at all during a particular period.

Arbitron also provides information about listeners to stations and advertisers through its qualidata service. *Qualidata* reports provide local-product-usage information and data on competing media such as television,

Sample page from the Arbitron Radio Diary. (Arbitron.)

newspapers, and direct mail. These reports help the radio station sales manager formulate a clear picture of where and how their listeners shop, what they purchase, as well as their lifestyle. With qualidata information, the sales manager is better able to develop a detailed profile of station listeners. For example, it may be determined that listeners are above average in income and educational background; it may also reveal that they have high employment status. In one case, by using qualidata information WMMR-FM of Philadelphia was able to show that its listeners ranked below average in percentage of credit card holders even though they ranked above average in income. Based on this data, WMMR's sales staff was able to convince advertisers from the credit industry that their station could deliver prime prospects.[18]

There are numerous ways to read and interpret the Arbitron book, and stations use this to their advantage; for that reason, it is not uncommon to find a number of different stations in one area claiming to be the best buy—but from whose point of view—the stations? the advertisers? the listeners? Ratings help deliver advertisers to stations. And they help deliver listeners to advertisers. But what, if anything, do they help deliver to listeners? Arbitron ratings tell us what people listen to.

Target Audience Estimates

Target Audience estimates appear in the format shown below. Six demographics appear on each page in the report.

The demographics are:
18 +, 18-34, 18-49, 25-49, 25-54, 35-64.

The day-parts are:

Mon-Sun	6AM-12Mid
Mon-Fri, Sat, Sun	6-10AM
	10AM-3PM
	3-7PM
	7PM-12Mid

Target audiences are reported for MEN, WOMEN, ADULTS and TEENS.

The estimates are:
Average Persons: Metro and TSA
Cume Persons: Metro and TSA
Average Persons Ratings: Metro
Average Persons Share: Metro

Included in the Target Audience section are estimates for Men, Women 18 + in the following day-parts:

Mon-Fri 6AM-Mid	Mon-Fri 6-10AM plus 3-7PM
Mon-Fri 6AM-7PM	Weekend 6AM-Mid

Average Quarter-Hour and Cume Listening Estimates

APRIL/MAY 1977

MONDAY-FRIDAY 10.00AM-3.00PM

Adults

STATION CALL LETTERS	ADULTS 18 + TOTAL AREA AVG. PERS. (00)	TOTAL AREA CUME PERS. (00)	METRO SURVEY AREA AVG. PERS. (00)	METRO SURVEY AREA CUME PERS. (00)	METRO SURVEY AREA AVG. PERS RTG.	METRO SURVEY AREA AVG. PERS. SHR.
WAAA	158	762	158	762	.3	1.2
WBBB	969	3883	914	3634	1.5	7.2
WCCC	551	2994	480	2314	.8	3.8
WDDD	314	2537	234	1951	.4	1.8
WEEE	399	1364	379	1244	.6	3.0
METRO TOTALS			12695	41675	20.6	

STATION CALL LETTERS	ADULTS 18-34 TOTAL AREA AVG. PERS. (00)	TOTAL AREA CUME PERS. (00)	METRO SURVEY AREA AVG. PERS. (00)	METRO SURVEY AREA CUME PERS. (00)	METRO SURVEY AREA AVG. PERS RTG.	METRO SURVEY AREA AVG. PERS. SHR.
WAAA	123	538	123	538	.5	2.5
WBBB	167	503	164	467	.7	3.3
WCCC	116	720	106	567	.4	2.1
WDDD	281	2358	215	1836	.9	4.3
WEEE	216	788	214	737	.9	4.3
METRO TOTALS			4965	17163	20.6	

STATION CALL LETTERS	ADULTS 18-49 TOTAL AREA AVG. PERS. (00)	TOTAL AREA CUME PERS. (00)	METRO SURVEY AREA AVG. PERS. (00)	METRO SURVEY AREA CUME PERS. (00)	METRO SURVEY AREA AVG. PERS RTG.	METRO SURVEY AREA AVG. PERS. SHR.
WAAA	145	678	145	678	.4	1.7
WBBB	565	1775	539	1656	1.3	6.3
WCCC	290	1583	271	1252	.7	3.2
WDDD	313	2487	233	1901	.6	2.7
WEEE	361	1137	345	1044	.9	4.1
METRO TOTALS			8503	27388	21.3	

STATION CALL LETTERS	ADULTS 25-49 TOTAL AREA AVG. PERS. (00)	TOTAL AREA CUME PERS. (00)	METRO SURVEY AREA AVG. PERS. (00)	METRO SURVEY AREA CUME PERS. (00)	METRO SURVEY AREA AVG. PERS RTG.	METRO SURVEY AREA AVG. PERS. SHR.
WAAA	108	427	108	427	.4	1.7
WBBB	507	1577	484	1494	1.7	7.8
WCCC	262	1400	244	1091	.8	3.9
WDDD	136	871	93	586	.3	1.5
WEEE	257	842	241	749	.8	3.9
METRO TOTALS			6234	19254	21.4	

STATION CALL LETTERS	ADULTS 25-54 TOTAL AREA AVG. PERS. (00)	TOTAL AREA CUME PERS. (00)	METRO SURVEY AREA AVG. PERS. (00)	METRO SURVEY AREA CUME PERS. (00)	METRO SURVEY AREA AVG. PERS RTG.	METRO SURVEY AREA AVG. PERS. SHR.
WAAA	117	491	117	491	.3	1.6
WBBB	595	2068	572	1985	1.7	8.0
WCCC	347	1834	318	1468	.9	4.4
WDDD	137	901	94	616	.3	1.3
WEEE	271	933	254	831	.7	3.6
METRO TOTALS			7151	22231	21.1	

STATION CALL LETTERS	ADULTS 35-64 TOTAL AREA AVG. PERS. (00)	TOTAL AREA CUME PERS. (00)	METRO SURVEY AREA AVG. PERS. (00)	METRO SURVEY AREA CUME PERS. (00)	METRO SURVEY AREA AVG. PERS RTG.	METRO SURVEY AREA AVG. PERS. SHR.
WAAA	31	204	31	204	.1	.5
WBBB	695	2676	656	2546	2.2	10.6
WCCC	359	1864	317	1480	1.1	5.1
WDDD	33	179	19	115	.1	.3
WEEE	174	498	159	447	.5	2.6
METRO TOTALS			6164	18739	21.0	

Average Quarter-Hour and Cume Listening Estimates—Men 18 +

Men

STATION CALL LETTERS	MON-FRI 6:00 AM-MID TOTAL AREA AVG. PERS. (00)	TOTAL AREA CUME PERS. (00)	METRO SURVEY AREA AVG. PERS. (00)	METRO SURVEY AREA CUME PERS. (00)	METRO SURVEY AREA AVG. PERS. RTG.	METRO SURVEY AREA AVG. PERS. SHR.
WAAA	64	692	64	666	.2	1.2
WBBB	273	3129	246	2890	.8	4.7
WCCC	273	3326	234	2742	.8	4.5
WDDD	186	2816	145	2191	.5	2.8
WEEE	95	1099	94	1041	.3	1.8
METRO TOTALS			5184	27663	17.7	

STATION CALL LETTERS	MON-FRI 6:00 AM-7:00 PM TOTAL AREA AVG. PERS. (00)	TOTAL AREA CUME PERS. (00)	METRO SURVEY AREA AVG. PERS. (00)	METRO SURVEY AREA CUME PERS. (00)	METRO SURVEY AREA AVG. PERS. RTG.	METRO SURVEY AREA AVG. PERS. SHR.
WAAA	77	641	77	641	.3	1.3
WBBB	316	2726	284	2503	1.0	4.8
WCCC	343	3105	293	2586	1.0	4.9
WDDD	208	2621	161	2009	.5	2.7
WEEE	125	1039	124	981	.4	2.1
METRO TOTALS			5920	27519	20.2	

STATION CALL LETTERS	MON-FRI 6-10 AM + 3-7 PM TOTAL AREA AVG PERS. (00)	TOTAL AREA CUME PERS. (00)	METRO SURVEY AREA AVG. PERS. (00)	METRO SURVEY AREA CUME PERS. (00)	METRO SURVEY AREA AVG. PERS. RTG.	METRO SURVEY AREA AVG. PERS. SHR.
WAAA	80	592	80	592	.3	1.3
WBBB	286	2467	255	2275	.9	4.1
WCCC	362	2825	306	2369	1.0	4.9
WDDD	224	2475	175	1914	.6	2.8
WEEE	129	949	127	891	.4	2.0
METRO TOTALS			6203	27206	21.2	

STATION CALL LETTERS	WEEKEND 6:00 AM-MID TOTAL AREA AVG. PERS. (00)	TOTAL AREA CUME PERS. (00)	METRO SURVEY AREA AVG. PERS. (00)	METRO SURVEY AREA CUME PERS. (00)	METRO SURVEY AREA AVG. PERS. RTG.	METRO SURVEY AREA AVG. PERS. SHR.
WAAA	40	403	40	377	.1	1.0
WBBB	272	2229	240	1984	.8	5.7
WCCC	167	1707	138	1378	.5	3.3
WDDD	149	1624	119	1252	.4	2.8
WEEE	111	825	110	783	.4	2.6
METRO TOTALS			4206	23558	14.3	

Footnote Symbols: (*) means audience estimates adjusted for actual broadcast schedule (+) means AM-FM Combination was not simulcast for complete time period.

ARBITRON

FIGURE 6-6 Sample Arbitron report. (*Arbitron.*)

MEDIA PROBE

You have just inherited a radio station and sufficient funds to permit you to operate it without worrying about whether the station's ratings and share-of-audience figures will be high enough to attract advertisers. In other words, you are free to program the station the way you would really like to program it. What will you do and why?

What they don't tell us is if they really like what they're hearing. Nor do they reveal what they would like to be able to hear. So radio delivers people what statistics say people will listen to. Whether this is what the people actually want from radio is another issue.

SUMMARY

In this chapter we explored radio and the recording industry. Radio has been called the adaptable medium, the one that can "tune itself" to the times. The history of radio attests to this skill.

Until 1844 the words "transportation" and "communication" were synonymous. Then in 1844 the first telegraph line and the Morse code came into being and the nature of our world was forever changed. The work of many inventors was pooled to create radio. Among those contributing ideas and innovations were Alexander Graham Bell (the telephone), Heinrich Rudolph Hertz (who demonstrated that energy could be sent through the air without wires), Guglielmo Marconi (sender of the first wireless signals across the Atlantic), and Lee De Forest (inventor of the audion).

After World War I, RCA was formed and it came to dominate communication in this country and abroad. As the size of the market for radio increased, a number of problems surfaced. Among these problems were the need for continuous programming and financial support of the medium. Stations KDKA and WEAF were helpful in providing solutions others would emulate: KDKA was the first station in America to provide continuous programming, and WEAF was the first station to sell advertising time. Gradually, station owners realized that networks would be vital to the future success of the medium, and the 1920s saw the birth of radio networking.

The Radio Acts of 1912 and 1927, and the Communications Act of 1934 reflect the efforts the government made to ensure that radio would continue its development and not drown in a sea of interference. Radio survived two wars, the depression, and television. Radio's ability to function as an entertainment, information, and advertising medium, and its ability to assess its strengths in the face of challenges and adapt accordingly account for its viability. To an extent, as we have seen, the state of radio is tied to the state of the recording industry and vice versa. Though challenged by MTV, radio still serves as a prime outlet for and promoter of recordings.

The future of radio, commercial and noncommercial, depends on its ability to continue to appeal to special segments of the market. Whether its success is measured in ratings, advertising revenues, or financial contributions, only time will tell what the medium's next big change will be.

KEY TERMS

Arbitron
Hertz
Network
Radio Act of 1927
Communications Act of 1934
Federal Communications Commission
Nickelodeon
Music Television
Mixing
Mastering
Stamping
Compact discs
Billboard
American Society of Composers, Authors and Publishers
Broadcast Music Incorporated

Payola
FM
AM
Corporation for Public Broadcasting
National Public Radio
Drive times
Program clock hour
Average persons
Average-persons ratings
Share of audience
Cume
Qualidata

NOTES

[1] Don Lawson, *FDR's New Deal,* Crowell, New York, 1979, pp. 47–48.

[2] Alexander Kendrick, *Prime Time: The Life of Edward R. Murrow,* Little, Brown, Boston, 1969, p. 173.

[3] *Radio Facts,* Radio Advertising Bureau, New York, 1983.

[4] Ibid.

[5] "New Discs Click with TV Flicks," *Time,* May 23, 1983, p. 42.

[6] Marc Kirkeby, "Video and Music," *ASCAP in Action,* Spring 1982, p. 22.

[7] "The New Sound of Music," *Newsweek,* June 13, 1983, p. 59.

[8] Clive Davis and James Willwerth. *Clive: Inside the Record Business,* Morrow, New York, 1975, p. 2.

[9] Greil Marcus, "The Beatles," in Jim Miller, ed., *The Rolling Stone Illustrated History of Rock & Roll,* Random House/ Rolling Stone Press, New York, 1980, p. 180.

[10] Don Hibbard and Carol Kaleialoha, *The Role of Rock,* Prentice-Hall, Englewood Cliffs, N.J., 1983.

[11] Edd Routt, James McGrath, and Fredrich Weiss, *The Radio Format Conundrum,* Hastings House, New York, 1978, pp. 2–3.

[12] "Reinventing Beautiful Music," *Radio Only,* April 1983, p. 17.

[13] "It's Beautiful," *Billboard,* January 20, 1983, p. 42.

[14] Nathaniel Sheppard, Jr., "Black-Oriented Radio: A Key in Chicago's Election," *The New York Times,* March 15, 1983, p. 24.

[15] "Public Radio Perks Up," *Newsweek,* March 12, 1979, p. 84.

[16] "NPR's Saddest Story Is Its Own," *The New York Times,* May 27, 1983, p. A14.

[17] Susan Stamberg, *Every Night at Five: Susan Stamberg's "All Things Considered" Book,* Pantheon, New York, 1982, p. 7.

[18] "Qualidata Helps Position WMMR Radio," *Beyond the Ratings,* June 1983, p. 1.

SUGGESTIONS FOR FURTHER READING

Barnouw, Erik: *History of Broadcasting in the United States,* 3 vols., Oxford University Press, New York, 1966–1970. *The history of radio has been documented in this fine three-volume series.*

Davis, Clive, and James Willwerth: *Clive: Inside the Recording Business,* William Morrow, New York, 1972. *Describes the recording industry from the point of view of top management. A particularly revealing look at Columbia Records.*

Denisoff, R. Serge: *Solid Gold: The Popular Record Industry,* Transaction Books, New Brunswick, N.J., 1975. *Provides an informative look at the history and current business practices of the recording industry.*

Fornatale, Peter, and Joshua Mills: *Radio in the Television Age,* Overlook Press, Woodstock, N.Y., 1980. *Describes the positioning of radio in the era of television. The focus is both on history and current practice within the industry.*

Johnson, Joseph S., and Kenneth K. Jones: *Modern Radio Station Practices,* 2d ed., Wadsworth, Belmont, Calif., 1978. *Presents a thorough examination of radio station operational procedures, which is of interest to students and professionals alike.*

Josephson, Larry, ed.: *Telling the Story: The National Public Radio Guide to Radio Journalism,* Kendall Hunt, Dubuque, Iowa, 1983. *Describes radio journalism in detail, including writing, editing, and the law. The accompanying audio tapes provide excellent examples.*

Kendrick, Alexander: *Prime Time: The Life of Edward R. Murrow,* Little, Brown, Boston, 1969. *Offers the reader a first-hand view of the* development of radio news during World War II.

Miller, Jim, ed.: *The Rolling Stone Illustrated History of Rock & Roll.* Random House/Rolling Stone Press, New York, 1980. *A comprehensive examination of many of the important artists and trends in the popular music world.*

Paley, William S.: *As It Happened: A Memoir,* Doubleday, New York, 1979. *Presents a fascinating first-hand account of the development of CBS.*

Routt, Edd, James McGrath, and Fredrich Weiss: *The Radio Format Conundrum,* Hastings House, New York, 1978. *A practical book which presents a detailed analysis of radio format programming. The book includes many excellent examples.*

Stamberg, Susan. *Every Night at Five: Susan Stamberg's "All Things Considered" Book,* Pantheon, New York, 1982. *In addition to detailing her role as a broadcaster, Stamberg provides a wealth of fascinating examples of radio journalism from the extensive files of National Public Radio.*

Sterling, Christopher, and John Kittross: *Stay Tuned: A Concise History of American Broadcasting,* Wadsworth, Belmont, Calif., 1978. *Presents a readable overview of the history and development of the radio medium.*

Weissman, Dick: *The Music Business,* Crown, New York, 1979. *A practical book. Presents a step-by-step procedure for becoming involved in the recording industry as an artist, executive, or engineer.*

CHAPTER 7

TELEVISION: THE IMAGE EMERGES

In its brief history television has become the American people's most important source of ideas, apart from interpersonal contact.
                                    Leo Bogart

CHAPTER PREVIEW

After reading this chapter, you should be able to:
- Explain what television means to you
- Identify the ways in which television affects daily life
- Enumerate and explain key happenings in the development of the television medium
- Compare and contrast the television experience with the radio experience
- Define and distinguish between networks, stations, and syndicates
- Identify the key players in the regulation game and explain their roles
- Identify and provide examples of how a station can serve the public interest
- Explain both the equal opportunity rule and the fairness doctrine
- Identify factors that have contributed to the problems currently facing public television
- Describe how cable television differs from broadcast television

Television is a target at which everyone likes to take aim: television is praised; television is faulted; television is blamed. Television serves us as a baby sitter, a dinner guest, a teacher, a companion. We are entertained by television. We are informed by television. To an extent, we might even be said to be created by television. In this chapter, we will not merely look at television; rather, we will attempt to understand television. To do that we must proceed through the mediated looking glass and examine the role television has played and will continue to play in our lives.

TELEVISION: AN "I" VIEW

Let us start by exploring what you think of television. What does the word "television" mean to you? To what extent do you equate television with a positive experience? A negative one? Why? What would a day in your life be like without television? How much time do you spend watching television, talking about television, or thinking about television? To what extent does television help you structure your life? For example, does it help you determine the hour at which you eat supper or go to sleep? Does it affect the amount of time you spend in the company of family members or friends? More significantly, does it affect the amount of time you spend talking to family members or friends? If television did not exist, what changes would occur in your life?

A life without television. An almost impossible idea. Television has become so ingrained in our existence that most of us could not imagine what life would be like without it. Television is such a critical factor in our lives that the New York State legislature passed a bill declaring the television set to be a "utensil necessary for a family" to survive in our society. Should a family have to declare bankruptcy, the television set is treated like other "necessities," including clothes, kitchen equipment, and furniture; it cannot be taken away. Do you agree with this policy? Why or why not?

It has been estimated that over 98 percent of American households have at least one television set, and more than half have several. The average American household has the television turned on over six and three-quarters hours a day, or almost half of our waking day. Americans spend more time watching television than doing anything else except sleeping. For some, the time spent watching television equals or surpasses the time spent working. According to media personality and critic Robert MacNeil, "If you fit the statistical averages, by the age of 20 you will have been exposed to something like 20,000 hours of television. You can add 10,000 hours for each decade you have lived after the age of twenty."[1] By the time you are 65, it is predicted that you will have spent about nine years of your life watching television. Sleeping habits are changed because of TV, mealtimes are altered because of TV, and leisure time is consumed. In fact, one study demonstrated that more than 40 percent of the leisure time we have available to us is spent watching television; that is almost three times the time we spend using all the other mass media.[2] To a great degree, television has affected the structure and the makeup of daily life.

The extent to which we have changed our lives to accommodate television was not expected. When television was introduced at the 1939 World's Fair, *The New York Times* stated: "The problem with television is that people must sit and keep their eyes glued to the screen: the average American family hasn't time for it." The reporter further stated that television posed no serious threat to other media. It was, in his eyes, a novelty, one we would soon tire of. As we know, he was wrong. In fact, time spent viewing television continues to increase. Not to watch television is to be out of step with the flow of life in America. Television provides us with a window on the world. Yet, we seem oddly un-

MEDIA PROBE

What does the word "television" mean to you? To your classmates? Let's find out. Place an X on one of the seven spaces in each of the scales below. The direction in which you mark each scale will, of course, depend upon which word most accurately describes your feelings about television. If you feel neutral, place your X in the middle space.

TELEVISION

good	___ ___ ___ ___ ___ ___ ___	bad
happy	___ ___ ___ ___ ___ ___ ___	sad
strong	___ ___ ___ ___ ___ ___ ___	weak
honest	___ ___ ___ ___ ___ ___ ___	dishonest
hot	___ ___ ___ ___ ___ ___ ___	cold
active	___ ___ ___ ___ ___ ___ ___	passive
valuable	___ ___ ___ ___ ___ ___ ___	worthless
sweet	___ ___ ___ ___ ___ ___ ___	bitter
fast	___ ___ ___ ___ ___ ___ ___	slow

You have just indicated your connotative meaning for the word "television." Unlike denotative (dictionary) meaning, which is objective, abstract, and general in nature, connotative meaning is personal, subjective, and emotional in nature. Your connotative meaning for a word varies according to your personal feelings for the concept you are considering. We can analyze your connotative meaning by assigning numerical values to each space. For each scale, number the positions 1 through 7 from left to right as follows:

good __1__ __2__ __3__ __4__ __5__ __6__ __7__ bad

Determine your scores and enter them on the form provided below.

SCALE	MY SCORE	CLASS AVERAGE	MALE	FEMALE
good/bad				
happy/sad				
strong/weak				
honest/dishonest				
hot/cold				
active/passive				
valuable/worthless				
sweet/bitter				
fast/slow				
Total				

How does your meaning for the word television compare with the meanings of other students? Was there a discernible difference that could be attributed to the sex of the student responding? What do you think accounts for the differences among the students' word scales?

MEDIA VIEW

JIMMY JET AND HIS TV SET

I'll tell you the story of Jimmy Jet—
And you know what I tell you is true.
He loved to watch his TV set
Almost as much as you.

He watched all day, he watched all night
Till he grew pale and lean,
From "The Early Show" to "The Late Late Show"
And all the shows between.

He watched till his eyes were frozen wide,
And his bottom grew into his chair.
And his chin turned into a tuning dial,
And antennae grew out of his hair.

And his brains turned into TV tubes,
And his face to a TV screen.
And two knobs saying "VERT." and "HORIZ."
Grew where his ears had been.

And he grew a plug that looked like a tail
So we plugged in little Jim.
And now instead of him watching TV
We all sit around and watch him.

Shel Silverstein, *Where the Sidewalk Ends*, New York: Harper & Row, 1974, p. 28–29.

MEDIA PROBE

For a three-day period, keep a record of the people with whom you interact. Note their names and occupation and describe them in one or two sentences. For the same three-day period, keep a record of the people (real or fictional) that you come into contact with through television. Also note their names and occupations and describe them in a sentence or two. Which list is longer? Which list contains a more varied array of occupations? Which list contains more interesting descriptions?

---

aware of how much of what we know, think, and feel about ourselves, other people, and life in general derives from television.

We have direct person-to-person contact with but a few people each day. Although television does not permit us to have direct person-to-person contact with others, it does allow us to extend our range by offering us the opportunity to have mediated contact with scores more people. But the personalities and characters we meet on television could affect the way we relate to the individuals who people our real-life environment. In fact, the people we meet through television could affect our image of the real world. To be able to understand and appraise what, if anything, television has done to or for us and those we know, to be able to understand and assess what, if anything, television has done to or for the society which we are a part of, we must take a step backward and examine the history of the medium, the operation of the medium, and the controversies sparked by the medium.

LOOKING BACKWARD

In 1882, Albert Robida, a French artist, drew a series of pictures that predicted what life would be like in the future. As Robida saw it, a "screen" on the wall would enable families of the future to take a course taught by a teacher who was not present, survey goods for sale, experience a "girlie" show, and watch a war—all while safe, secure, and comfortable in their living rooms.[3] As we now realize, Robida's musings proved to be prophetic; it wasn't too long before scientific advances made the dream of seeing at a distance—tele-vision—a reality.

During the late nineteenth and early twentieth centuries the electronic discoveries that made radio and film possible were joined by various mechanical scanning devices designed to permit the transfer of visual imagery. It is a fact that the technical devices that made television possible were developed years be-

MEDIA SCOPE

1884
Paul Nipkow experiments with a mechanical scanning disk and develops a method for breaking up and reassembling a visual image

1907
The word "television" is first used in Scientific American

1923
Vladimir Zworykin, funded by Westinghouse, invents the inconoscope, the "eye" of the early TV camera, and the first of the elements necessary in the development of an all-electronic television

1927
Philo Farnsworth applies for a patent on an "electronic vision system"

1928
The first experimental license is granted to RCA's W2XBS

1929
Vladimir Zworykin, now working for RCA, invents the kinescope, a cathode ray TV receiver, which completes his all-electronic TV system

1931
The placing of a TV Antenna atop the Empire State Building by NBC improves picture definition dramatically

1939
Commercial television is inaugurated at the New York World's Fair by RCA when Franklin Delano Roosevelt becomes the first head of state to appear on television

1941
The FCC authorizes commercial television. WNBT is the first commercial TV station on the air

1943
The duopoly ruling, prohibiting ownership of more than one AM or FM or one TV station in a single community forces NBC to sell one of its two networks

1947
John Cameron Swayze becomes TV's first big newscaster

1948
Milton Berle's Texaco Star Theatre, a variety show, is the most-watched program on television, the FCC orders a freeze on the granting of new TV licenses

1950
CATV is born in Lansford, Pa.

1951
The Today Show is launched; the first network connection between the East Coast and the West Coast is made

1952
The FCC issues its Sixth Order and Report: the freeze is ended; for the first time, TV is a major factor in national elections; the Ford Foundation creates the Educational Television and Radio Center (the forerunner of NET)

1953
The birth of "Little Ricky" on I Love Lucy makes national headlines and takes attention away from the Eisenhower inauguration; the Eisenhower-Nixon inauguration was the first to be carried live on TV

1954
The McCarthy hearings air on TV; Edward R. Murrow publicly challenges McCarthy on See It Now; the first color TV sets are sold, and the first color season begins

1955
The first big money quiz show, The $64,000 Question is on the air

TELEVISION: THE IMAGE EMERGES   195

1956	1959	1960	1961	1962	1963
Ampex demonstrates the videotape recorder; the networks give extensive coverage to the Eisenhower-Stevenson campaign	Quiz show scandals cause the networks to take a more active role in programming	The Nixon-Kennedy debates signal television's impact on the political process	Newton Minnow, chairman of the FCC, describes TV as a "vast wasteland"	The FCC rules that all new television sets must have UHF capacity; Congress passes the Educational TV Facilities Act	President John F. Kennedy is assassinated; the nation, united by television coverage, watches and grieves

1965	1967	1969	1970	1972
The Early Bird Communication Satellite is launched	Congress passes the Public Broadcasting Act, which appropriates money for the construction of facilities and calls for the formation of the Corporation for Public Broadcasting	TV covers the first moon landing: Americans see live coverage of Neil Armstrong's first steps on the moon	The Public Broadcasting Service (PBS) is formed	The Surgeon General issues the committee's Report on TV Violence

1975	1977	1978	1980	1983
Home Box Office begins the first satellite-interconnected pay network	ABC's Roots becomes the most-watched program to date; QUBE, a two-way TV system, is begun in Columbus, Ohio	The FCC gives permission for the development of superstations	An episode of Dallas becomes the most-watched show	The Winds of War becomes the most-watched program to date; The FCC gives the okay for broadcasters to offer the electronic information service, teletext

196 RADIO, TELEVISION, and FILM: THE ELECTRONIC WINDOW

MEDIA VIEW

Before electricity, a person's farthest range of vision was from the vantage point of a crow's nest on a ship or atop a lofty peak. Today our range of vision is limitless. Television is the telescope or window through which we can look at every corner of the earth. Sitting in our homes, we can watch the coronation of kings, death on the battlefield, flood and fire—wherever they are taking place. We can see through walls, across oceans and mountain ranges, and even examine the landscape of planets and moons.

Tony Schwartz, *Media: The Second God*, New York: Anchor Press, 1983, p. 34.

---

fore society at large would discover the new medium. In 1923, Vladimir Kosma Zworykin, a Russian-born American physicist who worked in the Pittsburgh Westinghouse Laboratories, patented the *iconoscope*—a camera tube that served as the core of an all-electronic television system. The iconoscope provided the first electronic means for breaking up a picture into tiny light and dark bits—the first essential task to be accomplished in a successful television system. Zworykin's kinescope came shortly thereafter in 1926. The *kinescope* was a receiving unit, a cathode-ray tube that carried an image composed of 30 horizontal lines—predecessor of today's 525-line standard. These two inventions were the technical base upon which television as we know it today was built.

At the same time that Zworykin was working, the self-educated son of a Utah sheep farmer, Philo Farnsworth, was also busy devising his own all-electronic television system. (In 1922, a young Farnsworth had amazed his Idaho high school teacher with his diagrams for such a system.) Farnsworth, unlike Zworykin, worked independently of corporate labs. In fact, he did most of his research in apartment laboratories—shades tightly drawn. Naturally, the secrecy fed suspicions and aroused curiosity about the nature of the work taking place behind those shades. So great was the suspicion that the police once raided Farnsworth's lab because they reasoned that someone using so many glass tubes must be manufacturing illegal drugs or alcohol. At the heart of Farnsworth's system was the "dissector"—a tube which scanned an image, one line at a time, accomplishing the break-up of the image into minute bits and the reassembling of it at the receiving end. In 1927, Farnsworth successfully transmitted his first picture—a dollar sign, a symbol of things to come. In 1930, at age 24, Farnsworth patented his TV system.[4]

The growth of television as a medium was slowed down by the 1929 stock market crash, the great depression, and years of arguing over patent rights. Still, by 1932, NBC had installed a television station in the newly built Empire State Building, and Vladimir Zworykin, no longer working for Westinghouse, was now employed as director of RCA's electronic research laboratory. Under the direction of David Sarnoff, the former Marconi operator who had heard the Titanic's distress signals, RCA set out to develop the commercial potential of the new medium. With the help of Zworykin and under a patent and royalty arrangement negotiated with Farnsworth, they began to make strides in that direction. Experimental broadcasts were aired from a converted radio station, Studio 3H in Radio City. Unfortunately, actors had to wear green makeup and purple lipstick and roast due to the intense heat of the lights.[5] Sarnoff arranged a demonstration of live television at the 1939 World's Fair in New York. While opening the fair, Franklin D. Roosevelt became the first president of the United States to appear on TV. In order to capitalize on the fair's introduction of television, RCA had TV sets with 5-inch and 9-inch picture tubes on display in department stores. Prices for these sets ranged from $200 to $600. The sets fascinated the public and drew large crowds.

YOU WERE THERE

FELIX THE CAT: STAR OF EARLY TELEVISION

The first "star" of television was Felix the Cat, a well-known cartoon character of the twenties. He made his debut before the TV cameras in 1929. RCA engineers needed someone to focus their camera on while they experimented with their equipment. They soon ran out of human volunteers—no one could stand the lights and the tedium for very long. So they mounted a foot-high statuette of Felix on a turntable and placed that in front of their camera. There he went round and round, hour after hour, day after day—and, in fact, year after year. What began as a temporary expedient became a fixture. Felix's career spanned most of the 1930's. His smiling visage became not only a symbol of early television, but also a sort of test pattern by which the engineers measured their progress . . . At Felix's debut in 1929, the RCA engineers were using a 60-line scanning speed and the image appears as if seen through a venetian blind. The 120-line picture of 1932 is much better, although still very fuzzy. The 441-line picture—typical of television as introduced at the 1939 World's Fair—is quite sharp. These, of course, are just three of the steps in television's progress. There were many in-between steps—and Felix appeared in most of them.

Judy Fireman, ed., *TV Book: The Ultimate Television Book,* New York: Workman Publishing Company, 1977, p.4.

Television sets might soon have become a common household item if it had not been for the intervention of World War II. The growth of the new medium would have to wait; the war had grounded the television industry. The nation's electronics manufacturing capacities were harnessed to produce radio equipment and radios necessary to the country's defense. As the war ended, however, television began to develop once again. In 1946, one year after the war's close, about 8000 TV sets were in the homes of the public. Only five years later, more than 37 million home receivers were in operation.[6] The quality of the television picture also began to improve with the passing years. The new technology that had been developed during the war was quickly applied to the television industry. But the most significant legacy of the war years for the future of television was the 1943 duopoly ruling that compelled NBC to divest itself of one of its radio networks; NBC chose to keep the Red network and dispose of the Blue network. This decision led to the creation of another viable national radio operation. the American Broadcasting Company, and also paved the way for the formation of the ABC Television Network.

The rapid growth of television caught both the industry and the FCC by surprise. Before World War II only six TV stations had licenses; in 1945, eight stations were on the air, and by 1948 there were 98 stations on the air. The FCC was swamped with applications for new TV station licenses. Remembering the chaos in broadcasting that had occurred during the early years of radio and fearful that, unless technical standards were worked out, the TV spectrum would be plagued by interference because of overcrowding, on September 30, 1948, the FCC imposed a freeze on all new applications for TV stations. They felt they needed the time to develop a master plan to control the frequencies, levels of power, and hours of operation of stations; only in this way could they be assured that one station wouldn't block out or interfere with the transmissions of other stations. For the four years during which the freeze was in effect, the FCC sought the counsel of technical experts and engineers.

The years of the freeze, 1948–1952, were a laboratory period for television. New York and Los Angeles each had seven stations and people in these cities saw a fully operating television system. Other cities like Austin, Denver, or Little Rock had no television, while most cities had only one station. The cities that had television were watched carefully, in the hope that they might somehow reveal what the future held in store for the television society. Would advertisers find a happy home awaiting them on television? Would the movie industry be affected by the new medium? What about life in general? Clues came quickly. The lipstick manufacturer Hazel Bishop had been doing an annual business of $50,000. When it began advertising on television, however, its sales for 1952 rocketed to $4.5 million. TV cities also reported changes. Movie attendance fell 20 to 40 percent—especially on Tuesday night, which was Milton Berle night. A sharp decline in attendance at sports events was also experienced. Likewise book circulation, restaurant receipts, and radio listening suffered declines. In television cities, television's influence on lifestyle and daily rhythms was beginning to be felt.

The 1948–1949 television season had also seen the arrival of national TV networking. In January 1949, the Midwest was linked by *coaxial cable* with the East. The West Coast link-up was accomplished in September 1951. For the first time, everyone in the United States was able to see the same thing at the same time.

On April 14, 1952, when the FCC issued its *Sixth Report and Order* and the freeze was lifted, a master plan had been produced. The FCC allocated space for twelve Very High Frequency *(VHF)* and seventy new Ultra High Frequency *(UHF)* channels. (Prior to World War II, television could only be sent out and received on the VHF band.) The commission

Family situation comedies, such as *The Danny Thomas Show*, were early favorites of the new networks and their growing audiences. (The Bettman Archive)

also compiled a list that assigned television channels to various U.S. communities and established rules designed to keep interference to a minimum. It should be noted that the Sixth Report and Order assigned three VHF channels to most larger markets, thus locking in the three-network structure of the industry which dominates to the present. Also, due largely to the efforts of Frieda Hennock, the first woman to serve on the commission, television channels were reserved for educational use. A boost for NBC was the fact that an all-electronic color system was adopted as the standard which would be compatible with the current black-and-white receivers. The standards adopted were those of RCA (NBC's parent company) and guaranteed that RCA would make more money than CBS. NBC launched its first season of color television in 1954–1955. It was the mid-1960s, however, before the broadcasters and the public followed its lead.

TELEVISION: THE IMAGE EMERGES

The ruling that seventy UHF channels were to be devoted to television didn't actually guarantee that viewers would receive seventy UHF channels. Few sets made in the 1950s were equipped with UHF receivers. If you wanted to receive the signal, you had to purchase a converter at a cost of $25 to $50. It wasn't until 1953 that Congress passed a law requiring that newly built TV sets be capable of receiving UHF channels. This didn't mean you could tune in UHF channels, however; it wasn't until 1976 that Congress passed another law requiring that manufacturers equip all television sets with automatic tuning devices for UHF as well as VHF. So, until relatively recently, UHF had been treated as the poor relation of the television industry. UHF stations had a smaller coverage area and advertising dollars went to the more powerful VHF stations. Of the approximately 750 commercial television stations in the United States today, less than 150 operate on the UHF band.[7]

From the beginning, television adhered to the pattern set by radio. Of special interest is the fact that the Radio Act had defined communication by radio as "any intelligence, message, signal, power, picture, or communication of any nature transferred by electrical energy from one point to another without the aid of any wire connecting the points." Thus, it could be said that radio had always been intended to include television.[8] The people and the companies that worked to develop and promote television were the same people and companies that had worked to develop and promote radio. As we will see, the programming concepts, economic structure, and pattern of regulation that had been adopted for radio were simply transferred, almost without alteration, to the television medium. In effect, television was perceived as radio with a picture.

The period from the late 1940s to the late 1950s has been dubbed the Golden Age of Television. Following the freeze there was a great rush to obtain station licenses. The in-

MEDIA PROBE

Unobtrusively observe a number of people listening to the radio. Describe their behavior. For example, do they talk while the radio is on? Do they engage in other nonlistening activities?

Now unobtrusively observe a number of people watching television and describe their behavior.

Do you agree that television is radio with a picture? Why or why not?

crease in the number of stations (by 1955, 439 stations were on the air) precipitated an increase in television set sales. In 1952, about 15 million homes, or 33 percent of the country, owned at least one television set; by 1960, 45 million homes, or 90 percent of the country, owned at least one TV set. No other mass medium had ever grown so quickly. In just ten years, television had become a pervasive force in American life.

The rapid growth and expansion of the industry was fed by a number of different factors. Early television had been hampered by the difficulty of storing programs. Shows were either broadcast live from network studios in New York or filmed on the West Coast. While live shows helped generate a sense of excitement for the medium, they also gave it an amateurish quality. For instance, now and then microphone booms would appear in the picture, a stage hand would pass in front of the camera, or lines would be forgotten. Live programs had several other drawbacks as well. They couldn't be run again, and they frequently had to be repeated for West Coast audiences. Film was expensive. In 1956 the problem was solved. The Ampex Company invented *videotape;* videotape is to television pictures what audiotape is to sound. The invention meant that television pictures could be prerecorded and edited before broadcast. This increased the artistic quality of the offerings. Expenses were

A Manhattan roofline bristles with the equipment of the new television age. (Charles Harbutt/Archive Pictures)

also cut. The cost of videotaping a program was much less than the cost of filming it. Tape could also be rerun and revised. By the start of the next decade, most of what had once constituted television's live programming was now shown on videotape.

The contents of television shows were copied from radio program formats. The quiz shows, westerns, police series, soap operas, variety shows, suspense dramas, news programs, and comedies of the decade were borrowed from the radio medium. In fact, television's early stars had first been radio personalities. Among those who transferred their allegiance were Red Skelton, George Burns and Gracie Allen, Jack Benny, and Arthur Godfrey. In like fashion, television's early hits had first been radio hits. Shows like *The Life of Riley, The Lone Ranger, Studio One,* and *The Aldridge Family* were taken from one medium and adapted to meet the requirements and demands of the other. Television commercials were sold just as radio commercials had been sold, and positioned between and within television programs just as they had been positioned between and within radio programs.

The dominant networks of the period were NBC and CBS. Both had network radio experience behind them, experienced talent, capital assets to rely on, and a large number of affiliated stations. ABC's basic problem was the lack of affiliates. After its merger with United Paramount Theatres in 1953 and the demise of the Dumont Network in 1955, this problem was eased.

THE EMERGING STRUCTURE

Three major networks dominate commercial television: NBC, CBS, and ABC. They are responsible for either producing or arranging the productions of most of the programming transmitted during prime time (7:30 to 11 P.M. on the coasts and 6:30 to 10 P.M. in the Midwest). Each of the three networks directly owns five licensed VHF stations in the largest key cities around the country; these network-owned-and-operated (O&O) stations enable the networks to reach 25 to 30 percent of all television homes in the United States. (A recent FCC proposal advocates raising the number of VHF stations a network can own to 12; the proposal would also lift nearly all ownership limitations in 1990). In addition to the five VHF stations they are permitted to own and operate, each network has about 200 to 250 affiliated stations (local stations that sign contracts with the network), so that approximately 90 percent of all the commercial stations in the United States are affiliated with one of the three networks.

The networks do not broadcast any programs themselves. Rather, they are program suppliers; they feed the shows they themselves produce or arrange to be produced to local stations (*O&Os* and *affiliates*), so that they may be broadcast to homes in each station's area. In effect, a network is a group of local stations electronically bonded together so that programs offered by a single source may be broadcast simultaneously by all. The electronic aspect of program distribution (a service that costs each network about $15 million a year) is handled by the American Telephone and Telegraph Company (AT&T) through its coaxial cable, microwave, and satellite facilities. Networks are not regulated by the FCC because networks require no government licenses. Stations, however, are regulated by the FCC and do require licenses.

Local television stations function as the heart of the American broadcasting system; the owners of the local stations make the final decisions regarding what will be broadcast on the television you watch each day. A local station is licensed by the FCC to provide television service to a particular market or community. The United States is divided into 212 markets ranging from number 1, New York City, with almost 6.5 million homes, to number 212, Miles City–Glendive, Montana, with about 10,000 homes. A local station that signs a contract with one of the networks is called an affiliate. Every affiliate has a stake in the network's programming schedule since what the network offers will affect the local station's audience size and thus its profitability. Affiliate stations are paid by the network to run a certain amount of the programming produced or supplied by the network. A local affiliate has the choice of accepting or rejecting the programming the network offers, but it is not permitted to run programming provided by the other two networks. On the average, an affiliate takes about 60 percent of its total programming from the network; the percentage tends to rise to close to 100 percent during the prime-time hours, although sometimes an affiliate may even decide to reject a number of prime-time offerings.

MEDIA PROBE

Imagine that you own a local television station. Based on this year's television schedule, which network would you most want to affiliate with? Why?

Examine this week's prime-time television schedule. Which programs of the network you chose to affiliate with would you accept to broadcast on your station? Which would you refuse to broadcast? Why?

There are a number of reasons a local station might choose not to broadcast a network program. First, regional differences could make a network offering less desirable to a particular station. For example, some kinds of programming might be more acceptable in the liberal Northeast than in the more conservative South. Second, the show might be judged to be too controversial. For instance, in April 1983, a number of affiliates refused to air *The Thorn Birds* because of the controversies that could be ignited by the portrayal of a priest's violation of his vow of celibacy. Third, a station might opt to broadcast a sports program featuring a local professional or collegiate team in place of a network offering. Or fourth, a station might believe it could attract more viewers by scheduling one of its own shows or a syndicated program instead of the network's selection.

The networks compete vigorously to generate enthusiasm among their affiliates to run the network schedule—especially the prime-time schedule. Each year the three commercial networks invite their affiliates to California for food, drink, and superlatives. In many ways, the gatherings resemble pregame pep rallys. The networks are estimated to spend somewhere between $750,000 and $1 million to create support for their programs—and with good reason. In many ways, the affiliates hold the keys to network success. Whenever an affiliate rejects a network offering, network ratings are adversely affected. Every time a station refuses to broadcast a network program and broadcasts something else in its place, the size of the audience for the network program is decreased. This directly affects the amount of money a network can charge a national advertiser for running a commercial during that program. If a substantial number of affiliates around the country refuse to air the same program, the potential audience for the show is decreased. Ultimately, the show's rating will be lowered significantly, and when the rating is decreased, the network suffers. As ratings go down, advertising rates go down as well. Consequently, every network tries to get all of its affiliate stations to consent to schedule its programs.

Networks court their affiliates even though the affiliates do not have to pay to schedule network programming. In fact, just the opposite is true: Networks pay their local stations to carry the network's shows. Stations are paid between 20 and 25 percent of what they would charge advertisers for a slot. For example, in an average city, a TV station might sell time at about $250 per rating point. So if a network offering carried a rating of 20, the station's income for running the show off the network's line would be $3000 (20 × 250 = $5000 per minute, × three advertising spots = $15,000, ÷ 20 percent = $3000), just for consenting to air a half-hour network show. This, however, is not all the local station stands to make. The local station is also free to sell its own advertising on the hour and the half-hour at full rate. From a purely monetary perspective, carrying a network schedule makes good sense. And as Harry Skornia writes in *Television and Society*, "If television can be said to have any values at all, it is those of the salesmen, big businessmen, manufacturers and showmen who control it—essentially materialistic values." If a local station is relatively confident that a network show will secure a high local rating, it will carry the show.

The networks provide their local stations with an array of programming (entertainment, news, and public affairs shows) that on the average attract a larger audience than locally originated programs probably would, and which few, if any, local stations could afford to produce on their own. For example, networks can afford to maintain large news bureaus in a number of American cities and around the world; no local station could afford to do that. Similarly, networks can afford to fund original entertainment series, miniseries, and specials. Often the network purchases the entertainment segment of its schedule from independent producers. These producers are either major film companies like Paramount, Warner, or Universal or production companies like Tandem Productions or Lorimar Productions. Networks spend over $2 billion a year for first-run programming. Local stations could never afford to do this. For these reasons, only about 5 to 10 percent of the typical affiliated commercial station's programming is locally produced; such programming is normally limited to sports and interview shows. On the average 65 percent of an affiliated commercial station's programs are fed from the network line. The remaining 25 to 30 percent is purchased from another source—program syndicates.

The *syndicates* are independent of both the networks and the local stations. Both affiliated and nonaffiliated stations purchase the rights to run programs from them. The purchased programs are either delivered to the local station on videotape or sent by satellite. Syndicate offerings include shows like *Merv Griffin*, *The Muppet Show*, *Family Feud*, and *Mary Hartman, Mary Hartman* and programs that have concluded their prime-time runs like *The Bionic Man*, *Wonder Woman*, *Mash*, and *I Love Lucy*. These latter programs may even have been aired originally by a number of the affiliates now buying them.

> **MEDIA PROBE**
>
> Identify the current syndicated offerings of the local stations in your area. How many of the offerings do you watch? Why?
>
> Examine current first-run programming. Which shows do you predict will be syndicated eventually? Explain your answers.
>
> Now, imagine that you own the local commercial station in your community. Which of today's first-run programs would you like to have air on your station once the series is syndicated? Why?

> **MEDIA PROBE**
>
> You are a member of the FCC. What do you think it means to serve the public interest, convenience, and necessity?
>
> You are a station manager. What do you think a television station should have to do in order to serve the public interest, convenience, and necessity?
>
> How, if at all, would your answer change if you were to respond as an advertiser might respond?
>
> How, if at all, would your answer change if you were to respond as the following viewers might respond: a senior citizen, a business executive, a parent, you?

Sometimes the syndication company produces its own programs, but more commonly it distributes programs produced by other firms. Traditionally, old network programs are the main type of program material sold through syndication. Recently, however, original programs produced for syndication have met with success and could signify a wider choice of new programming for the television viewer.

THE CONTROL AND REGULATION OF TELEVISION

Television, like radio, is a communication medium that uses a scarce and valuable public resource—the open airwaves. This means that television, like radio, is subject to a number of different controls and regulations.

Key players in the control and regulation game are the five commissioners who comprise the FCC (until June 30, 1983 there were seven members on this body). As in radio, it is the FCC that is responsible for ensuring that the television medium is technically controlled. The FCC assigns frequencies to individual stations, determines the power stations may use, regulates the time stations may be on the air, and works to guarantee that the locations of station transmitters and the type of transmission equipment stations use do not interfere with the effective operation of other stations. The FCC is also responsible for issuing, revoking, renewing, and transferring television station licenses. Specifically, the Communications Act of 1934 noted that "the Commission shall determine that public interest, convenience, and necessity would be served by the granting of a license . . . any station license may be revoked because of conditions . . . which would warrant the Commission in refusing to grant a license on an original application." The words "public interest, convenience and necessity" are the words that have generated the most controversy. Exactly what it means to serve the public interest, convenience, and necessity has been debated for years. While the FCC is not empowered to make the law, it is empowered to interpret and implement the law.

The same act that gave the FCC the right to deny a station a license if its programming did not meet the public interest also specifically forbade the FCC to interfere with the right to free speech or to intervene with program content decisions. How could the FCC involve itself in program regulation without interfering with the right of free speech? In 1946 the FCC issued the *Blue Book*, as it is now referred to, and in 1960 the FCC issued the *1960 Programming Statement*. Both identified program criteria the FCC would have liked to see stations abide by. Specifically, program categories defined by the FCC as "generally required for programming in the public interest" are: entertainment programs, opportunity for local self-expression, the development and use of local talent, programs for children, religious programs, educational programs, public affairs programs, editorialization by licensees, political broadcasts, agricultural programs, news programs, weather and market reports, sports programs, and minority audience programs. Both documents also placed responsibility for programming with the licensee, not the licenser. These documents, although similar in many ways, did contain significant differences. While the *Blue Book* had called for the development of unsponsored (sustaining) public service programs, the *1960 Policy Statement* did not. In its place was introduced a new item—*licensee ascertainment*. Licensee ascertainment requires stations to survey the needs and problems of their local areas so that they can better provide programs that address these needs and problems.

Once a station is licensed, it is more or less on its own, receiving little supervision from the FCC until license-renewal time. Until 1981, stations came up for renewal every three years. Then in 1981 Congress extended the period between renewals to five years. At renewal time there are three types of action the FCC can take if it determines that a station has not been operating in the public interest: (1) it can fine a station up to $20,000; (2) it can renew a station's license for a probationary period; or (3) it can revoke or decide not to renew a station's license. Statistics are on the station's side; 99.9 percent of all station licenses are renewed. And the trend in the 1980s has been toward deregulation, not regulation.

According to *New York Times* writer Sally Bedell, the current FCC chairman, Mark S. Fowler, "has beaten the drums for broadcast deregulation more insistently than any of his predecessors."[9] Media critic Les Brown supports this view. According to Brown, Mark Fowler came to the FCC "not to regulate or even deregulate, but in his words, to unregulate—to abolish the speed limit that was adopted for the public safety."[10] In Fowler's opinion, "The FCC must deal with the reality of broadcasting, a reality that begins with the fact that broadcasting is a business."[11] Fowler believes the FCC should not impose its judgments on broadcasters, but rather should "defer to a broadcaster's judgment about how best to compete for viewers and listeners because this serves the public interest."[12] In Fowler's words, "who are we in Government to dictate which program is good and socially desirable and which is bad and socially undesirable? We should let the marketplace decide."[13]

Two particular broadcasting regulations have generated a great deal of controversy over the years and have also become a focus of interest for Fowler. They are the *equal opportunity rule* and the *fairness doctrine*. Since it is contained in Section 315 of the Communications Act, the equal opportunity requirement is federal law. This requirement focuses on the ability of bona fide candidates for public office to have access to the airwaves. The law states that if one candidate for public office is sold or given time to appear on the air during a campaign, all other candidates for that office must be given the same opportunity. Thus, if a station sells a candidate one minute of time for $1000, it must use the same fee structure for all other candidates

MEDIA PROBE

What do you perceive to be the needs and problems of your local area? To what extent, if any, have local stations sought to create programming to reflect these needs and problems? If possible, provide specific programming examples from a composite week's schedule.

who wish to appear. Likewise, if the station permits one candidate to speak for a minute at no cost, it must also offer a free minute to other candidates. Equal opportunity refers to the "quality" of the time offered as well. It should be noted that regularly scheduled newscasts and on-the-spot coverage of news events are not subject to the provision.

The fairness doctrine had its origins in the requirement that broadcasters provide response opportunities to broadcast editorials. Gradually the policy was expanded into other broadcasting areas as well. The fairness doctrine states that broadcasters have an obligation to seek out and present contrasting viewpoints on controversial issues of public concern. Consequently, although the FCC is prohibited from censoring programming, this provision ensures it has the right to use programming as one measure of public service. The thinking is that adequate public service includes presenting different sides of controversial topics.

Under Mark Fowler's leadership, the FCC has asked Congress to remove both the equal time rule and the fairness doctrine. Do you think they should be modified or replaced?

In the past when stations came up for renewal, station owners were required to complete long, detailed questionnaires that were designed to reveal whether or not a station had fulfilled its public-interest obligations. Now the FCC has eliminated this form; in its place it has substituted a postcard-size form—hence the new label "postcard renewal." On June 27, 1984, in a sweeping deregulatory move, the FCC lifted its 16-minute an hour limit on ads, removed guidelines that required set amounts of news, information, and public affairs programming, and dropped requirements that stations maintain program logs and survey community needs. FCC chairman Mark Fowler defended the FCC's actions by noting, "At issue is whether the government trusts the common man's ability to make up his own mind about what he wants to watch."

Other groups of players in the control and regulation game are the networks and the National Association of Broadcasters. All three commercial networks belong to the NAB and until recently voluntarily adhered to the *NAB Television Code*. The code described the responsibilities of broadcasters, set general program content standards, and limited the amount of advertising that would be permitted during any hour. The programming guidelines contained in the code were generally phrased and led to many different individual interpretations. Here are some excerpts from the now defunct NAB code's guidelines:

In their totality, programs should contribute to the sound, balanced development of children...

Violence, physical or psychological, may only be projected in responsibly handled contexts, not used exploitatively. Programs involving violence should present the consequences of it to its victims and perpetrators.

The presentation of techniques of crime in such detail as to be instructional or invite imitation should be avoided.

Special sensitivity is necessary in the use of material relating to sex, race, color, age, creed, religious functionaries or rites, or national or ethnic derivation.

Subscribers shall not broadcast any material which they determine to be obscene, profane, or indecent.

The portrayal of implied sexual acts must be essential to the plot and presented in a responsible and tasteful manner.

The use of liquor and the depiction of smoking in program content shall be deemphasized.

A television station's news schedule should be adequate and well-balanced.

News reporting should be factual, fair and without bias.

Every effort should be made to keep the advertising message in harmony with the content and general tone of the program in which it appears.

In prime time on network affiliated stations, non-program material shall not exceed 9 minutes 30 seconds in any 60 minute period. . . . In all other times, non-program material shall not exceed 16 minutes in any 60 minute period.

Not all stations belonged to the NAB, and even if they did, not all stations chose to abide by the code. Those stations that did belong to the NAB and who were judged to be in violation of the code simply forfeited the right to display the NAB Television Seal of Good Practice. Since few, if any, viewers were conscious of whether or not a station displayed the seal, having the right revoked was a mild punishment. Also of significance was the fact that except for the provisions that focused on advertising limits, most of the code's guidelines might be construed in a number of different ways. In 1978, FCC commissioner Margita White noted: "It would make no sense to have seven government officials in Washington set standards of morals, taste and creativity. Does it make any more sense for the members of the NAB to pretend to do the same?" On the other hand, the code did offer a general standard against which the broadcasters and the public could evaluate programming. However, the future of the code is bleak. A March 1982 decision by a district court in Washington, D.C., ruled that the section of the Television Advertising Code that limited the number of products or services that could be advertised in a single commercial of less than 60 seconds in length was a violation of the antitrust laws. The NAB subsequently ordered suspension of all the advertising provisions of the code pending the outcome of an appeal.

Each of the networks also have departments—usually known as the Program Practices Department or Standards and Practices Department—whose responsibility it is to ensure that all the programming on the schedule measures up to the network's own performance standards. In reality, the members of these departments have the task of prejudging whether the programs they air will be acceptable to the majority of the viewing audience. During an average season, standards

> **MEDIA PROBE**
>
> Which excerpts from the old NAB Television Code do you agree with? Which do you disagree with?
>
> Identify the stations in your community that belonged to the NAB. To what extent do you find that station programming still reflects the code? Can you cite specific examples when the contents of a station's programming have been in violation of the code's guidelines?
>
> Which of the NAB Television Code excerpts were open to a wide range of interpretations? If possible, provide programming examples that illustrate the range of responses.

and practices departments evaluate scripts and programs according to criteria they themselves establish; thus the decisions they make sometimes involve highly subjective judgments. A constant flow of outlines, scripts, revisions, and resubmissions passes from program creators to the standards and practices editors (censors?) and back again. The standards and practices people are also responsible for overseeing the production and editing process as well. According to CBS, because of the diversity of material their editors are faced with, they have no written guidebook for them to refer to. Instead, CBS relies on the individual and collective judgments of the members of that department.

Following are excerpts from the *NBC Broadcast Standards for Television:*

> In general, programs should reflect a wide range of roles for all people and should endeavor to depict men, women and children in a positive manner, keeping in mind always the importance of dignity to every human being.
>
> Narcotic addiction should be presented only as a destructive habit. The use of illegal drugs or the abuse of legal drugs shall not be encouraged or shown as socially acceptable.
>
> The use of alcoholic beverages should be deemphasized and restricted to situations and cir-

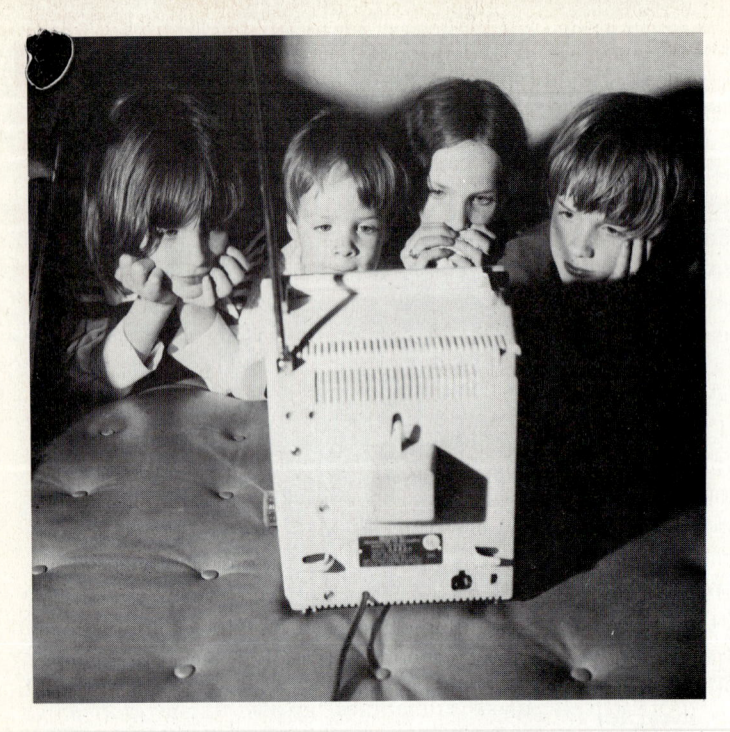

Various public interest groups lobby for high standards in children's television programming. (Jean Claude Lejeune/Stock Boston)

cumstances necessary to plot and/or character delineation.

Producers of programs designed for children are directed to avoid:
  a. placing children in situations that provoke excessive or prolonged anxiety;
  b. content that may give children a false and derogatory image of any ethnic, social or religious group, including their own;
  c. depictions of unlawful activities or acts of violence that glamorize such acts or make them appear to be an acceptable solution to human problems;
  d. depicting violence in a manner that invites imitation.

Local stations add their own policy book statements to supplement network policy statements. This book contains a description of the station's philosophy and operation standards and specifies those practices it would like encouraged and discouraged.

Additional players in the control and regulation game are the various public-interest organizations. Among the most widely known of these groups is Action for Children's Television (ACT) and the newer Coalition for Better Television chaired by the Reverend Donald Wildmon. Now over fifteen years old, ACT, led by Peggy Charren, has a paid staff of ten, more than 20,000 members, and a yearly budget of $400,000. Over the years, ACT has exerted influence on both the television industry and government regulatory agencies. Donald Wildmon's organization has been monitoring television programs and rating them and their sponsors for decency since 1977. The group uses organized economic boycotts as a weapon in attempts to pressure sponsors to withdraw backing from shows of which it does not approve.

The Federal Trade Commission is also involved in television regulation from time to time. The FTC, a body composed of five commissioners who serve staggered terms of seven years each, exists to look into matters where it is believed consumers are being deceived. If the FTC believes a company's advertisements are untruthful, it has the power to order the company to stop broadcasting the commercials. (The FTC will be covered in greater detail in Chapter 10.)

HOW THE STATION OPERATES

Television stations across the country have evolved staffing arrangements that reflect their size and needs. Large stations typically employ about 350 to 400 people and may be divided into a dozen or so different departments. In contrast, small stations may employ only 20 to 30 people and have only a few departments. Regardless of size, however, the typical station performs at least four primary activities: programming, sales, engineering and administration (see Figure 7-1). The general manager of the station is the person responsible for seeing that each of these functions are executed. The heads of the station's departments all report to the general manager.

The sales department is usually staffed by a sales manager and a number of sales representatives, although in a small station one person may be charged with fulfilling all sales functions. The sales department, whether large or small, is responsible for selling time to local and national advertisers, scheduling ads, and billing customers.

The engineering department is headed by a chief engineer and composed of all the people who keep the cameras, slide and film projectors, and other technical equipment in working order.

The programming department puts together locally produced programs and handles the programming functions of the station. The programming department is in charge of everything that goes out over the air, whether it is produced locally, fed by the network, or purchased from a syndicator. Thus, decisions regarding what programs should be broadcast and the times at which they should be broadcast are made by the programming manager and his or her staff in consultation with the general manager and other station personnel. Producers, directors, writers, camerapeople, on-the-air talent, announcers, floor personnel, makeup artists and costumers, and editors are part of the programming department. Depending on the size of the station, the news department may operate either under the auspices of programming or as an independent division. News is composed of the news director, reporters, and editors and writers responsible for the station's newscasts.

The administration and business depart-

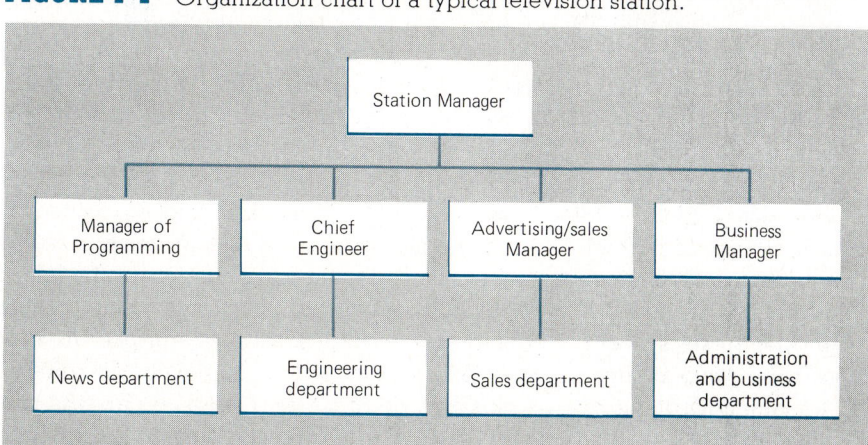

FIGURE 7-1 Organization chart of a typical television station.

ment helps the general manager run the station. The station's legal counsel, secretarial and clerical help, accountants, and bookkeepers work in this department.

THE PROMISE OF PUBLIC TELEVISION AND CABLE TV

During the past two decades two ideas have generated much excitement and interest: public television and community antenna TV. Let us examine the origins and outcomes of each of these innovations.

Public Television

Prior to 1967, noncommercial television was known as educational television, and unfortunately, programs aired on educational television stations had a reputation for being dull and uninteresting. The most common excuse offered by the stations for the amateurish quality and lack of creativity was money; in fact, the main problem facing these stations was how to obtain sufficient funds with which to operate. The Ford Foundation moved to alleviate this situation by underwriting the National Educational Television and Radio Center (NETRC). In 1959 it became known as National Educational Television (NET). Stations were provided with money to purchase kinescope recorders and were invited to submit to the NET program staff proposals for programs they felt they would be able to produce well if given the needed financial resources. Once proposals were approved, NET would arrange with the stations to produce the programs in their studios; each station would also make a kinescope of the show it produced. The kinescopes were then duplicated and sent to other educational television stations across the country. Kinescopes, of course, had quality problems, so it wasn't until after 1956, the year the Ampex Corporation demonstrated its new videotape recorder, that the technical deficiency problem could be alleviated. By the late 1950s, NET was distributing programs on videotape. It also moved its headquarters to New York City in the hope that being in the heartland of television would help improve programming.

In 1962 the federal government made its first financial commitment to educational television. The ETV Facilities Act of 1962 was passed. This act amended the Communications Act of 1934 to provide grants which could be used to support educational television facilities. Then, in June 1967, the Carnegie Commission on Educational Television released a report which had far-reaching ramifications. The report recommended a name change. From then on the medium was no longer referred to as educational television; its new appellation was *public television.* The commission noted that massive infusions of federal funds were essential if public television was to be kept alive and begin to fulfill its potential. Thus, it proposed that Congress create a nonprofit and nongovernmental group to be called the Corporation for Public Television. This organization would function as the channel through which federal and other monies could be distributed to support program development and individual stations. The commission also recommended "permanent funding" in an effort to avoid political interference with public television; it was suggested that funds could come from government passage of an excise tax of 2 to 5 percent on new television sets.

Following these recommendations, in 1967 Congress passed the Public Broadcasting Act; this act authorized money for the building of new facilities and created the *Corporation for Public Broadcasting,* a 15-member body appointed by the president and confirmed by the Senate with no more than eight persons from any one political party; it was the job of the CPB to oversee noncommercial television and radio. The CPB also established the *Public Broadcasting Service,* an agency designed to parallel the functioning of a commercial network; PBS would be responsible for schedul-

"To start with, gentlemen, I just want to say that if at times I strike you as being strange or weird or something, or whatever, it's because I'm probably the first member of this board to grow up with television."

(Drawing by W. Miller, © 1982 The New Yorker Magazine, Inc.)

ing, promoting, and distributing programming among member stations. The system was not actually a producer of programs; its job was to obtain them from other sources including public TV stations, production companies, and foreign countries. In fact, so many shows from Britain were aired that some said PBS stands for "Primarily British Shows." According to PBS, however, only 11 percent of its first-run schedule is made up of British shows. What is significant is that the Public Broadcasting Act did not contain any provisions for permanent funding. Instead, the law mandated that CPB be given $9 million for its first year of operation and further funds be appropriated by future Congresses. Though attempts were made to avoid political interference, politically motivated squabbles ensued. For example, in 1974, the Nixon White House expressed the belief that PBS programs were antiadministration. Consequently, a CPB funding bill was vetoed by the president. Public television was a controversial issue. And political, as well as organizational, problems continue to plague public broadcasting into the 1980s.

Today a three-tiered process exists: (1) the stations or other sources produce the programs; (2) PBS schedules and distributes the programs; and (3) CPB guides the operation and provides funding. Three basic models can be used to describe the way public broadcasting stations get their programs. In the first model, programming is paid for by corporations or foundations and is provided free of charge to all public broadcasting stations in the country. The large oil companies are frequent sponsors of PBS programs. For example, Mobil underwrites the making of *Masterpiece Theatre*. The prevalence of oil-company funding has led some to suggest that PBS really stands for the "Petroleum Broadcasting Service." In the second model, the Station Program Cooperative (SPC) selects programs to be carried by member stations. Member stations around the country are given ballots that include descriptions of potential programs. Stations vote for those programs they wish to carry. Once a decision is made, a station that wants to carry a program must pay part of the program's production costs. Approximately 30 to 40 percent of PBS's programming comes from the SPC. Frequently, even after the SPC has voted to underwrite a program, more money is required to fund the production fully. At this point, outside funds are solicited to make up the difference. Johnson & Johnson, for example, has helped to fund *Nova,* AT&T has helped to fund *The MacNeil-Lehrer Report,* and Exxon has helped to fund *Great Performances.* In the third model, stations fund the entire cost of a program. Owing to rising costs, this method of funding is being used with decreasing frequency.

After restudying public television, a second Carnegie Commission recommended that a new administrative structure and funding system be adopted. While these suggestions were being considered, the Reagan administration made additional cuts in the operating budget of PBS (Table 7-1). Today, Public broadcasting is short of funds, and many believe that its very existence is in jeopardy.

PBS programs have received numerous awards and high marks from critics. One show, *Sesame Street,* started a revolution in children's television; it proved that educational content could be presented in an entertaining way. Children raved about it and about *The Electric Company,* and *3-2-1 Contact.* Adults raved about *Life on Earth, NOVA, Cosmos, Upstairs, Downstairs,* and *Media Probes.* But not all of PBS's reviews have been raves. PBS has also been faulted for indicating a lack of commitment to local programs and issues and for practicing elitism, that is, offering programs that appeal to highbrow audiences only. However, a 1980 Neilsen survey demonstrated that 68 percent of *all* American households watch some public television each week.

To be sure, compared to network shows, public television does not measure up in the ratings game. But it was not designed to be a competitor of network television. Instead, it was designed to offer an alternative. Do you think it has succeeded in doing so?

To an extent, public broadcasting has, in the words of *New York Times* reporter Fred Flaxman, "become a charity case—complete with on-air telethons, premiums, direct mail solicitations, auctions, sweepstakes and extended sponsorship credits." To be sure, the present and future of PBS is open to question. As of 1982, Congress had authorized an

TABLE 7-1 Appropriations for Public Broadcasting

1980	$152,000,000
1981	$162,000,000
1982	$172,000,000
1983	$137,000,000*
1984	$130,000,000*

*Reagan budget

MEDIA PROBE

1. Analyze a full day's programming aired on your area's public television station. What types of programs are offered? To what extent, if any, do they differ from what is offered on network television? To what extent, if any, are they similar? What, if anything, should public and network television learn from each other?
2. Develop an argument in which you agree or disagree with each of the following statements:

Public television is good at what it does. It is no more elitist than the public library.

The audiences of CPB-supported stations tend to be wealthier and more educated than the general populace; they certainly possess the personal resources to support such stations, and they should do so, if they want to enjoy the benefits of public broadcasting. Taxpayers as a whole should not be compelled to subsidize entertainment for a select few.

eighteen-month experiment during which PBS stations would be permitted to air low-key forms of commercial advertising. And PBS president Lawrence Grossman proposed that PBS create a new cultural pay-TV service called the Public Subscription Network in order to ease the funding burden. Whatever the solutions, the debates that result should be interesting ones.

Cable TV

Though we will explore cable in greater depth in a later chapter, let us begin our consideration of it now.

Cable television is a system that delivers television by wire instead of through the open airwaves. Its signals are sent through coaxial cables stretched from location to location like telephone wires. Cable was begun as a means of bringing television to communities too small to support their own station or to improve reception in communities unable to receive clear TV because of their isolation (distance from television stations) or terrain (mountainous areas). It ended up doing much more than that.

Originally, cable made its home in those areas the TV signal, which travels in a straight line, was unable to reach; now, however, cable has found the welcome mat laid out for it in cities and suburbs. The appeal of cable is no longer merely the promise of television or improved reception. Instead, it is the opportunity it presents for programming of all kinds. While over-the-air TV is restricted to the available VHF and UHF frequencies, cable is not; in effect, cable is the television of abundance. All cable systems constructed in the United States must offer at least twenty-four channels; most cable systems now offer at least thirty-six channels, many sixty-four channels, and some more than double that amount. So, whereas conventional television has been dubbed the television of scarcity, cable television has been heralded as the television of diversity.

Cable television, originally developed to simply make reception possible in remote areas, is now the almost universal television of abundance and diversity. (Randy Matusow)

In 1965 the FCC issued a set of rules that slowed the growth of cable, but in 1972 the rules became less restrictive, and in 1980 the FCC more or less adopted a laissez-faire policy; virtually all rules governing cable have been dropped. Consequently, all expectations are that cable's growth and penetration into the mainstream of American television life will continue. Consider these statistics. In 1960, fewer than 2 percent of American TV households had cable television. In 1971, about 8.7 percent of the nation's TV households were cable subscribers. From 1970 to 1979 cable subscribers increased by about 9 million. In one year alone, 1979 to 1980, cable added about 3 million new subscribers. By 1981, over 23 million American homes were already hooked up to cable; that corresponded to approximately 28.3 percent of the country. This growth is continuing to accelerate. As of 1984 cable TV was nearing the halfway mark; Nielsen reported that 42.5 percent (35,783,000) of U.S. television households were wired for cable. The forecast is that cable's growth will continue until 75 to 80 percent of all TV households are connected. At that point we will have fulfilled cable's prophecy: we will have become a wired nation.

MEDIA PROBE

Using yourself if you have cable, or someone else if you don't, compile a log of viewing habits. Specifically, record those times when you viewed an offering not available on conventional television, the reason you chose to watch the program, and whether your expectations were fulfilled. Also, estimate the percentage of time you devote to watching programs not available on conventional television.

What do we watch on cable television? First, a cable system carries all the TV channels that we would watch normally through conventional television. Second, we can also watch programs that the cable system originates, including those shows created under a public-access programming agreement. In such an arrangement, the cable system, for a small fee, offers its studios and cameras to a group or individual wishing to present a program. Third, we watch programs derived from the importation of distant, independent stations, known as "superstations." Fourth, we watch shows provided by special programming services like Cable News Network and Nikelodeon. And finally, we may watch one or more pay-television services like Home Box Office, Show Time, or Cinemax. If we are a subscriber to an even more sophisticated cable system, we may not only watch cable television, we may actually "talk to" or interact with our cable television. In other words, some cable systems now offer a two-way capability enabling viewers to use TV to fulfill their shopping, banking, and home security needs. Two-way cable has been operating since 1977 when it had its start in Columbus, Ohio. Originated by Warner Communications, *QUBE*, allows viewers to answer multiple-choice and yes-no questions, ask for further information, shop by television, bank by television, and use electronic mail. Thus, television is beginning to play a larger role in the lives of Americans than it already does.

Research demonstrates that cable subscribers are generally younger and more affluent than conventional TV viewers; they also watch more television than those who are not hooked up to a cable. Likewise, those who have pay TV and other services watch even more than those who subscribe to the basic cable services only.

With such a plethora of offerings from which to select, cable offers the consumer the chance to become a selective viewer. In theory, if not in practice, cable viewers can mix and match programs to fit their special needs and interests.

How will cable affect the networks? Predictions vary. Some say the networks stand to lose 10 percent of their viewers to cable; other estimates are as high as 50 percent. Already, a 1981 Nielsen survey showed that in homes wired to pay TV, network ratings were 10 percent lower than the national average. The coming years may well represent an era of transition for television as we know it.

SUMMARY

Television means different things to different people. For some, television has a positive connotation, for others a negative one. Whatever our opinion of television, however, to varying degrees it helps structure each of our lives. Americans, in general, spend more time watching television than doing anything else except sleeping. In fact, television plays over six and three-quarters hours a day in a typical American household.

Two key inventions of the 1920s made television a reality: the iconoscope and the kinescope, the devices that made it possible to transmit and receive pictures electronically. Owing to the economic conditions of the times and years of arguing over patent rights, the growth of television as a medium was slowed. It was 1939 when commercial television was first introduced to America at the New York World's Fair. People were fascinated, but World War II intervened and again TV had to wait. After the war, things began to happen quickly—too quickly, the FCC feared, and in 1948 they ordered a freeze on the granting of TV licenses. In 1952, after a master plan for television's development was created, the freeze was lifted, and television quickly became part of American life, as radio had before it.

Three major networks dominate broadcast TV: NBC, CBS, and ABC. The networks are responsible for either producing or arranging the production of most of the programming transmitted during prime time; thus, they function as program suppliers. Networks are composed of groups of local stations (some O&O and some affiliated) that have been electronically bonded together. The local stations, however, function as the heart of the American broadcasting system because they have the final say regarding what we will and will not be able to watch on our TV set. Syndicates, organizations independent of both the networks and the local stations, also sell programs to the stations.

While networks are not licensed, stations are; as such they are subject to a number of different regulations and controls. Key players in the control and regulation game are the FCC, the networks, the stations themselves, the NAB, and various public-interest organizations.

Regardless of size, every station is headed by a general manager whose function it is to see that the stations' four main activities are performed: programming, sales, engineering, and administration.

Two alternatives to commercial, over-the-air broadcasting have generated interest and excitement over the years: public TV and cable TV. Both have their problems and their promises and could be responsible for altering the direction of television in the future.

KEY TERMS

Iconoscope
Kinescope
Duopoly ruling
Sixth Report and Order
VHF
UHF
Videotape
O&O
Affiliate
Syndicates
Licensee ascertainment
Equal opportunity rule
Fairness Doctrine
NAB Television Code
Public television
Cable television
Corporation for Public Broadcasting
Public Broadcasting Service
QUBE
Coaxial cable

NOTES

[1] Robert MacNeil, "Is Television Shortening Our Attention Span?" *New York University Education Quarterly,* Winter 1983, p. 2.

[2] George Comstock, *Television in America,* Sage, Beverly Hills, Calif., 1980, pp. 33–34.

[3] Erik Barnouw, *Tube of Plenty: The Evolution of American Television,* Oxford University Press, London, 1975, p. 4.

[4] See *The Story of Television: The Life of Philo T. Farnsworth,* Norton, New York, 1949.

[5] See Erik Barnouw, *A Tower in Babel,* Oxford University Press, New York, 1966.

[6] Sharon Lowery and Melvin L. DeFleur, *Milestones in Mass Communication Research,* Longman, New York, 1983, p. 16.

[7] Peggy Charren and Martin W. Sandler, *Changing Channels,* Addison-Wesley, Reading, Mass., 1983, p. 75.

[8] Barnouw, *Tube of Plenty,* op. cit., p. 60.

[9] Sally Bedell, "An FCC Chief in an Era of Broadcasting Change," *The New York Times,* February 22, 1983, p. C20.

[10] Les Brown, "Fear of Fowler," *Channels of Communication,* vol. 1 number 5, 1981–82, p. 21.

[11] Ibid.

[12] Ibid.

[13] Bedell, op. cit.

SUGGESTIONS FOR FURTHER READING

Barnouw, Erik: *A History of Broadcasting in the United States,* 3 vols, Oxford University

Press, New York, 1966–1968. *The most comprehensive historical survey of broadcasting; often referred to in the literature.*

———: *Tube of Plenty: The Evolution of American Television,* Oxford University Press, New York, 1975. *An abridgement of Barnouw's three-volume work, but still a thorough treatment of the history of the television industry.*

Bergreen, Laurence: *Look Now, Pay Later: The Rise of Network Broadcasting,* Doubleday, Garden City, N.Y., 1980. *A very readable account of the rise of network broadcasting in America.*

Carnegie Commission: *Public Television,* Harper & Row, New York, 1967. *The Carnegie Commission's Report, based on an eighteen-month study of public TV.*

Carnegie Commission: *A Public Trust: The Report of the Carnegie Commission on the Future of Public Broadcasting,* Bantam, New York, 1979. *A reexamination and reassessment.*

Kahn, Frank J., ed.: *Documents of American Broadcasting,* Prentice-Hall, Englewood Cliffs, N.J., 1978. *A valuable sourcebook and reference on critical issues in the electronic media.*

Sloan Commission on Cable Communications: *On the Cable: The Television of Abundance,* McGraw-Hill, New York, 1971. *Offers the reader facts and figures on the history and growth of the medium.*

Sterling, Christopher H., and Kitross, John M.: *Stay Tuned,* Wadsworth, Belmont, Calif., 1978. *Provides a chronological look at the development of TV.*

CHAPTER 8

TELEVISION: ASSESSING THE IMAGE

The living room has been converted into a kind of car: the TV screen is its windshield; every home is mobile; everybody is in the driver's seat; and we are all seeing the same sights simultaneously.

John Leonard

CHAPTER PREVIEW

After reading this chapter, you should be able to:
- Explain at least five principles of television programming
- Define the LOP theory
- Compare the programming practices of the three major commercial networks
- Distinguish between the following programming tactics: hamlocking, counterprogramming, blunting, and bridging
- Define and distinguish between a show's rating and a show's share of the audience
- Explain the advantages and disadvantages of the Nielsen rating system
- Compare a television news broadcast and a newspaper
- Identify factors that contribute to the American public's reliance on television news
- Explain why some critics believe that the main emphasis of television news is on entertainment rather than information
- Explain how the use of the Minicam has affected the news
- Identify the extent to which television affects your attitudes and behavior
- Compare "real life" with the image of life reflected on television
- Explain why some critics maintain that television is taking away childhood
- Compare the catharsis, stimulation, and null theories of television violence
- Provide examples of advertising practices directed at children that critics find objectionable
- Discuss how women, blacks, and the aged have been portrayed on television

In 1938, E. B. White wrote: "I believe television is going to be the test of the modern world, and that in this new opportunity to see beyond the range of our vision we shall discover either a new and unbearable disturbance of the general peace or a saving radiance in the sky. We shall stand or fall by television—of that I am quite sure." And so we have, and so we are. Television has taken us to the moon, on space shuttle flights, to the villages of Vietnam, to the conflicts of Central America, to the Olympics in Sarajevo, to the cosmos of Carl Sagan, and to the Archie Bunker of Norman Lear. Television has provided us with hours of shared laughter and shared tears. It permits us to see worlds of fact and worlds of fantasy; through television we are able to travel far beyond our own immediate experiences. As such, television may affect the way we see ourselves, the way we see others, and the way we think about our world.

We expect television to educate, comfort, entertain, and babysit. We use television to sell both products and sell ideas. We even rely on it to function as therapist and soothsayer. And, as we shall see in this chapter, all the while we criticize it. As one commentator observes, "Disparagement of TV is second only to watching TV." But disparagement for disparagement's sake serves no useful purpose. In contrast, a critical examination of the medium and a consideration of the practical ways we can use television to our advantage is of value. As Bill Moyers notes, "television can instruct, inform and inspire as well as distract, distort and demean. . . . This marvelous medium with all its potential for laughter and light, is worth fighting for."

Today, all signs indicate that television in one form or another will be with us for years to come. Will you be prepared to meet its challenge? Will you be able to use television to make your life better? We hope the information contained in this chapter will provide you with a good start.

PROGRAMMING: PRINCIPLES, PRACTICES, AND PRESSURES

The three networks spend over $1 billion a year on prime-time programming. A typical one-hour pilot costs over $1 million to produce. Thus, television executives who make successful programming decisions can find themselves elevated to the top level of management in the industry. This was the case with Fred Silverman. However, Silverman, as we now know, can also be used to illustrate the "fall from glory" that is apt to occur when programming decisions no longer pan out: Fred Silverman is the former network programming chief for CBS, ABC, and NBC. He explains the art of programming this way: "It's a screwy world—there is no science to what we do . . . you either start with a unique idea or a personality and you take it from there."[1]

MEDIA PROBE

The questions contained in the following programming aptitude test have been designed to let you match minds with actual television programmers. Write T if you think a statement is true and F if you think it is false. Also explain your answers.

1. A program should be visually pleasing.
2. A program should be devised according to a predictable formula.
3. A program should avoid controversy.
4. A program should appeal most to people in the 18- to 49-year-old age group.
5. A program should not contain totally new ideas.

Although there are no pat answers regarding television programming, the five items listed in the media probe are examples of the principles adhered to by typical programmers. For the most part programmers base the decisions they make on various assumptions they hold about the prime-time audience. For one thing programmers aim to secure the largest possible audience of 18- to 49-year-olds. Why this age group? Because this is the group that spends the most money and is most likely to appeal to advertisers. Next, programmers reason that viewers watch television, not specific programs, and that viewers tend to watch during certain hours no matter what is on. Given this premise, programmers aim to avoid flops rather than to select program winners. In other words, they program according to the least objectional program (LOP) principle, an idea best explained by its originator, NBC executive Paul Klein: "A very old law has become more and more useful in figuring our program popularity . . . Sir Isaac Newton's First Law of Motion, the one that says that a body at rest tends to stay at rest. Once a viewer chooses his program he may have to fiddle with a lot of knobs should he decide to switch channels, especially if it's an older color set. So a viewer in a chair tends to stay in his chair."[2]

It is believed that after an initial period of turning the dial to determine what's available, viewers tend to tune into one channel and stay tuned to that channel unless they hear something that upsets or offends them. Consequently, a "hit" show is not the one viewers like the most, but rather the one most viewers judge to be less objectionable than anything else on television at that time. Again, Klein's words are most telling; according to him a program's success is determined by "75 million thresholds of pain plus the law of inertia."[3] The LOP principle of programming results in a plethora of copycat programming—programming that reflects a bias toward the status quo; viewers, it is felt, are less apt to be disturbed by familiar ideas, ideas that do not challenge their beliefs and values. As T. F. Baldwin and C. Lewis note: "The character of television programs is determined by the three networks' notions of what will appeal to large numbers of people, sell products or services for advertisers, and not jeopardize the valuable licenses or the good will of affiliates by creating a negative audience response."[4] So the general rule, Don't offend anybody, applies, and to avoid generating controversy programmers have kept the offerings fairly predictable. Consequently, most television entertainment is written according to proven formulas. There are crime shows, situation comedies, variety show, talk shows, action-adventure shows, doctor-lawyer shows, game shows, family shows, soap operas, documentaries, and news shows.

The rewards for the television network executive who makes the right programming decisions can be enormous. Grant Tinker of NBC produced his then-wife's *Mary Tyler Moore Show*. (AP/Wide World)

MEDIA PROBE

Classify the network shows in this week's television schedule according to the categories described in the text. Log them into the following time frame: early morning, morning, midday, late afternoon, early evening, prime time, and late evening.

Are there any discernible differences in the types of programming presented by the networks? If so, what are they? Are there any *types of programming that heavily outweigh the others? Does any one network show more of a willingness to experiment? If so, in what ways?*

The LOP principle has other implications as well. Just because we watch something doesn't mean we are pleased with what we are watching. The size of the viewing audience has been used to confirm that we like what we get on television, but no evidence has been offered to demonstrate that we get what we like.[5] To further complicate matters, a recent study commissioned by the television industry's own National Association of Broadcasters has determined that viewers are becoming increasingly critical of the programming offered to them by the networks. Consequently, while Americans may be watching more television today than ever before, they are far less satisfied with it.[6] In addition, on April 25, 1983, a study released by Television Audience Assessment (TAA) showed that half of us leave the room at least once during a show, 40 to 50 percent of us are doing something else while the television is on, and approximately one-third of the audience deserts the typical hour-long program before it is over, switching to another channel or turning off the television.[7] According to TAA president Elizabeth J. Roberts, "We just don't use TV the way we used to. It may be that today's audiences expect more from television than audiences have in past years."

Another concern is whether LOP programming serves the public interest. If we consider that the public interest is what the public is interested in viewing, then those programs which attract the largest audience are holding the interest of the largest numbers of people and are therefore "serving the public interest." Television programmers, of course, would be apt to reason just this way. Others argue, however, that avoiding controversial issues and experimental program forms is not in the public interest. But there does appear to be a correlation between increasing profits and decreasing variety. And as profits rise, the networks simply become less willing to risk good time slots and what they perceive as ideal scheduling on "unusual" programs. Is this practice in the public interest? As long as standardized programming leads to higher profits, the network answer will be yes. And as long as the viewing audience is content to settle for liking what they get rather than getting what they like, such a programming practice will continue.

Many television programs are pretested at research facilities that measure viewers' reactions, including their galvanic skin responses—variations in the amount of sweat in the palm. At one such research center, the Preview House in Los Angeles, viewers are also requested to indicate their degree of approval for a pilot program by turning a dial at their seats. The dial is used to indicate how much they like or dislike what is being shown. In order to assess whether the audience's preferences are normal and representative, all assembled are first shown a *Mr. Magoo* cartoon. If the audience responds in a nonstandard or unusual manner to the cartoon, the results are adjusted up or down accordingly. A previewing show is scored in "Magoos," and it is judged a success if it earns a score of between 5.1 and 6.3 Magoos. Interestingly, research to date has shown that anything new or unfamiliar scores very low in Magoos.

Efforts at change have been made. In 1970, for example, the *prime-time access rule* was issued. The goal of this rule was to expand program diversity by requiring stations in the top fifty markets to schedule programs other than those produced or licensed by the three networks. In effect, the 7:30 to 8 P.M. (EST) time slot was taken from the networks and returned to the local stations. The impact of the rule is not clear. While independent producers did enter the prime-time television arena, most of the shows accepted for airing by the broadcasters have been game shows.

Programmers have devised various tactics to capture and maintain the desired audi-

MEDIA PROBE

Examine the programs offered in your community in the early evening, postnews time slot. To what extent do you think the prime-time access rule has had beneficial effects? Why?

---

ence. Among the strategies they employ are hamlocking, counterprogramming, blunting, and bridging. *Hamlocking* occurs when programmers sandwich a weak or brand new show in between two strong shows. This practice relies on the premise that once the set is on, the audience simply flows from one program to the next on the same channel; the belief is that the viewer will not get up to change the channel. As we have seen, this premise is debatable. *Counterprogramming* occurs when a decision is made to schedule a different kind of show from the type being offered by the other two commercial networks. In contrast, *blunting* means scheduling a program similar to those offered by the competing networks in the hope that the ratings of those programs will be reduced. In addition to these three programming strategies, networks also use *bridging* as a ploy; this involves selecting a show with a long running time and airing it just before the start of other prime-time offerings. By doing this, programmers hope that the audience will stay with the network schedule for the remainder of the evening. It is believed that as long as production costs are high, programmers will have to work to ensure that television programs are seen by large numbers of people: only in this way can the cost per viewer be kept reasonably low. Inevitably, this need becomes a quest to keep increasing audience size.

The Ratings Game

Separating the programs that will be on television from the programs that will not is part of a very critical economic game today. The goal of the game is to earn rating points, and each move taken toward that goal is peppered with risks and potential rewards. A program is deemed to be a success if it attracts viewers. After all, as Les Brown notes, "Advertisers buy audiences, not programs."[8] And as TV researcher William Melody reflects: "The programs are the bait used to lure the viewers into a position where they can be exposed to persuasive messages."[9] Advertisers, some believe, are the reason for television, not simply a by-product. It is advertising that provides the financing for television. So programmers are out to attract viewers to sell to advertisers.

This is where ratings enter the picture. The value of any particular commercial minute is directly related to the popularity of the show on which it appears. Each rating point is equal to 1 percent of the 84.9 million television households in America, or 84,900 homes. On an annual basis, one rating point represents about $27 million in pretax profit for a network. For this reason, the quest for ratings has become the dominant motivation and rationale for programming decisions. On the basis of ratings, viewers are sold to advertisers.

Two companies sell quantitative data on audience viewing behavior to the television industry: Arbitron (discussed in Chapter 6) and the A.C. Nielsen Company. Both Arbitron and Nielsen survey over 200 local television markets every year. Both use the diary technique to gather data, and both use similar techniques to select sample households. A computer chooses phone numbers at random from a listing of all telephone directories in an area. The targeted households are contacted by letter and by telephone and asked to keep a diary of their television viewing. Participating households receive one diary for every working television set in the home, and viewers are asked to record their viewing every quarter hour. Respondents are also requested to record the age and sex of all who are viewing. Space for the recording of addi-

What program is this isolated American family watching? The Nielsen ratings became the arbiter of survival for network television programming. (Gaylord Herron/Archive Pictures)

tional demographic data is left at the back of the diary; there respondents answer questions regarding family size and their city. Families keep diaries for seven days, after which they are returned to the rating company. About 50 percent of the diaries that are sent out are actually used. Periodically, Arbitron also employs personal interviews to gather more specialized data. The greatest difference between these two key rating services is that while Arbitron and Nielsen are both concerned with local audiences, only the A. C. Nielsen Company provides a second rating service for those interested in the performance of network programs.

In practice, Nielsen is the scorekeeper of network television. There are 1700 Nielson households in America; this sample represents the viewing habits of the more than 84 million American television households. Information about the viewing habits of Nielsen households is gathered by an electronic device attached to the television receivers (up to four) in the home. The device, called a *Storage Instantaneous Audimeter* (SIA), automatically records the precise time a set is on (one audimeter is attached to each set in a sample home) and the channel to which it is tuned. The audimeter compiles its record minute by minute. The information contained in the audimeter is carried over special telephone lines to a computer center in Florida, where the data collected from all 1700 audimeters are sent twice a day. In addition to the audimeters, Nielsen also collects data from about 2200 additional households through the diary method. The diaries, or *Audilogs,* supply supplemental information, including the age, sex, education, and income of the viewers of specific programs. After all data derived from audimeters and audilogs are collated and tabulated, a ratings book is sent to Nielsen clients. This national data, called the *Nielsen Television Index* (NTI), is published every two weeks. In New York, Los Angeles, Philadelphia, San Francisco, and Detroit, Nielsen also publishes overnight ratings on network shows. The "overnights" give data related to the number of households viewing. They do not take into account such variables as age, sex, or income.

Two key figures are contained in the data

YOU WERE THERE

THE BIRTH OF THE NIELSENS

Founded in 1923, Nielsen had among its clients firms like Campbell Soup and Johnson Wax. The audience size for their new radio advertising was a matter of concern to such clients, and they encouraged Nielsen to devise a way to measure it. Arthur Nielsen began to search around. An engineer by training, he was more inclined to mechanical devices which would keep track of listening than he was to dealing with the say-so of respondents. When two MIT professors came up with an instrument which could be attached to a radio and would record when it was switched on or off as well as any changes in tuning, Nielsen quickly acquired the rights in 1936. For the next three years the company worked on the development of the service, and by 1940 Nielsen was issuing radio ratings.

The service was costly, and as a result the Nielsen ratings were less in demand than those of its competitor, C. E. Hooper. Hooper used the more economical telephone-coincidental method, where a flurry of random telephone interviews produced estimates of what the public was listening to at the moment. After the Second World War Nielsen stayed with radio, while Hooper raced ahead to start up television ratings. But the Hooper company turned listless during the slack period of the 1948–1952 freeze. When Nielsen offered to buy out the Hooperatings in 1949, Hooper was losing not only money but also faith that national television would ever catch on. In March of 1950, for a half million dollars, Hooper sold his national rating services, telling friends that he had unloaded a worthless property. Nielsen immediately became the company with the best national figures, a prominence it has never lost. Profits came in due course. The competition between Nielsen and Hooper was a case of the tortoise outdistancing the hare.

All told, it took 17 years of development and 15 million dollars invested before A.C. Nielsen Company could break even on its Audimeter service. Companies without this sort of determination and capital fell out of contention long before. Nielsen succeeded in part because it was making enough money in its other operations that it could survive the drain of development costs. The firm was the world's leader at checking supermarket and drugstore shelves to see how well their clients' products were selling—a service of great importance to manufacturers who have to learn as quickly as possible about any snags in their long distribution channels and about how their sales compare to the sales of others. Income produced by the shelf-checking operation helped tide the company over as it became obvious that developing the ratings business was going to take time, since there were few forerunners and Nielsen would have to carefully feel its way.

It is an irony that the Nielsen ratings, which have come to count so much in the operation of modern media, count so little today in the operations of the A.C. Nielsen Company. Measuring television audiences amounts to only 11 percent of this large firm's business. Yet in the world of television, those ratings numbers are the be-all and end-all. "In television," writes ABC vice-president Bob Shanks, "everything depends on the question, How did it do in the ratings?" New York Times television writer Les Brown echoes this when he concedes, "In television only one notice matters, that from the ultimate critic, the A.C. Nielsen Company." The Nielsen ratings are the conduit of the public's choices, and when they arrive at the network offices, it is with considerable authority.

Jib Fowles, *Television Viewers Vs. Media Snobs,* Stein & Day, New York, 1982, pp. 57–59.

offered to Nielsen clients: the *rating* of a show and its *share*. The rating is the percentage of the total television households watching a show. The following formula is used to calculate a show's rating:

$$\text{Rating} = \frac{\text{number of households watching a program}}{\text{number of homes with television}}$$

A rating of 30 means that 30 percent of the homes with television are tuned to the program. Remember, these ratings represent households, not people, and are based only on homes with television sets. A share is also a percentage of the broadcast audience, but unlike a rating, it measures how well a program is doing compared to other programs aired at the same time; thus a share, a competitive statistic, indicates the percentage of viewership out of the actual number of sets in use. The following formula is used to calculate a show's share of the audience:

$$\text{Share of audience} = \frac{\text{number of households watching a program}}{\text{number of households using television at that time}}$$

In a three-network system a program needs to earn a share of at least 30 to be maintained; if it does not receive such a share of the television pie, it is felt that the show is not sufficiently competitive. Nielsen sells the derived data to the networks (they pay about $2 million a year for the service), stations, TV production companies, and of course advertising agencies (the largest group of Nielsen subscribers). The chief players in the game of television are the networks, the stations, and the advertisers; the people are simply counted. As Les Brown notes, "The consumer, whom the custodians of the medium are pledged to serve, is in fact served up."[10] The data generated from the people count—the count of consumers—determines what advertisers will be charged to run their commercials. Networks charge the highest rates for shows that appeal to the young adult market (18 to 34-year-olds); research shows that the people in this age group spend the most on the products being advertised. From an advertiser's perspective the next most valuable audience includes viewers between the age of 18 and 49. Together these two groups fill their households with what media critic Les Brown calls "the paraphenalia of middle-class life."[11]

The validity of the rating (and the share) system is taken for granted in the television and advertising industries. This does not mean the system is without its detractors; in fact, so much relies on the ratings that inevitably they have become a focus of criticism.

Critics have noted that the ratings have serious weaknesses. For one, the ratings are skewed in favor of television viewers who are 18 to 49 years old, the group advertisers perceive as containing their prime prospects. Second, 50 percent of the people asked by Nielsen to serve as Nielsen families say no; we don't know whether there is a significant difference in the viewing habits or characteristics of people who agree to have their viewing monitored and those who refuse such an offer. Likewise, in the case of both the Nielsen and the Arbitron diaries, we don't know if returners behave differently from the non-returners. Further complicating the evaluation of the data is a third factor. According to *TV Guide* author David Chagall, it is quite likely that about 300 Nielsen families are not counted in any biweekly rating period. Various factors can account for this: audimeter lines may malfunction, TV sets may break, or families may go on vacation. Nielsen also employs what statisticians refer to as a "low-confidence level" in reporting information. There can be an error of as much as plus or minus 2.6 in any rating number supplied by Nielsen. This represents a total of about 2

MEDIA PROBE

Given: One rating point equals about 17 Nielsen households, and one Nielsen household represents about 84,900 real houses.

Imagine you are asked to be a Nielsen viewer. Would you accept the offer? Why or why not?

Imagine you and the others in your class are Nielsen families. Your program choices will help determine what shows stay on the air. Compile a list of shows you would watch, noting the day, time, and channel for each. Compute the rating and the share for each show earned in your class.

What do you think are the advantages and the disadvantages of using such a rating system to determine which programs live or die?

---

million viewers who should be added to or subtracted from the show's total audience. Criticisms have also been leveled against Nielsen for relying on too small a sample. Here an analogy to medical blood tests is offered by the Nielsen company to refute the complaint: "When a doctor wants to count your red corpuscles, he doesn't drain the body but merely takes a small sample of blood."

Defenders note that the Nielsens have had a positive effect on commercial television. According to Marvin Mord, vice president of research for ABC Television, the Nielsens "serve to stimulate programmers to perform better all the time." Others argue that the Nielsens perform no such service; instead, they really turn the consumer of television into the product of television. The Nielsen figures have been assailed for other reasons as well. At any given moment in prime time, over 38 million television sets in America are turned on. Nielsen data reflects such a figure. What the Nielsen data cannot tell us, however, is whether viewers are interested in the program or are even in the room. In fact, research shows that almost 20 percent of the time a television set plays in an American household, it plays to no one; the room is empty.[12] In addition, it is possible that the Nielsen figures are invalid for another reason; people who know their viewing is being measured may consciously change their viewing behavior. Others complain that the entire rating structure is dated because ratings are generally based on households instead of individuals. It is felt that the household structure of audience measurement precipitates invalid results at a time when multiple sets make viewing preferences an individual decision. The main criticism, however, is that far too much emphasis is given to the ratings. Instead of programming to meet the needs of diverse groups in the population, television is transformed into a popularity contest with look-alike programming. Minority interests are all but ignored. Finally, the ratings reveal only which of the offerings are the most popular. They do not reveal what anyone thinks about the total offering. The A.C. Nielsen Company readily acknowledges this: "these are quantitative measurements. The word 'rating' is a misnomer because it implies a measurement of program quality—and this we never do. NEVER!"[13] In light of this, the research firm Television Audience Assessment recently unveiled a new methodology that measures a program's appeal (enjoyment), and impact (emotional or intellectual involvement) on viewers instead of merely recording the number of people tuned in to a program. What has not yet been demonstrated for advertisers, however, is that those viewers who respond favorably to quality shows also respond more favorably to the commercials that accompany them. It is certain that the ratings will remain a point of contention for years to come.

FOCUS ON TELEVISION NEWS AND THE ELECTRONIC JOURNALIST

Is the definition of news changed by the medium through which it is presented? Should it

MEDIA PROBE

Compare a daily newspaper with two televised news programs, one local and one national. What do they have in common? Where do the two media diverge? How does the medium affect the way the processer (reader or viewer) experiences the news?

---

be changed? How, if at all, does television alter the definition and the substance of the news? According to former NBC anchorman David Brinkley, "News is what I say it is. It's something worth knowing by my standards."[14] In addition, Brinkley believes that a story should not be aired on television "unless it is interesting to at least ten percent of the audience. Preferably more. But at least ten percent."[15] Why is "interest" of such critical importance? Do you think it is the task of the television journalist to communicate to viewers what they "need to know" or what they are "interested in knowing"? How do the differences between a televised news show and a newspaper affect what is deemed newsworthy?

The news as reported on television and in a newspaper can be distinguished in a number of ways. Pictures play more of a critical role in televised news reporting than they do in print news reporting. In fact, a thirty-minute news broadcast contains fewer words than the front page of *The New York Times*. According to Av Westin, author of *Newswatch*, the impact of the two media is very different. "Time is our equivalent of a newspaper's space, and it takes time to allow tears to flow down the cheek of the mother of children killed in the Palestinian massacre, time to allow the President of the United States to say that the economy is a mess. Visual and audio impact is what television is all about . . . that outweighs the 'sacrifice' of the more detailed information that a newspaper can deliver." Thus, on television the camera becomes the arbiter of what is considered to be newsworthy. If a camera crew is able to get to an event, cover it, and relay the film or tape to the station in time for the newscast, then the event stands a chance of being judged newsworthy. If not, it does not. As a result, much of the news that appears on television has been "scheduled" to occur at times and places convenient to crews and reporters; consequently, much of the news we are presented with through television did not occur "spontaneously." Rather, we are offered a large percentage of pseudoevents—events which are planned for the purpose of being reported. For this reason, when viewing a news broadcast, it is important to ask whether the event would have occurred at all, or if it would have occurred differently, if TV were not there to report it.

When reading a newspaper, you can skip around, read what is of interest to you, and, if you desire, ignore the rest. In contrast, the television viewer must process the news as it is delivered and in the order in which it is delivered. Unlike the newspaper reader, the viewer cannot opt to skip over an item and go on to something else. To be sure, you can mentally tune out for a period of time, but if you do, you can never be certain that you will tune in at an appropriate juncture. Thus, news commentator Brinkley concludes that the right question for the electronic journalist to answer is, Who really cares about this? Providing people with just the news they are interested in receiving has critical drawbacks, however. Television news helps set our national agenda; it helps determine the issues we will think about and discuss with others. It also helps determine those issues we will *not* be thinking about or discussing with others. And as Fred Friendly pointed out in *Due to Circumstances Beyond Our Control*, "What the American people don't know can kill them."

Research indicates that despite the fact that Americans have more opportunities to receive more news than ever before, they are actually less knowledgeable about their

MEDIA VIEW

DETERMINING WHAT GOES INTO A BROADCAST AND WHAT DOESN'T

In order to handle the pressure and irrevocable fact that television news operates on the basis of elimination rather than inclusion, I developed a series of questions to determine what should go into a broadcast and what should be left out.

Is my world safe?
Are my city and home safe?
If my wife, children and loved ones are safe, then what has happened in the past twenty-four hours to shock them, amuse them or make them better off than they were?

The audience wants these questions answered quickly and with just enough detail to satisfy an attention span that is being interrupted by clattering dishes, dinner conversation or the fatigue of the end of the working day.

Is my world safe? I mean that both literally and figuratively. Does the story deal with the safety of the world? If the nation's vital interests are affected, could it mean war? Does the story have geopolitical or economic implications that concern world safety? . . .

Are my city and home safe? Next to the world and nation, personal concerns center on the home and its immediate environment, the city. People need to know about events that directly affect their lives. . . .

If my wife, children and loved ones are safe, then what has happened in the past twenty-four hours to shock them, amuse them or make them better off than they were? Though a story in this category rarely takes the lead, it certainly belongs on the program. . . . This is family news.

Av Westin, *Newswatch: How TV Decides the News,* Simon & Schuster, New York, 1982, p. 62–63.

---

world. Over half the American population has no idea who the senators and representatives who represent them are. Over half of all 17-year-olds in the country are under the impression that the president appoints the members of Congress.[16] According to Ron Powers, the author of *The Newscasters,* television news shows are partly to blame for reinforcing this ignorance. He cites a sign posted on the wall of one network affiliate as a case in point: "Remember, the vast majority of our viewers have never seen a copy of The New York Times. The vast majority of our viewers do not read the same books and magazines that you read. . . . In fact, many of them never read anything."[17]

The latest Roper surveys indicate that two-thirds of the American public report their main source of news to be television. In contrast, only 44 percent rely on newspapers as a primary news source.[18] Television has surpassed all other media on this question since 1963. And according to the newest Roper Poll, 41 percent of the American people now get all of their news from television alone. Thus, according to a spokesperson for the Television Information Office, TV is "steadily increasing its lead as the single most relied upon news medium."[19] Likewise, television has led as the most believable medium since 1961. Asked in the current Roper Poll which they would believe if presented with conflicting stories, 53 percent of respondents chose television, 22 percent chose newspapers, 6 percent chose radio, and 8 percent chose magazines. Currently, television enjoys a better than two-to-one advantage over newspapers. In addition, a large proportion of the people interviewed for the latest Roper survey rated television's coverage of all types of news as "excellent" or "good." And when queried as to which medium they would most

MEDIA VIEW

FACES

Perhaps an entertainer, with good lines or the right music, can appear on television one time and become that rare article, the overnight hit. In television news no such lightning strikes. The newsman must be on the screen night after night, long enough for the public to decide if the personality is hollow.

To a degree TV news is built around the star system. Far less than the rest of the schedule, but inescapably based on it. Yet search as I might, I can find no pattern to the success of the most visible faces in the industry.

Walter Cronkite. David Brinkley. John Chancellor. Harry Reasoner. Mike Wallace. Edwin Newman. Eric Sevareid. In looks, voice and approach no two are alike. But there is a common denominator. They are believable. No machine known to science can measure the human waves that come across the screen. But believability is the test.

Local stations have tried bringing an actor to read the news, with consistently poor results. On the other hand, if Walter Cronkite walked into a local newsroom today and said, "Hello, I'm applying for a job as your ten o'clock anchor person," I have an idea how the management would react. They would say, "This guy has to be kidding." Walter might be hired as their news director or even to manage the station. But not to appear on camera. What made Walter Cronkite a star, at the network level, was not his physical appearance but his inner integrity. Over the years the viewers came to believe him.

Television is a copycat medium. What works in one place is soon tried in another. The impression is heightened by the fact that on any night the network anchor teams are working with generally the same bulk of news. The nuances of staging and direction are lost on the viewer. He knows he can change the dial and hear the same story three, or more, times.

So, conditions being equal, the contest often comes down to a quality easily named, hard to define: believability, charisma, personality, warmth.

Dan Rather, *The Camera Never Blinks,* New York, Ballantine Books, 1977, pp. 315–316.

---

want to keep if they could have only one, since the first Roper survey was conducted in 1959, most Americans have responded, "television." As Robert MacNeil, of *The MacNeil/Lehrer Newshour,* comments, "TV has created a nation of news junkies who tune in every night to get their fix on the world."[20] The question is, If TV news is our window on the world, what kind of a fix are we being given?

It has been charged that the very words "television news show" reveals that the main purpose of television news is to entertain rather than to inform. Herbert Schmertz, vice president for public affairs of the Mobil Oil Corporation, says TV "is too concerned with the ratings. They won't do a complex story unless it is visually exciting. TV news is too superficial; this is what happens when a premium is placed on entertainment values."[21] A number of media researchers support this view. Neil Postman, for example, notes that all news shows begin and end with music; in fact, there is even music at each commercial break. What purpose does the music serve? It helps create excitement, it builds expectations; and it heightens interest. But unlike the music that accompanies a film, the theme music of a particular news show is not varied according to the emotion the content calls for; instead the music is unrelentingly upbeat and bright. The same music is played whether the story is about fighting in Lebanon, unemployment in the United States, or a sports team's victory. The goal is for the news to "be perceived as

YOU WERE THERE

WHAT IT'S LIKE TO ANCHOR THE NEWS

Anchoring the news is essentially the same in every market, big or small. You're at a desk, you've got a script, you face two cameras and a TelePrompTer, and you do the news. The Sunday I anchored my first network news show was just like any other time—right down to the fumbles.

NBC had decided to change to open sets, meaning that on a wide shot you were seen head to toe. For several days I debated whether or not to wear slacks so I wouldn't have to worry that, while reading the news, I might inadvertently move my legs to an embarrassingly revealing position. My mother insisted slacks were too casual and in the end I decided she was probably right. To protect myself in case I forgot and crossed my legs, I took a piece of thick masking tape—the kind reporters say mends everything but broken hearts—and taped my ankles together. It worked exceedingly well, holding my legs neatly together every time I inadvertently tried to move them. The first open show went without a hitch. When I finished, pleased with my performance, I stood up to shake hands with the crew. I had completely forgotten the tape and tumbled flat on the floor. Luckily the monitors were off, so the entire country did not get to see me literally fall on my face. . . .

A story can break too late for the editor to polish his script or turn the tape in on time. When you consider that you're putting together a half hour show *live* with news coming in from all over the world, it is a miracle that so many news shows are produced without incident. One evening I came to the last story, a taped piece which was to run three minutes and forty seconds, and I said, "And now this story from California . . . " I paused, waiting for the crew to cut to Los Angeles. Nothing happened. All I saw on the monitor was my increasingly worried face.

Finally the director cut to black. I picked up the phone and said, "What are we going to do?"

"Ad lib," said the producer.

"I'm alone. There's no one to ad lib with."

The producer answered by putting me back on the air.

"Well, you've probably figured out by now that we don't have that spot ready," I announced. "So what I think I'll do for those of you who might have missed the first part of this news broadcast . . . " and I turned the script over and just reread the news until it was time to sign off.

Jessica Savitch, *Anchorwoman,* New York: G.P. Putnam's Sons, 1982, pp. 150–153.

---

warm . . . as appealing to the mood of the audience."[22]

Also supporting the entertainment emphasis of the news is the attention given to attractive and likable anchorpersons and overdesigned news production areas commonly referred to as the "studs and sets" formula. All of this is not done for naught, however. A study printed in *Journalism Monographs* found that 41 percent of the viewers selected their news program on the basis of the anchor's personality and characteristics while only 9 percent selected the program because of its news quality or program format. The remaining 50 percent of the viewers selected a program because of the channel it appeared on or for no particular reason.[23] Thus, news shows are counseled to promote the messenger or anchor above the message or news. As media critic Donna Woolfolk Cross asserts, even the title "anchorman" supports this notion. According to Cross it derives from sports and refers to the last runner of a relay team, the one whose final effort decides the race.

Television news shows, like programming

in general, are involved in a race—a ratings race. What impact does the quest for higher ratings have on televised news? For one thing, according to Frank Mankiewicz and Joel Swerdlow, authors of *Remote Control,* television news has developed a number of unwritten rules that news producers adhere to. Among these is the rule that unattractive faces not appear on camera in good-guy roles. For another, media consultants like McHugh and Hoffman of MacLean, Virginia, and Frank Magid Associates of Marion, Iowa, have assumed enormous importance in television news. In fact, they are commonly referred to as "news doctors." For a fee, these firms will conduct surveys designed to reveal which types of news programs, features, and anchorpersons viewers prefer. They will then compile a list containing those suggestions they believe stations should adopt if they are to reflect viewer preferences. Usually consultants advise the station to hire a warm, attractive, young person to serve as anchor—regardless of whether they are schooled in news reporting or not. In fact, many consultants now suggest that "news has become too important to be left to the newsmen." Today, the newsperson is as much a celebrity as the people he or she covers. As a case in point, one newscaster reportedly unhappy with the way the day's newscast was developing admonished the program manager during a commercial break: "You've got to get the camera closer to me. I have to make love to that camera. That's what I do—make love to those women right through that lens."[24] And noting how the role of the female anchor has experienced a corresponding change, columnist Russell Baker wrote the following:

> The faces of television newswomen are never wrinkled....The faces of television newswomen always seem to have arrived fresh from the presser two seconds ahead of the camera.
>
> Several years ago, to be sure, there was a woman with a wrinkled face on the networks, but they put her aside. "That woman is wrinkled," said a vital executive, and they cut the juice to her camera.
>
> I still miss that woman. She was evidence that women who had undergone human experience grew faces like everybody else in spite of being on television.[25]

But now it is felt that great profits stand to be made in news. Equally as important, it is realized that a highly rated news show can provide a significant boost to a station's entire schedule.

What other steps have been taken to up the ratings of news shows? In general consultants have advised that the length of news stories be shortened, so that on the average, stories occupy ninety seconds or less of air time. Thus, more news is covered in less time. Today only the most unusual events are permitted three minutes of air time, roughly equivalent to 350 words of news copy. And those stories which are accorded less than thirty seconds of air time were probably covered in less than 100 words. The average story length is sixty seconds. According to one critic, the world of television news is made up of short bursts of unrelated information. During a typical thirty-minute show, about fifteen to twenty stories are covered. In practice, according to veteran TV newsman Av Westin, "Television news is obsessed with time."

Consultants have also advised that reporters be positioned at the scene of a story. This tactic has received a boost from the increased use of *electronic newsgathering equipment (ENG)*—especially the Minicam—the small lightweight, expensive, but highly portable camera which enables crews to broadcast stories directly from the scene. According to Ed Godfrey, news director of WSB-TV in Atlanta, "The minicam has added at least an hour more of reporting time to the news show's day." Because of the Minicam's ability to send live pictures to the station via microwave transmitters, and because videotape,

230   RADIO, TELEVISION, AND FILM: THE ELECTRONIC WINDOW

Women are making great professional strides in TV newsrooms. (Catherine Ursillo/Photo Researchers)

MEDIA VIEW

THE WOMEN ON THE NEWS

One day in 1973 the news director of an Austin, Tex., television station approached the anchorwoman of the news program and said, "Don't try to look so pretty because you're going to alienate the women in the audience."

"I said, 'Okay.'" Sara Lee Kessler remembers, "and started buying suits instead of dresses."

Eight years later, the news anchorwoman at a Kansas City, Mo., station spurned the studio's makeup and wardrobe departments in favor of her own clothing and lighter makeup. Christine Craft was taken off the air and made a reporter. Her failing, she alleged in a subsequent lawsuit, was that she didn't look pretty enough.

This might lead one to remark how times have changed, but in fact they have not. Given two competent on-the-air newswomen, fortune has always favored the fairest. The difference is that television now is less afraid to admit it.

Last January a district-court jury awarded $325,000 in damages to Craft for what it concluded was a fradulent representation by her employers when they first hired her. But it is significant that this award was only for fraud—that Craft's concurrent complaint of sexual discrimination was thrown out by the judge before the trial began. Left intact was the industry perception that the best women anchorwomen are the ones who let the audience know they are both anchors and women. . . .Many newswomen openly resent that something beyond their ability to broadcast the news controls their careers, even though they have chosen to work in a medium of appearance and of entertainment.

Joel Pisetzner, "The Women on the News," *The Record,* July 29, 1984.

unlike film, requires no processing, reporters are able to stay out later and cover stories that might not have received coverage previously. Live-from-the-field, see-it-when-it-happens journalism boosts ratings. But ratings do not provide an accurate reflection of news values or ethics. The following example is by Eric Levin:

> On June 24, 1975, for instance, when an Eastern Airlines jet crashed near Kennedy Airport in New York, killing 113 of the 124 people aboard, WNBC-TV got to the scene first with its minicams and garnered the highest ratings in town that night. Anthony Prisendorf, the reporter who stood in front of those live cameras, remembers the crash as "the worst story I ever covered." By sheer accident he happened to be near the airport when the jet went down. When his crew set up—in the record time of seven minutes—he found himself "close, much too close" to the action. "It was horribly grim," he recalls. "Bodies were writhing right in front of us. Once you set up the live feed, you're rooted to the spot. All I could do was tell the cameraman to keep the shot wide. Meanwhile, in my walkie-talkie I could hear the control room saying, 'Beautiful. Keep it coming.'"

While we can agree with newscommentator Ted Koppel that "never has any generation of Americans had greater reason to claim they were eyewitnesses to history," we can't help but wonder if at times the camera should blink.

Robert Rutherford Smith, author of *Beyond the Wasteland: The Criticism of Broadcasting,* emphasizes that too frequently television news stresses the drama inherent in events. The question he ponders is whether the dramatic and the important are one and the same. Rutherford questions the extent to which the important information contained in television news broadcasts is sacrificed to the demands of the dramatic. If so, then the concerns expressed that the news business has crossed over into the realm of show business may, indeed, be valid.

MEDIA PROBE

In March 1983, two camera operators were approached by Cecil Andrews who asked them, "How would you like to see someone burn?" He proceeded to soak his jeans with lighter fluid and then ignited them with a match. Imagine that you are one of the camerapersons. Would you record the resulting events? Explain your answer. (For your information, the camera operators who witnessed the actual event filmed the event for thirty-seven seconds before one of them tried to extinguish the blaze. Andrews, a 37-year-old unemployed roofer who said he was protesting unemployment, suffered second- and third-degree burns over more than half his body.)

TELEVISION VERSUS REAL LIFE

A character in Paddy Chayefsky's award-winning movie *Network,* states:

> Television is not the truth.... We lie like hell.... We deal in illusions, man. None of it is true. But *you* people sit there day after day, night after night.... We're all you know. You're beginning to believe the illusions we're spinning here. You're beginning to think that the tube is reality and that your own lives are unreal. You do what the tube tells you to do. You dress like the tube, you eat like the tube, you raise your children like the tube. In God's name, you people are the real thing; we're the illusion!

Critics of the television medium assert that too frequently we do not see life as it is; rather, we see it as television presents it to us. To what extent do you think television reflects, distorts, or creates reality? Let us now examine a number of the reflections provided by life with television.

How does television affect your attitudes and your behavior? How does it affect your

MEDIA PROBE

On the average, how much time do you spend with television per day? (How does your TV consumption time compare with the national average? On the average Americans watch TV six hours and forty-eight minutes each day.)

What programs do you habitually watch each week? What do you like about these programs? Be specific.

Have you ever applied what you have seen on television to your own life? How?

Divide your life into three approximately equal stages. (For example, if you are 18 years old, your life would be divided into these segments: age 1–6, age 7–12, and age 13–18, and if you are 24 it would be divided into these segments: age 1–8, age 9–16, and age 17–24.) From each life period, select a television program that you believe exerted some influence on the way you thought and felt about yourself, your daily existence, or the people with whom you interacted. Explain how each program and its characters affected you. Cite particular examples.

Compare and contrast the image you have of each of the following with the image portrayed on television. Which do you prefer and why?

A doctor
A teacher
A family
A teenager
Marriage
The elderly
The police
The poor
The rich
Business executives

If you could trade places with any television personality or character, past or present, who would it be and why?

---

perception of yourself? your perception of others? What is its cumulative impact on your life? For many, what is experienced in real life does not compare favorably with what is shown on television. For example, going to a doctor in real life is often very different from the experience as portrayed on TV. The television doctor rarely misdiagnoses a patient, and traditionally he or she is portrayed as a very confident practitioner who is usually successful at effectuating a cure—one that is for the most part quick and painless. Fees for the physician's services are rarely, if ever, discussed. How does this affect your opinion of your own physician's competence? Television programs devise images, some true, some false; whether valid or invalid, however, these images affect the attitudes we hold and the way we act. For example, while television cannot be said to "cause wealth," it can be said to affect the attitudes we have about the wealthy and the lifestyle they are shown living. Although the situation comedy family may not accurately reflect the American family, it still serves as the standard against which we evaluate our own families. Do you know any families that appear to be as loving, adventuresome, and successful as the ones you see in sit-coms? In like fashion, although television may not cause violence, it may well affect the way we think about the role played by violence in our society. As has been noted, "Television is a powerful educational medium even when it isn't trying to be, even when it's only trying to entertain."[27] Television exerts a considerable force in helping us formulate an image of our world. But we're not always sure that the image that we develop accurately reflects the way things really are, or for that matter whether it should.

Like adults who are drawn to shows in the mold of *Love Boat* and *Fantasy Island,* children

MEDIA PROBE

Imagine that you are an extraterrestrial who has landed on Earth. You know nothing about life in America and you decide to familiarize yourself with the people and the American way of life by watching TV. Using this week's *TV Guide* as a resource, compose a description of life in America as portrayed through TV programming.

To what extent was the description you developed a positive one? A negative one? To what degree does the image that emerged reinforce life as you know it? Contradict life as you know it? Again, which do you prefer—the image or the reality? Why?

---

appear to use television to escape the real world and enter a world of fantasy. In fact, much of their world is brought to them by television. The author Jerzy Kosinski reports an experience he had while teaching public school. Kosinski had invited a group of 7- to 10-year-olds to sit in a large classroom and listen to him tell a story. Since the room was equipped with TV cameras and monitors, the children had a choice: they could either pay attention to the "in-person" Kosinski or watch and listen to the "on-television" Kosinski. During the course of the story telling, by prearrangement, an adult burst into the room and began to argue with and assault Kosinski. A third camera recorded the children's reactions. No child voiced a protest; in fact, only a sparse few watched the "real-life" Kosinski being hit and pushed. The majority kept their eyes glued to the TV monitor.[28] In a subsequent interview with Kosinski the children explained that they preferred viewing the video screen because it provided closeups of the attack. There is a *New Yorker* cartoon that parallels the Kosinski experience. It depicts a parade crossing an intersection; apartment houses abound at each corner. The windows in the apartment houses are large and the reader can see the people in the apartments watching the parade. Only they're not viewing the parade through the windows available to them; instead they are watching the parade on the electronic window—television. To what extent do you see elements of such behavior manifested in your own lives or the lives of people you know?

IS TELEVISION TAKING AWAY CHILDHOOD?

What differentiates children's television from adult television? According to media critics Neil Postman and Josh Meyerwitz, the correct answer is "Nothing." Both Postman and Meyerwitz assert that everything on television is available to everyone. Thus television makes it impossible to keep secrets, and without secrets, they contend, there can be no such thing as childhood. Since a television is rarely if ever put away in a closet or stored in a drawer children have the potential to be privy to everything it shows. Through such an occurrence, the innocence of childhood may

MEDIA VIEW

CHANNELS

Channel 1's no fun.
Channel 2's just news.
Channel 3's hard to see.
Channel 4 is just a bore.
Channel 5 is all jive.
Channel 6 needs to be fixed.
Channel 7 and Channel 8—
Just old movies, not so great.
Channel 9's a waste of time.
Channel 10 is off, my child.
Wouldn't you like to *talk* awhile?

Shel Silverstein, *A Light in the Attic*, New York: Harper & Row, 1981, p. 87.

> **MEDIA PROBE**
>
> What are some of the "secrets" television reveals to children about life? Identify particular information or attitudes children might not come to know or experience if it were not for television.

> **MEDIA PROBE**
>
> Imagine that you are the parent of a young child. Your child asks if he or she can watch a program you know will contain violence and, at the least, one assault. Would you let your child watch the show? Why or why not?
>
> Your child tells you that two people are fighting outside your home. He or she asks your permission to watch the fight. Do you give your consent? Why or why not?

be lost. In effect, television helps to reveal the backstage of adult life to children: through television children come to know the secrets of sex, the dangers of violence, the causes of marital conflict, the incompetence and dishonesty of our leaders, as well as the myriad diseases that can afflict the human body.[29] But television does not stop there. Television also reveals the joys of consumerism to children—the satisfaction that stands to be gained from purchasing a wide array of products.

Television has also helped to merge the tastes of children and adults. The *1980 Nielsen Report on Television* revealed that children and adults rated the following programs among their most favored syndicated shows: *Family Feud, The Muppet Show, Hee Haw, M*A*S*H, Dance Fever, Happy Days Again,* and *Sha Na Na.*

Even when portrayed on television, today's children are usually depicted as young adults; their language, clothes, and opinions do not appear to differ significantly from those of adults. In effect, television has helped to make children into little adults.

TELEVISION VIOLENCE AND CHILDREN

What is the child's relationship to television? What is the parent's role in guiding that relationship?

The typical child between the ages of 2 and 5 spends almost as much time watching television as an adult spends at his or her place of employment—between 30 and 40 hours a week. For much of the child's time, television functions like an electronic baby-sitter; that is, the parent is not directly supervising the youngster. By the age of 12, the average child has spent over 12,000 hours watching TV. And by the time a child graduates high school, with the aid of television, he or she will have witnessed about 15,000 televised murders. What is the cumulative effect of such exposure? Will the children who see x number of murders each week on television find it easier to take someone's life? According to media researcher Harry J. Skornia:

> If I were to attempt to destroy a nation internally, I would brainwash that nation into accepting violence. I would educate the masses to hate and kill and burn and destroy. I would condition people to tolerate violence as an acceptable type of behavior and condone its use as the most effective means to solve problems. I would provide specific lessons in the use of guns and knives and show how cars can be used as instruments of death. I would present this information entertainingly—in the form of television.[30]

The possibility that the content of television can stimulate aggression on the part of young viewers has received more attention than any other issue. If television teaches by example, then perhaps children (as well as adults) are influenced by its lessons.

Do not surmise that children watch only

"children's programming." The statistics on children's television-viewing habits reveal quite the opposite. In addition to Saturday morning cartoons, children watch television most of the same hours adults watch television. According to Mankiewicz and Swerdlow, between 10:30 and 11 P.M. there are still 5.6 million children between the ages of 2 and 11 watching television each night. From 11 to 11:30 there are still 3 million children watching. And from 11:30 to midnight, over 2 million are still before the set.

In 1969, Senator John Pastore requested the Surgeon General of the United States to appoint an advisory panel to identify what harmful effects, if any, television programs have on children. The resulting inquiry lasted almost three years. During that time an array of research projects and papers were commissioned and a controversial report was issued. The report noted that the committee had found a preliminary and tentative causal relationship between televised violence and aggressive behavior. In 1982, a follow-up study by the National Institute of Mental Health confirmed the original findings and reaffirmed that a link between televised violence and antisocial behavior does exist. And as late as April 1983, Dr. Leonard D. Eron of the University of Illinois at Chicago testified before the House Judiciary Committee's Subcommittee on Crime that "heavy exposure to televised violence is one of the causes of aggressive behavior, crime and violence in society." According to Dr. Eron, television violence "affects youngsters of all ages, of both genders, at all socioeconomic levels and all levels of intelligence." Through the years, the people testifying change, but the roles remain set: social scientists assert that television exerts an improper influence on its viewers, and network representatives, among them also social scientists, maintain there is nothing to be concerned about. For example, Dr. Alan Wurtzel, former director of news, developmental and social research for ABC-TV, testifying before the same committee as Dr.

> **MEDIA PROBE**
>
> Select three programs children are likely to watch. For each program record the violent or aggressive acts occurring during the program using this definition of violence: "The overt expression of physical force against others or self, or the compelling of action against one's will on pain of being hurt or killed."[31]

Eron, cited a 1982 study that indicated that only 1 percent of a group of 400 researchers studying television's social effects agreed that television was "the cause" of aggressive behavior.

On what, if anything, are researchers able to agree? It is acknowledged that television does not appear to have a uniform effect on all children. It is believed that TV violence has its greatest impact on those who are "predisposed" to respond in an inappropriate way. In fact, to date, the most widely quoted statement on the effect of televised violence on children was made by Wilbur Schramm, Jack Lyle, and Edwin B. Parker, authors of *Television in the Lives of our Children*; "For *some* children, under *some* conditions, *some* television is harmful. For *other* children under the same conditions, it may be beneficial. For *most* children, under *most* conditions, *most* television is probably neither harmful nor particularly beneficial." Given this statement, some are quick to ask: "If some television programs cause some children to act violently some of the time, are we justified in eliminating all such content from all children's programming all of the time?" What do you think?

In general, there are three theoretical perspectives on televised violence: the catharsis theory, the stimulation theory, and the null theory. Supporters of the *catharsis theory* contend that the viewing of scenes of aggression helps to purge the viewers' own aggressive feelings. In other words, experiencing violence vicariously may make the individual less likely to commit a violent act. In contrast, the supporters of the *stimulation theory* maintain that seeing scenes of violence helps to stimulate an individual to behave more violently. The last group, the supporters of the *null theory*, maintain that fictionalized violence has no influence on real violence. The pendulum on television and violence appears to swing back and forth between the positions represented by these groups.

Much of the research cited in support of the stimulation theory was conducted by Albert Bandura, a psychologist of Stanford University, and his colleagues. Bandura has reported the results of numerous laboratory studies in which children were shown violent films or television programs and then led to a closely monitored room to play. There the children were faced with a number of choices: they could play with dominos, game boards, or a large rubber doll called a "bobo doll." Invariably, children who had witnessed violent action sought out the "bobo doll," using it to help them enact or replicate the aggressive experiences they had just witnessed on the television screen. Children, more than adults, imitate what they see.

The work of Seymour Feshback and his colleagues represents the other end of the television-and-violence continuum. In the report *Television and Aggression* Feshback noted that among youths predisposed to delinquency, a diet of violent, adventure-oriented programs actually decreased hostile behavior. Other studies conducted by Feshback confirmed the hypothesis that fantasy violence (depicted during the course of a television movie) could help reduce aggressive impulses.

Stanley Milgrim and his associate Lance Sholland represent the continuum's null position; they assert that there is no connection between mediated aggression and aggression in real life. As described in their book *Television and Antisocial Behavior*, in order to study the effects of television under natural but controlled conditions, they had several special episodes of the program *Medical Center* prepared. The episodes were identical except for one or two scenes. The basic plot revolved around a medical attendant who had quit his job but, owing to financial needs, asks to be rehired. He is informed by Dr. Gannon that the position has been filled. Subsequently, he sees Dr. Gannon on a telethon tell viewers that collection boxes to fund the building of a new clinic have been placed around the city. In one version of the specially prepared segment, the medical attendant smashes open some of the collection boxes. Subjects were recruited at random and told they would receive a free transistor radio for previewing the show. After viewing the episode, subjects were told to proceed to a nearby office to pickup their gift. When each subject arrived, he or she was greeted by a sign that stated there were no more radios left. Also in the office was a collection box for Project Hope, similar in design to the one used in the television show. Each subject's behavior was videotaped. Results suggested that subjects who had been exposed to the episode containing the scene in which the attendant smashed the collection boxes were no more likely to imitate his behavior than those who had viewed the episode with that particular scene omitted. Thus, depicted violence was judged not to influence behavior.

Yet, television has long been accused of promoting aggressive behavior in children. Recently, an ABC News poll, commissioned for the program *Viewpoint,* indicated that seven out of ten people polled felt that there was too much violence in TV entertainment shows. Two-thirds expressed the belief that TV violence tended to encourage violence among children and teenagers. This belief is also supported by Dr. Thomas Radecki, chairman of the National Coalition on Television Violence: "The last 20 aggression researchers . . . agree . . . that there is a direct causal relationship between the culture of violence promoted by television and real life violence in our homes, streets and schools." According to the latest survey by the National Coalition on Television Violence, the incidence of

MEDIA VIEW

TV ISN'T VIOLENT *ENOUGH*

Today, as a physician, I still sneer at TV violence, though not because of any moral objection. I enjoy a well-done scene of gore and slaughter as well as the next viewer, but "well-done" is something I rarely see on a typical evening in spite of the plethora of shootings, stabbings, muggings and brawls. Who can believe the stuff they show? Anyone who remembers high-school biology knows the human body can't possibly respond to violent trauma as it's usually portrayed. . . .

The human skull is tougher than TV writers give it credit. Clunked with a blunt object, such as the traditional pistol butt, most victims would not fall conveniently unconscious for a few minutes. More likely, they'd suffer a nasty scalp laceration, be stunned for a second or two, then be extremely upset. I've sewn up many. . . .

Children can't learn to enjoy cruelty from the neat, sanitized mayhem on the average series. . . .

"Truth in advertising" laws eliminated many absurd commercial claims. I often daydream about what would happen if we had "truth in violence"—if every show had to pass scrutiny by a board of doctors who had no power to censor but could insist that any action scene have at least a vague resemblance to medical reality ("Stop the projector!. . . .You have your hero waylaid by three Mafia thugs who beat him brutally before he struggles free. The next day he shows up with this cute little band-aid over his eyebrow. We can't pass that. You'll have to add one eye swollen shut, three missing front teeth, at least 20 stitches over the lips and eyes, and a wired jaw. Got that? Roll 'em. . . .")

Seriously, real-life violence is dirty, painful, bloody, disgusting. It causes mutilation and misery, and it doesn't solve problems. It makes them worse. If we're genuinely interested in protecting our children, we should stop campaigning to "clean up" TV violence. It's already too antiseptic. Ironically the problem with TV violence is: it's not violent enough.

Mike Oppenheim, "TV Isn't Violent *Enough,*" *TV Guide,* February 11, 1984, p. 20–21.

---

violence on prime-time network TV reached a new high in the first quarter of 1983. Dr. Radecki has accused the networks of trying to downplay the effects of TV violence on society; he has called on Congress to reject efforts by broadcasters to deregulate their industry and said that, instead, laws should be passed requiring safeguards for the public.

In contrast to the stance taken by Dr. Radecki, the networks and the Television Information Office emphasize that there is no convergence on the issue of violence and television in the academic community; indeed, they emphasize that the existing research literature on the topic is peppered with inconsistencies. They maintain that the early surveys revealed no significant relationship between overall exposure to television and aggressive behavior. But overall exposure to television and exposure to television violence are not really one and the same thing.

The issue of television violence has even made its way into the courts—in a number of cases as the defendant and in one particular case as the defendant's excuse. In the movie *Born Innocent,* an adolescent girl encarcerated in a reform school was shown being raped with a plumber's helper by other girls in the school. Four days after the film was aired in 1974, 9-year-old Olivia Nieme was attacked by teenagers, who raped her with a bottle.

MEDIA PROBE

Dr. Thomas Radecki, chairman of the National Coalition on Television Violence, has proposed that violent cartoons should be prefaced by a warning of their content or that a warning be aired constantly in a corner of the picture. Do you agree or disagree with this proposal? Why?

Olivia's mother and her lawyer, Marvin Lewis, claimed that the television airing of the movie provoked the attack. They charged NBC and its affiliate station KRON-TV, with negligence and demanded $11 million in damages. NBC based its defense on the First Amendment. Its lawyers argued that the only legal basis for holding someone responsible for what he or she wrote or aired on television was if the content was libelous or obscene, or if they had had the intent to incite lawless action. Floyd Abrams, the defense attorney for NBC, was persuasive in his insistence that NBC neither advocated nor intended to incite rape with its broadcast. After years of court proceedings and entanglements, the negligence suit was dismissed by Judge Robert Dorsee, who ruled that the plaintiff had failed to prove that the network had intended its viewers to copy the violent sexual attach shown in the move.

On June 4, 1977, 15-year-old Ronald Zamora killed his 82-year-old neighbor, Elinor Haggert, while burglarizing her home. Zamora's attorney, Ellis Rubin, pleaded that Ronnie was temporarily insane at the time of the murder because he was "suffering from and acted under the influence of prolonged, intense, involuntary, subliminal television intoxication." Zamora's parents and psychiatrists testified for the defense. They argued that Ronnie was addicted to television and obsessed with *Kojak*. It was contended that the murder was a conditioned response. Dr. Michael Gilbert stated that "the [murdered] woman's statement 'I'm going to call the police' was a symbol of everything Zamora had seen on television, and he reacted to rub out the squealer." Zamora's lawyer characterized television as an "accessory to the crime." He noted: "I intend to put television on trial." Despite his attorney's efforts, Ronnie Zamora was found guilty. The jury failed to accept the argument that television had precipitated a murder. Ironically, a television camera had videotaped the proceedings as part of an experiment authorized by the Florida Supreme Court to see if trials could be televised without excess publicity interfering with the course of justice.

Some media reform groups, including the Coalition for Better TV (CBTV), which is backed by the Moral Majority and headed by the Reverend Donald Wildmon, use boycotts to pressure broadcasters to eliminate what they consider to be unacceptable content from television programming. Does the idea of generating a list of "approved" television shows frighten you? Why? Who do you think should determine the kinds of effects to be encouraged or discouraged on television? It is our belief that learning to monitor and control your own viewing is preferable to delegating control to others.

Despite all the clamor, most parents believe that television enhances the lives of their chil-

MEDIA VIEW

AND NOW THE GOOD NEWS...

When 'Starsky & Hutch' was on the air, there was one scene when they got in the car and used their seat belts.... Within the next six days maybe 100,000 people bought seatbelts. When Fonz on 'Happy Days' went in and got a library card, something like 500,000 people went in and got library cards. Television is very powerful. I hope we can use it constructively.

Norman Lear

TELEVISION: ASSESSING THE IMAGE

dren, and they contend that their children are better off with television than without it. In fact, in a national survey, eight out of ten parents polled asserted that the advantages of television for children outweighed the disadvantages. They noted that it is up to parents to use television as a constructive medium rather than to think of it as a "boob tube." To do this children must be turned into active viewers; they must be encouraged to consider questions like: What makes some televised stories more interesting than others? What types of programs would you dream up if you were free to do so? and What outcome would you predict for this show based on what you know at this time? It is also felt that television can be used to promote positive outcomes. If children tend to imitate what they see, television should be able to be used to help them learn prosocial behaviors like how to cooperate, how to exercise self-control, and how to demonstrate concern for others. Studies have shown that after children view a television show on an issue like sharing, they tend to perceive and mirror the behavior of the model provided in the show. But the verdict is still out; in fact, research on prosocial behavior and television is really just gaining favor.

ADVERTISING AND CHILDREN

Television has also been criticized for its advertising practices. Action for Children's Television (ACT), headed by Peggy Charren, has asked the Federal Communications Commission to limit television advertising in a number of specific ways. ACT petitioned the FCC to prohibit "host selling," in which the star of the children's show makes a personal pitch for the product. This practice was stopped by the industry before the government intervened. ACT also lobbied to achieve a general prohibition of commercials on children's shows and sought to require broadcasters to air at least 14 hours of shows targeted to specific age groups of children a week. The government did not act, but again, on its own, the industry cut the maximum level of advertising to children from 16 minutes to 9.5 minutes per hour on weekends and 12 minutes per hour on weekdays. Still, Charren has expressed concern that the NAB code permits broadcasters to air more commercials during the children's prime-time viewing hours than during adult prime time.

Charren's concern stems from her belief that young children aged 2 to 8 are unable to differentiate a program's content from its commercial messages. Research conducted in the 1970s supports this view. The attention of children under age 7 did not change when commercials came on the screen. while the attention of older children did.[32] Additional research indicated that only half of the children who were able to differentiate commercials from the programming showed any awareness of their selling intent. In fact, it was judged that only a quarter of the time were children able to both recognize and realize the purpose of a commercial.[33] On the basis of such research, Charren and her followers maintain that children cannot appreciate the commercial motives (the selling intent) inherent in TV advertising and that misleading impressions are often created by these commercials despite their disclaimers. ACT's position is that commercials aired on television should be directed to adults rather than to children.

More recent research appears to refute these findings. Marion and Charles Winick in their book *The Television Experience: What Children See* note: "One generalization that emerged very clearly was the very considerable awareness of commercials as something apart from program, at all age levels, even the very young. The youngest child in this study, two years old, left the room regularly every time a commercial was shown." But even if children are able to recognize some distinctions between commercials and programs, does this mean they are able to understand

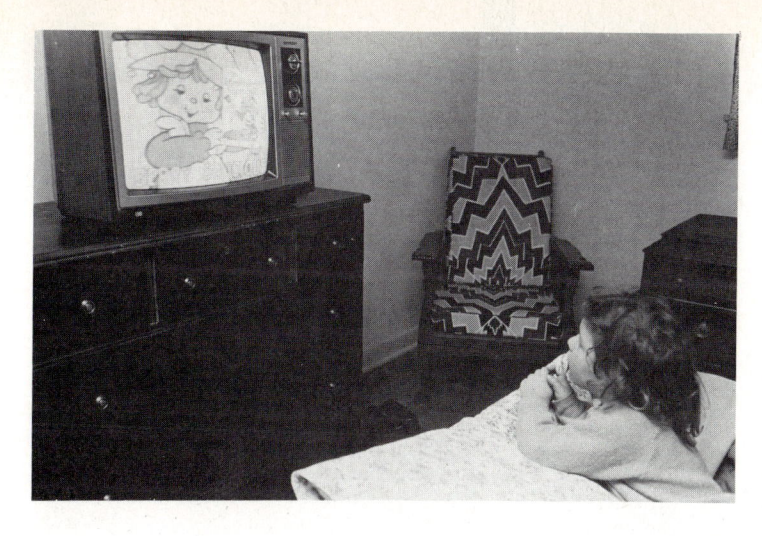

In many families the television set is a kind of baby sitter. The side effects of heavy TV watching are being widely studied. (Randy Matusow)

and process the selling intent? What do you think?

A second pressure group that has sought to reform children's advertising is the Counsel on Children, Media and Merchandising (CCMM), headed by Robert Choate. Choate's primary concern is the poor eating habits encouraged by children's ads. Researchers have noted that food products comprise a large portion of children's television advertising. For example, by analyzing children's television programming, F. E. Barcus determined that 34 percent of the commercials aired on network-affiliated stations were for cereals, 29 percent for candies and sweets, 3 percent for snack foods, 1 percent for other foods, and 15 percent for eating places, especially fast-food chains. Nonfood product commercials were for toys (12 percent) and other items (6 percent). Thus, it was concluded that 82 percent of the commercials directed to children were designed to sell manufactured food products, the majority of which were highly sugared. Researchers also discovered that heavy viewers of children's programming are less knowledgeable than light viewers regarding the nutritional aspects of food.[34]

We have to consider the other side as well. In his book *The Best Thing on TV: Commercials,* Jonathan Price asks: "Why do parents who buy tires, wines, film, cards, transmissions, cars they first saw on TV, get so upset when children ask for something *they* saw on TV? Maybe it's like a bad habit. Kids doing it reminds us that *we* do it." Also in defense of advertising to children, Peter Allport, president of the Association of National Advertisers, notes, "Fundamentally we feel—and feel we can document—that advertising to children is a service to children. Hence, any cutback in time devoted to advertising to children is in no way beneficial to children." Broadcasters and advertisers assert that the elimination of children's advertising would precipitate the end of children's program-

MEDIA PROBE

Spend a Saturday morning watching children's programming. Paying particular attention to the commercials, compile a list of what is being sold to children. For each item, indicate whether the advertising message used to sell the product was appropriate or inappropriate in your opinion, and why. Also identify those items on the list that you believe are harmful to children, and how you would reform advertising practices if you were free to do so.

ming. They stress that the economic realities of children's programming parallel the realities of adult programming.

Recognizing that further regulatory action was unlikely, Robert Choate has written: "The handwriting on the wall is clear. Parents must help their children to comprehend the totality of the message in the more than 20,000 commercials per year they view." The acknowledgment of this need has resulted in the development of educational programs designed to promote "critical viewing skills" in children, thereby rendering them less vulnerable to the persuasive techniques used in television advertising and more aware of the potentially adverse effects of programming. The networks have helped in this regard. For instance, one such program was funded by the American Broadcasting Company.

IMAGES OF WOMEN AND MINORITIES

There are two basic ways that television can bias our attitudes toward women and minority groups in society: by not giving them their fair share of roles; and by not treating them with respect when they are given roles. Research reveals that no group on television is accorded as many roles or treated with as much respect as the white male. In contrast, women, blacks, and other minorities have been either underrepresented in programming or shown in a very unflattering light.

During the early years of television, blacks were typically cast as objects of amusement or buffoons (*Amos 'n Andy* or Farina and Buckwheat in *Our Gang*), or household servants (Beulah or Rochester). Bob Johnson, president of the Black Entertainment Network, notes: "When I was growing up watching television there were only two black children on the screen, Buckwheat and Farina on the 'Little Rascals.' ... We didn't have the reinforcement of Timmy on 'Lassie' or 'Leave It to Beaver,' 'Father Knows Best,' or any of the

MEDIA PROBE

Spend an evening watching prime-time television and a Saturday morning watching children's television. On each occasion, keep a record of the number of men and women characters in each show. For each individual, note

1. Whether the character has a leading or subsidiary role
2. The race of the character
3. The approximate age of the character
4. Whether the character is likable and why
5. The appearance of the character

other programs that showed warm and cordial family ties for young white kids."

During the 1960s the civil rights movement received national attention, and television reacted by adding more black characters to its shows. Still, portrayal was and continues to be a problem. According to critic Brenda Grayson, "One of the hottest trends today is the distortion and satirization of black family life in weekly situation comedies.... Rather than providing a humanistic perspective of this minority's lifestyle and culture, these series often mock it."

Historically, women have also been restricted to stereotypical roles, performing as scatterbrained wives (*I Love Lucy, Burns and Allen, I Married Joan*) or model housewives and mothers (*The Donna Reed Show, Father Knows Best, Leave It to Beaver*). Although women make up 52 percent of the American population, males on television still outnumber females three to one. In addition, more often than not, men are depicted as leaders, doers, and problem solvers. Females, in contrast, are frequently left occupationless. Far too often we are given no idea of the job they may perform when not in the home; instead, females are depicted as overly concerned with romance, marriage, and babies. So while males generally are shown in highly prestigious roles (doctors, lawyers, law enforcement officers), women are frequently relegated to marital and family roles. In addition, as women age on television they become less successful; as men age on TV they become more successful. Even in children's cartoons women are depicted as nagging housewives or helpless. Except for the occasional "superheroine," most women are generally defined by their relationship to a male. Even on cartoons men occupy more diverse jobs; in fact, one researcher, Linda Busby, counted 42 different male jobs and only 9 different female jobs. To date, sexual stereotyping is the rule, not the exception. Women are still depicted as more emotional than men, though there have been some improvements over the past decade. We have had shows that spotlight the new, liberated, competent female television character, but still she is usually young, she is usually beautiful, and she spends a large portion of her very busy time schedule falling in love. So while television today may present us with images of working women, only infrequently are these working women mothers or older.

George Gerbner, television researcher and dean of the Annenberg School of Communication at the University of Pennsylvania, believes that television affects the attitudes we have toward the elderly, and he documents his beliefs with statistics. Gerbner notes that only 2 percent of all dramatic characters on television are over 65 years old. Thus, according to Gerbner, older people are not merely misrepresented on television; they are almost nonexistent. This is the case even though the elderly are quickly becoming the fastest growing minority in America and currently comprise more than 14 percent of the population. In the rare instances when they are portrayed on television, the elderly are usually depicted as doddering, forgetful, or crime victims. Television, unfortunately, exaggerates the extent to which older Americans are targeted as crime victims. So, in addition to presenting senior citizens in a denigrating manner, television also succeeds in terrifying them. Can you point to instances when older women or older men have occupied leading roles and been treated with respect? Perhaps, with time, their numbers will increase.

Since we know that the more time people spend watching television, the more they are apt to make television's version of life their own version of life, the following questions relevant to each of the groups just considered merits our attention: If some of the basic lessons we learn about life are learned from the television, what are we currently being taught about women, blacks, and the elderly? Can the images be changed? Or have we watched so much television that we now expect real life to reflect the television shows we watch rather than vice versa?

SUMMARY

Television, while watched more and more by the American people, has also been a subject of increasing concern. Among the factors that have contributed to a growing criticism of television are programming practices, the rating system, and the possible side-effects of the medium.

Programmers base the decisions they make on a number of assumptions: (1) the 18- to 49-year-olds are the most important group; (2) the LOP principle is valid; (3) a show should not offend its viewers, (4) proven formulas should be followed, and (5) a show should be visually appealing. In order to enhance their chances of capturing and maintaining the largest possible audience, programmers have also used a number of strategies, including hamlocking, counterprogramming, blunting, and bridging.

Program ratings measure the extent to which programming efforts have been successful. Two companies sell quantitative data on audience viewing behavior to the television industry: Arbitron and the A. C. Nielsen

Company. However, the A. C. Nielsen Company is generally looked to as the scorekeeper of network TV. Two figures computed by A. C. Nielsen provide what is considered to be critical information: the show's rating and the show's share of the audience. Though generally accepted and relied on by the TV industry, the Nielsens have been a favorite target of media critics.

TV news, the extent to which television reflects or distorts reality, and the effects of television on children and our perception of various societal groups have also been favorite subjects for debate.

KEY TERMS

LOP principle
Prime-time access rule
Hamlocking
Counterprogramming
Blunting
Bridging
A.C. Nielsen Company
Storage Istantaneous Audimeter
Audilogs
Nielsen Television Index
Rating
Share
Electronic newsgathering equipment
Catharsis theory
Stimulation theory
Null theory

NOTES

[1] Jeff Greenfield, "The Silverman Strategy," in James Monaco (ed.), *Media Culture*, Dell, New York, 1978, p. 53.

[2] "The Men Who Run TV Know Us Better Than You Think," in Rod Holmgren and William Norton (eds.), *The Mass Media Book*, Prentice Hall, Englewood Cliffs, N.J., 1972, p. 328–329.

[3] Ibid.

[4] T. F. Baldwin and C. Lewis, "Violence in Television: The Industry Looks at Itself, in G. A. Comstock and E. A. Rubinstein (eds.), *Television and Social Behavior, vol. 1: Media Content and Control*, U.S. Government Printing Office, Washington, D.C., 1972.

[5] Frank Mankiewicz and Joel Swerdlow, *Remote Control*, Ballantine, New York, 1978, p. 45.

[6] "Watching More and Enjoying Less," *Broadcasting*, April 18, 1983, p. 99.

[7] Ben Brown, "We're More Picky About Our TV Fare," *USA Today*, April 25, 1983, pp. 1–2.

[8] Les Brown, *Televi$ion: The Business Behind the Box*, Harcourt Brace Jovanovich, New York, 1971, p. 58.

[9] William Melody, *Children's Television: The Economics of Exploitation*, Yale University Press, New Haven, Conn., 1973.

[10] Les Brown, op. cit., p. 16.

[11] Les Brown, *Keeping Your Eye on Television*, Pilgrim, New York, 1979.

[12] Peggy Charren and Martin W. Sandler, *Changing Channels*, Addison-Wesley, Reading, Mass., 1983, p. 22–27.

[13] "Everything You've Always Wanted to Know About TV Ratings," A. C. Nielsen Company, New York, p. 3.

[14] George McKenna, *Media Voices: Debating Critical Issues in Mass Media*, Dushkin, Guilford, Conn., 1982, p. 14.

[15] David Brinkley, "A Question for Television Newsmen: Does Anyone Care?" *TV Guide*, March 19, 1977 A 5.

[16] "Uninformed Voters," *The Wilson Quarterly*, Summer 1979, p. 29.

[17] Ron Powers, *The Newscasters*, St. Martin's, New York, 1977, p. 79.

[18] Television Information Office, "Trends in Attitudes Towards Television and Other Media: A Twenty-Four Year Review," Roper Organization, Inc., New York, 1983, pp. 4–5.

[19] "Once Again Public Votes TV Number-One News Medium," *Broadcasting*, April 11, 1983, p. 34.

[20] "The Face of TV News," *Time*, February 25, 1980, p. 65.

[21] "TV News Gets Bigger, But Is It Better?" *U.S. News and World Report*, February 21, 1983, p. 50.

[22] Ron Powers, "When News Gets Lost in the Stars," *Channels of Communication*, vol. 1, no. 2, 1981, p. 341.

[23] Mark R. Levy, *The Audience Experience with Television News*, Journalism Monographs, no. 55, Association for Education in Journalism, 1978, p. 7.

[24] "Sex and the Anchor Person," *Newsweek*, December 15, 1980, p. 65.

[25] Russell Baker, "Wrinkles on TV," *The New York Times Magazine*, March 8, 1981, p. 20.

[26] Eric Levin, "Do Minicams Distort the News?" *TV Guide,* April 15, 1978, pp. 30–32.

[27] Donna Woolfolk Cross, *Media Speak: How Television Makes Up Your Mind,* Coward-McCann, New York, 1983, p. 95.

[28] David Sohn, "A Nation of Videots: An Interview with Jerzy Kosinski," *Media and Methods,* April 1975, p. 19.

[29] Neil Postman, *The Disappearance of Childhood,* Delacorte, New York, 1982, p. 95.

[30] Harry J. Skornia, "The Great American Teaching Machine—of Violence," *Intellect,* April 1977, p. 347.

[31] George Gerbner, "Violence in Television Drama: Trends in Symbolic Functions," in G. A. Comstock and E. A. Rubinstein (eds.), op. cit., p. 31.

[32] S. Ward and D. B. Wachman, "Children's Information Processing of Television Advertising," in P. Clarke (ed.), *Models for Mass Communication Research,* Sage, Beverly Hills, Calif., 1973.

[33] E. L. Palmer and C. N. McDowell, "Program/Commercial Separators in Childrens' Television Programs," *Journal of Communication,* vol. 29, no. 3, 1979, pp. 197–201.

[34] See F. E. Barcus, *Food Advertising in Children's Television: An Analysis of Appeals and Nutritional Content,* Action for Children's Television, Newtonville, Mass. 1978; and C. Atkins, B. Reeves, and W. Gibson, "Effects of Television Food Advertising on Children," paper presented at the Association for Education in Journalism, Houston, Texas, 1979.

SUGGESTIONS FOR FURTHER READING

Adler, Richard P. (ed.): *Understanding Television: Essays on Television as a Social and Cultural Force,* Praeger, New York, 1981. *Documents ways in which TV helps structure social and cultural patterns.*

Brown, Les: *Televi$ion: The Business Behind the Box,* Harcourt Brace Jovanovich, New York, 1971. *Offers an anecdotal account of a "typical" year in the TV business.*

Comstock, George: *Television in America,* Sage, Beverly Hills, Calif., 1980. *Describes what studies reveal about television in the United States.*

Charren, Peggy, and Martin W. Sandler: *Changing Channels,* Addison-Wesley, Reading, Mass., 1983. *A practical book. Presents an analysis of the flaws and the potential of television.*

Cross, Donna Woolfolk: *Media Speak: How Television Makes Up Your Mind,* Coward-McCann, New York, 1983. *Examines how TV influences the American psyche.*

Eastman, Susan Tyler, Sydney W. Head, and Lewis Klein: *Broadcast Programming: Strategies for Winning Television and Radio Audiences,* Wadsworth, Belmont, Calif., 1981. *Provides an overview of all significant aspects of broadcast programming including audience strategies, ratings, and the particular tactics of programming executives.*

Fowles, Jib: *Television Viewers vs. Media Snobs,* Stein & Day, New York, 1982. *Describes why Americans regularly watch TV, and reveals how the medium serves its viewers.*

Liebert, Robert M., Joyce N. Sprafkin, and Emily S. Davidson: *The Early Window: Effects of Television on Children and Youth,* 2d ed., Pergamon, New York, 1982. *Provides an account of the theory and research on TV and the child; interprets the social, political, and economic questions that surround the issues.*

Mankiewicz, Frank, and Joel Swerdlow: *Remote Control: Television and the Manipulation of American Life,* Ballantine, New York, 1978. *Explores the impact television has had on all levels of society.*

Newcomb, Horace (ed.): *Television: The Critical View,* Oxford University Press, New York, 1976. *A collection of essays that provide interesting reading on the genres and the meaning of TV.*

———: *TV the Most Popular Art,* Doubleday, Garden City, N.Y., 1974. *Offers the reader insight into TV genres and speculates as to why these types of programs became so popular.*

Powers, Ron: *The Newscasters,* St. Martin's, New York, 1977. *A critical analysis of TV newscasts and newscasters.*

Postman, Neil: *The Disappearance of Childhood,* Delacorte, New York, 1982. *Explores the extent to which TV can be accused of depriving children of childhood.*

Westin, Av: *Newswatch: How TV Decides the News,* Simon & Schuster, New York, 1982. *A behind-the-scenes account of TV journalism.*

Window Dressing on the Set: Women and Minorities in Television. A Report of the U.S. Commission on Civil Rights. Washington, D.C., August 1977. *Documents that women and minorities continue to be underrepresented in dramatic programs and on the news, and discusses their continued stereotyped portrayals.*

CHAPTER 9

MOVIES: THE WINDOW SCREEN

The cinema is as rich, broad, complicated and simple as life itself.
Arthur Lennig

CHAPTER PREVIEW

After reading this chapter, you should be able to:
- Describe the role movies play in your life
- Explain why movies are a social and psychological happening
- Enumerate and explain key developments and stages in the history of the movies
- Compare the three-part structure of the movie industry with the industry structures of other mass media
- Explain the present legal status of censorship of the movies
- Discuss the significance and purpose of the MPAA movie ratings
- Identify the steps involved in the production and release of a film
- Explain how awards, critics and reviewers, and film festivals can contribute to the success of a film
- Identify the basic shots, camera angles, and camera movements film directors use to communicate with audiences
- Discuss why many documentaries and short films remain "invisible" today
- Explain the relationship of film to video
- Compare the television experience and the film experience

It's Saturday night. What to do? Study? Read a book? Fiddle with the computer? Watch television? Same old thing. A friend calls. "Let's go to a movie." But there are movies on TV, movies on the pay channel, movies on videocassette! Why go out, pay four or five bucks for a ticket, another dollar for eatables, take a chance on getting stuck in somebody's old chewing gum.... But out you go, and the film industry racks up another ticket sale (see Figures 9-1 and 9-2).

MOVIES: THE PERSONAL EXPERIENCE

The movies have been around for about a hundred years now. For most of those years, and for most people, the movies have been a special experience. But what kind of a moviegoer are you?

Moviegoing is much more a matter of conscious choice and personal preference than such media-consuming activities as watching television and listening to the radio. In many ways, moviegoing might be compared to purchasing records: most people listen to music, but some people devote time and money to developing a record collection. And age seems to affect patterns of moviegoing more than sex does. For some reason, movies are largely made for and consumed by young people, especially teens and young adults. And attendance patterns vary considerably from one individual to another. Some people describe themselves as film "freaks" or "buffs," while others are quite indifferent to the medium. Into which of these groups do you fit?

However you as an individual feel about movies, they continue to have a large and influential place in the mass media and mass culture of America. Let's examine why.

Why Movies Are Special

First of all, moviegoing is getting out. Movies become special because of the effort of choosing and spending time and money getting to them. We tend to discount television and videocassettes just because they are easily at hand. We tend to value "going out" because of the effort and specialness of it.

MEDIA PROBE

The following questions will help you assess the role moviegoing plays in your life:

- How many movies have you seen in the theater in the last thirty days? Name them and rate them (one to four stars, tops). Have two friends do the same thing.
- How do the number of films you have seen compare to the number of films your friends have seen? To what extent do you and your friends rate films similarly? Why do you think this is so?
- Do you know people who go to the movies much more frequently than you do? Do you know people who go to the movies much less frequently than you do? Why do you believe they have adopted these viewing patterns?
- To what extent, if any, do you find there is a pattern of sex differences in those who attend more or less regularly than you do? To what extent, if any, is there an age difference in those who attend more or less regularly than you do?
- Can you distinguish any patterns from your observations? What are they?
- Did you attend more movies when you were younger? Why?
- Do you now see more movies than you want to, or fewer? Would you just as soon watch a movie on TV as in the theatre?
- Is moviegoing "special" for you or just another going-out activity?

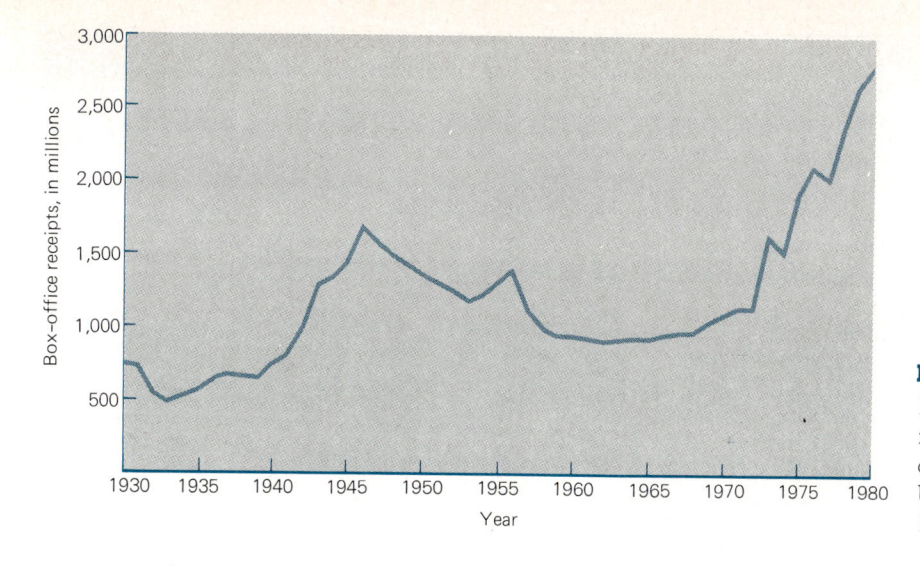

FIGURE 9-1
Movie box-office receipts in millions of dollars in the United States, 1930–1979.

Second, the movie theater is a kind of magical place, big and dark, familiar yet strange, perfumed with the evocative scent of stale popcorn. The ritual of buying the ticket, getting the eats and drinks, perhaps waiting with the crowd to get in, builds a sense of anticipation which intensifies our response to the film. (It also intensifies our disappointment when the film doesn't work for us.) We also share the experience with a group of individuals who become one in their reaction to the film.

Third, the movies are big! The screen is big, the stars are big, the budget is (usually) big, and what we experience is "bigger than life" or seems to be. In a purely physical sense, movies are the most intense, dominating, involving form of mass-media entertainment. The darkened theater, the giant screen, the enveloping sound, and the response of the audience are combined into a perceptually powerful form of presentation.

The movie industry has been counted out a number of times in its almost 100-year his-

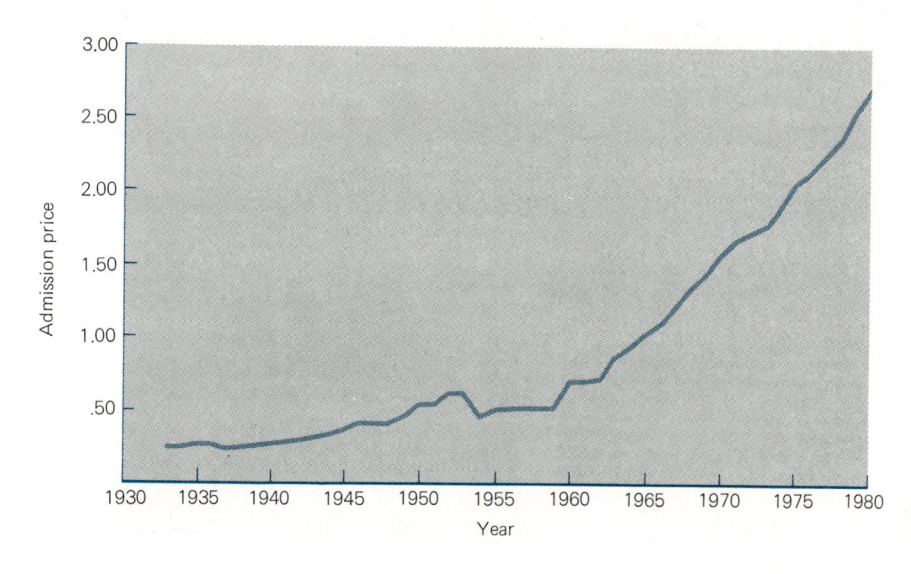

FIGURE 9-2
Average price of a movie ticket in the United States, 1933–1980.

MOVIES: THE WINDOW SCREEN

MEDIA PROBE

What makes a film buff? This is a rate-yourself test. Award yourself 1 point every time you answer yes.

Do you ever go to the movies alone?
Do you regularly read a particular movie critic?
Do you ever go to see foreign films?
Have you ever taken a film course?
Have you ever made a film or videotape?
Are you the first one in your group to suggest a movie?
Do you go back and see favorite films a second or third time?
Did you look forward to this section of the course?
Do you pay attention to the names of directors and writers?
Do you have a favorite type (or genre) of film?
Do you like to watch "old" movies?

A score of 7 to 11 indicates a high preference for moviegoing.

A score of 0 to 3 indicates that you are not a serious moviegoer.

A score of 4 to 6 is average.

---

tory. Radio was going to finish the movies, then the depression was going to, or television, or cable and the videocassette. Although film did suffer a temporary decline in the 1950s owing to the increased popularity of television, and cable and cassettes have made their presence felt, the dismal fate prophesied for the film industry has never materialized. Says Joel H. Resnick, president of the National Association of Theatre Owners: "The doomsayers missed the boat. They forgot the American people have two great loves: cars and going out to the movies." In fact, movies today—that is, those feature films produced for theatrical release—are one of the basic program supports for television, cable, and videocassette. According to Goldman, Sachs and Company, about 24 percent of the studios' U.S. revenue from theatrical films in 1983—some $1.07 billion—came from pay-TV and videocassettes. Theatrical movies are somehow more real, more authentic, than any product "made for 'TV'"—even the multimillion-dollar multinight miniseries. It is the movies that make "real" stars, not television or theater, or the recording industry.

MEDIA VIEW

"It's only a movie." What beautiful words. At the movies, you're left gloriously alone. You can say it stinks, and nobody's shocked. That's something you can't do with a Dickens novel or a Beethoven symphony or even a poem by Browning, and because you can't, because they're all pre-selected and pre-judged and graded for greatness, you don't talk about them with the other kids the way you do about the movies.

Pauline Kael, quoted in Clark McKowen and William Sparke, *It's Only a Movie*, Prentice-Hall, Englewood Cliffs, N.J., 1972, p. 45

MOVIES: A SOCIAL AND PSYCHOLOGICAL HAPPENING

A major movie is a community event: it is announced in the news media (as well as in advertising); it is discussed and anticipated by its potential audience, as well as by others who may not be film goers at all; and it becomes a personal experience—one that will be shared in social interactions for months to come. Some examples of the "event" movie are *The Exorcist, The Godfather, Jaws, Raiders of the Lost*

MEDIA VIEW

GOING TO THE MOVIES

The June 6, 1983, issue of *USA Today* notes that there is an average of one movie theater for each 27,264 persons in the USA. No wonder we have to wait in line for the best movies. But that's not the case in these ten metropolitan areas, where the ratios are the lowest in the country.

RANK METRO AREA	RESIDENTS PER THEATER
1. Killeen/Temple, Texas	8,390
2. Des Moines, Iowa	8,420
3. Columbia, Mo.	9,692
4. Billings, Mont.	9,722
5. Sioux Falls, S.D.	9,973
6. Sarasota, Fla.	10,057
7. Eau Claire, Wis.	10,174
8. Lewiston/Auburn, Maine	10,302
9. Yakima, Wash.	10,367
10. Anniston, Ala.	10,649

Source: U.S. Department of Commerce.

For nearly seventy years, the movies have had the power to create larger-than-life plots and characters that affect the fantasy and cultural lives of whole generations. The *Star Wars,* trilogy, including *Return of the Jedi,* has certainly had that impact. (AP/Wide World)

Ark, and, more recently, *E.T.* and *Return of the Jedi.*

The movies also serve important psychological functions, not only for the individual, but for the community. Society has a need for fantasy, for identification with larger-than-life characters, for heroes and gods and powerful forces of good and evil, who dramatize for us the great virtues and vices which are rarely experienced directly in our individual lives. These dramas give us hope that good *will* triumph over evil, that justice *will* be done. The power of the movies to create such larger-than-life characters—gods and goddesses in a secular world—has been present in American culture for over seventy years and shows no sign of abating. In different eras moviegoers identified with the characters played by Judy Garland in *The Wizard of Oz,* Humphrey Bogart in *Casablanca,* Dustin Hoffman in *The Graduate,* or John Travolta in *Saturday Night Fever.* Or, as one 4-year-old proclaimed intensely to his nursery school classmates, "Luke Skywalker. . . . that's me!"

When a movie effectively taps into powerful psychological needs, we forget ourselves and pass through the frame of the picture and into the world of the film, be that world in a distant galaxy or in an antebellum southern mansion called Tara. And the experiences we have in this transported state are as vivid,

MEDIA PROBE

Identify one movie you believe you will possess for the rest of your days. Why did you select this film? More specifically, what about it caused you to attach yourself to it? Why does it appeal to you? For instance, do you identify with a character, emotion, or idea expressed in the film? Has the film prompted you to think thoughts or caused you to feel feelings you did not realize you could experience so deeply?

MEDIA VIEW

THE DREAM.... ACCORDING TO INGMAR BERGMAN, FILMMAKER

No other art-medium—neither painting nor poetry—can communicate the specific quality of the dream as well as the film can. When the lights go down in the cinema and this white shining point opens up for us, our gaze stops flitting hither and thither, settles and becomes quite steady. We just sit there, letting the images flow out over us. Our will ceases to function. We lose our ability to sort things out and fix them in their proper places. We're drawn into a course of events—we're participants in a dream. And manufacturing dreams, that's a juicy business.

By Slij Bjorkman, Torsten Manns, and Jonas Sima, *Bergman on Bergman,* Paul Britten Austen (trans.), Simon & Schuster, New York, 1973, p. 44.

---

as real, as any in our lives. The experience possesses us, and we will possess it for the rest of our days.

Since the early days of film, viewing a movie has been compared to dreaming. As with a dream, a movie causes us to become involved in an adventure from which we cannot easily escape. Our eyes become fixed upon the screen—the one light area in the darkened theatre—and the channel through which the dream will be shared. To be sure, as critic Hollis Alpert has written, "the movies are the stuff American dreams are made of."

Finally, as you have discovered by now, behind every mass medium there looms a complex industry which generates the media products we consume. The motion picture industry is no exception. The motion picture industry has a fascinating history stretching back more than 100 years. It has a way of doing business unlike any other medium, and it has a special (and more interactive) relationship to the other mass media. In this chapter, we will explore the history, the business structure, and the intermedia relationships of this creative and exciting industry.

THE BEGINNINGS OF CINEMA: FROM DREAMS TO PIONEERS

The nineteenth century was preoccupied with possibilities for the image. The photographic process was invented by Joseph Niepce in 1822 and rapidly developed into an art by his collaborator, Louis Daguerre. At the same time, numerous inventors were producing gadgets for the parlor which reproduced motion from drawings and, later, from still photographs. Most importantly, in 1824, Peter Mark Roget (author of *The Thesaurus of English Words and Phrases*) published a scientific paper setting forth his theory on *persistence of vision* which argued that a series of sequential still pictures rapidly scanned would produce the illusion of motion because the brain "retained" each image for a fraction of a second. Despite the fact that contemporary perceptual psychology would find Roget's theory a crude oversimplification of the process of motion perception, its practical application was correct: a series of still pictures *can* be perceived as moving. Since this is the fundamental principle of cinema, let's take a minute to explore how it works.

Every time you attend a film, you actually spend half of your viewing time looking at a blank screen. The reason you fail to perceive the screen as blank is because the process of seeing is delayed: the eye's retina (the part of the eye responsible for sending visual images to the brain) retains images for about 1/30 to 1/10 of a second after an object is out of sight. Thus every time you view a film you experience an optical illusion—the illusion of

MEDIA SCOPE

1822 — Joseph Niepce invents photographic process

1824 — Peter Mark Roget publishes theory of persistence of vision

1834 — George Horner's Zoetrope produces appearance of motion from drawings

1839 — Louis Daguerre develops silver plate photography, the daguerreotype

1872 — Eadweard Muybridge simulates motion through sequential photographs

1882 — Etienne Marey records first series photographs of live action with a single camera

1888 — George Eastman begins making film attached to flexible celluloid base

1889 — William Dickson, Edison lab assistant, invents Kinetoscope for viewing sequential photographs

1893 — Kinetoscope receives U.S. patent

1894 — Andrew Holland opens first Kinetoscope parlor in New York

1895 — Lumière brothers project film in Paris, using Cinématographe

1896 — Edison buys rights to Armat projector with "Latham" loop, markets same as Vitascope; George Melies uses motion picture camera to make images "disappear"

1903 — Edwin S. Porter creates first western, The Great Train Robbery

1907 — D. W. Griffith hired by Biograph; actor turns director

1909 — Motion Picture Patents Company formed

1910 — Birth of the star system: Carl Laemmle hires Florence Lawrence from Biograph

1912 — Adolph Zukor's Famous Players releases feature-length Queen Elizabeth with Bernhardt.

1914 — Chaplin hired by Keystone, stars in Making a Living

1915 — Griffith releases The Birth of a Nation

1916 — Griffith releases four-hour $2-million Intolerance; film fails

1918 — Chaplin earns first $1-million salary from First National

1919 — Chaplin, Pickford, Fairbanks, Griffith form United Artists to produce and release their pictures.

1922 — Hays office set up by MPPDAA in response to Arbuckle scandal

1926 — Valentino dies

1927 — The Jazz Singer released by Warner Brothers, first feature sound film with talking

1929 — Tough motion picture code authority formed

1934 — Legion of Decency formed

1936 — Chaplin releases last "Tramp" picture, Modern Times

MOVIES: THE WINDOW SCREEN   253

1939
Gone With the Wind becomes top award-winning and box office film

1940
Orson Welles' Citizen Kane amazes, shocks film world

1942
Casablanca released as America enters World War II

1946
The Best Years of Our Lives sweeps Academy Awards

1947
Hollywood Ten jailed for refusing to testify in HUAC communist witchhunt

1948
Supreme Court strikes down "vertical integration" of major studios; television boom begins

1952
Cinerama process—a widescreen, multi-camera process—introduced; Bwana Devil released as first 3-D film

1953
The Robe introduces anamorphic wide-screen process, initiates "blockbuster" films; The Moon Is Blue released without Production Code approval

1956
Fellini's La Strada wins Academy Award as Best Foreign Film

1959
French "New Wave" begins with Truffaut's The Four Hundred Blows

1960
British "New Cinema" begins with Saturday Night and Sunday Morning

1964
Richard Lester's A Hard Day's Night initiates Beatles' cycle of films

1967
Bonnie and Clyde and The Graduate top the box office

1968
MPAA ratings system replaces Production Code; 2001: A Space Odyssey begins sci-fi cycle.

1969
Easy Rider initiates wave of motor cycle and drug films

1970
Financier Kirk Kerkorian liquidates famous MGM studio and real-estate holdings

1972
Coppola's The Godfather dominates box office and popular culture images

1973
Supreme Court, in Miller vs. California, lays down criteria for determining obscenity

1975
Time, Inc., establishes Home Box Office for cable distribution of films

1977
Woody Allen's Annie Hall sweeps Academy Awards

1980
Robert Redford wins Best Director award for first film: Ordinary People

1981
Michael Cimino's Heaven's Gate becomes top Box Office loser: over $40 million

1982
HBO, Columbia Pictures, and CBS form Tri-Star studios

1983
Gandhi takes five of six top Academy Awards

254 RADIO, TELEVISION, and FILM: THE ELECTRONIC WINDOW

movement. A movie camera, like a snapshot camera, takes only still pictures. When the pictures are viewed, however, the movie projector's gears and claws jerk the film in front of the lens in a stop-and-go fashion. Each frame is stopped in front of the light for a split second (1/24 of a second today). Light is alternately blocked and let through by the projector shutter as a frame of film is pulled into place. During the time that light is blocked, the audience is viewing an empty screen but fails to realize this. Why? The persistence-of-vision principle is working; audience members are watching afterimages. (By the way, for a certain period of time each day, you walk around with your eyes closed. Without realizing it, you blink. But you do not perceive these moments of darkness. Why? The answer again lies in the persistence-of-vision principle). So we understand that movies are nothing more than a series of still pictures presented before the eye in rapid succession.

However, over sixty years passed from Roget's pronouncement before the possibility of cinema was realized. A combination of factors had to come together before the first motion picture could be produced: (1) a strong, steady light source—the electric light; (2) a tough, flexible, transparent medium for the photographs—George Eastman's celluloid; and (3) a mechanism which would draw the film in front of the light source rapidly enough to produce the illusion of motion, yet stop each frame for an instant behind the lens. The device was produced independently in at least four countries, with Edison of the United States and the Lumière brothers of France as the primary claimants. Edison's basic patent was dated 1893, but years of patent fights were to follow.[1]

The first films were a mere minute long, but they were a sensation to the viewers. The Lumière brothers were the first documentarists. They lugged their camera to the entrance of the Lumière factory and photographed the employees going home. They photographed waves crashing on the shore and, in one of

MEDIA VIEW

One of the minor ironies in cinema history emerges from the fact that Edison always wanted movies to "talk." More specifically, he wanted a visual accompaniment to the earlier invention, the phonograph, and assigned lab assistant William Dickson to develop a machine to project images in synch with the music. In 1889 he succeeded in developing the Kinetoscope, which permitted a single individual to view the film through a peephole. Edison took full credit for the invention. In another irony, Edison failed to consider the possibilities of the projected image, preferring to collect his revenues a penny at a time. His delay in developing this next stage permitted other inventors to stake out patent claims which would be upheld in court.

Condensed from David A. Cook, *A History of Narrative Film,* Norton, New York, 1981, pp. 6–7.

YOU WERE THERE

1896: *THE NEW YORK TIMES* REVIEWS FIRST SCREENING

When the hall was darkened last night, a buzzing and roaring were heard in the turret and an unusually bright light fell upon the screen. Then came into view two precious blonde young persons of the variety stage, in pink and blue dresses, doing the umbrella dance with commendable celerity. Their motions were all clearly defined. When they vanished, a view of the angry surf breaking on a sandy beach near a stone pier amazed the spectators.... A burlesque boxing match between a tall, thin comedian and a short, fat one, a comic allegory called "The Monroe Doctrine," an instant of motion in Hoyt's farce, "The Milk White Flag," repeated over and over again, and a shirt dance by a tall blonde completed the views, which were all wonderfully real and singularly exhilarating.

Lewis Jacobs, *The Rise of the American Film,* Teacher's College Press, New York, 1968, p. 3.

MOVIES: THE WINDOW SCREEN   255

their more sensational early efforts, a locomotive pulling into a station. Viewers in the front rows are reported to have screamed with alarm.

Edison became the first studio impresario. He built a large (and remarkably ugly) rotating structure, the famed Black Maria, in West Orange, New Jersey. The entire studio swiveled to face the sun, admitting the bright light required for the slow film stock of the day. Into the studio, Edison brought the famous, the fascinating, and the bizarre, to be photographed by the new medium: Sandow, the Strong Man; John C. Rice and Mary Irwin in *The Kiss* (1896), which caused a scandal at the time; and the sensation of the World's Columbian Exposition of 1895, Fatima, the belly dancer. More about her later.

The first excitement at seeing motion on the screen quickly faded, and filmmakers turned to telling stories. Films were now one reel in length—about twelve minutes—and the camera looked at the action like a spectator in the theater—dead center about eight rows back. One of the early masters of this stage of development was George Melies, a witty French magician who realized the camera's capacity for creating illusions and exploited this in a series of clever and charming films in the early 1900s. Perhaps the most famous of these was *A Trip to the Moon*. But, despite his lively imagination, it never occurred to Melies to move the camera.

The next step was taken by Edwin S. Porter, an American film director who carried the medium forward a giant step with his revolutionary 1903 film, *The Great Train Robbery*. Among the devices Porter used in this film were the medium closeup, the camera *pan*, rear projection, and, most importantly, the "meanwhile, back at the ranch" shot. Porter also discovered the possibility of presenting *parallel action*, that is, action occurring in different places at the same time. This innovation permitted the director to shoot two or more story lines, apparently occurring simultaneously, and draw them together for a con-

MEDIA VIEW

The movies, an industry built on an illusion, has probably had more than its share of tricksters, fakers, charlatans and con men, and Edwin S. Porter belongs right up there with them. Before directing at Biograph, Porter had supported himself by a string of odd jobs, perhaps the oddest of which was as a touring projectionist in the islands of the Caribbean. Porter would show up in a village with a battery-operated Edison projector, a few pirated films, and introduce himself as Thomas Edison, Jr., son of the famed inventor. He would show his film, take up a collection and head on down the road.

Condensed from Gerald Mast, *A Short History of the Movies,* Bobbs Merrill, Indianapolis, 1976, pp. 36, 41–3.

clusion. To this day, it remains one of the basic devices in filmic storytelling. Ironically, Porter himself did not really grasp the significance of what he had done and went back to making conventional pictures. Despite Porter's "retreat," the challenge of effective "cinematic" storytelling was met by a man who would make a far greater contribution to the history of cinema—D. W. Griffith.

David Wark Griffith, an out-of-work stage performer and would-be writer, took an acting job with Biograph Studios in 1907—a great comedown for a theatrical performer at the time. After appearing in *Rescued from the Eagle's Nest* (directed by Porter), Griffith soon realized that the creative potential in cinema existed behind the camera, and he moved into the role of director. In the next ten years, almost single-handedly, he took the crude communications medium of the cinema and turned it into an art form. With his master cameraman, Billy Bitzer, Griffith poured his creative intuition into the development of cinema language, which was powerful, effective, and even subtle. He drew the camera ever closer to his actors, experimented with lighting and framing, refined acting styles, and developed longer and more

The silent film classic *Birth of a Nation* demonstrated the growing sophistication of the cinematographic arts. (Cinemabilia)

complex stories. This process culminated in 1915 with the first great masterpiece of cinema, *The Birth of a Nation*.[2] Although viewed today as bad history and racist, the film constituted a significant film history milestone.

Sharing the Wealth: A System Develops

As Griffith was rising to preeminence among directors, a new institution was developing which would dominate American cinema for the next forty years: the major studio. If, as we have seen, the development of cinema technology was difficult, then so was the development of a financial system for sharing the costs of producing films and the income from them. Originally, the simplest and most direct system was used. Studios produced films, bore the cost, reproduced prints of the films, and sold them to the exhibitors who showed the films. There were two problems with this system, however:

1. Once the exhibitor had "used up" the film he was showing (usually in a week), he was stuck with a costly and useless property.

2. There was nothing to prevent the exhibitor from copying and reselling the print. (In fact, this became the illegal but standard practice!)

In 1903 the Miles brothers of San Francisco set up a film exchange, buying prints from the studios and leasing them to exhibitors for a fraction of the purchase price. This solution benefited all parties and rapidly spread across the country. At the same time, permanent theaters were being designed and built primarily for showing films, and these quickly became known as nickelodeons by reason of the 5-cent price, then the standard. With the multiplication of theaters came the demand for more films, and the fledgling industry began a period of rapid expansion. Thus, the basic three-part structure of the industry came about and remains essentially unchanged to the present. It consists of (1) production: the making of the film either by a studio or by an independent producer; (2) distribution: the complex process of releasing the picture; and (3) exhibition: the showing of the picture to the public. It would not be long before it would occur to someone that con-

YOU WERE THERE

WEST COAST PREMIERE OF *BIRTH OF A NATION*

I'll never forget that first big showing. It was here in Los Angeles, and the picture was still called *The Clansman*. The audience was made up largely of professional people and it was our first big showing—the whole industry's first big showing.

I have never heard at any exhibition—play, concert, or anything—an audience react at the finish as they did at the end of *The Clansman*. They literally tore the place apart. Why were they so wildly enthusiastic? Because they felt in their inner souls that something had really grown and developed—and this was a kind of fulfillment. From that time on the picture had tremendously long runs at high seat prices.

Joseph Henabery, quoted in Kevin Brownlow, *The Parade's Gone By*, Knopf, New York, 1968, p. 49.

---

trol of all three parts would lead to a guaranteed source of revenue.

The Struggle for Control: The "Trust"

As the industry grew, and the financial potential of the movies became more apparent, so did the desirability of gaining control of the industry. This was near the end of the great age of monopolies in America (the Sherman Anti-Trust Act was written in 1890) and the great robber barons of the nineteenth century showed the way to the rising young cinema entrepreneurs: get control of the competition! As was mentioned previously, Edison made an early attempt at this through equipment patents. A much more serious attempt was made in 1909, with the formation of the Motion Picture Patents Company, or MPPC, also known as "the Trust." Nine companies, including the Edison Company and Pathé, the French company which held the Lumiére patents, came to an agreement whereby they would share rights to equipment use and deny it to outsiders. They made an exclusive agreement with the Eastman Kodak Company. Kodak would sell raw film stock only to MPPC producers. Having gained virtual control of the production side of the business, MPPC then required "exclusivity" of its exhibitors. That is, if an exhibitor wanted to rent Trust films, he or she could not rent films from any other distributor. Further, the exhibitor was required to lease equipment from the Trust and to pay a weekly fee for the right to do so. In 1910, MPPC bought up all major film exchanges across the country and forced the competitors out of business. Finally, MPPC decreed that a picture was to be one reel (ten to twelve minutes) in length, leading to such curiosities as a ten-minute silent version of *Hamlet*. The Trust, it seemed, had locked up the industry.

But they locked it up too tight, excluded too many producers and exhibitors who were bitten with the movie bug and who were not about to be forced out of business. Chief among these were Carl Laemmle of the Independent Motion Picture Company (IMP) and William Fox, a film renter in New York. The independents went abroad for film stock and equipment and continued to produce and release pictures. In addition, they imported foreign pictures of greater length with considerable success. (Language was not a problem—they simply spliced in English title cards in place of the French or Italian cards.) In particular, Adolph Zukor's production company, Famous Players, imported the world-famous Sarah Bernhardt in a four-reel silent version of the play *Queen Elizabeth* (1912). People flocked to the anomaly of a silent-stage play recorded on film. It proved the box office potential for "feature length" films, and MPPC lost a round in its struggle for survival.

They lost again when they attempted to resist the rise of individual film stars. The producers realized early on that certain individuals had special appeal to the audiences—box office drawing power—and they also realized that they would have to pay a premium if the identity of these individuals became known. Consequently, the MPPC studios attempted to hide the identity of their stars: Mary Pickford was "little Mary" and Florence Lawrence was "The Biograph Girl." In 1910, Carl Laemmle lured Lawrence from the security of Biograph Studios (one of the MPPC companies) by increasing her salary and permitting her pictures to be released under her own name. Thus, Florence Lawrence became the first of the long list of special individuals we know as "stars." Mary Pickford followed quickly, along with "Bronco Billy" Anderson (who had two small parts in *The Great Train Robbery*), Gloria Swanson, Charlie Chaplin, Douglas Fairbanks, William S. Hart (Rio Jim), and a host of others.

The war of the Trust and the independent producers was waged in the courts and in the streets. Although MPPC won most of the early battles, their clear violation of the antitrust laws and changing public sentiment regarding trusts led to a government suit which ended the monopoly. By 1915, the Trust began to disband and the independents were growing into major studios.

The Major Studios and Vertical Integration Although the independent producers had won the struggle against the patents company, this did not mean that they were opposed to control over the industry. They just wanted that control for themselves. Adolph Zukor led the way. Paramount Pictures, formerly Famous Players Lasky, already a large producer and distributor of films, began to purchase motion picture houses around the country and initiated the practice of block booking: if an exhibitor wanted to lease a certain Paramount picture, the exhibitor was obliged to take with it a whole block of less desirable films. The other film producers quickly followed Paramount's example, and the system of *vertical integration* was set in place, to last until the 1950s. *Vertical integration* meant that all aspects of the industry (production, distribution, and exhibition) were under a single control. It was, obviously, a form of limited monopoly, and it

---

MEDIA VIEW

It's the jungle. It appeals to my nature. . . . It's more than a place where streets are named after Sam Goldwyn and buildings after Bing Crosby. There's more to it than pink Cadillacs with leopard-skin seat covers. It's the jungle, and it harbors an industry that's one of the biggest in the country. A closed-in, tight, frantically inbred, and frantically competitive jungle. And the rulers of the jungle are predatory and fascinating and tough. (*John Huston, 1950*)

The new Hollywood is very much like the old Hollywood. (*David Chasman, executive vice president, MGM, 1981*)

Quoted in David McClintick, *Indecent Exposure*, Dell Publishing Company, New York, 1982, p. 10.

contributed to the development of a limited number of dominant studios which came to be called "the Majors."

MODERN TIMES

Traditionally, films are identified with particular time periods or styles. Considered carriers of our culture, films help provide us with a mirror of our changing society.

The Twenties: Hollywood Triumphant

With the end of World War I in November 1918 and the return of the troops from Europe, American society was plunged into a period of intense social change, and the movies represented a leading edge of this change. In the words of a popular song of the time, "How you gonna keep 'em down on the farm, after they've seen Paree?" From a society dominated by small-town and rural America, traditional values, and Victorian morality, America was plunged into the jazz age—the Roaring Twenties, prohibition (a hangover from the old morality), speakeasies, bathtub gin, and the rise of the gangs. The values of the young characterized the popular arts, marked by the writings of F. Scott Fitzgerald and Earnest Hemingway, the hot jazz records of Louis Armstrong and Bix Biederbeck, and the rapidly multiplying stars of the newly matured movie industry.

The system which dominated movie making for the next thirty-five years had reached its maturity. The industry was controlled by the major studios and the great box office stars. Hollywood was the glamour city and scandal center for the nation, and the dream of thousands of young people was to make their way to California and be discovered.

American films were important abroad as well. Given the ease of converting titles from one language to another, American films

THE MAJORS AND THE MINORS: 1930

THE MAJORS

Metro-Goldwyn-Mayer (from merger of Metro Pictures, Goldwyn Pictures, Louis B. Meyer Productions, and Loew's theatre chain)
Paramount (from merger of Famous Players Lasky and the Paramount distribution exchange)
Warner Brothers (from a takeover of First National Studios by Warner Brothers)
Twentieth Century-Fox (from a merger in 1935 of Fox Film Corporation and Twentieth Century Pictures)
RKO (from Radio-Keith-Orpheum, a subsidiary of RCA, formed to market the RCA photophone sound system)

THE MINORS (NO THEATER CHAINS)

Universal (found by Carl Leammle in 1912)
Columbia (founded by Harry Cohn in 1924)
United Artists (formed by Chaplin, Pickford, Fairbanks, and D. W. Griffith in 1919)

B-PICTURE STUDIOS

Republic (specialized in westerns)
Monogram (specialized in gangster films)
Grand National (specialized in comedies)

---

dominated the screens of Western Europe, and the passionate young revolutionaries in Russia studied the prints of Griffith's films until they fell apart. The preference for American films, particularly comedies, was so strong in Europe that native film production had difficulty establishing itself. This was particularly true in England and, oddly enough, Italy. One film historian estimates that in the period after the war, 70 percent of the films screened in Italy were American-made. Chaplin was the greatest star in the world and a particular favorite in France.

260 RADIO, TELEVISION, AND FILM: THE ELECTRONIC WINDOW

MEDIA VIEW

THE GREATEST STAR: CHARLIE CHAPLIN

An internationally famous vaudeville star in 1913, Chaplin, aged 24, was hired by Mack Sennett for $150 a week to star in a series of one-reel films. In a little over a year he made 35 keystones varying in length from a half reel (six minutes) to six reels. He then made 14 films for Essanay in 12 months (1915–16). At Essanay he enjoyed a measure of directorial and authorial freedom plus the tidy salary of $1,250 a week. Next, he made 12 films for Mutual in 18 months (1916–17), and received $670,000. Then he made eight films for First National in the next five years (1918–22), several of them exceeding the two-reel length of most of his previous films. He received a million dollar contract (the first such ever) plus bonuses and percentages of the profits. Finally, he had eight feature films for United Artists over the next 30 years (1923–52), all of which made money. From any point of view—salary, creativity, longevity, consistency, or universal appeal—Charlie Chaplin was the greatest star the cinema has ever produced.

Gerald Mast, *The Comic Mind*, Bobbs Merrill, New York, 1973, pp. 62–63.

Some European films did make their way to American screens. Germany in particular, which went through a brilliant period of filmmaking following World War I, contributed *The Cabinet of Dr. Caligari, Variety, The Last Laugh, The Joyless Street, Metropolis,* and *M,* among others. Discriminating audiences in the larger cities sought out these films. The cash-rich American studios were not above hiring away both stars and directors from the European studios, which made for additional European influence on American films. Thus came to our shores Emil Jannings, Pola Negri, Victor Seastrom, Asta Nielsen, Mauritze Stiller, and his young star, Greta Garbo.[3]

For the most part, however, Hollywood preferred to manufacture its own stars. The exotic Theda Bara, perhaps the movies' first sex goddess, is a good example. Born Theodosia Goodman, a banker's daughter from Cincinnati, Theda Bara (an anagram for Arab Death) became "the Vampire" who lured men to destruction by her dark powers. She contributed the term "to vamp" (seduce) to the language.

The greatest romantic star of the 1920s was, far and away, Rudolph Valentino, whose "Latin lover" glances devastated the women, young and old. Born Rodolpho Guglielmi di Valentina d'Antonguolla, an Italian-American dancer from the Bronx, New York, he

Douglas Fairbanks, Sr. and Charlie Chaplin were the principal founders of United Artists in 1919. (Cinemabilia)

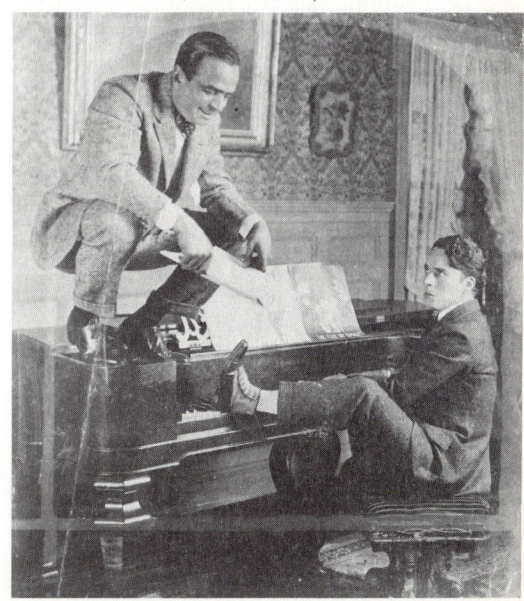

> **MEDIA PROBE**
>
> Who do you believe is the top male romantic star of our own time? What are the special qualities which make him attractive to you? To what extent is there wide agreement on your choice?
>
> In your opinion who is the female "sex goddess" today? Does she play similar roles from film to film? To what degree has the women's movement made the notion of a "sex goddess" repellent to today's audiences? To you?

> **MEDIA VIEW**
>
> It may be concluded that a film in which the speech and sound effects are perfectly synchronized and coincide with their visual images on the screen is absolutely contrary to the aim of the cinema. It is a degenerate and misguided attempt to destroy the real use of the film and cannot be accepted as coming within the true boundaries of the cinema. Not only are dialogue films wasting the time of intelligent directors, but they are harmful and detrimental to the culture of the public. The sole aim of their producers is financial gain, and for this reason they are to be resented.
>
> Paul Rotha, quoted in *The Film Till Now*, Spring Books, London, 1967, p. 408.

was catapulted to fame by *The Four Horsemen of the Apocalypse* (1920) but may be best known for his title role as *The Sheik* (1921). He died in 1926 at the height of his fame, shortly after completing *The Son of the Sheik*. The funeral was a national event, and mourners, mostly women, visited his grave in vast numbers for decades.

The Coming of Sound and the 30s

Until this point in history, the growth of the movies could be described as an evolution—technical, artistic, financial, administrative—but the advent of sound was a revolution which affected all parts of the industry. As we have seen, sound existed with film from the very beginning, with the Edison-Dickson Kinetograph. Several other processes had been developed in the intervening years, films were made, and theaters were specially equipped to show them. But the major studios adamantly resisted the coming of sound.

In 1926, Warner Brothers, a minor studio willing to gamble on making the big time, bought the rights to Vitaphone, a technically superior sound-on-disc process developed by Western Electric. Warners thought of the process as a way to bring the richness of full orchestra to silent films. (The silent films were *never* silent, as we all know, but normally accompanied, at least by a piano, sometimes by a small pit orchestra.) In October of the same year, Warners released *Don Juan*, a John Barrymore costume drama with a full orchestral score, and the film ran successfully in major cities across the country. Of course, theaters had to be extensively (and expensively) rewired to accommodate the new system.

The release of *The Jazz Singer* in 1927 confirmed (and indeed increased) the impact of the new medium. Originally intended only as another silent movie with songs and music, the irrepressible Al Jolson burst into speech in the middle of his famed rendition of "Mammy": "Wait a minute, wait a minute! You ain't heard nothing yet." Ostensibly speaking to the nightclub audience in the film, Jolson was also addressing the film audience, and they were electrified. The "talkies" had arrived. The worldwide success of *The Jazz Singer* forced the hands of the major studios, and the rush was on. In just three years, the silent picture was dead.

The early talkies were just that, using the sound as a novelty, with the actors awkwardly clustered around hidden microphones or moving pointlessly from one microphone to another on the sound stage. A more serious

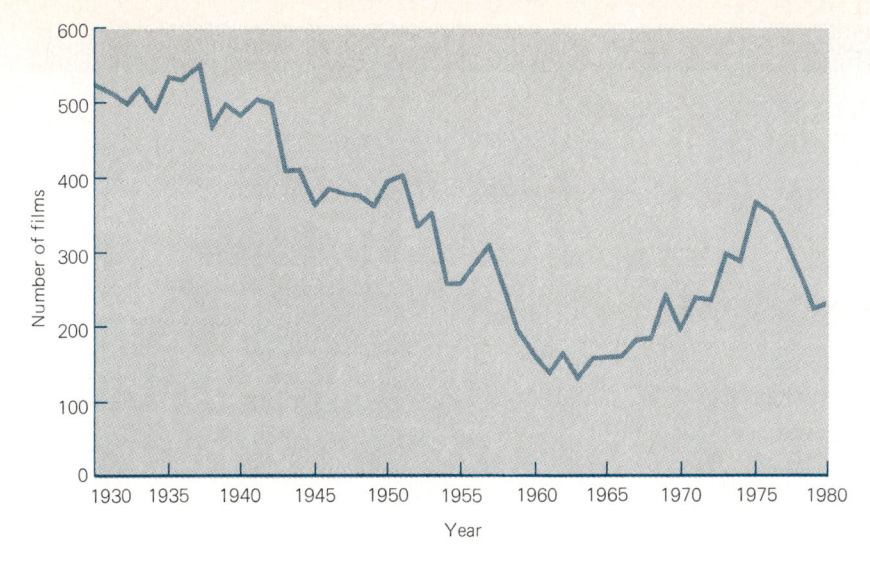

FIGURE 9-3
Number of films produced in the United States, per year, 1930–1979.

problem occurred when the studios realized that the speaking voices of many of the great stars did not match their screen images. Some voices were too high, some too effeminate, too raspy, too shrill, or too heavily accented. (The coming of sound to the movies is parodied wonderfully in the 1952 musical classic *Singing in the Rain*.) Speech coaches rushed to Hollywood from all over the nation, but many careers could not be saved. Among these were the great silent comedians. Keaton spoke and was soon forgotten. Chaplin understood that the Little Tramp must never speak and released two films in the sound era in which he did not speak a word. (*City Lights* has a music track but no dialogue, as well as many jokes about sound, including the final gag of the film in which the Tramp is forced into a situation in which he must sing a song.)

Quickly, however, the studios discovered

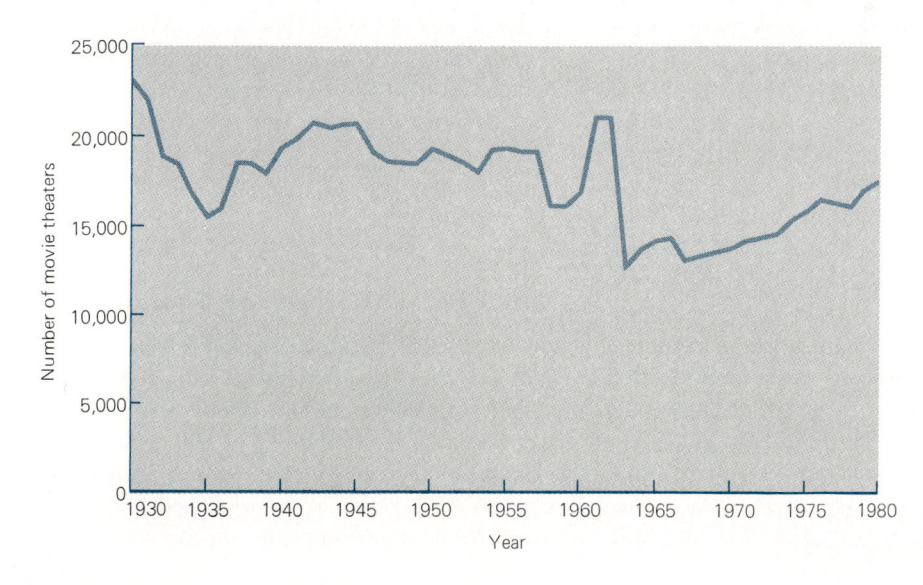

FIGURE 9-4
Number of movie theaters in the United States, 1930–1980.

MOVIES: THE WINDOW SCREEN 263

YOU WERE THERE

SCARLETT O'HARA: A DEPRESSION HEROINE?

In *Gone With the Wind* a young girl comes to womanhood against the backdrop of a great national calamity, the Civil War. By cunning and determination she not only survives, but transforms defeat into good fortune. Scarlett O'Hara secures a place for herself in Atlanta society after three marriages, several family deaths and the destruction of the South.

Gone With the Wind appeared at the end of the decade that had contained the Depression; its narrative line subscribes to the traditional American pattern of getting ahead; it was overwhelmingly popular.

Just before the intermission, after Scarlett has returned to the gutted fields of Tara, she digs her hands into the rich, red soil, stands and tells the camera, "As God is my witness, I will never go hungry again!" Those words were on the lips of a whole population in the early thirties. Scarlett was swearing to rise from the ashes, not of the Civil War, but of the Great Depression.

American Film Institute Education Newsletter, Sept–Oct. 1978.

---

two new genres of film which depended on sound for their effectiveness—the musical and the gangster film. The success of *Broadway Melody* of 1929 generated a series of sequels and imitations advertised as "all talking, all singing, all dancing." The gangster films followed in the early thirties with *Little Caesar* (1930), *Public Enemy* (1931), and *Scarface* (1932). Sound was essential to convey the blaze of the tommy gun, the snarl and threats of the tough guys, and the screech of auto tires. In fact, the success of these early gangster films hastened the formation of the Legion of Decency.

For a couple of years, it appeared that the movies might be "depression-proof," but as the depression deepened, the movies took a financial downturn, fighting back with lowered admission prices, double features, giveaways, and bingo. The dual pinch of the revived Production Code and the Legion of Decency, a Catholic organization devoted to purifying the cinema, whitewashed the screen, and the favorite genre became the "crazy comedy," usually featuring eccentric members of the wealthy class acting irresponsibly. From such films as *It Happened One Night* (1935) to *Bringing Up Baby* (1938) and comedy teams like the madcap Marx Brothers and Laurel and Hardy, who had successfully made the transition from silents, the suffering nation sought escape through laughter. Films featuring music and dance continued to gain in popularity with *42nd Street* (1933), *Gold Diggers* series (1933, 1935, 1937) and other films of Busby Berkeley, the incredibly inventive dance director of Warner Brothers. Fred Astaire and Ginger Rogers kept RKO Studios alive with a series of films from *Flying Down to Rio* (1933) to *The Story of Vernon and Irene Castle* (1939). Sound and the creative imagination of Walt Disney led the animated film to new heights, culminating in three brillant feature-length stories: *Snow White* (1937), *Pinocchio* (1941), and *Fantasia* (1940).

The Forties: Hollywood Goes to War

In 1940, the mood of the United States was isolationist—the problems in Europe were "none of our business." The attack on Pearl Harbor on December 7, 1941, brought a total reversal of that attitude, and Hollywood geared up for a major propaganda effort. A single film which perfectly captures the tran-

MEDIA VIEW

AS TIME GOES BY, *CASBLANCA* GAINS MORE AND MORE FANS

Only moments after it opened—with a long shot of a revolving globe ("With the coming of the second world war, many eyes in imprisoned Europe . . . ")—this tale of intrigue and frustrated romance galvanized the audience's emotions.

"Casablanca" became a box-office hit and won the Academy Award as best picture. Its stars, Humphrey Bogart and Ingrid Bergman, were launched on their way as screen immortals.

The movie went on to capture an enduring place in the hearts of American moviegoers and critics, a pantheon occupied by only a handful of legendary films from the 1930's and 1940's—movies such as "King Kong," "The Wizard of Oz," "Gone With the Wind," and "Citizen Kane." For many, "Casablanca" is the definitive World War II picture.

The popularity of "Casablanca" has grown during the four decades since its release. It draws standing-room-only crowds at revival theaters and invariably tops any competition during frequent TV showings. The movie has inspired at least four full-length books and hundreds of critical essays, as well as Woody Allen's "Play It Again, Sam."

"We used to think of it as a young people's picture, since college students rediscovered it in the 1960's. Now it seems to have become everybody's picture," said Howard Koch, who shared an Oscar for the movie's screenplay with Julius and Philip Epstein. Recalling the film's often turbulent genesis recently at his home in Woodstock, N.Y., the 80-year-old writer offered his theory on the durability of "Casablanca."

"I think it's a little more than nostalgia. Today it is very hard for people to find values they can identify with," said Koch, a staunch liberal who was blacklisted in Hollywood during the 1950's and is now active in the "nuclear freeze" movement. "So they go back to 'Casablanca' and a time when there were values worth living and worth dying for."

Koch also pointed out that "Casablanca" embodies all the virtues of the old Hollywood studios—a superbly crafted film with a top-flight cast and first-rate talent behind the cameras.

Lou Lumenick, "Play It Once Again!" *The Record,* November 26, 1982.

---

sition is 1942's *Casablanca.* Rick, the cynical, cool, tough American (Bogart's ultimate role), is converted in the course of the film to the cause of the Allies, gives up the girl, and strides off into the fog with his French ally to do further battle with the Nazis. The movie remains one of the most popular and memorable of all American films.

Hollywood had three major tasks during the war: to show our troops as heroes defeating the evil Nazis and Japanese; to help the folks at home carry on by showing their pluckiness and loyalty and providing entertainment and comic relief; and to bring images of the war through the newsreel and documentary series. Perhaps the best-known documentary films made during this time were the *Why We Fight* series, using documentary footage put together by major Hollywood directors such as Frank Capra, John Ford, and John Huston. The Huston documentaries, in particular, were so graphic that the War Department, fearing a negative impact on public morale, refused to release them. On the home front, the MGM musicals were the cream of the entertainment crop, often dealing with a nostalgic past and highlighting the American virtues of home and

Judy Garland in *Meet Me in St. Louis.* (Bettman Archive)

Myrna Loy and Frederic March in *The Best Years of Our Lives.* (Cinemabilia)

family. *Meet Me in St. Louis* (1944) was among the best and most typical of these.

At the same time, the B-picture studios were releasing a remarkable series of low-budget black-and-white pictures which revealed the dark underside of American culture. Called *film noir* (black film), these films cataloged the lives of losers, gamblers, thieves, and killers—not as glamorous gangsters but as sleazy lowlifes. The recurring themes were cynicism, betrayal, and death, and the police portrayed in these films were seldom better than the criminals. The action of these films took place mainly at night, in alleys, dimly lit bars, cheap hotels, and docksides. The grayness mirrored this dark look in American culture. Of these films, perhaps the best example is *The Killers* (1946), which was

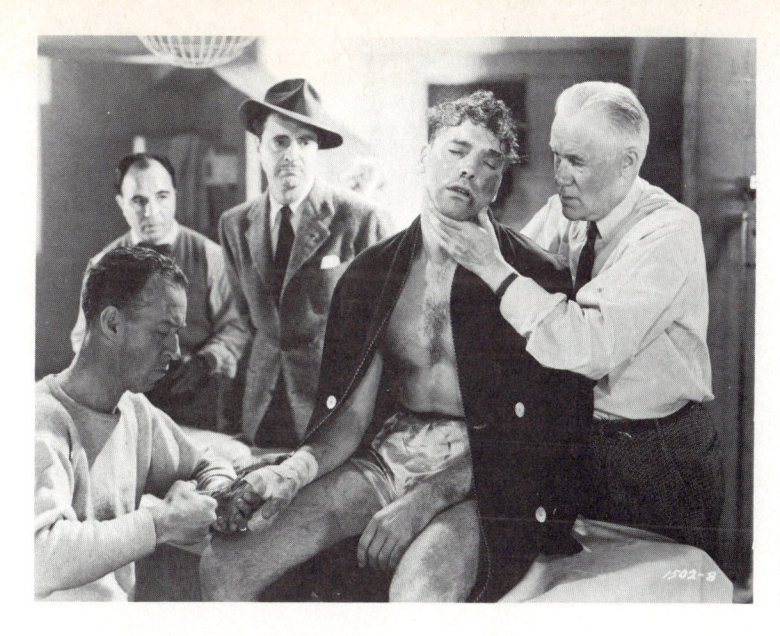

Burt Lancaster made his movie debut in *The Killers,* a movie in the mid-forties *film noir* genre. (Bettman Archive)

based on the short story by Hemingway. It was directed by Robert Siodmak with Burt Lancaster making his film debut in this movie.[4]

The end of the war signaled the "return to normalcy" as a theme, best captured in the candid and touching *Best Years of Our Lives* (1946), which swept the major Academy Awards for the year. The film retains its sense of decency and candor today. For the first time in many years, filmwise Americans were also being exposed to foreign films in small, expensive (tickets were $2!) "art houses," and the experience was a revelation. First came the neorealism of Italian films like *Open City* (1946). These were dramas with the force and the conviction of documentaries. These films featured earthy and often scantily clad Italian actresses (Anna Magnani, Silvana Magnano, Sophia Loren, Gina Lollabrigida) and scenes of sexual candor not seen on American screens since the 1920s. French sex comedies followed in the 1950s, the best known of which features Brigitte Bardot, the ultimate French sex goddess. The darker, brooding Swedish films of Ingmar Bergman also came to the American screen about this time. The British cinema produced a brilliant series of comedies featuring a whole stable of convincing British character actors.

Finally, the proliferation of nuclear weapons, and increasing knowledge of and fear about the effects of nuclear warfare, radiation, fallout, and so on, generated a series of science fiction films, which dealt with these themes in fantasy and provided a kind of hope for the viewers. One such influential film was *The Day the Earth Stood Still* (1951), technically archaic compared to present standards but still effective in its threat/plea for "peace, or else."

MEDIA PROBE

Science fiction has remained an important film genre since the early 1950s. Some titles include *2001: A Space Odyssey,* the *Star Trek* movies, the *Star Wars* series, and *E.T.: The Extraterrestrial.* What messages do you believe these films deliver about science and technology? About the moral responsibility and wisdom of scientists? About political systems? About the future?

The popularity of 3-D movies eventually waned as audiences wearied of the cumbersome glasses. (Nancy Pierce, Photo Researchers)

The Fifties: A Confrontation with Television

Television became the dominant mass medium in the United States in the years between 1948 and 1952. As sales of television sets soared Americans discovered a new and compelling "at home, at hand" medium—free! At first, Hollywood chose to ignore television. The major studios refused to lease any of their vast film holdings to television. Television, desperate for cinematic material, leased or bought westerns from the old B-picture studios and British films of the 1930s, mostly detective stories.

As it became clear that television was not going to go away, the major studios geared up for war. The first response was 3-D, a process involving colored glasses and the color filtering of prints to produce the illusion of three dimensions. Arch Oboler's *Bwana Devil* (1952) was the first of a brief spurt of 3-D films; the fad had virtually ended by 1954 when the limited dramatic possibilities of the process had been explored. (In the 1970s the process was resurrected for a series of soft-core pornographic films, and in the 1980s for a couple of science fiction films, in each case with very limited success.)

Next the studios embarked on a campaign emphasizing the slogan "Movies are better than ever." What they really meant was "bigger than ever" as Hollywood unveiled a series of wide-screen processes intended to underline the contrast between the tiny television screen and the large movie screen. Epic films got production emphasis with lots of scenery to fill the giant screens. "Big" westerns and Biblical tales predominated. But box office erosion continued. As the graphs indicate, movie attendance peaked in 1948 and has steadily declined since then, although rising ticket prices have kept the box office figures inflated. The decline in attendance is even more dramatic when considered against the sharp rise in American population during the baby boom years.

In point of fact, the role of movies in the popular culture mix in America was changing. Television had become the family medium; its contents, especially in the 1950s,

MEDIA PROBE

Joseph M. Boggs in *The Art of Watching Films* notes: "The motion picture has progressed step by step from drawings, to photographs, to projected images, to sound, to color, to wide screen, to 3-D." He reports that experiments were conducted that attempted to add the sense of smell (Smellarama) to the film experience by releasing frangances through the theater—odors designed to reinforce or intensify the visual image projected on the screen. And he goes on to add that in his *Brave New World*, Aldous Huxley had predicted that future motion pictures would go even further, highlighting "toucharama"—a complex electrical system positioned at each patron's seat, a device that would enhance the visual image on the screen by adding a sense of touch to it. What do you think of motion pictures that rely on such special devices to achieve an effect? To what extent do you approve or disapprove of them? Why? Can you think of any type of artificial device that could be used to enhance the viewing experience today?

---

were very much G-rated. Film was becoming the medium for young people who wanted more sex, more action, more reality, and more social criticism.

The 1960s: The "Film Generation"

By the end of the 1950s, the United States was rapidly entering a period of cultural revolution, with popular taste dominated by an increasingly affluent and critical young-adult group—a group that was raised on the antiestablishment rhythms of the new rock and roll. As young teenagers they had reveled in the antiparent, antisystem images of movies such as *The Wild Ones* (1953), *Blackboard Jungle* (1955), and most of all, Nicholas Ray's *Rebel Without a Cause* (1955), starring James Dean. With only three feature films to his credit, Dean perished in a fiery high-speed car crash, which fixed his public image at a high point of adulation.

The invasion of the Beatles in 1963 and the success of their first film, *A Hard Day's Night* (1965), marked the youth takeover of popular culture. *The Graduate* (1967), the most popular film of the 1960s, most clearly captures the sense of the times. The adult world was characterized as uptight and repressive, while the world of young people was marked by a determined but rather aimless quest for "freedom." *In the Heat of the Night* (1967), which took the Academy Award for Best Picture and also received two other top awards, galvanized black audiences when Sidney Poitier slapped the upper-class white villain across the face. The intoxication of the early days of the revolution gave way to a darker, more pessimistic national mood. The polarization of the nation, the confusion of values, and the sense of hopelessness is perfectly caught in the low-budget, box office sensation of 1969, *Easy Rider*, which spawned a whole generation of freedom-of-the-open-road, drug-doing, disaster seekers on the screen. The sordid revelations of the Watergate scandal and the resignation of President Nixon left the "hippie generation" both vindicated and villainess.

The late 1960s and 1970s mark the gradual decline in the importance of women on the screen. This decline may be seen in several ways, perhaps most graphically in the Quigley Publications poll, an annual survey of exhibitors to name the year's top box office stars. "The lists neatly trace the decline of female stars: whereas women make up 50 percent of the top stars of the 1930's, for example, they comprise little over 10 percent during the 70s and this ten percent stems from the indomitable presence of Barbra Streisand."[5]

What could take the place of the conventional romantic relationship which had formed the emotional dynamic of American films for fifty years? Hollywood's answer was the "buddy film." In the buddy film the central emotional dynamic lies in the relationship between two male figures, a relationship neither sexual nor friendly, but usually marked by a joking, tough often violent, competitiveness which issued into a grudging respect and a tight male bonding. Two 1969 hits clearly illustrate the buddy film: *Butch Cassidy and the Sundance Kid,* the box office champion of the year, and *Midnight Cowboy,* which won the Academy Award for Best Picture of the Year. In *Butch Cassidy* the Katherine Ross character, Etta Place, floats between the two men, commits herself to neither, has primarily a mothering role to the two "boys," and finally disappears from the picture altogether. In the much darker *Midnight Cowboy,* Joe Buck (Jon Voight) unsuccessfully aspires to be a male prostitute in New York City but is used and manipulated by women and finally settles for a tender (but nonsexual) and ultimately tragic relationship with Ratso Rizzo (Dustin Hoffman).

The buddy film trend continued with *M*A*S*H* (1970), *Papillon* (1973), *All the President's Men* (1976), *Apocalypse Now* (1979), *Ordinary People* (1980), and more recently, the Eddy Murphy–Nick Nolte hit, *48 Hours* (1983).

Films Today: Forms of Escape

Trend spotting is a popular pastime for mass-media film critics. Any three successful films which appear to have something in common may look like a trend. Considering films over a larger historical perspective, however, we find that movies serve different functions for the audience in different times. Film goers wanted escape during the great depression, patriotism during the war, ideological support during the 1960s. When things look bleak in the real world, film goers look to the movies for escape. Realism in films gives way to magic and style. Escape can be found in a nostalgic retreat into the past, in adventures in the future, or in magical manipulations of the "way things are" to bring about an unlikely happy ending. Rocky Balboa, a third-rate club fighter, becomes heavyweight champion of the world. Luke Skywalker becomes a Jedi Knight and repeatedly rescues Princess Leia from the dark forces of the Empire. The star of *Flashdance,* a welder by day and a bar dancer by night, is plucked from obscurity for the corps de ballet. We know these things do not happen, but we want to believe that they can.

In the difficult decade following Watergate, Americans faced a loss of faith in their political system, an oil shortage, rampant inflation, high unemployment, and a general sense that the American Dream was fading. George Lucas's *American Graffiti* (1973), a surprise box office hit, demonstrated the viability of nostalgia at the box office, first signaled by *Summer of '42* (1971) and echoed by *Grease* (1978) and a number of lesser imitators. The amazingly successful *Star Wars* series ignored the more serious possibilities of the science fiction genre and concentrated on exciting action and special effects, cute minor characters, and the mystical workings of the Force.

Dealing with the War and Watergate

Hollywood's long silence on the Vietnamese war indicates the ambivalence about the war which divided the nation. Only John Wayne's independently produced and hawkish *Green Berets* (1968) treated the war directly and it was largely ignored by film goers. Peter Davis's *Hearts and Minds* (1974) won the Academy Award for Best Feature-Length Documentary and achieved a respectable theatrical release, but *The Deer Hunter* (1978), directed by fledgling Michael Cimino, was the first Hollywood

"Sure it was lousy, but it was better than reality."

(Drawing by Stevenson, © 1979 *The New Yorker* Magazine, Inc.)

film to bring the war to the screen. This film was closely followed by *Coming Home* (1978) and Francis Coppola's long-awaited and trouble-plagued *Apocalypse Now* (1979). As a measure of public acceptance, *The Deer Hunter* and *Coming Home* took five of the six top Oscars in that year.

All the President's Men (1976), a journalistic detective story ripped from the front pages, details the dogged investigation by *Washington Post* reporters Woodward and Bernstein (played by Robert Redford and Dustin Hoffman) which ended with the Nixon resignation in 1974. From that point, interest in Watergate as a subject for film was relegated to the level of TV movie.

Women and the Working Class In 1976 there emerged a decided preference for blue-collar heroes on the part of film audiences. Three of the five nominees for Best Picture—*Bound for Glory*, *Taxi Driver*, and *Rocky*—featured working-class heroes in leading roles. Sylvester Stallone's appealing pugilistic story took the top award and threatens to engender sequels for a long time. The runaway success of *Saturday Night Fever* (1977), with John Travolta as the disco dancer trying to escape his environment, confirmed the trend. Recent blue-collar films—*Norma Rae* (1979), *Urban Cowboy* (1980), *Coal Miner's Daughter* (1980), *An Officer and a Gentleman* (1982)—have included women in the central roles.

Despite the continuance of the buddy film trend, a number of "feminist" films have received good box office attention recently. In addition to *Norma Rae* and *9 to 5*, *An Unmarried Woman* (1978), *It's My Turn* (1980), and to some degree, *Kramer Vs. Kramer* (1979) have probed feminist issues. Ironically, the most popular feminist film to date has been *Tootsie* (1982), with Dustin Hoffman as the out-of-work actor turned actress, who discovers the world from a woman's point of view.

Molly Haskell, a feminist film writer, notes that recently there have been better roles for female stars, with Meryl Streep and Jessica Lange in a series of memorable performances, Diane Keaton alternating between comedy and serious roles, Jill Clayburgh representing the rise of the professional woman, and Jane Fonda in a wide range of roles. While all these are "bankable," as Haskell notes, none of them are as big as any one of the ten male stars.[6]

Minor Trends The success of *Saturday Night Fever* reminded the film industry that dancing is a highly cinematic activity, and a series of films featuring forms of dance have followed, including *The Turning Point* (1977), *Grease* (1978), *All That Jazz* (1979), *Fame* (1980), and *Flashdance* (1983).

Another trend which has proved to be big box office in recent years involves the resurrection of comic book heroes, beginning with *Superman,* the top grossing film of 1978. The man in the red cape was quickly followed by *Buck Rogers in the Twentieth Century* (1979)—a rather unsuccessful attempt to salvage expensive props and footage from the failed TV series *Battleship Galactica*. Other films featuring comic book heroes are *Flash Gordon* (1980) and the *Superman* sequels. (A Superwoman film is currently in production.) The comic strip heroes provide, at their best, a blend of fantasy and nostalgia, which attracts audiences of all ages and provides the base for an enormous box office gross.

Undoubtedly the most bizarre attempt to cash in on the comic strip hero trend was 1981's *Tarzan: The Ape Man.* Budding sex symbol Bo Derek, with her husband John as director, attempted to resurrect the durable Tarzan (the subject of dozens of films dating back to 1919) as a foil for a comic, feminist, sex film adventure. Most of the crew was fired or quit during the shooting, and the resulting mishmash is of interest primarily to film students who want to examine the details of a disaster.

CENSORSHIP: TOO CLOSE FOR COMFORT

Films have been subject to *censorship* attempts from the very beginnings of the medium. Because films have the power to bring us close to the subject and to depict human behavior graphically, they have an equal power to offend and outrage the guardians (often self-appointed) of taste and morality. One of Edison's first films, *The Kiss* (1896)—a minute-long recreation of a famous stage scene of the time—shocked prudish audiences and generated attempts to have the film withdrawn. To our eyes, *The Kiss* is a pretty mild business in which the principals spend most of their time puckering up, but we must remember that this was at the height of the Victorian age and standards have changed considerably.

An even more bizarre example of early censorship concerned Edison's *Fatima* (1897). Fatima was the famed Little Egypt of the Chicago Centennial Fair of 1895, and Edison, with a keen eye for the sensational, brought the bellydancer into the Black Maria and made another short film. In response to the instant outcry upon the film's release, Edison released a second version, with a kind of white-picket-fence pattern super-imposed over the crucial areas of the dancer's body. The censored film is far more "provocative" than the original. Again to our eyes, Fatima is a heavy-set, fully clothed woman, moving repetitively in a kind of modified hula, but she raised the temperatures of the audiences of the time.

It is worth noting that American censors have been concerned almost exclusively with sex and nudity. Protests have been made about violence and sometimes sacrilege, but it was sex that was censored. European censors have been considerably more concerned about violence and more permissive about sex and nudity.

An important Supreme Court decision in

MEDIA VIEW

All-Time Box Office Grossers

TOP GROSS LIST	ADJUSTED FOR INFLATION
1. *E.T.: The Extra-terrestrial* (1982)	*Gone With the Wind* (1939)
2. *Star Wars* (1977)	*Star Wars* (1977)
3. *The Empire Strikes Back* (1980)	*Jaws* (1975)
4. *Jaws* (1975)	*The Sound of Music* (1965)
5. *Raiders of the Lost Ark* (1981)	*E.T.* (1982)
6. *Tootsie* (1982)	*The Godfather* (1972)
7. *Grease* (1978)	*The Empire Strikes Back* (1980)
8. *The Exorcist* (1973)	*The Exorcist* (1973)
9. *The Godfather* (1972)	*The Sting* (1973)
10. *Superman* (1978)	*Grease* (1978)
11. *The Sound of Music* (1965)	*The Ten Commandments* (1956)
12. *The Sting* (1973)	*Dr. Zhivago* (1965)
13. *Close Encounters of the Third Kind* (1977)	*Raiders of the Lost Ark* (1981)
14. *Gone With the Wind* (1939)	*Ben-Hur* (1959)
15. *Saturday Night Fever* (1977)	*Mary Poppins* (1964)

Source: *USA Today*, May 24, 1983.

1915 opened the door to censorship activities. In a suit concerning *Birth of a Nation*, the Court ruled in *Mutual Film Corporation v. Ohio* that the movies are a business and therefore not protected by the First Amendment. Censorship boards for states and hundreds of local communities were set up and either refused release to films which offended them or simply cut out the objectional portions. Some films arrived back at the distributor's exchange considerably shortened.

The Hays Office: Puritanism and Public Relations

In the late teens and early 1920s Hollywood had become known across America as "sin city." Publicity agents did little to discourage this, often manufacturing scandal where none was to be found. In 1921 things went too far. A beloved comedian, Fatty Arbuckle, was charged with the rape and murder of a young starlet, Virginia Rappe, at a wild party in San Francisco. The Hearst papers played up the sordid details of the affair and the nation was outraged. Although he was acquitted after three trials for lack of evidence, Arbuckle's career was ended two years later. The Hollywood producers had to respond. They formed the Motion Picture Producers and Distributors Association of America (MPPDAA), hired Will Hays, the former U.S. postmaster general and a Presbyterian elder and conservative Republican, to head the organization, and promulgated a code for the movies. Although the office did little actual censorship and functioned largely as a public relations organization for films, it did serve to stave off federal intervention and censorship. The crucial notion in the code was that films should contain "compensating values," whereby ten reels of sin could be made acceptable by one reel of repentance or just rewards.

Since nothing was really done by the Hays office, the tides of public protest were rising again by the 1930s. A strict Production Code had been written in 1929 by a Catholic layman and a Jesuit priest, and Hays set up the Office of Production Code Administration to review and approve scripts, scenes, and the completed picture. Release of a film without Production Code approval would generate a heavy fine. The strictures of the code were severe. As film historian David Cook points out:

> The Code prohibited the showing or mentioning of almost everything germane to the situation of normal human adults. It forbade depicting "scenes of passion" in all but the most puerile terms, and it required that the sanctity of the institution of marriage and the home be upheld at all times (married couples, however, were never to be shown sharing a bed). Adultery, illicit sex, seduction or rape could never be more than suggested, and then only if they were absolutely essential to the plot and were severely punished at the end. Also prohibited were the use of profanity and racial epithets, any implication of prostitution, miscegenation, sexual aberration, or drug addiction; nudity of all sorts; sexually suggestive dances and costumes; "excessive and lustful kissing" and excessive drinking.[7]

Also forbidden were details of crime, any justification of crime, attacks on religion, cruelty to children or animals, and excessive brutality.

The Legion of Decency

Despite the fact that the Production Code was written by Catholics and administered by another Catholic (Joseph Breen), the American bishops were suspicious of the Hays office and, in 1933, set up the Legion of Decency. The legion rated films according to a scale of acceptability (from Unobjectionable for All, through Objectionable in Part, to the dread Condemned). The ratings were published weekly and church members were required to pledge to respect them. If the weapon of the Production Code Administration was prior censorship, the weapon of the Legion was boycott or the threat of boycott. Between them, they sanitized the silver screen and their power lasted into the 1950s.

The Supreme Court Decisions: Censorship in Check

In 1952, the state of New York opposed the release of the Italian film *The Miracle*. The movie, written by Federico Fellini and directed by Roberto Rossellini, tells the story of a feeble-minded peasant woman seduced by a stranger whom she thinks is St. Joseph. Bitterly attacked by the archdiocese of New York and Cardinal Spellman as sacrilegious, the film generated much controversy but few ticket sales. At the Supreme Court, the justices reversed the 1915 decision by ruling that films *were* a medium for the communication of ideas and thus deserved the protection of the First Amendment. They also held that "sacrilege" is too vague a concept to be used in the censoring of a film.

In 1961, a high court ruling upheld the legality of prior censorship. In effect, the court rejected the argument that the First Amendment precluded prior censorship of movies. This ruling, which presently covers the rights and limits of film censorship, was enunciated in *Miller v. California.* (June 21, 1973). Justice Burger, who wrote the majority opinion, attempted to clear the legal underbrush and gave three practical criteria for censors to make their decision:

1. Whether the average person, applying contemporary community standards, would find that the work, taken as a whole, appeals to the purient interest
2. Whether the work depicts or describes anything in a patently offensive way that is specifically defined by an applicable state law prohibiting it

> **MEDIA PROBE**
>
> In the words of Justice Tom Clark: "It cannot be doubted that motion pictures are a significant medium for the communication of ideas." In your opinion should films fall within the range of speech protected by the First Amendment? Why or why not? Can you cite specific ideas advanced by motion pictures? In what ways have these ideas influenced you? people whom you know?

3. Whether the work, taken as a whole, lacks serious literary, artistic, political, or scientific value

While providing a clear legal basis for censorship, *Miller v. California* made the practice of censorship almost impossible to defend in court.[8] The U.S. Supreme Court attempted to clarify its position on prior censorship of motion pictures in the 1965 *Freedman v. Maryland* case. In a unanimous decision, the Court reversed the conviction of Baltimore theater manager Ronald Freedman for exhibiting the film *Revenge at Daybreak* without a license. Holding that Maryland had failed to provide adequate procedural safeguards "against undue inhibition of expression," the Court shifted the burden of proof from the exhibitor to the censors.

From Control to Advice: The MPAA Ratings

In the meantime, producer-director Otto Preminger began releasing a series of films which violated the previously sacrosanct Production Code, but nevertheless achieved resounding commercial success. The films included *The Moon Is Blue* (1953), which used the term "professional virgin," *The Man With the Golden Arm* (1955), which showed drug addiction, and *Anatomy of a Murder* (1959), which dealt with rape. The Production Code had lost its teeth. At the same time, the Legion of Decency, which had been gradually liberalizing with the times, split over the issue of nudity in *The Pawnbroker* (1966), with half the panel acknowledging the seriousness of the theme and the dramatic necessity of the brief nude scene, the other half demanding the "condemned" rating as a stance against screen nudity. The film was condemned but widely honored and viewed; the Legion of Decency lost credibility and, despite reorganization as the National Catholic Office for Motion Pictures, waned in influence and no longer issues ratings.

By the late 1960s, American films were becoming more violent, more overtly sexual, and more socially critical. Public outcry against the movies was, once again, mounting. The Motion Picture Association of America (the former MPPDAA) abandoned the Production Code for a *rating system,* which is still in place. With a G rating for the totally innocuous, and an X rating for the overtly sexual or excessively violent, most films (about 85 percent) fall into the PG (parental guidance advised) or R (restricted to those 17 and older) categories, largely on the basis of nudity. The G rating is considered to be death at the box office, so even an obvious children's fantasy like *E.T.: The Extraterrestrial,* contains the phrase "penis breath" in order to earn the more commercial PG. On July 1, 1984, PG-13, the first rating to be introduced since the voluntary industry movie rating system began in November 1968, went into effect. PG-13 carries the following explanatory statement in all advertising and movie preview trailers: "Parents are strongly cautioned to give special guidance for attendance of children under 13. Some material may be inappropriate for young children." According to Jack Valenti, MPAA president, PG-13 "gives a resting place for films that were bursting out of PG but not leaping high enough to get into R." As with the original Production Code, the MPAA ratings are generally viewed as a public relations device with

MEDIA PROBE

JACK VALENTI ON ART AND GOOD TASTE

We simply cannot discard the right of the artist to film what he chooses, in the way he chooses. Sometimes to shock is to seize the truth, and sometimes to unsettle is to make a visible revelation. Moreover, one must buy a ticket to see a movie; no one is forced to enter a movie theatre.

We have created a film-rating system which tells parents in advance what kind of movie is playing at the local theater, and allows them to judge whether or not they should take their children. This system rates films on the acceptability of the material, as it pertains to children. With the cooperation of the National Association of Theater Owners, viewing of certain films is restricted to adults.

But even this film rating does not repeal the basic rules of public decency. No responsible person ought ever to defend the fakery of those who construct vulgarity and call it art. When discipline and discretion disappear, we will have gone culturally berserk. There is such a think as good taste, and if one has to ask what it is, he plainly doesn't have it.

The majority of creative film-makers and executives are allied in their judgment that excellence, not hokum, is what endures. But the public has a responsibility, too: the obligation to stay away from trash and give their patronage to quality.

To what extent do you agree with what Valenti has written? Do you think you have good taste? Why or why not? How do you differentiate a "trashy" film from a quality film? In your opinion, is it enough for films to be classified as either G, PG, PG-13, R, or X, or should viewers also be told why the film was given the rating?

---

little important influence on the content of the films or the intended behavior of the audience.

THE MOVIE BUSINESS

Film is a medium of communication, cinema is an art form, movies are entertainment, but the motion picture industry is a business—a business like no other. With the breakup of the old studio system and the rise of independent production, every major film is virtually a company unto itself. It has been said that the true art of the movies is putting together the deal, that is, the complex and interlocking series of agreements which will guarantee the financing required.

The Property

The deal usually begins with the *"property,"* that is, the subject matter of the film. (See Figure 9-5.) This may be no more than a one-sentence idea, but someone must own the rights to that idea. The ideal property, however, is "presold," that is, it has been before the public in some form and proved popular. Examples include popular novels, Broadway plays, television series, old movies, comics, and sometimes even recordings, such as "Take This Job and Shove It." Presold properties are expensive, however, with the current high-price record held by *Annie*. (Columbia Pictures paid $9.5 million for the rights to the long-running Broadway musical.) Commonly, however, the property is a story or scenario that may have been floating around Hollywood for years.

The Package: Making the Deal

Although there are a hundred variations on how a film deal is put together, the person who makes the deal is usually the producer, the person who is responsible for the financial side of the film. The producer's job is to attend to the business side of the movie. During the years when the big studios controlled

MEDIA VIEW

DECLARATION OF PRINCIPLES OF THE CODE OF SELF-REGULATION OF THE MOTION PICTURE ASSOCIATION

This Code is designed to keep in close harmony with the mores, culture, the moral sense and change in our society.

The objectives of the Code are:

1. To encourage artistic expression by expanding creative freedom and
2. To assure that the freedom which encourages the artist remains responsible and sensitive to the standards of the larger society.

Censorship is an odious enterprise. We oppose censorship and classification by governments because they are alien to the American tradition of freedom. . . .

The creators of motion pictures undertake a responsibility to make available pertinent information about their pictures which will assist parents to fulfill their responsibilities.

But this alone is not enough. In further recognition of our obligation to the public, and most especially to parents, we have extended the Code operation to include a nationwide voluntary film rating program which has as its prime objective a sensitive concern for children. Motion pictures will be reviewed by a Code and Rating administration which, when it reviews a motion picture as to its conformity with the standards of the Code, will issue ratings. It is our intent that all motion pictures exhibited in the United States will carry a rating.

MEDIA VIEW

The playground opens early. Mechanics push out the giant arc lights that simmer in the morning gloom. There is the muffled sound of carpenters, the slam of a door on a coffee van. A giant image flickers on the other side of a vacant hanger, and solemn men sit and debate how best to mix the sound that will match that image. This playground is a factory.

Studio executives pass the guards and put their glossy cars carefully into the parking spaces that are marked with their names. When each man quits the studio, his name will be painted over. This playground is no place for permanency.

On the fifty-fourth floor of the Bank of America tower on South Flower Street, men settle in their open-plan offices. They are blind to the dizzying view that stretches from ocean to mountains to the bleached, white bones of the Hollywood sign. They talk seriously of points and profit. They examine credit ratings and collateral. The bankers care about the playground because it is a business.

In Cincinnati a group of lawyers meet. They want to shelter their income from taxes. For that reason a banker in Los Angeles will advance money. From that money an executive will assemble his profit. Carpenters hammer for it, stars act for it, writers invent for it, and directors shape it. The playground will come to life. . . .

This playground is a machine, an assembly line, a brokerage for artificial images. But it is also a sizeable part of the emotional reality of our past. It bred the images we share. We remember crying at the movies almost more than real tears. Our adolescent ideas grew on the models in the films we were offered. The playground helped shape our culture and our assumptions. What it produces is consumed on a mighty scale. The playground manufactures popular culture.

Michael Pye and Lynda Myles, *The Movie Brats,* Holt, Rinehart & Winston, New York, 1979, pp. 3–4.

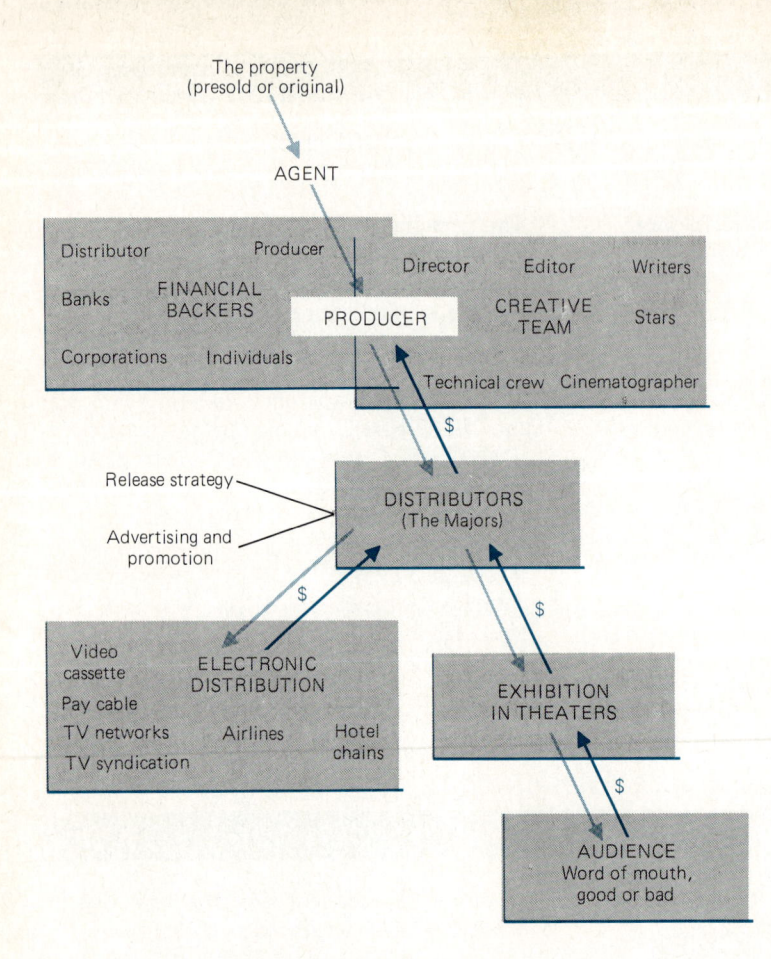

FIGURE 9-5 A model of film production and release.

filmmaking, the producer was an employee assigned by a studio to oversee the spending of studio funds. As the reign of the big studios came to an end, the independent producer assumed responsibility for the whole organization of the film—including finding the story or property. Once the producer acquires the rights to a property, he or she then attempts to build a cast and crew. The director, the person responsible for shooting the film, is normally chosen first. Then the producer and the director look for a writer (often a series of writers) to put together a shooting script. The writing is usually going on while the deal is being put together, and as each major person is added changes are called for, and adjustments are made to elements in the script that the new person does not like.

Finally, the producer and the director look for a "bankable" star, one whose presence in the film will virtually guarantee exhibitor bidding and ticket sales. Current bankable stars are John Travolta, Richard Gere, Dudley Moore, Barbra Streisand, and, above all, Richard Pryor. Recently bankable but fading after a series of weak performances at the box office are Clint Eastwood and Burt Reynolds. Many major stars who appear in hit after hit never become bankable—their success is tied to the film in which they appear. Examples of nonbankable major stars are: Dustin Hoffman, Meryl Streep, Robert De Niro, Roy Scheider, Donald Sutherland, Dolly Parton,

YOU WERE THERE

THE (CONDENSED) HISTORY OF A DEAL

In the fall of 1982, George Roy Hill, the movie director (*The Sting, Butch Cassidy*), traveled to Switzerland to meet the English novelist David Cornwell, better known as John Le Carrè. Hill wanted to direct Le Carrè's just completed novel, *The Little Drummer Girl.* Attorney Morton Leavy, an entertainment/literary lawyer, who represented both Hill and Le Carrè, convinced Warner Brothers to buy the film rights to the book and assign them to Pan Arts Corporation (Hill's production company), which had a financing and distribution deal with Warners. The deal was made.

The motion picture agent for John Gregory Dunne (novelist and screenwriter) and Joan Didion (novelist, screen writer, and Mrs. Dunne) had heard a rumor of the deal and discovered that there was "interest" at Pan Arts in having Dunne/Didion as the script writers.

Though Hill and Le Carrè preferred a British screen writer, their choice was unavailable, and Pan Arts turned to Dunne/Didion. They read the manuscript, agreed to do the script, and worked for two days with Hill, blocking out the story.

The Dunnes' agent proposed asking for $500,000 guaranteed for the writers, based on the assumption that the budget for the film would exceed $20 million. The Dunnes, having only five days to settle before a planned vacation, agreed to ask for a guaranteed $300,000 for a first draft and one set of changes, against a final fee of $450,000, the same amount they had received on their previous picture.

Hill, through Pan Arts, offered $250,000 for a first draft and a set of changes, against a final fee of $450,000. Although the $50,000 difference would have been made up in the second draft, neither Hill nor Dunne budged, and in Dunne's words "this mutual display of ego and hubris finally caused the negotiations to fall apart." Dunne returned the manuscript to Pan Arts, and Hill sent the Dunnes a case of expensive French wine and a card with a single word: "Thanks."

See John Gregory Dunne in *Esquire*, August, 1983.

Jane Fonda . . . the list is long. The presence of such stars in the deal are guarantees of financial support for the film but not for ticket sales.

When the property is put together and the writer, director, stars, and a price tag is arrived at, the producer has a "package." The producer then goes with the package to the sources of finance: banks, studios, distributors, cable networks, and videocassette releasing firms. With some films, early perceived as big box office, licensing agreements for related products such as T-shirts, toys, and record albums can often generate significant revenues. Licensing agreements for the famed *Star Wars* trilogy have been estimated at over $500 million. Despite the high production cost of *Annie* (well over $40 million), master dealer Ray Stark had put together licensing agreements worth $50 million even before the film was released.

The Finances: Megabucks and Megarisk

It should be clear to you by now that any mass-media enterprise is identified by one characteristic: high cost. Even if a movie can

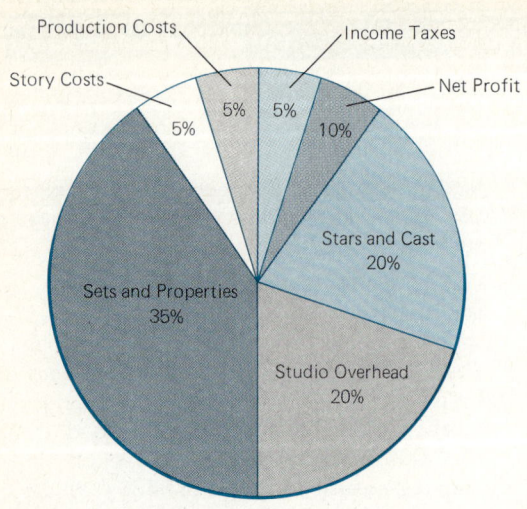

FIGURE 9-6 Costs of making a movie.

be produced for "peanuts" (less than $1 million), the cost of distributing the film will run many times that amount.

The average production cost presently runs around $12 million with a range running from $40,000 (*Chan Is Missing*) to more than $50 million (the *Superman* series). The budget (see Figure 9-6) for the average picture breaks down as follows:

ITEM	PERCENT OF TOTAL COST
Story costs	5
Stars and cast	20
Sets and properties	35
Studio overhead	20
Production costs	5
Income taxes	5
Net profit	10

MEDIA VIEW

"PROFIT PARTICIPANTS" SELDOM SEE ANY PROFITS

Hollywood—In the entertainment industry, "net profits" almost always means "no profits." With rare exceptions, no matter how much a film or television series earns, so-called profit participants never see any money. This is a major reason that salaries of actors, directors and others have risen so much in the last few years.

"I've been a 'profit participant' too many times not to realize that those things aren't worth the paper they're written on," says actor James Garner, whose pay as the co-star of *Victor/Victoria* was $650,000 plus 5 percent of the net profits. "Everyone knows you can't depend on paper promises. You have to get your money up front."

The problem, actors and others say, is that studios charge an arbitrary overhead fee on all projects (usually 15 percent to 25 percent of the total budget) regardless of the actual administrative and studio expense; get a distribution fee as high as 50 percent; and charge continuing interest on all costs until the break-even point is reached. And the definition of when a film or series has reached that point is subject to negotiation and can be different on every project.

Studio chiefs such as Sidney J. Scheinberg, the president of MCA, Inc., say that their accounting practices are open and above board and that profit participants who complain have merely negotiated a bad deal for themselves.

(Garner is suing MCA because he has not received any proceeds from his 35.5 percent share of the net profits from the highly successful "Rockford Files" TV series.)

"The studios can do just about anything they want and get away with it," Mr. Garner charges. "We're helpless unless we can get Hollywood to change its accounting practices."

The Wall Street Journal, July 21, 1983.

> ## MEDIA VIEW
>
> People who make films... must be pitchpersons first. They must be able to go out and sell themselves and their ideas to strangers. Or they must have rich families and friends, or access to people with so much money that they embrace the possibility of tax-loss carry-forwards. Then, once the film is made, the moviemaker must be able, in industry terminology, to "sell it," to get someone to put it into theatres and then to persuade people to come to those theatres in huge numbers. It makes no difference if a movie is great if no one sees it.
>
> Vincent Canby, "If You Want to Make Movies, Learn to be a Salesman," *The New York Times*, April 24, 1983.

The producer can acquire the rights to a property (the material on which the film will be based) and have it developed into a shooting script for relatively little financial risk, but once the shooting starts, the major portion of the funding must be available. The funding is based on the estimate of audience potential for a given property, and it may come from a number of sources, including private financing, corporate financing, or financing by a distributor. For big-budget pictures, the money usually comes from one of the seven major producer-distributors, since they have both the know-how to market (and thus to estimate the market value of) the picture, and the cash flow from previous films to spread the risk.

The situation in the late 1970s, then, was one in which six (Columbia, Paramount, 20th Century Fox, United Artists, Universal and Warner Brothers) of the seven major producers had a distribution unit (MGM being the only exception). The dominance of these major producer-distributors is demonstrated by the fact that, although the market share in terms of movie rental revenues has remained quite high, "it has been estimated that the percentage of rental revenues which the major producer-distributors receive is 83% for the top six firms and 92% for the top eight firms."[9]

It is easy to see from these figures that the majors have found a way to retain control of the industry despite the antitrust actions of the courts.

In recent years, the major producers have opted to fund and distribute relatively few films, aiming for big box office and foreign distribution to secure their profits. This leaves exhibitors short of films to show and therefore less able to bargain with the distributor. Deals for good box office films are so favorable to the distributor that the theater owner is left with a very small margin of profit. Oddly enough, one solution for these exhibitors has been to develop multiscreen theaters (thus reducing the cost of personnel) and to rely on sales of popcorn and sodas and return from video games to make their money. It has been estimated that 60 to 80 percent of exhibitor profit comes from these nonticket revenues.

Distribution: Strategy and Second Guessing

If the production of the average film costs $12 million the cost of releasing the film may double that. Release costs include the lab costs for the number of prints to be made (at $2000 a print), advertising and promotion for the film, and, of course, overhead and profit for the distributor. These costs will be influenced by the "release strategy" of the distributor, which may be crucial to the film's ultimate success or failure. Timing the release is as crucial as the form of the release. (Do you open "wide,"—that is, at many theaters across the nation—or "tight,"—that is, at a few select theaters? For major pictures, distributors aim for a release near the two peak film-viewing periods—Christmas or early summer, when schools are not in session.

MOVIES: THE WINDOW SCREEN   281

MEDIA VIEW

NOT COMING TO A THEATER NEAR YOU

When Steve McQueen died in 1980, the press eulogized him as one of Hollywood's last superstars. His movies, some of the most profitable and widely seen in the past decade, made millions for the studios releasing them and for the actor himself. There is one startling exception. McQueen made a movie in 1976 that has never been released commercially—an adaptation of Henrik Ibsen's classic play *An Enemy of the People,* co-starring Bibi Andersson and Charles Durning.

This film is only one among hundreds of unreleased films that are gathering dust in Hollywood's vaults, movies which include: Robert Altman's *Health,* a satiric look at a healthfood convention, starring Carol Burnett, Lauren Bacall, Glenda Jackson and James Garner; *Second Hand Hearts,* starring Robert Blake and Barbara Harris and directed by Hal Ashby; *Just a Gigolo,* starring David Bowie and Marlene Dietrich; *Tilt,* with Brook Shields as a teenage pinball wizard; *Phobia,* a thriller directed by John Huston; and *The Picasso Summer,* with Albert Finney and Yvette Mimieux. Some of these movies may have had a very limited release in three or four theatres, and some may have been shown on television years after they were made. But they have never been seen as they were meant to be seen—in your local neighborhood theatre. They are orphans of a billion-dollar industry.

How can a studio spend several million dollars making a movie and then decide not to release it? The basic explanation is economic. In the past few years movie advertising and distribution costs have skyrocketed—to such an extent that studios have decided even a picture with Steve McQueen or Faye Dunaway may be cheaper to shelve than to release. To open a film nationwide now costs a minimum of $3 million, sometimes as much as $8 to $10 million.

Stephen Farber, "Not Coming to a Theatre Near You," *Ambassador,* April 1981, p. 39.

Once the film is released, word-of-mouth becomes the most influential form of advertising. If the word is good, the film will have "legs," that is, it will retain or even build an audience after its release. If a film's audience begins to slip in the second week, no matter how large the first week grosses, the chances of its becoming a box office hit are almost nil.

Release Patterns: The Channels Multiply

It is monumentally difficult to get a movie made, both because of the enormous sums involved in most productions, and because of the complexity of the deals that must be made. And sometimes, once a film is made, it does not get released. The producers, in effect, admit to a terrible mistake and take a tax write-off, often more valuable to them financially than a marginal film.

If a film is reasonably successful in theatrical release, its release on videocassette and video disc follows almost immediately. This is intensely distressing to exhibitors, but they have no control over the distributors, and the distributors want to get their money back as quickly as possible. The next stage of release is sale to cable companies like HBO or Showtime. Even if a film has bombed in theaters, there is a place in the cable schedules which, despite repeat showings, require a large number of films monthly. If a film has performed so poorly that no sale to cable television is possible, there is the possibility of sale to airlines for use as in-flight movies, to hotel chan-

MEDIA VIEW

Hollywood, July 8, 1983—During the last two weeks, this summer's blockbuster movie "Return of the Jedi" has been stolen six times, from theaters in three states and in Britain. The movie industry is certain that the objective in each case was to turn these 35-millimeter prints into illegal home video cassettes to be shipped around the world.

"A low estimate of the film industry's loss from piracy is $100 million a year," said Richard Bloeser, the former Federal FBI agent who heads the film security office of the Motion Picture Association of America. "It could be as high as $500 million a year."

Industry officials say illegal film laboratories turn the stolen prints into videotapes that are then duplicated and sold to the public in the United States and usually rented by the public in stores abroad. The price charged for a videotape varies according to how long the film has been out. The price for a pirated tape of "Jedi" at present ranges from about $85 to $150, Mr. Bloeser said.

Aljean Harmetz, " 'Jedi' Prints Stolen for Cassette Piracy, Movie Industry says," *The New York Times,* August 9, 1983, pp. 1, 10

---

nels, and to prisons—the end of the line in film releasing. It should also be noted that many films today are shown for the first time on cable. For example, in January 1983, Universal Studios offered *Pirates of Penzance* for pay per view on the same date as its theatrical release.

Theatrically successful films will be leased to networks for prime-time airing and finally will make their way into the syndication market, to be leased (usually in blocks with other films) to individual stations.

Some films have a remarkable life on television. Although *The Wizard of Oz* only did marginally well in theatrical release, it has become an annual event on CBS, and over the years has garnered seven of the top fifty ratings for films on television. No other movie appears on the list even twice. The king of syndication ratings is *Casablanca*.

PROMOTING THE FILM: OUTSIDE INFLUENCES

The three factors which "sell" a film are, in ascending order of importance: the anticipation of the potential viewer, the promotion campaign which addresses that anticipation, and the word-of-mouth reaction of early viewers. In special circumstances, other factors can promote a film, among them awards and festival prices and critical acclaim.

Awards

It is safe to say that every filmmaker likes to receive awards—but some awards are better than others. Chief among awards that promote a film are the Academy Awards. One of the top five awards can add 20 percent to a film's gross, and a sweep of major awards can double a film's pre-Award gross. (Such was the case for *Ordinary People*, but not for *Gandhi*.) New York Critics Awards are somewhat influential in the East, but serve primarily as a predictor for the later Academy Awards. The Golden Globe Awards (by foreign journalists) are of such little importance that they are rarely mentioned in advertising.

Critics and Reviewers

In the words of a thousand embittered creative people, "everybody's a critic." And to be sure, all viewers are critics.

According to movie critic Vincent Canby, every viewer "brings into the motion picture

MEDIA PROBE

After attending a film, listen to the comments of audience members as they leave the theater. To what extent do people appear to have diverse opinions regarding the value of the movie they just viewed?

By what standards do you judge a film?

---

theatre a different set of habits, perferences and prejudices, as well as physical equipment. Some of us are near sighted, some farsighted, some hard of hearing, and some have ears almost too sensitive for modern movie sound." As Canby concludes, "it's a wonder that any two people ever agree on what they've just seen." Unlike regular viewers, some people make a living by criticizing films. Almost every newspaper and general-interest magazine has a film critic, and more and more television stations are doing film reviews. Some of these people are merely reviewers. They summarize the film and react to it, pretty much as they think their audience will react. Essentially, their function is to give information about the film.

Some critics are primarily word stylists. They use the occasion of a review to display their literary talents, usually in panning the film (John Simon is a classic example). Some writers are serious critics, who are given the space and time to explore films in depth.

Recently, PBS initiated a half-hour weekly review series called *Sneak Previews* with Roger Ebert and Gene Siskel, film reviewers for two Chicago newspapers. The series was so successful that Ebert and Siskel left the show and began to syndicate their own show, *At the Movies*, to commercial television stations; *Sneak Previews* continues with Jeffrey Lyons and Neil Gabler.

The Influence of Critics

In the New York theater, critics can and do make or break plays. A play with poor reviews will often close the next night. Rave reviews can signal the beginning of a long and lucra-

---

MEDIA VIEW

WHAT THE CRITICS HAD TO SAY ABOUT A FILM THEY SAW

In the first thirty seconds, this film gets off on the wrong foot and, although there are plenty of clever effects and some amusing spots, it never recovers. Because this is a major effort by an important director, it is a major disappointment. (*Stanley Kauffmann in* The New Republic)

The world's most extraordinary film. Nothing like it has ever been shown in Boston before, or, for that matter anywhere. (*Majorie Adams in* The Boston Globe)

———is some sort of great film and an unforgettable endeavor. (*Penelope Gilliott in* The New Yorker)

———is not the worst film I've ever seen. It's simply the dullest. (*Petter Dibble in* Women's Wear Daily)

———is just such a bolt of brilliant, high-voltage cinema. (*John Allen in* The Christian Science Monitor)

A regrettable failure...(*John Simon in* The New Leader)

Each critic was writing about the same film: *2001: A Space Odyssey.* What did the critics write about 2010? Was there as much disparity?

tive run. Almost the opposite is true for films! Negative reviews from serious critics often serve to indicate a film's popular appeal. For example, critics savaged the Burt Reynolds vehicle, *Smokey and the Bandit* (1977), which rapidly moved to fifteenth place on the All-Time Box Office Grossers list, and has generated two sequels and dozens of imitations.

On rare occasions, a critic can resurrect a film which has been overlooked by the system. *The Great Santini* (1979) had already been sold to HBO (under the alternate title, *The Ace*) after release at a single New York theater. A highly favorable review from Vincent Canby of *The New York Times* began to build box office for the film, which led to wider distribution, respectable box office, and an Academy Award nomination for newcomer Michael O'Keefe as Best Supporting Actor.

Critical reviews are often important for foreign films, which have a difficult time getting American distribution. In one celebrated case, a single rave review by influential *New Yorker* critic Pauline Kael got wide American distribution for Bernardo Bertolucci's controversial *Last Tango in Paris* (1973). In wide release, the film got mixed reviews and Kael later admitted that she didn't think the film was all that great. She gave the favorable review in order to get U.S. distribution for the film.

Film Festivals

Film festivals can sometimes be influential in getting distribution for a film. Top prizes at the major European festivals (Cannes, Berlin, Venice) usually guarantee a U.S. release for foreign films. The fourth major festival, the New York Film Festival, is not a prize-granting festival but does serve as a showplace for foreign films which might not otherwise be seen here. The impact of the festivals on American films is rather minimal. For example, despite highly favorable reviews and reactions at the New York Film Festival, Jon Demme's engaging *Handle With Care*, which died on its first release, was released again after the festival (as *Citizen's Band*) and died again. It may safely be said that the awards and festivals are only influential for the small segment of the mass audience which has a special interest in films.

FILM WATCHING: A VIEWER'S GUIDE

Film is a form of communication. The message a film sends, and the message a viewer receives is dependent, at least in part, on the shots a director chooses to use. In fact, the shot is itself the basic unit of film communication: it is the base upon which a film will be built; it is the means through which a director speaks to the audience. The director must decide where to place the camera, how to move it, what to reveal to the viewer, and what to conceal from the viewer. *Film shots* are divided into *scenes* (a single shot or group of shots usually unified by time and place), and scenes are divided into *sequences* (a grouping of scenes unified by a common purpose or setting).

The movie itself, however, is composed simply of a number of different shots, shots that are taken from different positions and angles, cut, and then joined together. Let us now explore the key types of shots, camera angles, and movements a director uses to communicate.

Basically there are five shots from which a director selects: the extreme long shot, the long shot, the medium shot, the close-up, and the extreme close-up. The *extreme long shot* is almost always an exterior shot that reveals the entire area of action or a locale. It is used to impress viewers with the vast scope of an event and to communicate grandeur or a sense of space. The *long shot,* sometimes referred to as an establishing shot, reveals where the people or objects are located. The *medium shot,* depicts a character or subject in

Truffaut, the prolific French director, at work. (Mary Ellen Mark/Archive Pictures)

its immediate surrounding. Typically, it depicts a figure or figures from the knees or waist up. Sometimes called a two-shot, the medium shot is a functional shot, and the most effective shot to use when two people are talking to each other. The *close-up* focuses in on a relatively small object—the face of the main character for example; it reveals very little, if any, locale. By magnifying its subject, the close-up, tends to elevate the importance of that which it depicts. An *extreme close-up,* a variation of the close-up, will focus in on its subject to an even greater extent; thus, it may show us the eyes or the clenched teeth of a character. The basic order of shots is a long shot (the director establishes where things are), a medium shot (the director shows you who is involved), a close-up (the director reveals the focus of his or her attention), and a long shot (the director reminds you of what surrounds the focus of his or her attention). While this basic order of shots is widely used, there are many exceptions to this basic order. For instance, one way to achieve a shock response is to start with an extreme close-up of a daisy in bloom, cut to a medium shot that reveals that the daisies are being carressed by a woman, and finally, a shocking long shot—showing that the daisies and the woman are all that remain in a bombed-out neighborhood. If this sequence had been shot in normal order its impact would have been lessened.

The shots described above may be taken from one of three basic angles: normal angle, low angle, and high angle. *Normal angle* shots are taken from the eye level of the subject and place the audience on the same level as the subject. Subject and audience could be said to share a symmetrical relationship; viewers are led to look at the subject as their equal. In contrast, in the *low angle shot,* the camera looks up at the subject; thus, the low angle shot heightens the importance of the subject, making it appear superior and making the viewers feel less secure; in effect, a low angle shot compels viewers to look up to the subject. For this reason, a low angle sets up a complementary relationship between viewers and audience, one in which the subject is in a one-up position. The *high angle shot* has just the opposite effect. In a high angle shot, the camera looks down at the subject; thus, the viewer is led to look down on the subject too. The high angle shot places the viewer in the one-up position; the audience member is made to feel superior while the subject is made to appear smaller or inferior. When a director changes the camera's angle, a message is being sent to viewers to change their perspective and the way they feel about the subject as well.

As a viewer, in addition to being able to identify shots and camera angles, you should also be able to recognize a number of commonly used camera movements: a pan shot, a tilt shot, a tracking shot, a dolly shot, and a hand-held shot. In a *pan shot,* the camera is moved from left to right or vice versa. It can be used to show a vast expanse of scenery, to introduce a character as part of the environment, or to follow a moving object. A vertical (up and down) pan is called a *tilt shot.* Such a shot gives viewers a trip up or down a person, thing, or object. When the director uses a *tracking shot,* tracks are laid, and the camera is mounted on a rubber-tired vehicle and moved along the rails, enabling the director to follow a moving object or person. If the ground is smooth, the director may opt to simply have the camera pushed along the floor on a rubber-wheeled dolly—thus, we have the dolly shot. When the director uses neither a track nor a dolly, but instead has someone carry the camera around, this is called a *hand-held camera shot;* most frequently used in filming documentaries or news, this type of shot is used to add a sense of reality to a feature film.

DOCUMENTARIES AND SHORT FILMS

It has been estimated that 80 percent of the cinema footage (including film and video) shot in the United States in any one year is *not* feature film footage. Hundreds of *documentary* and instructional films are shot by professional filmmakers, schools, corporations, and other institutions. The Pentagon is far and away the major filmmaker in the United States. In addition, hundreds of experimental (avant-garde or art) films and videotapes are made each year. Very few of these productions reach a mass audience. Many are amateurish or mechanical, many are brilliant and even award-winning efforts by gifted filmmakers, films made with care and passion which will be seen by a tiny audience and never heard of again.

One of the exceptions to the rule of the invisible documentary was 1974's *Hearts and Minds,* a feature-length documentary which explored the background, impact, and lingering effects of the U.S. involvement in Vietnam. Documentarist Peter Davis made no attempt to conceal his opposition to the Vietnamese war but was able to interview top spokesmen for the Kennedy, Johnson, and Nixon administrations as well as disillusioned veterans, peace movement activists, and North Vietnamese civilians. The ambitious and emotionally powerful film was so realistic that veterans of the Vietnamese war were reported to be unable to watch the film because it reminded them too strongly of their own experiences. *Hearts and Minds* received the Academy Award for Best Feature-Length Documentary and was accorded wide theatrical release across the United States.

Another documentary which received fairly

MEDIA PROBE

Select a comic strip or comic book to work with. Cut out examples of close-ups, medium shots, and long shots, high angle shots, low angle shots, and normal angle shots. Label each and be prepared to discuss the effect each type of shot had on the way you responded to the story.

Using a nursery rhyme like "Little Miss Muffet" or "Humpty Dumpty" turn it into a short film script. That is, divide the lines of the nursery rhyme into shots—being certain to indicate the type of shot, shooting angle, and camera movement you intend to use for each line or line segment.

wide distribution following its Academy Award was Barbara Kopple's *Harlan County, U.S.A.* (1977), a harrowing study of a coal miner's strike in Kentucky. In the process of shooting the film, Kopple and her crew were threatened, shoved, and shot at, which did nothing to diminish the intensity of their involvement.

More typically, a feature-length documentary receives a brief theater release, often in an art house, in the two cities (New York and Los Angeles) which qualify it for Academy Awards. Then it is consigned to the back shelves of film distribution libraries, for rare rentals to film societies and film classes. Sometimes a documentary is resurrected by public television stations or PBS and thus reaches a much larger audience. Such was the fate of Ira Wohl's *Best Boy* (Academy Award for Best Feature-Length Documentary, 1979), a touching story of an elderly couple preparing their 52-year-old retarded son for life after their deaths.

Despite the skill and dedication lavished on these films, the documentary is generally perceived by the public as an educational experience, and the public goes to the theater and watches television primarily for entertainment. The result is that, without awards, and without money for publicity, few documentaries are even known to the public, much less available for their viewing. Some documentaries which have appeal for particular audiences, such as 1983's much-praised *Say Amen, Somebody*, which traces the rise of gospel singing in American black churches, may circulate within this smaller context. Other documentaries like *The Flight of the Gossamer Condor* receive support from corporations whose products are featured in the film. (In this case, DuPont's Mylar was the basic material used for construction.)

If oblivion is the fate awaiting most feature-length documentaries, it is almost inevitable for short films, either documentary or animation. Formerly a staple of the "A Feature" show, with newsreel, cartoon, docu-

MEDIA PROBE

Do you ever think of television commercials as if they were movies? Make a list of five commercials which strike you as using advanced film techniques. Try to identify the techniques used and their intended effects. Then turn the sound off and study the visual techniques employed in the commercials. To what extent does turning down the sound help you to examine the filmmaker's technique? Next, count the number of separate shots that occur in a single commercial. Do you think the commercial is too busy or effective? Why? Finally, make a list of commercials which are done in a single shot, using no editing techniques. Do you think they are effective or ineffective? Why?

mentary and feature, the short cinema form exists now largely in the category of "art" and is dominated by the new video technology.

Finally, it is worth mentioning that some of the best filmmakers in America shoot television commercials. Some commercials have enormous shooting budgets, making them—foot for foot—the most expensive films ever shot. (The current record: $750,000 for a one-minute commercial for Great American Soups featuring dancer Ann Miller.) These filmmakers have a minute or less to reach their audience and put across their message; the competition they face from rivals is formidable. Some ads are cinema at their best.

FILM AND VIDEO: TWO MEDIUMS OR ONE?

From a technical viewpoint, film and video are totally different mediums. The film medium consists of a complex set of processes: physical (the film itself passing through the camera, the developing machine, the editor, the projector); chemical (the photosensitive particles in the emulsion reacting to light, being chemically fixed, and gradually fading and changing over time), and electrical (the power drives for the equipment, plus the light source for the projector). Video is an electronic process, whereby the light and sound images are converted to electronic equivalents by the camera, recorded on magnetic tape, and transformed by the monitor or reciver back into light and sound images. Film wears out with use and colors change, but videotape may be used repeatedly without loss of picture quality and the images do not fade.

Standard theatrical film is circulated in a 35-mm format. It contains the equivalent of about 1000 lines of television information. A home television receiver reproduces about 280 lines of information, roughly equivalent to super 8-mm film. Thus, at present, the theatrical film image contains about four times as much information as a transmitted television image. This means, in effect, that a film image is four times as well defined as a television image.[10] High-resolution video systems of 1000-line-plus magnitude have been developed but are not presently available to the public. In addition, the video medium is currently undergoing rapid miniaturization, making the equipment lighter, more flexible to use, and cheaper to produce. The film technology has nearly reached the limits of its development.

Cinema: One Medium, Many Channels

From the point of view of the film producer and the viewer, as well as the student of mass media, the difference between the technologies of the mediums is not important. The growth of the electronic channels of distribution—television, cable, videocassette—have been a boon to filmmakers and audiences alike. Only the exhibitors suffer. As we have seen, the financing of a picture now normally involves sales to a cable company, a television network, and a film syndicator.

MEDIA PROBE

Conduct an analysis of your local movie theater. What is the size of the "house"? How many screens does it contain? Is it locally owned or a chain? Is it a first-run theater? A specialty house?

Either call or arrange to meet the theater's manager. How many employees does he or she have? What kind of projection system does the theater use? Are the projectionists union members?

Does the manager have any hand in booking the films? Is the manager happy with the bookings the theatre has had? Does he or she notice any difference in the character of the crowds for different films?

Does the manager seem enthusiastic about the movie business? Does he or she think the business is getting better or worse? Why?

These revenues may almost equal the production cost of a low-budget film.

At home, movie lovers may now view their favorite films repeatedly and even build a collection of cassettes, either prerecorded or recorded off the air. In June 1983, the U.S. Supreme Court refused to rule on a lawsuit by Buena Vista Studios (The Disney Corporation) against the makers of VCRs, charging that home recording is a violation of copyright laws. It is the general opinion, however, that the home video-recorded movie is primarily used for "time-shift" functions, that is, to record a program in order to watch it at a more convenient time. (This also permits the user to fast-forward past the commercials.)

The primary concern today is developing films people will go to see. As Paramount's Bob Evans notes: "The habit of going to *the movies* is over. But the desire to see *a movie* is bigger than ever." Thus, while pay-TV probably will not put the neighborhood theater out of business, it may compel theaters to change for the better. Time will tell.

SUMMARY

The movies occupy an important place in our popular culture. While some individuals and some segments of the audience (particularly people in the teen through young-adult demographic categories) prefer movies more than others, movies do affect us all. Since major films are social events, even nonmoviegoers are aware of these films, their subjects, and something of their meanings. Those who do go to movies expose themselves to the most psychologically powerful of the mass media.

The 100-year history of the motion picture industry has seen a continual development of the technology of the medium, including better lighting and projection, sound systems, color film stock, wide screen and 3-D techniques, and multiscreen projectors. Technological development of the medium has probably peaked. This history has also seen repeated struggles to gain a monopolistic control over the industry. While this has not succeeded, the motion picture in America have been dominated since the 1920s by the major studios, despite successful antitrust actions by the government.

Censorship has marked another on-going struggle between the movies and society. City and state governments have set up censoring boards, but the industry's various efforts at self-regulation have managed to stave off federal censorship. At the present time, Supreme Court rulings extend the protection of the First Amendment to films, while still protecting the rights of states and local communities to censor. The present criteria for legal censorship are difficult to apply successfully, however.

The electronic channels for distribution of motion pictures, including videocassettes, cable telecasting, and television broadcasting, once seen as a threat to the movies, are now becoming important sources of supplemental revenue for film distributors, though not for exhibitors. The financial operations of the industry, for the most part, continue to be vast, complex, shady, and shot through with "creative bookkeeping." Yet, despite the enormous financial risks, the industry continues to thrive, enriching both itself and the American popular culture.

KEY TERMS

Persistence of vision
Pan
Parallel action
Vertical integration
Legion of Decency
Censorship
MPAA rating system
Property
Film shots
Film scenes
Film sequences
Extreme long shots
Long shot
Medium shot
Close-up
Extreme close-up
Normal angle shots
Low angle shots
High angle shots
Pan shot
Tilt shot
Tracking shot
Hand-held camera shot
Documentary

NOTES

[1] Arthur Knight, *The Liveliest Art,* New American Library, New York, 1957, pp. 15–18.
[2] Lewis Jacobs, *The Rise of the American Film: A Critical History,* Teachers College Press, New York, 1968, pp. 102–119.
[3] Arthur Knight, op. cit., pp. 91–93.
[4] Paul Schrader, "Notes on Film Noir," *Film Comment,* vol. 8, no. 1, 1972, pp. 8–13.
[5] Cobbett Steinberg, ed., *Reel Facts: The Movie Book of Records,* Vintage, New York, 1982, p. 57.
[6] Molly Haskell, "Women in the Movies Grow Up," *Psychology Today,* January 1983, pp. 18–25.
[7] David A. Cook, *A History of Narrative Film,* Norton, New York, 1981, pp. 266–267.
[8] George Gordon, *Erotic Communications,* Hastings House, New York, 1980, p. 266.
[9] John Larmett, Elias Savada, and Fredric Schwartz, Jr., "Analysis and Conclusions of the Washington Task Force on the Motion Picture Industry: 1978," in Garth Jowett and James M. Linton, eds., *Movies as Mass Communication,* Sage, Beverly Hills, Calif. 1980, p. 39.

[10] Sidney Head and Christopher Sterling, *Broadcasting in America,* 4th ed., Houghton, Mifflin, Boston, 1982, p. 69.

SUGGESTIONS FOR FURTHER READING

Bawden, Liz-Anne, ed.: *The Oxford Companion to Film,* Oxford University Press, New York and London, 1976. Excellent reference work on international film, including important directors, stars, writers, films, and other topics.

Brownlow, Kevin, ed.: *The Parade's Gone By,* Knopf, New York, 1968. Fascinating first-hand recollections from the early days of Hollywood.

Cook, David A.: *A History of Narrative Film,* Norton, New York, 1981. More than a history, this text is crammed with information on the movies.

Film Comment: A bimonthly publication of the Film Society of Lincoln Center. Represents top critical writing on films from a New York point of view.

Pye, Michael, and Linda Miles: *The Movie Brats: How the Film Generation Took Over Hollywood,* Holt, Rinehart, & Winston, New York, 1979. Informal and controversial, but compelling look at the "new" Hollywood directors, including Coppola, Lucas, Scorsese.

Steinberg, Cobbett S., ed.: *Reel Facts: The Movie Book of Records,* Vintage, New York, 1982. Contains every movie list imaginable, including all film awards, top grossers, and so on.

Weekly Variety: Published by Variety, "must" reading for all show business professionals.

Warshow, Robert: *The Immediate Experience,* Athenaeum, New York, 1972. Classic critical study of the movies and other popular media.

PART FOUR
PERSUASION: MORE THAN WINDOW DECORATION

CHAPTER 10

ADVERTISING: THE PROPELLING POWER

Papa, what is the moon supposed to advertise?
　　　　Carl Sandburg, The People Yes

The ad is the meeting place for all the arts, skills, and all the media of the American environment.
　　　　　　　　Marshall McLuhan

CHAPTER PREVIEW

After reading this chapter, you should be able to:
- Identify the average number of advertisements you come into contact with each day
- Define advertising and distinguish it from personal selling and publicity
- Explain four ways advertisements may be categorized
- Show how early methods of advertising foreshadow present-day practices
- Distinguish between space brokers and modern advertising agents
- Evaluate your own susceptibility to advertising
- Describe the role research plays in advertising
- Explain what it means "to target" an audience
- Define demographics, psychographics, and motivation research
- Compare the Thematic Apperception Test, the Paired-Picture Technique, the Word Association Test, and the Sentence Completion Test
- Provide examples and analyses of product claims
- Demonstrate how Maslow's Needs Hierarchy can be used in advertising
- Demonstrate how Spranger's Value Profile can be used in advertising
- Evaluate the effectiveness of sexuality as an attention getter
- Explain why advertisers rely on celebrity and "unsolicited" testimony to add credibility to their messages
- Identify the parts of an advertisement
- Compare the strengths and weaknesses of the following advertising media: newspapers, magazines, radio, television, billboards, and direct mail
- Explain how a typical advertising agency operates
- Explain the role the Federal Trade Commission, the industry, and consumers play in the regulation of advertising
- Discuss each of the following: Should the advertiser be an advocate or a reporter? Should advertisers try to sell us things we do not really need? Do ads present stereotyped portrayals of males and females? Should liquor advertising be curtailed? Should politicians be marketed like products?

What do you think of when you hear the word *advertising*? Do pictures of particular products appear in your mind's eye? Do you reflect on familiar jingles or slogans? Do you have an urge to "reach out and touch someone," "be a pepper," "catch the Pepsi spirit" and/or have a Coke because "Coke is it"? Do you ever think about all the money that is poured into advertising—more than $70 billion a year? In this chapter we will examine the role advertising has played and continues to play in our lives, and we will also look at the method behind the magic.

THE ENVIRONMENT: DISPLAY WINDOW FOR ADVERTISING

Open your mail—you find an advertisement. Turn on the radio—you hear an advertisement. Watch television—you hear and see an advertisement. Turn the pages of a newspaper or magazine—advertising beckons. Ride down the street—advertising billboards and window signs follow. Seek refuge in a movie theater, and before the feature is run what appears? Advertisements. Traverse the aisles of a supermarket, and what do you notice decorating the wheeled shopping carts? Advertisements. All day, every day, people who want to sell you something compete to capture your attention. In fact, given the pervasiveness of the mass media in our society, it is estimated that you and each member of your family may be confronted with as many as 1450 ads a day. Advertising messages color your world, turning it into a display window for goods and services. Today, thousands of advertisers are jockeying for position, trying to do the same thing at the same time—obtain a piece of your mind. Try as we might, we cannot easily free ourselves from advertising's reach. Advertising is simply an inevitable and inescapable part of our lives in America. Our environment has become almost a blizzard of advertising messages.

MEDIA PROBE

For a twenty-four-hour period attempt to avoid coming into contact with any advertising messages.
If you were unable to accomplish this assignment, explain why. If you were successful, note the steps you had to take to achieve the goal.

But advertising messages do more than merely reach us: whether we are willing to admit it or not, they also affect us and our way of life. If they didn't, our mass media would be in trouble, for in our society, advertising is the fuel that makes them work. This is not to suggest that advertising is only an economic force, because it is more than that. Advertising is also a cultural force—a force that influences our values and our quality of life.

Advertising: What It Is and What It Isn't

Before we begin our examination of advertising, it's important to establish a working definition. Just what is meant by the term "advertising"? How would you complete this sentence: Advertising is———

Through the years, practitioners and theorists have completed this sentence in many different ways. For example, for some time it

MEDIA VIEW

Advertising: what is it? Education. Modern Education, nothing more or less. The airs schoolmasters and college dons give themselves are extraordinary. They think they're the only people who teach. We teach ten times as much.

A reflection by H. G. Wells' fictional advertising man, Dickon Clissold.

YOU WERE THERE

"I CAN TELL YOU WHAT ADVERTISING IS"

One spring afternoon in 1904, in an office building... two men were chatting. One was Ambrose Thomas, one of the founders of the Lord and Thomas agency. The other was a bright young man named Albert Lasker, who... would soon be running the agency.
...

Following a polite knock, an office boy came in with a note and handed it to Thomas. Upon reading it, Thomas snorted and gave it to Lasker. The note said: "I am downstairs in the saloon, and I can tell you what advertising is. I know that you don't know. It will mean much to me to have you know what it is and it will mean much to you. If you wish to know what advertising is, send the word 'yes' down by messenger." It was signed by a John E. Kennedy.

Thomas asked Lasker if he had ever heard of the man, and when Lasker said he hadn't, Thomas decided Kennedy was probably mad and wasn't worth wasting time on. But Lasker, who was dissatisfied with the concept of "keeping your name before the public," was willing to take a chance. He sent down for Kennedy, and the two spent an hour in Lasker's office. Then they headed for the saloon downstairs, not to emerge until midnight.

Kennedy was a former Royal Canadian Mounted Policeman, a dashing, mustachioed chap who in 1904 was employed as a copywriter for an elixir known as Dr. Shoop's Restorative. What he said to Lasker that day resulted in his being hired on the spot for the unheard-of salary of $28,000 a year. Within twenty-four months, he was making $75,000.

What did he say to Lasker? Simply this: "Advertising is salesmanship in print."...

Under Albert Lasker's leadership, Lord and Thomas became the biggest, most successful agency of its time.

From John O'Toole, *The Trouble With Advertising*, Chelsea House, New York, 1981, pp. 15–16.

---

was felt that advertising was a means of "keeping your name before the public" (attributed to the N. W. Ayer Agency). Advertising has also been called "salesmanship in print" (attributed to John E. Kennedy, it became the creed of Albert Lasker, the unofficial father of modern advertising). McCann Erikson officials have described advertising as "truth well told," and practitioner and author William Weilbacher has written that advertising can be defined as "a fraction of the incoming messages that the individual receives."

While each of the preceding definitions is valid, we believe the following working definition will more fully clarify what advertising is and what it is not. It is based on the one offered by the American Marketing Association: Advertising is the paid, nonpersonal, and usually persuasive presentation of ideas, goods, and services by identified sponsors through various media. Let's take this definition apart and analyze its components. The key words in it are "paid," "nonpersonal," "persuasive," "identified," and "through various media."

First, advertising is usually paid for. Various sponsors pay for the ads we see, read, and hear over the various media. This distinguishes advertising from publicity, which is free. Second, advertising is nonpersonal. The offer is *not* made in person in the presence of the seller. Advertising is not face-to-face communication. Although you may *feel* the message is aimed directly at you, in reality it is directed at large groups of people. This helps

> **Don't let your glasses blur your vision.**
>
> Whether a glass holds 12 ounces of beer, 5 ounces of wine, or 1¼ ounces of spirits, the alcohol content is the same. It's important to know this because the size and shape of a glass can give people a distorted impression of how much alcohol they're actually drinking.
>
> So when you're in the mood to celebrate, remember how much alcohol is in your glass and that moderation always keeps things in focus.
>
> **Have a safe and Happy New Year.**
>
> **The House of Seagram**

The line between product advertising and public interest advertising can sometimes blur. (The House of Seagram)

to distinguish advertising from personal selling efforts. Third, advertising is usually persuasive. Directly or indirectly it urges people to do something. An attempt is made to convince people that the product, idea, or service advertised can benefit them. According to author and advertising practitioner John O'Toole, advertising can be viewed as salesmanship functioning in the paid space and time of mass media.[1] As such, its primary function is not simply to catalog goods or services, or present receivers with a list of the items' good and bad points, but to promote them so that they are judged to be not merely worthwhile but indispensable.[2] Fourth, the sponsor of the ad must be identified. From the ad, we can determine if the sponsor is a corporation, like General Motors or Procter & Gamble; an organization, like the Democratic or Republican National Committee; a not-for-profit enterprise, like the World Council of Churches; or an individual, like singing star Diana Ross. Fifth, advertising reaches us through traditional and nontraditional mass media. Included in the traditional mass media are newspapers, magazines, radio, television, and film; nontraditional media include the mail, matchbook covers, billboards, and skywriting.

In summary, ask yourself the following

questions in order to determine whether a message is or is not advertising:

Is it paid for?
Is it nonpersonal?
Is it persuasive?
Is there an identified sponsor?
Is it being carried through the mass media?

Our definition can be applied to all types of advertising regardless of the nature of the target audience, the subject of the advertisement, or the media used.

Categorizing Advertising: What's the Message?

How can advertisements be categorized? First, we can categorize advertisements by the nature of the audience to whom the ad is directed. *Consumer advertising* is directed at people who are expected to use a product or service for personal reasons. *Business advertising* is addressed to people who are expected to use the product or service for business reasons or to resell the product or service.

Second, advertisements can also be categorized according to whether the advertiser is national or local. Do not be misled here; the distinction is not merely a geographical one. *National advertising* refers to those advertising messages that are paid for by the owner of a product or service that is or will be sold through various stores or distributors. In effect, the job of the national advertiser is to create demand for a product or service. Thus, when the Chrysler Corporation urges us through magazines, television, radio, newspapers, or billboards to buy a Chrysler, this is national advertising. In contrast, *local (retail) advertising* is paid for by a dealer who sells directly to the consumer. Local advertising's message is, "This is something you should buy here—now." A particular Chrysler dealer who urges you to come in to make your best deal today is an example of a local advertiser.

Third, advertising can also be categorized on the basis of the medium relied on to carry the message. The main media include newspapers, magazines, radio, television, signs and billboards, and direct mail. Newspapers get the largest share of the advertising dollar among the traditional mass media (28 percent), followed by television (21 percent), magazines (9 percent), and radio (7 percent). *Direct mail* accounts for about 14 percent and outdoor advertising about 1 percent. About 20 percent is accounted for by other forms of advertising, including displays in stores and specialty advertising.[3]

A fourth method of categorizing advertising is based on what the ad is expected to do. For example, *primary advertising* is expected to create a demand for generic products or services, while *selective advertising* is expected to stimulate demand for a particular product. Thus, advertisements that advise you to "drink milk" represent primary advertising in action. In contrast, advertisements that ask you to "buy Tuscan milk" represent selective advertising.

Finally, while some advertising is intended to create a demand for a product, generic or selective, other advertising does not aim to sell a product; instead it is designed to sell ideas. When Mobil places an ad for its gasoline, it is placing a product ad; but when it uses advertising to tell us about the need for oil and gasoline deregulation, it is placing a nonproduct ad. Nonproduct advertising

MEDIA PROBE

For the next day keep a log of the first ten to twenty advertisements you come into contact with. Record the following information for each: the product, service, or idea advertised; the audience to whom the ad is directed; the type of advertiser; the medium through which it was advertised; and the apparent purpose of the ad.

Times Square, New York, illustrates the saturation potential of advertising in our society. (F. B. Grunzweig, Photo Researchers)

comes in various forms and is sometimes referred to as corporate, institutional, or *image advertising*. In additon to this type of advertising, we also have *public-service advertising*. While most advertising is commercial and intended to help the sponsor make a profit, this type of advertising is noncommercial and is sponsored by or for a charitable institution, civic group, religious or political organization. A special kind of public-service advertising is "advertising prepared in the public interest"; it is designed to support noncontroversial causes of interest to the public. The subjects of such ads range from nutritional concerns to child abuse, pollution, and appeals to hire the handicapped. The time or space and talent needed to develop and transmit these advertising messages may be donated by the advertising agencies, television and radio stations, magazines, and newspapers. In the United States, the majority of public-interest advertising is coordinated by the Advertising Council, a volunteer association formed during World War II. In 1980, media in the United States contributed almost $600 million to such efforts.

THE DEVELOPMENT OF ADVERTISING

In order to understand and assess the role played by advertising in America today, we should briefly examine the role it played in the past. To be sure, advertising predates America. In fact, the desire to advertise may be part of human nature itself.

The earliest advertisements were probably those of the town criers or the signs that marked the location of shops and inns. Whether you lived in ancient Egypt, Rome, or Greece, no doubt you would have heard and responded to the shouts of street vendors who peddled their wares. For example, this

MEDIA VIEW

Prime among the magical advertising tools, in terms of tested effectiveness, is the jingle: the clever little tune and arresting lyric that compel us to buy everything from acne cream to cars.

The first jingles were the cries of street vendors, consisting of simple rhymes listing produce and products. Their reasoning for using the rhymes in this fashion was simple. By offering their wares in a sing-song fashion, they made their product line more memorable. To prove this, on a more personal level, think back to your own early years. Chances are excellent that you learned the letters of the alphabet with a song, a song you can probably still recite to this day. It was only natural that 20th-century advertisers would latch on to this time-proved technique.

You can talk to a consumer from now until eternity and get no results. It is only when you touch some responsive chord that you have the power to influence buying decisions. Music enables you to emotionalize your product and its benefits: your entire selling proposition. Through music, you are selling from the heart, to the heart.

Buddy Scott, "The Magic of Jingles," *Broadcasting*, vol. 105, no. 6, Aug 8, 1983, p. 24.

---

verse (or one quite like it) is said to have been used in ancient Athens:

> For eyes that are Shining, for cheeks like the dawn,
> For Beauty that lasts after girlhood is gone,
> For prices in reason, the woman who knows,
> Will buy her cosmetics of Aesclyptos.[4]

Town criers were also used to announce the arrival of ships bearing precious cargoes of wine, spices, and metals. Frequently, a musician accompanied the crier's chants, helping to ensure that he stayed in the right key.

The transmission of information—a key idea of advertising—extends far back into antiquity. For instance, the following inscription was etched on a Pompeiian wall:

> Traveler
> Going from here to the twelfth tower
> There Sarinus keeps a tavern.
> This is to request you to enter,
> Farewell.[5]

To it may be traced current ads for hotels and motels like Sheraton and Holiday Inn. In like fashion, one actual Roman ad should remind you of ads for today's circuses, boxing matches, or health clubs:

> There will be a dedication or
> Formal opening of Certain Baths.
> Those attending are promised Slaughter
> of Wild Beasts, Athletic Games, Perfume
> Sprinkling, and Awnings to keep off the Sun.[6]

Outdoor signs survived the fall of the Roman Empire and were transformed into the decorative art of inns. Because literacy rates were low, these signs were symbolic of the goods to be found within: a goat indicated a dairy, a mule driving a mill stood for a bakery, and a spinning wheel announced a weaver. This practice enabled those who could not read to identify the nature of a store.

The most significant event in the history of advertising was the invention of movable type by Johannes Gutenberg in 1440. This innovation led to the use of printed posters, handbills, and newspaper ads. About forty years after the introduction of movable type, the first English advertisement was printed by Caxton of London. It announced a prayer-book for sale and was posted on church doors. *Siquis,* the forerunner of our present want ads, also emerged about this time. Also known as "if anybodys," they usually began with the words, "If anybody desires" or "If anybody knows of." In addition to advertising available positions and services or lost articles, *siquis* were also used to advertise products like tobacco and perfume.[7] However, it was not until the early seventeenth century that the newspaper was born, giving advertising an important push forward.

The first newspaper advertisement appeared in the back of a London newspaper in 1650; it offered a reward for the return of twelve stolen horses. Gradually, ads were used to help sell products like chocolate, real estate, medicine, and coffee. The following is an example of an ad that appeared in 1657:

> In Bartholomew Lane, on the back side of the Old Exchange, the drink called coffee, which is a very wholesome and physical drink, having many excellent virtues . . . is to be sold both in the morning and three o'clock in the afternoon.

Among the virtues noted in the copy were the following:

> It closes the orifices of the stomach, fortifies the heat within, helpeth digestion, quickeneth the spirits, maketh the heart lightsum, is good against eye sores, coughs, or colds, rhumes, consumption, headache, dropsie, gout, scurvey, King's evil, and many others.[8]

Advertising attracted the attention of critics in the eighteenth century. In 1759, Dr. Samuel Johnson, writing in the *Idler,* noted: "Advertisements are now so numerous that they are very negligently perused, and it is therefore become necessary to gain attention by magnificence of promises and by eloquence sometimes sublime and sometimes ridiculous."

In colonial America, advertising appeared in many vehicles, including newspapers, pamphlets, broadsides, and almanacs. Benjamin Franklin was the first American newspaper publisher to realize that advertising could provide a major portion of a newspaper's revenue. So significant were Franklin's achievements that he has been dubbed "the father of American advertising." Besides publishing periodicals that contained advertising, Franklin also used advertising to promote his own products, including, of course, the Franklin stove. The following copy is attributed to Ben Franklin:

> Fireplaces with small openings cause draughts of cold air to rush in at every crevice and 'tis very uncomfortable as well as dangerous to sit against any such crevice. . . . Women, particularly from this cause (as they sit so much in the house) get cold in the head, rheums, and deflexions which fall into their jaws and gums, and have destroyed early, many a fine set of teeth in these northern colonies.[9]

How do you think the ad created by Franklin compares with today's ads for storm windows and fireplace air circulators? To be sure, both stress the health and comfort benefits to be derived from their use. Besides being an adept copywriter, Franklin is also credited with the following innovations: He surrounded the ads with white space to separate them from each other; he made ads more readable by giving each ad its own large headline; and he used illustrations to enhance copy. Other patriots followed Franklin's lead and used advertising to promote their own products; for example, Paul Revere used advertising to sell false teeth, and George Washington used advertising to sell real estate.

The growth of the penny newspaper soon made advertising big business in America. Volney B. Palmer, the first advertising agent in the United States, started his brokerage service in Philadelphia in 1841. Palmer made his money by contracting to buy large volumes of advertising space at a discount from newspapers and then reselling the space to advertisers at a higher rate. Palmer, however, did not actually prepare the ads. It was not until 1890 that N. W. Ayer and Son, another Philadelphia concern, offered to aid in the preparation of ads as well. N. W. Ayer and Son is credited with being the first *advertising agency* to function in much the same way as agencies function today; that is, the agency planned, created, and executed advertising campaigns for clients in exchange for a commission paid by the media or fees received from clients.[10]

It remained for magazines to make the sale of products on a national scale a reality. James W. Thompson, the founder of today's J. Walter Thompson agency, is the person responsible for persuading American magazines to accept advertising. Like Volney Palmer, he bought up space magazines had available and resold it to advertisers and other space agents.[11] The readers of many of the national magazines were women, and consequently the most frequently advertised products were soaps, cosmetics, and patent medicines. It was not long before advertisers realized that these ads were capable of creating new markets by influencing the buying habits of readers. Between the end of the Civil War and 1900, advertising expenditures increased from $50 million to $540 million.[12]

MEDIA PROBE

Working individually or in groups, select and photocopy an advertisement for a particular type of product like soap, cosmetics, coffee, tobacco, or patent medicines from: a 1920 newspaper and magazine; a 1940 newspaper and magazine; a 1960 newspaper and magazine; and a newspaper and magazine of today. Compare and contrast the ads noting differences and similarities in such things as language used, appeals made, and illustrations. Do you think the earlier ads would be effective today? Why or why not?

As the years passed, advertising in magazines and newspapers continued to flourish.

As we know, newspapers and magazines were soon forced to compete with the new electronic media. In the 1920s radio came on the scene, and shortly thereafter television "supplied" and entered the picture. These media would force advertising to evolve from a craft that used words and supporting pictures to promote products into one that relied on spoken words and moving pictures as well as written words to accomplish its objectives. Just as advertising expenditures had built the financial base that spurred the proliferation of America's newspapers and magazines, so advertising would help pay for radio and television.

Since World War II, advertising has experienced a steady ascent: $2.8 billion in 1945; $9.1 billion in 1955; $15.2 billion in 1965; $23.1 billion in 1972; $54.6 billion in 1980; over $60 billion in 1981; and over $70 billion today. Advertising now accounts for about 2 percent of the gross national product. Through the growth years, the purpose of advertising—to inform as well as persuade—has remained unchanged. And there is little doubt that advertising plays an essential role in our economy. Besides supporting commercial broadcasting, advertising also pays for almost three-quarters of the cost of the newspapers and magazines we read. Without advertising we would have to pay considerably more than we currently pay to read these periodicals, and some plan would have to be devised to support commercial radio and television as well. In addition, the demand for advertising will undoubtedly contribute to the growth of cable programming in much the same way.

As is apparent, the media are not the only businesses advertising supports. As English historian and essayist Thomas Macaulay wrote: "Advertising is to business what steam is to industry—the sole propelling power. Nothing except the Mint can make money without advertising." Thus, for business, advertising is a tool that facilitates the presentation and sale of goods to consumers. And for consumers, advertising is a tool that familiarizes them with the marketplace.

History has shown that advertising is the most efficient way to introduce new or improved products and keep an existing product in the public's mind. The only substitute for advertising is personal selling, and a huge amount of money would be needed to fund armies of personal sales representatives. The cost of an average personal business sales call is now estimated to be over $90. If we multiply that number by the estimated audience for a hit television program, or even the circulation figures of a newspaper or magazine, the cost is mind-boggling. The cost of using advertising to reach the public is much less. In fact, you can reach 1000 prospects through advertising for less than 10 percent of what it costs to talk to one prospect through personal selling.[13]

To various degrees, advertising influences the products you choose to buy by bringing you information about new products, existing products, or product improvements. To various degrees, advertising induces you to reuse products you have tried, and it attempts to dispel misconceptions. Advertising acquaints you with the differences (real or perceived) between product brands as well as the distinguishing characteristics of companies and institutions. Advertising reveals what a particular product should do for you when used, and by so doing it gives you criteria for evaluating the products you currently use. Advertising is simply an important part of your world.

THE METHOD BEHIND THE MAGIC

Few people would dispute the belief that advertising sells products and ideas, brings about changes in behavior, influences the outcome of elections, and affects the attitude people have toward various businesses and organizations. Yet, many people have failed to explore the extent to which advertising affects their individual buying decisions, lifestyle choices, and day-to-day activities.

If you are like most people, you probably believe you are immune to advertising influences. But as Jeffrey Schrank points out:

> The personally immune, consider most ads (especially those on TV) dumb, silly, "beneath my dignity," and generally a waste of time. Members of this group can sometimes be heard to say, "Ads seldom influence my opinion; I am an informed consumer who knows true value when I see it." Ads, this group believers, are evidently aimed at those unfortunate [people] . . . who rush out and purchase promiscuously. Strangely enough, 90 percent of the nation's adults believe themselves members of the "personally immune." This same 90 percent accounts for approximately 90 percent of all purchases of advertised products—obviously something is amiss.[14]

Can you recall the last time you felt yourself to be influenced by advertising? Was it a month ago? a week ago? this morning? Are there some products you are convinced that no amount of advertising could convince you

MEDIA PROBE

Use the accompanying scale to rate advertising's power to influence the buying habits, beliefs, and attitudes of: (1) men in general, (2) women in general, (3) a close friend, (4) an older relative, (5) a young child, and (6) yourself.

Strong Influence
1   2   3   4   5   6   7
Weak Influence

According to your evaluation, who do you believe is most susceptible to advertising's influence? Least susceptible? Where did you position yourself on the scale when compared to others on the list? Why?

YOU WERE THERE

Prune sales were declining about one percent monthly when the Prune Advisory Board decided to hire an advertising agency to lift the lowly prune to new heights of acceptability.

The agency ran the following radio ad in eighteen American cities:

(door chimes)

WOMAN: Yes? Who is it?
MAN: Hi. I'm your new neighbor, Steven Williams in 107.
WOMAN: Oh, how nice to meet you . . . well come on in . . . it's a pleasure.
MAN: Thank you.
WOMAN: I see you've got a measuring cup. Now let me guess . . . you ran out of sugar.
MAN: No.
WOMAN: You're a bachelor. . .
MAN: No (laughter), as a matter of fact—I was wondering if I could borrow some prunes.
WOMAN: Prunes? (laughter) I'm sorry. . .
MAN: Well, yeah . . . I thought a couple. . .
ANNOUNCER: There are still a lot of people who laugh at prunes. But now quite a few are finding out how good they really are. Because pound for pound, prunes have eight times the Vitamin A of the leading fresh fruit . . . and more iron, niacin, and Vitamin B2 than the five leading fresh fruits. They're also a great natural source of quick energy.
WOMAN: He wants to borrow a cup of prunes? (uncontrollable laughter)
MAN: Thanks anyway . . . maybe I'll try 105.
WOMAN: Yeah . . . (laughter)
ANNOUNCER: California prunes, the funny fruit that does so much for you.

If you were to position yourself at the prune display in a supermarket in any of the eighteen cities targeted for advertising and ask people why they are buying prunes, you would hear some strange answers. You would certainly have a difficult day and perhaps even collect a few strange looks, and maybe a bruise or two, but you would *not* hear people reply, "Because of that persuasive ad I heard on the radio." Yet, sales increased an amazing 18 percent in the cities where the ad was used. Prune sales in cities where the ad was not used continued their typical 1 percent decline.

Jeffrey Schrank, *Snap, Crackle, and Popular Taste: The Illusion of Free Choice in America*, Dell, New York, 1977, pp. 85–86.

---

to purchase? Why? For example, do you think advertising could persuade you to buy prunes? What would the content of the ad have to contain for it to do so? For some reason, prunes have a negative connotation for most people. They are the subject of many a joke and are a difficult item to order at a restaurant without producing snickers from those seated around you. Yet, advertisements sponsored by the Prune Advisory Board were successful in changing people's buying patterns with regard to prunes, just as campaigns conducted on behalf of milk producers have also resulted in increases in milk consumption; and users of both products changed their behavior without fully understanding if, why, or how their behavior had changed. How did advertising help bring about the desired changes? Why is advertising able to exert such a profound influence on our actions?

Discovering What Makes You Tick: Meet the Target

What makes people change or maintain their buying habits? What makes them alter or keep the attitude they hold toward an institution, idea, or product? What makes people respond to some advertising messages but not others? By seeking to answer questions like these, advertising practitioners have refined their ability to influence us. As John O'Toole points out, "In reality, advertising is not about products, but about a person and his (or her) life—and how the products can fit into that life to make it easier, richer, or more rewarding."[15] If advertising is about people, then it stands to reason that one of the most important elements of effective advertising, if not *the* most important element, is an understanding of people. Thus, one goal of advertising professionals is to get to know the consumer, the target of their efforts, as well as possible. As practitioner Stephen Baker notes, "To an advertising professional the consumer must be a close acquaintance."[16]

There are different types of research the practitioner can rely on to help find out what makes the consumer tick: *demographics* (the study of the numerical characteristics of the population), *psychographics* (the classification of consumers based on psychological makeup including personality, lifestyle, and attitude), and *motivation research*. But why is research necessary at all? Because although we may be exposed to hundreds of ads daily, experts tell us that we're actually only aware of 75 to 150 ads a day. This means that over 75 percent of all advertising is ignored, unnoticed, or leaves no memorable impression on us.[17] Consequently, for a message to gain entrance into our minds, advertisers need to rely on information that permits them to plan strategically. They need to understand us in order to know what to say to us, as well as how and where to say it; in other words, advertisers need to target their audiences. To target an audience they need to create a composite picture of it. In effect, the audience is broken down into one individual whom the practitioner knows inside and out. For this reason, when you see ads that do not appeal to you, it just might be because the ad is not aimed at a group of people to which you belong. You are not the ad's target; it was not meant for you.

Using Demographics In order to become acquainted with the members of the target audience, practitioners rely, in part, on demographic data. This type of information segments or classifies the target audience by using criteria like age, sex, annual income, level of education, occupation, marital status, religion, and race. For example, about ten years ago, *Media Decisions* profiled females in the 12-to-19-year-old market, which at the time represented about 33 million individuals who spent over $25 billion annually. The report indicated that although they comprised only about 14 percent of the female population, they purchased over 20 percent of the beauty products sold. It also noted that the members of this group were better educated than their predecessors, and because a large percentage of their mothers worked many of the teenagers functioned as surrogate shoppers.[18] Data like this can guide the advertising practitioner in making product-targeting decisions as well as decisions regarding the types of appeals and media to employ.

Using Psychographics Practitioners who conduct psychographic research classify people on the basic of their personality, attitude toward life, and purchasing patterns. Measures of leadership potential, conformity, and friendliness are analyzed. Psychographic data can be used to develop a profile of a heavy user of a product in much the same way demographic research can. For example, a decade ago women who were heavy users of bank credit cards were profiled in this way: they lead an active lifestyle, belong to various social groups, and are concerned with their appearance; they view the homemaking role as managing and purchasing rather than as cooking and cleaning; they tend to be liberal and liberated and are innovators in that they are willing to take risks and try new things.[19]

Using Motivation Research Motivation researchers probe the reasons why people buy particular products. It is their task to try and explain what makes consumers react to

MEDIA VIEW

THE REMARKABLE 80-20 RULE

A basic yet effective approach to segmentation is to divide the entire United States population into two parts on the basis of income, one part being about 4 times as large as the other.

"The one beer to have when you're having more than one" campaign for the Schaefer brewery once again brought this marketing truism to the attention of the advertising community, although the same statistics had been staring marketers in the face for more than a quarter of a century. As it happened, this brewery had drifted into a comfortable but static third-place position among the local brands that dominated the huge beer market around New York City in the 1950s. It was not until 10 years later that its advertising agency, BBDO, discovered that about 20 percent of heavy beer drinkers guzzled about 80 percent of all the beer sold.

It appeared that the heavy beer drinker was happy with the way his beer tasted in the first cold glass; it was the taste of his second and third that bothered him. Each drink seemed to lose a little, not measuring up to the first. Since Schaefer's beer is less bitter, heightened enjoyment could be a genuine promise.

The new advertising campaign, based upon this approach, helped to push Schaefer into the Number 1 position in New York City and near the top in its entire marketing area.

Following the Schaefer experience, other advertisers found that their prime users, too, were concentrated in a realtively small target area, covering about 20 percent of the market. AT&T discovered that 80 percent of all telephone calls were made by 20 percent of their customers. A food company simplified its product line when researchers told its officials that the average housewife, obviously a creature of habit, repeats 20 percent of the recipes 80 percent of the time. When a paint distributor learned that 20 percent of his orders were responsible for 80 percent of his business, he changed his media schedule to concentrate on his most important customers....

Figures released by the U.S. Bureau of the Census shed some light on the 80–20 percent marketing phenomenon, at least as far as the general population is concerned. It appears that for over the last two decades about half of the total United States income was received by a little more than 20 percent of American households.

Stephen Baker, *Systematic Approach to Advertising Creativity*, McGraw-Hill, New York, 1979, p. 42.

---

various products and different types of appeals. Frequently, in order to obtain such information, they rely on projective techniques and depth interviews. Projective techniques are used because sometimes individuals are unable or unwilling to reveal their own feelings directly, but it was found they do so *indirectly* if they are asked to attribute to others the emotions or attitudes they themselves have. Motivation research was developed by Dr. Ernest Dichter, a Viennese psychologist who understood its commercial applications.

Among the projective techniques used in motivation research are the Thematic Apperception Test (TAT), the Paired-Picture Technique, word association tests, and sentence completion tests. The TAT consists of a series of cards containing different photographs, pictures, or drawings. The subject is shown a card and asked to make up a story about what he or she sees: explain the situation, the events leading up to it, the outcome, and the thoughts and feelings of those represented in the pictures. For example:

Such a picture might show a woman taking a

MEDIA PROBE

Using some of the demographic and psychographic categories supplied above, summarize in paragraph form a demographic and psychographic profile of yourself. Then identify five products (if possible specify brands) for which you believe you would be a target, and explain your choices.

---

prepared cake mix from a supermarket shelf. When the respondent is asked to tell the story portrayed by the picture, she may say: "This is a woman who works, and she is buying a ready-mix cake because she doesn't have time to bake one from scratch," thus perhaps indicating that she feels that using ready-mixed foods is a lazy way of cooking and can only be justified by such circumstances as not having enough time to cook because of other obligations to the family. Other responses to the same picture may reveal that those interviewed believe the use of ready-mixed cakes is "smart," "modern," "thrifty," or the sign of a "poor cook." Because the respondent is talking about someone else (the lady in the picture), there is believed to be less personal emotional involvement, and thus a clearer portrayal of actual feelings emerges. These feelings are projected into the picture by the respondent.[20]

Similar to the TAT, the Paired-Picture Technique uses two pictures; one may depict a woman reaching for perfume, and another may show the same woman reaching for cologne. The respondent would then be requested to tell a story about each. In this way information about product attitudes would be gathered.

When a word-association test is used, the words to be studied are interspersed between a list of neutral words. The respondent is asked to listen to each word and supply another word as quickly as possible. The words he or she gives in response are then analyzed in order to determine what they reveal about his or her attitudes.

Sentence completion tests have also been used to study respondent feelings and attitudes. For example, partial sentences like these might be used:

Mouthwashes are———
Smokers usually———
A woman who uses hair dye is———
A man who wears designer clothes is———

How would you and people you know respond to each of these? What do your responses tell us about your attitudes?

Depth interviews or focus group interviews are also used to gain insight and "meet" the consumer. While a depth interview typically involves an interviewee who has a discussion with one respondent—a representative of a group of consumers—about the subject of research, in the focus group experience, the attitudes and feelings of consumers "typical" of the target market are probed by a trainer-leader who guides the discussion.

Techniques like those discussed above help advertisers cut their risks. All this is not to say that research is foolproof, for it is not. There are a multitude of errors that can be made during research. The researchers, for instance, can ask the right people the wrong questions, or the wrong people the right questions, or interpret the responses people give incorrectly. For example, advertising writer Edward Buxton tells the story of a large and famous food company whose goal was to make a better chocolate cake mix. First, they put home economists to work to create every conceivable kind of chocolate cake; they came up with over forty-five different varieties including Swiss chocolate, sweet chocolate, semisweet chocolate, dark chocolate, light chocolate, chocolate mint, chocolate fudge, and chocolate malt. Next, they explored a plethora of cake textures—light, heavy, moist, and so on. Then came more variations. Finally, after testing the outcomes for more than a year on small panels of "typical" consumers, they came up with "the per-

YOU WERE THERE

My partner, Ron Travisano, was working at Marschalk when they got a cake mix that was almost too good for the marketplace. All you had to do to make a cake was add water, but the product was going nowhere. They ran tests and then they ran more tests. They found out that the average housewife hated the product because if she couldn't do something physical in the making of the cake, she felt that she was being cheated. If all she had to do was add water, well, she felt that she really was nowhere as a homemaker and a cook. The product was just too slick.

So they pulled it back and did whatever you do to cake mixes and they fixed it so now to make a cake you had to break an egg. In the instructions they said if you break an egg into this mix and add water, you're going to have one hell of a cake. But without the egg the product is nothing. It worked. The very act of breaking an egg told the housewife that she was a cook again. The product worked, sold like hell. It was unbelievable.

Ron also was involved with a problem dealing with a first-aid cream, a Johnson & Johnson product. This stuff was a painless antiseptic for cuts, scratches, things like that. Now here's Johnson & Johnson, a hell of a good company, and they go and invent an antiseptic that doesn't drive you up the wall when you put it on. They send it out on a test and nobody buys the stuff the second time around. The company can't figure out what's wrong. They ran tests again and they discovered that people have to feel pain before they'll accept the fact that they're getting healed. They have to feel a burning sensation. And what's wrong with this stuff? It's obviously no good because when you put it on it doesn't burn. Forget that the cut is healing, there wasn't any burn.

Jerry Della Femina, *From Those Wonderful Folks Who Gave You Pearl Harbor*, Simon & Schuster, New York, 1970, p. 37.

---

fect chocolate cake." At this point, they tested again. They sought input from hundreds of "heavy users"—people who ate cake three or more times a week—the serious cake eaters. They asked them to compare their creation with other chocolate cakes in a blind taste test. This nationwide test took months, but they were willing to take the time because they wanted to be certain that their mix would be popular across the United States. And the tests showed the cake to be a winner. The cake eaters loved it. So the new product was launched. Several million dollars had gone into this effort and when it appeared in stores . . . it bombed. Looking back over the information given can you detect what the research mistake was? It took months before the company discovered where they had failed. You see, they had researched their chocolate cake among "cake lovers" in general. But this was too broad a group. They should have researched it among chocolate cake lovers. It seems there is a great difference in the reactions of these groups. Heavy chocolate cake eaters apparently like a darker, richer, moister cake than do just heavy cake eaters, who may eat chocolate cake only occasionally.[21] People in advertising need to study consumers carefully—very carefully—because only in this way can they find out what you really want and give it to you.

Understanding the Techniques and the Appeals Used in Advertising

Advertising relies on simple principles of human persuasion. Whether or not advertisers are successful depends to a large degree on whether they are able to get us to know, feel, or understand what they want us to know, feel, and understand. Advertisers stand the best chance of realizing their goals if they find a way to give form to our deep-lying desires, meet our needs, or solve a problem (or problems) we face. Consequently, according to theorist Jim Fowler, the task of advertising is "to tug at our psychological shirt sleeves and slow us down long enough for a word or two about whatever is being sold."[22] What techniques do advertisers use to slow us down? What types of claims and what kinds of appeals do they use to convince us that what they are selling is for us, or what they are advocating is in our best interest?

First, in almost every ad created, a *product claim* is made. The product claim is simply what the ad reveals about the product. The following hypothetical examples represent the types of claims advertisers use repeatedly as they attempt to win us over:

> "Our Brand soap helps get your skin cleaner and fresher. Its special ingredient, GT-20, fights acne."

Unfortunately, this ad contains no useful information. Many ads use adjectives like "cleaner" or "fresher" without saying cleaner or fresher than what. For example, Ford once ran an ad that read, "Ford's LTD is over 700 percent quieter." While you are apt to think the ad means that the Ford LTD is quieter than cars of comparable size and price, according to critic Jeffrey Schrank, what's really meant is that the inside of the car was 700 percent quieter than the outside.[23]

> "Brushing with Our Brand toothpaste helps fight cavities."

Words like "helps," "fights," and "acts against" are used over and over again. Remember, they do *not* mean "eliminate" or "stop." It would be correct to say that brushing with water helps stop cavities too. One of the most useful tools in advertising is a weasel word like those above. *Weasel words* weaken statements and deprive them of significance. Weasel words got their name because of their resemblance to the weasel, which is able to suck the content out of a raw egg without damaging the egg's shell. Though the egg may look like a perfect one, it is hollow. In like fashion, an advertising statement containing a weasel word may look like a statement of real advantage, while in reality it is a statement without meaning.

> "New, improved Our Brand chocolates now contain twice as many pieces per package."

"New" does not necessarily mean better, and twice as many pieces of chocolate does not mean twice as much chocolate.

> "Our Brand gives you more."

What exactly does Our Brand give you more *of*? More trouble? More calories? This type of claim is called an unfinished claim.

> "Our Brand—no other brand is quite like it."

Of course no other brand is quite like it; no other brand can have its name. This claim is called a "we're different" or "we're unique" claim.

> "Shouldn't your family be using Our Brand?"

This technique relies on the audience to supply a response that, hopefully, will affirm the product's goodness.

> "Our Brand is the very best."

Today, many products are parity products; that is, they literally possess no discernable or significant differences. When this is the case, advertisers find ways to make the product appear to be special and exclusive. They sometimes claim to be the best, a claim that, according to legal tradition, any parity product can make because in reality it is no better or worse than its competition.

"The truly amazing thing about our new and improved product is that it's seventy-three per cent more effective than our previous product, which, in turn, was eighty-five per cent more effective than our original product, which, it must be admitted, wasn't really effective at all."

(Drawing by Ed Fisher, © 1982 *The New Yorker* Magazine, Inc.)

Second, advertisers also recognize that human behavior is motivated. They realize that if they are to convince you to do or believe what they would like you to do or believe, the messages they create must appeal to your needs, values, and goals. One popular device used to analyze human motivation is Abraham Maslow's Needs Hierarchy.[24] Maslow pictured motivation as a pyramid, with our most basic needs at the base and our most sophisticated needs at the apex. As we can see in Figure 10-1, human beings are motivated to take care of survival—shelter, food, water, procreation—first and foremost. Once this is taken care of, we then go on to secure our other needs: the need for security, for love and fulfilling relationships, for self-respect and the respect of others, and finally, at the peak of Maslow's hierarchy, the need for self-actualization. When we satisfy this need, we realize our potential; that is, we take steps to become everything we are capable of becoming.

How can the advertising practitioner use Maslow's hierarchy? Advertisers rely on the fact that salient needs make salient motives. For instance, the army's slogan "Be all that you can be" appeals to our need for esteem as well as our need for self-actualization. Many of the telephone company, soft-drink, cosmetic, and deodorant ads appeal to our need for affiliating, loving, and belonging. In like fashion, many ads for insurance or trav-

FIGURE 10-1 Maslow's Needs Hierarchy.

- Self-Actualization Needs
- Esteem Needs
- Love and Belonging Needs
- Security and Safety Needs
- Survival Needs

ADVERTISING: THE PROPELLING POWER

MEDIA PROBE

1. For each of the following situations identify the types of motivational appeals you could use to persuade a target audience to behave or believe as you would like. First, select a primary target group. Second, using Maslow's Needs Hierarchy (Figure 10-1), select the level and appeal you believe would be most effective. Third, explain your choices.
   (a) You want to convince ——— to stop smoking.
   (b) You want to convince ——— to drink orange juice.
   (c) You want to convince ——— to purchase life insurance.
   (d) You want to convince ——— to buy a camera.
   (e) You want to convince ——— to wear designer jeans.
2. Select five examples that illustrate how the levels represented in the hierarchy are used in current advertising messages.

eler's checks are designed to appeal to our survival, security, and safety needs.

Edward Spranger developed another model for identifying our values.[25] According to Spranger, while there may be more than one set of values that influence our behavior, there is probably one value that is dominant. To learn more about the values that guide your life, try the Spranger Value Profile exercise in the accompanying Media Probe.

Using his Value Profile, Spranger identified the following types of people:

Theoretical: values the pursuit and discovery of truth, the intellectual life
Economic: values that which is useful, practical
Aesthetic: values form, harmony, beauty
Social: values love, sympathy, warmth, and sensitivity in relationships with people
Political: values competition, influence, personal power
Religious: values unity, wholeness, a sense of purpose above human beings

What is the dominant value that guides your

MEDIA VIEW

What is a good advertisement? There are three schools of thought. The cynics hold that a good advertisement is an advertisement with a client's OK on it. Another school accepts Raymond Rubicam's definition, "The best identification of a great advertisement is that its public is not only strongly sold by it, but that both the public and the advertising world would remember it for a long time as an 'admirable piece of work,'" I have produced my share of advertisements which have been remembered by the advertising world as "admirable pieces of work," but I belong to the third school, which holds that a good advertisement is one which sells the product *without drawing attention to itself*. It should rivet the reader's attention on the product. Instead of saying, "What a clever advertisement," the reader says, "I never knew *that* before. I must try this product.". . .

Your most important job is to decide what you are going to say about your product, what benefit you are going to promise. Two hundred years ago Dr. Johnson said, "Promise—large promise—is the soul of an advertisement." When he auctioned off the contents of the Anchor Brewery he made the following promise: "We are not here to sell boilers and vats, but the potentiality of growing rich beyond the dreams of avarice."

David Ogilvy, *Confessions of an Advertising Man*, Atheneum, New York, 1963, pp. 90, 93.

MEDIA PROBE

SPRANGER VALUE PROFILE

1. Six different types of people are described in the box below. Read each description and then rank them from 1 to 6. Place the number 6 next to the description that most closely resembles you, the number 5 next to the one that quite closely resembles you, and so forth down to number 1—the description that least fits you.

	A. You value the pursuit and discovery of truth—the intellectual life.
	B. You value that which is useful and practical.
	C. You value form, harmony, and beauty.
	D. You value love, sympathy, warmth, and sensitivity in relationships with people.
	E. You value competition, influence, and personal power.
	F. You value unity, wholeness, a sense of purpose above human beings.

2. Place the numbers you entered in the box in the appropriate place on the graph below. Connect the dots. What you have is your personal value profile—a visual representation of six dimensions of your personal system of values.

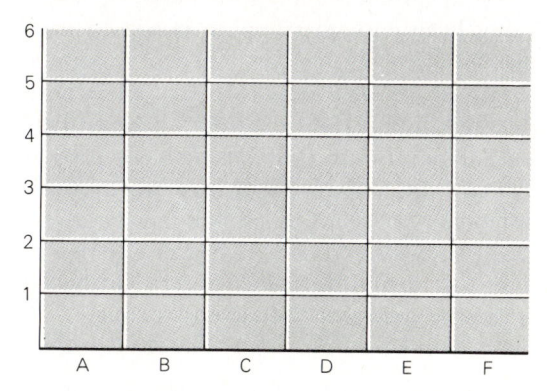

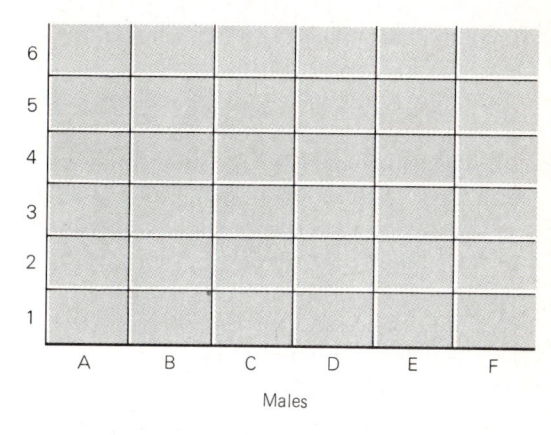

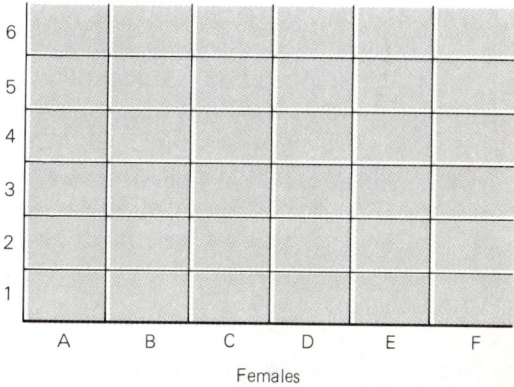

3. Compare the rankings of males and females in the class. Use the accompanying charts to aid you in answering this phase of the exercise. Simply enter the number of males and females who made each choice in the appropriate column. To what extent, if any, is there a difference in ranking by sex? Why?

4. Finally, select three ads you like that are directed at men, three ads you like that are directed at women, and three that might be directed to members of either sex. To what extent do your choices and the results of the male-female analysis reflect the value profiles you devised?

ADVERTISING: THE PROPELLING POWER

life? How is this reflected in the way you respond to advertisements? Different people have different ideas about the satisfactions they are after when they consider purchasing a product, so products are designed with satisfactions that match the needs and values of particular groups of consumers.

Sexuality is also a bait advertisers use to attract a consumer's attention. One ad begins with a nicely shaped female announcing, "I don't wear panties anymore." Once she has you transfixed, she elaborates: "Under all my dresses, under all my slightly tight pants, I wear underalls." However, the actual use of sex or nudity as an appeal is relatively rare because it tends to obliterate product information and brand recall.

Advertisers also cast ads with the consumer in mind. They are aware that we tend to believe, trust, and respond to people we judge to be credible sources. Can you identify several people used as spokespersons for products that you believe possess high credibility? Can you identify others that you believe could serve as effective product spokespersons? Explain your reasons for your choices. For the most part, advertisers tend to select celebrities who are widely known, easily recognized, and well liked to endorse their products. Bill Cosby (Jell-O), Karl Malden (American Express), Robert Young (Sanka), Robert Conrad (First Alert), Jane Russell (Playtex), Florence Henderson (Wesson Oil), Brooke Shields (Calvin Klein), and Ed MacMahon (Alpo) are among those personalities who have been judged by consumers to have high credibility. Studies have also shown that "unsolicited" testimonials by ordinary or average people can be as effective as star testimony. We have all seen or heard advertising in which "real people" offer sincere testimonials for products ranging from shampoo to deodorant soap, poultry stuffing, and dogfood. It seems that in addition to looking up to a well-known figure or personality for guidance, we sometimes like to look to people like ourselves for advice. Which type of testimonial do you respond to more readily: the celebrity or the person on the street? Why?

Leonard Old was one average individual who starred in a Prell commercial. To the innocent observer watching him on a television commercial for the first time, Leonard Old was simply a sincere consumer seen dipping his hands in two dishes of shampoo suds, one his shampoo and one, it turns out, the sponsor's product, Prell. But when Leonard Olds tells the story, a somewhat different picture emerges: "The guy had me put my hands in the two soap dishes and asked me, which one feels this way or that way? They didn't say the one on the left is the Prell, but when I put my hands in the bowls it turned out the Prell one was warm and the other was pretty obviously cold. I assumed the warm one was the one to choose. You were kind of led along and you reacted almost exactly the way they wanted you to. You had to be pretty damn dumb not to recognize what was going on."[26] Should testimonial advertising be believed? Although the FTC has stiffened the requirements for testimonial advertising (for example, your authors had to sign a statement asserting that they produced the photo appearing in the ad on the next page by themselves) the validity of some testimonial advertising is still open to question.

The techniques and appeals used in advertising have enough stopping power to have made advertising not just a potent economic force but a potent social force as well. Believe it or not, a time did exist when there actually was no mouthwash. Advertising has helped to change that, though. To be sure, whether you personally are ready to admit it or not, advertising has affected the American psyche. In light of this development, Art Buchwald wrote the following "Holiday Greeting":

May you never have iron-poor blood or an Excedrin headache. May your breath be always fresh, and may you never perspire in case someone in the family has made away with the deodorant. God grant that you have the wisdom to choose the right toothpaste. I pray that your soap will give you twenty-four-hour protection, and that you never develop dishpan hands.

May you get more shaves with your blade than with any other brand. May your cigarettes always be mild and their tar content low. May your beer always be cold. May the wax stay on your floors, and the stains on your linen disappear in seconds. May your peanut butter never stick to the roof of your mouth.

May your bank be ever ready with a loan to tide you over the rough places in life, and may you never get stuck in the mud because you used the wrong gasoline. May your spark plugs spark, and your battery never run down. And may you win thousands of dollars at gas station sweepstakes.

Finally, I wish each and every one of you instant tuning, a clear, ghost free picture, and on this holiday may all your TV tubes be bright.[27]

The Parts of the Advertisement

An advertisement is usually composed of most, if not all, of these: the headline, the illustration, the body copy, the motto or slogan, and the logotype. Let us briefly examine the function of each.

The purpose of the *headline* is to get the attention of the audience—the specific audience to whom the ad is directed. The headline is also the key factor in getting people to read the body copy. So critical is the headline that when copywriter and author John Caples listed the fifty things he had learned in fifty

ADVERTISING: THE PROPELLING POWER 315

YOU WERE THERE

When I was a struggling graduate student, I participated in a "hidden-camera" commercial. I was alerted in advance that while the "interview" would appear to be a routine consumer survey of a number of products, it was in truth a hidden-camera commercial for Scope. If I was "good," my friendly informant told me, I could earn a lot of money. I had never used Scope, but I was not about to let that stand between me and down payment on next semester's tuition.

When I arrived for the interview, I was led into a small room in which one wall was covered by an enormous mirror. "Sit over there," said my interviewer, motioning to a chair directly facing the mirror. "Now, then," he went on pleasantly, "we're just going to have a nice chat about some of the different products you use every day." He went on to ask several questions about what brand of toothpaste, laundry detergent, soap, and shampoo I used. I waited for him to get around to Scope. Sure enough:

"What kind of mouthwash do you use?"

"Well," I began, leaning toward him earnestly.

"*Don't move the chair!*" he shouted, bounding around his desk to shove the chair, with me in it, back to its original position. I smiled, and pretended to see nothing unusual in this bizarre behavior.

"Speak up clearly," he said. "now, again, what kind of mouthwash do you use?"

"Scope," I chirped obediently.

He sat up and adjusted his tie. "I can't *hear* you. What kind of mouthwash do you use?"

"SCOPE," I bellowed in what I hoped was the direction of the "hidden" microphone.

"Good. Would you mind leaning slightly forward and to the left when you answer? Now," he said, his voice changing to practiced, resonant, pear-shaped announcer's tones. "Why do you prefer Scope over the other brands?"

I was prepared. "Why, it leaves my breath so much cleaner and fresher!"

"Repeat that statement using the word *Scope* instead of *it*," he said. "And lean a bit more to the left when you answer."

I did so.

At the end of the interview he announced grandly, "Guess what? Behind that big mirror is a camera. You're being filmed!"

"No!" I said, arranging my features into an expression of shock. "What a surprise!"

"Would you repeat that a little louder and lean to your left?"

As it turns out, this commercial was never aired.

Donna Woolfolk Cross, *Media Speak*, Coward-McCann, New York, 1983, pp. 33–35.

---

years in advertising, he gave first place to the following statement: "The headline is the most important element in most advertising. David Ogilvy also supported this view; in fact, Ogilvy insists that the headline is likely to represent "eighty cents of your client's dollar." The *illustration*, like the headline, is designed to attract attention. The headline and the illustration should support each other; together they should complete a thought. In other words, they are interdependent and, to be effective, should operate as a team. The job of the *body copy* is to stimulate interest in and create a desire for what is being advertised. Its task is to amplify, explain, and capitalize on the headline. To be effective body copy must be easy to understand and believable. The *slogan* or motto summarizes or encapsulates the campaign theme. For example, "You're in good hands with Allstate," "The coffee-er coffee" (Savarin), or "the wings of man" (Eastern Airlines). Finally, the *logotype*,

It is in the marketplace itself that the effectiveness of product advertising is ultimately tested. (Tyrone Hall, Stock, Boston)

or signature cut, is a special design of the name of the advertiser which is used repeatedly in the advertising. Remember, it is the total communication power of an advertisement that determines whether or not it will hit or miss its mark.

THE MEDIUM BEHIND THE MESSAGE

Advertising fuels the mass media by providing much of the revenue the mass media need to function. Commercial radio and television stations, as we know, depend entirely on

MEDIA PROBE

Based on what you understand regarding the parts of an ad, and the techniques advertisers use—the claims they make, the appeals they rely on, and the types of research on which they base their decisions—create an ad for a safety pin.

MEDIA PROBE

Select an ad that you like from each of the following media: newspapers, magazines, radio, television, billboards, and direct-mail. Which do you like best? Why is it your favorite?

Next, again use the above media, select an ad that you dislike. Which ad do you dislike the most? Why?

To what extent do you think the medium the ad appeared in affected your choices? Why?

advertising, while typical newspapers and magazines rely on advertising for about 70 percent of their operating budgets. This is not to suggest, however, that the relationship of advertising and the media is a one-way affair. In fact, the situation is quite the contrary. The media do not simply "feed off" advertising; instead, advertising and the media serve each other. After all, were it not for the mass media, advertising messages would not reach the people. We could say that the media are vital links, that each "medium that carries an advertiser's message is the vital connection between the company that manufactures a product and the consumer who might wish to buy it."[28]

Each advertising medium communicates with its audience in a somewhat different way. The question advertisers need to answer is, which medium or combination of media will most effectively communicate the message the client wants to send to the target audience? The importance of making the right decision cannot be overemphasized; the largest part of all advertising expenditure goes toward the purchase of advertising media space and time. Only by exploring the strengths and weaknesses of each medium will we be able to understand why effective media planning is such a balancing act.

The Print Media

Let us begin with newspapers. How do you read a newspaper? Do you skim it? Search for

ADVERTISING: THE PROPELLING POWER   317

a favorite section? Check the index? Look at the ads? Research reveals that most people read the newspaper in a fairly ordered way. During the time the average person spends reading a newspaper, he or she either opens or looks at 84 percent of the paper's pages. This is one of the reasons why newspapers take the greatest share of the nation's advertising dollar—almost 30 percent—and why they are able to derive an estimated $15.6 billion from advertising revenues.[29] In addition, the advertising source cited most often as bringing a purchase item to the attention of consumers is the newspaper.[30] So it is understandable why advertisers feel that newspapers provide them with the opportunities they need to gain the attention of readers. Advertisements today comprise about 64 percent of the printed matter of the paper and account for 70 percent of the paper's income. Were it not for advertising, the cost of purchasing a newspaper would skyrocket.

Newspapers also offer advertisers great flexibility. For example, they have very short deadlines: only about 48 hours notice is required for the placement of an ad. The printed message can be almost any size and shape and can appear in black-and-white, spot color, or full color. Interestingly enough, newspaper advertising has also been judged to be the most believable of all the major media. Newspaper ads can also be reread, easily clipped, and shared. Advertising in a newspaper means you are advertising in an active, not a passive, medium. The newspaper does have certain drawbacks, however. It has a short life and is not usually circulated among many different readers. The advertiser has little or no control over where the advertisement is placed on a page. Also, the bulk of advertising appearing in newspapers is local rather than national, with department stores leading the way in newspaper advertising spending.

In contrast to newspapers, the workhorse of advertising, magazines handle only about 9 percent of the national advertising volume.

MEDIA PROBE

1. Examine the ads in three different magazines obviously intended for different types of readers. Compare the products and services advertised in each magazine. To what extent do they differ? Supply examples.
2. Select one particular product or service that is advertised in each of your selected magazines. To what extent have the advertising techniques and appeals used in the ads been altered to reflect each magazine's target audience?

Yet, more manufacturers advertise in magazines than in any other mass medium—principally because magazines are the most selective of all media except direct mail.

In addition to offering their advertisers accurate demographic information, magazines also offer great opportunities to use high-quality graphics to advantage. They also have a long life and are kept around the home, office, or waiting room for longer periods than other media. Research studies also reveal that magazines rarely just "lie around" without being picked up; rather, people return to read magazines regularly. For example, over 75 percent of the men and women who read magazines refer back to or reread something in a magazine they have previously read.[31] Thus, unlike newspapers, magazines offer relative permanence. However, while some magazines offer regional additions, most magazines are so widely distributed that it is difficult to fit copy to local conditions. Another limitation is that magazines have long closing dates (usually about three months), making it difficult, if not impossible, to make last-minute changes in advertising. Consequently, the immediacy of newspapers is sacrificed with magazines. Also, as in newspapers, the ratio of advertising to editorial content is high (about 50 percent of the magazine is advertising), leading to heavy advertising competition.

The Electronic Media

We will start by examining radio. Radio has been termed the ubiquitous medium; it goes everywhere and seems to be everywhere. As advertisers have come to realize that radio leads all other media in both daily and weekly reach (daily radio reaches 81.5 percent; weekly radio reaches 95.8 percent), radio's advertising revenues have steadily increased.[32] Part of radio's appeal derives from the fact that it is broadly selective. Different types of programming attract different types of audiences, so the advertiser is able to select the stations that appeal to the kind of audience the client is after. In effect, radio offers advertisers the chance to "narrowcast," as opposed to broadcast, their messages. As practitioner Tony Schwartz points out: "if we want to reach the elderly, we buy time on Station A, we reach teenagers on Station B, young Blacks on Station C, Hispanics on Station D."[33] Also, according to statistics supplied by the Radio Advertising Bureau, the biggest spenders, the well-educated, and working women spend more time with radio than with television, newspapers, or magazines. And radio offers one of the lowest costs per thousand—so the budget needed for an effective radio schedule is less than that needed for newspapers, magazines, or television. In addition to all this, radio gives free rein to the imagination.

This is not to suggest that radio does not present disadvantages. Radio is heard, not seen. Although the use of imagery and "theater of the mind" techniques can compensate to an extent, advertisers do assert that some products simply need to be seen in order to be understood. Also a radio ad can't be cut out and saved like a newspaper and magazine ad can. Still, this drawback didn't stop McDonald's from introducing the idea of radio coupons:

CLARA: What are you doing, Glen?
GLEN: Making McDonald's radio coupons.

MEDIA VIEW

SPEAKER 1: Radio? Why should I advertise on radio? There's nothing to look at. No pictures.
SPEAKER 2: Listen. You can do things on radio you couldn't possibly do on TV. All right. Watch this. Okay people. Now when I give you the cue I want the 700 foot mountain of whip cream to roll into Lake Michigan which has been drained and filled with hot chocolate. Then the Royal Canadian Air Force will fly overhead towing a ten ton marachino cherry which will be dropped into the whip cream to the cheering of 25,000 extras. All right: Cue the mountain. . . . Cue the Air Force. . . . Cue the Marachino Cherry. . . . Okay 25,000 cheering extras. . . . Now, you want to try that on television? You see radio is a very special medium because it stretches the imagination.

Stan Freeberg, The Radio Advertising Bureau.

CLARA: Radio coupons?
GLEN: Don't you listen to the radio, Clara? Place a dollar bill on a piece of paper and draw a dotted line around it.
CLARA: Then what?
GLEN: Then take a pencil, crayons, whatever, and draw a picture of a Big Mac on it.
CLARA: Why, Glen?
GLEN: 'Cause everytime you buy a Big Mac, you can turn in your homemade coupon—and get a free regular-size soft drink.
CLARA: Why so many coupons, Glen?
GLEN: 'Cause I love Big Macs—and I love free soft drinks.
CLARA: A free soft drink at McDonald's is great but . . .
GLEN: Yeah?
CLARA: Glen, your drawings are silly.
GLEN: They're impressionistic, Clara.
CLARA: Glen, you're a bad artist.
GLEN: I'm paid well.
CLARA: Glen, you're clipping McDonald's.
GLEN: That's the whole idea, Clara.
CLARA: Cut it out, Glen!

GLEN: OK, Clara!
ANNOUNCER: You heard it on radio, folks! Make your own dollar-bill-sized coupon. Draw a Big Mac on it—pencil, ballpoint, colors—whatever. When you buy a Big Mac, turn in your coupons for a free regular-size soft drink. Get cuttin', Washington. Offer ends September 17th.
SINGERS: (music up) At McDonald's . . .
GLEN: (clip-clip-clip!) Clara, that's a beautiful coupon!
SINGERS: We do it all for you.

Let us next consider television. In 1970, the average cost of a nationally televised thirty-second commercial was $30,000. That figure more than doubled by 1980 and by 1983 approached $100,000, with many commercials priced at much more than that (see Figure 10-2). Television attracts the largest volume of national advertising (more than $8 billion in 1980). A large percentage of that comes from the packaged-goods industry (food and drugs). Since 1951, Procter & Gamble has led the way in spending. Despite the high cost of TV advertising, television's large audience brings the cost per 1000 down to a comparatively low level. About 50,000 television commercials are produced in the United States each year.

Advertisers can purchase time on television through a network (network TV) or from individual stations (spot TV). Network TV allows advertisers to reach virtually everyone, while spot advertising increases the flexibility of the medium, permitting advertisers to air their messages in particular cities at particular times. Television also is adept at promoting viewer empathy. For example, AT&T spots do not order people to make long-distance calls; instead, they make us *feel like* making long-distance calls. TV commercials can make us laugh and they can make us cry. Their combination of sight and sound is almost unbeatable. But television also presents some problems. Though they may be repeated frequently, the advertising messages aired on television come and go so quickly. Also, the increased profusion of commercials has produced clutter: more and more commercials are jammed together, precipitating confusion as well as anger in viewers. An average viewer is exposed to over eighty TV commercials a day.

Like radio advertising, television advertising interrupts programming; television, however, is more intrusive. Consider this: Which medium do you find it easier to tune out—television or radio? If you are like most people, you can shut out a radio commercial more easily than you can shut out a TV commercial. For some reason people simply have stronger likes and dislikes for TV spots than they do for those aired on or appearing in other media. It may be getting somewhat easier to tune out television commercials, however, and this fact is beginning to make advertising executives anxious. The reason? Almost 25 percent of today's TV households now own remote-control channel switchers, devices advertising executives refer to as

FIGURE 10-2 The rising cost of commercials. Average gross costs of a thirty-second live-action commercial for a nationally advertised product or service. The gross costs to the client include all soundtrack and postproduction costs for a ready-to-air spot. (*Hooper White*).

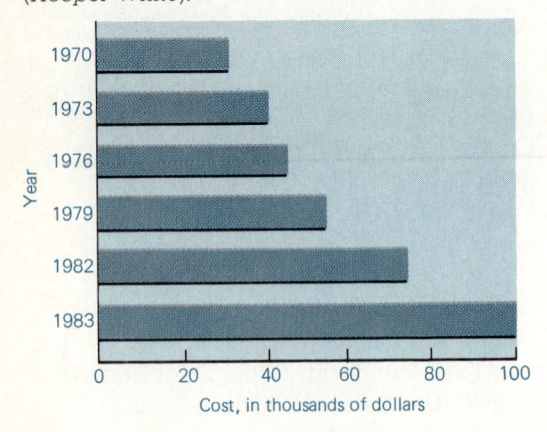

YOU WERE THERE

The first thing you notice when you walk onto a sound stage where a commercial is being filmed is the organized chaos. There will usually be as many as twenty people, all going in different directions, each doing something different.

Two men are wrestling with a large lamp (called a "deuce"), trying to get it up ten feet in the air. Another man is on a ladder, holding a long pole with a microphone attached to one end. Over in the corner a man is sitting behind a card table with a tape recorder on it, working hard at what turns out to be the morning newspaper's crossword puzzle.

The set itself looks like a middle-class American kitchen, with two crucial exceptions—a wall is missing and there's no roof. In the set you see two women dressed in slacks and blouses—one with her hair up in curlers, talking to a man in a rumpled shirt and blue jeans. In front of them is a large camera resting on what appears to be a trolley with two swivel seats; this is called a "dolly."

Another man is moving quietly around the set with his light meter, checking the light levels. "Let's hit the table with a deuce," he calls out.

A light is turned on and aimed at the kitchen table. "That's it, now I'm reading a perfect four." (This means that his exposure reading for the camera lens is f/4.) He turns to the man in the rumpled shirt.

"We're all set, Steve."

"Thanks, Pete—okay, gang, let's make movies."

Suddenly, all attention is turned to the area in front of the camera. The man with the light meter climbs onto the dolly and sits in position to look through the lens of the camera. Rumpled Shirt stands next to the camera to see the action. A young woman comes up to him.

"We have five seconds for this scene, Steve."

"Right! Everyone set?"

Curlers are removed from the first woman's hair, while someone quickly puts a final touch of lipstick on the other woman. The two women take their positions on the set—one standing by the sink, the other sitting at the table.

A young man moves in front of the camera. He is carrying a small board on which is printed the name of the production company, the name of the commerical, and the number of the scene. This is called a "clapstick" because the top of the board is hinged so that it can be raised and "clapped" down at the beginning of each take. This creates a visible mark on the film, which can be matched to the sound of the clap on the audio tape that is recording the sound. This will be used to synchronize the sound track to the film.

"We're ready, Steve."

"Roll—sound."

The man behind the tape recorder turns it on.

"Speed!"

A button is pushed on the camera.

"Rolling."

The young man with the clapstick calls out, "Sound one."

Bang! The stick is clapped.

"Okay, Judy and Chris, we've got five seconds for this scene. Let's not rush it—and action."

The woman by the sink moves to the table with two cups of coffee.

"All set for the party tomorrow night, Helen?"

"Almost, but I could sure use a helping hand cleaning up."

The action stops abruptly with a loud "Cut!" from Steve. "That was fine," he says, "but Judy, you looked a little uncomfortable crossing to the table with the coffee. Let's do another take."

A young woman dressed in blue jeans leaves a group of people who have been standing in the background watching the scene. She walks toward the camera.

ADVERTISING: THE PROPELLING POWER

"Steve, the client wants Chris to deliver her line with a little more sparkle."

"No problem, she's just warming up—Chris, could you be a little more up this time, a little more like you're trying to con Judy into helping you?"

"Sure, Steve."

"All right, let's do another take."

This scene is typical of what you might find at the filming of a television commercial.

H. Ted Busch and Terry Landeck, *The Making of a Television Commercial*, Macmillan, New York, 1980, pp. 1-3.

"commercial zappers." And recent research shows that between 6 and 19 percent of all commercial breaks are being zapped—turned off or switched away. What are commercial zappers switching to? According to the results of a survey conducted by Television Audience Assessment (TAA), two-thirds of Music Television's (MTV's) viewers said they turned to that cable channel during commercial breaks in other programs. TAA also reports that about 15 percent of broadcast television viewers and 40 percent of cable subscribers said they "always" or "often" change channels during commercial breaks.[35] Imagine going to the expense of writing, producing, and airing a commercial only to have nobody watch it.

Direct-Mail Advertising

When advertisers do not use one of the preceding media, but instead mail their ads directly to prospective customers, it is called direct-mail advertising. Direct mail is the only medium in which it is the advertiser's job to supply the circulation. Thus, the mailing list is a critical factor that will determine the success or failure of the advertising effort.

Direct-mail advertising offers the advertiser great flexibility. The direct-mail piece may be as simple or as sophisticated as the advertiser desires. It can be personalized to reflect the needs and wants of the recipient. On the other hand, it also offers the greatest chance for error. The piece of direct mail pictured on the next page was sent to us; to this day we have not opened it.

Despite such occasional errors, direct mail outperforms other media in terms of responses, inquiries, and sales. While direct mail is the most expensive medium on a strict cost-per-1000 exposure basis (it costs about 14 times more per 1000 than magazines and newspapers), it is the most effective because the advertiser can be very selective in targeting his or her message to the most likely customers only. And the direct-mail advertiser knows quickly whether the advertising effort will be successful or not. On the average, the direct-mail advertiser receives 15 percent of the responses he or she will receive, within a week of a mailing. A successful direct-mail result can be expected to yield between 0.7 percent and 5.0 percent of the names mailed to; that's roughly equivalent to 7 to 50 orders per 1000.

Outdoor Advertising

One of the oldest forms of advertising, outdoor advertising is also one of the most enduring. Outdoor ads are seen all day, every day. They cannot be turned off like television, tuned out like radio, or thrown out like newspapers, magazines, and direct-mail pieces. In addition, the audience for outdoor advertising is younger and more affluent than the national average. According to the Institute of Outdoor Advertising, outdoor audiences are also on the go: they do more; they buy more.

Errors in direct mail plague the medium.

MEDIA VIEW

DIRECT MAIL PACKS WOWIE! ZOWIE! PUNCH

Mr. Read Er
Your Street
Anytown, USA

Dear Mr. Er.

Congratulations! You and the entire Er family can tell your neighbors on Your Street that you have won the opportunity to read about direct mail! That's right! You've been selected from among all of the families in the Anytown metropolitan area to learn why marketers spend more than $10 billion a year to send 38 billion pieces of mail to you, the Ers of Anytown, and others!

What's more, the SPECIAL non-negotiable PERSONAL CHECK-like coupon below entitles the Ers to get this bonus information!:

Volume!
Strategy!
Growth!
Psychology!

Sound like a reason to keep reading? We hope so! Otherwise this direct solicitation is already a flop!

Why Direct Mail Is Attractive To Advertisers!!
Because it is measurable! Unlike advertisers that use TV commercials or magazine ads, those that use direct mail know precisely how hard their ads work! If they spend $260,000 to send out a million pieces (a typical, inexpensive mailing), and they get back 20,000 answers (an adequate response), they know:

- How effective the ad is—2 percent!
- How much each response cost—$13!

ADVERTISING: THE PROPELLING POWER 323

"Money is being diverted into direct mail because of that kind of measurability," says John W. Booth, senior vice president of New York's Direct Marketing Group.

The $10.6 billion spend on direct-mail in 1981 . . . represented 17 percent of all advertising spending!

Why Advertisers Like To Use Your Name and Address All Throughout Their Mailings!!

"It works better," says Edward Pfeiffer of the Direct Marketing Association.

Sure, a letter addressed to you by a computer is no more personal than one addressed to "occupant!" But, even a sophisticated reader like yourself, Mr. Er, is more likely to open and respond to a computer-personalized mailing!

"What we think it is," says Janet Rothstein of Publishers Clearing House, "is people like seeing their names."

This isn't just idle speculation! One of the big advantages of direct mail is that advertisers can send out various versions of the same mailing and test which works best!

That's right, Mr. Er, the letter you get on Your Street may be different from the letter received by your Anytown neighbors!

Why Those Letters, Especially The Sweepstakes Entries, Frequently Contain All Sorts of Stickers and Tokens and Other Junk!!

At Publishers Clearing House, Rothstein says the key is involvement!

"By the time they get down licking stickers and sticking them down somewhere," she says, "they're going to get interested in our product message."

Why Subscribers And Non-subscribers Have Different Ways to Respond on Publishers Sweepstakes Entries!!

The law says that everybody has an equal chance, and, in fact, everybody does!

But, says Booth of the Direct Marketing Group, "Clearly the psychology behind the sweepstakes is that the individual believes that if they do not buy something . . . ,"they won't win!

Yes, acknowledges Charles Pintchman of The Reader's Digest Association Inc., people probably do think that way! However, he says, the reason for separate entries in the Reader's Digest contest is that the magazine wants to process subscription orders as soon as they arrive, instead of waiting for the sweepstakes to end!

Why Direct-Mail Letters Tend To Have A Lot Of Exclamation Points!!

Drama!

USA Today, July 1, 1983, p. 3B.

Since the two basic types of outdoor advertising—the poster panel and the printed bulletin—can be purchased individually or in a variety of packages, outdoor advertising also gives the advertiser great flexibility. The flexibility can be geographic (the advertiser's buy can range from the entire state to a small section of a city) or demographic (the advertiser can concentrate the message in areas frequented by young people, upper-income people, or a specific ethnic group).

Also, while the other media are heard and viewed in the home for the most part, buying is usually done out of the home. Thus, outdoor advertising helps fill the gap between the ad heard in the home and the purchase that is made out of the home. Still, outdoor advertising does have inherent disadvantages. For one thing, people pass by outdoor displays very quickly with little or no opportunity to slow down. This limits the amount of copy that billboards can contain. Also outdoor advertising has little value for advertisers trying to reach a small segment of the market, say, for example, women aged 25 to 49.

The function of each medium described above is to transmit the advertiser's message to the "right" audience. New media, like cable television (one of the newest media to

The billboard sells billboard advertising because advertisers respond to advertising, too. Communications have a circular influence in our society. (Randy Matusow)

be used by advertisers), are constantly appearing. Balloons, the telephone, the fronts of shopping carts, coptermedia (thousands of lightbulbs are mounted in a frame 40 feet by 8 feet, creating a flying electric sign that is pulled by a helicopter), and theater-screen advertising all pose their challenge to the traditional advertising media. Whatever the medium, however, the goal is the same—to connect the advertising message with as many members of the target market as possible.

THE ADVERTISING AGENCY: INDUSTRY NERVE CENTER

The advertising agency is the nerve center of the advertising business. It is an independent business, composed of creative and business people whose job is to develop, prepare, and place advertising in media for clients who are seeking to find the most appropriate target audiences for their products and services. Though the agency works for the advertiser, it gets most of its money from the media. This practice stems from the days when advertising practitioners were agents of the media who represented newspapers and magazines in the sale of their space to advertisers or space brokers. It was Frances Wayland Ayer, the founding father of N. W. Ayer and Son, who moved the advertising agent beyond the "order taker" function and into the area of advertising preparation.[36] Not long after, agencies began dreaming up advertising copy for clients, recommending media, and conducting market research. In exchange for their efforts, agencies were paid a percentage of the total advertising dollar (usually 15 percent).

How does an advertising agency work? Today's full-service agencies perform three key functions: planning, development, and quality control. First, it is up to the agency to find out all it can about the client it represents, the client's product, and the market so that it can develop an effective advertising plan. Second, it is the agency's job to create the ad-

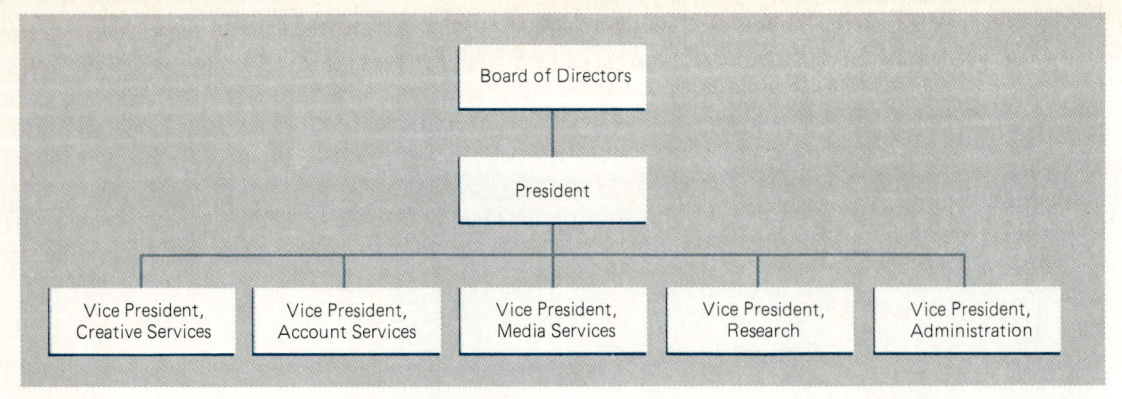

FIGURE 10-3 Organization chart of a typical advertising agency.

vertisements and choose the media that will serve as the channels of communication when these messages are presented to selected target audiences. Third, the agency needs to take steps to verify that the advertising is working; only if this is done can it amend the advertising plan as needed. Although the precise way an agency functions may vary, most agencies have five predominant service groups in operation: (1) the creative group, (2) the media group, (3) the account management group, (4) the research group, and (5) the financial services group (see Figure 10-3).

The job of the creative group is to provide the copy and the design for an advertisement. People who create the words of the ad are called copywriters. Copywriters usually work closely with agency artists, graphic designers, and production staff. The primary task of the agency artists and graphic designers is to lay out the ad or create a storyboard; in this way they indicate how the various parts of the ad fit together. The print or broadcast production people are responsible for supplying the finished art or the finished commercial. Most advertising agencies organize their creative group in one of two ways: writers and art directors work independently of each other, or writers and art directors work together as a team.

The media group is charged with matching the profile of the target market with the audiences of an array of media. The members of this department are responsible for evaluating media based on a number of criteria, including efficiency and cost, and then recommending which medium or combination of media a client should use.

The account management group is composed of account executives whose task it is to attract advertising to the firm, interpret a client's problem to the agency's creative and media people, and then to explain the developed campaign to a client. They are the liaison between agency and client, funneling information in both directions.

The people in research try to provide the creative department with an accurate description of the target market. They also pretest ideas and evaluate the effectiveness of the agency's advertising efforts.

Finally, the financial services group administrates the overall operation of the agency.

WHO WATCHES THE ADVERTISERS? THE REGULATORS

In order to help protect the consumer, a variety of controls ranging from regulation by the federal government, to self-regulation, to regulation by consumers and consumer groups have evolved. Basically, the restrictions placed upon advertisers by these groups

MEDIA VIEW

Roy Whitter of the Young and Rubicam agency was soliciting an account for a company advertising manager who asked him what he would do if he rejected the proposed campaign. Whitter answered, "If you reject our best idea, we'll present our second best idea." The advertising manager asked what would happen if the company didn't like any of Young and Rubicam's ideas. Whitter replied, "Then we'll do it your way, because you might as well waste your money with us as with somebody else."

G. Allen Foster, *Advertising: Ancient Market Place to Television,* Criterion Books, New York, 1967. p. 191.

---

have been designed to protect the consumer from deceptive or misleading advertising.

The *Federal Trade Commission* (FTC) performs the major role in the regulation process. Established in 1914, the FTC is composed of five commissioners who are appointed by the president of the United States with the advice and consent of the Senate for seven-year terms. This body is empowered to monitor "truth in advertising"; that is, they are on watch for ads that contain false and misleading claims. In effect, the FTC compares an actual product with the product as represented in ads. They ask advertisers to submit documentation that supports the performance claims they make. If a company refuses to document its claims, it can be sued by the government. For example, the STP Corporation had advertised that adding a can of STP Oil Treatment to a car's engine would save 20 percent in oil consumption. When the STP Corporation failed to submit documentation to prove this claim, they were fined $700,000.

Next, consider the Campbell Soup case. For one of its commercials, Campbell Soup placed marbles at the bottom of a soup bowl. The marbles forced the solid ingredients in the soup to the top of the bowl where they could be readily photographed and would give the impression that the soup contained more ingredients than it actually did. Campbell Soup argued unsuccessfully that without the marbles the ingredients would sink to the bottom and give the impression that the soup contained fewer ingredients than it did. The FTC found Campbell's argument unpersuasive and Campbell Soup agreed to stop the practice.

What exactly are the FTCs powers? After conducting an investigation, the FTC may decide to issue a complaint against an advertiser. Basically, the FTC has four options from which to choose.

1. It can issue a cease-and-desist order. Such an order prohibits the further use of the objectionable advertising practice. The advertiser signs an agreement to comply voluntarily. No guilt is admitted.
2. It can issue a consent order. At this point, the advertiser again, without admitting guilt, agrees to halt the advertising and not to indulge in such practices.
3. It can require corrective advertising

MEDIA PROBE

Find one ad that you judge to be untruthful and another ad that you judge to be completely truthful and bring them to class. Explain your reasons for each selection. To what extent do people in your class agree with your choices? Was it easier for you to find an ad you thought was misleading or one you thought honest? Why do you suppose this was so?

ADVERTISING: THE PROPELLING POWER

whereby a percentage of the company's advertising for a period of time must be devoted to explaining that the ad they ran was false or misleading.
4. It can ask the Attorney General to try the advertiser on a misdemeanor charge. Decisions by the FTC can be appealed through the federal court system.

Testimonials have been of particular interest to the FTC in recent years. The FTC requires that an endorsement by an expert or authority must be based on actual experience with the product being advertised. Thus, Bill Cosby must actually eat Jell-O pudding. The FTC also requires that if an ad indicates that an endorser because of training or experience is superior to others in making judgment about the product, the endorser's actual qualifications must justify this portrayal. This means that an actor cannot be dressed as a doctor and advise you to use Anacin.

A number of advertisers—including American Express, the Sugar Association, Ocean Spray (cranberry juice), Profile (bread), and Listerine—have been required by the FTC to run corrective advertising. The FTC ordered the corrective advertising in order to help erase the false impressions advertising had created. Listerine's case is particularly noteworthy because it was the first corrective-advertising case to face court review. For over fifty years, Listerine had been advertised as a cold and sore-throat remedy. Finally, the FTC was able to prove that the product did not relieve colds or sore throats. The maker of Listerine was compelled to spend $10.2 million on ads that included this statement: "Listerine will not help prevent colds or sore throats or lessen their severity."

The powers of the FTC are limited, however. The commissioners are charged with regulating "unfair and false advertising in the public interest." But this mandate is confined by law to "material fraud in connection with the sale of a product." Thus, the FTC's powers do not extend to how persons (for instance, women or members of an ethnic group) are portrayed in ads as long as the portrayal does not constitute an extra claim for a product. This is why the FTC did not take action when Spanish groups were angered over corn chip advertising that featured the "Frito Bandito," a classic Mexican stereotype, or when women's groups protested the way women were portrayed in ads. It should be noted that in recent years Congress has made it difficult for the FTC to define "unfair" broadly.

In addition to government regulation, the advertising industry also attempts to regulate itself. One self-regulatory organization is called the *National Advertising Review Board* (NARB). It is composed of fifty members—thirty representing national advertisers, ten representating advertising agencies, and ten representing the public. Complaints about particular ads are referred to the board by the National Advertising Division (NAD) of the Council of Better Business Bureaus; the NAD receives them from the public, the industry, or other sources. Only after a complaint has been reviewed and investigated by the NAD, and it has been unable to resolve it, is the complaint passed on to the NARB. Once informed of a complaint, the NARB appoints a five-member panel to serve as a court of appeals for the advertiser cited for a misleading ad. While this body is not empowered to order an advertiser to stop running an ad or to impose a fine, it does publish the panel's reports, favorable or unfavorable, and can refer the matter to an appropriate regulatory agency. It can let it be known that in the judgment of the advertiser's peers, an ad that is currently running is harmful to advertising, the public, and the offender. The threat of adverse publicity is usually an inducement to compliance.

In addition, the American Association of Advertising Agencies (AAAA), as well as the Association of National Advertisers, and the American Advertising Federation, are also engaged in monitoring industry practices. For example, the AAAA denies membership rights to any agency judged unethical. Its creative code establishes those principles member agencies should adhere to.

Lastly, consumers also play a role in the regulation process. Besides voicing their feelings informally, consumers have organized several formal channels through which their opinions on advertising are made known. Among the most important are the Consumer Federation of America and the National Consumer League. In addition, nonprofit testing organizations like Consumers Union rate products and issue findings on a monthly basis. But perhaps the greatest of all consumer powers is the choice you have to say yes or no to an ad. After all, in the end, it is the response of consumers that will lead to success or failure for a product. In the end, it is the consumer who either is or is not moved by advertising. As one advertising professional put it: "If we know they [the consumers] like sugar, we put sugar in it. If we know they like toys, we put toys in it. If we know they like speed, we put power in it. We give people exactly what they want." Careful consumers do not permit advertisements to exploit them. Instead, they take steps to ensure that the consumer, and not the advertiser, remains in charge. Consumers play an important role in the dynamics and the mechanics of a purchase. A human being is more than a buying machine.

WHERE DO YOU STAND?

Advertising has been criticized on many grounds. For example, some argue that advertising forces prices up; others say advertising leads to unnecessary purchases; and still others note that it creates in us wants that we will never be able to realize. Advertising has also been charged with manipulating us to buy things we can't afford, and it has been condemned for making us believe that insecurities will vanish and sex appeal, social status, and a "good time" will be ours if only we do what the ad advises or requests. Advertising has also been attacked for debasing our language and our lives, for being offensive and in bad taste, and for contributing to conformity. We believe it is important for us to examine some of the current questions raised about advertising so that we are better able to assess the state of the profession today.

The Advertiser: Advocate or Reporter

Some critics feel that advertising should function not as an advocate but rather as an unbiased arbitrator; that is, they believe advertisements should lay out the "facts" impartially so that we, the consumers, are in the position to make informed and wise decisions. Others counter that advertising is neither impartial nor unbiased. Instead, they affirm that advertising is the advertiser's mouthpiece, and as such its task is to present the advertiser's story or product as attractively and as persuasively as possible. For example, where a house is the subject of an ad, the advertiser, they believe, should not mention the house's defects. To be sure, in their opinion the ad as written would never read: "Brick Colonial, seven small rooms, two baths of which one needs new tile, old trees but the elm is dying, gardens which require much maintenance, brick patio which doesn't drain well, and a roof which will need replacement in two years." Instead, it would read: "brick Colonial, seven rooms, two baths, quiet neighborhood, old shade, gardens, brick patio."[37]

The Bait: Wants Versus Needs

Some critics of advertising complain that ads make us purchase things we do not *need* to have. The defenders of advertising counter that advertising has no power to *make* us buy anything. What do you think? Should adver-

CREATIVE CODE

American Association of Advertising Agencies

The members of the American Association of Advertising Agencies recognize:

1. That advertising bears a dual responsibility in the American economic system and way of life.

To the public it is a primary way of knowing about the goods and services which are the products of American free enterprise, goods and services which can be freely chosen to suit the desires and needs of the individual. The public is entitled to expect that advertising will be reliable in content and honest in presentation.

To the advertiser it is a primary way of persuading people to buy his goods or services, within the framework of a highly competitive economic system. He is entitled to regard advertising as a dynamic means of building his business and his profits.

2. That advertising enjoys a particularly intimate relationship to the American family. It enters the home as an integral part of television and radio programs, to speak to the individual and often to the entire family. It shares the pages of favorite newspapers and magazines. It presents itself to travelers and to readers of the daily mails. In all these forms, it bears a special responsibility to respect the tastes and self-interest of the public.

3. That advertising is directed to sizable groups or to the public at large, which is made up of many interests and many tastes. As is the case with all public enterprises, ranging from sports to education and even to religion, it is almost impossible to speak without finding someone in disagreement. Nonetheless, advertising people recognize their obligation to operate within the traditional American limitations: to serve the interests of the majority and to respect the rights of the minority.

Therefore we, the members of the American Association of Advertising Agencies, in addition to supporting and obeying the laws and legal regulations pertaining to advertising, undertake to extend and broaden the application of high ethical standards. Specifically, we will not knowingly produce advertising which contains:

a. False or misleading statements or exaggerations, visual or verbal.

b. Testimonials which do not reflect the real choice of a competent witness.

c. Price claims which are misleading.

d. Comparisons which unfairly disparage a competitive product or service.

e. Claims insufficiently supported, or which distort the true meaning or practicable application of statements made by professional or scientific authority.

f. Statements, suggestions or pictures offensive to public decency.

We recognize that there are areas which are subject to honestly different interpretations and judgment. Taste is subjective and may even vary from time to time as well as from individual to individual. Frequency of seeing or hearing advertising messages will necessarily vary greatly from person to person.

However, we agree not to recommend to an advertiser and to discourage the use of advertising which is in poor or questionable taste or which is deliberately irritating through content, presentation or excessive repetition.

Clear and willful violations of this Code shall be referred to the Board of Directors of the American Association of Advertising Agencies for appropriate action, including possible annulment of membership as provided in Article IV, Section 5, of the Constitution and By-Laws.

Conscientious adherence to the letter and the spirit of this Code will strengthen advertising and the free enterprise system of which it is part. *Adopted April 26, 1962*

Endorsed by

Advertising Association of the West, Advertising Federation of America, Agricultural Publishers Association, Associated Business Publications, Association of Industrial Advertisers, Association of National Advertisers, Magazine Publishers Association, National Business Publications, Newspaper Advertising Executives Association, Radio Code Review Board (National Association of Broadcasters), Station Representatives Association, TV Code Review Board (NAB) tising concentrate only on our functional basic human needs, or should it be allowed to stimulate our psychological and physical wants? For example, while we need to eat food, we do not need to eat "gourmet" food; while we need to shelter our bodies from the elements, we do not need to wear designer clothes to do this. Should advertising be censured for persuading us to behave "irrationally"? Is it wrong to acknowledge that we all desire more than the basics of food, clothing, and shelter? Is it wrong for advertising to try to sell us things we don't need—things that might help to make our lives more pleasureable, easier, or happier? As practitioner John O'Toole confesses: "Yes, I sell people things they don't need. I can't, however, sell them something they don't want. Even with advertising."[38] Where do you stand?

We believe it is important to note that while advertising may successfully persuade us to try a new product or service, it works no magical spell that mesmerizes us into continuing to be loyal to the product if we do not find it satisfactory.

The Sexual Image: Male and Female

What do advertisements reveal about the role of men and women in our society? How are members of each sex portrayed? For example, are women shown as homemakers while men are depicted as performing professional roles? Are women concerned that "their colors be more colorful and their whites whiter than white" while men are shown studying how they can enhance their economic investments? When ads put men and women in their place, into what type of place are they put? Are women shown serving, while men are shown receiving? A decade ago, it was written that "Advertising is an insidious propaganda machine for a male supremacist society. It spews out images of women as sex mates, housekeepers, mothers, and menial workers—images that . . . make it increas-

> **MEDIA PROBE**
>
> Watch television commercials and collect newspaper and magazine ads that include male and female models. To what extent does there appear to be one kind of male look that predominates? One kind of female look? Describe the typical male model and the type of activity in which he is engaged. Do the same for the typical female model. What conclusions, if any, are you able to draw?

ingly difficult for women to break out of the sexist stereotypes that imprison them."[39]

The Move to Curtail Liquor Advertising

It has been charged that advertising contributes to excessive alcohol consumption and that consequently beer and wine commercials should go the way of cigarette commercials and be banned from radio and television. (See Figure 10-4) Some critics go even further and advocate the prohibition of alco-

FIGURE 10-4 Alcohol advertising. (*M. Shanken Communications; USA Today, August 15, 1983.*)

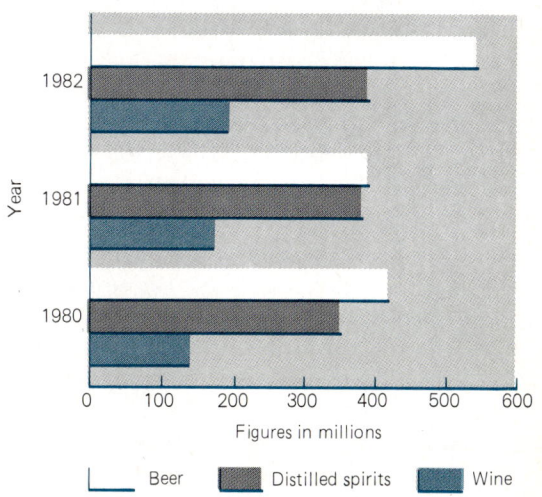

MEDIA PROBE

For each of the following questions prepare a position statement that describes your stand on the issue.

1. In your opinion, do advertisers have a moral obligation to disclose all the facts or just the facts that will accomplish their objectives? Why? Do you think advertising should tell you what a product is or how good it is? Should it present you with basic facts or a "floorshow"? Why or why not?
2. In your opinion, does advertising cause us to buy things we do not need or want? Why or why not?
3. In your opinion, has the way males and females have been portrayed in advertisements made it easier for us to stereotype them? Why or why not?
4. In your opinion, does advertising encourage "vulnerable groups" including teenagers and heavy drinkers to increase their intake of alcohol? Why or why not?
5. In your opinion, has political advertising ever influenced the way you or people you know voted? Do you think politicians should be marketed like products? Why or why not?

Supply examples of advertisements from various media to support each position you take.

---

holic-beverage advertising in newspapers as well.

Politics and Advertising: The Candidate as Product?

One recent study revealed that more voters based their decision on information received from television advertising than on information received from any other source.[40] One reason for this is that people confuse political commercials with news shows. Political media consultant David Garth notes, "A lot of times when we poll we ask people if they saw our commercials. They say, 'No, we saw you on the news. That was the news . . .' We use our commercials as a news vehicle."[41]

What are the differences that distinguish political advertising from traditional advertising? For one thing, in politics the product is a person. For another, while advertising may persuade you to buy a product once, unless you are satisfied with the way the product performs, you won't purchase it again. In contrast, when a political ad convinces you to vote for a candidate, you may be stuck with your "purchase" for many years to come. As newscaster Robert MacNeil writes: "If a TV commercial makes you like the image of one brand of toothpaste enough to buy a tube, it is no great matter if you find you don't like the stuff after all. You can quickly revert to the brand you like. If a TV commercial makes you like the image of a politician, it may be six years before you can change him, and he is next to impossible to throw away."[42]

The way you answer the questions posed above and in preceding sections of this chapter should help you decide how you believe the display window that is advertising should operate. Fairfax M. Cone, of Foote, Cone and Belding, Inc., noted, "Advertising is neither moral nor immoral. But being a representation by individuals, it is subject to all their character traits."

SUMMARY

Advertising is the paid, nonpersonal, and usually persuasive presentation of ideas, goods, and services by identified sponsors through various media. Each advertising message can be categorized in the following ways:

by audience (consumer or business); by advertiser (national or local); by medium or media used; and by what the ad is expected to do (create a demand for a generic product or service, a particular product or service, or sell an idea).

Exploring the history of advertising can help us understand the field as it is practiced today. The most significant event in the history of advertising was the invention of movable type by Johannes Gutenberg in 1440. This invention led to the use of printed posters, handbills, and, eventually, newspaper advertising. But it was the growth of the penny press that made advertising big business and led to the creation of brokerage services and full-scale advertising agencies. As new media came on the scene, the advertising industry continued to boom. Today, besides supporting commercial broadcasting, advertising also pays for approximately three-quarters of the newspapers and magazines we read.

Through the years, advertising has sought to fulfill a dual purpose: to inform and to persuade. To accomplish these goals, advertisers plan strategically; they rely on demographic, psychographic, and motivation research to facilitate this effort. Advertisers use research in order to identify the techniques, appeals, and media a particular target audience will respond to. The importance of making the right decisions regarding the target audience, the ad's message (verbal and nonverbal), and the medium or media used cannot be overemphasized.

The typical advertising agency has five predominant service groups in operation: the creative group (the people responsible for providing the design and copy for an ad); the media group (the people responsible for placing an ad in appropriate media); the account management group (the people who serve as the link between an agency and its client); the research group (the people who test, interpret, and evaluate agency efforts); and the financial services group (the people responsible for the overall operation of the agency).

In order to help protect the consumer from deceptive or misleading advertising a variety of controlling agencies ranging from the federal government (the FTC), to industry regulators (the NARB and the AAAA), to consumer groups have evolved.

However you feel about advertising, it is important that you consider the issues that reflect present concerns about the field; taking the time you need to do this will enable you to better assess the state of the profession today.

KEY TERMS

Advertising
Consumer advertising
Business advertising
National advertising
Local advertising
Direct-mail advertising
Primary advertising
Selective advertising
Image advertising
Public-service advertising

Siquis
Advertising agency
Demographics
Psychographics
Motivation research
Product claim
Weasel word
Federal Trade Commission
National Advertising Review Board

NOTES

[1] John O'Toole, *The Trouble With Advertising*, Chelsea House, New York, 1980, p. 17.

[2] S. R. Bernstein, "What Is Advertising? What Does It Do?" *Advertising Age*, November 21, 1973, p. 8.

[3] These are 1980 figures. See Courtland L. Bovee and William F. Arens, *Contemporary Advertising*, Richard D. Irwin, Homewood, Ill., 1982, p. 463.

[4] Quoted in S. W. Dunn and A. M. Barban, *Advertising: Its Role in Modern Marketing*, 4th ed., Dryden, Hindsdale, Ill., 1978.

[5] Frank Presby, *History and Development of Advertising*, Doubleday, New York, 1929, p. 8.

[6] James S. Norris, *Advertising*, Reston, Va., 1980, p. 3.

[7] Presby, op. cit., p. 17.

[8] Maurice I. Mandell, *Advertising*, 2d ed., Prentice-Hall, Englewood Cliffs, N.J., 1974, pp. 23–24.

[9] Dunn and Barban, op. cit., p. 23.
[10] Bovee and Arens, op. cit., p. 22.
[11] Louis Kaufman, *Essentials of Advertising*, Harcourt Brace Jovanovich, New York, 1980, pp. 10–11.
[12] S. R. Bernstein, op. cit., pp. 6–7.
[13] Bovee and Arens, op. cit., p. 11.
[14] Jeffrey Schrank, *Snap, Crackle and Popular Taste: The Illusion of Free Choice in America*, Dell, New York, 1977, p. 84.
[15] O'Toole, op. cit., pp. 89–90.
[16] Stephen Baker, *Systematic Approach to Advertising Creativity*, McGraw-Hill, New York, 1979, p. 41.
[17] See Eward Buxton, *Promise Them Anything*, Stein & Day, New York, 1972, p. 89, and Jim Fowles, "Advertising's Fifteen Basic Appeals," *ETC*, vol. 39, no. 3, 1982, p. 274.
[18] "The Teens," *Media Decisions*, August, October, and November, 1976.
[19] Joseph T. Plummer, "Life Style Patterns and Commercial Bank Credit Usage," *Journal of Marketing*, April, 1971, pp. 35–41.
[20] Laurence C. Lockley, "The Use of Motivation Research in Marketing," *Studies in Business Policy*, no. 97, National Industrial Conference Board, New York, 1960, p. 4.
[21] Buxton, op. cit., p. 219.
[22] Fowles, op. cit., p. 273.
[23] Jeffrey Schrank, op. cit., p. 101.
[24] Abraham Maslow, *Motivation and Personality*, Harper & Row, New York, 1954, pp. 90–92.
[25] Edward Spranger, *Types of Men*, P. Prigors, (trans.), M. Numeyer, 1928.
[26] Mark N. Grant, "I Got My Swimming Pool by Choosing Prell Over Brand X," *More Magazine*, 13, November, 1976.
[27] Quoted in Stuart Chase, *Danger: Men Talking*, Parents Magazine Press, New York, 1969, pp. 191–192.
[28] Bovee and Arens, op. cit., p. 142.
[29] 1981 Facts About Newspapers, p. 7.
[30] "How America Shops and Buys, Newspaper Advertising Bureau, Inc., 1983.
[31] Dunn and Barban, op. cit., p. 553.
[32] Radio Facts, 1983.
[33] Tony Schwartz, *Media: The Second God,* Anchor, New York, 1983, p. 54.
[34] Hooper White, "Has the Tide Run Out On the New Wave?" *Advertising Age,* March 7, 1983, p. M4.
[35] Susan Spielman, "Is TV Spot Zapping Zooming?" *Advertising Age,* June 27, 1983, pp. 1.
[36] See James V. O'Gara, "The Advertising Agency—What It Is and What It Does," *Advertising Age,* November 21, 1973, p. 34.
[37] John Crichton, "Morals and Ethics in Advertising," in Lee Thayer (ed.), *Ethics, Morality and the Media,* Hastings House, New York, 1980, p. 109.
[38] O'Toole, op. cit., p. 53.
[39] Vivian Gornick and Barbara K. Moran, *Women in Sexist Society,* New American Library, New York, 1971, p. 304.
[40] Donna Woolfolk Cross, *Media Speak,* Coward-McCann, New York, 1983, p. 170.
[41] Quoted in Sidney Blumenthal, *The Permanent Campaign,* Beacon, Boston, 1980, p. 79.
[42] Robert MacNeil, *The People Machine: The Influence of Television in American Politics,* Harper & Row, New York, 1968, pp. 193–194.

SUGGESTIONS FOR FURTHER READING

Arlen, Michael J.: *Thirty Seconds,* Farrar, Straus & Giroux, New York, 1980. *A humorous, engrossing, and in-depth look at the creation of a television commercial.*

Baker, Stephen: *Systematic Approach to Advertising Creativity,* McGraw-Hill, New York, 1979. *Treats the study of advertising as a whole, with the creative as the pivotal force.*

Betancourt, Hal: *The Advertising Answerbook,* Prentice-Hall, Englewood Cliffs, N.J., 1982. *A reference guide containing tips and suggestions.*

Bogart, Leo: *Strategy in Advertising,* Harcourt, Brace & World, New York, 1967. *A provocative commentary on advertising fads and fancies.*

Bovee, Courland L., and William F. Arens: *Contemporary Advertising,* Richard D. Irwin, Homewood, Ill., 1982. *A thorough survey of the field of advertising.*

Brower, Charlie: *Me and Other Advertising Geniuses,* Doubleday, New York, 1974. *The former president of BBDO looks at advertising.*

Busch, H. Ted, and Terry Landeck: *The Making of a Television Commercial.* Macmillan,

New York, 1980. *A comprehensive analysis of the world behind the TV ads and the people who make up that world.*

Buxton, Edward: *Promise Them Anything,* Stein & Day, New York, 1972. *An insider's view of Madison Avenue.*

Clymer, Floyd: *Early Advertising Art,* Bonanza Books, New York, 1955. *A delightful collection of old advertisements.*

Della Femina, Jerry: *From Those Wonderful Folks Who Gave You Pearl Harbor,* Simon & Schuster, New York, 1970. *An insider looks at advertising. Funny and readable.*

Dunn, S. W., and A. M. Barban: *Advertising: Its Role in Modern Marketing,* Dryden, Hinsdale, Ill., 1978. *A thorough text that introduces you to the complex and dramatic world of advertising.*

Engle, Jack: *Advertising: The Process and the Practice,* McGraw-Hill, New York, 1980. *A readable text that pays attention to retail, industrial, trade, professional, and international advertising.*

Ernst, Sandra: *The Creative Package: A Working Text for Advertising Copy and Layout,* Grid, Columbus, Ohio, 1979. *A how-to book that introduces you to the process of planning and creating advertising messages.*

Foster, G. Allen: *Advertising: Ancient Market Place to Television,* Criterion Books, New York, 1967. *A vivid and entertaining account of advertising methods from prehistoric times on.*

Galanoy, Terry: *Down the Tube,* Henry Regnery, Chicago, 1970. *A lighthearted and informative look at the wacky world of early television commercials.*

Glatzer, Robert: *The New Advertising,* Citadel, New York, 1970. *A behind the scenes look at twenty successful advertising campaigns.*

Kleppner, Otto: *Advertising Procedure,* 7th ed., Prentice-Hall, Englewood Cliffs, N.J., 1979. *A thorough examination of the planning, creation, use, and place of advertising in society.*

Ogilvy, David: *Confessions of an Advertising Man,* Atheneum, New York, 1963. *David Ogilvy reveals how he got clients, how to write effective copy, and how to get to the top.*

———: *Ogilvy on Advertising,* Crown, New York, 1983. *Another look at how this master won clients and created successful campaigns; anecdotal in approach.*

O'Toole, John: *The Trouble With Advertising,* Chelsea House, New York, 1981. *A practitioner's view of advertising—a look at what's right and wrong with advertising, how it works, and how it can work even better.*

Price, Jonathan: *The Best Thing on TV,* Viking, New York, 1978. *Commercials get their due; a perceptive look at how commercials are made, who watches them, and what they're supposed to accomplish.*

Reeves, Rosser: *Reality in Advertising,* Knopf, New York, 1961. *A how-to book by former chairman of the board of Ted Bates and Company.*

Rowsome, Frank, Jr.: *They Laughed When I Sat Down,* Bonanza Books, New York, 1959. *An informal history of eighty years of advertising in words and pictures.*

Schrank, Jeffrey: *Snap, Crackle and Popular Taste,* Dell, New York, 1977. *The Chapter on reading ads, "Advertising: The Engineers of Illusions," should not be missed.*

CHAPTER 11

PUBLIC RELATIONS: THE PRACTICE OF COMMUNICATION

I never saw a public relations person who, when open about everything, did his company any damage, assuming the company was a responsible one.
   Andy Rooney, CBS award-winning essayist

CHAPTER PREVIEW

After reading this chapter, you should be able to:
- Define public relations
- Explain why we all practice public relations
- Discuss what public relations is and is not
- Provide examples of public relations in action
- Discuss public relations activities
- Discuss the roots of modern public relations
- Define "public," "opinion," and "public opinion"
- Describe the way public opinion breaks down
- Identify strategies used to influence public opinion
- Explain what is meant by P + I + A + B
- Describe how Johnson & Johnson and the Mobil Corporation attempted to counter negative public opinion
- Explain what it means to lie and what it means to tell the truth
- Demonstrate an ability to use your own sense of ethics to respond to public relations problems
- Itemize the criteria John W. Hill found useful in determining those actions that are in the public interest
- Compare public relations and propaganda

Public relations. Two simple words. A growing field. But what do the words mean? What does the field involve? Why should we care? Let's begin to find out by considering some questions about you and public relations.

EXPLAINING PUBLIC RELATIONS

Do you practice public relations? More specifically,

Do you care what other people think of you? Why?
Do you ever find yourself actively seeking the approval of other people? Who? Why? Under what conditions?
Have you ever tried to secure the help of others in achieving your own goals? How?
Was there ever a time when not having others support you caused you problems? In what ways?

If you care what others think of you, if you actively work to gain the approval of persons important to you, if you try to create conditions that will motivate others to help facilitate your own growth and development, and if you succeed in eliminating those obstacles that could prevent you from achieving your goals, then whether you are consciously aware of it or not, you are practicing public relations.

To various extents we all practice public relations. From the day we realized that how we acted, what we said, and how we looked affected how others viewed us, most of us have taken steps to encourage others to view us positively. In other words, we have used our own brand of personal public relations to build and reinforce as favorable an image or reputation of ourselves in the minds of others as we could. This is essentially what professional public relations is all about. Just as we need help to accomplish our aims and reach our objectives, so do all profit and non-for-profit organizations. Today, few, if any, individuals or organizations can succeed without receiving support from others. As public relations counselor Philip Lesly writes: "Perhaps the most important force affecting all organizations and governments today is the opinion of the people."

Emergent Definitions: A Potpourri of Concerns

Webster's New Collegiate Dictionary defines public relations as "the business of inducing the public to have understanding for and goodwill toward a person, firm, or institution." Philip Lesly develops the idea of goodwill even further. He notes that with the aid of public relations, institutions and people are able to learn what others think of them, determine what they must do to get the goodwill of others, devise ways to win that good will, and carry on programs designed to secure goodwill. Thus, for Lesly, public relations is a bridge to goodwill.[1]

Public relations practitioners assert that it is unfortunate that we do not think about the value of goodwill often enough. In fact, they report that sometimes it seems that people only realize the importance of goodwill once it is missing. Just as individuals learn to appreciate good health the hard way—when they have lost it—so institutions, corporations, or personal clients learn to appreciate goodwill the hard way—when it is absent and a crisis is upon them.

MEDIA PROBE

1. Identify specific instances in your own life when not having the goodwill of your peers, instructors, or supervisors caused problems for you.
2. Identify specific instances in your own life when having the goodwill of your peers, instructors, or supervisors facilitated things for you.

MEDIA VIEW

Increasingly, corporate leaders are becoming convinced that an organized and systematic program to win friends and influence people—that is, PR—is the remedy for the varied tribulations that beset their companies....

The corporation, more than ever, is operating in what David I. Margolis, president of Colt Industries Inc., calls a "pressure-cooker" environment. It is under siege from consumerists, environmentalists, women's liberation advocates, the civil rights movement, and other activist groups. Their demands are being steadily translated into an unprecedented wave of intervention by federal and state governments into the affairs of business. Even without government interference, the activists are forcing changes in corporate operating policies that range from a halt in loans to South Africa to curtailment of infant milk formula sales in less developed countries.

The corporation also faces intensified competition in the marketplace, the growing threat of takeover by outsiders, and new challenges in employee relations. And all the while, the corporate community continues to be plagued by a negative public image. Only 22 percent of the general population has confidence in business leadership, down from 55 percent at the beginning of the decade, according to pollster Louis Harris. "A PR problem today does not simply mean loss of good will," says John J. Bell, senior vice-president for communications at the Bank of America. "It threatens a corporation's ability to achieve its business goals."

"The Corporate Image: PR to the Rescue," *Business Week,* January 22, 1979, p. 47.

MEDIA VIEW

IMAGE AGENCIES THRIVE ON CRISES

The executive begins by defending his company against charges of pollution before a skeptical city council. Then he rushes to meet with angry representatives of minority groups who complain of employment discrimination. After that, he fields rumors that his plant is about to lay off hundreds of workers. Just as a horrid day is about to end, an explosion hits the plant and in the resulting chaos the executive must deal with TV cameramen and reporters clamoring to cover the story.

That's a day in Crisisport, a mythical world devised by Burson-Marsteller, where actors push executives into tough situations (managers from, Standard Oil of Indiana's Amoco are currently being run through the mill in Chicago). Crisis management, especially in the wake of criticism surrounding confusing public pronouncements in the Three Mile Island nuclear accident, is becoming a sought-after skill, and public-relations firms, whose main job used to be to encourage favorable news coverage of clients, are increasingly being called on to provide the training. Such crisis-coping is not the only growth area for public-relations firms these days. Companies are turning to them for help in lobbying, aiding corporate mergers and dealing with employee programs....

In the last several years corporate executives have come to rely more heavily on public-relations counselors. "Public relations has been a defensive type of business," said William Durbin, chairman of Hill & Knowlton (who announced Friday that he planned to step down as chairman). "But quite a few companies are becoming increasingly aware that they don't like to be surprised. They want to know what is going to hit them one year down the road."

Chief executives, who often have backgrounds in marketing or finance, find themselves spending 25 percent or more of their time dealing with the press, Congress or pressure groups. Often the chief executive is at a loss on how to handle his new public role.

Besides writing speeches, public-relations agencies coach executives on how to face the public, often in circumstances similar to the Burson-Marsteller program. Ruder & Finn, Hill & Knowlton and other leading agencies have mock television studios where executives can prepare for interview by sitting under lights and facing a panel of hostile questioners. The performance is videotaped and criticized. . . .

"The environment in which business operates today is becoming so complex that no matter how good an internal staff is it can't cover all the bases," said C. Ramon Greenwood, senior vice president for public affairs of the American Express Company.

A week after the accident at the Three Mile Island nuclear generating plant Metropolitan Edison, operator of the facility, retained Hill & Knowlton, an international operation with 672 employees. The electric utility had agreed that all statements to the press would be issued by the Nuclear Regulatory Commission. So the normal press responsibilities—and the blame for dissemination of confusing material—went to the Government. The agency's job was to present the company's views to its employees and to the nearby community. Its Washington and New York offices also helped monitor press reports coming from the national wire services and other media. The Washington office monitored Congressional hearings on the accident, and when officials from the utilities holding company were called to testify, the agency helped brief them.

"We advised them on what they might expect," said Richard C. Hyde, senior vice president of Hill & Knowlton. "So that they would go into those hearings as well prepared as possible."

Some of the largest firms monitor social trends and political developments. The 60-member Washington staff of Hill & Knowlton observes Congressional action and sometimes attends committee hearings, reporting on what happens and how it might affect clients. Some staff members of large agencies register as lobbyists, supplying Congressmen with information supporting a client's case on issues ranging from product labeling to tax equity for Americans abroad.

American industry's craze for takeovers has been a boon to public relations. Firms work closely with lawyers and financial officers, advising on how to phrase responses and deal with the press. Manning, Selvage & Lee, the seventh largest firm with billings of $4.67 million, works with management to prepare a step-by-step plan that is activated in the event of a takeover. Some clients have been Pabst, Endicott Johnson and Elgin National Watch.

In the case of takeover defenses, Manning surveys shareholders and, working with the client's chief financial officer, prepares reasons why the shareholder should not tender his shares. Plans are made to reach the shareholders quickly, with addressed envelopes kept at the ready for a speedy mailing.

Another big growth area for the agencies has been employee communications. In the past, corporations tended to limit their efforts to chatty house organs. In recent years public-relations agencies have been advising companies on programs using videotape and other techniques to explain why productivity increases can help save jobs and how inflation affects the company. When layoffs are ordered, some companies make an effort to announce the move ahead of time and present the company's view.

Stan Luxenberg, "Image Agencies Thrive on Crises," *The New York Times,* July 29, 1979, p. F9.

As we see, it is becoming more and more apparent that companies need to take steps to prevent the loss of good will, as well as implement programs to help them anticipate and alleviate trouble effectively. Decisions regarding how to win, regain, or maintain the goodwill of relevant groups of people are made every day, and are an overwhelming force in contributing to the success or failure of individuals and institutions.

So what is public relations? Public relations is planned, purposeful communication that is designed to influence and persuade significant publics. Theorist Lawrence Nolte supports this perception. He writes that by public relations we mean "an activity whose purpose is to affect the attitudes and opinions of the public."[2] And E. J. Robinson also reflects this view in his definition.[3] According to Robinson, public relations is an applied social and behavioral science that

1. Measures, evaluates, and interprets the attitudes of the various relevant publics
2. Assists management in defining objectives for increasing public understanding and acceptance of the organization's products, plans, policies, and personal
3. Equates these objectives with the interests, needs, and goals of the various relevant publics
4. Develops, executes, and evaluates a program to earn public understanding and acceptance

Public Relations News mentions many of these same points in its definition, one that has earned widespread acceptance: "Public relations is the management function which evaluates public attitudes, identifies the policies and procedures of an individual or organization with the public interest and plans and executes a program of action to earn public understanding and acceptance." John Marston, practitioner and author of *Modern Public Relations,* refined this definition by adding the words "and communication" after the words "a program of action."[4]

But what do these definitions tell us about the practice of public relations? First, they tell us that management is responsible for the public relations function. Second, they tell us that the public relations arm of an organization is responsible for identifying public attitudes and needs. And third, they tell us that it is the responsibility of the public relations arm of an organization to take steps to realize those needs. So we could say that *public relations* is the planned, two-way communication effort through which an individual or organization strives to win the understanding, acceptance, support, and cooperation of the public. Note the inclusion of the words "two-way communication." As we shall see, public relations is not simply a one-way street. Public relations does not just benefit the individual or organization that desires public support and cooperation. Public relations is not self-centered. Rather, public relations is also a channel through which the public can make known its concerns and needs. For this reason, public relations helps individuals or organizations and their relevant publics adapt to each other. If done well, public relations can help establish and nourish multidirectional lines of communication between individuals or organizations and their publics.

What Public Relations Is and What It Is Not

Public relations is a familiar but misunderstood term. Despite the fact that it is all but impossible to function in society today without paying attention to public relations, prejudices about the field persist and misconceptions abound. Let us clear up some of those misunderstandings by examining the world of public relations.

The world of public relations is an ever-expanding one. As our world increases in complexity, it becomes more important for the institutions of our society to be able to communicate with selected groups of people (other businesses, employees, customers, stockholders, communities, and the government), and more important for the people to have their feelings and opinions transmitted and listened to by the institution. But public relations is not just words. Public relations is not just empty phrases. Rather, public relations is action; public relations is behavior. In other words, from a public relations perspective, what an institution says should not be contradicted by what the institution does. Public relations should not be an effort to make people believe what is untrue. But far too frequently that is the conception people have. As Stephen A. Greyser noted in his address to the Thirty-Third National Conference of the Public Relations Society of America: "It is important for public affairs/public relations professionals to recognize how and why it could be said in the 1920's that 'the business of America is business' and why that view is less widely accepted today."[5] Today's public relations professionals know that the attitudes and beliefs of people matter. Today's public relations professionals know that a favorable climate of opinion is needed if an institution is to secure public understanding and acceptance. But how is this achieved? What are the tools used by the practitioner to secure public understanding and acceptance?

Where is the hand of the public relations professional found? Examples are numerous.

> A new 500-bed medical center needs assistance in developing a community relations program...
>
> A high tech software manufacturer can't afford an advertising blitz but wants exposure for a new product line...
>
> A controversial chemical manufacturer wants media training prior to a grilling by 60-MINUTES...
>
> A corporate giant panics when a national product recall threatens to damage the reputation of a well-known household name...

MEDIA PROBE

1. Using this week's newspapers, magazines, and television and radio offerings, locate concrete examples of public relations in action.
2. After examining your examples, identify the tools that were used to conduct the activity that is public relations.

> What do all these organizations have in common?
>
> They all need public relations.[6]

Public relations has been called upon to improve the image of the potato chip, and it has been used to try to convince us to use the Susan B. Anthony dollar. It has been useful in helping companies handle crises when the practitioner is skilled.

Though some of these examples might cause you to chuckle, public relations is a serious business. Whenever we read about, view, or listen to a story about a product recall or ingredient scare we have encountered public relations. Whenever we listen to a speech by a corporate official or political figure, read a release about an organization or public figure, or see a segment on the news provided free of charge by a corporation, we have met public relations. Whenever we attend a grand opening or other celebration, we are experiencing public relations. When a corporation contributes to public television, public relations is at work. When we attend a charity dinner or read an annual report, we are tasting the effects of public relations. When we attend a press conference, participate in a demonstration, or visit a lobbyist's office, we are witness to public relations. And when we conduct or ponder the results of an opinion poll, we are measuring or considering a measurement of public relations.

Each of the preceding stimulus events is designed to influence public understanding,

"We ought to consider taking Freedley off crisis management."

(Drawing by Stevenson, © 1981 *The New Yorker* Magazine, Inc.)

MEDIA VIEW

PUBLIC RELATIONS: TWO VIEWS

The potato-chip industry plans a $200,000 campaign to brighten the snack food's image, but already the drive is in trouble. In an editorial, the St. Louis Post-Dispatch says potato chips "have almost no redeeming nutritional value." It added that polishing the potato chip's image "is like trying to portray Attila the Hun as a pioneer in urban renewal."

From "The Wall Street Journal."

In show business, when a performer's reputation is in trouble, his managers often hire a public relations firm. In what is believed to be a first in the annals of government currency, the Federal Reserve hired a PR agency for the Susan B. Anthony dollar: DWJ Associates, located in Manhattan. The fee was $150,000.

"Our job was to get the good story out about the coin," said Michael Friedman, executive vice-president of the PR firm. "But we made a false assumption. We assumed that there would be good stories to get out. There weren't. The negative thing got rolling, and it never stopped..."

"We were looking for any little piece of good news about the coin, so we could feed it to the networks and the wire services. But nothing good ever happened. Anywhere."

Friedman has his own theory of why the coin failed. He feels that, especially in a time of inflation, the Anthony dollar didn't *look* like a dollar; it was so small that people refused to take it seriously.

"Look, I used it, but I stopped after six months," Friedman said. "I got sick of it. I got sick of walking into the bank and having the tellers say 'Here comes that nut.' I got sick of fighting with cab drivers."

DWJ Associates has scrapebooks filled with news stories about the Anthony dollar. Getting space in the papers wasn't the problem. The problem was that people had already made up their minds that they wanted nothing to do with it.

Bob Green in "Heads You Lose," *Esquire,* April 1981, p. 14.

PUBLIC RELATIONS: THE PRACTICE OF COMMUNICATION

Public relations, by its very nature, thrives on special events—openings, announcements, fanfare. (Elizabeth Hamlin/Stock, Boston)

and affect the attitudes and opinions of relevant people. But public relations is composed of a group of activities; it is never just one. In the case of public relations, the whole is more than the sum of its parts.

Traditionally, the following activities are included as part of the public relations function: publicity (the placement of newsworthy information in print or broadcast form in the media); opinion research (taking the pulse of the public, conducting polls, surveys, and tests to determine the mood of the public); press agentry and special-event management (the planning or staging of events designed to attract public attention); promotion and fund raising (the effort to attract personal and financial support for a person, product, institution or idea); lobbying (the petitioning of the government to support legislation in the best interest of the client); public affairs (performing political, educational, and civic service functions in order to cooperate with and support the community); institutional advertising (aiding in the creation of advertisements designed to sell ideas or images); gift giving (the act of screening, evaluating, and making recommendations for the dispersement of grants); creating the printed voice of the institution or person (writing speeches, reports, and brochures designed to appeal to selected groups of people), and counseling (advising clients on courses of action prior to, during, and after the decision-making process).

The point is that each of these activities plays its part in performing the public relations function, but no one of them alone or clustered in a combination with two or three others approximates the total function. So public relations is not only *publicity*. It does not consist solely of succeeding in having stories appear in or on the news media. Neither is public relations only *press agentry* or *lobbying*. Public relations involves more—much more. In fact, each day you are surrounded by diverse examples of public relations in action. It's time to begin paying attention to public relations–related communication.

THE PUBLIC RELATIONS PRACTITIONER

The label "public relations" was not used until the twentieth century, but the practice

MEDIA PROBE

Working as a group or individually, interview a local independent or corporate public relations practitioner about his or her job, and prepare a report for the class. In your report, provide specific examples that illustrate the types of work performed by the individual.

> ### YOU WERE THERE
>
> **BUSINESS AND THE PRESS: THE CREDIBILITY GAP**
>
> Television newsman Martin Agronsky, anchoring a "special report" on the fertilizer industry, announces, "We take you now to Donaldsonville, La., and Joan Levetter."
>
> Joan Levetter, standing in front of a plant that makes ammonia, a component of chemical fertilizer, interviews a plant official, then sums up: "If we didn't supplement our soil with nitrogen-bearing compounds, millions of the world's cupboards would be bare and food prices would skyrocket. Fertilization is not merely desirable, it is essential. This is Joan Levetter reporting. Martin?"
>
> Back in the studio, Agronsky looks at what appears to be a TV monitor on which he presumably sees correspondent Levetter. He says, "Thank you, Joan," and continues his narration.
>
> Just another dull television news feature? So it must have seemed to TV viewers in San Francisco, New Orleans, Cincinnati, and other cities. But, "And One to Grow On" is no ordinary TV news feature. For one thing, it was produced not by any news organization, but by the chemical fertilizer industry. For another, the news room, anchor desk, and TV monitor were all fake. Agronsky only pretended to be able to see and talk with reporters in the field. And they weren't reporters. "Joan Levetter," for one, is actually an actress under another name.
>
> The Fertilizer Institute, which is the trade association of manufacturers of chemical fertilizers, says it made "And One to Grow On" to help disassociate fertilizers in the public's mind from the unfavorable publicity that has tarnished pesticides. It says it chose a television newscast format to give the 18 minute film immediacy and credibility, and it omitted any reference to the Fertilizer Institute's sponsorship to enhance the film's acceptance by TV as a "public service" program.
>
> A. Kent MacDougall, "Business and the Press: The Credibility Gap," *Washington Journalism Review*, July/August 1981, pp. 20–25.

of public relations extends far back in history—probably to the time that social groups first formed. Direct evidence exists that public relations was being practiced over 4000 years ago. A cuneiform tablet excavated in Iraq served as a bulletin to tell farmers how to harvest, sow, and irrigate their crops; in many ways, this tablet was a forerunner of the many notices released by the United States Department of Agriculture. The commentaries of Julius Caesar are also cited as skillful examples of public relations in action since they helped persuade people that Caesar was a great and able leader and thus paved the way for his takeover of Rome. The Greeks and Romans also used public relations skills to promote their cultures. In both countries people were paid by ruling governments to write poetry or develop verbal arguments that would help mold public opinion. Thus, the roots of political communication and lobbying delve deep into history.

But public relations was not used just to convey information or advance political ambitions or culture; it was also used to promote religion. One of the earliest public relations organizations was the Society for the Propagation of the Faith, an organization whose goal it was to increase membership in the Roman Catholic church.[7]

In the United States, during the colonial period and the Revolutionary War public relations techniques were used to garner support for the independence movement. For

The Boston Tea Party was really a public relations event, with Yankees in Indian guise dramatizing resistance to the Stamp Act. (Culver Pictures)

example, Samuel Adams led the communications phase of the revolution by organizing committees of correspondence to write letters protesting English rule, by holding meetings that gave colonists the opportunity to voice their opposition to colonial status, and by staging events (the Boston Tea Party, for one) that dramatized the plight of the colonists. These events precipitated publicity that carried the arguments of the colonists to the public. In the decades that followed American independence, similar techniques and media would be relied upon—newspapers, magazines, phamphlets, public meetings, speeches, and songs.

One of the first men to understand the advantages of the newspaper (then, the penny press) as a means to reach the public was Phineas Taylor Barnum, the owner of a circus museum. A man who displayed a sharp ability to stage events that gained him free press attention and intrigued the public, Barnum was a nineteenth-century precurser of today's professional publicist and the acknowledged king of public relations pioneers.[8] Among the people Barnum made famous were the midget, Tom Thumb and the "Swedish nightingale," Jenny Lind. Thumb traveled with Barnum and his entourage to Europe in 1844, where they were received by Queen Victoria. Some years later, he and Barnum would also be invited to visit Abraham Lincoln in the White House. Credited with coining the phrase, "There's a sucker born every minute," Barnum's keen understanding of people and what aroused public interest paved the road for the generations of press agents that followed him.

The era of the industrial revolution was exemplified by people like William Vanderbilt, J. P. Morgan, and John D. Rockefeller, individuals who were reputed to be more concerned with making a profit than benefiting humanity. For instance, when queried about the public's reaction to his closing a New York-to-Chicago passenger train, Vanderbilt responded, "The public be damned! I am working for my stockholders; if the public wants the train, why don't they pay for it?" It is not surprising that Vanderbilt and others like him were cursed by Americans, called "robber barons," and targeted for exposure by the muckrakers. Two of the best known muckrakers were Upton Sinclair, author of *The Jungle*, in which the deplorable conditions of the meat-packing industry were attacked and Ida M. Tarbell, author of *The History of Standard Oil*, a work that exposed the unfair business practices of the nation's leading petroleum firm, a company headed by John D. Rockefeller.

This era hastened the emergence of practitioners whose task it was to alter the public's opinion of these large corporations. One of the best known of these public relations practitioners was Ivy Ledbetter Lee. Lee stressed that the key to public acceptance and support of business was an honest information program. In 1906, while working on behalf of the anthracite coal industry, Lee sent to newspaper editors his "Declaration of Principles."

> This is not a secret press bureau. All our work is done in the open. We aim to supply news. This is not an advertising agency; if you think any of our matter ought properly to go to your business office, do not use it. Our matter is accurate. Further details on any subject treated will be supplied promptly, and any editor will be assisted most cheerfully in verifying any statement of fact.... In brief, our plan is frankly and openly, on behalf of business concerns and public institutions, to supply to the press and public of the United States prompt and accurate information concerning subjects which it is of value and interest to the public to know about.[9]

In time, Lee would also represent the family of John D. Rockefeller, Jr. Because of the efforts he made to humanize the Rockefellers and the favorable publicity he generated for them the family's reputation improved. Lee represented his clients well before the court of public opinion, so well that the Rockefeller family came to be recognized as one of the nation's outstanding philanthropic sources. Called "the father of modern public relations," Ivy Lee did not believe in the suppression of bad information; instead, he believed if you were candid and truthful, in due course, public confidence and trust would be won. Among the public relations tools Lee developed was the written handout, an addition that made the reporters job easier and also increased the likelihood that positive information about a client would be printed.

Other practitioners soon followed in Lee's footsteps. With the advent of World War I, even the government made use of public relations by establishing the Committee on Public Information headed by George Creel. The *Creel Committee* effectively mobilized public opinion in support of the war and stimulated the sale of war bonds.

Two practitioners trained by Creel would go on to become famed practitioners in their own right: they are Edward L. Bernays, author of *Crystallizing Public Opinion,* the first book on the field of public relations, and Carl Byoir, founder of the public relations firm Carl Byoir and Associates. Begun in 1930, this firm is still one of the world's leading public relations organizations.

Also during the 1930s, George Gallup, Elmor Roper, and others added another dimension to the practice of public relations by developing modern public opinion marketing and survey techniques. With the addition of these tools, public relations counselors could now evaluate public attitudes quantitatively.

In addition, the great depression of the 1930s provided American corporations with an impetus to tell their side of the story. Among the companies that created public relations departments to help them fill that need were Bendix, Eastman Kodak, and U.S. Steel. Because practitioners were successful in regaining the trust of the American people in big business, the field as a whole earned respect and enjoyed a strong position during World War II and the subsequent decade.

Then once more public trust in large institutions waned during the 1960s. The conflicts of the period paved the way for a new consumer movement, a renewed equal rights movement, and an awakened concern for the environment. As before, public relations practitioners were called upon to help.

The 1970s saw public relations become a first-line responsibility. Corporations aban-

MEDIA PROBE

THE PUBLIC RELATIONS PERSONALITY CHECKLIST

Rate each item yes or no. Each yes counts for four points. A no doesn't count. Anything below 60 is a poor score. A score between 60 and 80 suggests you should analyze your weak areas and take steps to correct them. Scores above 80 indicate an effective public relations personality.

Good sense of humor
Positive and optimistic
Friendly, meet people easily
Can keep a conversation going with anybody
Take frustration and rejection in stride
Able to persuade others easily
Well-groomed, businesslike appearance
Flair for showmanship
Strong creative urge
Considerate and tactful
Adept in use of words
Able to gain management's confidence
Enjoy being with people
Enjoy listening
Enjoy helping other people resolve problems
Curious about many things
Enjoy reading in diverse areas
Determined to complete projects
High energy level
Can cope with sudden emergencies
See mistakes as learning experiences
Factual and objective
Respect other people's viewpoint
Perceptive and sensitive
Quickly absorb and retain information

Cantor, "The Public Relations Personality Checklist," *Public Relations Journal,* June 1983, p. 30–31.

---

doned the posture of confrontation and adopted instead the policy of conciliation and compromise.

In general, the public of the 1980s is better informed and more aware than the publics of preceding decades. And so are the public relations practitioners who are charged with the responsibility of communicating with them. To be sure, today's public relations field is an accepted and well-established one.

COMMUNICATION AND PUBLIC RELATIONS

If *public opinion* were unimportant or inconsequential, there would probably be no public relations. But public opinion does matter, and efforts to influence it is what public relations is all about. Just how important is public opinion? In the eyes of public relations educator Walt Siefert, it is all-important; in fact, Seifert is fond of noting that for all practical purposes, "the United States Supreme Court is not the highest court in our land." In Seifert's eyes, "Our highest court is the court of Public Opinion, which meets every hour."[10] So in our society, public opinion is quite an influential force. Positive public opinion can help an aspiring candidate win an election, raise the selling price of a stock, fill the coffers of a charitable organization, attract employees to an organization, and increase the likelihood that community members will view an organization as a good corporate neighbor. In contrast, adverse public opinion can spell failure for a political candidate, a product, a not-for-profit corporation, or a business. But what exactly is public opinion? And what must the practitioner understand about public opinion if he or she is to hope to sway it? Let us examine these questions next.

In order to understand the concept of public opinion, we will begin by dividing the term into its two components, that is, *public* and *opinion*. A public may be thought of as a group of people who have something in common and are united by that common bond. Particular publics are affected by and in turn can affect the operation of organizations or institutions; in addition, they may participate in the definition and dialogue about current public issues. We are all indentified with several publics. For example, you may now be part of a community, school, investor, political, religious, or employee public. As such, you belong to a group of individuals who are interested in a common subject, higher wages, better dividends, or an improved quality of life, for instance.

Now, what is an opinion? We all have opinions, and at one time or another, we all talk about our opinions. An opinion is simply what you get in response to a question you pose to another individual about a controversial topic. From the individual's utterances—that is, from his or her expressions of opinion—you are then able to infer his or her *attitudes* toward the subject. For opinion to become public opinion a consensus about the controversial issue must develop within a group or public. Thus, public opinion is the sum of individual opinions on an issue or issues affecting the group. When enough individuals have the same opinion, we can then talk of public opinion. At this point, let us see the various way public opinion can break down.

Rate the following statements on a 7-point scale.

1. Grades should be abolished.

Fully agree	Mostly agree	Slightly agree	Neutral	Slightly disagree	Mostly disagree	Fully disagree
___	___	___	___	___	___	___

2. Capital punishment should be prohibited.

Fully agree	Mostly agree	Slightly agree	Neutral	Slightly disagree	Mostly disagree	Fully disagree
___	___	___	___	___	___	___

3. Abortion should be prohibited.

Fully agree	Mostly agree	Slightly agree	Neutral	Slightly disagree	Mostly disagree	Fully disagree
___	___	___	___	___	___	___

4. The federal government should provide all citizens with national health insurance.

Fully agree	Mostly agree	Slightly agree	Neutral	Slightly disagree	Mostly disagree	Fully disagree
___	___	___	___	___	___	___

5. Only individuals who live in your community should be permitted to work in your community.

Fully agree	Mostly agree	Slightly agree	Neutral	Slightly disagree	Mostly disagree	Fully disagree
___	___	___	___	___	___	___

Analyzing the results indicated on the scales should reveal the status of public opinion on each of the preceding issues. On which issues did students agree with each other? On which issues were they equally divided? On which issues were they passive or neutral? If 90 percent support a position, only 5 percent are neutral and only 5 percent oppose the position, we can be relatively comfortable saying that public opinion favors it. If only 5 percent support a position, 5 percent oppose it, and 90 percent are neutral, we can say that there is currently no public opinion on the subject. And if 50 percent favor a position, while 50 percent oppose it, then we can say that public opinion is equally divided. So we see that on some issues we achieve a consensus, on some issues opinions are polarized, and for others minds have not been made up. The strength of an individual's opinion may also be analyzed by examining how disposed he or she felt toward the concept being measured. While a number of us may approve or disapprove of an issue, we may do so to varying degrees. Thus, while the direction of our ratings may be similar, the comparative strength or *intensity* of our ratings may be different. Not all people who support a position support it equally. Finally, some of the statements made above may have had more relevance to some people than to others. We call those statements that were most important or significant to you and your lifestyle *salient* to you. The important thing to keep in mind is that public opinion can and does change, sometimes very rapidly. And in order to influence public opinion you need to know how to communicate with and influence people.

As public opinion has grown in importance so have efforts to sway it. The key tool practitioners rely on to help them bring about changes in public opinion is persuasion. According to Cutlip and Center, the basic objective of most public relations efforts is to alter or neutralize hostile opinions, crystallize unformed or latent opinions, or maintain favorable opinions by reinforcing them.[11] To guide them as they work, practitioners use a number of different strategies, not the least of which is the public relations plan, a document that sets forth the goals and objectives, methods and media of a particular public relations program. In any campaign there are at least five questions practitioners need to answer.

MEDIA PROBE

Select an issue on which public opinion has changed during recent months. Who appears to be responsible for the change? Identify the individuals, groups, or organizations involved. How did these forces contribute to the change? For example, what messages did they send, through what media, to what receivers, with what effect? Who opposed their efforts? Why do you think they were successful, while those in opposition to them were not?

1. How do we hope to affect public opinion? What are our objectives? Whose support and cooperation do we need to achieve our goals? Who are our target publics?
2. In how many different ways and using how many different media can our objectives be accomplished?
3. What are the potential risks and benefits of each of the preceding choices?
4. Which choices should we select?
5. How will we evaluate the effectiveness of our efforts?

Setting objectives, developing strategies, and planning are essential if the public relations effort is to succeed. Most coordinated public relations efforts rely on a variety of media to achieve their goals; for example, they might use advertising, public speeches, and presentations, feature articles and films, print and broadcast news releases, press conferences, brochures, newsletters and reports, bulletin

YOU WERE THERE

THE "RESELLING" OF TYLENOL

On December 19, 1982, this report was broadcast on the CBS *Evening News.*
MIKE WALLACE: On the evening of September 30, 1982, millions of Americans heard some startling, sad news.
DAN RATHER: Good evening. This is the CBS *Evening News,* Dan Rather reporting. A bizarre and terrifying story today in the Chicago suburbs of Arlington Heights and Elk Grove Village. A 12-year-old girl and two men who were brothers are dead after taking poison capsules of Extra-Strength Tylenol.
WALLACE: The Tylenol poisonings have triggered one of the biggest FBI manhunts in recent history. But this is not a crime story; it is a business story—the reselling of Tylenol—about the crucial decisions made by the people at Johnson and Johnson, Tylenol's parent company.

Before the cyanide-laced extra-strength capsules caused several deaths, Tylenol had been the leading pain reliever, with a 37 percent share of the total analgesic market. It had a solid reputation with physicians and consumers, and then urban terrorism—terrorism that strikes in the home where we had felt safe and secure—lashed out at Tylenol and its users, causing the company's market share to plummet to 6 percent. But Johnson & Johnson came back and survived the biggest scare in history, averting a corporate catastrophe and leading the way in packaging improvements. The story of Johnson & Johnson's handling of the Tylenol murders has been widely praised and hailed by some as a textbook case in turning around a nightmare and demonstrating how responsible big business can be when the public welfare is at stake.

To help Johnson & Johnson cope with the crisis, James Burke, chief executive officer at Johnson & Johnson, set up an emergency executive committee that met twice daily for six weeks. At the same time, Burson Marsteller, the company's public relations firm, was busy conducting daily research interviews with people in order to gauge the public's attitude toward Tylenol. Research results showed that the people were afraid to use Tylenol, but also that they did not blame Johnson & Johnson for what had occurred; instead, most people said they viewed Johnson & Johnson as a victim. Initially, Johnson & Johnson had made a decision to communicate from a knowledge base. They cooperated with the media, the FBI, and the FDA, and because company surveys had shown that advertising at this time might offend the public further, they also cancelled all advertising for Tylenol capsules. Interestingly, research revealed that at this time, advertising was not really necessary anyway. Owing to a plethora of publicity about the cyanide murders, more people knew Tylenol's story than could name the president of the United States; over 90 percent of the people questioned knew of the tragedy, and 90 percent also knew it involved Tylenol capsules only. Then, at a cost of $100 million, Johnson & Johnson made the decision to withdraw all Tylenol capsule products from the marketplace. The company offered either to exchange these capsules for Tylenol tablets or to provide holders with a full cash refund. This move helped to establish the company's totally responsive public posture. In addition, Johnson & Johnson set up special phone lines and trained phone crews to field inquiries from concerned consumers; they also sent out 450,000 electronic messages of warning to members of the medical community.

As weeks passed and the crisis atmosphere subsided, the real problem facing Johnson & Johnson was how to get their product back into the marketplace. With no Tylenol capsules on the shelves, Johnson & Johnson's competitors were ready to move into the lucrative vacuum their absence created. At this point, James Burke and his committee made the brave decision to keep the Tylenol name and relaunch the product, this time in a tamper-resistant container. For their plan to succeed, they first had to restore faith in their product among doctors, retailers, and consumers. It was at this juncture that Johnson & Johnson mobilized a task force of 2500 Johnson & Johnson employees; their task was to make thousands of visits to members of the medical and retail publics. They were successful. Doctors agreed to recommend Tylenol to patients once it returned to the market and retailers agreed to keep the shelf space empty while awaiting the product's return. At this point, Burson Marsteller and Johnson & Johnson made another key decision: they reasoned that since the media had unwittingly contributed to Tylenol's problem by giving it so much publicity (and making it the key news event in 1982), the media also held a potential solution. It was, they believed, the nation's journalists who could provide Johnson & Johnson with a much-needed coast-to-coast information network. After making and running a number of public-service announcements, Johnson & Johnson decided to use a thirty-city media teleconference as the nationwide platform from which they would relaunch Tylenol. Such a satellite hookup usually takes ninety days to plan; Johnson & Johnson gave themselves but one week. During this brief time they developed the conference's format, produced videotape segments, drafted mailgram invitations, and prepared 7500 press kits. Even though expensive, the total cost of the conference was less than a thirty-second spot on the Super Bowl.

The results? The November 11, 1983, teleconference attended by 600 reporters received extensive media coverage on both network and local TV and radio stations; in addition, the average newspaper across the country provided 32 column inches of coverage. Following this media event, Jim Burke and Johnson & Johnson executives made television and radio appearances on a number of shows, including *The Phil Donahue Show, Today, Nightline,* and local news programs. To prepare their executives to meet the media, Johnson & Johnson arranged for all involved to attend an executive TV workshop. At the same time, Johnson & Johnson also took steps to give their product back to consumers by printing 80 million free Tylenol coupons.

What is noteworthy is that through each phase of the crises, from tragedy to comeback, Johnson & Johnson made every effort to communicate with its employee and stockholder publics. The company used letters, employee publications, specially produced videotapes, and a special brochure to keep people apprised of the situation.

On January 2, 1984, Johnson & Johnson resumed running TV ads for Tylenol. Print advertising began again in early February 1984. Today, Tylenol is again the number one product in its field.

Adapted from discussions with Larry Foster, vice president, Johnson & Johnson, and Jim Dowling, president, Burson Marsteller.

---

boards and posters, displays and press kits, internal television, teleconferences and video conferences, open houses, exhibitions, tours, task forces, entertainment, and person-to-person contacts to influence those they seek to reach. What is especially impressive is the range and variety of media and activities employed.

According to Lloyd Newman, executive vice president of the public relations firm Manning, Selvage and Lee, Inc., before you begin a project, you need to decide exactly why you want to conduct the program. In his opinion, it is critical to ask two basic questions: What do you hope to accomplish? What do you want your audiences to do? Newman has devised a formula which he advocates as a guide to affecting behavior: $P + I + A + B$. *Programs* convey *Information*, which creates *Attitudes*, which affect *Behavior*.[12]

Since organizations today are very sensitive to the way they are portrayed in the media

Corporate sponsorship is a grassroots image-building device. (Robert Houser/Photo Researchers)

and perceived by the people who work for them, invest in them, live in the communities in which they are located, or simply know of them, they frequently rely on public relations practitioners to help shape and communicate what they are all about. According to practitioner-author Fraser P. Seitel, before the public relations people can go to work three questions must first be answered: (1) What is the client's present image? (2) What image would the client like to have? (3) What must the client do to win a new image?[13]

The Mobil Corporation appears to have considered each of these questions when the energy crisis of the 1970s, compounded by increasing oil prices, precipitated a surge of negative criticism on the part of the public, criticism aimed directly at Mobil and the nation's other large oil companies. According to Herbert Schmertz, Mobil's vice president for public affairs, Mobil concluded that they were having a problem communicating directly and accurately with the American people, in large part because of the way they were being portrayed in the media. Determined to compel the media and the public to take the company more seriously and treat it with respect, Mobil devised a two-phase plan. First, the company decided that assuming a low profile was no longer a viable option. Therefore, company executives were coached and sent to appear on talk shows, news programs, and call-in programs where they would be in a position to present the company's side of the story. At the same time, Mobil published print ads that stated the company's position on a number of key issues before the public, including energy and the role of business. Through their program of issue, or *advocacy*, advertising (advertising that reveals the sponsor's viewpoint on matters of controversy) Mobil's personality was prominantly displayed to the American people. Second, Mobil committed itself to developing a long-term program of constructive criticism of the press. Whenever Mobil believed itself to have been misinterpreted by the press, it bought and sought space or time to communicate its side of the argument. To date, few corporate advertising-communication campaigns have sparked more controversy than that of the Mobil Corporation.

<u>Are the media giving us the facts?</u>

4. The myth of the open airwaves

There is a simple, yet overwhelming, difference between the print media and television journalism. Newspapers and magazines offer regular access to their pages to those who wish to rebut what has been printed. The major television networks do not.

Access to television is supposed to be governed largely by the Federal Communications Commission's Fairness Doctrine. That doctrine owes its existence to the theory that the airwaves are a scarce resource and must therefore be allocated among potential users. The doctrine requires owners of broadcast licenses "...to encourage and implement the broadcast of all sides of controversial public issues..." and to play "...a conscious and positive role in bringing about the balanced presentation of the opposing viewpoints." In theory, the Fairness Doctrine doesn't preclude anything. In reality, the networks have turned it into a doctrine of unfairness.

Under a mandate to present all sides of a public issue,' the networks confine debate through controls imposed by their own news departments. Through their news staffs, the networks exercise total control over the agenda of issues, and who may speak to the public. Unfortunately, the result of this network control, with no system or forum for rebuttal, has resulted in a narrow and selective discussion of major public issues—and the systematic exclusion or distortion of many viewpoints.

Mobil has often been denied the opportunity to rebut inaccurate television news broadcasts. Frequently, the broadcasts appeared at times when critical energy legislation was under debate in Congress—legislation regarding oil company divestiture, natural gas deregulation, oil decontrol, and the "windfall profit" tax. At such times, the networks' systematic exclusion of ideas and information impaired the public's ability to rationally decide fundamental policy issues.

Other companies have experienced similar frustrations in their attempts to gain adequate airtime to rebut erroneous television newscasts. Kaiser Aluminum & Chemical Corporation had to threaten a slander suit and had to ask the FCC to order ABC to give it time to respond to charges made on a 1980 *20/20* segment, before ABC finally gave the company the opportunity for an unedited reply. It took more than a year, however, before the rebuttal was aired on prime-time TV.

In response to a 1979 CBS *60 Minutes* broadcast, Illinois Power Company produced its own tape to point out the network's distortions. Called "60 Minutes/Our Reply," the power company's rebuttal exposed the bias of the broadcast by including CBS film footage not included in the original segment. The program has been widely shown to various groups across the country, but it has not been aired on television.

The networks not only block rebuttals, they refuse to air advertisements on "controversial" issues, and have rejected Mobil advocacy commercials since 1974—despite evidence that public support for issue advertising is strong (Network policies would preclude the very message you are currently reading.) A 1980 survey by the Opinion Research Corporation found that 85 percent of the American public think corporations should be allowed to present their views on controversial matters in television commercials. And most independent stations and network affiliates have opened their doors to advocacy advertising, without creating the chaos the networks profess to fear.

As the Supreme Court affirmed in its 1978 *Bellotti* decision: "The press does not have a monopoly on either the First Amendment or the ability to enlighten."

Next: The myth of the threatened First Amendment.

Mobil®

> **MEDIA PROBE**
>
> The following appears in a Mobil Corporation publication:
>
> > We think that by speaking out, we have made the public more aware of who we are and what we stand for. And people have come to respect what we say and the way we say it. Even when they disagree, they respect our honesty. We have made our critics look to see whether their guns were loaded before shooting from the hip.
> >
> > We think we have also changed some minds among opinion leaders in government, academia and elsewhere. And among the public at large.
>
> Do you agree or disagree with the company's statement? Why?

> **MEDIA PROBE**
>
> How do you define the word "lie"? To whom would you lie? What types of conditions, if any, do you believe justify telling a lie? How often do you lie? How often are you caught lying? Would you lie to the public?

THE ETHICS OF PUBLIC RELATIONS

The code of professional standards adopted by the Public Relations Society of America (see pages 354–355) states that it is the practitioner's responsibility to tell the truth at all times. Indeed, having a reputation as a credible communicator is essential to the successful practice of public relations. But what does it mean to tell the truth? And to whom must you be truthful? Let's see if we can begin to answer these questions.

In order to discover what it means to be truthful, we first need to determine what it means to lie. A person who lies does not merely deliver wrong information; rather, his or her aim is to deceive the public *intentionally*. In her book *Lying*, author Sissela Bok notes that liars hope and expect to succeed in misleading one or more individuals to believe something that they themselves do not believe. In effect, what a liar does is invite receivers to accept a statement or statements that the liar knows to be false. In a very real sense, the liar's goal is to exploit the receiver.

It is the unusual person who after telling a lie is able to limit his or her lying to that single episode. In order to cover the lie, frequently the liar must tell more lies. As Sissela Bok writes, "The liar always has more mending to do." Like the counterfeiter who rarely if ever prints only one false bill, the liar often thatches lie upon lie. But lying, like communication in general, has serious consequences. For example, imagine how an editor would react if it turned out that information contained in a release provided to him or her by a public relations practitioner was false and that the practitioner knew it was false when the release was sent. Information exchanged between the two from that point on would be practically worthless. Once we have been lied to by someone, future messages sent by that person are received with suspicion rather than trust. Yet, as you no doubt realize, resisting the temptation to lie, cheat, and hide the truth is not always easy to do, especially if clients or superiors ask you to do so. A few public relations people (unfortunately their behavior tends to taint the whole profession) ask reporters to write news releases that are untrue, delay the delivery of bad news, omit part of the story, or to participate in a cover-up. Jim Montgomery, writing for *The Wall Street Journal,* reported: "In public relations, ethical conflicts pose continuing problems. Lies, stonewalling, cover-ups to protect the company often are a way of life." He further notes that such stresses have caused public relations positions to rank sixth among jobs having the highest admission rates to mental institutions.[14]

On the other hand, there are practitioners who counter that they rarely find themselves

MEDIA VIEW

PUBLIC RELATIONS SOCIETY OF AMERICA

This code, adopted by the PRSA Assembly, replaces a similar code of Professional Standards for the Practice of Public Relations previously in force since 1954 and strengthened by revisions in 1959, 1963 and 1977.

DECLARATION OF PRINCIPLES

Members of the Public Relations Society of America base their professional principles on the fundamental value and dignity of the individual, holding that the free exercise of human rights, especially freedom of speech, freedom of assembly and freedom of the press, is essential to the practice of public relations.

In serving the interests of clients and employers, we dedicate ourselves to the goals of better communication, understanding and cooperation among the diverse individuals, groups and institutions of society.

We pledge:

To conduct ourselves professionally, with truth, accuracy, fairness and responsibility to the public;
To improve our individual competence and advance the knowledge and proficiency of the profession through continuing research and education;
And to adhere to the articles of the Code of Professional Standards for the Practice of Public Relations as adopted by the governing Assembly of the Society.

CODE OF PROFESSIONAL STANDARDS FOR THE PRACTICE OF PUBLIC RELATIONS

These articles have been adopted by the Public Relations Society of America to promote and maintain high standards of public service and ethical conduct among its members.

1. A member shall deal fairly with clients or employers, past and present, with fellow practitioners and the general public.
2. A member shall conduct his or her professional life in accord with the public interest.
3. A member shall adhere to truth and accuracy and to generally accepted standards of good taste.
4. A member shall not represent conflicting or competing interests without the express consent of those involved, given after a full disclosure of the facts; nor place himself or herself in a position where the member's interest is or may be in conflict with a duty to a client, or others, without a full disclosure of such interests to all involved.
5. A member shall safeguard the confidences of both present and former clients or employers and shall not accept retainers or employment which may involve the disclosure or use of these confidences to the disadvantage or prejudice of such clients or employers.
6. A member shall not engage in any practice which tends to corrupt the integrity of channels of communication or the processes of government.
7. A member shall not intentionally communicate false or misleading information and is obligated to use care to avoid communication of false or misleading information.
8. A member shall be prepared to identify publicly the name of the client or employer on whose behalf any public communication is made.
9. A member shall not make use of any individual or organization purporting to serve or represent an announced case, or purporting to be independent or unbiased, but actually serving an undisclosed special or private interest of a member, client or employer.
10. A member shall not intentionally injure the professional reputation or practice of another practitioner. However, if a member has evidence that another member has been guilty of unethical, illegal or unfair practices, including those in violation of this Code, the member shall present the information promptly to the proper authorities of the Society for action in accordance with the procedure set forth in Article XIII of the Bylaws.
11. A member called as a witness in a proceeding for the enforcement of this Code shall be bound to appear, unless excused for sufficient reason by the Judicial Panel.
12. A member, in performing services for a client or employer, shall not accept fees, commissions or any other valuable consideration from anyone other than the client or employer in connection with those services without the express consent of the client or employer, given after a full disclosure of the facts.
13. A member shall not guarantee the achievement of specified results beyond the member's direct control.
14. A member shall, as soon as possible, sever relations with any organization or individual if such relationship requires conduct contrary to the articles of this Code.

OFFICIAL INTERPRETATIONS OF THE CODE OF PROFESSIONAL STANDARDS FOR THE PRACTICE OF PUBLIC RELATIONS

Interpretation of Code Paragraph 2 which reads, "A member shall conduct his or her professional life in accord with the public interest."

The public interest is here defined primarily as comprising respect for and enforcement of the rights guaranteed by the Constitution of the United States of America.

Interpretation of Code Paragraph 5 which reads, "A member shall safeguard the confidences of both present and former clients or employers and shall not accept retainers or employment which may involve the disclosure or use of these confidences to the disadvantage or prejudice of such clients or employers."

This article does not prohibit a member who has knowledge of client or employee activities which are illegal from making such disclosures to the proper authorities as he or she believes are legally required.

Interpretation of Code Paragraph 6 which reads, "A member shall not engage in any practice which tends to corrupt the integrity of channels of communication or the processes of government."

1. Practices prohibited by this paragraph are those which tend to place representatives of media or government under an obligation to the member, or the member's employer or client, which is in conflict with their obligations to media or government, such as:
   a. the giving of gifts of more than nominal value;
   b. any form of payment or compensation to a member of the media in order to obtain preferential or guaranteed news or editorial coverage in the medium;
   c. any retainer or fee to a media employee or use of such employee if retained by a client or employer, where the circumstances are not fully disclosed to and accepted by the media employer;
   d. providing trips for media representatives which are unrelated to legitimate news interest;
   e. the use by a member of an investment or loan or advertising commitment made by the member, or the member's client or employer, to obtain preferential or guaranteed coverage in the medium.
2. This Code paragraph does not prohibit hosting media or government representatives at meals, cocktails, or news functions or special events which are occasions for the exchange of news information or views, or the furtherance of understanding which is part of the public relations function. Nor does it prohibit the bonafide press event or tour when media or government representatives are given an opportunity for on-the-spot viewing of a newsworthy product, process or event in which the media or government representatives have a legitimate interest. What is customary or reasonable hospitality has to be a matter of particular judgement in specific situations. In all of these cases, however, it is or should be understood that no preferential treatment or guarantees are expected or implied and that complete independence always is left to the media or government representative.
3. This paragraph does not prohibit the reasonable giving or lending of sample products or services to media representatives who have a legitimate interest in the products or services.

Interpretation of Code Paragraph 13 which reads. "A member shall not guarantee the achievement of specified results beyond the member's direct control."

This Code paragraph, in effect, prohibits misleading a client or employer as to what professional public relations can accomplish. It does not prohibit guarantees of quality or service. But it does prohibit guaranteeing specific results which, by their very nature, cannot be guaranteed because they are not subject to the member's control. As an example, a guarantee that a news release will appear specifically in a particular publication would be prohibited. This paragraph should not be interpreted as prohibiting contingent fees.

MEDIA PROBE

You are employed as a public relations officer and ghostwriter for a senator. You are well paid, earning approximately $80,000 a year. As part of your job you prepare papers and news releases for publication and speeches for delivery; it is your task to make the programs and policies advocated by the senator sound appealing and attractive to the public. Throughout your nine months of service you have been firmly committed to the goals and strategies of the senator and his staff. Thus, no problems arose. Now, however, the senator has taken a stand on an issue that you believe is not in the public's interest. In fact, you vehemently oppose his stance. Despite this, you are asked to speak in favor of the senator's position at meetings around the country, to draft materials to be sent to a variety of newspapers and magazines, and to develop persuasive speeches for the senator to deliver. If you do not complete any part of the assignment, you will be fired. On the other hand, if you fail to develop effective and persuasive communications you could also lose your job. What would you do? Why? In your opinion, is lying to yourself the same thing as lying to the public? Why?

---

involved in ethical conflicts. And others counsel that often there are valid reasons to stick with a job even if by doing so you violate your own conscience. For instance, James E. Grunig and Todd Hunt in *Managing Public Relations* advise: "We believe ethical practitioners should stay on the job and argue for ethical organizational behavior, even if they are not always successful. If an ethical practitioner quits, he or she will be replaced by an unethical practitioner. In that case, no one will be left to advocate ethical behavior." What do you think?

Public relations firms have also come under fire for aiding the regimes of repressive countries, in part by trying "to shine the tarnished images of nations accused of human rights violations." John Cooney, writing in *The Wall Street Journal,* notes that because the public relations agencies accept large fees, sometimes more than $1 million a year, they "are viewed as cynical mercenaries willing to fight for any cause if the price is right." Further, Cooney adds, "The PR people themselves tend to brush aside the question of ethics. 'Whom you work for is a business decision, not a moral one," a publicist says. Another adds huffily, 'I have nothing to feel guilty about.'"[15]

We should point out that there is nothing wrong with persuasion. The very nature of our democracy depends on people having the opportunity to try to convince others, either by appeals to logic or by appeals to emotion, that what they are advocating is right and in the public's interest. John W. Hill, founder of Hill and Knowlton, has identified five criteria he believes are useful in determining what is in the public interest.[16] With regard to a proposal, Hill asks us to consider

1. The number of people it will affect
2. The number of people it will harm
3. The number of people it will benefit
4. The significance of its effects
5. Its probable long-range effects

MEDIA VIEW

You work for a large public relations agency. For a fee of $800,000 you are asked to overhaul the image and reputation of Haiti in the United States by attempting to encourage tourism, trade, and foreign aid. Would you accept? Why? In your opinion should the decision you make be a business one or an ethical one? Why?

In order for people to be able to use these criteria as they should be used—that is, to help them make credible decisions—they must be provided with accurate and truthful information to work with—and this is where the techniques of the persuader and the *propagandist* diverge. Whereas the propagandist considers the interests of the source exclusively, viewing the receivers as individuals who may be used in order that desired ends be achieved, a good public relations practitioner does not. Ethical practitioners will not work to deceive the public and subvert truth; instead they will try to persuade in such a way that a democratic consensus is achieved, one that is earned in honest and straightforward ways, not by suppression of facts or the release of false and misleading data. Sound public relations is simply not directed at making people believe what is untrue. Thus, whether or not public relations plays a socially beneficial or socially harmful role in society depends on how it is used.

A MESSAGE FOR OUR TIME

Negative information about individuals, companies, institutions, and products appears to predominate in today's world. As Stephen A. Greyser notes, we are greeted daily with product recalls, examples of corrective advertising, special-interest-group blacklists, rumors, and general image problems. Given the current state of affairs, we believe the message for public relations is clear. Today's public relations professionals have a unique opportunity to try to discover ways to make persons or organizations more responsive to the changing concerns and needs of their publics.

The number of efforts made to influence the attitudes and beliefs of particular groups of people increases every day. We can barely survive and we certainly will be unable to thrive unless we take time to understand how organizations affect people and how people affect organizations. We can barely survive and we will certainly not thrive unless we learn how to formulate and analyze the informative and persuasive messages sent and received in the name of public relations—communications that can make the difference between a favorable, neutral, and unfavorable climate of opinion. As Lawrence Nolte notes: No longer can a public relations program be based entirely on adapting the environment (the complex of social, technological, economic, and political trends and events) to the organization. Now it must give equal attention to adapting the organization to the environment." Reflecting this concern with the environment, one company's chief executive officer recently told practitioner Jay S. Mendell: "Our corporations are floating like corks in a toilet bowl and pretty soon the environment is going to pull the chain."[17] Not a pretty image, but a realistic appraisal of current conditions, and an important message. As the environment changes, so should

> **MEDIA VIEW**
>
> As I look back on the years that I have been in the business, I can think of products which were not as good as our clients said they were; statements about disappointing financial results that were not as candid as they should have been; errors in judgment that were described in carefully worded public statements that disguised the true facts. It is this tendency which led Richard Nixon to suggest (on tape) that it was time to call in the public relations people to solve the Watergate problem. He thought his problems were merely perception, not reality. And this is how public relations has won its reputation of being all fluff and no substance, of being a cover up, of trying to make bad things look good. That is public relations at its worst.
>
> David Finn, Chairman of the Board, Ruder, Finn and Rotman, Inc.

the public relations programs. While it is noteworthy that never before have the attitudes and actions of groups of people had more of an impact on the success or failure of individuals, businesses, social, religious, and political institutions, it is also noteworthy that never before has public relations had the opportunity it now has to demonstrate that it is prepared to meet these challenges.

SUMMARY

To the extent that we care what others think about us and actively work to gain their approval, we all practice personal public relations. Doing what we do for ourselves for a business or other client is what professional public relations is about.

As practiced today, public relations includes all of the following activities: publicity, opinion research, press agentry, special-event management, promotion and fund raising, lobbying, public affairs, institutional advertising, gift giving, creating a printed voice, and counseling. Though it has been defined in a number of different ways, the following definition appears to encompass critical dimensions of the field: Public relations is the planned, two-way communication effort through which an individual or organization strives to win the understanding, acceptance, support, and cooperation of the public.

The roots of modern public relations extend far back in time, perhaps even more than 4000 years ago. As long as people wanted to inform or influence others, they used public relations techniques to help them realize their goals. But it was Ivy Ledbetter Lee, the father of modern public relations, who stressed that an honest information program was basic to achieving public acceptance of a proposal. The Code of Professional Standards adopted by the Public Relations Society of America echoes this belief. Despite this, today's practitioners must also be prepared to meet and resolve a number of ethical conflicts.

Underlying the practice of public relations is the theory that the court of public opinion is the highest court in our land. This theory postulates that if you give everyone in society a chance to participate in the decision-making process, you do get better decisions. Once they enter the court of public opinion, individuals and the companies or clients they represent are free to take part in the public debate on controversial issues and to use a variety of media and methods to try and attain their desired ends.

KEY TERMS

Public relations
Public opinion
Publicity
Opinion research
Lobbying
Press agentry
Creel Committee
Public
Opinion
Attitude
Advocacy advertising
Propagandist

NOTES

[1] Philip Lesly (ed.), *Public Relations Handbook*, Prentice-Hall, Englewood Cliffs, N.J., 1971.

[2] Lawrence W. Nolte, *Fundamentals of Public Relations*, Pergamon, New York, 1979, p. 4.

[3] E. J. Robinson, *Communication and Public Relations*, Amocom, New York, 1974.

[4] John E. Marston, *Modern Public Relations*, McGraw-Hill, New York, 1979, p. 6.

[5] Stephen A. Greyser, "Changing Roles for Public Relations," *Public Relations Journal*, vol. 37, no. 1, 1981, pp. 18–25.

[6] "Public Relations in the 80's: Trends and Challenges," *PR Casebook*, October 1983, p. 4.

[7] Lawrence W. Nolte, op. cit., p. 33.

[8] Ronald P. Lovell, *Inside Public Relations*, Boston, Allyn and Bacon, 1982, p. 19.

[9] Cited in Sherman Morse, "An Awakening in Wall Street," *American Magazine*, vol. 62, September, 1906, p. 460.

[10] Walt Seifert, "Our Highest Court: Public Opinion," *Public Relations Journal,* December 1977, p. 24.

[11] Scott M. Cutlip and Allen H. Center, *Effective Public Relations,* 5th ed., Prentice-Hall, Englewood Cliffs, N.J., 1978, p. 111.

[12] *Editor's Newsletter: Trends and Techniques in Business Communication,* vol. 11, no. 1, January 1981, p. 1.

[13] Fraser P. Seitel, *The Practice of Public Relations,* Merrill, Columbus, Ohio, 1980, pp. 50–52.

[14] Jim Montgomery, "The Image Makers," *The Wall Street Journal,* August 1, 1978.

[15] John E. Cooney, "Vox Unpopular," *The Wall Street Journal,* January 23, 1979.

[16] Raymond Simon, *Public Relations: Concepts and Practices,* 2d ed., Grid, Columbus, Ohio, 1980, p. 61.

[17] Jay S. Mendell, "The Practitioner as a Futurist," *Public Relations Journal,* vol. 36, no. 2, December, 1980, p. 17.

SUGGESTIONS FOR FURTHER READING

Cutlip, Scott M., and Center, Allen H. *Effective Public Relations,* 5th ed., Prentice-Hall, Englewood Cliffs, N.J., 1978. *The leader in the field; contains a wealth of information.*

Harlow, Rex F.: "Building a Public Relations Definition," *Public Relations Review,* vol. 2, no. 4, Winter 1976, pp. 33–41. *Highlights key components of a definition.*

Lesly, Philip (ed): *Public Relations Handbook,* 2d ed., Prentice-Hall, Englewood Cliffs, N.J., 1978. *Covers all aspects of the field; embodies the expertise and skills of key practitioners.*

Marston, John: *Modern Public Relations,* McGraw-Hill, New York, 1979. *Discusses public relations principles and cases in detail.*

Moore, H. Frazier, and Bertrand R. Canfield: *Public Relations: Principles, Cases and Problems,* 7th ed., Irwin, Homewood Ill., 1977. *Balances theory and practice.*

Newman, Lloyd N.: "Public Relations Phase II: Advisor Becomes Decision-Maker," *Public Relations Journal,* vol. 36, no. 12, December 1980, pp. 10–13. *A clear discussion of the roles the practitioner needs to be ready to assume.*

Nolte, Lawrence W.: *The Fundamentals of Public Relations,* Pergamon, New York, 1979. *Shows the role played by public relations in our social, political, and economic environment.*

Seitel, Fraser P.: *The Practice of Public Relations,* Merrill, Columbus, Ohio, 1980. *Cites theoretical concepts and applies them to the real world.*

Simon, Raymond: *Public Relations: Concepts and Practices,* 2d ed., Grid, Columbus, Ohio, 1980. *Not a handbook, but a valuable resource for those interested in the essential nature of public relations.*

PART FIVE RESEARCH AND MASS COMMUNICATION: THE OTHER SIDE OF THE WINDOW

CHAPTER 12

Each new endeavor is a creative effort building on past efforts. . . . A good study opens the door to many new studies.
Maxwell McCombs

RESEARCHING THE MASS MEDIA: LOOKING FOR ANSWERS

CHAPTER PREVIEW

After reading this chapter, you should be able to:
- Explain the role of research
- Compare five basic research approaches: the historical approach, the experimental approach, the field study, the survey method, and content analysis
- Provide examples of topics that researchers, using the five preceding research approaches, might formulate
- Discuss how each of the studies included in this chapter illustrate a particular research method
- Describe at least one alternate strategy used to explore mass-media research
- Illustrate how research is tied to changing views of the mass media and the mass-communication process
- Define the hypodermic, or magic-bullet, theory of mass communication
- Define the two-step flow theory of mass communication

Though formal study of the mass media is still relatively new, it is gradually coming into its own. During the last fifty-year period alone, thousands of studies focusing on the media have been conducted, studies that reveal that the media have the capacity to function as both positive and negative influences in our lives. Propelled by an ability to reach and affect virtually every member of our society, the mass media of today are dynamic forces that merit careful and thorough investigation and research.

THE ROLE OF MASS-MEDIA RESEARCH

Why research the mass media? Why not simply acknowledge that the mass media exist and go about our lives without worrying about them? To be sure, many of us do just that. We live our lives in a media-rich society without ever stopping to consider how each medium that is part of that society affects us, influences the way we work and play, or perhaps even helps to alter the course of world history. Serious students of the mass media think otherwise, however. They understand that the only way that we can advance our knowledge about the media is to ask and answer questions, and asking and answering questions is the role of research. When we engage in research, we try to find out what a medium is about, how it is used, what its effects are, and what its potential is. Without adequate research, we are not in a very good position to suggest ways to make the media better or more useful communication tools. What researchers hope to do is to add pieces to an incomplete puzzle, a puzzle which in light of the rapid development of the mass-media field may never be completed. But unfilled spaces in the puzzle, that is, unanswered questions, are precisely what make the mass-media story so exciting and interesting. In fact, they are what make becoming media-wise a challenge. Let us now prepare to meet the mass-media challenge by enhancing our understanding of the role research has played in the development of communication theory.

MASS-MEDIA RESEARCH: KEY TO CHANGING THEORIES

Research has provided us with the accumulated knowledge we need to formulate, alter, and revise the way we think about mass communication. For example, during the field's early days, it was believed that mass communication was capable of affecting audiences in extremely powerful and antisocial ways. Since it was believed that the mass media controlled audiences much like puppeteers control marionettes, people were understandably alarmed. According to the "*hypodermic*" or "*magic-bullet*" theory of mass communication, as it was dubbed in the hands of skilled men and women, the mass media could hit and inject people with messages just as a bullet can penetrate a target.

In other words, the reigning assumption of the day was that a given message reached and influenced every member of the audience in virtually identical ways, eliciting responses also essentially similar in nature. And since information was perceived to flow directly from the media to intended targets, it was believed that the media could control audience behavior. The thirteen Payne Fund studies conducted from 1929 to 1932 seemed to lend support to this magic-bullet model by demonstrating that motion pictures did indeed

FIGURE 12-1 The hypodermic, or magic-bullet, theory of mass communication.

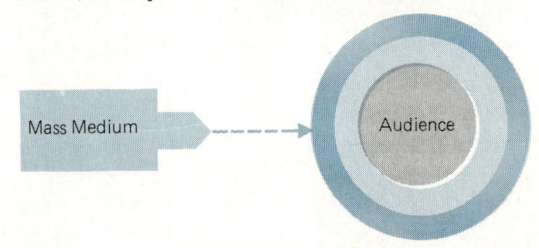

MEDIA VIEW

All research . . . has as its underlying purpose the advancement of knowledge. Everything we know today is the result of an inquisitive mind that doubted, that wondered, that wanted to find something new. Every significant step into the future will come with "careful search; studious inquiry; critical and exhaustive investigation or experimentation having for its aim the revision of accepted conclusions in the light of newly discovered facts." A researcher looks at a person, a phenomenon, a condition, a relationship or situation; examines all the previous information on the subject; searches for additional facts through observation or experimentation; carefully evaluates the new evidence; and finally draws a set of conclusions. The research cycle is complete and knowledge concerning a particular area is moved one step forward.

Presley D. Holmes and James E. Lynch, "Research: Methods, Trends, Ideas," in Keith Brooks, *The Communicative Arts and Sciences of Speech*, Charles E. Merrill Books, Inc., Columbus, Ohio, p. 411.

---

have a dramatic influence on children, even motivating them to adopt certain play, dress, and speech habits as well as affecting the way they handled themselves during their person-to-person encounters.

Later researchers, however, would dispel the validity of the magic-bullet theory by demonstrating the power that other people and subgroups exerted in influencing how individuals responded to mass-media messages. For example, Hadley Cantril in his 1940 work *The Invasion from Mars: A Study in the Psychology of Panic* explored the panic precipitated by the 1938 radio broadcast of *The War of the Worlds*.[1] Cantril's investigation revealed that while the broadcast frightened some people, it had failed to frighten others; this discovery helped to challenge the belief that audience reaction to a mass medium was necessarily uniform.

In another research project Lazarsfeld, Berelson, and Gaudet tried to discover how and why people decided to vote as they did in the 1940 election.[2] Results of extensive surveys indicated that while many people received information about the candidates directly from the mass media, a significant number of others received information from other people. Thus was born *the two-step flow* theory of mass communication, that is, the belief that information flows from the media to some people directly, but that it also flows from those people to an even wider circle of people. In addition, it was noted that the people who relayed information to others functioned as opinion leaders, since they were capable of affecting the informational environments of the individuals with whom they interacted (see Figure 12-2). It is important to note that, in practice, more than just a single relay person may be involved in the transfer and interpretation of the information. Thus, social relationships between people—that is discussion and rediscussion of ideas—was found to be a significant factor in the mass-communication process.

Hovland, Lumsdaine, and Sheffield further exposed the limitation of mass communication to elicit the desired effects.[3] At the outset

FIGURE 12-2 The two-step flow theory of mass communication.

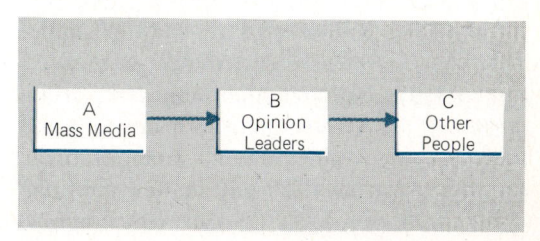

A
Mass Media → B
Opinion Leaders → C
Other People

of World War II, Hollywood was given the charge by U.S. Army Chief of Staff George C. Marshall to prepare films that would explain "to our boys why we are fighting and the principles for which we are fighting."[4] However, while effective in teaching soldiers factual material, the resulting films proved to be ineffective in altering either the attitudes of our soldiers or their motivation to fight.

Each of the three studies demonstrated that mass communication did not affect receivers uniformly, as had originally been hypothesized; rather, owing to each receiver's unique qualities and to group influences, it had a varied impact. Three basic factors were cited as helping to account for this variability: *selective attention* (receivers selectively expose themselves to certain kinds of information); *selective perception* (once exposed to messages receivers will interpret them in ways that support their predispositions); and *selective retention* (receivers selectively recall those portions of messages with which they agree). Thus, we were led to understand that it is not just what the mass media do to people that we ought to be concerned with, but what the people do with the mass media as well. Receivers are not merely targets; rather, they are active participants in the mass-communication process.

Today, mass-media researchers are hard at work attempting to answer more questions about the mass media and their effects. In addition to validating some of the data, explanations and insights provided to us by studies past, we can anticipate new data, new explanations, and new insights to be revealed. Indeed, according to Shearon Lowery and Melvin L. DeFleur, the current trend in research seems to signal a return of the pendulum to the belief that media influence is greater than we expected, indicating not that the magic-bullet theorists were right, but suggesting that perhaps research methods used previously had been inadequate to determine the influences the media actually have. So generalizations about the mass media cannot be set in stone; instead, we need to recognize that media generalizations may remain applicable for specific time periods only. At this point let us examine some recent media studies in an effort to become better acquainted with the types of research people conduct.

MEDIA RESEARCH: A POTPOURRI OF APPROACHES

There are five basic research approaches that are used repeatedly by people who choose to study the mass media: (1) the historical approach, (2) the experimental approach, (3) the field study, (4) the survey, and (5) content analysis. After a brief description of each option, we will provide an example of it in operation.

Historical Research

Researchers who use a *historical approach* to study the mass media offer us interpretations of the past; their main aims are to gather, record, and evaluate facts relevant to a person or event that they themselves may or may not have known or experienced personally. Historical researchers rely on interviews, letters, newspapers, magazines, audio, kinescope or videotape recordings of the period or individual being studied, as well as previous literature on the subject. But because the subjects of historical research are set in the past, the events or persons being studied cannot be controlled by the researcher directly; for this reason, special care must be taken to ensure that researcher prejudices do not bias the investigations. However, when historical researchers are successful in attaining the objectives they set for themselves, they help us add to our storehouse of experience and, at the same time, provide us with standards against which to measure our own progress. It should also be noted that when it succeeds, historical research not only offers us insights into what we should do but also presents us with warnings regarding things we should not do.

STUDY IN FOCUS

THE HISTORICAL APPROACH

It was June 1959. That morning, Colby College had presented Edward R. Murrow with an honorary doctorate, and we were traveling—the two of us—in his new Thunderbird down the Maine Turnpike. That section of the highway had only recently been opened, and I now appreciated what Eric Sevareid said about the only danger equal to that from bombs during the Battle of Britain had been Murrow's driving. Murrow at the wheel of that gleaming black Thunderbird with the wine red upholstery indeed seemed dangerous. The cigarette-stained index finger resting indifferently on the steering wheel struck me as less than adequate for the 90-mile-an-hour speed.

When the stretch of new highway ended and traffic on the approaches to Portsmouth became congested, Murrow drove less demoniacally. We were riding with the top down and began talking. I remember little of our conversation—often I have wished I remembered more—but at one point I asked him if, as a boy, he ever felt he was put in the world for a special purpose. He seemed, from the start, to have been driven.

He waited so long to answer I wondered if he would. Had I been impertinent? Then he said, "No, I never had that. I've just tried, whatever I did, to do it the best I could."

It was September 1983. Diane Sawyer was addressing the annual meeting of radio and television news directors. She had been doing some research on Murrow and was impressed as much by the care he took with words as by his courage. She said:

> He believed that his words could make a difference, that ultimately we in our profession have the power to use words and pictures to improve the human condition.... I came away with the conviction that Murrow and Collingwood and Sevareid and Shirer were not accidents, like a shower of comets in the sky. They were the kind of journalists they were because of the kind of people they were. Educated and experienced and respectful of facts.

The two incidents—a quarter century apart—are not unrelated. It was Murrow's striving to be his best, as much as courage and intelligence, more than commanding voice and striking appearance, which made him, in Fred Friendly's phrase, "the Polaris, the true North Star." It is Murrow's example, more than any other's, that inspires the best of contemporary broadcast journalists and, one suspects, the best of them for generations to come. "We shall live in his afterglow," Eric Sevareid said, "a very long time."...

All broadcasting is changing. Technology and the profit to be made from news programs have produced a revolution. Murrow would be astounded at the changes and, in some respects, appalled. But one thing not changed, challenging conscience, is the tradition for which he, more than anyone else, is responsible. So responsible that it is called the Murrow tradition.

What is this tradition? It can be summed up in one word, integrity, which is more than accuracy, more than reliability, more than intellect. It requires what Diane Sawyer suggests is the vital element, soundness of character. It derives from the quality of Murrow as a person, the man who remembered from childhood the Bible reading: "Whatsoever thy hand findeth to do, do it with thy might."

An appraisal of Murrow, and his meaning, must include his background. His father was a farmer turned locomotive engineer, his mother a devout Quaker. Grace was said at mealtime, and Murrow and his two older brothers, as Alexander Kendrick relates, took turns reading from the King James version of the Bible on Sunday. Murrow's younger brother, Dewey, told Kendrick, "They branded us with their consciences."

Murrow had a live conscience. All his life, he asked himself: What should I do?

There was inculcated a sense of honor. Writing from London, Murrow assured his parents that if anything happened to him or his brothers in the war, they would act as they were taught to act as boys and "bring no shame upon the name." After the war, Godfrey Talbot, a commentator for the BBC, said of Murrow: "In the halls of Broadcast House, the name of Ed Murrow is there in gold."

Another major influence was Ida Lou Anderson, Murrow's speech instructor at Washington State. A cripple, she taught him courage. She also gave him a philosophy. She introduced him to Marcus Aurelius, whose advice was "to live not one's life as though one had a thousand years, but live each day as the last.". . .

Someday—if not already—someone will go through Murrow's broadcasts to document the influence of the King James Bible on his writing. "And I was very frightened" seems to be a paraphrase of "And I was sore afraid." The clause "that righteousness exalteth a nation" clearly shows Bibilical influence.

So what is Murrow's legacy?

There are no discoveries. His legacy is his example, which needs in this confusing, revolutionary time to be kept ever green. For in the midst of rapid change, his verities—the standards he set—can be lost. That would be the nation's loss. The majority of Americans have come to depend on broadcast journalists, not only for lively features and ball scores, but for information essential for a healthy society. That dependence may be too great, but the heavy reliance on radio and television for news of what is happening is a fact. Broadcasters may lose their sense of responsibility; they cannot escape responsibility itself.

Ed Murrow felt, and lived, his responsibility. He was what he demanded of the reporters he hired: steady, reliable and restrained. "Just provide the honest news." Is this the demand being made today?

He set standards in writing. By choosing the right words—no matter his avowal that words did not exist to describe what he saw—he showed how effective writing can be without frills. He believed his words could make a difference.

He had honor. He had conscience. And always, whatever he undertook to do, he did his best.

Murrow was forever setting standards for himself, and these are the standards for broadcast journalists today.

And tomorrow.

Edward Bliss, Jr., "The Meaning of Murrow," *Feedback*, Winter 1983, pp. 3–6.

For example, a researcher using a historical approach might decide to explore the history of the woman newscaster in network television. In order to complete such a project, the researcher would probably have to dig through the archives of the Museum of Broadcasting, examine critical reviews received by newscasters, read the writings of the newscasters, apply for permission to read network records, interview network and station executives and personnel, speak to the women newscasters and their colleagues (if they are still alive), as well as examine news program ratings and station practices—all in an effort to compile an accurate record that would be of value and interest to television broadcasters and the viewing public today.

Experimental Research

In contrast to historical researchers, experimental researchers who work in laboratories do exercise at least some control over the situations they explore. In fact, *experimental research* permits investigators to exercise rather tight control over three key factors: (1) the environment, (2) the variables being studied, and (3) the subjects.

When conducting an experiment researchers are free to arrange the environment (the laboratory) any way they desire. (The control that they exert over the environment has led some critics to complain that the results obtained in the laboratory setting cannot be generalized to real-world settings.) Experimental designs permit researchers to control the number and types of variables they will manipulate during the course of their study. And since the researchers themselves select the subjects to be used in their study, it is within their power to limit the number and types of people they will involve in their experiments.

In addition, the goals of most experimental researchers differ from those of most historical researchers. Experimental researchers usually seek to demonstrate that cause-and-effect relationships exist. For example, a researcher might set out to discover if mail anchors have more credibility than female anchors when delivering hard-news stories. In order to answer this question, the researcher might expose two groups of people of similar age and sex distribution to a portion of a news broadcast; one test group would watch a male anchor deliver the news, and the other test group would watch a female anchor deliver the news. After viewing the news segment, groups would then be asked to complete news-anchor credibility scales, and the resulting group ratings would then be compared to see if there was a significant difference in the ratings received by the male and the female anchor. Experiments like this one incorporate two basic types of variables into the research design: the independent variable (that which is being manipulated), in this case the sex of the news anchor, and the dependent variable (the variable that is observed and whose value is assumed to depend on the independent variable), in this case the credibility ratings.

Field Research

Field research differs from experimental research in that it is conducted in the field, not in a laboratory. In other words, the field researcher uses the real world as a natural setting for his or her work. Consequently, subjects in field studies may not even be aware that their behavior is being observed or measured. For example, a researcher might choose to use a field approach to study whether a male or female voice-over has more impact on the sale of a product. To do this, the researcher would arrange to have a male announcer read the commercial message for the product in one test market and a female announcer read the same commercial message in a similar but different test market; then, following each message's airing, the researcher could monitor and compare resulting product sales in an effort to determine whether to continue airing the spots using the male or female voice-over. Unfortunately, it is virtually impossible for researchers to control all the intervening variables that could affect the outcome of such an experiment when it is conducted in the field.

In addition to running experiments, field researchers also rely on observations and focus groups (group interviewing) to aid them in understanding the attitudes and the behaviors of the people they are studying.

Survey Research

Another research approach relied on to advance our understanding of mass-media uses and effects is *survey research*. Surveys are conducted in interpersonal settings (face-to-face), mediated settings (via the telephone), or by mail. Typically, researchers use the survey as a tool to help them accomplish two basic goals. First, a survey can aid researchers in describing current conditions or attitudes; for example, during election periods pollsters regularly conduct surveys in an effort to measure public opinion on a number of key election issues as well as to determine the comparative popularity of the candidates. Second, a survey can help researchers explain and assess why certain situations exist; for ex-

STUDY IN FOCUS

SURVEY RESEARCH

A survey of 181 callers to three talk radio shows found that 24 percent called to use the program as a forum and 27 percent called to chat. As predicted, those seeking companionship were more frequent callers.

Even in the early days of empirical mass communication research there was a concern with the motives that led people to the media and the gratifications that audiences derived from the experience. Radio was center stage and researchers focused on the medium's audience.[1] Herzog, for example, studied radio quiz programs and soap operas and found that women used the latter as a means to escape from the reality of daily routines but also saw it as a source of information on how to cope with life's problems.[2] Suchman also looked at the motives that led to people's interest in serious music on radio.[3]

Interest in audience analysis shifted toward television[4] when that medium took the prime time audience and radio adopted a news and music format. Radio was seen primarily as a companion for commuters and a source of background music. Uses and gratifications research actually emerged as a serious stream of academic scholarship in the past decade or so, a time when the specialization occurring in radio had introduced talk radio formats to audiences across the country.

The talk radio format allows audience members to actively participate, and this has intrigued researchers interested in the way these formats are used by listeners and callers. One of the first researchers to investigate this area was Crittenden, who conducted research amongst callers and listeners to "Speak Out," a talk show broadcast over WAAC in Terre Haute, Indiana.[5] He concluded that calling the station allowed people to place issues before the public and might even prompt action. Callers were predominantely lower-middle class or working class people who otherwise might not have had access to community leaders. Talk radio has also been found to serve as a forum for people who appear as guests or who initiate public service announcements on these programs.[6] Thus, talk radio may be used as a forum by callers and guests.

Other researchers have focused on the companionship aspects of talk radio, presenting it as a surrogate for social interactions. Turow found that callers to WCAU in Philadelphia were older and less affluent than were the majority of other Philadelphians. The proportion of widowed callers was also higher. Turow maintains that living alone may tend to produce a sense of social isolation which makes talk radio appear particularly attractive.[7] Avery, Ellis and Glover reported that many listeners to talk radio are retired and have low or moderate incomes; lacking other contacts, they use this medium as a "window on the world."[8]

Our research focused on the motivation of talk radio show callers. To what extent do callers use this format as a forum and a companion, and which gratification prompts the most frequent use? We might expect callers in isolated circumstances to call more frequently for companionship because the situation is a continuing factor. Since loneliness is an ongoing aspect of their lives, the desire to seek "surrogate companionship" may also be ongoing. Talk radio also has much to recommend it as a forum. People can announce their views to an audience of thousands while remaining anonymous.

METHODOLOGY

A survey was administered to people calling several talk radio shows, and information was obtained to examine their intentions, etc. The survey was administered to a total of 181 persons calling in to four programs on three radio stations in the summer of 1979 in Cleveland, Ohio. Respondents and programs constitute a reasonable sample of the variety represented by available programming.[9] The survey was necessarily short because management feared that a longer instrument would hamper the flow of callers through the show. People contacting the talk radio shows were asked: "Are you calling to give or receive information or did you want to chat?" Possible answers included: to chat, to give/receive information, both (to chat and to give/receive information), and "I have never thought about why I called." Those reporting that they wanted to chat or both were considered to be companionship-seeking. The first question was followed by an open-ended question: "Is there some other reason why you called?" If a caller indicated that he/she wanted either to express an opinion or to set the record straight, using words to that effect, he/she was considered to be seeking a forum. Callers also were asked: "How many times have you been on the air?"

RESULTS

Of the 181 people who called one of the four shows, 71 were first-time callers, while 110 were repeat callers. Thirty-six had called on fewer than four previous occasions, 40 had called 4–25 times, and 34 had called more than 25 times. The frequency varied greatly from show to show. Some 61 said that they wanted to give or receive information, while 49 reported they wanted to chat. Twenty of those indicating an interest in information-sharing had complaints relating to previous interactions with the station. Only nine of those reporting a desire to chat fit into this category. Some 99 of the repeat callers reported that they had discussed their experiences with the station. Twelve had never mentioned these matters.

Were those seeking companionship more frequent callers than those calling for other reasons? The range was from one to more than 100 for both groups of callers. As expected, those who called "seeking companionship" were more frequent callers; the mean for this group was 30.73, while the mean frequency of those calling for other purposos was 22.96 (t − 2.6; p < .01). The high means reflect the five people in each group who reported calling at least 100 times. The median for the first group was 5.82 and the median for those seeking companionship was 11.19. Many people called to talk about a specific incident or individual, while others were anxious to express a certain viewpoint such as anticommunism, declining morals, etc. The latter tended to be "one-issue" callers who frequently contacted the station as often as three times a day, according to station personnel.

Some 44, or 24.3 percent of the 181 people surveyed, called to use the program as a forum. Four claimed they wanted to give facts, six wanted to express an opinion about the station, 10 wanted to give their opinions about the Cleveland Browns, and 24 said they wanted to express an opinion but provided no further details. Only seven persons said they wanted to solicit information.

Thus, while substantial numbers of people called to use the talk radio format as company and as a forum, the gratification prompting the greatest frequency of calling was companionship seeking. Just as Herzog found radio soap operas functional outlets for escape some 40 years ago,[10] today's talk radio formats are providing a similar outlet for today's isolated listeners.

---

[1]Paul F. Lazarsfeld and Frank N. Stanton, eds., *Radio Research,* 1941 (New York: Duell, Sloan and Pearce, 1942); Lazarsfeld and Stanton, eds., *Radio Research,* 1942–43 (New York: Duell, Sloan and Pearce, 1944).

[2]Herta Herzog, "What Do We Really Know About Day-Time Serial Listeners?" in *Radio Research,* 1942–43, eds. Paul F. Lazarsfeld and Frank N. Stanton (New York: Duell, Sloan and Pearce, 1944), pp. 3–33; Herta Herzog, "Professor Quiz: A Gratification Study," in *Radio and the Printed Page,* ed. Paul F. Lazarsfeld (New York: Duell, Sloan and Pearce, 1940), pp. 64–93.

[3]Edward A. Suchman, "An Invitation to Music," in *Radio Research, 1941,* eds. Paul F. Lazarsfeld and Frank N. Stanton (New York: Duell, Sloan and Pearce, 1942).

[4]See Robert T. Bower, *Television and the Public* (New York: Holt, Rinehart and Winston, Inc. 1973);

Ronald E. Frank and Marshall G. Greenberg, *The Public's Use of Television* (Beverly-Hills, CA Sage Publications, 1980).

[5] John Crittenden, "Democratic Functions of the Open Mike Radio Forum," *Public Opinion Quarterly* 35: 200–210 (Summer 1971).

[6] Also the national director of Neurotics Anonymous noted: "Talk radio is very effective in explaining our program. We've used it across the country and the response has been good." Ruth Hutton Fred, executive director of Jewish Family Services in Houston, Texas, said her "Ask Ruth" show has had an inestimable value in parent education, counseling and referral. See Margaret McEachern, "The Town Meeting Is Not Dead—It's Alive and Well on Radio," *Today's Health* 48: 32–33 (July 1970).

[7] Joseph Turow, "Talk Show Radio as Interpersonal Communication," *Journal of Broadcasting* 18: 171–179 (Spring 1974).

[8] Robert K. Avery, Donald G. Ellis and Thomas W. Glover, "Patterns of Communication on Talk Radio," *Journal of Broadcasting* 22: 5–17 (Winter 1978).

[9] Surveys were conducted at WBBG, WCSB and WZZP. WBBG was then an all-talk station featuring continuous open-mike programming. WZZP was a hard rock station with an audience consisting largely of adolescents; surveys were completed during a talk program broadcast over this station on Sunday evening. WCSB is the Cleveland State University student station; conversations were conducted during a Wednesday evening program that featured an open-mike format.

[10] Herta Herzog, "What Do We Really Know About Day-Time Serial Listeners?" op. cit.

Harriet Tramer and Leo W. Jeffres, "Talk Radio—Forum and Companion," *Journal of Broadcasting*, vol. 27, no. 3, Summer 1983, pp. 297–300.

ample, advertisers and station owners may conduct a survey to determine if viewer or consumer lifestyles may be used to predict program or product success. In addition, let us not forget that in broadcasting and in advertising, companies like Nielsen, Arbitron, and Simmons are continually feeding their clients with current audience data gathered with the assistance of survey techniques.

Content Analysis

The last research approach we will examine is content analysis. The goal of the content analysts is to describe the content of communication objectively, systematically, and quantitatively.[5] For example, using a content analysis approach researchers can investigate topics like the number of women and men

Polling the public—or at least those passersby willing to stop and answer questions—is a time-honored marketing tool. (AP/Wide World)

Telephone surveys are more targeted than sidewalk polls. Data can be more systematically analyzed. (Randy Matusow)

STUDY IN FOCUS

CONTENT ANALYSIS

The media still do not perceive public relations as an issues-oriented profession, and their coverage tends to focus on the people and activities of the profession rather than its impact in the public arena [see table, "Analysis Of 1982 Articles" and graph, "Coverage By Categories"].

While media interest in the profession has increased significantly, with coverage doubling in the past year, there is little evidence that practitioners have made headway in educating the media to the broad and complex role public relations plays in today's society.

Other likely reasons for the sparse reporting on public relations' involvement with social, political and economic issues: Public relations people, of necessity, take a behind-the-scenes approach that does little for their own visibility; and practitioners are still talking primarily to themselves about their broader responsibilities instead of addressing such external audiences as the media.

These findings are among the results of a recent media analysis by the Public Relations Society of America that examined 877 news clips received from February 1981 through

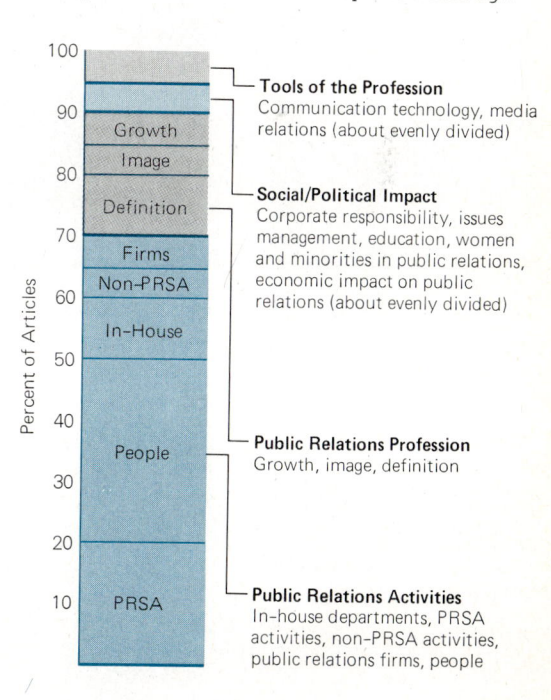

Tools of the Profession
Communication technology, media relations (about evenly divided)

Social/Political Impact
Corporate responsibility, issues management, education, women and minorities in public relations, economic impact on public relations (about evenly divided)

Public Relations Profession
Growth, image, definition

Public Relations Activities
In-house departments, PRSA activities, non-PRSA activities, public relations firms, people

RESEARCHING THE MASS MEDIA: LOOKING FOR ANSWERS 375

Analysis of 1982 Articles *(Ranked by three measures)*

ARTICLE TOPIC*	NUMBER OF ARTICLES	ARTICLE TOPIC	COLUMN INCHES	ARTICLE TOPIC	PERCENT OF CIRCULATION
People	119	PR Firm Activities	980	People	24
PRSA Activities	102	Definition	795	PR Firm Activities	18
PR Firm Activities	53	Image	769	PRSA Activities	15
Definition	39	People	756	Image	13
Image	35	PRSA Activities	725	Media Relations	6
PR Activities (non-PRSA)	28	PR Activities (non-PRSA)	550	In-House PR Departments	5
In-House PR Departments	16	Media Relations	381	Growth	3
Media Relations	15	Growth	338	Definition	3
Growth	13	In-House PR Departments	327	Communication Technology	3
Economic Impact	10	Communication Technology	238	Economic Impact	3
Communication Technology	9	Economic Impact	187	PR Activities (non-PRSA)	3
Corporate Responsibility	5	Corporate Responsibility	148	Women and Minorities in Public Relations	2
Issues Management	4	Issues Management	126	Issues Management†	
Women and Minorities in Public Relations	3	Women and Minorities in Public Relations	46	Corporate Responsibility†	
Education	2	Education	15	Education†	

*Based on 453 articles
†Less than 1 percent

[Bar chart showing percent by region (Northeast, North central, South, West) for categories: Public relations profession, Public relations activities, Tools of the profession, Social and political impact, Total articles]

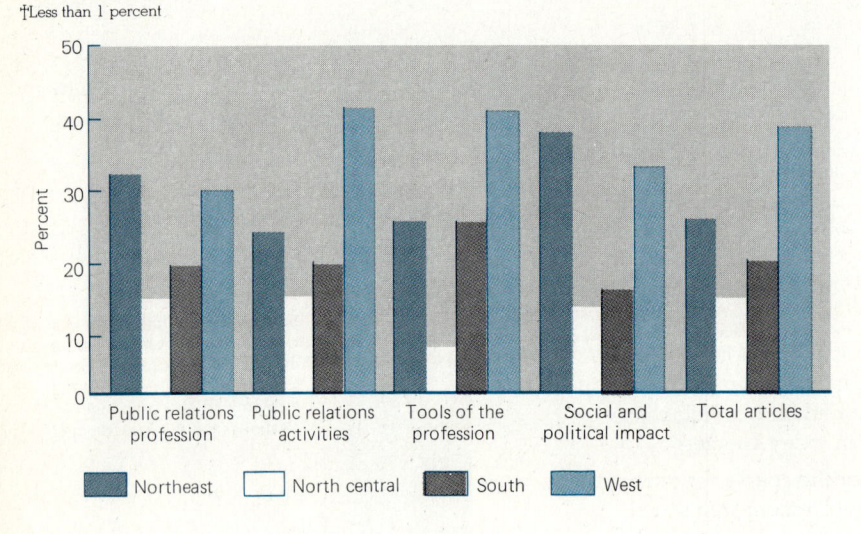

July 1982. Total circulation represented by the clips was 66.9 million, and exposure was estimated at 167.5 million readers.

Clips (424 received in 1981, 453 in first half of 1982) were divided into four categories with subcategories:

1. public relations activities (PRSA activities, people, agency activities, non-PRSA activities);
2. public relations profession (growth, definition, image);
3. tools of the profession (communication technology, media relations);
4. social impact (corporate responsibility, issues management, education, women

and minorities in public relations, economic impact on public relations).

Only 5 percent of the clips focused on social-impact issues, while 70 percent reported news of public relations people and their activities. Twenty percent included news about the profession and the remaining 5 percent dealt with the tools of the profession.

COVERAGE EXPLAINED

Coverage of the profession in general (total clips studied) was greatest in the West (39 percent), but the biggest number of clips on the social impact of public relations (37 percent of clips in this category) came from the Northeast [*see table, "Geographic Coverage By Subject Category"*]. *Reporting from the West was dominated heavily by reports of public relations people and their activities, which could cast some doubt on the long-held theory that East Coast gatekeepers control national media coverage. On the other hand, the heavy concentration of public relations firms and corporate public relations departments in the East could influence this finding.*

The study also revealed that over 50 percent of total clips studied were published in the general media, compared with non-public relations trade media (40 percent) and public relations trade media (10 percent).

The tone of media coverage appears to be improving, according to the study. Only 1 percent of all coverage was negative, while 85 percent appeared neutral. The remaining 14 percent was positive. One interpretation of these data is that editors and reporters are still trying to form solid opinions on a profession that has exploded rapidly in the last few years.

Kathy M. Hyett, "How the Media Cover Public Relations," *Public Relations Journal,* March 1983, pp. 30–31.

---

holding major roles on prime-time television series, the number of violent acts committed in cartoons aired on Saturday mornings and directed at child audiences, or the amount of newspaper space each presidential candidate received in a major newspaper the week before the election.

The prior Study in Focus contains an example of how content analysis can help researchers answer the questions they pose.

Exploring Research: An Alternative Approach

Of course, the preceding categories are not the only ones we can use to explore the types of mass-media research being conducted. In fact, one popular alternative strategy is to divide the mass-communication process into its constituent parts and suggest studies that might help to explain each part of that process. A popular model used to further this effort is Harold Lasswell's "Who Says What in What Channel to Whom with What Effect?" Each component in Lasswell's model corresponds to a prime media research area. For example:

- "Who" suggests that we should analyze the speaker, the reporter, or the medium owner.
- "Says what" suggests that we should examine the content of the message being carried over a medium during the communicative process.
- "In what channel" suggests that we should analyze the medium itself.
- "To whom" suggests that we need to examine the audience for this particular content.
- "With what effect" suggests that we should explore the impact that the media exert on audiences and society.

We've now explored the types of research that people conduct in an effort to help fill in the mass-media puzzle. What can we conclude? We hope you understand that as the nature of our society changes and as we change in response, we can expect the gen-

MEDIA PROBE

Divide into groups. Each group will be assigned to work with one and only one of the components of Lasswell's model. Next, each member in a group will select one of the following areas of the field: books, newspapers, magazines, radio, television, film, advertising, or public relations; it will be his or her task to locate a research study in that field that focuses on the group's assigned research variable. Finally, each individual is to summarize the selected study and explain how it advances our knowledge of that ingredient in the mass-communication process.

eralizations we are able to make about the media and our relationships to them to change also. However, one thing is certain: The task awaiting researchers is still as relevant and valid as it ever was in years gone by. Just as in the past, the present demands researchers who are willing to ask questions about, speculate about, examine, test and assess the impact of the media on us and our world. Are you one of those people?

SUMMARY

Mass-media researchers have a goal—to add pieces that will help enhance our understanding of the media, the uses we make of them, the way they affect us, and the impact they have on our world and the institutions that are a part of our world. Mass-communication researchers rely on five basic research methodologies: the historical approach, the experimental approach, the field study, the survey, and content analysis.

Researchers who use a historical approach aim to fill in a mass-communication puzzle piece by offering us an interpretation of the past. In contrast, the aim of researchers who use an experimental approach is to demonstrate the existence of a cause-and-effect relationship. Experimental researchers have more control over the situation they are exploring. Field researchers use the real world as a setting for their work. Because they use real-world locations their findings are somewhat more generalizable than are the results of experimental researchers. Survey researchers advance our knowledge of uses and effects by detailing current conditions and attitudes. Finally, the content analyst describes the basic content of mass communication objectively, systematically, and quantitatively.

Whatever the question asked or the method used to answer it, it is research that holds the key to the formulation and revision of mass-communication theories.

KEY TERMS

Historical research
Experimental research
Field research
Survey research
Content analysis
Hypodermic, or magic-bullet, theory
Two-step flow theory
Selective attention
Selective perception
Selective retention

NOTES

[1] Hadley Cantril, *The Invasion from Mars: A Study in the Psychology of Panic,* Princeton University Press, Princeton, N.J., 1940.

[2] Paul F. Lazarsfeld, Bernard Berelson, and Hazel Gaudet, *The People's Choice,* Columbia University Press, New York, 1948.

[3] Carl I. Hovland, Arthur A. Lumsdaine, and Fred D. Sheffield, *Experiments on Mass Communication,* Princeton University Press, Princeton, N.J., 1949.

[4] Frank Capra, *The Name Above the Title: An Autobiography,* Macmillan, New York, 1971, p. 327.

[5] Bernard Berelson, *Content Analysis in Communication Research,* Free Press, New York, 1952, p. 18.

SUGGESTIONS FOR FURTHER READING

Babie, E. R.: *The Practice of Social Research,* Wadsworth, Belmont, Calif., 1979. *A useful volume; often referred to in the literature.*

Berelson, Bernard: *Content Analysis in Communication Research,* Free Press, New York, 1952. *This work has become a standard in the field.*

Bormann, Ernest G.: *Theory and Research in the Communicative Arts,* Holt, Rinehart & Winston, New York, 1965. *An examination of research functions, contexts, and methodologies.*

Kerlinger, F. N.: *Foundations of Behavioral Research,* 2d ed., Holt, Rinehart & Winston, New York, 1973. *Comprehensive and understandable introduction to the field.*

Lowery, Shearon, and Melvin L. DeFleur: *Milestones in Mass Communication Research: Media Effects,* Longman, New York, 1983. *The first analytic history of the beginnings, development, and current status of the scientific study of the effects of mass communication.*

PART SIX

THE FUTURE: THE WINDOW WIDENS... OR DOES IT?

CHAPTER 13

THE NEW TECHNOLOGY: DEMASSIFYING THE MEDIA

Perhaps in some future century the history of the late twentieth century, like that of the fourteenth, will mark a great transition of civilization, a cusp between old and new. It could be called: the electronic renaissance.
    Frederick Williams

CHAPTER REVIEW

After reading this chapter, you should be able to:
- Compare our reaction to contemporary technological innovation with the way we reacted to innovations of the past
- Discuss how our "demassified" media differ from the traditional mass media
- Describe how the home video revolution could affect your life
- Explain how satellites are affecting our media menu
- Account for the increased popularity of video recorders
- Compare the capabilities of videocassette and videodisc machines
- Discuss the potential benefits and drawbacks of two-way cable
- Define and distinguish between teletext and videotex
- Assess the worth of video games

Recent advances in technology are turning our homes into quite interesting places. Many of us now live in "home entertainment and information centers." Home-tech systems have transformed our traditional living quarters into totally electronic, wired environments. More and more of us stay home today, content to plug ourselves into the myriad services available to us. What is apparent is that the widespread utilization of such technological innovations cannot help but affect the way we live, think, and interact with others. And, to be sure, not everyone is happy about it. But as media critic Les Brown points out, if we are to attain some perspective on current happenings, we must look not to the present, which is a notoriously poor guide to the future, but rather to the past, for it is the past that is capable of reminding us "that we have lived through this, or something like it, before."[1] As a case in point, consider the following observation: "It seems to us that we are getting perilously near the ideal of the modern Utopian whose life is to consist of sitting in armchairs and pressing a button. It is not a desirable prospect: we shall have no wants, no money, no ambition, no youth, no desires, no individuality, no names and nothing wise about us."[2] No, the menace spoken of is not the contemporary computer; neither is the fear expressed a present-day one. Rather, the statement first appeared in an 1890 publication, and the object of reference was the telephone.

Well, we plugged ourselves into telephones, and we survived. And in the days, years, and decades ahead we shall continue to fear new technologies (perhaps unnecessarily), but we are, as we shall see, plugging ourselves into them nonetheless. Whatever technologies succeed we shall celebrate; whatever technologies fail, we shall simply forget. What is certain, however, is that change is in the wind.

THE CHANGING MEDIA ENVIRONMENT: PLUGGING IN, TUNING OUT

For much of their existence the traditional media were unchallenged and secure in their preeminant positions as suppliers of news and entertainment to the mass market. Today, however, alternatives to our traditional media (books, magazines, newspapers, radio, and television) have appeared on the scene. These alternative media (among them cable television, videocassette recorders, and videodiscs) are "demassifying," or individualizing, our society and providing us with countless entertainment and information options. Our *demassified media* attempt to speak to us on a more personal level, hoping to convince us that they understand and can relate to our personal needs and wants. And we are buying it. As a result, the once invulnerable mass audience has begun to fragment, and individuals who are in the financial position to do so are beginning to assume more control over the media in their lives. Thus, for some of us, today's television set no longer simply receives broadcast programs; instead, our sets have add-ons that connect us via electronic plugs to such devices as an interactive cable, a computer, and teletext. Even our mediated landscape is changing: cables and satellite dishes now dot the scene that was once crisscrossed by television antennas. The Big Three networks, once also thought of as invulnerable, now find their ability to attract mass audiences threatened by the new machines—machines that are capable of offering a wide range of advanced specialized services to consumers. Consequently, consumers are beginning to zap commercials, tune out regular network programs, and plug into the other available news and entertainment facilities—all at hand in their own homes. Though it ruled for years, network television may face some very real challenges from the

MEDIA VIEW

WE ARE CHANGING

Not just in our institutions, the automobiles we buy, or the fashions we wear, but in how we behave as human beings.... The contemporary explosion in communications technologies—computers, satellites, tape, disc, microprocessors, and new telephone and radio services—are perceptibly changing the nature of our human environment. As we have done so many times in the history of our species, WE ARE IN THE PROCESS OF ADAPTING TO ENVIRONMENTAL CHANGE. This is not so much a "future shock" type of thesis as it is one of recognition and observation of change. After all, change is nothing unique or new to us humans. We are already the consequences of many millennia of environmental adaptation. Change is the name of our game.

Frederick Williams, *The Communications Revolution,* New American Library, New York, 1983, p. ix.

---

new technologies. But the networks are not alone: as we become less mobile, as there is less reason for us to leave our homes, as we come to rely on single, all-inclusive home communication centers, other media are affected as well.

As French sociologist Jacques Ellul notes: "All technological progress exacts a price; that is, while it adds something on the one hand, it subtracts something on the other."[3] What will be the price exacted by our changing media environment? Will we give up some media completely in return for others? Will some of our present media be rendered obsolete? If so, will there come a day when we will miss them? However we feel about the changing media environment, one thing is certain: we cannot and we should not ignore

MEDIA PROBE

Advances in mass-media technology are bringing about changes in our lives and the lives of people we know. In what ways, if any, have media innovations effected changes in the way you use the media, feel about the media, and behave? What kinds of technical media hardware do you wish you had today? Why?

---

the changes. After all, it is the media technology of today that will help us give shape to all of our tomorrows. You might say we are experiencing a technological revolution.

THE HOME VIDEO REVOLUTION

We are the inheritors of a technological cornucopia that promises to deliver to us a wider range of entertainment and information than people have ever had before. As we noted in Chapter 7, cable television has truly become a part of our media environment: more than 40 percent of U.S. households have cable and are capable of experiencing the breadth of programming brought into their homes via satellite and cable. *Direct satellite-to-home*

MEDIA PROBE

Which of the following do you own or have direct access to?

———A direct satellite-to-home transmission system
———A videocassette recorder
———A videodisc player
———A two-way cable system
———A teletext system
———A videotex system
———Video games

MEDIA VIEW

This excerpt, written in 1976, took a look into the future. In your opinion, has this already become our present?

> The chief characteristics of . . . the American culture were immediacy, impact, and sensation. In electronic terms the culture was merely self-indulgent. The future meant instant gratification, which is what instant photographs and videotapes were all about. It was not until copper wires had been replaced with broad-band optical fibers that communications became somewhat more refined. Broad-band optical fibers, activated and enforced by laser propulsion, meant that their users could link up with central information services in order to hear what they wished to hear instead of what someone else wanted them to hear. For example, a universal television retrieval system came into being, attached to the telephone. Wired to a home computer terminal, the system contained a constantly updated encyclopedia of information available to anyone with the ability to push a button. Security systems became computerized and could detect and isolate burglaries instantaneously. All shopping was performed through the computer-telex and all mail and newspapers were now effected through computer-television.
>
> The large TV screen, modern so short a time before, was replaced with a three-dimensional wraparound wallscreen. Even middle-class homes were glutted with voice-activated typewriters, picture phones, hologram-projection machines, and laser burglar alarms set not to kill but to stun. The well-to-do sported decorative computer watches on their wrists and laser scanners in their libraries. Most homes were solar-powered. Videophiles had become videomaniacs.
>
> The home had now become a total environment—the ultimate cocoon—and life, its bemused inhabitants believed, was terribly modern. More important, and for the first time, an intimate dialogue had been initated between man and the machine. The computer had eliminated the merely mechanical. All essentially mechanical movements, in fact, were becoming obsolete, although they had not yet been taken, as you will see, to their logical conclusions.
>
> Almost no one "traveled" anymore. More and more business was conducted from the home. Students were educated in the home; and as an alternative to the horrors of enforced holidays, the three-dimensional wraparound screen allowed one to be in, say, the South of France, and the sound-around system made soft Mediterranean noises. The wraparound screen also enabled one to link up with live concerts, sporting events, or any other public function. Computer units had become microminiaturized, operating on a less-input, more-output ratio. The computer, or Central Processing Unit as it came to be known, controlled everything. The demand for communication between computers was filled by the laser. The portable C.P.U., worn as a watch, was a peripheral device linked by matching light frequencies to the main C.P.U., and it provided a time-divisional highway along which multiplexed information was transmitted. The tiny device functioned as a calculator, watch, telephone, and memory bank. You didn't have to know what you wanted from the C.P.U.; it calculated that for you. It always knew what you wanted because it knew you.

Jon Bradshaw, "The Shape of Media Things to Come," *New York,* April 19, 1976, p. 63.

transmission is also well on its way to becoming a viable option, and *two-way interactive cable,* already introduced in a number of cities, is expected to spread. In addition, the marriage of the computer and the television set is turning the home into an information network well-fed and nourished by *teletext* and *videotex* systems. And of course no longer is our media-consumption time governed or orchestrated: VCRs and videodisc machines let us watch what we want when we want to. An array of computer games also stands ready to please us just in case we should find our present media environment deficient and seek other outlets. Our homes, transformed into self-contained home communications centers, could well become veritable "media cocoons."

How we use the communications innovations of today may well determine whether or not we succeed in constructing an improved, more individually pleasing media environment, as well as whether or not we prevail in building a new kind of future for ourselves.

Let us now look at some of the innovations that comprise our newly enriched media menu.

Satellites

In 1962, the launching of the first communications satellite heralded the birth of satellite technology; during the intervening years, instantaneous nationwide and worldwide communication became realities. It was Home Box Office's use of the satellite to deliver programming to client systems in 1975 that helped cable television really take off. Now, in addition to cable, commercial and public networks also use satellites to transmit programs to their subscribers. In fact, much if not all of our television programming is delivered to stations via satellite for retransmission to home TV sets either over the air or by means of a cable. Since they are unaffected by atmospheric conditions and less expensive than other signal transmission systems, satellites are increasingly becoming the way of the future.

Satellite signals are picked up by a dish-shaped antenna; presently more than 2000 such receivers, called *earth stations,* are in operation throughout the United States. The cost of an earth station has dropped from about $100,000 to about $300 or less. Thus, whereas once only cable or other communications companies could afford them, today the number of individually owned earth stations is increasing. No bigger than an umbrella and easily mountable on rooftops, the receiving dishes enable viewers to watch television direct from the station. Such earth sta-

---

MEDIA VIEW

A DISH ON EVERY ROOF

DBS is television without the middleman. Providing the first wholly national TV service, direct broadcast satellites can beam television programs directly to individual homes, skipping the local broadcaster or cable operator. What makes this possible is the gigantic "footprint"—or coverage area—of communications satellites, coupled with the development of relatively small and inexpensive receiving dishes or earth stations.

A receiving dish about one meter in diameter is installed on the subscriber's roof or in his yard, so as to have a direct line of sight to the satellite. A wire runs from the dish to the first of two converter boxes, where the signal is "down-shifted" from the extremely high frequencies on which the satellite broadcasts to the VHF signals a TV set can receive. A second converter box unscrambles the signal and serves as a channel selector. That box also contains an "addressable converter," allowing the DBS operator to turn a channel on and off, which facilitates pay-per-view service.

"DBS: The Space Race Is On," *Channels of Communication,* November-December 1983, p. 12.

> **MEDIA PROBE**
>
> It is believed that in the near future direct satellite broadcasting will be in a three-way race with cable and over-the-air TV for a majority of the audience. Based on your own research, who do you think will win the race and why?

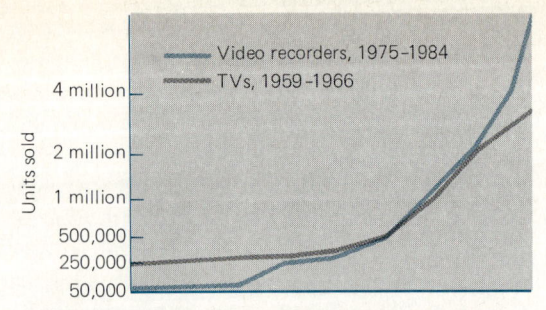

FIGURE 13-1 The growth pattern of VCRs compared with the growth pattern of television sets. (*Anthony Hoffman, Craline & Co.*)

tions have even been featured as possible gift items in recent Nieman Marcus catalogs.

As a result of the direct broadcast satellite, programs can now be beamed directly to individual homes. This emerging video option could well benefit the 20 to 30 million homes situated in areas judged to be too sparsely populated to be worth wiring for cable. And since satellites know no national boundaries, dish antenna owners are able to pick up programming from as far away as Brazil; they are also able to receive network "feeds" from correspondents long before newscasts air, obtain an ever-increasing number of programs from every broadcast source available, and even secure, direct from NASA, pictures of explorations of distant planets.[4]

In addition to enhancing viewing options, the satellite also makes feasible the creation of myriad private networks, each customized to fit the needs of the user. Today, by using satellite technology, virtually anyone can mount a nationwide news conference, symposium, or rally; consequently, videoconferences are very much a part of our present.[5]

Videocassette Recorders

The home *videocassette recorder* was introduced in 1975 by the Sony Corporation. Called Betamax, it sold for about $2300. In 1976, JVC, another Japanese firm, put its video home system, the VHS, on sale. Thus began the battle to see who would emerge as ruler of the home VCR market. You see, the Beta and VHS systems are incompatible. Though other competitors are also currently seeking a share of the market, Sony and JVC are still the most appealing to consumers.

Today, more than 10 percent of American homes own a VCR. It is expected that by 1990, 51 percent of American homes will own a recorder (see Figure 13-1). Their increasing popularity has been compared to color TV, which took off from 1959 to 1966. Since almost everybody knows somebody who owns one, the major force believed to be responsible for the success of the VCR (like the major force responsible for color TV sales) is the snowball effect; in other words, potential buyers are introduced to the product by friends who already have the product. A gradual drop in prices (some models now sell for less than $400) also accounts for an increase in the VCR's popularity.

How do owners use the VCR? The most common use continues to be the recording of programs for later viewing. In effect, the VCR operates as a time-shift machine. In January 1984, the Supreme Court ruled that home videotaping did not constitute a copyright infringement, thus ensuring that the time-shift practice would continue. To be sure, in the coming months Congress probably will find itself pressured to consider bills that impose fees on both VCR and videotape sales in an effort to compensate copyright holders.

VCRs are also used to play purchased or rented prerecorded programs; though some

"The Supreme Court says we can tape this if we want."

(Drawing by Stevenson, © 1981 *The New Yorker* Magazine, Inc.)

are instructional in nature ("How To Play Baseball" "How to Give First Aid"), approximately 80 percent of all tapes are movies, of which 20 percent are estimated to be pornographic.[6] Such movie tape sales are benefiting the film business. The copyright owner receives 20 percent of the wholesale price of such videotapes—a larger proportion than they receive from cable airings.

A number of media observers believe that the home VCR may well be the best thing to happen to the movie business since the invention of television. Do you agree? Approximately 10 percent of VCR owners also use accompanying portable video cameras to produce their own home movies.

The VCR has enhanced our viewing flexibility, increased the uses we make of our television sets, and widened the repertoire of programs from which we may select what we wish to watch. As a result, diverse rather than merely mass interests stand a chance of being satisfied. We are now free to create our own prime-time schedule, fill it with instructions, news, or entertainment, and scan through it or edit out the commercials. The VCR is an instrument that is helping to shape the way we live. But it is not alone: so is the videodisc.

Videodiscs

Unlike videocassette machines, which have recording and playback capabilities, videodisc machines, which are also plugged into TV sets, are playback-ready only. Consequently, videodisc machines don't allow their owners to dub onto blank discs or produce their own programs. The disc resembles a 33⅓ rpm record. At least in one form (presently there is no compatibility among competing brands) the replacement of the traditional stylus by laser beam technology has rendered the disc virtually indestructable. Since no stylus ever touches the disc, the disc cannot wear out.

Discs are changing not only our entertainment environment but our information environment as well. A single disc can store 3200 books, half a million pages—the equivalent of 54,000 individual frames of information on each silvery side. In effect, what the disc provides is a data compression system capable of storing a wealth of audio, video, or print

MEDIA PROBE

Some movie studios are thinking about eliminating HBO or pay TV releases of films, opting instead to proceed directly from theater releases to videocassette releases to network broadcast releases—all in an effort to give the cassette version a longer life.

1. Imagine that you are the studio executive in charge of making such a decision. What would you decide to do and why?
2. Imagine that you work for HBO or some other pay TV service. What arguments would you raise to forestall such a move?
3. Now, think of yourself as an HBO patron. How would such a change in procedure affect you?

information in a very small space. The videodisc is the most efficient form of information storage currently servicing the home market. And all the information contained on the disc is machine-readable, easily accessible, and of higher picture and sound quality than is available from most VCRs. Offering individuals even more control over what they watch than the VCR, laser discs enable viewers to call up any of the images by merely touching a button, because each of their 54,000 frames is separately numbered.

Whether we use them for education, persuasion, or entertainment, the shiny videodisc is another tool that is not only altering our media environment but also changing the way we see, learn, and behave. Because we are able to interact constantly with the disc, the passivity engendered by traditional television watching is no longer a problem.

The possibilities for videodiscs are limited only by the imagination. Among the information being considered for disc storage or already in disc form are the contents of an entire museum, an encyclopedia, visual trips or surrogate tours, dramatizations of children's books, Army recruitment appeals, and cardiopulmonary resuscitation training lessons. But again, a key dimension of videodisc technology is its potential for increased program choice. While millions of viewers must be "countable" (the ratings must be high) to guarantee the viability of a commercial television program, only a few thousand discs need to be sold for the disc to "make it." Despite its features, however, for the time being VCRs continue to outsell disc players 10 to 1. But the prognosis for disc players is a good one. In fact, in the years ahead, of all the new machines brought to us by advances in technology, videodisc players are expected to sell the fastest. These predictions are indicated in Figure 13-2.

Two-Way Cable

Another of our recent technological gifts is two-way interactive cable. Begun in 1977 in Columbus, Ohio, interactive systems are now in operation in a number of cities including Cincinnati, Houston, and Pittsburgh. Presently installed in over 500,000 homes, two-

MEDIA VIEW

When the disc's interactive abilities are used, you can "climb" it, from one branch to the next. Whether the content is a sales pitch, lesson, concert, catalogue, game, or story, the disc branches out where you choose to go. It's a trick, of course, but the plastic disc appears to be possessed of the intelligence to respond to you.

Along with the video-game, the interactive disc is ending the age of passive television-watching. "There are *some* people who can't remember not having radio," observes Jeffrey Silverstein, a young disc designer. "My generation can't remember not having television. The kids now can't remember not *controlling* television."

Paul Mareth, "The Video Disc," *Channels of Communication,* March–April 1984, p. 24.

way cable, working in conjunction with the computer, has made it possible for subscribers to feed back information to the "head-end" of their cable systems. Speaking of two-way cable, Vivian Horner, vice president for programming of Warner Amex, noted: "We have witnessed the coming and going of the passive television era. There will always be television which is simply there to view. But I believe that we have almost inadvertently entered the age of interactive television.... We are standing on the very edge of an entirely new relationship with video. It is probably, in its impact, at least as great as the invention of the printing press."[7] Described by some as "electronic democracy," two-way cable systems make it possible for viewers to participate in instant referenda on diverse topics and public issues: Should the host shave his head? Should capital punishment be banned? Should the mayor be recalled from office? Though this aspect of interactive cable used to receive the most attention, the focus of such systems is being rethought. Receiving additional stress instead are the pay-per-view and market research aspects of interactivity. In addition, most two-way systems can provide a range of other services to their subscribers: shopping, banking, bill paying, fire and theft protection, and medical diagnoses are among the benefits subscribers may sign up for.

Though it only gets into the home by permission (subscribers pay to participate), many have hesitated to endorse it because they fear that the abuse potential for interactivity is just too great. One media critic who has expressed such a concern is Les Brown: "Like a sighted person playing heads or tails with a blind person, the cable company is free to deceive by reporting a false tally on issues in which it has an interest and thus may influence legislation as it chooses."[8] Others complain that since two-way capability makes it feasible for the cable system to monitor what channels we tune to, interactive cable has turned the tables on us; in effect, critics claim, we have become the watched—we are no longer just the watchers.

Certainly one potential nightmare is that the stored information would be misused, perhaps even shared with other people or companies without our knowledge or consent. But there are also potential dreams. We might really end up with participatory television; we now have the means to be connected to the creative aspects of entertainment programming. In other words, the day may not be too far off when we decide how a story will end, help develop a plot line, or based on clues provided in the course of a show race to

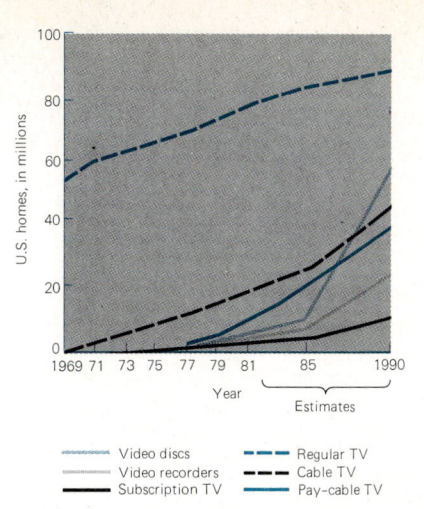

FIGURE 13-2 Growth in new distribution channels for television, 1969–1990. *(Data from Television Bureau of Advertising, National Cable Television Association, and* Television Digest, *Reprinted from* Business Week, *December 17, 1979.)*

MEDIA PROBE

What do you think? Does the fact that interactivity makes it possible for the cable company to store information on your purchasing habits, lifestyle, program preferences, and/or political and moral opinions infringe in any way on your rights to privacy and personal freedom? If you had the opportunity to subscribe to such a system, would you? Why or why not?

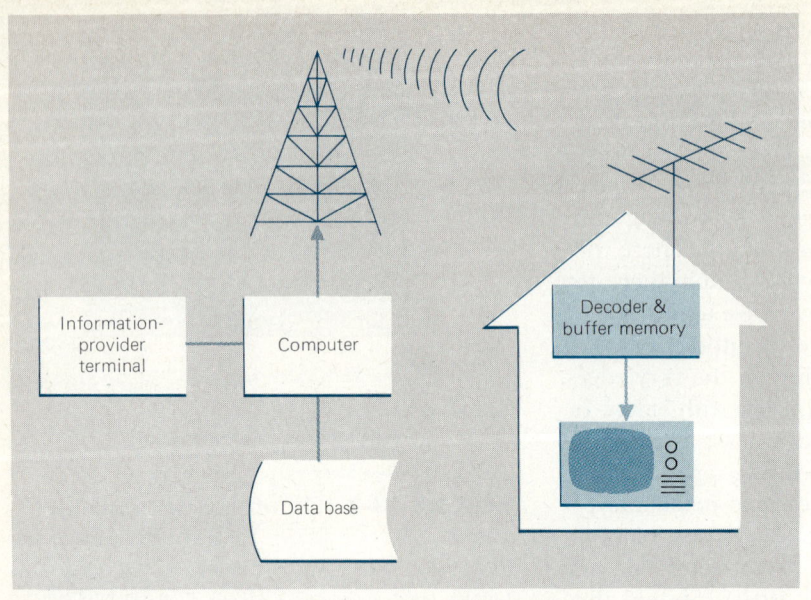

FIGURE 13-3 Teletext. Teletext is a service in which data are provided to subscribers from the source via television signals. The subscribers receive the data on their home television sets. *(John Tydeman, "Videotex: Ushering in the Electronic Household," The Futurist, World Future Society, Washington, D.C., 1982, p. 999.)*

solve the mystery for ourselves. Of course, while whether "entertainment by consensus" is a dream or a nightmare is open to debate, one thing is certain, interactive television is adding a new dimension to our media experience.

Teletext and Videotex

Of all the new technologies, teletext and videotex are the most innovative. Again, by uniting the home television set and the computer, we have recreated a traditional entertainment medium as a tool of the information age. Teletext and videotex refer to systems that supply textual and graphic data by totally electronic means. Teletext is a one-way system, delivering its verbal and visual information to the television receiver as part of the standard, over-the-air broadcast signal (see Figure 13-3). Mixed into the signal in such a way, only a user with a special decoder and a keypad can display the available information.

Videotex is an interactive system (see Figure 13-4). By hooking the home TV set into either a telephone line or a two-way cable, and connecting it to a central computer, users are able to send as well as receive signals. Beside the potential for interactivity, the main difference between teletext and videotex is that videotex is connected to a much larger computer; whereas most teletext "magazines" typically transmit about 100 pages of data, videotex can transmit much more. In addition, unlike the teletext user, the videotex user has the ability to "call up" instantaneously information existing in the system's data bank. The teletext user must wait until a transmission cycle is completed before a page of specifically requested information appears on the home screen.

But whether we are talking about teletext

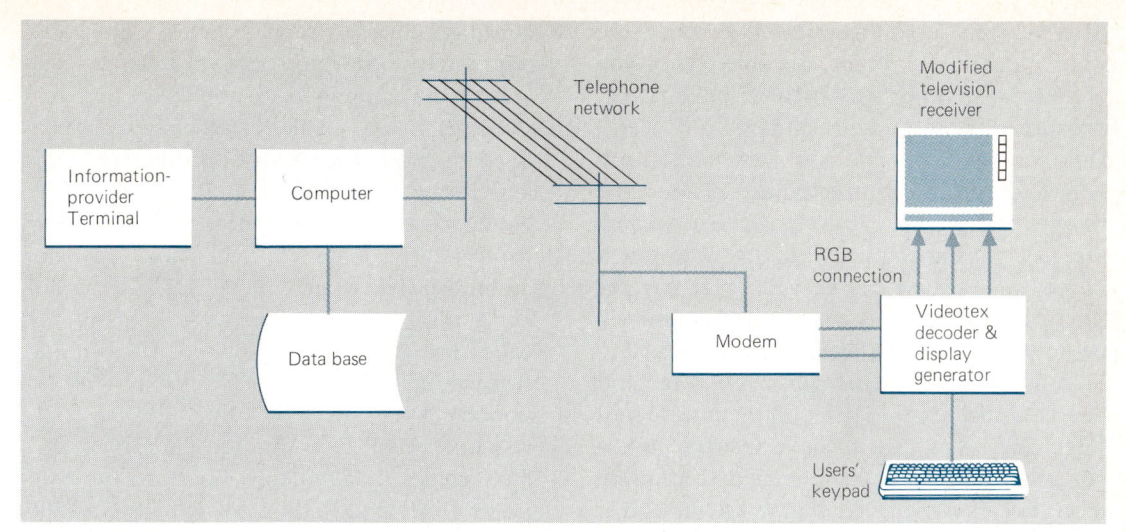

FIGURE 13-4 Videotex. Videotex is a two-way system allowing subscribers to access information via telephone cables, cable TV, or a combination of the two; subscribers can also respond via a home computer (John Tydeman, "Videotex: Ushering in the Electronic Household," The Futurist, *World Future Society, Washington, D.C., 1982, p. 1001.*)

or videotex, one-way or two-way capability, what is significant is that the electronic delivery of information—ranging from hard news to weather and traffic reports, classified ads, book and movie reviews, and electronic mail, frivolous data and profound observations—is here. No longer is the TV just a picture tube; it can now also function as an information screen.[9] In fact, the basic ingredient of both types of systems is old-fashioned print—flashing across your television and available to you at your request. In effect, each day you can create your own special-interest newspaper. The consumer has truly become his or her own gatekeeper.

MEDIA PROBE

If you were to subscribe to a teletext or videotex service, what kinds of information would you want available to you? What kinds of services? Why?

Will teletext and videotex be successful? According to Gary Arlen of *Channels of Communication*, "A classic catch-22 plagues teletext's development. Viewers cannot decide if they want to buy a decoder until they see

Customized computer systems can become a family project. (Catherine Ursillo/Photo Researchers)

THE NEW TECHNOLOGY: DEMASSIFYING THE MEDIA   393

what teletext looks like, and they can't see what it looks like without a decoder."[10] Nonetheless, with the support of advertising, broadcasters took the plunge (or leap), launched teletext, and are now pressuring manufacturers to begin building decoders for the general public. With regard to videotex, the key question appears to be how much money will subscribers be willing to pay for the service? Estimates are that customers will be asked to pay between $25 and $30 a month to cover both the subscription fee and the potential cost of telephone time. Thus, since teletext is free to anyone who buys a computer, and videotex carries a continuing price tag, it is believed that even though it can't do as much, teletext will probably be the winner in the electronic publishing numbers game.

Video Games

What's the fastest growing sport in America? It's not soccer. It's not baseball. It's not football. It's not racketball. It's not tennis. According to futurist John Tydeman, it is video games.[11] Included in the general category *video games* are coin-operated games housed in arcades, cartridge-based games that are playable on special machines in our homes, and computer games that make use of the more sophisticated home computer. Americans dish out approximately $1 billion a year (more than they spend on movies and records) in order to satiate their video game appetite.

Building on the newest advances in electronic technology, video games have come a long way since the first modern offering hit the consumer market and became a blockbuster. That was in 1979 and the name of the game was Space Invaders. What Space Invaders announced to the world was the "natural marriage of computers, science fiction and war."[12] The goal of the game was to shoot to kill in an effort to repel invaders. Fast-paced and totally absorbing, Space Invaders kept consumers coming back for more and heralded in the age of the electronic game-playing wars. Soon the likes of Pac-Man and Donkey Kong were also populating the video game scene. Within a short time, however, game players began to seek more involving and more vivid duels; the new media technology was prepared to meet the demand. Arcades are presently populated with interactive videodisc laser games, among them, the popular Dragon's Lair. And advances have also been made in computer games—we now have games that not only build on the computer's increased ability to generate quality graphics and sound but also rely on recent innovations in game design. Today we can actually participate in role-playing games, games in which we are expected to respond in character, that is, as a character living in the self-contained world of the game would respond. In effect, the game has been transformed into a complex situation, one that requires us to adopt a set of values (probably those of the game-maker) and act accordingly.

The debate over the worth and value of video games is a continuing one. Parents, doctors, and some media-effects researchers attack the games for distracting students from schoolwork, being too violent, and plunging the participant into an unreal world devoid of actual person-to-person contacts. For example, Patricia Greenfield, a professor of psychology at the University of California, notes that when she asked one boy why he liked video games better than television he answered, "On TV, if you want to make someone die, you can't."[13] Defenders of the games counter that the games do have pro-social aspects: they note that the games help improve eye-hand-brain coordination, develop inductive reasoning abilities, improve spatial perception, and pave the way for play-

MEDIA VIEW

THE NAME OF THE GAME

In what kinds of scenarios do computer games immerse their afficionados? One (game made for the Apple) is called Castle Wolfenstein. The game's plot is explained when you "boot" the floppy disc containing the program into your computer: You are a prisoner of the Nazis in World War II, held in an old castle. You get hold of a smuggled gun, kill the men guarding your dungeon, and go through the castle unlocking trunks and searching them for weapons, uniforms, and enemy plans. As you manipulate your persona through the castle, you encounter Nazi guards who shout at you in German. When you kill one of them, you hear his screams through your computer's speaker. You win by escaping from the castle. (I've played for hours, and have yet to see the bright sunshine and doves that supposedly accompany an escape)....

In playing Adventure . . . the persona finds himself in a world full of murderous dwarfs, unbridgeable caverns, and dark passageways. There are treasures to be found, but only if the adventurer gives the proper commands to the computer, not only telling it where to move the persona ("Go south") but having the persona interact with the environment. "Kill dwarf," you might say, and the computer will respond, "With what?" Then you might say, "Use ax," and if you have picked up an ax in your travels, the computer will tell you that you have killed the dwarf.

Steven Levy, "Fantastic Worlds of the Computer Game," *Channels of Communication*, November–December 1983, p. 8.

MEDIA PROBE

On December 29, 1982, *The MacNeil/Lehrer News Hour* focused on "Pac-Man Perils," the possibility that video games might breed antisocial behavior and violence. During the course of the program, Rabbi Steven Fink stated:

I'm against the violence in the games. I think that the primary value that the games teach is kill or be killed. And that is what concerns me.... These games are very different from cowboys or Indians or even children playing soldiers. In those games they emphasize imaginary kinds of skills. There's nothing imaginary about the zapping of space ships or little monsters on the screen. And I think that the ultimate effect of these games is that they will add to the dehumanization and objectification of human beings.... When children spend hours in front of a screen playing some of these games that are inherently violent, they will tend to look at people as they look at these little blips on the screen that must be zapped—that must be killed before they are killed. And it is my concern that ten, twenty years down the line we're going to see a group of children who then become adults who don't view people as human beings but rather view them as other blips to be destroyed—as things.

Have you played Pac-Man? Do you agree with this opinion? Why or why not? Which do you think outweighs the other—the perils or the benefits of video game playing? Why?

For those who stand to be priced out of the information market, the government may have to provide information subsidies as it now provides food stamps. (Sylvia Plachy/Archive Pictures)

ers to develop positive attitudes toward computers and computer literacy skills.

Of course, what remains constant (at least for the moment) is that no matter how frustrating, upsetting, or elating the game experience has been, the entire experience comes to an end when time runs out (in the case of coin-operated machines) or the computer is turned off.

THE IMPACT OF THE NEW TECHNOLOGY

It is a given that the technological innovations we have examined will affect us in a number of different ways. First, we see ourselves becoming increasingly demassified. Messages are now more individualized; we need only open ourselves to the information we desire and we can now even schedule when we receive it. Communication "on demand" is a reality. Second, the home of the future is here. We now have the power to create a home media environment perfectly suited to our interests and needs; all we need for work, school, play, and home management can be attained within our own households. Third, the capacity of the technology knows no real limits; it is the wants, interests, and imagination of creator and consumer that impede or promote future developments. That is the promise of the new technology. What are the problems?

Each of the innovations we have examined also has potentially negative effects. For one, the opportunities we now have for random exposure to information are decreasing.[14] Some years ago, writing in *The Wall Street Journal*, Douglas Cater appeared to recognize this happening when he posed the following question: "Is the fractionalization of audiences a net social gain? . . . What happens when each minority group can tune in to its own prophets?"[15] With demassification this might well occur. No longer will the media function as Elmer's glue and bind all of our interests equally.[16] We might each plug in to only small tips of an iceberg of information; shared knowledge might indeed become a thing of the past. In addition, the gap between those who have the money to afford the new technology and those who must be content with what they can derive from the old technology could widen. Thus, another class division would be added to our society: the information rich (the haves) versus the information poor (the have-nots). Access to in-

396   THE FUTURE: THE WINDOW WIDENS...OR DOES IT?

formation would not be a right—available to all who needed and wanted it. Instead, it would become an earned privilege, within reach of only those who could bear the price. So while the new technology might be liberation for some, for those who stand to be priced out of the information market, it might be merely one more reminder of society's lack of information equity. Consequently, it could well become necessary for the government to provide information subsidies much the way it provides food stamps and welfare. Finally, having everything we need at our fingertips at home could turn us into information caterpillars—creatures who have no need to leave the comfort of their cocoons. Inhabiting self-contained abodes, we might cease to be social animals.

But no one really knows how the scenario will develop. All we do know is that these issues must be considered. Whatever the outcome, the years ahead are sure to be interesting. Welcome to tomorrow!

SUMMARY

Technological advances are transforming the way we live our lives. Our homes, for example, are being turned into totally electronic, wired environments capable of providing us with a plethora of mediated services. Challenging the supremacy of the traditional media, alternative media, like direct broadcast satellites, cable television, video casette recorders, videodiscs, teletext, and videotex, are demassifying our society by offering us countless entertainment and information options.

Whether we are able to adapt to and use the communications innovations of today may well determine whether or not we succeed in creating an improved, more individually pleasing media environment, and whether or not we prevail in building a new kind of future for ourselves.

KEY TERMS

Direct satellite-to-home transmission
Earth stations
Videocassette recorder
Two-way interactive cable
Teletext
Videotex
Video game
Demassified media

NOTES

[1] Les Brown, "Perspective: Beyond Boom and Bust," *Channels of Communication,* November–December 1983, pp. 5–6.
[2] Asa Briggs, "The Pleasure Telephone: A Chapter in the Prehistory of the Media," in Ithiel de Sola Pool (ed.), *The Social Impact of the Telephone,* MIT Press, Cambridge, Mass., 1977, pp. 40–59.
[3] Jacques Ellul, "The Technological Order," *Technology and Culture,* vol. 3, 1962, p. 394.
[4] Peggy Charren and Martin W. Sandler, *Changing Channels,* Addison-Wesley, Reading, Mass., 1983, p. 121.
[5] Lisa Moss, "Videoconferencing: The Electric Meeting Comes to Order," *Channels of Communication,* November–December 1983, p. 24.
[6] David Lachenbruch, "Home Video: Home Is Where the Action Is," *Channels of Communication,* November–December 1983, pp. 42–43.
[7] Quoted in "High Tech, High Stakes," *Inside Story,* May 12, 1983.
[8] Les Brown, *Keeping Your Eyes on Television,* Pilgrim, New York, 1979, p. 52.
[9] Kenneth Edwards, "Delivering Information to The Home Electronically," Michael Emery and Ted Curtis Smythe (eds.), in *Readings in Mass Communication* (5th ed.), Brown, Dubuque, Iowa, 1983, p. 244.
[10] Gary Arlen, "Teletext: Teletext Takes to the Air," *Channels of Communication,* November–December 1983, p. 41.
[11] John Tydeman, "Videotex: Ushering in the Electronic Household," *The Futurist,* February 1982, p. 54.
[12] Steven Levy, "Fantastic Worlds of the Computer Game," *Channels of Communication,* November–December 1983, p. 6.
[13] Fox Butterworth, "Video Game Specialists

Come to Harvard to Praise Pac-Man Not to Bury Him," *The New York Times,* May 24, 1983, p. A22.

[14] Thomas E. Baldwin and D. Stevens McVoy, *Cable Communication,* Prentice-Hall, Englewood Cliffs, N.J., 1983, p. 356.

[15] "A Communication Revolution?" *The Wall Street Journal,* August 6, 1973, p. 44.

[16] Wilson P. Dizard, Jr. *The Coming Information Age,* Longman, New York, 1982, p. 142.

SUGGESTIONS FOR FURTHER READING

Baldwin, Thomas E., and D. Stevens McVoy: *Cable Communication,* Prentice-Hall, Englewood Cliffs, N.J. *A thorough overview of the fascinating cable communications industry.*

Dizard, Wilson P., Jr.: *The Coming Information Age,* Longman, New York, 1982. *A scholarly examination of the technological, economic, and political implications of the new age of information. The author describes the high-technology machines that will power the era.*

"Field Guide to the New Media," *Channels of Communications,* November–December 1983. *A carefully researched primer on the new electronic media. Examines both state of the art and state of the market. Explores where things stand and why. Interesting reading.*

Salvaggio, Jerry L.: *Telecommunications,* Longman, New York, 1983. *A collection of critical essays focusing on the social and cultural side-effects accompanying new forms of telecommunications.*

Williams, Frederick: *The Communications Revolution* (rev. ed.), New American Library, New York, 1983. *A readable guide to the new technologies. Explores both the possibilities and the implications of recent developments.*

CHAPTER 14

NOT THE LAST WORD: YOUR ROLE BEYOND THIS BOOK

Media are both a door to the mind and a window on the world. They provide insight and "outsight"—the introduction to hitherto unperceived realities.

Tony Schwartz

CHAPTER PREVIEW

After reading this chapter, you should be able to:
- Identify your career goals and skills
- Compare opinions expressed regarding the future of the media
- Describe the key changes you see occurring in your media environment
- Assess the extent to which you are able to use the media effectively

We hope you now realize that this book was as much about *you* as it was about the media that permeate your world. As we noted at the outset, the media have a way of affecting our lives: they shape us, the people with whom we relate, and our environment. Consequently, as we come to know the media better, we also come to know ourselves, other people, and our society better. To be sure, each of the media we have studied has exerted an influence on the nature and quality of our existence. Helping you to understand that influence was one of our major goals. Yet, even mastering the content of this book is only a beginning; if you are to comprehend how both existing and new media are helping to alter the way you behave as a human being, you need to acknowledge that what you really have facing you is a lifetime assignment. To aid you in meeting this challenge, let us examine a number of strategies you can use to enhance your understanding of the media and make your present and future relationships with the media as rewarding and fulfilling as possible.

WHERE DO YOU GO FROM HERE? LOOKING FOR A CAREER

As you complete this text, you may be mulling over the following questions: Would I like a career in mass communication? Would I be interested in working in the book, magazine, newspaper, radio, television, film, advertising, or public relations industry? Although you may not feel ready to answer these questions with a definitive yes or no, the time is right for you to begin taking stock of your career options and preferences.

MEDIA PROBE

Which of the mass communication industries interest you as a career? Put a 1 beside those industries that interest you the most, a 2 beside those that interest you somewhat, and a 3 beside those that do not interest you at all at this time.

```
_____ Books              _____ Television
_____ Newspapers         _____ Film
_____ Magazines          _____ Advertising
_____ Radio              _____ Public Relations
_____ Recordings
```

Explain your reasons for your rankings. What is it about each area that attracts or repels you?

If you put a 3 beside all areas, that too is revealing. It means that you have chosen or believe you will choose a career outside of the media. On the other hand, if you have given a 1 or 2 rating to any industry, you may want to think over the subsequent career development suggestions. By the way, even if you do plan to work in a field unrelated to mass communication, you may find some of these job-search ideas helpful to you.

Career Search—Career Research

How much control do you feel you will be able to exert over your future career? If your family owns an advertising agency and you want to enter that field, you probably will be in a position to exercise quite a bit of control. Most of us, however, are not in such a position; therefore we have a much greater challenge facing us. When you undertake a career search, in order to be successful at it, you really need to mount a two-pronged research effort: you have to research yourself and the industry that interests you. Since by taking this course, you've already begun the second, let's backtrack and start with the first—you.

Researching Yourself Stop for a moment. Dream a little. Suppose money were no object and you were in a position to do anything or become anyone you wanted to. What would you choose to do? Who would you choose to be? Make yourself a list of several such dreams. Next, try to create for yourself a scenario for each of the media positions you are considering. For example, what would it be like to be a famous movie star? A famous television director? A best-selling novelist? An investigative reporter? A radio station executive? A book editor?

Each of us has 168 hours available to us each week—no more and no less. What you are in the process of considering is how you would like to spend the work portion of that available time. Far too often, people seem to fall into a job without ever first having explored other options open to them. The career dreams that you just had need not be a one-time occurrence. We suggest that several times each year you take the time to write down such career dreams in order to assess whether or not you are on the career path that is right for you—the one that will let you use the work portion of your weekly budget of 168 hours in a productive, fulfilling, and rewarding way.

Continue your self-examination by answering these questions:

- Do you want the security of an established firm behind you, or would you prefer the challenges and accompanying risks of an emerging firm? What working circumstances do you desire? Would you enjoy a desk job? Being out in the field? Working with others? Working alone? On the air? In a management position?
- What kinds of people do you want to work with? Do you enjoy being around competitive people? Thinkers? Caring people? Humorous ones? What starting salary are you looking for? Under what conditions will you accept less?
- What salary do you want to be making five years after you enter your chosen position? Do you want to be rich? If so, how much are you willing to risk for money?

Answering these questions should help you identify some of the criteria you need to consider before deciding on a career.

Your skills are another factor which could

MEDIA PROBE

Score yourself on each listed skill, with 1 representing the lowest possible rating, and 5 representing the highest possible rating.

———Learning   ———Writing
———Managing   ———Researching
———Analyzing   ———Instructing/Explaining
———Directing   ———Listening
———Organizing   ———Negotiating
———Delegating   ———Persuading/Convincing

Place a check next to the items you scored highest and lowest. To what extent are your skill area highs and lows correlated with the career preferences you identified earlier? Are your skills and career preferences in sync or out of sync? What skills would you need to work on in order to make it in your chosen field?

affect your job-search success quotient. When we speak of skills, we are not just referring to equipment knowledge or content mastery (though these are part of it); rather, we are also speaking of more basic proficiencies such as those included in the preceding exercise.

It is important to realize that your personality could affect the way you work as well. For example, do you work better surrounded by people or do you work better on your own? Are you a self-starter who prefers to be left to your own devices, or do you prefer to have goals set for you and have someone there to guide you as you work toward attaining those goals? Four personality variables are identified below. Which characterizes you best? Give it a 4. Which characterizes you next best? Give it a 3, and so on till you have given a 1 to the one which least typifies your behavior.

———Dominant. You want control. You feel conflict is natural. You deal with people in straightforward and direct manner.

———Talkative. You want to be liked. For the most part you are happy and optimistic. You have a good sense of humor.

———Patient. You want security. For the most part, you are cautious and careful, dependable and steady.

———Compliant. You seek to avoid criticism. You are precise and accurate in your work. For the most part you are conservative, preferring to avoid risks.

Which adjective do you believe best describes you? How does this mesh with your career choice? For example, while that "talkative" person might do well in media sales, management might be a better choice for the "dominant" individual. Of course, we all probably display each of these qualities to various degrees. Some careers, however, might require that we emphasize a particular trait while deemphasizing others. To what extent is your career choice in or out of step with the personality traits you perceive yourself to have?

Finally, in order to complete this phase of your research into yourself, take a few minutes to finish this sentence in as detailed and as specific a way as possible:

Before I retire, I would like to———

You have now compiled a body of data you can use as you continue your career research.

Of course, in order to really understand any medium you need to meet and talk to the people who work in or write about that industry. Consequently, as you get closer to looking for that first job, you may want to schedule some informational interviews with key people, that is, interviews during which you seek information, not necessarily a position. To aid you in that effort, in the following section a number of industry leaders offer their opinions regarding where each of their fields is heading. We hope their views on the future of the media will help you understand the role the media will play in your own life in the years to come, as well as the career possibilities open to you.

WHERE WILL THE MEDIA GO FROM HERE?

What does the future hold for the media we have examined? In this section, a number of well-known practitioners and educators answer that question. Contained in their answers are clues to the type of mediated environment you may be entering.

The Future of Books

John Tebbel, author and book historian, has this to say.

"For more than a hundred years, the decline and fall of the book has been regularly predicted. The novel is periodically certified as dead or dying by qualified custodians of literature, yet it continues to thrive and even proliferate. Books were threatened first by the bicycle in the nineties, which were not so gay, then it was the automobile, motion pictures, radio, and television. Now it is the computer which will make all reading unnecessary except what is projected on the flickering green screen.

"Those who are familiar with the history of science and technology will not be misled by these requiems for the book. It teaches us that while new technologies may surpass old ones, and usually do, the old coexists with the new for indefinite periods. We have bicycles, movies, automobiles, radio, television, and the computer today, all flourishing—and we have books, about 40,000 titles published in

MEDIA PROBE

After reading the comments on each medium summarize what you believe the experts are saying about the medium's future.

the United States alone every year, nearly 2 billion copies sold. This is scarcely material for an obituary.

"The reason for these steadily increasing figures is the best guarantee of their survival. People tend to think of books in terms of trade publishing, that is, general nonfiction and fiction as advertised and sold in retail stores. In reality, that is only a small part of the market. The largest part of publishing is educational, scientific, medical, and technical. For this kind of information, there is at present no substitute. Information is transmitted by the computer screen, to be sure, but no computer bank constructed or envisioned can begin to equal what is available in books. If the great libraries of the world were available to home computer users, as they conceivably might be some day, it would still not seriously dent the usefulness of books.

"We should remember that television and computer screens are stationary installations. The book is portable, from desk to couch to chair to bed to the bathroom, the beach, the train, the bus, the airplane. Nothing in the foreseeable future suggests that its competitors can begin to match such portability.

"Books may change (and indeed, have already done so) in terms of their physical composition, in the sense of computer typefaces. Technology has changed the means of producing them, too. But the general shape and character of the book remains the same and is likely remain so in the lifetimes of those now living. They continue to play a major role in our society as dispensers of information and entertainment. They are also the last free forum remaining to us, uncontrolled by advertisers, special interests, or the government. The freedom books provide, however, is constantly under assault by both government and numerous special interests, and there has already been serious damage.

"Those are the two large question marks for the future. How successful will attempts to control what people read become? No one knows; the answer is embedded in complicated social factors. The other question mark is the rising tide of illiteracy. It continues to grow, and whether the image, moving or stationary, will dominate in the end remains an open question."

J. Robert Moskin, senior editor of the Aspen Institute for Humanistic Studies, outlines some of the possible effects of the new electronic technology on the future of books and book publishing that were discussed by a panel of diverse experts in a two-day seminar at the Jerusalem International Book Fair in late April 1983.

"In the future, a book may be bought as a bubble-wrapped package containing a dust jacket together with a computer chip from which the reader prints out the text at home. "Publishers may not stock inventory but print books when customers order them.

"Information will be acquired rapidly from computerized databanks, but literature and poetry will remain in printed form.

"The use of language may be changing under the impact of staccato TV talk.

"Although most cultural and political life has always taken place outside the home, the new electronic technology may be creating an isolating living room culture."

The Future of Newspapers

Dr. Leo Bogart asks, "Will newspapers still be published a century from now?" He goes on to say:

"There will be newspapers in 2084, but they will be quite different from those of today, in an age of vastly expanded communications resources. It is easy enough to project from existing trends to a society of far better educated people living longer, healthier, more rewarding lives. We can visualize a global economy becoming steadily more productive upon an ever-expanding base of new technology, fueled by new sources of energy and stimulated by new adventures in space.

"It is harder to foresee the changes in human values, aspirations, and behavior patterns than those in the material aspects of life. The division of labor between the sexes will be progressively less distinct; the ranks of the disadvantaged will be diminished as minorities find their way into the mainstream. With a growing population of vigorous older people, the definitions of work and leisure will be blurred. The relationship between home and the workplace will be different, as home communications systems allow more personal business, shopping, and work activity to take place at home. All this will change the balance of cities and suburbs, and thus the physical appearance of the country itself. Daily life will be very different when everyone can fly through the air with the greatest of ease and the wristwatch picturephone is a commonplace. Developments like these, and others now unimaginable, will change the public's preoccupations and interests, change the content of the news, change people's loyalties and identifications, and thus change the constituencies for news media.

"The functions of all existing media will be transformed by the development of artificial intelligence, of two-way interactive linkages, and of ready access to vast amounts of stored information and entertainment. Not only will individuals be able to get what they want when they want it, but advertisers will be readily able to identify the individuals or households at whom they want to aim their messages. So where will newspapers fit in?

1. "Newspapers will still appear in a printed format, simply because there is no more efficient way of encompassing and packaging a great mass of complex information for easy and speedy retrieval.
2. "The substance on which newspapers are printed will not be based just on woodpulp, but on an amalgam of raw materials selected to minimize both expense and effects on the environment.
3. "Newspaper organizations will be comprehensive information providers, rather than publishers. They will generate not a single uniform product, but a variety of products available to users through different means. These will include text and pictures (still and motion) in a video format (with the option of a wall-screen or a lap-board) and with a facsimile in-home printer for those willing to pay the extra price and to bear the inconvenience of maintaining a paper-recycling machine under the bed.
4. "Newspapers will market a high share of the input available to them. Editorial copy that is now discarded, as well as the entire morgue of prior information, will be routinely sold in electronic or printed form to the limited number of customers who have a use for it, and new additional data sources will be developed.
5. "High quality color will be universally available. Electronic controls will provide perfect register and tones for papers printed at ultra-high speed.
6. "Decentralized production will make possible the up-to-the-minute, round-the-clock newspaper. Papers will be printed in small plants at many locations, with both editorial matter and advertising continually fresh and updated throughout the day by telecommunication.
7. "There will be a revival of newspaper competition. Readers will have their choice of a variety of national dailies appealing to different tastes and interests. The development of low-budget production facilities and pooled distribution systems will make it possible for small-circulation papers to compete at the community level as well. No clear distinction will remain among newspaper, magazine, and book publishers, broadcasters, filmmakers, and telecommunications companies, all of whom

will compete directly, offering timely information in both electronic and printed form.

8. "Distribution systems will be competitive and comprehensive, delivering non-daily publications, advertising, product samples, and packages through professional, full-time adult career forces making the rounds of their assigned territories a number of times each day.

9. "Newspapers will include a high proportion of individually customized content. Detailed marketing and media information on individual households will be routinely available. Inkjet printing methods will make it possible to tailor each paper to the recipient's characteristics and wishes, with optional charges for supplements to the basic package. Advertising will be highly targeted, with ad copy and art beamed to fit the profile of each reader household.

10. "Newspapers will still be a mass medium, providing a common core package of the information that most people need to orient themselves to the society around them. This will include the news they could not possibly anticipate, as well as the special details that express their own individuality.

11. "Readers will pay a larger share of the newspaper's income than they do now, and advertisers less. This seems inevitable as newspapers provide the reader with additional values and as advertising itself becomes more competitive and more selective. By the year 2084, the classification of advertising as national or local will be meaningless, and a high proportion of product marketing will be done on an international scale.

12. "Newspaper content will be geared to a more sophisticated reader. A better educated, more widely traveled population will demand authoritative reporting and good writing. But they will still come to the newspaper with the same expectations that have attracted readers for some three hundred years past: to satisfy their curiosity about what's new, to widen their horizons, to learn what's useful, and to find an unexpected laugh or two along the way. Of one thing we can be sure. Since their origins, newspapers have generated and spread ideas, stimulated controversy, sought the truth, and exposed inequity. A century from now, those tasks will be no less essential, and the need to do them with conviction, grace, and style will be no less urgent."[1]

The Future of Magazines

Tom Lashnits, associate editor of *Reader's Digest,* writes about magazines.

"When I arrived in New York in the early 1970s, my ambition was to become an editor. Visions of Luce and Wallace and Hearst danced in my head, and there was no doubt in my naive mind that editors were the most important people in the world, at least in the publishing world. Of course, I was wrong. Even then the influence of the editor was ebbing from its heyday in the early twentieth century. Today the situation has changed entirely. Now the most important people in publishing are the accountants, the M.B.A.s, the market researchers. Editors, for example, no longer decide what goes on the cover of a magazine; the marketing people do.

"But I think over the next decade the limitations of market research will be recognized—regarding all products, actually, but particularly in publishing. Market research gives you a rough idea of what an audience wants and a scientific basis for making (or justifying) your decisions. But what thoughtful publishers have found out is that the numbers may be right, but the predictions can still be dead wrong. We all know this from the spotty records of political pollsters and weather forecasters. Market research will always be a valuable tool, but it will no longer be a media god.

"A magazine is a living breathing organism and must meet its readers' needs in more fundamental, more emotional, and more empathetic ways than a market researcher's numbers can identify. So I believe—and I don't think it's just wishful thinking—that over the next decade the editor will regain his or her position as the interpreter of reader interest and the keeper of a magazine's heart and soul.

"Five years ago I would have told an ambitious young person breaking into publishing to get a job on the business side. Today I'd say, "Be an editor."

"Just as the last two decades have seen the rise of the marketing man or woman, they have seen the demise of the general-interest magazine—*Saturday Evening Post, Look, Colliers*—and the emergence of special-interest magazines about your city, your hobby, or your computer. Even the general-interest magazines that have made a comeback, like the *Post,* have done so as special-interest publications. I believe this trend toward specialization will continue, and that as old magazines fall by the wayside, new ones will start up to fill the changing needs and desires of the American audience.

"The magazine business is in many ways a trendy one, and it will no doubt continue this way. There were underground magazines in the 1960s, then back-to-nature magazines in the early 1970s, followed by fitness magazines, women's magazines, business magazines, women's business magazines. Meanwhile, the established publications that have survived have consolidated their audiences and evolved to reflect the changing tastes of their readerships.

"What's in the future? Whatever the next trend, the magazines that will continue to thrive will be the ones that do what magazines do best, the magazines that do what other media cannot or will not do. Magazines have an advantage over other media in that they arrive at your doorstep in a semipermanent form, whereas TV, for example, is as evanescent as the airwaves—unless you're willing to make a large investment in videotape equipment. Even then, you benefit from random access in magazines—meaning that you can dip into a magazine at any point, instantly finding a particular article on a particular page—rather than waiting while a tape fast-forwards to the spot where you guess you can retrieve your information.

"Magazines are cheap. They also offer better graphics than TV and newspapers and all but the most expensive books.

"Magazines that flourish will, therefore, offer information that is worth saving and going back to—be it self-help advice, consumer tips, how-to instructions, career guidance, or an inspirational message. Magazines will have to stay relatively inexpensive to compete successfully with their new high-tech competitors. Magazines will have to exploit their graphic potential, excelling in design, print quality, colorful photographs, memorable illustrations.

"And magazines will have to continue to offer an intelligent perspective on the world. A TV program is often more entertaining than a magazine article; but a magazine article is always more intelligent.

"Finally, a magazine must retain its sense of audience. A reader of a magazine is not alone. He or she shares a common frame of reference, a shared perspective on the world, an overlapping pool of interests with fellow readers—as often reflected in a letters-to-the-editor column. There is, in the best magazines, a sense of community—whether you're a *Cosmopolitan* type of woman, a *Playboy* kind of guy, a confident executive who reads *Business Week.*"

Warren Burkett, associate professor at the University of Texas at Austin, has this to say about magazines in the future.

"Depend on human ingenuity for continuing use of magazines, and magazine writers, over the next two decades or more. Count also on both traditional and untraditional forms. Writers and publishers will continue to find ways of doing what newspapers and other media cannot do or will not do. We even may see a return of the so-called general magazine.

"The magazine form, as others have observed, is too useful in its flexibility, durability, organization, and transportability to be discarded. Advancing technology will make four-color pictures economical for many more small publications, perhaps mandatory in a competitive world. Holograms, the latest attempt to achieve three-dimensional graphics, will likely be refined and improved, but they are not necessarily the final word picture.

"Magazines may grow even more specialized by region, by topic, by audience, or by occupation. If market research turns up nests of affluent, left-handed skeet shooters, someone will make them a magazine. More of these magazines will likely be distributed as free or controlled-circulation publications. New presses are making shorter production runs profitable for editor-publishers as well as for the printers.

"Magazine articles, with some exceptions, will continue to grow shorter. This would fit the growing awareness of what is to some researchers a shortening attention span among readers or a more distracted society. These stories will satisfy readers using magazines for entertainment or notification. Some magazines operate now on the theory that their readers are so affluent that they get their subscription money's worth if only one or two stories a year provoke intense reader interest. So the place of the "blockbuster" story will remain secure.

"Readers who want to spring from printed "notification" to more detail will be able to request longer and more complete stories, even down to the level of basic references and research notes. These should be available from either the magazine publisher's data base by computer or from a third party, such as a commercial data base or the author's computer. At a price, of course. Thus authors' payments may reflect more directly reader interest.

"In the United States and Canada, magazines have been regarded generally as a "class act." The designs have been clean, elegant, and uncluttered, except in the most inept instances. This contrasts greatly with most overseas magazines, especially from Europe and Japan, where the appearance of trashiness may be acceptable as "high graphics." The first inroads of European publishers in the United States followed traditional American patterns; English editions of later arrivals follow more conventional European design and may force changes in American design patterns if they are successful.

"New forms of magazines also seem possible. They may be economical for some writers and publishers. One of these is "computer" publishing, where the article and illustrations go into a data base and a reader calls the story into his or her computer when ready. This will be cheaper than sending magazines out as computer disks, as some futurists propose. This may help magazine writers emerge from near-anonymity to develop an audience for their particular subject, region, or style. Speed of delivery, based on perceived need for information—such as in business or other cases of intense interest—will be a key factor in widespread development of this method. Some operators of data banks and networks may emerge as primary employers of editors, writers, and researchers.

"Another new form of the magazine could evolve from music television. Text integrated with audio and video appear to be a powerful magazine form that could be delivered on video tape through newsracks or computer access to specialized reader-viewers. We might be able to order this with or without advertising. This would permit those readers who have voiced objections to advertising content to put their money where their magazine is. Either way, both print and electronic publishers will be asking readers to pay more of the editorial and production costs of the new magazines.

"Foreseeable improvements in printing technology driven by computers, and optics research, promise some people an individual magazine. It may be delivered in a neighborhood news center by print or microfiche. Affluent holders of a certain zip code, professional affiliation, or credit standing could have a free or minimal cost allowance to "draw out" stories and ads of their choice.

"This individuation—one magazine, one reader—is the ultimate specialization. Yet it is not too far removed from what happens now among hundreds of business and government executives who receive daily, weekly, and monthly "digests" tailored to their interests. Clever editors, aided by pagination and computerized layout programs, will find ways to make this work. Others, probably by the thousands, will continue searching for the elusive "general" magazine.

"The safer bet for young editors and publishers lies in specialization. The new general-interest magazine lies beyond the grasp of present editors—except, perhaps, at *Reader's Digest*. Yet somewhere out there, perhaps slouching toward a high school or college journalism class, is an editor or publisher possessing some higher level of cognizance, abstraction, and integration in his or her view of our world. It has been said that the magazine is an idea transformed into printed word. Respect for human ingenuity says that somebody will find in the new technology a unified grasp of presentation and values that will draw together the mass audiences of shared readership."

The Future of Radio

Richard M. Brescia, senior vice president of CBS Radio Networks, writes on the future of radio:

"We all know that radio continues to be the

Print and broadcast. Whatever new technologies emerge, these media are likely to remain basic to communications. (Alan Becker/Photo Researchers)

ubiquitous medium. Just about everybody tunes in, and listeners can easily find just what they want to meet their needs at any time of the day by drawing from a full menu of news, information, and entertainment formats. It is radio's tremendous ability to provide those choices that will, I believe, insure its popularity in the years to come.

"The medium's resiliency was tested in the 1950s with the advent of television and again in the 1960s and 1970s, when FM radio came into its own. In both situations, the way in which the medium was being used changed. In the 1950s television, the new family-oriented "mass-appeal" medium, caused radio to shift programming gears and become more individualized. Aided by the development of the transistor and miniaturization, both the "portable" and "personal" characteristics of radio were enhanced. Later, innovation and experimentation began on the FM band, focusing sharply on the younger segment of the listening marketplace. This was characterized by scheduling fewer commercials per hour, longer music sweeps, and additional album cuts not normally heard in the past. The younger listeners adopted FM as their band on the dial. FM was no longer the stepchild; eventually listenership surpassed that of AM in 1974.

"While some say the shift in audience was caused by technology (stereo broadcasting), I do not believe that was a primary cause. Programming innovation, not technology, enabled broadcasters to attract their new target audiences to the FM band. The effect this boon has had on AM listenership and on those stations and networks that program to them has been dramatic. Many of these AM broadcasters entered the 1980s in a kind of midlife crisis. Some decided to abandon music altogether, surrendering that venue to the better-sounding FM dial. Others followed the lead of those who had shifted earlier to all news or telephone talk in an attempt to successfully reposition themselves to fill a new void in the marketplace and attract a new and older target audience. Still other AM stations stayed with music as the major source of their sound but abandoned the competition for younger listeners by adopting formats of nostalgia (for example, big bands) or country and western.

"There are always marketplace pressures demanding change or adjustment that keep radio in a constant state of flux. The successful radio broadcaster therefore must have a sense of history—what happened and why. He or she must be on top of current listener needs and trends and must also have the courage and flexibility to deal with change for the future.

"Broadcasting—radio and television—is also a cyclical business. In many instances we're reinventing the wheel. With that in mind, I think it's worth considering that all the dynamics which have taken place in the 1950s, 1960s, and 1970s will form the model for the way the medium will respond to similar situations in the future. As competition—from TV, cable, VCRs, computers, and other radio broadcasters—for listeners' time increases, the good broadcaster will adapt. New formats will evolve, old programming strategies may be revived, but the nature of the medium will not change. Radio will remain personal, portable, and adaptable to the individual's needs by time of day.

"In terms of programming, we must continually look for avenues to keep us in tune with our target audience. Research will play a vital role. It will not replace individual judgment, nor will it remove the challenge of innovation. It will help us make better decisions, and the broadcast manager of the future must have a solid grip on its value. I believe we can also anticipate continued experimentation and see creative approaches to audience maintenance on both the AM and FM bands.

"A movement away from the pure sound of "sameness" twenty-four hours a day toward a kind of block programming by daypart will create fertile ground for both talent and the creative program director. This mix of types or tones of formats, offered to coincide with listening habits by daypart, will keep the radio pot boiling. The FM dial, long noted for its extended music blocks, will experiment by placing increased emphasis on the talk segments (more news, personality chatter, and, yes, even talk) geared to their young-adult audience's interest.

"Network radio will continue to play an important role in helping local affiliates satisfy the public's need to know by providing timely news coverage with their unique expertise in reporting world and national news. Interesting features, play-by-play sports, and special music programming will continue to emphasize network's value to the successful radio broadcaster.

"Radio management must also hone their

business skills to successfully compete in the future where an already crowded marketplace will present even greater competition. Developing a sound business plan that incorporates solid revenue goals, cost management, people development programs and a continuing plan for the future is a must. Most important though will be the understanding that we are in business to serve a community, whether it be through entertainment or the dissemination of information. The segment of the public we choose to target in on is our customer base and we must keep that notion primary in all our plans.

"Similarly, the sales environment of the future, in which decreasing average-quarter-hour audience shares (a result of increased competition) will be in conflict with the need to increase rates, will demand that the radio salesperson develop creative approaches to selling commercial time. Awareness of what we are as stations, networks, or services as opposed to what are our "numbers" (that is, ratings) will become more important. Using a conceptual sell, plus a qualitative analysis of those numbers and the way these ingredients relate to the marketing needs of our other customers (the advertiser), is what will count.

"The future broadcasters should bring to the profession a broad base of knowledge and interests which will enable them to understand and tackle the varied aspects of our business. A liberal arts education with an emphasis on writing and reading is invaluable in developing and practicing good communication skills. The broadcaster, like any other professional, must be able to present ideas clearly and listen to those of others.

"Radio, as always, will offer career opportunity in a dynamic industry. The medium will remain ubiquitous because it is time-sensitive to listeners' needs, and because it is timely all the time, the future looks bright."

Robert Mounty, executive vice president of NBC Radio, writes as follows:

"Radio is the closest thing we have to face-to-face, mouth-to-mouth communication. It offers total mobility. It offers ubiquity. For me, it's really hard to imagine radio not being a very important communication medium.

"I predict that in the years ahead radio will remain a primary medium for the distribution of information. As far as I can tell there is also no reason why radio cannot remain a very viable advertising medium. In fact, in many ways radio is the more stable of our electronic media. At this particular moment, for example, radio can be looked upon as firmly established; everybody knows what it is. The competition that it faces develops from within the radio medium itself.

"Let's take a look at TV. I am a believer that the viewer does not care whether a TV program is being transmitted via the cable, over the air, via a network, or via satellite. They know, though, that all radio goes out via the airwaves. And while you probably would not bring your TV with you onto the beach, to your backyard, or even to a barbeque, your radio goes with you.

"We now have 9000 radio stations. Legislation is going to create 800 to 1000 new FM stations. There are also discussions of proposals for additional legislation that would allow stations on the AM band to expand from 1600 to 1800 mHz. We are talking in the next ten years of having 11,000 radio stations. And yet, this is not necessarily a traumatic thing for radio.

"Compare this to TV. Cable brought us TV sets that contain between 50 and 150 channels. Yet there is nothing to put on them. To be sure, cablecasters have coined buzz words like narrowcasting, but in actuality, this has not happened. The only cable station making money is HBO and it does not have narrow appeal; it has mass appeal. In order for it to succeed, cable must decide how to narrowcast. I see this as the main challenge facing video.

"Radio, however, has already met this challenge. It did so when it adopted format radio—programming that was locally oriented and especially targeted to meet the needs of specific age groups. In radio, I see this trend continuing. I predict that radio stations will become more effective at reaching a more highly targeted audience, not only in music areas, but in other areas as well. Radio, you see, has the ability to zero in on small groups of people—groups of people too small for TV because of this medium's production costs.

"Since FM is currently dominant, you can expect AM stations to experiment more. But if AM stations are wise they will be careful to avoid competing with a superior facility, that is, FM.

"To conclude, I firmly believe that while in time, the Rockies may crumble and Gibraltar may fall, radio is here to stay!"

The Future of Television

Bert R. Briller, from the Television Information Office of the National Association of Broadcasters, writes on television's future.

"As I plug in my electronic crystal ball to forecast the future of television, two words take form and float out of the mist: endless possibilities. TV's future, like TV itself, is constantly evolving, generating new forms and discarding others. And what was only a vague dream ten years ago is now a vivid reality.

"The future will have its science fiction aspects, but these will be shaped by economic realities and long-standing cultural needs. These social forces are part of television's heritage and will be part of the medium's future.

"The New Technologies The major impact on television and its viewers over the last decade has been the rapid growth of cable and related new technologies. In 1984 about 40 percent of all the TV households in the country have cable, and this figure is predicted to rise to around 55 percent by the end of the decade.

"Along with cable have come other new technologies—such as videocassette recorders, teletext, and satellite transmission—that have and will continue to have a major influence on home viewing.

"Not only will the number of channels continue to increase, but so will the uses these channels are put to. More and more people will be able to shop and bank through their home screen or use it as a newspaper or encyclopedia to look up information. Digitalized TV receivers will allow viewers such options as split-screen, stop-motion and the ability to zoom in on part of the picture. Along with stereo sound, the new TVs will provide the kind of capabilities only advanced audio systems and VCRs previously could.

"The explosion of VCR ownership and rental tapes will also change the way many families entertain themselves. From first-run motion pictures to exercise lessons, the home screen will provide families with hours of fun at relatively inexpensive cost. Much of VCR use will be for time shifting—recording a show to watch at a more convenient time.

"I also see a great expansion of the new technologies into the all-important area of education. Teachers will be able to utilize, as they already are beginning to, videodiscs, video games, and cassettes to convey information. Teachers will be playing more of a role in teaching students *how* to think and *how* to do research. They will serve more as role models and transmitters of values. Young people will be learning in a much freer and self-directing way, and more at their own pace—the slow learners not overwhelmed, the fast learners not bored.

"The time is nearing when high-definition television, which greatly improves picture quality, will be readily available to television owners. Transmission capabilities should improve with the increased use of optical fibers, instead of copper coaxial cable. And program distribution by satellite, which is less costly than cable for programming sent more than 300 miles, should also increase.

"How Much Is Too Much?" Yet amid all these rosy predictions are a few thorns. Most of the ventures described above require large-scale investments that companies are not always willing to underwrite unless *their* crystal balls predict a big payoff. Wiring a major urban area can cost upward of $100 million. High rates and an uncertain economic climate, both at home and abroad, could make such outlays feasible only for the largest and strongest financial institutions. Even then, there's no guarantee that every cable system will be profitable.

"Only a few years ago, cable's potential was considered virtually unlimited. Today that is no longer the case, and the shaking-out process has already begun within the industry. There have been narrowcasting failures like CBS Cable and the Satellite News Channel; RCA and Rockefeller Center closed down the Entertainment Channel; and ailing networks like the Cable Health Network and Daytime merged into a new service, Lifetime. Tele-First Entertainment, which planned to deliver programming in scrambled form for automatic VCR recording and playback in subscribers' homes, fizzled out after a half-year test. CBS took a $15 million write-down to stop manufacturing videodiscs, and RCA took a $175 million write-down to get out of the videodisc player business.

"There are other signs which presage a possible bumpy road for some of the new technologies. Both Western Union and CBS have announced that they have withdrawn plans to build direct broadcast satellite systems. (DBS would bypass conventional TV stations and deliver programs directly to homes which have their own satellite dishes.) RCA has said it will slash its DBS investment and postpone the start-up of its planned service. In all three cases, the need to expend huge sums of capital for what could turn out to be small returns prompted the pullback.

"The other side of the financial equation, which could put a damper on technological expansion, is weak effective demand—the consumer's hard-pressed pocketbook. Just how much is the average TV viewer willing or able to pay for all these new services? One DBS permit holder, Comsat, estimates that the viewer with a satellite will need about $300 dollars of receiving equipment and on top of that will have to pay monthly subscription fees of $20 to $25. While VCR prices have fallen to the point where more and more households can afford them (January 1984 sales were up 80 percent over the previous year), one must ask how many of these households will wish to shell out additional money for more and more services.

"Over-the-Air Television" Despite the foreseeable growth of the new technologies, the three commercial networks, their affiliated stations, and the independent stations are optimistic about the future. They feel that cable will enjoy a comfortable complementary role alongside traditional over-the-air TV.

"Although much has been made of the networks' declining share of the TV audience (BBDO ad agency predicts it will fall to 65% by 1990), the three networks believe their total audience delivery will decline very little in absolute terms. They'll be getting a smaller share, but the pie will have grown.

"The primary reason for this view is that the networks will probably maintain their preeminence in selecting, financing, and delivering mass-appeal programming. They'll continue their vast investments in programming yielding large audiences that draw advertiser support. Added to this is the knowledge that only broadcast television will continue to be *the mass medium* reaching virtually every household in America.

"James Duffy, ABC-TV president, concurs that the outlook for the networks is bullish. He predicts that network gross income will increase from $7.6 billion in 1984 to at least $10.3 billion in 1988. An RCA study shows similar growth. According to Herbert S. Schlosser, RCA executive vice-president, advertiser-supported domestic video entertainment markets (the networks, local TV stations, and the still-small advertiser-supported cable industry) will grow from about $13 billion in 1982 to more than $32 billion by 1990.

"Local TV stations, both networks affiliates and independents, will also maintain their advantage of providing strong program services in their communities, in addition to serving as a conduit of popular network and syndicated programming. It is doubtful that cable, with more than 5000 systems now in operation, will develop the facilities of personnel to compete effectively with local stations, especially in such important areas as local news coverage.

"While cable slugs it out with standard over-the-air broadcasting, with the new technologies aiding both camps, the eventual winner will continue to be the average TV viewer. For the home viewer, the only real problem will be deciding how much video is enough. From hookups with home computers and VCRs to add-ons like pay cable and stereo sound, the television set will be able to perform wondrous feats of entertainment and education as never before. Some new TV systems will allow subscribers to change program content to fit their needs and interests—to expand the sports or business news, for example.

"As I gaze into my crystal ball one last time, a final surprising image stuns me. It is 1990, and in homes across the country I see viewers watching a rerun of *I Love Lucy,* which I first saw in October 1951! In glorious black-and-white, no less. Some things will never change: the masks of comedy and tragedy which the Greek dramatists developed still work their ancient magic. What builds an audience is not the *novelty* of the delivery system, but its *content* of information and entertainment."

Joel Persky, chairman of the department of radio, TV, and film at Texas Christian University, has this to say.

"Television will be, as it has been in the past, an important force in society and the lives of those who spend thousands of hours each year before the box. However, the big change in our consumption of this electronic medium will be the shift from passive observer to active participant.

"With the marriage of computers and televisions, the viewer will no longer sit contentedly and absentmindedly before the box. In the future we will interact with, rather than be massaged by, the box. By means of videodiscs, videocassette recorders, electronic game machines, and personal computers we will no longer merely watch. We will talk to, be talked at, and dialogue with the box. We will receive our mail, order our groceries and clothing, vote for political candidates, and a multitude of other activities that are limited only by the imaginations of computer programmers.

"The commercial networks, once the undisputed rulers of the box, will find their hegemony cracked, if not broken. The networks will not disappear, but their precious and almighty share of the audience will diminish. I predict that this shrinkage will be in the neighborhood of 1 million viewers per year.

"Viewers will not have to rely upon the networks for their television fare—which has always been only fair. Viewers will have alternative viewing possibilities. They will watch cable, MTV, MSG, CNN, PTL, SIN, ESPN, VEU, HBO, and dozens of as-yet-unknown programming sources. They will use their VCRs for time shifting. They will buy or rent videocassettes by the thousands. They will play games. They will program their PCs and sets themselves.

"When the box is being used for these other activities, then it is not being used to watch the networks. Ratings will drop and the network programmers will try innovative ways to lure the viewers back. The new programs will be series based on successful and trendy movies, resurrections of old series, miniseries, docudramas, quiz shows, and the like. The network efforts will fail, and viewers, disillusioned by these highly touted efforts, will cling to their alternative programming possibilities. The networks will lose more of the audience. Shrinkage will accelerate.

"The technology of television is undergoing dramatic changes. The sets we currently have in our homes are not very different from the sets our parents owned. The technology of television has not changed very much in the medium's first thirty years.

"In the past we bought television sets. In the future we will buy components. This evolutionary move is not unlike the move in the purchase of radios. First we bought radio sets. Now we buy stereophonic components and assemble our own "sets." In the future we will buy large-screen TVs, flat-screen TVs, holographic TVs, units with stereophonic or quadraphonic sound systems, units with controls that will allow us to slow-down, speed-up, choose various camera angles and other production values of the program. We will all become TV directors.

"Television will, in the future, play the same role in our society that it has in the past—only it will play that role with greater force and clarity. It will continue to shape our view of the world, shape our opinions of people as yet unmet and probably disliked, shape our relationships with parents and children and lovers. It will continue to make us instant experts on subjects far too complicated to be treated in any way but superficially. It will continue to desensitise us to violence, the problems of minority groups, and the plight of the underclass. It will continue to give us false feelings of superiority. It will continue to give credibility to our prejudices.

"The future is an exciting time for the development of television. It is also a frightening time for television. I write this brief piece on the medium's future in the year 1984—that should be a warning to us all."

The Future of Cable

John Tatta chairman of the board at Cablevision, writes on the future of cable.

"I have been asked to comment on the changes that can be expected in the cable industry over the next ten to fifteen years and the future of the cable medium in general.

"Up until now, we have seen an impressive growth of cable across the country, as it presently serves around 40 percent of television households. Homes passed by cable are approximately 54 million and about 33 million subscribers presently have service. Much of this growth has been fueled by pay television options, and the industry now posts 18 million pay subscribers paying for 27 million pay cable units. Subscriber pay penetration is 59 percent, while unit penetration is close to 85 percent.

"The latter figure dramatically reflects the interest consumers have shown in the availability of optional services, particularly movies and sports. Cable's multiplicity of channels, creative development of services and increasing marketing sophistication have resulted in the relatively quick growth of "foundation" movie services, regional sports networks, performing arts and adult programming, perceived by subscribers as welcome additions to the frequent sameness of commercial network fare. Once cable entered the home, usually in the more recent periods of growth as a result of attractive packaging of the pay offerings, subscribers began to appreciate some of the specialty services included in their basic or family tiers. Services such as Cable News Network, Nickelodeon for children, Music Television for teenagers, the Entertainment and Sports Network covering twenty-four hours of sports, plus others added to the perceived value of the total cable package. Although there has been the inevitable shaking out of some program service offerings, which is to be expected in an early stage of a fast-growing industry, construction of the vast urban markets is continuing and the future looks bright.

"Set against this growth to date is the fact that we have seen only the tip of the iceberg of cable's capabilities. Although competing delivery technologies have been growing as well and in particular, filling in areas that have not as yet been cabled, cable remains as a unique telecommunications resource for the future. In addition to having the broadest channel capacity of the various new methodologies, with the promise of additional national and regional programming services and potential interactive data and information offerings, cable remains the medium with the highest potential for service as a local telecommunications resource.

"Given the habit structures of the American viewing public, it is understandable that a young industry poised for growth would focus its marketing programs on broad-based entertainment and sports fare, as the name of the game has been getting into as many homes as possible and generating the revenues necessary for viability in this capital-intensive industry. However, as the industry begins to establish a more secure base, it will mature into a phase wherein its local telecommunications resource potential can be increasingly tapped and recognized.

"Cable systems are franchised locally and, in spite of their carriage of national or regional services, do derive a substantial part of their character from local surroundings and needs. For example, in lower Fairfield County in Connecticut, Cablevision and its partner Scripps-Howard Broadcasting Company, detected a community frustration at the lack of sufficient local news coverage and filled the gap with a highly professional and eventually award-winning news program. While the movie and sports programming packages were key marketing elements, the news programming very quickly established a respected presence of the system in the community. A related local talk program added to the perception of a system interested in its community and this type of programming is now surfacing in other Cablevision systems.

"As individuals in the local community become more sophisticated in the use of video equipment, whether as consumers of new videobased appliances and related equipment or through the training programs offered by cable systems, they will increasingly look to the systems' access channels for expression of their interests and creative potential. In what has been called the growing age of high-tech, high-touch, cable system operators will begin to appreciate the high-touch value of the development of local programming, including coproductions with various community groups....

"As we look over the next ten or fifteen years, then, we will continue to see the development of the broad-based movie and sports services, enhanced by the revenues generated from increased outlets as more cable is built. Additionally, more national and regional specialty services will appear, perhaps more cautiously introduced in a more mature industry phase, but introduced nevertheless as the collective cable subscriber base expands. We will begin to see the further marriage of cable and computer technology, resulting in increased access to data bases and the development of local telecommunication loop capacity. But side by side with these services will be the expanding local services and the increasing perception of the cable system as the local station or the electronic community marketplace.

"This will be an exciting period for young people studying for careers in the new media environment and for those in general who will benefit from a familiarity with and an appropriate orientation toward the potential that cable will increasingly offer for community expression and the development of fresh programming ideas. I have been privileged to participate in the initial and exciting first phase of the development of the cable medium. My message to those looking to enter the field at this point in time is my strong feeling that the best is yet to come."

The Future of Film

John Darretta, associate professor of communication arts at Iona College, writes on film past and future.

"Although the novel, the dramatic story in print, has not yet disappeared and still attracts a large number of literate adventurers, words about its imminent demise grow daily.

After all, the cinema—with its vibrant new appeal for persons learned or otherwise—was supposed to have eradicated the printed story. So, too, go the present projections about television and its role in the demise of the filmed story. Albeit, the remote future with its convergence of video, computers, optic fibres, holography and "come-what-next" technology will see a different mode of moving information for the purposes of learning, labor, and leisure. Presently, however, print media does well, and cable television screens and computer monitors still make abundant use of the written alphabet. So what does the near future hold for the art, science, and industry of film? Changes, yes. But changes that are only intermediate steps toward that new and different medium of the distant future.

"Films in the 1980s obviously reveal a technological bias. One used to talk about the effect of a film (philosophical, psychological, humanistic); now, one "relates" to the "special" effect (technological, physical, scientific). But the situation is not a new one in recollection of the film industry's technological answers to the threats of television in the 1950s: wider screens, curved screens, 3-D Aromarama, brighter colors, broader sounds. Then, television screens were small (as were, in a relative sense, most living rooms and dens); theaters, on the other hand, were large. "Bigness" in terms of physical properties was film's answer to television. Throughout the 1960s and 1970s movies and movie houses had their up and downs, ins and outs, renovations and bifurcations, but they were not interred. The outcome of the battle between movies and television was a draw: movies and commercial television could coexist; after all, they were for different times, different places, and varied interests.

"Today's film audience is witnessing the second onslaught against television and its extended possibilities through VCRs, cablecasting and satellite dishes. The defense, once again, is to fight technology with technology. But that is a losing battle. Television screens get larger, stereophonic video speakers match the "full" sounds of movie theaters, 3-D films are transmitted over airwaves. Also, VCRs, disc players, and alternative forms of transmission offer flexible viewing times free of commercial scheduling or interruptions. Is that not a decisive blow against movies and movie houses? Evidently not, as new shopping malls allow "quads" to multiply into "octaves," where more first-run film choices (some in 70-mm and six-track Dolby stereo) are available in one location at one time than even the most up-to-date home video system could provide. Here, the consumer advantage is that the material is "brand new" and "top of the line," not "last season's fad" or a "designer copy." Then, too, current plans call for larger theater screens (Imax offers an area 75 feet by 100 feet; Envirovision utilizes a 360-degree hemisphere) in all the sizes and shapes used for commercial promotions and national travelogs at the World's Fair or Epcot Center (where one can also see Kodak's new 3-D process). The attack is reminiscent of the 1950s, only on a larger and grander scale.

"Video's new weapon, however, is a formidable one: electronic effects enhanced by computer technology. Most of today's blockbuster films utilize video to their utmost advantage, which has left technicians, critics, and scholars with the very probable speculation that in the near future film stock will give way to videotape. The elements of screen size, shape, clarity of image, illusion of depth, purity of sound in relation to each medium are much discussed and evaluated in professional film and video journals. Debates and pronouncements addressing these elements will continue throughout the next decade. However, we know the ultimate answer: science and technology can (and will) reproduce larger, clearer, and deeper images through electronic means.

"Physical properties aside, the real future of film hinges on other aspects: the psychological and social aspects arising from where the viewing is done, the integrity and acuity of the filmmaker's vision. Then, too, the deliverance of the essential message of a fictive or informative art does not rest solely on the means of mechanical transmission (this is not to say that the artful use of a medium cannot enhance meaning), be it the projection of an image by ambient or radiant light. Identical narrative meanings can be conveyed by drama, ballad, novel, film, or telefilm, whether they are read, seen, or heard.

"One integral advantage of going to a movie theater is that the experience is a communal one. It removes the individual or the family unit from what could become the insular and antisocial closure of the television room. Communal laughter, communal fear, communal hatred, communal admiration, among other emotions and attitudes, are formed by and experienced in the social milieu of the large movie house, where hundreds of individuals can participate in simultaneous reactions. It is not just the physical dimensions of the room that matter (watching a film alone in a huge theater—not unlike watching television alone, except that one is in the dark—is certainly different from watching with a small group, which is very different from watching with a large crowd), it is participation in the almost palpable emotional and spiritual intensity of the crowd that fills the room that is important.

"As for cinematic content, the next ten years will, in line with the pendulum of public taste, witness a swing back to the film medium as a provider of important values and personal visions of humanistic concerns. Just as the advent of sound technology in film saw a concentration on the auditory, so, too, electronic and computer technologies will continue to give the film audience a barrage of special technical effects. When the use and technique of such have been mastered and balanced (as they become hackneyed to the audience), there will be a renewed interest in the central story matter and content value of film. Social concerns, conflicts of the human heart, questions of the probing mind will again become dominant forces that will draw viewers to theaters. This renewal will occur even sooner if television producers continue to favor soporific, facile, and inconsequential storylines.

"Nonetheless, films of important and intelligent content must be made by artists with strong and honest visions, by artists well versed in literatures, philosophies, histories, and theologies, and not only the technologies and techniques of filmmaking. Furthermore, it should be the obligation of secondary schools and of university film departments to create and offer programs and courses that balance film theory and technique with traditional studies in the liberal arts. It should be their function to train future viewers, as well as filmmakers, in the understanding and use of such an enormously pervasive and powerful medium.

"The visual narrative—whether projected from film stock or transmitted by videotape—will continue to be one of the most important contributors to modern culture. Increasing numbers of people with more time for watching films and telefilms will be offered a pleasing and effective way to learn and to grow. Concurrently, technologies will continue to make the production, photographing, editing, copying, distribution, and transmission of visual materials faster, cheaper, and more accessible to the public. Because of this, the future will see an accelerated need for film writers, photographers, editors, directors, actors, technicians, marketers, distributors, archivists, and educators.

"Cinema has entered a new era in its history. As with the movement from the silent era to the sound era, it will be saddened by losses and encouraged by new possibilities. With its continual integration of the old and the new and its evolving conjunction of art and technology, film has always been an open medium. Perhaps it is this quality that allows the exhilaration and optimism that perpetually surrounds each cinematic change and movement."

On the same subject Jean Firstenberg, director of the American Film Institute, writes:

"I look at the world of film not as a business but as a means of communication and as a cultural force in our society. Basically, filmmaking is storytelling. As a result, filmmakers must know how to tell stories and have stories to tell. Film plays a critically important role in how our society views itself and how it changes. The film world itself, however, is changing as technology changes. I think people will be making films forever because it is such an effective way to reach other people. The question of how films are produced and how they are distributed will be greatly affected by the technological breakthroughs. For example, I would not be surprised if the technology of videotape were able at some time to solve high-resolution requirements and satisfy the needs of artists so videotapes could be shown in movie theaters.

"At the American Film Institute we are interested in film not only as entertainment but for its highest purpose, which is to enlighten. This is not to say that it is not appropriate for a film only to entertain; but it is also essential that we try to use film in its entirety. It is important for films to reach out to large groups in our society. I think that film as a social force (where people leave their homes to watch it) is a very effective tool for society. That interaction in and among people is very positive.

"Looking toward the future, the American Film Institute is really interested in encouraging the recognition and respect for film as an art form. Although filmmaking can be a very commercial enterprise and a very successful one, by the same token it is an artistic endeavor. We seek to encourage that endeavor because it is not only exciting but very powerful. The filmmaker as artist has a responsibility to improve the cultural offerings of our society. So we are particularly interested in training people to recognize film as culture. We encourage people to seek out those kinds of filmmaking efforts.

"There are always trends and films run in cycles. What we have now is a new phenomenon in the business environment which requires larger-grossing pictures. However, I feel there is always a place for many kinds of films. It is essential that filmmakers have the opportunity to gain experience, whether they are in Hollywood, New York, or across the country. An environment has to be created to encourage filmmaking. It should be done by the American Film Institute and the National Endowment for the Arts. State governments should also encourage filmmakers to become interested in their states by establishing state film commissions. In the future there should be far more philanthropic work for the cinema arts. Traditionally film has not been accorded the same respect as other art forms. Consequently, what we are trying to do is have people recognize that film is not only a business, but also an art form like literature, poetry, or painting.

"If you look at the history of film you notice that the only thing that is constant is change. I have no doubt that technology will continue to develop in the future. After all, rockets go off and technology moves. I am concerned, however, that the creative work be nurtured as well. We must be able to combine technology with art in order for film to make significant contributions to our culture."

The Future of Advertising

David Ogilvy predicts thirteen changes in the field of advertising."

1. "The quality of research will improve, and this will generate a bigger corpus of knowledge as to what works and what doesn't. Creative people will learn to exploit this knowledge, thereby improving their strike rate at the cash register.

2. "There will be a renaissance in print advertising.
3. "Advertising will contain more information and less hot air.
4. "Billboards will be abolished.
5. "The clutter of commercials on television and radio will be brought under control.
6. "There will be a vast increase in the use of advertising by governments for purposes of education, particularly *health* education.
7. "Advertising will play a part in bringing the population explosion under control.
8. "Candidates for political office will stop using dishonest advertising.
9. "The quality and efficiency of advertising overseas will continue to improve—at an accelerating rate. More foreign hares will overtake the American tortoise.
10. "Several foreign agencies will open offices in the United States and will prosper.
11. "Multinational manufacturers will increase their market shares all over the noncommunist world and will market more of their brands internationally. The advertising campaigns for these brands will emanate from the headquarters of multinational agencies but will be adapted to respect differences in local culture.
12. "Direct-response advertising will cease to be a separate specialty and will be folded into the "general" agencies.
13. "Ways will be found to produce effective television commercials at a more sensible cost."

Joel J. Blattstein, executive vice president of Schein/Blattstein Advertising, Inc., has these observations.

"The other day I was skimming through some 1950s issues of the *National Geographic* magazine (the grist of flea markets and garage sales everywhere) when I was stopped by an article entitled, "New Light on the Changing Face of Mars."

"A recent project had concluded that green patches splotching the red face of our planetary neighbor strongly suggested broad expanses of vegetation. *Life!* Several astronomers went even further to posit that those mysterious "canal" markings were irrigation systems and, yes, quite possibly the work of intelligent beings.

"It was fascinating. Science's most brilliant minds offering highly educated speculations that were later to be proven utterly (and for most Earthlings, I think, disappointingly) false. Photographic fly-bys, followed by the sensational landing of a soil analyzer, put to rest the notion of green men with antennas on their pointy little heads.

"There was something else in this particular issue, dated September 1955, that presented the same kind of intriguing naiveté. The advertising.

"The artwork consisted of trite cartoons; contrived, static photography; or illustrations used to simulate contrived, static photography. The typography was limited to a handful of styles, all dull. And the copy? About as daring and creative as the fine print in an insurance policy.

"Of course, to accuse members of an earlier generation of naiveté is to be naive oneself. Interplanetary messengers did not exist for the astronomers of the 1950s. They worked with what they had and what they knew; their theories were, in fact, state of the art. For then.

"Similarly, advertising professionals of that era produced what they considered to be the ultimate in advertising. They worked with what they had and knew . . . all that had developed as of that moment. What they did *not* have was the technology and social sophistication that ensued. They did not have high-tech computers. The Pill and its "new morality." Satellite-relayed TV. Videocassette recorders. Computerized type design and typesetting. Laser photo-engraving. Or Michael Jackson.

"What does all this tell us about formulating a prediction about the state of advertising over the next decade or so? It tells us to be very, very careful. For the unknown—the *x* in the formula—can jump up at any moment and make our prediction seem as naive as those we've just derided.

"But surely there must be some way we can get a preview of that *x;* some idea where the changes will come from. Indeed, there are several areas to watch.

"First, *technology.* Computer-generated graphics have already begun revolutionizing TV commercials. Used for titling, animation, and a host of special effects, computer graphics can cut time and production costs and create sensational impact. In addition, this powerful new tool has created a brand-new and rapidly growing job category: computer artist.

"Cable technology has added its impact to the creation of advertising. Its narrowcasting nature, the ability to isolate smaller and more specialized audience segments (for example, sports, religious, health, foreign language, children's programming), has encouraged commercials that are more tailored to the viewer's specific wants and needs. Its enhanced selectivity has also prompted an increase in the amount of special-interest direct-marketing (mail-in and 800-number) commercials for categories like magazines, records, sports, and hobbies. In addition, cable's relatively inexpensive rates have spurred the creation of ninety-second or longer spots. Certainly a challenge there for copywriters and art directors to maintain viewer interest!

"The next area is the *economy.* A broad topic, to be sure. But an analysis of the ripple effects it has produced of late tells us much about what is to come.

"For example, consider the current general trend of business operations. Despite the occasional zigs and zags of the national economy, business has embarked upon a belt-tightening course that seems relatively fixed. Overall, it means that companies are requiring that their advertising dollars work harder. "More bang for the buck" is the new mantra.

"Specifically, it shows up in a demand for ads that are more benefit-oriented and less creative—creative in the sense of aesthetic splendor or verbal and visual flair. We can expect a long and bitter battle between hard-sell tacticians and those who believe that hard-sell advertising produces dull ads and precludes the possibility of finding brilliant, new solutions to tough marketing problems.

"The move towards heightened cost-effectiveness is also evident in the increasing use of direct-marketing techniques to target audiences more effectively, test ad efficiency, create leads, and track sales. The day is just dawning for direct-marketing copywriters, artists, and management people who know how to implement direct mail, direct-response print, and direct-response TV.

"Another ramification of watching the bottom-line is a gradual shift in media emphasis. Owing to the skyrocketing time costs of network TV, many advertisers are redirecting parts of their budgets to the less costly media of magazines, newspapers, radio, direct mail, cable TV, and spot TV.

"*Demographics* is another area to be watched while peering toward the future. Yes, you will find more and more women at work and heading households in the years ahead. What good advertising will address itself to in the years ahead, is recognition of their accomplishments, their worth, and their need for help in playing several roles at once.

"We should also be paying attention to the fact that we are developing a senior-citizen "bulge." Heightened awareness of proper nutrition and exercise, coupled with miraculous medical advances, is prolonging life and increasing its quality. You will therefore see more and more advertising—for basic, everyday products and services—created specifically for media with high concentrations of seniors, with specially tailored copy approaches.

"Naturally, the post-World War II baby boom is the classic example in population study. This famous generation's birth, teen buying habits, marriages, house and car buying, parenting, etc. directed the fortunes of entire industries. Are you watching today's *Sesame Street* generation (of which you are likely a charter member) with astuteness? You should be, because their *psychographics*—their patterns of behavior—are increasingly influencing the rest of the population: people of all ages are emulating their lifestyles, the way they dress, what they drink, the music they listen to, the cars they buy, their attitudes toward sex. In a nation that lionizes and idolizes its young, the young very often set the pace. . . .

"And certainly important, at least from a creative standpoint, is the fact that we will continue to see strong use of "hot" graphics: bold designs; glowing colors; catchy headlines in large type with few words; punchy, quick body copy. All this is acknowledgment of the fact that Sesame Streeters learned to read via such tactics and quickly tune out most things that do not excite them visually. Taking cues from the fads that turn them on—like music video, New Wave design, breakdancing, and purple hair—advertising is now searching for new ways to arouse them with sight and sound. And the search will continue, as long as *they* continue to be a major economic force. . . .

"On the subject of psychographics, a basic and much-discussed question arises: When it comes to social behavior and lifestyles (and therefore, buying habits), exactly what role does advertising play? Is it active or *reactive*? Does it help create the times or just mirror them?

"I believe that, for the most part, advertising is simply a mirror. Changes in accepted sexual behavior, fashion trends, alcohol consumption, leisure and sport activities, et al. arise from societal changes. Such changes start at the grass roots—the people—as national social attitudes and economic conditions evolve. The changes then find their way into the popular media as movies, magazines, music, soaps, and sitcoms. Then, once they have become accepted values, advertising will utilize these changes in its appeals. Of course, at that point, advertising *will* play a role in spreading the change to the as-yet unconverted.

"But as for advertising initiating change all by itself, no way. It's simple logic. Given the tremendous amounts of money at risk, the advertising industry follows an extremely cautious and conservative route. For the most part, it does not adventure into new territory, but seeks to present imagery and ideas that have already been accepted and are therefore comfortable, natural, and easy for the consumer to relate to. In addition, considering the stringent codes of advertising acceptability employed by major media (not to mention governmental regulatory bodies), any advertising featuring a daring departure in sexuality, nudity, or social behavior is unlikely to see the light of day. In point of fact, acceptability is defined by what the mainstream of America finds acceptable.

"Therefore, do not look to the companies and their advertising agencies to see where change will come from in the years ahead. Look to the areas we've just discussed. Focus on the trends now in place and try to project their future development. And use your insights and general knowledge of the world around you to spot the seeds that are destined to blossom.

"As certain as I am that what I have just written is valid and worthy of consideration, I am also certain that—thirty years from now—someone will dust off the predictions I have made herein and wonder how I ever could have been so naive."

The Future of Public Relations

The following observations on the future of public relations were offered by David Finn, chairman and chief executive officer of Ruder, Finn and Rotman during an interview with the authors.

"If you had asked me ten or twenty years ago where public relations would be today, I'm not certain that I would have said that we'd be where we are. It's very hard to predict the future. I'm a member of the board for the Institute for the Future, the largest think tank devoted exclusively to futures research. I've been involved with this organization for ten or fifteen years, and as a result I've become acutely aware of how difficult it is to look ahead. What I really admire about the institute's philosophy is that they don't try to predict the future; what they try to do, instead, is identify trends and directions so that we can make decisions that will, in effect, create our future. In other words, I believe we make the future; the future does not happen without us. I think of the future not as a child of prophecy, as it was viewed in ancient times, but as a child of planning—a guide of planning.

"In my opinion, it is the students who are going to forge a new direction for public relations. I know we feel that at this company. We hope that we are attracting young people who will be innovators and come up with ideas which we cannot predict at this time.

"For example, twenty-five years ago, we started an arts division. We had no reason for feeling that such a division belonged in public relations, but we believed personally that support of cultural projects would be a legitimate public relations interest of corporations. We were really there before it started, and we created a department to encourage that kind of behavior. Now there are many people in that field in corporate life. There is no other agency that has a department like ours, though. We did it because we wanted to, and we liked it. In effect, we created a field. It turned out to be a very exciting field, which we think has great growth possibilities. Now more and more corporations recognize that it is in their interest to be involved in the cultural life of a country, or their community, or their employees; it is also to their advantage to introduce cultural values into the workplace and the community. We now find that cultural institutions are seeking public relations counsel. Museums and performing arts groups are hiring us to help them with their public relations. Sometimes they call on us to help them find corporate support or build membership; other times they ask us to help attract attendance or create national visibility for their programs.

"The exciting thing about public relations to me is that the field is really still in its infancy. Advertising, in comparison, is in its maturity. Thus, any advertising agency knows that in order to get business, it has to take business away from another advertising agency. This is because, with very few exceptions, everybody who is going to be an advertiser has an advertising agency, the exceptions being new companies. But new companies are not big. So big advertising agencies are looking for big clients, and to win big clients they have to compete with each other; they have to get business away from each other. This is not the case with us. At least half of our business comes from people who never had a public relations firm working for them before, and, unlike advertising, there's a whole world out there that does not have public relations people working for them. So I think that this field has a long way to go and grow, partly by moving into new ground. Cultural institutions are one promising field that excites us; universities are another. We've worked for about ten universities over the last few years. Universities are now turning more and more to outside firms to help them capitalize on their expertise and their knowledge. We are also attracted to foundations. Foundations have been very withdrawn in their public stance. In fact, until recently, foundations had no interest in public relations. But what happened a few years ago was that two schools of thought arose about foundations—and both of them were critical. The first said that they were the plaything of liberal capitalists—people who made a lot of money, who now had liberal ideas, and were going to fund liberal causes, progressive causes, and not conservative causes. There was criticism in Congress to apply certain controls over these foundations that would limit their abilities to skew their contributions. The other criticism was that foundations were a tax device by rich people to avoid taxes; wealthy people were taking money away from the government, tax money that would have been distributed on the basis of elected officials' decisions and judgments, using the tax dollars to achieve their own personal goals. So it became necessary for foundations to start speaking up; they had to let people know what they were really doing. One of the things we started telling foundations was that when they give a grant, they ought to publicize this fact. That would help to make people aware of the kinds of things they were doing. There is a whole new world of public relations out there.

"In addition, government agencies are using public relations more and more. Also, public relations abroad is in a much less developed stage than it is in our own country. What I'm getting at is that there are enormous opportunities all over the world.

"So I ask, what will young people develop? Will they develop public relations in sports? That's another field burgeoning. How about public relations for the sciences? As we become an increasingly complex society, and the nature of the services and the technologies created becomes much more remote for the average citizen, how is democracy going to work? What about issues on which the experts disagree? What happens when more and more information adds more and more confusion instead of clarity? What happens, for example, when institutions and environmentalists disagree?

"We have an ethics committee here. We always have an outside scholar sit in with us on the ethics committee. We meet once a month, and we try to come to grips with ethical problems. Some of the ethical problems we considered were: How do we feel about nuclear power plants? How do we feel about acid rain? It's difficult to ask and answer such questions, but by discussing them, we learn more. After all, who really knows what the public interest is? The dilemma about our relationship as citizens and as professionals is a very serious one that needs to be looked at. All of these complicated issues in science represent an area of opportunity for public relations.

"Broadcasting represents another such area. For example, with all the technology developing, what will happen to television? This is a question we need to grapple with.

"Public relations to a certain extent means trying to bring clarity to situations. I don't believe that our role should be like a lawyer's; that is, I don't believe that every side deserves to have an advocate. Therefore, I believe that you can't represent everybody. Unlike a lawyer, who is subject to a jury or judge to make a final judgment, we are the judge—as citizens. So I believe that we should only advocate things we believe in and not advocate things we do not believe in. That imposes an obligation on us to really think through what we do believe in.

"What role will public relations play in the new technologies? I don't know. It's up to young people to develop their own ideas. One of the definitions of public relations that I like is that it's a search for meaning. A lot of what we're doing isn't simply communicating; instead we often try to figure out who we are and what we're about as an institution or an organization. Once we know that, then we can speak up to help express ourselves and convey a sense of our personality, our spirit, our goals, and our direction. At a deeper level, public relations gets into some basic questions about what we are as a society and how (in the business world) a corporation can play a role not just as a good citizen (which I think is a term overused), but on the basis of what lies underneath it—usually in the mind of the executive at the top. Our role is to help the CEO achieve something that he or she may not even be able to verbalize. To do this, we really need to listen with a third ear. Only then can we find out what really is underneath it all.

"Then there is the whole field of research. In our business, we have the largest research division in public relations in the world; we have 32 full-time research professionals on staff out of a total staff of about 200 interviewers. We strongly believe that research is playing an important role in public relations, not because it enables us to measure results but because it enables us to systematize the work we do. We now take two to three months to get a perspective on a company; we interview people in a systematic way—people who work for the company, people who do business with the company, bankers, creditors, employees, whoever—asking them a systematic list of questions, digesting that, and developing a plan based upon that kind of research. We're also doing public-issue research as a contribution that a company or organization can make to knowledge. One client of ours, for example, has done a series of studies on the fear of crime and its effect on American life. This company is a multinational company that has nothing to do with crime. But it's been a good public relations program for them. It's a real contribution. It's useful; it's of value of society and the company. And we do many things that are even more abstract than that.

"It's the opportunity to do exciting things that is so wonderful about this business. And if you think about all these new fields and our growing research department (our department is growing by 35 percent a year), I think that the opportunities for growth are extraordinary. I like to say that public relations is the one function in corporate life which has the broadest horizon. Our job is to find interest within our clients which we can work with. With that in mind, we can work for any segment of society. We have a real opportunity to use our imaginations, to conceive entirely new programs, to conceive new ideas, to make something out of nothing, to do things that never happened before. To me, that's the most satisfying part of this business."

WHERE DO YOU GO FROM HERE? LIVING WITH THE MEDIA

The world you are living in today is far different from the world that your grandparents and parents were born into; for that matter, it is probably far different from the world you were born into. In each of the last four decades, more new forms of communication have evolved than in the previous 3600 years.[2] And things are still changing—more quickly than ever before. In fact, if there is one media happening you can count on, it is change. But to deal effectively with change, we must acknowledge it.

In her book *Passages,* Gail Sheehy emphasizes: "We are not unlike a particularly hardy crustacean. The lobster grows by developing and shedding a series of hard, protective shells. Each time it expands from within, the confining shell must be sloughed off. It is left exposed and vulnerable until, in time, a new covering grows to replace the old one."[3] It might be said that our relationship to the media is somewhat similar. As technological advances are made, we too pass through various media stages. Thus, while print used to be our prime means of non-face-to-face communication, today the electronic media are fulfilling this function. According to media critic Tony Schwartz, we have now become a "post-literate society."[4] Of course, there are

Life in the future will be even more of a multimedia event than it is now. (Alice Kandell/Photo Researchers)

differences between our relationship to the media and the lobster's relationship to its shell. Unlike the lobster, who must totally shed its protective casing before it can grow another one, we never fully let go of preceding media even though we embrace others. Certainly, we are not an nonliterate society; the printed word still exists. What is happening though, is that we are shifting and realigning our media allegiances.

Take the time you need to explore how your media allegiances are changing, if indeed they are. After all, as Sheehy writes, "we must be willing to change chairs if we want to grow. There is no one right chair. What is right at one stage may be restricting at another or too soft."[5] Sheehy's analogy holds when we think of our relationship to the media. We now know that we must be prepared to change media chairs. The media we relied on to fulfill our needs and wants in the past may not be totally adequate to fulfill our present or future needs and wants. But as we increase our use of new media or change the amount of time we spend with existing media, we may begin to perceive that we, too, are changing; perhaps we look at ourselves differently, have acquired different attitudes or values, or simply look at others in a different way. What is important is that we try to understand the changes so that we can realistically assess the impact that the media, both new and old, are having upon us.

Use the following exercise to help you keep up to date on your personal media environment.

MEDIA VIEW

Characterizing this as a post-literate society does not mean that print and the written word are dead. Those who speak of the "space age" do not mean that airplanes and automobiles have disappeared, and those who call this the "age of the auto" do not mean that every train has dissolved to dust and all the horses have dropped dead. The postliterate society means simply that the shift in the communication of non-face-to-face information from the written word to the electronic media is now dominant and has a deep and fundamental significance.

Tony Schwartz, *Media: The Second God,* Anchor, New York, 1983, p. 10.

NOT THE LAST WORD: YOUR ROLE BEYOND THIS BOOK 425

MEDIA PROBE

1. Describe your relationship to each of the media listed below ten years ago, five years ago, and today. Discuss this relationship in terms of the amount of time you spend with each medium, the way you use it, and how your perceive its effect on you.

   Books
   Newspapers
   Magazines
   Radio
   Broadcast television
   Film
   Cable television
   Videocassette recorders
   Videodiscs
   Video games
   Computers

2. Describe yourself ten years ago, five years ago, and today in terms of the typical way you respond to advertising and public relations messages.
3. Based on your analyses, answer these questions:
   a. Which medium or media are you most loyal to? Why?
   b. Identify factors (personal or environmental) that might account for the stability and/or change in the ways you process the media and/or advertising and public relations messages.
   c. What are some of the social and professional circumstances surrounding your use of each medium? your use of advertising and public relations?
   d. What consequences and what rewards have you experienced as a result of the way you use the preceding media?
   e. What steps you do think you can take to increase the positive effects of the media in your life and diminish their negative effects upon you? In other words, how can you use the media more effectively?

Be sure to repeat this exercise every few years.

Only if we analyze the positive and negative outcomes of our media passages can we hope to understand how the media we have created are helping to change us, the way we work, the way we learn, the way we spend our leisure time, even the way we interact with others. Knowing our rationale for seeking out particular media and comprehending how those choices affect us are essential if we are to become better at processing the media and their messages. As we see it, if the media are influencing us, perhaps even transforming us, it is incumbent upon us to do our best to determine how.

The mass media can help us improve the quality of our lives or they can detract from the quality of our lives; they can help us cope with problems or they can present problems. They can increase our freedom by functioning as our windows on the world, or they can limit our freedom by turning us into technological slaves. It all depends on whether we use them wisely. Those of us who do accept this challenge, those of us who do continually strive to become media-wise, are taking steps to improve our chances of passing smoothly from one stage of media development to the next. To be sure, as our media menu increases, our lives will become more complicated, but they will also become more interesting.

SUMMARY

Each of the media we discussed in this book affects us and the way we live our lives to some extent. Because of their pervasiveness, it is incumbent upon us to work to analyze how the media influence us; doing this, however, is a continuing assignment, not one that can be completed this week, this month, or even this year. It will take a lifetime.

Perhaps you are considering a career in media. If so, the time to begin your planning is now. On the other hand, perhaps you are wondering how the media will change and how you will change in the years ahead. The time to begin assessing that is also right now. But whatever the role you expect to play in the media, one thing is certain—the media will be playing a role in your life as well. Exactly what kind of role they will play, however, depends on how wisely you are able to use them.

NOTES

[1] Leo Bogart, "Newspapers in 2084," *Editor & Publisher,* March 31, 1984, p. 370.
[2] Frederick Williams, *The Communications Revolution,* rev. ed., New American Library, New York, 1983, p. 24.
[3] Gail Sheehy, *Passages: Predictable Crises of Adult Life,* Bantam, New York, 1976, p. 29.
[4] Tony Schwartz, *Media: The Second God,* Anchor, New York, 1983, p. 7.
[5] Sheehy, op. cit., p. 31.

SUGGESTIONS FOR FURTHER READING

Greenfield, Patricia Marks: *Mind and Media: The Effects of Television, Video Games, and Computers,* Harvard University Press, Cambridge, Mass., 1984. *Explores results of new research in an effort to discover how the media can be used to promote social growth and thinking skills.*

Schwartz, Tony: *Media: The Second God,* Anchor, New York, 1983. *Thoughts on how we can use and control media to our advantage.*

Sheehy, Gail: *Passages: Predictable Crises of Adult Life,* Bantam, New York, 1976. *Shows how perceived crises may be turned into opportunities for creative change.*

Williams, Frederick: *The Communications Revolution,* rev. ed., New American Library, New York, 1983. *A guide to the possibilities of the present and the future.*

Zimmermann, Caroline A.: *How to Break Into the Media Professions,* Doubleday, Garden City, N.Y., 1981. *Step-by-step instructions for getting that first job.*

GLOSSARY

A *A. C. NIELSEN* A market research firm; the largest commercial ratings service used by broadcasters.

ADVERTISING The paid, nonpersonal, and usually persuasive presentation of ideas, goods, and services by identified sponsors through various media.

ADVERTISING AGENCY The organization responsible for the planning, creation, and execution of advertising campaigns.

ADVOCACY ADVERTISING Advertising that reveals the sponsor's viewpoint on matters of controversy.

AFFILIATE A local broadcasting station that signs a contract with a network.

ALTERNATIVE NEWSPAPERS Special-interest newspapers that promote the interests of those who feel alienated from the mainstream.

AM RADIO Amplitude modulation; the older form of radio transmission.

AMERICAN SOCIETY OF COMPOSERS, AUTHORS, AND PUBLISHERS (ASCAP) A music-licensing organization that collects fees from those who use the music of its members for profit.

ARBITRON A professional research service that measures radio and television audiences.

ATTITUDE A disposition toward a person, thing, or issue; measured on a pro-con continuum.

AUDILOGS Diaries that provide supplementary viewer information.

AUTHORITARIAN THEORY The belief that the

press operates solely with the permission of, and to serve the purposes of, the ruling government.

AVERAGE PERSONS The estimated number of persons listening to a station at least five minutes during any quarter hour in a time period.

AVERAGE-PERSONS RATINGS The ratio of the number of people listening to a particular station to the number of people in the entire market.

B

BEAT REPORTER A journalist whose task it is to cover a particular area.

BILLBOARD The trade publication of the sound recording industry that tabulates record popularity.

BLUNTING The scheduling of a program similar to those offered by the competing networks.

BREAK THE BOOK The process of deciding how the space of a magazine will be used.

BRIDGING The airing of a show with a long running time just before the start of prime-time offerings on other stations.

BROADCAST MUSIC INCORPORATED (BMI) The sister organization to ASCAP; also a music-licensing organization.

BUSINESS ADVERTISING Advertising addressed to people who are expected to use the product or service for business reasons or to resell the product or service.

C

CABLE TELEVISION Community antenna television; a system that delivers television by wire instead of through the open airwaves.

CATHARSIS THEORY The theory that the viewing of aggressive scenes helps to purge viewers of their own aggressive feelings.

CENSORSHIP Interference with the distribution of certain materials to the public.

CHANNEL The means or pathway through which a message is transmitted from source to receiver.

CIRCULATION The total number of copies of a publication delivered to newsstands, vending machines, or subscribers.

CLOSE-UP A shot taken at a very short distance from the subject to permit a close and detailed view of an object or action.

COAXIAL CABLE A cable composed of an inner wire core surrounded by a layer of plastic, a metallic layer of webbed insulation, and a layer of plastic; used to transmit television signals.

CODEX A type of binding in which a volume of parchment pages were bound on the left side; today, a manuscript volume, usually of an ancient classic.

COMMUNICATION The process of sharing meaning; our link to the rest of humanity.

COMMUNICATIONS The means we use to send messages; the tools we use to communicate.

COMMUNICATIONS ACT OF 1934 An act of Congress that created the Federal Communications Commission, the body charged with regulating broadcasting in the United States.

COMPACT DISCS Recordings that are played by a laser instead of a stylus.

CONSUMER ADVERTISING Advertising directed to people who are expected to use a product or service for personal reasons.

CONTENT ANALYSIS A research procedure that explores the content of communication objectively, systematically, and quantitatively.

CONTEXT The communication setting.

COPYRIGHT LAW A statute that allows creators and publishers of a work to control who can use the work and to set conditions for that use.

CORPORATION FOR PUBLIC BROADCASTING The network office of the Public Broadcasting Service.

COUNTERPROGRAMMING The scheduling of a different kind of show from the type being offered by the other two networks.

CREEL COMMITTEE The Committee on Public Information formed during World War I to mobilize public opinion in support of the war.

CUME Figures that reveal the total number of people who have tuned in at all during a particular period.

D

DEMASSIFIED MEDIA Media that cater more to small audiences and individualized needs and wants.

DEMOGRAPHICS The study of the numerical characteristics of the population.

DIME NOVELS Cheaply priced nineteenth-century books emphasizing action.

DIRECT-MAIL ADVERTISING Advertising that is mailed directly to prospective customers.

DIRECT SATELLITE-TO-HOME TRANSMISSION The transmission of signals from an orbiting satellite on a home TV set.

DRIVE TIMES Prime radio time; the time during which most people are traveling to and from work, normally from 6:30 to 9 A.M. and 4:30 to 6:30 P.M.

DOCUMENTARY A film that attempts to portray a real-life situation in a factual way.

DUOPOLY RULING Federal Communications Commission rule that prohibits ownership of more than one AM, one FM, or one TV station in a community.

E

EARTH STATIONS Dish-shaped antennas that receive satellite signals.

EFFECT The outcome of communication.

ELECTRONIC NEWSGATHERING EQUIPMENT (ENG) The small, lightweight, portable cameras that enable crews to broadcast stories directly from the scene.

EQUAL OPPORTUNITY RULE Contained in section 315 of the Communications Act of 1934; the law states that if one candidate for public office is sole or given airtime during a campaign, all other candidates for that office must be given the same opportunity.

EXPERIMENTAL RESEARCH Laboratory research that permits individuals to exercise control over the environment, the variables being studied, and the subjects; the measuring of the relationship between two types of variables under closely observed and controlled conditions.

EXTREME CLOSE-UP A shot taken at an extremely short distance from the subject to permit a very close and detailed view of it.

EXTREME LONG SHOT A shot that reveals the entire area of action or a locale.

F

FAIRNESS DOCTRINE Federal Communications Commission rule that states that broadcasters have an obligation to seek out and present contrasting viewpoints on controversial issues of public concern.

FEDERAL COMMUNICATIONS COMMISSION Federal agency created by Congress in 1934 to regulate broadcasting by assigning frequencies and licensing persons or groups to broadcast.

FEDERAL TRADE COMMISSION The five-member governmental body empowered to monitor truth in advertising.

FEEDBACK The return of information to the source of a message; the means by which a source determines whether the message sent was received and understood as intended by its receivers.

FIELD RESEARCH Research that takes place in real-life settings; the study of the behavior of subjects who are not in a controlled environment.

FM Frequency modulation; has a higher fidelity than AM radio.

FIELD OF EXPERIENCE Each person's storehouse of experiences.

FILM SCENES A single shot or group of shots usually unified by time and place.

FILM SEQUENCES A grouping of scenes unified by a common purpose or setting.

FILM SHOT The period of time elapsed from the point a camera starts rolling to the point it stops rolling.

FIRST AMENDMENT The legal basis for both the libertarian and social-responsibility theories of the press; guarantees freedom of speech, the press, and religion.

FREE SHEET PAPER Paper that is devoid of the less desirable impurities found in groundwood paper; usually used in hardcover trade editions.

FREEDOM OF INFORMATION ACT The 1967 law that protects the public's right to know what is happening in the government by requiring every federal executive branch agency to publish instructions regarding what a member of the public must do to get information.

FREEDOM OF THE PRESS The right of the press to be free of governmental control; guaranteed by the First Amendment.

G

GAG ORDER Court order that restrains participants in a trial from divulging information to the media or prevents the media from covering court events.

GATEKEEPER Any person who has the ability to limit, expand, emphasize, or deemphasize, interpret, or reinterpret the information sent over or received from a mass medium.

GRAVURE A printing process usually used in art books and other heavily illustrated works.

GROUNDWOOD PAPER A type of paper usually used in mass-market paperbacks.

GROUP COMMUNICATION The process by which several persons communicate; one-to-few interaction.

H

HAMLOCKING The scheduling of a weaker or brand-new show between two strong shows.

HANDHELD CAMERA SHOT A shot taken with a handheld camera.

HERTZ The basic unit of frequency; the cycles per second at which the radio station broadcasts.

HIGH-ANGLE SHOT A shot taken with the camera looking down at the subject.

HISTORICAL RESEARCH Research that provides an interpretation of the past.

HYPODERMIC THEORY The belief that information flowed directly from the media to intended targets, who all responded in essentially the same way to the information; for the most part, replaced by the two-step flow theory.

I

ICONOSCOPE A camera tube that served as the core of the first all-electronic television system.

IMAGE ADVERTISING Nonproduct advertising that focuses on issues confronting a particular company or industry.

INVERTED PYRAMID A format in which the reporter gives the most important facts first, those next in importance second, and so on to those least in importance.

INVESTIGATIVE REPORTER A journalist whose work involves extensive digging and checking.

J

JAZZ JOURNALISM A new cycle of sensationalism that started at the close of World War I; characterized by an easy-to-understand style, it relied on vivid photographs for impact.

K

KINESCOPE The receiving unit in early electronic TV receivers; a cathode ray tube that carried an image composed of thirty horizontal lines.

L

LEAD The beginning of a news story; contains such information as who, what, when, how, and where.

LEGION OF DECENCY A Catholic organization formed in 1933 that rated films according to a scale of acceptability.

LETTERPRESS A method of printing in which ink is applied to a raised surface, which then contacts the paper.

LIBERTARIAN THEORY The belief that the press exists to serve the people, that people are rationale decision makers, and, therefore, that the government must not interfere with the medium's operation.

LIBEL Published or broadcast material which is false and damages the reputation or good name of a person.

LICENSEE ASCERTAINMENT The requirement placed upon stations to survey the needs and problems of their local areas so that they can better provide programs that address these needs and problems.

LINOTYPE A machine that sets type mechanically.

LOBBYING The petitioning of the government to support legislation in the best interests of a client.

LOCAL ADVERTISING Advertising paid for by a dealer who sells directly to the consumer.

LONG SHOT An establishing shot; reveals where the people or objects are located.

LOW-ANGLE SHOT A shot taken with the camera looking up at the subject.

LOP PRINCIPLE The theory that states that viewers will watch the least objectionable program.

M *MAGAZINE FORMULA* The concept that guides the magazine through the editorial process and gives the magazine its distinctive personality.

MAGIC-BULLET THEORY See Hypodermic Theory.

MASS COMMUNICATION The multistage process by which an organization using technical devices or intermediate transmitters sends messages widely and rapidly to large, scattered, heterogeneous audiences whom they do not know personally and who have a limited opportunity to provide feedback.

MASTERING The transfer from tape to disc.

MEDIUM SHOT A camera shot that depicts a character or object in its immediate surroundings.

MESSAGE The content of the communicative act.

MIXING The merging of the various tracks of a recording down to two tracks.

MOTIVATION RESEARCH Research designed to determine why people buy particular products; the effort to identify the needs and desires being met.

MPAA RATING SYSTEM The rating system of the Motion Picture Association of America; devised in the late 1960s, with minor changes it is still in place today.

MUCKRAKERS Term coined by Theodore Roosevelt to describe the reform-minded journalists of leading magazines in the late nineteenth and early twentieth centuries.

MUSIC TELEVISION A video version of the top 40 tunes.

N *NAB CODE* National Association of Broadcasters Code that describes the responsibilities of broadcasters, sets general program content standards, and limits the amount of advertising that should be permitted during any hour; ruled in violation of the antitrust laws in 1982.

NATIONAL ADVERTISING Those advertising messages that are paid for by the owner of a product or service that is or will be sold through stores or distributors.

NATIONAL ADVERTISING REVIEW BOARD (NARB) A fifty-member self-regulatory organization.

NATIONAL PUBLIC RADIO (NPR) A network of noncommercial radio stations created in 1969 by the Corporation for Public Broadcasting; functions as a program distribution service for member stations.

NETWORK An organization comprised of broadcasting stations connected by wire, satellite, or microwave that broadcast the same programs, often simultaneously.

NEW JOURNALISM A colorful, dramatic, and highly personal style of reporting in which journalists, like novelists, incorporate dialogue, flashbacks, the thoughts of people, and their own thoughts and opinions into the articles they write.

NEWS Events that because they fulfill the criteria of prominence, proximity, consequence, timeliness, and/or human interest are reported to a mass audience through a mass medium.

NEWS COOPERATIVE An association that services a number of different papers.

NEWSPAPER GROUP OR CHAIN Two or more newspapers with common ownership.

NEWS HOLE The amount of space available in a newspaper after all the advertisements are set.

NICKELODEONS The early permanent amusement centers that specialized in recordings and films; a popular name for the coin-operated phonograph popular at the turn of the twentieth century.

NIELSEN TELEVISION INDEX (NTI) A ratings

book describing the data derived from audimeters and audilogs.

NOISE Anything that interferes with the ability to send or receive messages.

NORMAL-ANGLE SHOT A shot taken with the camera at eye level.

NULL THEORY Adherents maintain that fictionalized violence has no influence on real violence.

O *OBJECTIVITY* The traditional ideal of journalism, characterized by factual reporting uninfluenced by the attitudes and values of those doing the reporting.

OFFSET PRINTING A photographic printing process.

O & O Network owned and operated station; five VHF broadcasting stations may be owned and operated by each of the three commercial networks.

OPINION Response to a question about a controversial topic; gathered in surveys or polls.

OPINION LEADERS Those who, when exposed to media content, knowingly or unknowingly influence other people's opinions about the content.

OPINION RESEARCH Polls or surveys conducted to find out the public's beliefs or feelings about a subject.

P *PAN* The following of action by the camera.

PAN SHOT A shot in which the camera is moved from left to right or vice versa.

PAPERBACK EXTRAS Instant books produced almost as quickly as newspapers and magazines.

PAPYRUS The earliest form of paper; a cardboardlike material used by the ancient Egyptians.

PARALLEL ACTION Action occurring in different places at the same time.

PARCHMENT A writing material made from animal skins.

PAYOLA Special favors offered to disc jockeys in exchange for airtime.

PENNY PRESS The first mass newspapers; a term descriptive of the mass-appeal press of the early to mid-nineteenth century.

PERSISTENCE OF VISION The quality of the human eye that enables it to retain an image for a split second after the image has vanished; the psychological principle upon which the movie is based.

PERSONAL COMMUNICATION The process by which an individual communicates with one other person; one-to-one interaction.

POCKET BOOK A paperback book that is pocket size.

POSTAL ACT OF 1879 A statute that gave special mailing rates to magazines, thereby enabling editors and publishers to reach national markets.

PRESS AGENTRY The planning or staging of events designed to attract public attention.

PRIMARY ADVERTISING Advertising designed to create a demand for generic products or services.

PRIME-TIME ACCESS RULE Issued in 1970; returned the 7:30 to 8:00 P.M. (EST) time slot to local stations in an effort to expand program diversity.

PRIOR RESTRAINT The attempt by the government to halt the printing or distribution of information.

PRIVACY LAW The statute that enables citizens to protect themselves adequately from the prying media.

PRODUCT CLAIM The claims that an advertisement makes about a product.

PROGRAM CLOCK HOUR The time within which a radio programmer must incorporate a number of different programming elements, including music (if that is the format), talk, news, station IDs, weather, and commercials.

PROPAGANDIST An advocate who considers the interests of the source exclusively, viewing receivers as individuals who may be used to certain ends.

PROPERTY The subject matter of a film; the creative idea submitted to a producer.

PSEUDO-EVENT A term coined by historian Daniel Boorstin to describe a happening planned, fabricated, or incited so a reporter can cover it.

PSYCHOGRAPHICS The classification of consumers according to psychological makeup.

PUBLIC A group of people who have something in common and are united by a common bond.

PUBLIC BROADCASTING SERVICE An agency that parallels the functioning of a commercial network.

PUBLIC COMMUNICATION The process by which an individual addresses a large audience; one-to-many interaction.

PUBLICITY The placement of newsworthy information in print or broadcast form in the media.

PUBLIC OPINION The sum of individualized opinions on an issue.

PUBLIC RELATIONS The planned, two-way communication effort through which an individual or organization strives to win the understanding, acceptance, support, and cooperation of the public.

PUBLIC-SERVICE ADVERTISING Advertising that supports nonprofit causes and organizations; provided as a free service to the public by the print or broadcast media in which the ad appears.

PUBLIC TELEVISION Noncommercial television.

Q *QUALIDATA* Reports that provide local-product-usage information and data on competing media.

QUBE The first two-way cable system started in 1977 by Warner Communications.

QUERY LETTER A letter written by an author to an editor containing a brief but intriguing description of a proposed manuscript; a means of selling an idea.

R *RADIO ACT OF 1927* An act of Congress that established that the airwaves were a natural resource which had to be conserved and protected and formulated the concept that stations had to operate in the "public interest, convenience or necessity"; also created the Federal Radio Commission.

RAG-CONTENT PAPER Expensive paper used primarily in the printing of Bibles.

RATING The percentage of the total number of television or radio households tuned to a given program.

RECEIVER The person who is the target (intended or unintended) of the source's efforts during the communication process.

REGIONAL AND DEMOGRAPHIC EDITIONS Editions of large-circulation magazines that are created to match the needs and interests of segments of the magazine's total readership.

ROYALTY Compensation paid to originators of works for each copy of their work sold or used.

S *SANS SERIF* The second most frequently used typeface; does not contain cross strokes at the ends of lines.

SEDITION ACT Federal law passed in 1798 prohibiting the publishing of "false, scandalous, or malicious writing" against Congress or the president. The Sedition Act of 1918 made it illegal to publish anything that showed contempt for the federal government or the American flag.

SELECTIVE ADVERTISING Advertising that is designed to stimulate demand for a particular product.

SELECTIVE ATTENTION The selective exposure by receivers to information with which they agree and avoidance of information with which they disagree.

SELECTIVE PERCEPTION The interpretation by receivers of received messages in ways that support the receivers' predisposition and prior knowledge.

SERIF The most common typeface; characterized by cross strokes at the ends of lines.

SHARE The percentage of total listeners or viewers who are tuned to a particular program.

SHIELD LAW A statute that protects reporters from having to reveal their sources of information.

SIGNATURE A small booklet usually composed of thirty-two pages.

SIQUIS The forerunner of our present want ads; also known as "If anybody's."

SIXTH AMENDMENT Guarantees a defendant the right to a fair trial before an impartial jury.

SIXTH REPORT AND ORDER Lifted the 1948–1952 freeze on TV station licensing; put forth a master plan for the development of television.

SOCIAL-RESPONSIBILITY THEORY The belief that while the press has the right to criticize the government, it also has the obligation to inform the citizenry properly and to respond to societal needs and interests.

SOURCE The person who originates and transmits a message to others during the communication process.

STAMPING The molding of the actual record.

STIMULATION THEORY The theory that the viewing of scenes of aggression stimulates individuals to behave more violently.

STORAGE INSTANTANEOUS AUDIMETER (SIA) A device that automatically records the precise time a television set is on and the channel it is tuned to; used to compute ratings.

SUMMARY LEAD See Lead.

SURVEY RESEARCH A research procedure that employs the questionnaire as a key tool.

SYNDICATES Organizations independent of both the networks and the local stations.

T

TABLOID Technically, a publication usually half the size of a standard newspaper page; commonly used to refer to a splashy, heavily illustrated newspaper.

TELETEXT A one-way service in which textual and graphic data are broadcast as part of a television signal.

TILT SHOT A vertical pan.

TRACKING SHOT A shot taken with a camera that is moved along rails.

TRADE BOOK Books produced for mass audiences and sold primarily through bookstores and book clubs.

TWO-STEP FLOW THEORY The belief that while information flows from the media to some people directly, it also flows from some people directly exposed to the media to more people; *see also Opinion Leader.*

TWO-WAY INTERACTIVE CABLE A system that makes it possible for receivers to feed back information to the "head-end" of their cable systems.

U

UHF The ultrahigh frequency band of the electromagnetic spectrum; channels 14 to 83 on the TV set.

UNIVERSAL COPYRIGHT CONVENTION The agreement that supported international copyright protection.

V

VERTICAL INTEGRATION A form of limited monopoly; the control of all aspects of the film industry by a single studio.

VHF The very high frequency band of the electromagnetic spectrum; channels 2 to 13 on the TV set.

VIDEO GAME Coin-operated games housed in arcades; cartridge-based games playable in the home; computer games.

VIDEOCASSETTE RECORDER (VCR) Telecommunication recording and playback machine.

VIDEOTAPE Invented by the Ampex Company; tape through which visual images are magnetically recorded.

VIDEOTEX A two-way service that enables users to receive information and respond through the telephone network, a cable TV system, or a combination of the two.

W

WEASEL WORD A word that turns a statement of real advantage into one without meaning.

WIRE SERVICE Organizations which function as a primary source of news stories and photos for newspapers, television, radio, and cable stations that pay for the service.

Y

YELLOW JOURNALISM The late-nineteenth-century era of sensationalized journalism characterized by an emphasis on violence, sex, and human interest.

INDEX

Page numbers in *italic* indicate illustrations.

Abbott, Emma, 64
ABC (American Broadcasting Company), 154
ABC News, 98, 114
ABC Television Network, 198
Abrams, Floyd, 101, 105, 239
Academy Awards, 283
Ace (publisher), 31
Ackerman, Martin, 128
Action for Children's Television (ACT), 208, 240
Adams, John, 60
Adams, Samuel, 346
Addison, Joseph, 120
Adler, Bill, 45
Adventure (computer game), 395
Advertising, 295–332
   development of, 300–304
   future of, 418
   in magazines, 126, 128, 132, 303, 318
   media for, 317–325
   methods of, 304–317
   of movies, 283–285
   national, 72, 73, 78
   in newspapers, 70–71, 73, 78–79, 302, 317–318
   on radio, 70–71, 150, 156, 182–183, 319
   in recording industry, 168
   in suburban dailies, 73
   in throwaway shoppers, 76
   on TV, 70–71, 199, 203, 207, 240–242, 320–322
   (*See also* Ratings)
Advertising agencies, 325–326
   organization chart of a typical agency, *326*
Affiliates (TV stations), 201–202
Agee, Philip, 112–114
Agents, literary, 37
Agronsky, Martin, 345
Airlines, magazines for, 131
Alcoholic beverages, advertising for, 331

Alexander, Charles, 120
Alger, Horatio, 27
Alien and Sedition Acts of 1798, 60
All-news radio, 177, 184
All-talk radio, 177
All the President's Men (film), 271
All Things Considered (radio program), 180, 181
Allen, Nathan, 122
Allport, Peter, 241
Alternative newspapers, 77
Alton Telegraph (newspaper), 97
AM radio, 177–179, 409
American Association of Advertising Agencies (AAAA), 328–330
American Booksellers Association (ABA), 28, 41, 45
American Broadcasting Company (*see* ABC)
American Film Institute, 418
American Library Association, 29, 46
American Magazine or a Monthly View of the Political State of the British Colonies, 119, 120
American Marconi Corporation, 149
American Marketing Association, 297
American Newspaper Industry Association, 109
American Revolution, newspapers during, 58
American Society of Composers, Authors and Publishers (ASCAP), 171
American Society of Newspaper Editors (ASNE), 105, 109, 112
American Telephone and Telegraph Company (*see* AT&T)

Amos 'n' Andy (radio program), 157
Ampex Corporation, 164, 200
Anchor (TV news), 229
Anderson, Ida Lou, 370
Andrews, Cecil, 232
Angle, Jim, 181
Annie (musical), 276
Apple, R. W., 34
Applebaum, Stuart, 42
Arbitron, 146, 185–188, 221, 222
Arbuckle, Fatty, 273
Arlen, Gary, 393
Armstrong, Edwin Howard, 148, 178–179
Ashenfelter, David L., 108
Associated Press (AP), 89–90
Association magazines, 130–131
Association of American Publishers, 46
AT&T (American Telephone and Telegraph Company), 150, 202, 212, 320
Atkin, Charles, 88
Atkinson, Samuel, 120
Atwater, Gordon A., 47
Audiences, 8, 9
Audilogs, 222
Audimeters, 222
Audion, 147, 148
Audit Bureau of Circulation, 119, 130
Authoritarian-style press, 95
Authors:
   in book promotion, 41–42
   in magazines, 137–138
   Maxwell Perkins and, 38–39
   publicity escorts for, 43
   of romance novels, 31–32
   royalties for, 30, 37–39
   tours for, 41–42
   Kurt Vonnegut on, 37
Avon (publisher), 31
Ayer, Frances Wayland, 325
Ayer, N. W., and Son, 303

437

B-pictures (films), 266–267
Bagdikian, Ben, 73, 88
Baird, Russel N., 129, 136, 139
Baker, Russell, 230
Baker, Stephen, 307
Baldwin, T. F., 219
Bandura, Albert, 237
Bantam Books (publisher), 31–33, 41, 42
Bara, Theda, 261
Barcus, F. E., 241
Barnes, A. S., and Company (publisher), 25
Barnes, Alfred Smith, 25
Barnouw, Erik, 149
Barnum, Phineas Taylor, 346
Bay Psalm Book, 22, 24
Beadle, E. F., 27
Beadle's Dime Novels, 22, 27
Beatles, The (music group), 148, 171–172
Beer advertising, 307
Behrens, Dave, 92
Bell, Alexander Graham, 147, 148
Belsen, James A., 82
Berg, A. Scott, 39
Berg, Alan, 178
Berger, Larry, 176
Bergman, Ingmar, 252
Berkeley, Busby, 264
Berkeley, William, 24
Berkley (publisher), 31
Berliner, Emile, 148, 163
Bernard, Walter, 140
Bernays, Edward L., 347
Bernhardt, Sarah, 259
Bernstein, Carl, 81, *82*, 83
Bernstein, Fred, 139
Bernstein, Richard, 45
Berry, Dave, 32
Best Boy (film), 288
Best-sellers, 22, 27–28, 42–45
Best Years of Our Lives (film), 267
Betamax, 388
Between Fact and Fiction (book), 106
Bible, 22, 24, 40
Bickerstaff, Isaac, 120
Bicycle network (radio), 179, 180
Billboard (magazine), 169
Binding of books, 23, 24, 40
Birth of a Nation (film), 257, 258, 273
Bishop, Hazel, 199
Black Maria (movie studio), 256
Blacks, 77–78, 170, 242
Blakiston Company, 25
Blattstein, Joel J., 419

Bliss, Edward, Jr., 162, 370
Block, Martin, 173
Bloeser, Richard, 283
Blume, Judy, 46
Blunting (TV programming), 221
Bly, Nellie, 64
Body copy (advertising), 316
Bogart, Humphrey, 265
Bogart, Leo, 191, 403
Boggs, Joseph M., 269
Bok, Sissela, 112, 355
Bonneville Broadcasting Systems, 177
Book Industry Study Group, 21
Book-of-the-Month Club, 22, 30, 45
Books, 19–52
  best-sellers, 22, 27–28, 42–45
  binding of, 23, 24, 40
  and bookstores, 22, 24–25, 44
  censorship of, 45–49
  development of, 21–26
  educational, 20, 35, *36*, 47–49
  future of, 402–403
  popular, 26–28
  production of, 23, 39–41
  trade, 35, 41
  (*See also* Publishing; *specific titles*)
Bookstores, 22, 24–25, 44
Boorstin, Daniel, 49, 91
Born Innocent (film), 238–239
Bosse, Malcolm, 44
Boston *Globe* (newspaper), 135
Boston *Herald* (newspaper), 135
Boston News-Letter (newspaper), 58
Boston Tea Party, *346*
Boston Women's Health Book Collective, 46
Bowker, R. R. (publisher), 31
Bradshaw, Jon, 386
Branch, Jim, 112
Brandeis, Louis, 98
Branzburg, Paul, 104
Branzburg v. Hayes, 104
Brend, Thomas, 24
Brennan, William, Jr., 49
Brescia, Richard M., 408
Breslin, Jimmy, 94
Bridging (TV programming), 221
Briller, Bert R., 411
Brinkley, David, 226
Brinkley, John R., 155
British Broadcasting Corporation (BBC), 13
Broadcast Music Incorporated (BMI), 171
Brown, Les, 205, 222–224, 384, 391

Browning, Robert, 27
Bryant, William Cullen, 25
Buchenwald concentration camp, 161–162
Buchwald, Art, 314
Buckingham, Joseph, 121
"Buddy films," 270
Bureaucracies as mass communicators, 8–9
Burgoon, Judee, 88
Burgoon, Michael, 88
Burke, James, 351
Burkett, Warren, 406
Burnett, Carol, 97
Burson-Marsteller, 339, 351
Burton, William, 120
Busch, H. Ted, 322
Business:
  in magazines, 123
  magazines for, 130
Butch Cassidy and the Sundance Kid (film), 270
Buxton, Edward, 308
Byoir, Carl, and Associates, 347
Byte (magazine), *130*

Cable television, 213–214, 385–387, 420
  future of, 414–415
  movies on, 282–283
  MTV, 164–165
  two-way, 390–392
Cablevision, 415
Caesar, Julius, 345
Cake mixes, 309
California Test Bureau, 25
Call-in radio talk shows, 177
Campbell, John, 58
Campbell Soup, 327
Canby, Vincent, 281, 283–284
Cantril, Hadley, 367
Caples, John, 315
Capote, Truman, 94
Carnegie Commission on Educational Television, 180, 210, 212
Carter, Hodding, 72, 76, 114
Carter, Jimmy, 53
Cary, Alice, 123
Cary, Phoebe, 123
Casablanca (film), 265
Casket, The: Flowers of Literature, Wit and Sentiment (magazine), 120
Castle Wolfenstein (computer game), 395
Catcher in the Rye (novel), 46
Cater, Douglas, 396

Catholics, 274, 345
Causley, Stephen A., 97
CBS (Columbia Broadcasting System), 31, 131, 152, 207
Celebrities, 76, 97
Censorship:
  of books, 45–49
  military, during Civil War, 63
  in movies, 272–276
  prior restraint as, 105–106
Center for Communication, 134
Central Intelligence Agency (CIA), 112
Cerf, Bennett, 29, 30
Chagall, David, 224
Channels in communication, 5
Chaplin, Charlie, *261*, 263
Charren, Peggy, 208, 240
Chastain, Thomas, 45
Chicago Daily News (newspaper), 71
Children:
  magazines for, 122
  TV for, 208, 212, 233–242
Children's Magazine, 119
Choate, Robert, 241, 242
Christian Science Monitor, The (newspaper), 72
Chrysler Corporation, 299
CIA and the Cult of Intelligence, The (book), 106
Cinderella (book), 48
Circulation:
  Audit Bureau of Circulation, 119, 130
  of college papers, 77
  of magazines, 118, 126–127, 130
  of newspapers, 71, 73, 76, 77, 79
  of *Time* magazine, 125
Citizen Kane (film), 65
City editor, 90
Civil War, 62–67, 123
Clansman, The (film), 258
Clark, Lewis Gaylord, 121
Clark, Thomas, 102
Click, J. W., 129, 136, 139
Coalition for Better TV (CBTV), 208, 239
Cohn, James J., Jr., 106
College newspapers, 77
College students, 13, 54
Collier's (magazine), 118, 119
Color separations, 40
Color television, 199
Colum, Terry, 108
Columbia Broadcasting System (*see* CBS)
Columbia Phonograph Broadcasting System, 152

Columbia Phonograph Company, 163, 164
Columbia Records, 148
Comic-book heroes in movies, 272
Commercials (*see* Advertising)
Commission on Freedom of the Press, 96
Communication, 4–8
  (*See also specific forms*)
Communications Act of 1934, 156, 175, 204, 210
Compact disc players, *167*
Compact discs, 167
Compaine, Benjamin, 31, 129
Computers, 390–394, 413, 420
Condé Nast, 132
Cone, Fairfax M., 332
Conflict of interest in newspaper industry, 109–112
Conrad, Frank, 149
Constance Missal, The (book), 23
Constitution, U.S.:
  copyright laws derived from, 25
  (*See also* First Amendment)
Consumer Magazine & Farm Publication Rates and Data, 136
Consumers, 130, 329
Contemporary hit radio, 175–176
Content analysis, 374–377
Contests, 42–45, 64, 109
Context of communication, 6–7
Cook, David A., 255, 274
Cooney, John, 358
Coop advertising, 183
Cooper, James Fenimore, 25
Copyright Act of 1790, 26
Copyright laws, 22, 25–26
"Corantos," 55
Cornetti, Angelo, 64
Corporation for Public Broadcasting (CPB), 179, 180, 210–211
Corporation for Public Television, 210
Corrective advertising, 328
Cosby, William, 58
Cosmographs, 68
Cosmopolitan (magazine), 123
Counsel on Children, Media and Merchandising (CCMM), 241
Counterprogramming (TV), 221
Country music, 172, 177
Cousins, Norman, 134
Covers of magazines, 139
Craft, Christine, 231
Creel, George, 347
Creelman, James, 66

Crisis (magazine), 59
Critics and reviewers, 42, 283–285
Cronkite, Walter, 228
Cross, Donna Woolfolk, 229, 316
Culkin, John, 3
Cullum, Leo, *42*
Curtis, Cyrus, 119, 123
Curtis Publishing Company, 128

Dailies (newspapers), 71–76
Daily Graphic (newspaper), 68
Daily Mirror (newspaper), 68
Daily News, The (newspaper), 68
Dalton, B., Bookseller, 44
Dance in movies, 272
"Dance With Me Henry" (song), 170
Danny Thomas Show, The (TV program), *199*
Darretta, John, 415
Davis, Clive, 167
Davis, Peter, 287
Davis, Sid, 69
Day, Benjamin H., 60
Day, Clarence, 49
Daye, Stephen, 24
DBS (direct broadcast satellites), 387, 412
Dean, James, 269
"Deep Throat," 103
Deer Hunter, The (film), 270–271
DeFleur, Melvin D., 368
Defoe, Daniel, 118
De Forest, Lee, 147, 148, 179
deGraff, Robert Fair, 31
Dell (publisher), 34
Della Femina, Jerry, 309
Demographics, 306, 421
Dennie, Joseph, 120, 121
Depression (1930s), 70, 156, 163, 264
Derow, Peter, 140
Design of magazines, 139–140
Dessauer, John, 23, 39
Detroit News (newspaper), 108
Diamandis, Peter, 140, 141
Diario Los Americas (newspaper), 77
Dickens, Charles, 26
Dickson, William, 255
Dictionaries, censorship of, 48
Didion, Joan, 94, 279
Digital technology in sound recording, 166–167
Dime novels, 22, 27
Direct broadcast satellites (DBS), 387, 412

INDEX **439**

Direct-mail advertising, 322, 323
Disc jockeys, 173–*174*
Disney, Walt, 264
"Diurnals," 55
Documentary films, 265, 287–288
Dodd, Mead (publisher), 25, 47
Dodd, Moses, 25
Donovan, Hedley, 135
Dorsee, Robert, 239
Doubleday, Nelson, 28
Doubleday (publisher), 47
Douglass, Frederick, 77
Dowling, Jim, 352
Dr. X, 104
Dreyfuss, Joel, 45
Duffy, James, 412
du Maurier, George, 27
Dumont Network, 201
Dunn, William G., 118, 128
Dunn & Bradstreet, 137
Dunne, John Gregory, 94, 279
Durbin, William, 339
Dutton, E. P., & Company (publisher), 25
Dutton, Edward, 25
DWJ Associates, 343
Dyer, Wayne, 42
Dylan, Bob, 171, 172

Eagle Forum, 48
Earth stations, 387–388
East/West Network, 131
Eastman Kodak Company, 258
Ebert, Roger, 284
Ebony (magazine), 119
Ed Sullivan Show, The (TV program), 170, 171
Edison, Thomas, 148, 163, 255, 256, 272
Editing and editors:
 of books, 35–39
 of magazines, 134–141
 of newspapers, 65, 80–84, 89–90
Educational books, 35, 47–49
 (*See also* Textbooks)
Educational radio, 179, 182
Educational Research, 48
Educational television, 199, 210, 242
 (*See also* Public television)
80-20 rule (advertising), 307
Elderly, the, on television, 243
El Diario–La Prensa (newspaper), 77
Electronic communications (*see* Radio; Television; Video)
Electronic news-gathering equipment (ENG), 230

Ellsberg, Daniel, 106
Ellul, Jacques, 385
Emery, Edwin, 55
End of the Presidency, The (book), 33
Entertainment by mass media, 11
Entertainment Tonight (TV program), 76
Epstein, Edward J., 106
Equal opportunity in television broadcasting, 205–206
Eron, Leonard D., 236
ETV Facilities Act of 1962, 210
Evening Telegram (newspaper), 68
Expense accounts, 111–112
Experimental research, 370–371
Exxon, 131, 212
Eye on the Media (TV program), 98

Fair play in newspaper industry, 112
Fairbanks, Douglas, Sr., *261*
Fairness doctrine in television broadcasting, 205–206
Fame (*see* Celebrities)
Families (magazine), 134
Farber, Myron, 104, 105
Farm Journal (magazine), 128–129
Farmers Museum, The (weekly), 120, 121
Farming, magazines for, 131
Farnsworth, Philo, 197
Farrar, John, 35
Fatima (film), 272
Federal Bureau of Investigation (FBI), 107
Federal Communications Commission (FCC), 179, 198, 199, 201, 202, 204–206, 213
Federal Privacy Act, 108
Federal Radio Commission, 155
Federal Trade Commission (FTC), 208–209, 327
Feedback in communication, 9
Felix the Cat, 198
Feminism (*see* Women)
Fertilizer Institute, 345
Feshback, Seymour, 237
Fibber McGee and Molly (radio program), 156–157
Field of experience, 5
Field research, 371
Film festivals, 285
Film noir, 266–267
Films (*see* Movies)
Findley, Ellen, 84

Fink, Steven, 395
Finn, David, 359, 422
Fireman, Judy, 198
Firestone, Mary Alice, 97
First Amendment, 59–60, 96, 98, 100–106
 (*See also* Censorship)
Firstenberg, Jean, 418
Flashdance (film), 165
Flax pulp, 23
Flight of the Gossamer Condor, The (film), 288
FM radio, 178–179, 408–409
FOI (journal), 46
Folio (magazine), 132
Ford Foundation, 210
Ford Motor Company, 310
Foreign-language newspapers, 77
Forever (novel), 46
Formats (radio), 175–178
Foster, G. Allen, 327
Foster, Larry, 352
Fowler, Jim, 310
Fowler, Mark, 205
Fowles, Jib, 223
Fox, William, 258
Franklin, Benjamin, 22, 24, 57–58, 120, 302
Frederick Douglass's Newspaper, 77
Free-sheet paper, 40
Freeberg, Stan, 319
Freedberg, Sydney, P., 108
Freedman, Morris, 48
Freedman v. Maryland, 275
Freedom of Information Act (FOIA), 106, *107*
Freedom-to-read statement, 46
Freedom's Journal (newspaper), 77
Friedman, Michael, 343
Friendly, Jonathan, 91

Gabler, Mel, 48
Gabler, Norma, 48, 49
Gag orders, 103
Games in newspapers, 80
Gangster films, 264
Garland, Judy, 104, *266*
Garland, Phyl, 77–78
Garner, James, 280
Garth, David, 332
Gatekeepers in communication, 9
General Magazine and Historical Chronicle for the British Plantations in America, 119, 120
General Motors, 131
Generic advertising, 183
Gerbner, George, 243

440 INDEX

Gibbs, Georgia, 170
Gillett, Charlie, 172
Ginn and Company (publisher), 31
Glamour (magazine), 137, 139
Glessing, Robert, 77
Go Ask Alice (book), 46
Godey, Louis, 121
Godey's Lady's Book (magazine), 121
Godkin, E. L., 119
Golding, William, 19, 46
Gollob, Herman, 44
Gone with the Wind (film), 264
Good Morning America (TV program), 76
Goodrich, Samuel, 122
Government, 95–109
  (*See also* Constitution, U.S.; Regulation, governmental; Supreme Court, U.S.)
Graham, George, 120
Graham's Magazine, 120
Grand Ole Opry (radio), 170
Grapes of Wrath, The (novel), 46
Gravure printing, 40
Grayson, Brenda, 242
Great Santini, The (film), 285
Great Train Robbery, The (film), 256
Greeley, Horace, 60–62
Green, Bob, 343
Green, Dan, 41, 44
Greenfield, Patricia, 394
Gregg Company, 25
Grey, Zane, 29
Greyser, Stephen A., 342, 359
Gribbons, Joseph, 138
Griffith, David Wark (D. W.), 256–257
Grossman, Lawrence, 213
Groundwood paper, 40
Group communication, 7
Grunig, James E., 358
Grunwald, Henry Anatole, 136
Gubser, Charles, 109
Gutenberg, Johann, 22, 23

Haas, Robert, 30
Hale, Sara Joseph, 121
Hall, Dennie, 111
Hall, W. F., Printing Company, 34
Hamblin, Dora Jane, 126, 127
Hamilton, Andrew, 58
Hamlocking (TV programming), 221
Handle With Care (film), 285

Harlan County, U.S.A. (film), 288
Harlequin (publisher), 31
Harmetz, Aljean, 283
Harper, Fletcher, 25
Harper, James, 25
Harper, John, 25
Harper, Joseph, 26
Harper, Wesley, 25
Harper & Brothers (publisher), 22, 23, 25, 26
Harper's Monthly (magazine), 119
Harris, Benjamin, 58
Harrison, Benjamin, 26
Hart, Abraham, 26
Harvard University, 65
Haskell, Molly, 271–272
Hayden Planetarium, 47
Hays, Will, 273
HBO (Home Box Office), 282, 387
Headlines:
  for advertisements, 315–316
  in newspapers, 93–94
Hearst, William Randolph, 63, 65, 66
Hearst Corporation, 131
Hearts and Minds (film), 287
Hefner, Hugh, 119
Henabery, Joseph, 258
Hennock, Frieda, 199
Hentoff, Nat, 48
Herald Tribune (newspaper), 61
  international edition, 72
Hertz, Heinrich Rudolf, 147
Hibbard, Don, 173
Highet, Gilbert, 20
Highland, Jean, 34
Hill, George Roy, 279
Hill, John A., 25
Hill, John W., 358
Hill & Knowlton, 339, 340
Hill Publishing Company, 25
Historical research, 368–370
Hodgins, Eric, 136
Holly, Buddy, 170
Hollywood (*see* Movies)
Holmes, Presley D., 367
Holt, Rinehart, & Winston (publisher), 31
Home Box Office (HBO), 282, 387
Homer, 138
Homosexuality, 111
Hooper, C. E., 223
Horner, Vivian, 391
Host selling, 240
Huckleberry Finn (*The Adventures of Huckleberry Finn*) (novel), 46–48

Hulse, Jerry, 111
Hunt, Todd, 358
Huston, John, 259, 265
Hyett, Kathy M., 349, 377
Hynds, Ernest, 71
"Hypodermic" theory, 366–367

Iconoscope, 197
Illustrated Daily News (newspaper), 68
Illustration in advertisements, 316
In Cold Blood (book), 94
Independent Motion Picture Company, 258
Interactive cable, 390–392
International Wireless Conference, 154
Interpersonal communication, 7, 8
Intrapersonal communication, 7
Inverted pyramid style of writing, 63, 93
Investigative reporting, 91–92
Irwin, Leslie ("Mad Dog"), 100

Jacobs, Lewis, 255
Jacoby, Susan, 43
Jarvis, Al, 148, 173
Jascalevich, Mario, 104, 105
Jazz journalism, 68–70
Jazz Singer, The (film), 262
Jefferson, Thomas, 24, 59, 96
Jenkinson, Edward, 49
Jingles (advertising), 301
Johnson, Bob, 242
Johnson, Samuel, 302, 312
Johnson & Johnson, 212, 309, 351
Jolson, Al, 262
Journalism:
  evolution of, 54–78
  jazz, 68–70
  new, 94
  in penny press, 60–62
  photo-, 125
  reporters, 90–92, 103–105, 109
  in Spanish-American War, 66
  on TV, 225–232
  in twentieth century, 67–71
  writing the news, 92–95
  yellow, 62–67
  (*See also* News; Newspapers)
Judson, Arthur, 152, 153
Juke boxes, 163
Jurors, pretrial publicity effect on, 100–103

Justice, U.S. Department of, in *Pentagon Papers* case, 106
JVC, 388

Kael, Pauline, 250, 285
Kaleialoha, Carol, 173
Kandy-Kolored Tangerine Flake Streamline Baby (book), 94
Kansas City Star (newspaper), 154
Kaplan, Peter W., 178
KDKA (radio station), 148, 149
Kendrick, Alexander, 159, 369
Kennedy, John E., 297
Kennedy, John F., 19, 69–70
Kent, Rockwell, 29
KFKB (radio station), 155
Kiker, Douglas, 70
Killers, The (film), 266, *267*
Kinescope, 197, 210
Kinetograph, 255
King, Larry, 178
King Features Syndicate, 65
Kipling, Rudyard, 27
Kirkeby, Mark, 165
Kiss, The (film), 272
Klein, Paul, 219
Klopfer, Donald, 29
Knickerbocker (magazine), 121
Knipe, Judy, 34
Knopf, Alfred (publisher), 29
Koch, Chris, 88
Koch, Howard, 265
Kodak, 258
Kosinski, Jerzy, 234
KRON (TV station), 239

Ladies' Home Journal (magazine), 119, 123
Ladies' Magazine, 121
Laemmle, Carl, 258, 259
Lancaster, Burt, *267*
Landeck, Terry, 322
Lashnits, Tom, 134, 405
Lasker, Albert, 297
Lasswell, Harold, 377
Last of the Mohicans, The (novel), 25
Last Tango in Paris (film), 285
Law (*see* Government; Regulation, governmental)
Lawrence, Florence, 259
Lea and Blanchard (publisher), 26
Lead (journalism), 93
Lear, Norman, 48, 239
Learning through mass media, 14

Leavy, Morton, 279
Le Carré, John (David Cornwell), 279
Lee, Harper, 46
Lee, Ivy Ledbetter, 347
Legion of Decency, 264, 274, 275
Lennig, Arthur, 247
Lennon, John, 172
Leonard, John, 217
Lesly, Philip, 338
Lessing, Erish, 138
Letterpress printing, 40
Levetter, Joan, 345
Levin, Eric, 232
Levy, Steven, 395
Lewis, C., 219
Libel by newspapers, 96–98
Libertarian-style press, 95
Libraries, 20, 27
Library of Congress, 24
Licensee ascertainment, 205
Life (magazine), 118, 119, 125–127
Linotype machine, 24
Liquor advertising, 331
Listerine, 328
Literacy, newspaper promotion of, 58
Literary agents, 37
Literary factories, 28
Little, Ray, 34
Little Drummer Girl, The (book), 279
Locomotive Engineer (magazine), 25
Logotype, 316
Lone Ranger, The (radio program), 152
Look (magazine), 118, 119, 125–126
LOP (least objectionable program) principle (TV programming), 219–220
Lord of the Flies (novel), 46
Lorimer, George Horace, 123
Los Angeles Free Press (newspaper), 77
Los Angeles Times (newspaper), 111
Louchheim, Jerome, 153
Louisville Courier-Journal (newspaper), 98
Lowe, E. T., Publishing Co., 34
Lowery, Shearon, 368
Loy, Myrna, *266*
Luce, Clare Booth, 49
Luce, Henry, 125
Luedtke, Kurt M., 109
Lumenick, Lou, 265

Lumière brothers, 255
Luxenberg, Stan, 340
Lyle, Jack, 236
Lynch, James E., 367

Macauley, Thomas, 303
McClure's Magazine, 119, 121, 123
McCombs, Maxwell, 365
McConey, Ward, 64
McCord, James W., Jr., 82
MacDougall, A. Kent, 345
McGraw, James H., 25
McGraw-Hill (publisher), 22, *25*, 29, 130
McGraw Publishing Company, 25
McGuffey's *Readers*, 27
McLuhan, Marshall, 145, 295
McMahon, Ed, 133
Macmillan (publisher), 47
MacNeil, Robert, 192, 332
McQueen, Steve, 282
Macroediting, 135–136
Magazine Publishers Association (MPA), 118, 126–127
Magazines, 117–142
    advertising in, 126, 128, 132, 303, 318
    circulation of, 118, 126–127, 130
    contemporary, 126–132
    development of, 118–123
    editing of, 134–141
    future of, 405–408
    general-interest, 120–121, 123–126
    graphic design in, *140*
    organization of, 132–134
    organization chart of a typical magazine, *132*
    preferences for, of college students (chart), 13
    production of, 39
    teenagers' use of (chart), 11
    (*See also specific titles*)
"Magic-bullet" theory, 366–367
Magnetic tape recording, 164
"Magoos," 220
Mail and Express (newspaper), 68
Make Believe Ballroom (radio program), 173
Malls, bookstore chains in, 22
Manning, Anita, 44
Manning, Selvage & Lee, 340
Manutius, Aldus, 23
Mapes, Glynn, 75
March, Frederic, *266*
Marcil, William, 71
Marconi, Guglielmo, 147, 148

442 INDEX

Marconi Wireless Telegraph and Signal Company, 147, 149
Marcus, Greil, 171
Mareth, Paul, 390
Margolis, Esther, 41
Marquee value, 139
Marylas, Daisy, 44
Maslow, Abraham, 311
Mass audience, specialization of, 9
Mass communications, 8–10
 (*See also* Mass media)
Mass media, 10–14
 advertising in, 317–325
 research on, 365–378
 (*See also specific media*)
Massachusetts Spy (newspaper), 59
Mast, Gerald, 261
Mastering (sound recording), 166
Mathews, Paul, 49
Mathews, T. S., 136
Maynard, Robert, 78
MCA, Inc., 280
Means, Marianne, 69
Media (*see* Mass media)
Media Decisions (magazine), 306
Melies, George, 256
Men, mass-media use by (chart), 11
Men at Work (music group), 165
Mencher, Melvin, 90
Menudo (music group), 168, 173
Meredith Corporation, 131
Mergenthaler, Ottmar, 24
Mergers and takeovers:
 in book publishing, 22, 30–31
 among newspapers, 68
Messages, 5
Metz, Frank, 45
Meyers, John A., 125
Meyerwitz, Josh, 234
MGM, 265
Miami News, The (newspaper), 90
Microediting, 135–136
Midnight (newspaper), 76
Midnight Cowboy (film), 270
Miehle offset press, 34
Milgram, Stanley, 237
Miller, Arthur, 101
Miller v. California, 274
Milton, John, 55
Minicams, 230–232
Minorities on television, 242–243
Minority press, 77–78
Miracle, The (film), 274
Mitford, Jessica, 41
Mixing (sound recording), 166
Mobil Corporation, 353–355
Modern Library (publisher), 27

Montgomery, Jim, 355
Moore, Christine, 47
Moral Majority, 46
Morning Edition (radio program), 180
Morris, William, 47
Morse, Samuel, 146, 148
Morse Code, 146
Moskin, J. Robert, 403
Motion Picture Association of America (MPAA), 275, 277
Motion Picture Patents Company (MPPC), 258–259
Motion Picture Producers and Distributors Association of America (MPPDAA), 273
Motion pictures (*see* Movies)
Motivation research, 306–307
Mott, Frank Luther, 62, 66, 68, 121
Mounty, Robert, 410
Movable type, 23
Movies, 247–290
 business of, 276–282
 documentary films, 265, 287–288
 as experience, 248–250
 future of, 415–418
 history of, 252–273
 preferences for, of college students (chart), 13
 production and release of, *278, 280*
 promotion of, 283–285
 social psychology of, 250–252
 teenagers' use of (chart), 11
 viewer's guide to, 285–287
 women in, 269–272
 (*See also specific titles*)
Moyers, Bill, 218
Ms. Magazine, 119
MTV (Music Television), 164–165
Muckraking in magazines, 123–125
Munsey, Frank A., 68
Munsey's Magazine, 119, 121, 123
Murdoch, Rupert, 76, 77
Murrow, Edward R., 148, 159, 162, 369
Music, 163–173
Music Television (MTV), 164–165
Mutual Broadcasting System (MBS), 153, 178
Mutual Film Corporation v. Ohio, 273
My Lai massacre, 103
Myles, Lynda, 277

Nation, The (magazine), 119
National advertising, 72, 73, 78
National Advertising Division (NAD), 328
National Advertising Review Board (NARB), 328
National Association of Broadcasters (NAB), 206–207, 220
National Association of Educational Broadcasters, 179
National Broadcasting Corporation (*see* NBC)
National Catholic Office for Motion Pictures, 275
National Coalition on Television Violence, 237
National dailies, 71–73
National Educational Television (NET), 210
National Enquirer, The (newspaper), 76, 97
National Police Gazette, The (magazine), 122
National Public Radio (NPR), 148, 179–182
National Tattler, The (newspaper), 76
Nautical Quarterly (magazine), 138
Navy, U.S., 108
NBC (National Broadcasting Corporation), 114, 148, 154, 197–199, 207, 229, 239
Near v. Minnesota, 106
Needs Hierarchy, 311
Nelson, Thomas (publisher), 47
Network (film), 12
Networks:
 radio, 151–154
 TV, 199, 201–204, 214, 218–225
Neuharth, Allen, 72
New American Library (publisher), 31
New England Courant (newspaper), 57, 58
New England Palladium (newspaper), 59
New journalism, 94
New National Era, The (newspaper), 77
New Right, 46
New York Film Festival, 285
New York Herald (newspaper), 68
New York Herald Tribune (newspaper), 71, 104
New York Journal (newspaper), *63*, 66
New York Magazine, 140

INDEX **443**

New York Mirror (newspaper), 120
New York Morning Post (newspaper), 60
New York Press (newspaper), 68
New York Sun (newspaper), 60, 68
New York Times, The (newspaper):
    best-seller list of, 43–44, 47
    book reviews in, 42, 45
    in Dr. X case, 104
    libel suit against, 96–97
    as national daily, 72
    under Adolph S. Ochs, 62, 67–68
    and *Pentagon Papers* publication, 106
    Henry Raymond as publisher of, 62
    as *White House Transcripts* collaborator, 34
New York Times Company, 131
New York Times News Service, The, 89
New York Tribune, The (newspaper), 61, 68
New York Weekly Journal (newspaper), 58
New York World (newspaper), *63*, 64, 66
New Yorker, The (magazine), 119, 126
Newhouse (Condé Nast), 131
Newman, Lloyd, 352
News, 55
    on radio, 159, 177, 180, 184
    on TV, 225–232
    (*See also* Journalism; Newspapers)
News cooperatives and associations, 63
"News doctors," 230
News hole, 78, 88
Newsday (newspaper), 73, 91
Newspaper Advertising Bureau, 79
Newspaper Readership Project, 76, 88
Newspapers, 53–116
    advertising in, 70–71, 73, 78–79, 302, 317–318
    contemporary, 71–78
    development of, 55–77
    ethics in operation of, 109–114
    future of, 403–405
    legal restraints on, 95–109
    news gathering by, 89–95
    organization of, 78–84
    organization chart of typical paper, *79*
    penny press, 60–62
    preferences for, of college students (chart), 13

Newspapers (*Cont.*):
    production of, 80
    radio news opposed by, 159
    teenagers' use of (chart), 11
    versus TV news, 226
    (*See also* Journalism)
Newsweek (magazine), 125
Nickelodeons, 163, 257
Nielsen, A. C., Company, 221–225
Nielsen, Arthur, 223
Nielsen Television Index (NTI), 222
Nieme, Olivia, 238–239
Niepce, Joseph, 252
1984 (novel), 46
Nixon, Richard M., 33, 34, 211
Noise, 5–6
Nolte, Lawrence, 359
Nonfiction novel, 94
North American Phonograph Company, 163
Novels:
    mass production of, 28
    and new journalism, 94
    romance, 31–32
    Kurt Vonnegut on novelists, 37

Oakland Tribune (newspaper), 78
Ochs, Adolph S., 62, 67–68
Odyssey, The (Homer), 138
Of Mice and Men (novel), 46
Of Time and the River (novel), 39
Offset printing, 40
Ogilvy, David, 312, 316, 418
Oil companies, 124, 211
Old, Leonard, 314
One-shot magazines, 131
Oppenheim, Mike, 238
Optical fibers, 386
Orwell, George, 46
Osborne (publisher), 25
O'Toole, John, 297, 306
Our Bodies, Ourselves (book), 46
Outdoor advertising, 322–325

Pac-Man (video game), 395
Paine, Thomas, 59
Paired-Picture Technique, 308
Paley, William S., 152, 153
Palm Sunday (book), 37
Palmer, Volney B., 302
Pan Arts Corporation, 279
Paper for books, 40
Paperback extras, 22, 33
Paperbacks, 22, 31–33, 40
Papyrus, 23

Parallel action (movies), 256
Paramount Pictures, 259
Parchment, 23
Parity products, 310
Parker, Barbara, 49
Parker, Edwin B., 236
Parley, Peter, 122
Parley's Magazine, 122
Pastore, John, 236
Pawnbroker, The (film), 275
Payne Fund, 366
Payola, 174–175
Penguin Books (publisher), 31
Pennsylvania Evening Post (newspaper), 59
Pennsylvania Gazette (newspaper), 58
Penny press, 60–62
Pentagon Papers, The (book), 46, 91, 106
People for the American Way, 48
People Magazine, 76, 139
"Perfect" binding, 40
Perkins, Maxwell Evarts, *38–39*
Persistence-of-vision principle, 252–255
Persky, Joel, 413
Personal communication, 7
Petersen, Clarence, 20, 32, 33
Peterson, Theodore, 126
Petroleum refining industry, 124
Phelps, Jim, 133
Phil Donahue Show, The (TV program), 42
Philadelphia Inquirer (newspaper), 91
Phillips, Sam, 170
Phonograph records (*see* Recording industry)
Phonographs, 163
Photography:
    in picture magazines, 125
    in tabloids, 68
Photojournalism, 125
Phrenology Review (magazine), 122
Pickford, Mary, 259
Pico v. Island Trees Board of Education, 49
Piracy:
    of books, 25–26
    of movies, 283
    in recording industry, 164
Pisetzner, Joel, 231
Pittsburgh Courier (newspaper), 78
Plate, Thomas, 92
Playboy (magazine), 119
Playboy Enterprises Inc., 131
Plugola, 174–175
Pocket Books (publisher), 22, 31

444 INDEX

Poe, Edgar Allen, 120, 122, 123
Politics, advertising in, 332
Poor Richard's Almanack, 22, 24
Pope, Generoso, 76
Popular music, 169–173
Pornography, censorship of, 46
Port Folio, The (magazine), 120
Porter, Edwin S., 256
Postal Act of 1879, 123
Postal services for magazines, 119, 123, 134
Postman, Neil, 228, 234
Powers, Ron, 227
Prell shampoo, 314
Preminger, Otto, 275
Prentice-Hall (publisher), 22, 29
Presley, Elvis, 170
Pretrial publicity, 100–103
Preview House, 220
Price, Jonathan, 241
Prime-time access rule, 220
Printing of books, 23, 24, 40
Printing presses, 23, 32, 80
Prior restraint on newspapers, 105–106
Prisendorf, Anthony, 232
Privacy:
 right to, 113–114
 versus right to know, 98–100
Production:
 of books, 23, 39–41
 of magazines, 140
 of newspapers, 80
Production Code (movies), 273–274
Profit participants, 280
Programming:
 radio, 151–154, 156–162, 175–178, 180, 183
 TV, 201, 202, 204–205, 209, 211–212, 218–225
Progressive, The (magazine), 106
Propagandists, 359
Prune sales, 305
Pseudo-events, 91, 226
Psychographics, 306, 421
Psychology Today (magazine), 136
Public Broadcasting Act, 180, 210, 211
Public Broadcasting Service (PBS), 210–212
Public communication, 7
Public interest:
 advertising for, 300
 in TV programming, 204–209, 220
Public opinion, 348–350
Public relations, 337–360
 communication and, 348–355

Public relations (*Cont.*):
 definition of, 338–344
 ethics of, 355–359
 future of, 422–424
 practitioners of, 344–348
Public relations magazines, 131
Public Relations News (newspaper), 341
Public Relations Society of America, 356–357, 375–376
Public Television, 210–212
Publicity escorts, 42, 43
Publick Occurrences Both Foreign and Domestick (newspaper), 58
Publisher's Clearing House, 133
Publishers Weekly (magazine), 42, 44, 45
Publishing, 33–45
 booksellers in early America, 24–25
 modern, 28, 30–31
 organization chart of typical house, *35*
 (*See also* Books; *specific publishing companies*)
Pulitzer, Albert, 65
Pulitzer, Joseph, 53, *63*–66
Pye, Michael, 277

Qualidata reports, 185
QUBE (cable TV), 214
Queensboro Corporation, 150
Query letters, 137–138
Quigg, H. D., 90
Quigley Publications, 269

Rack jobbers, 168–169
Radecki, Thomas, 237, 239
Radio, 145–188
 advertising on, 70–71, 150, 156, 182–183, 319
 educational, 179, 182
 federal regulation of, 154–156
 future of, 408–411
 history of, 146–154
 news on, 159, 177, 180, 184
 in newspapers' decline, 70
 organization chart of a typical station, *182*
 preferences for, of college students (chart), 13
 programming, 151–154, 156–162, 175–178, 180, *183*
 radio stations, 154, 182–188
 and recording industry, 163–171
 restructuring of, 173–178
 survey research on, 372–373

Radio (*Cont.*):
 talk, 41, 177, 372–373
 teenagers' use of (chart), 11
 (*See also specific programs; specific stations*)
Radio Act of 1912, 154
Radio Act of 1927, 148, 154–156, 200
Radio Advertising Bureau, 160, 319
Radio Corporation of America (*see* RCA)
Rag-content paper, 40
Random House (publisher), 22, 29, 30
Rather, Dan, 228, 351
Rating system (movies), 275
Ratings:
 for radio, 184–188
 for TV, 203, 221–225, 230–232
 (*See also* Arbitron)
Ray, Garrett, 109
Raymond, Henry, 62
RCA (Radio Corporation of America), 149, 150, 163, 179, 197, 199
RCA Corp., 31
RCA Victor, 163, 164
Readers of books, 20–21
Reader's Digest (magazine), 119, 125, 133
Reader's Digest Association, Inc., 131
Reagan, Ronald, 90, 105, 114
Real People (TV program), 76
Receivers in communication, 4
Record, The (newspaper), 80
Record Industry Association of America, 164, 165
Record players, 163
Recording industry, 163–173
 organization chart of a typical company, *168*
Records and tapes, 12, 13, 163
Redbook (magazine), 136
Reference books, censorship of, 48
Regensteiner Press, 34
Reggae music, 173
Regulation, governmental:
 of advertising, 326–329
 of radio, 154
 of TV, 204–209
Report of the Warren Commission on the Assassination of President Kennedy (book), 22, 33
Reporters, 90–92, 103–105, 109
Research:
 at magazines, 137
 on mass media, 365–378

INDEX **445**

Return of the Jedi (film), *251*, 283
Reuters, 89
Review, The (magazine), 118, 119
Reviews:
    of books, 42
    of movies, 283–285
Reynolds, Dean, 90
Rienzi (book), 26
Right to know versus privacy,
    98–100
Rivers, William, 134
Roberts, Chuck, 69
Roberts, Elizabeth J., 220
Roberts, Sidney, 69
Robida, Albert, 194
Robinson, E. J., 341
Rock music, 169–173
Rockefeller, John D., 124
Rockefeller, Winthrop, 128
Rockefeller family, 347
Roget, Peter Mark, 252
Role-playing games, 394
Romance novels, 31–32
Romeo and Juliet (play), 64
Rooney, Andy, 337
Roosevelt, Franklin Delano, 148,
    158, 197
Roosevelt, Theodore, 123
Roper Polls, 227
Ross, Harold, 126
Rotary presses, 32
Rotha, Paul, 262
Royalties for authors, 30, 37–39
Rubicam, Raymond, 312
Rubin, Ellis, 239
Rudman, Kal, 175
Russworm, John B., 77
Rutland, Robert, 65

Sacramento Observer (newspaper), 78
Sadat, Anwar, 93
St. Louis Dispatch (newspaper), 64
Salinger, J. D., 46
San Francisco Examiner (newspaper),
    65
Sandburg, Carl, 295
Sans serif type, 40
Sarnoff, David, 151, 152, 197
Satellite communications, 72, 89,
    385, 387–388
Saturday Evening Post, The
    (magazine), 118–120, *122*, 123,
    128
Savitch, Jessica, 229
Sawyer, Diane, 369
Say Amen, Somebody (film), 288
Schaefer beer, 307

Schaum Publishing Company, 25
Schenck, V. M., 28
Scherman, Harry, 30
Schlafly, Phyllis, 48
Schmertz, Herbert, 228, 353
Schoolmaster's Assistant (book), 27
Schramm, Wilbur, 236
Schrank, Jeffrey, 304, 305
Schuster, Max, 29
Schwartz, Tony, 197, 425
Science-fiction movies, 267
Scope mouthwash, 316
Scott, Buddy, 301
Scribner, Charles, 25
Scribner's, Charles, Sons
    (publisher), 25, 38–39
Scripps, Edward Wyllis, 65–67
Seifert, Walt, 348
Seitel, Fraser P., 353
Senders in communication, 4
Senior citizens, 243
Sennett, Mack, 261
Sensationalism, 64, 68, 76
Sentence-completion tests, 308
Serif type, 40
Sesame Street (TV program), 212
Sevareid, Eric, 369
Seventeen (magazine), 132
Sex and sexuality:
    in advertising, 314, 331
    in movies, 272–273
Shapley, Harlow, 47
Shatzkin, Leonard, 45
Sheehy, Gail, 424
Shepard's Citations, 25
Sheppard, Sam, 100–103
Shield laws, 104
Sholland, Lance, 237
Shopping malls, 22
Shots (movies), 285–287
Showtime, 282
Signatures (book production), 40
Signet (publisher), 31
Sigourney, Lydia, 123
Silverman, Fred, 218
Silverstein, Shel, 194, 235
Simecka, Milan, 45
Simon, Richard, 29
Simon & Schuster (publisher), 22,
    29, 31, 41, 44, 48
Simons, Howard, 82
Sinclair, Upton, 123, 346
Singletary, Michael, 89
Siquis (advertising), 302
Siskel, Jean, 284
Sixth Amendment, 100–105
Skornia, Harry J., 203, 235
Slander, 96

Slogans (advertising), 316
Sloyan, Patrick, 93
Smith, Anthony, 71
Smith, Robert Rutherford, 232
Smith, Roger M., 33, 34
Smokey and the Bandit (film), 285
Sneak Previews (TV program), 284
Snow White (book), 48
Soap operas, 157–158
Social-responsibility theory, 96
Society for the Propagation of the
    Faith, 345
Society of Professional Journalists,
    46
Sony Corporation, 388
Sound films, 262–264
Sound recording (*see* Recording
    industry)
Sound Recording Act of 1972, 164
Sound studios, 166
Southern Literary Messenger
    (magazine), 123
Space Invaders (video game), 394
Spanish-American War, *63*, 66
Spanish-language newspapers, 77
Special-interest magazines, 122
Special-interest newspapers, 77
Spectator, The (magazine), 120
Speed Graphic (camera), 113
Spence, Gerry, 98
Spranger, Edward, 312
Stamberg, Susan, 180, 181
Stamford Daily, The (newspaper),
    104
Stamp Act of 1765, 59
Stamping (record production), 166
Standard Oil Company, 124
Star, The (newspaper), 76
Star Wars (film), 270
Stark, Ray, 279
Station Program Cooperative, 211
Steam press, 23
Steele, Richard, 120
Steffens, Lincoln, 123, 124
Steinbeck, John, 46
Stewart, Paul, 43
Storage instantaneous audimeter
    (SIA), 222
Stowe, Harriet Beecher, 27, 123
STP Corporation, 327
Strachan and Henshaw printing
    press, 32, 34
Street Railway Journal (magazine), 25
Students, 13, 54
Subscribers to magazines, 133
Suburban dailies, 73–76
Suburban Newspapers of America,
    73

446 INDEX

Sullivan, H. B., 97
Summary lead (news writing), 63
Sunday papers, 71
Supermarkets:
  magazines sold in, 133
  supermarket tabloids, 76
Supreme Court, U.S.:
  on censorship in movies, 272–275
  on libel, 96–97
  on *Pentagon Papers,* 106
  on pretrial publicity, 100, 103
  on prior restraint, 106
  on reporters' source protection, 104
  on VCR usage, 388
Survey research, 371–374
Susan B. Anthony dollar, 343
Sussman, Barry, 82
Swanberg, W. A., 64
Sweeney, Kate, 64
Sweepstakes for magazine subscribers, 133
Syndicates (TV), 203–204
Syndication:
  of movies, 283
  of radio programs, 184

Tabloids, 68, 76
Takeovers (*see* Mergers and takeovers)
Talese, Gay, 54, 62, 67, 94
Talk radio, 41, 177, 372–373
Tanner Company, 184
Tape recorders, 164
Tapes (*see* Records and tapes)
Tarbell, Ida, 123, 124, 346
Tarzan: The Ape Man (film), 272
Tatler, The (magazine), 120
Tatta, John, 414
Taylor, Charles, 135
Teaching and learning through mass media, 14
Tebbel, John, 23, 26, 28, 120, 402
Technology, 383–397
  of sound recording, 165–167
  of TV, 383–396, 411–412
Teenagers, mass-media use by (chart), 11
Telegraph in journalism, 61, 63
Teletext, *392–393*
Television (TV), 191–245
  advertising on, 70–71, 199, 203, 207, 240–242, 320–322
  BBC test on nonuse of, 13
  book promotion on, 41
  cable (*see* Cable television)

Television (TV) (*Cont.*):
  for children, 208, 212, 233–242
  in daily life, 192–194
  educational, 199, 210, 242
  future of, 411–414
  magazines affected by, 118, 126–129
  movies competing with, 268–269
  networks, 199, 201–204, 214, 218–225
  new technology in, 383–396, 411–412
  news on, 225–232
  newspaper purchase of stations, 70–71
  organization chart of a typical station, *209*
  preferences for, of college students (chart), 13
  programming, 201, 202, 204–205, 209, 211–212, 218–225
  radio affected by, 159
  ratings for, 203, 221–225, 230–232
  versus real life, 232–234
  structure of, 201–204
  teenagers' use of (chart), 11
  TV sets, 192, 197–198
  TV stations, 198, 200–210
  Kurt Vonnegut on, 37
  women and minorities on, 230, 231, 242–243
  (*See also* specific programs)
Television Advertising Code, 207
Television Audience Assessment (TAA), 220, 225, 322
Television Information Office, 238
Terrorism, newspaper coverage of, 114
Testimonial advertising, 314, 328
Textbooks, 20, *36*, 48
  (*See also* Educational books)
Thematic Appercection Test (TAT), 307
Thom, James Alexander, 114
Thomas, Ambrose, 297
Thomas, Isaiah, 59
Thompson, James W., 303
Thoreau, Henry David, 146
Thorn Birds, The (TV program), 202
3-D movies, *268*
3M Company, 164
Three Mile Island nuclear facility, 340
Throwaway shoppers, 76
Time (magazine), 39, 43, 119, 125, *129,* 136

Time Inc., 131, 132
Tinker, Grant, *219*
TM Companies, 183
To Kill a Mockingbird (novel), 46
Tokyo Kikai Seisakusho (TKS), 80
Tootsie (film), 271
Torre, Marie, 104
Towne, Benjamin, 59
Trade books, 35, 41
Trade journals, 130
Tratec (publisher), 25
Travisano, Ron, 309
Treadwell, Daniel, 23
Trerice, Paul, 108
Triangle Publications, 131, 132
Trilby (novel), 27
Truffaut, François, *286*
"Trust, The" (Motion Picture Patents Company), 258–259
Turf Register (magazine), 122
TV Guide (magazine), 119, 127
Twain, Mark, 46, 102
Two-step-flow theory, 367
2001: A Space Odyssey (film), 284
Two-way cable, 390–392
"Tydings," 55
Tylenol, 351–352
Typography of books, 40

Ultra-high-frequency (UHF) television, 199–200
Uncle Tom's Cabin (novel), 22, 27, 123
Underground press, 77
Ungar, Sanford, 181
United Independent Broadcasters Network, 152, 153
United Paramount Theatres, 201
United Press International (UPI), 89–90
United States Safety Deposit Corporation, 45
United Stations (radio), 184
Universal Copyright Convention, 26
U.S. News & World Report (magazine), 125
US Urban Press, 73
USA Today (newspaper), 72
USS Ranger (ship), 108

Valenti, Jack, 275, 276
Valentino, Rudolph, 261
Value Profile, 312, 313
Vanderbilt, William, 346
van der Zee, James, *41*

INDEX   **447**

Van Doren, Philip, 27
VCRs (videocassette recorders), 14, 388–389, 411
Velikovsky, Immanuel, 47
Verdery, Dave, 177
Vertical integration in movie business, 259
Very-high-frequency (VHF) television, 199–201
VHS, 388
Victor Talking Machine Company, 163
Victrolas, 163
Video, 288–289, 385–396
  (See also Television)
Video games, 394–396
Videocassette recorders (VCRs), 14, *388*–389, 411
Videodiscs, 389–390
Videotape, 200–201, 210
Videotex, 392–*393*
Vietnam war, 106, 270–271, 287
Village Voice, The (newspaper), 77
Violence on TV, 235–240
Vonnegut, Kurt, 37

Waldenbooks, 44
Wall Street Journal, The (newspaper), 71–72, *74–75*, 97, 114, 128
Wallace, DeWitt, 125
Wallace, George, 90
Wallace, John, 47
Wallace, Lila, 125
Wallace, Mike, 351
War of the Worlds, The (radio program), 157, 367
Warlord, The (book), 44
Warner Brothers, 262, 279
Warner Communications, 214
Warren, Samuel, 98
Warren Commission report, 22, 33
Washington, George, 59
Washington Post (newspaper), 34, 81–*82*, 91, 106
Washington Post Company, 131

Washington Star (newspaper), 71
Watergate scandal, 81–83, 91, 95, 103, 271
WDAF (radio station), 154
WEAF (radio station), 148, 150
Weasel words (advertising), 310
Webster, Noah, 59
Webster Publishing Company, 25
Webster's New World Dictionary (book), 48
Weeklies (newspapers), 76
Welles, Orson, 148, *158*
Westerns (novels), 22
Westin, Av, 226, 227
Weyler, Valeriano, 66
WGY (radio station), 151
WHA (radio station), 179
WHB (radio station), 154
Whipple, A. B. C., 138
White, E. B., 218
White, Luke, 24
White, Margita, 207
White, Theodore H., 103
White House Transcripts, The (book), 33, 34
Whitney, Ruth, 137, 139
Whitter, Roy, 327
Who Killed the Robins Family? (novel), 42–45
Whole Book of Psalmes, The, 22, 24
Why We Fight (film), 265
Wicker, Tom, 69–70
Wilburt, Mike, 167
Wildman, Donald, 208
Wiley, Charles, 25
Wiley, John, & Sons (publisher), 25
Williams, Frederick, 385
Willis, Nathaniel, 122
Wilson, Harold, 125
Wine press in printing system, 23
Winick, Charles, 240
Winick, Marion, 240
Winston-Salem Chronicle (newspaper), 78
Wire editors, 89–90
Wire services, 89–90

Wizard of Oz, The (film), 283
WJZ (radio station), 151
WMMR (radio station), 186
Wolfe, Thomas, 39
Wolfe, Tom, 94
Wolsey, Roland, 78
Women:
  in advertisements, 331
  magazines for, 119, 121–122
  mass-media use by (chart), 11
  in movies, 269–272
  supermarket tabloids read by, 76
  on TV, 230, 231, 242–243
Wonder, Stevie, 166
Woodward, Bob, 81–*82*
Word-association tests, 308
Working class in movies, 271
World War II:
  book industry during, 29–30
  movies during, 264–266
  Pocket Books during, 31
World's Fair (1939), 197
Worlds in Collision (book), 47
Writers (*see* Authors)
Writing, ancient, 23
WSM (radio station), 170
Wurtzel, Alan, 236

Xerox Corporation, 31

Yellow journalism, 62–67
"Yellow Kid, The" (cartoon), 65
Youth's Companion (magazine), 122

Zamora, Ronald, 239
Zenger, John Peter, 58–59
Ziff-Davis Publishing Company, 131, 132
Zigli, Barbara, 21
Zukor, Adolph, 258, 259
Zurcher v. The Stamford Daily, 104
Zworykin, Vladimir Kosma, 197